Turbulent Era

A Diplomatic Record
of Forty Years

1904 – 1945

VOL.
II

Joseph C. Grew, 1952

Turbulent Era

A Diplomatic Record
of Forty Years

—————————— 1904–1945 ——————————

Joseph C. Grew

EDITED BY WALTER JOHNSON

Assisted by Nancy Harvison Hooker

VOLUME II

BOOKS FOR LIBRARIES PRESS
FREEPORT, NEW YORK

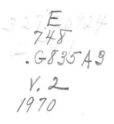

Table of Contents for Volume II

▼

List of Illustrations

13. Joseph C. Grew, 1952, *frontispiece*

following page 858

14. The American Embassy, Tokyo — the Residence
15. The American Embassy, Tokyo — the Chancery
16. At the graves of the sailors of Perry's Expedition
17. The Author speaking at a dinner of the America-Japan Society
18. Mr. and Mrs. Grew with their granddaughters
19. Letter of "explanation" from Yosuko Matsuoka
20. Mr. and Mrs. Grew before the shrine to Townsend Harris
21. Unveiling of a plaque to the memory of Townsend Harris
22. The Author and William Turner on the *Gripsholm*
23. The Dumbarton Oaks Conference, 1944

PART FOUR

The New Turkey

1927–1932

THE TURKISH REVOLUTION not only succeeded in freeing the Turkish homeland from foreign domination but was followed by a period during which the new leaders of Turkey embarked upon a reconstruction of Turkish society and government. Even before the Nationalist Turks had concluded their favorable peace settlement at Lausanne, the internal revolution had been launched.

The Nationalist movement in Turkey was inspired and carried through by a small group of leaders who, after overthrowing the existing regime and defeating numerous foreign enemies, established a republican form of government which only thinly veiled the autocracy of their leadership. The Republic of Turkey was not the natural product of democratic growth within the country. "Therefore we must look for the growth and development of this republic not in the psychology of the masses, as we should do in studying the French or American democracies, but in the policies of its few leaders," Arnold J. Toynbee and Kenneth P. Kirkwood have noted. "We must bear in mind throughout our study that the Republic, at least during these first years of its life, is a strange and exotic thing, not securely rooted in the hearts of the people, but loosely planted among an acquiescent and only momentarily enthusiastic population of peasants." [1]

"Modern Turkey," Mr. Grew observed in 1930 in his diary, "is working out a problem which never before has been at-

[1] Arnold J. Toynbee and Kenneth P. Kirkwood, *Turkey* (London: Ernest Benn, 1926), p. 160.

*tempted in so short a space of time. Realizing that in the ex-
acting demands of modern competition, parity with European
nations could only be achieved though the adoption of western civilization and western culture, the new Turkish Republic has thrown off the retarding trammels of orientalism as
practiced under the regimes of Abdul Hamid and his predecessors. The Sultanate and the Caliphate have been abolished,
and with them has gone, too, the old-time fez which was sym-
bolic of the unprogressive past. The Government has separated
itself from Islam; the old Moslem schools, where the youth of
the country spent its formative years chanting the Koran
and were largely hindered from acquiring a western education, have been suppressed; the women have been unveiled
and will, according to present indications, eventually receive
the vote; polygamy has been abolished and western codes of
civil, criminal and commercial law have been adapted to the
Turkish needs; the Latin alphabet has supplanted the old Arabic script — and all this has been done not as a process of slow
development, but in the very few years that have elapsed since
the Republic was founded. One by one the old branches, dead
and rotting, have been chopped off, almost overnight, from the
central tree-trunk where the sap is healthy and capable of contributing to new and healthy growth. This amazing revolution
is due to a keen and forceful nationalistic spirit, much of the
same intensity as that which inspired our own country in 1776,
but it is due in greatest measure to one man, the father of this
country, Mustafa Kemal who, having driven the foreign in-
vaders from this land, set about to cure 'The Sick Man of
Europe' and to make him permanently well and strong."*

*Since the vowel-values of Turkish are variable, it has been
difficult to establish a rule of spelling for Turkish names. With
the advice of an expert in the language, the editor has tried to
adopt one acceptable spelling for the names of people and
places and to use this spelling consistently in the book.*

XXV

Arrival in Turkey
AUGUST, 1927 – JANUARY, 1928

August 1–7 [1927]

Here they come again, the "Immortal Memoirs," withheld from hungry eyes these three and a half years. Once again these vivid pictures of current events, political upheavals, wars, rumors of wars, diplomatic discretions and indiscretions, Machiavellian intrigues, Oppenheimian plots and counterplots, will unfold before the eyes of the favored few who are privileged to read these sacred chronicles of history in the making. Anyone found guilty of revealing them to the Hearst Press will promptly be struck from the list of recipients. So on with the record, let discretion be unconfined.

It was four weary soldiers who took themselves on the good ship *Leviathan* . . . on Sunday afternoon, July 31. First there had been the closing of the house in Washington and the packing, then the glorious but strenuous celebration of the 25th anniversary of the Harvard Class of 1902, and finally the lovely wedding of Lilla to Pierrepont Moffat [1] at Hancock on July

[1] After attending Harvard University, Jay Pierrepont Moffat became private secretary and assistant to the American Minister at The Hague, where he served from 1917 until 1919. He was assigned after examination to be Third Secretary to the American Legation at Warsaw in September, 1919. In 1921, he became Second Secretary of the Legation in Tokyo, in 1923, Second Secretary of the Legation in Constantinople, and in 1925, he was assigned to the Department of State, serving as a White House Aide. Soon after his marriage to Lilla Grew, he was sent to Berne, Switzerland, as First Secretary. In 1932, he returned to the Department as Chief of the Division of West European Affairs. From 1935 to 1937, he was Consul General at Sydney, Australia, returning again to the Department in 1937, where he remained until 1940 as Chief of the Division of European Affairs. His brilliant career was abruptly ended by his death in 1943 at his post as Minister to Canada.

27th, out under the trees, its simplicity being perfect only because Alice had with great foresight prepared every detail with perfect precision. Finally we all went to Laura Curtis' at Roslyn, Long Island, and spent our last two days there with Jim Curtis, Dick and Janet Aldrich, Garrard Winston, Newbold Noyes and Eppes Hawes.[2] Our departure from New York was in true Oppenheim atmosphere because some gentle Armenian at a recent meeting had advocated the shooting of the new Turkish Ambassador to the United States, or me, or both, as a practical method of turning the attention of a sympathetic world to the sorrows of the Armenian race, so, reluctantly, we were accompanied to the theatre . . . and to the dock by a secret service agent and a member of the New York bomb squad, one of whom stood at the door of our cabin until sailing time. But there was not a sign of trouble.[3]

The ship sailed at 1 A.M. Monday, August 1st. . . . Alice, Anita and I stayed up until we had nearly reached the Narrows, which took over an hour as the ship was berthed up at 46th Street and the *Aquitania* backed out into the stream just ahead of us, impeding our progress for some time. The old

[2] James Curtis was a lawyer and at one time Assistant Secretary of the Treasury. Richard Aldrich was, for a time, a congressman. Garrard Winston was once Under Secretary of the Treasury. Newbold Noyes was a newspaperman, and Eppes Hawes, the daughter of Senator Hawes. — J. C. G.

[3] The American Committee Opposed to the Lausanne Treaty had protested vigorously to the State Department and to the President against an exchange of ambassadors between the United States and Turkey. James Gerard, one of the leaders of the opposition, made public on June 22, 1927, a letter which he had sent to Secretary Kellogg attacking the *modus vivendi* of February 18, 1927, under terms of which normal diplomatic and treaty relationships between the two countries were to be resumed. Gerard stated that this agreement contravened the authority of the Senate, and he could "but express amazement that the State Department should be willing to resort even to processes which are novel, to say the least, to show favor and partiality to the Turks, to whom we have no obligations and who fought against us, but that it should be unwilling to do the things which it can legitimately do for the Armenians, to whom we have fixed obligations and who fought on our side. . . .

"Likewise, it is difficult to understand why we should send an 'Ambassador' to Turkey — a primitive Asiatic country, with a population of 5,000,000, when we have reduced to a Legation our Embassy to Austria." See the *New York Herald Tribune*, June 23, 1927, p. 13.

Statue of Liberty was wrapped in dense fog and only the bea-
con could be seen shining through the mist. Was this sym-
bolical, I wonder? However, the little ceremony which the
girls and I perform — of repeating Scott's lines on passing the
old lady coming up the bay [4] — requires no supplementary
rite on going out. For myself, the old stanzas of Kingsley,[5]
which my mother read to me on September 11, 1902, on the
eve of setting out on my first real adventures, still fill the bill
— the world, thank heaven, is still young and the trees still
green. I feel like a boy out of school, shaking the dry, dry dust
of the old Department after these three strenuous, hectic years.
We can call our souls our own once more.

Chamberlin had his runway built athwart the ship just behind the bridge and Commodore Hartley, on whom I had
called on boarding the *Leviathan*, told me that the aviator
might take off at any time after daybreak.[6] So I was up at 5.30
after three hours of sleep and watched us pass through two
terrific thunderstorms with fierce thunder and lightning before the weather conditions moderated about 8. Chamberlin
took off at 8.14, was in the air even before reaching the end of
the runway and then celebrated his success like a small boy,
turning somersaults and cartwheels all around the ship before
he made off for Long Island, 90 miles distant, followed by two
destroyers which had been following us and another plane
which had come out to meet him. There was nothing new in
this feat as it has been done countless times before from the
decks of battleships, but this was the first time from a liner

[4] Breathes there the man, with soul so dead,
Who never to himself hath said,
This is my own, my native land!
Whose heart hath ne'er within him burn'd,
As home his footsteps he hath turn'd,
From wandering on a foreign strand?
                     Sir Walter Scott, *The Lay of the Last Minstrel.* — J. C. G.
[5] When all the world is young, lad,
And all the trees are green;
                                    Charles Kingsley, *Water Babies.* — J. C. G.
[6] Clarence Chamberlin, who had gained recognition by his transatlantic flight
in June, 1927, flew from the *Leviathan* to Teterboro, New Jersey, carrying mail.

and it marks, no doubt, a new era in transatlantic travel and mail transportation.

The voyage was uniformly smooth, very hot the first three days, chilly the last three. The ship excellent: good service, good food, luxurious accommodations, the Line having given us suite 161–163, two big rooms, bathroom, trunk room and hall. Our friends consisted of Uncle Godfrey Cabot, who asked to join us at our table and was a fund of interesting information and anecdotes throughout, Senator and Mrs. Dave Reed, with the former of whom I played most of the time, Judge and Mrs. Chauncey Parker, Mrs. Hampson Gary and her daughter, the three Misses Patten and their sister Mrs. Corbin, Robert Kelley, Chief of the Eastern European Division of the Department, Percy Grainger the pianist and composer, and two Consuls, James Bowcock from Munich and Harry Anslinger from the Department.

Nothing marred the peacefulness of the voyage, in spite of the fact that Elsie was greatly worried because one of the waiters near our table looked like an Armenian. But he proved peaceful too. . . .

Geneva, Venice, Brindisi, Athens,[7]
September 9–18 [1927]

. . . Early on the 15th we went aboard the *Cleopatra* of the Lloyd Triestino which sailed at noon to the minute, steaming out past the whole lovely waterfront of Venice. The Captain, to whom I introduced myself, promptly hauled the American flag to the foremast and invited us to sit beside him at table. He was a jovial soul and wrestled nobly, if somewhat inadequately, with the English language. An Egyptian Prince, the President of the Italian Chamber of Commerce in Constantinople, Fernandez Diaz, and an assortment of English, Germans, Greeks, Italians, French, Poles, Armenians, Egyptians, Swiss, Austrians and Turks made up the passenger list. The food was good, our accommodations small. Movies every night.

[7] The Grews visited in London, Geneva, and Venice, before sailing for Istanbul.

The first day and night the sea was absolutely smooth. We stopped for an hour at Brindisi and took a short walk ashore. On leaving Brindisi the wind had freshened and a fair sea rolled in from the Mediterranean as we crossed from Italy to Greece. . . .

The next day, the 17th, the sea was quite calm again; we were among the Greek islands, passing by the town where Byron died, through the Gulf of Corinth and thence through the Corinth Canal. It is not long — only three or four miles — but cut through a high hill, so that the cliffs rise almost perpendicularly and it is so narrow that a ship six feet broader than ours could hardly get through. Twenty years ago, before the canal was built, ships had to go all the way around the Peloponnesus.

We came into the Piraeus just before sundown, some two hours late, for the ship's engines are dirty and the Captain said her scheduled speed was reduced considerably but that she would be laid up before her next trip. I am sorry because we had planned to go up to Athens during our two-hour scheduled stay. The Captain said this was impossible as he wished to sail at the earliest moment. . . . However, I was glad that Alice and the girls were able to see Athens, the Acropolis and the Parthenon very clearly from the ship as we entered the Piraeus. The whole city lies clearly revealed from the roadstead. I had seen it in 1905.

The next morning found us entering the Dardanelles after passing the island and town of Tenedos. To me it was intensely interesting because I remembered the Gallipoli campaign [February, 1915 to January, 1916] in detail. We took advantage of the Captain's standing invitation to come up to the bridge and saw everything from that vantage point. The first landmark was the sunken hulk of the French battleship *Bouvet*. How well I remember the news of her sinking [on March 18, 1915]. Then the cemeteries, Australian and French, laid out on the sloping hillsides and the Australian monument, permanent memorials, visible to all who enter the Dardanelles, of that terrible and fruitless campaign. Then Chanak, the narrows and the forts. No wonder the warships couldn't get through. Forts and gun emplacements everywhere, although now dismantled in accordance with the Treaty of Lausanne. An international commission now controls the Straits. We, not being signatories of the Treaty of Lausanne, enjoy all the advantages and shoulder none of the responsibilities. I sometimes wish that the standards of governments and gentlemen were the same. . . .

The lights of Constantinople hove into view after dark, disappointing me in my hope that we should have that magnificent picture of the city at sunset. We anchored off Galata and soon the Embassy launch (the Admiral's [Mark Bristol] former barge) bearing the entire Embassy staff came up beside us but the staff could not come aboard until the Turkish quarantine authorities had comfortably finished their dinner and boarded the ship first. A half-hour of waiting. Finally, having accomplished our passport formalities in the smoking room, we descended to the barge and were very pleasantly welcomed by the staff. At Galata our Cadillac car, with new Turkish chauffeur and Kavass [Embassy guard] on the box, was waiting, just as we had stepped out of it in Washington scarcely three months ago. We drove to the Embassy, up the steep hill into Pera [the principal residential section of the European colony in Istanbul].

First impressions are generally inadequate. Outside, the Embassy shone in whitened splendor for it had recently been scoured from roof to cellar. Inside, what met our view was a large ornate hall from which opened the dining room, a salon and the Ambassador's office. Upstairs, a fine marble staircase led to another large and equally ornate hall, in which my beloved Bechstein piano was already installed, whence opened on one side a smoking room and a big living room, at the back a card room, and on the other side a corridor leading to Alice's bedroom, my dressing room and two large bathrooms. On the floor above was a large bedroom for Anita and Elsie and another for Miss Lewis, and servants' and storerooms galore. But what immediately enchanted us was the enormous terrace opening from the living room — such a terrace as a hotel might be proud of. It faces due west, looking straight down upon the Golden Horn and over to Stamboul, crowned by its many mosques and minarets, a wonderful vantage point for the glorious sunsets of Constantinople. Below is the Embassy garden, flanked by the chancery wing with offices for all our staff (with direct access to my own study); to the right is the Constantinople Club and tennis court and little dinner tables out under the stars, and next door the Pera Palace Hotel; to the left a restaurant and open-air café with an orchestra playing every night till 12.30 (Alice thinks she *may* get used to it). Such is our new habitation, owned by the Government of the United States, tenanted free of charge by her Ambassador and his family.

Did I say "free of charge"? Alice took one look at it and promptly dived into the bazaar, returning laden with rugs, screens, damasks, tapestries. Bare walls must be covered, worn furniture must be upholstered, great open spaces must be sheltered by screens, tatterdemalion curtains must be replaced. The interior of our splendid building is almost hopelessly run down, but we shall have an Embassy to be proud of before we are through. All this, I suppose, will be our free gift to the penurious Government of the United States. It is our privilege.

We arrived on Sunday evening, September 18th. I immediately inquired whether the Minister for Foreign Affairs, Tewfik Rushdi Bey, would receive me on Thursday the 22nd in Angora,[8] whither the express train goes on Monday, Wednesday and Friday nights. He replied in the affirmative. Monday, Tuesday and Wednesday were spent in gradually getting unpacked and straightened out. Our lift van had arrived safely and all our things, practically undamaged, were already in the Embassy. It was a question of unpacking the trunks and shift-

8 On October 13, 1923, the National Assembly declared Angora to be the capital of Turkey. Many of the foreign governments, however, did not immediately move their embassies or legations from the former capital of Constantinople. Mr. Grew kept part of his staff in Angora and traveled frequently to the capital, although he lived in the Embassy in Constantinople most of the year.

ing our things from one room to another, according to the wisdom and vision of the General-in-charge. Alice hardly spoke to me or to any of us during these three days; she planned and plotted and directed; useless to ask her to look at a sunset or to gaze at the mosques and minarets of Stamboul until her problem was solved. Meanwhile I got acquainted with my staff: Sheldon Crosby (Counselor), F. Lammot Belin and Ernest Ives (First Secretaries) — Jefferson Patterson (Second Secretary) being on leave — Colonel Frederic Smith (Military Attaché), Gardner Richardson (Commercial Attaché), Keeler (Assistant Trade Commissioner), Thomas Cole (Chief Clerk), Duncan Laing (File Clerk), Hyman Goldstein (Codist), Mrs. Roums and Ali Nour Bey (Translators), Miss Maher and Miss Bell (Stenographers), the several kavasses, Hamza, Hassan, Achmed, Shakir, Balthazar, Dimitrow (Messenger), Nubar (Fireman), Onnik (Embassy servant) and the gatekeepers Giovanni Kermitch and Petro Nilerovitch, and by no means last or least Miss Betty Carp. Carpie is known throughout the Foreign Service — whether for her inimitable letters or her sunny personality or merely her extraordinary ability and efficiency in getting things done, I know not, but the name of Betty Carp is respected and admired. She will keep my personal files, buy railway tickets, keep my bank accounts and draw all checks, return cards on visitors, buy supplies, engage servants, do errands of any kind or description, and that's only part of her manifold duties. The Embassy is indeed fortunate to have her on its staff, as well as Ali Nour Bey, our efficient translator. I have chosen Miss Frances Maher as my personal stenographer.

One afternoon I played golf with Mott Belin on the dry and rough, but interesting, 18-hole course, established by the British Army during its occupation of Constantinople. They had a whole system of water pipes laid down to water the greens, but the moment the evacuation had taken place the Turks tore up the pipes to use elsewhere. Furthermore, Turkish cavalry occasionally uses the course (including putting greens) for its maneuvers. Still, one can play and have a lot of exercise and fun. Mott Belin beat me one up. . . .

Hussein Bey [Chief of the Turkish Department at Robert College], my old friend of Lausanne, came to call. He has grown a beard on the ground that everybody who had them before had shaved them off and he didn't wish the appendage to become extinct. . . .

Constantinople, September 21 [1927]

Time has flown — it often does — and here I am on the night train from Constantinople to Angora (marked on the outside of the two sleeping cars and dining car, "Express d'Anatolie; Londres-Paris-Angora") feeling much more on a sightseeing tour than traveling for the purpose of establishing relations with a new Government. My visit to the Minister for Foreign Affairs tomorrow will be purely incidental; happening to find myself in the capital of Turkey, of course I shall look in on him — that's the way I feel; I ought really to be carrying a Turkish Baedeker.

That sunset, seen from the deck of the little steamer which carried us from Galata to Haidar Pasha, was indescribably beautiful. Only a painter could enumerate the colors of it, but what will always stand out in my memory — and I suppose we shall see the same thing very often — was the deep mauve in which Stamboul was bathed, with its mosques and minarets silhouetted against that flaming sky. On the left were Pera and the Bosporus, on the right Stamboul and the Sea of Marmora, and ahead Scutari and Haidar Pasha where the Anatolian Railway begins. The water nearly approached, I think, the color of lapis lazuli and the tops of the waves were very nearly carmine. That sounds crazy but it didn't look so. It took my breath away for sheer beauty. . . .

Angora, Thursday, September 22 [1927]

The Anatolian Express arrived at Eskishehr at 3.45 A.M. I was awake and saw our aged conductor with the distinguished white moustache buying meerschaum beads, cigarette holders and pipes from the vendors at the station according to our instructions of the night before, for Eskishehr is famous for its meerschaum mines and the prices are fantastically low. On the return trip he would give back whatever we didn't want. Then came the dawn and I was once again in country like Wyoming, with rolling prairie on every side. About 10 Angora came into view, clustered around its ancient fortress, gleaming in the sun, the brown, uninhabited prairie approaching to its very doors. The "Express d'Anatolie," which began to run but a few weeks ago, had taken less than fifteen hours. Ives told me that the first time he came up — and that was less than three years ago — it took twenty-five hours, and Julian Gillespie [Commercial Attaché], who has been in the Embassy for a long time, took, on his first trip to Angora, fifteen days.

A few kilometers out of Angora we passed Mustafa Kemal Pasha's farm.[9] He has built some comfortable-looking buildings and is evidently experimenting with all sorts of vegetables, fruits and grains. Finally, the station. I could picture it from Howland Shaw's [Chief of the Division of Near Eastern Affairs] description. Djelal Shakir Bey, Assistant Director of Protocol, and Shemseddin Bey, a Secretary in the Foreign Office, attired in their London best — silk hats, spats and morning coats — were kind enough to be there and to welcome me to Angora in the name of the Minister for Foreign Affairs. So, en poste at last. If any local color was missing, it was furnished on our short drive to the Embassy, for we passed a peasant driving three superb Angora goats. Ives said they were the best specimens he had ever seen; certainly they are far different from the ordinary variety with their curly white wool — at least it looks like wool — and their long markhor-like horns. . . .

The American Embassy, which has been rented from the Evkaf (the Pious Foundation, now merged with the Government) looks not unlike some of the villas that have been springing up in recent years around Woodley Road in Washington. The little garden surprised even Mrs. Ives, who, I

[9] On June 21, 1934, a law was passed requiring the adoption and use of family names. The National Assembly granted Mustafa Kemal the surname of Atatürk, meaning "First and Foremost Turk." Hereinafter in the footnotes and introductions of these volumes he is referred to as Kemal Atatürk.

gather, had shepherded it into existence, for the entire grounds were covered with grass, some of the trees were doing exceedingly well, and the flowers — marigolds and a lot of others — were blooming. But due to the long dry spell, the water supply has been inadequate for the past six days, necessitating the purchase of water from nearby springs. Anyway, I had a good bath. From the vantage point of our three bedrooms, two baths, living room, balcony, study, salon and three offices, I looked across to the little building which first housed the American Delegation — as it was then called. . . . The stretch of ground between these villas and the railway station used to be a swamp whence come anopheles mosquitoes bearing malaria broadcast. But it has been drained and dried and on its edge stands, in solitary grandeur, the residence of the Director of the Municipal Park. Alas, while the residence and the director may remain, the park has been found impractical because nothing will grow in the salty soil, so it is being cut up and sold in individual building lots.

After a bath and change I drove in a comfortable automobile with Ives and Malik Bey, our interpreter, out through the dusty city to Tchan-Kaya, a greener and fresher suburb where reside the Gazi, Ismet Pasha,[10] Tewfik Rushdi Bey and many members of the Government and of the Assembly, as well as the British, Czechoslovak and Polish diplomatic missions. On the way we passed the immense Russian Embassy and the German Embassy, the latter composed of fourteen separate buildings, still in process of construction. Saw also the residence of Mouhtar Bey, the appointed Turkish Ambassador to the United States. . . .

Tewfik Rushdi Bey, the Minister for Foreign Affairs, had set 5.30 for my call. The Foreign Office is a ramshackle building, dark and dingy and crowded but is soon to move to new quarters. Ives and I were ushered in to the Minister's cubbyhole — one could hardly call it a room — and for the first mo-

[10] In 1934, Atatürk selected the surname of Inonu for his Prime Minister, Ismet Pasha. Ismet Inonu became president of the Turkish Republic after Ataturk's death on November 10, 1938.

ment the surprise of his personality made me wonder if this indeed was Tewfik Rushdi Bey about whom I had heard so much from Admiral Bristol and others. . . .

The Minister greeted me cordially and said that he was glad to receive me as the representative of the United States and especially so as I had signed the Lausanne Treaty; also that he had heard Ismet Pasha speak of me often in complimentary terms and refer to my grasp of all details of the Lausanne Conference.

I replied that I had come to know something about Turkey at the Lausanne Conference; that I had great sympathy and admiration for Ismet Pasha, who had certainly grasped the details of a very complicated conference; that I was deeply interested in Turkey's development during the last few years and that I was particularly happy when the President had appointed me to this post. I then said that I had so often heard Admiral Bristol speak of Tewfik Rushdi Bey that I felt I had known him already.

The Minister appeared pleased at this remark and said that Admiral Bristol had understood the trials and tribulations of Turkey and that it was due to his sympathy and understanding that the situation between the two countries was as it existed today.

I said that Admiral Bristol's work had been fully recognized in the United States and that he had been appointed to one of the most important posts in his own career, Commander of our Asiatic Squadron. . . .

Kemal Aziz Bey [secretary to Tewfik Rushdi Bey] brought in a note which interrupted the conversation, after which I handed to the Minister my note of September 19, requesting that I be informed of the date on which I might present my letter of credence to the President of the Republic and enclosing a copy of the letter of credence from the President of the United States and copy and French translation of my proposed speech. . . .

The Minister then said that he would make every effort to

have me received before the meeting of the People's Party [11] in Angora on October 15 and would inform me several days in advance so that I should have plenty of time to make reservations beforehand. I told him that I proposed to return to Constantinople tonight as there were many things requiring my attention there in connection with settling my family. The Minister said he wanted to have my audience arranged before other waiting Ambassadors so that I should take prior rank. I asked him what other Ambassadors were waiting. He replied that a new Persian Ambassador was coming but could not remember what others. (No announcement has been made in the press of the date of the arrival of the Persian; I know of no other prospective changes.) The Minister said that he wished this priority in view of the fact that Turkey had been deprived of an American Ambassador for such a long time.[12] I referred, in the course of this conversation, to the fact that I had telegraphed to Sheldon Crosby to inquire whether it would be desirable to arrive in Turkey so long before the President's return to Angora; that Mr. Crosby had wired me of his talk with the Minister in which Tewfik Rushdi had expressed the hope that I would come as soon as possible, and that I had then come immediately. I expressed my appreciation of the Minister's cordial message of welcome. . . .

I then inquired whether Mouhtar Bey was in Angora. The Minister replied that he was doing all he could to hasten his departure and that he would leave for the United States before the end of this month. I asked whether I might cable this

11 On December 6, 1922, Atatürk had announced that the Defense of Rights Group, which supported him in the National Assembly, would be extended into a political party to be known as the People's Party. With Atatürk at its head, the People's Party of the Republic was the only existing political party in Turkey in 1927.

12 The last American Ambassador to Turkey had been Abram Elkus who had held his post until April 20, 1917, when the Sublime Porte had broken diplomatic relations with the Government of the United States. After the armistice of Mudros, Lewis Heck had been appointed American Commissioner to Turkey. Almost eight months later on August 12, 1919, Rear Admiral Mark Bristol had become High Commissioner representing all departments of the United States Government.

information to Washington. Tewfik Rushdi replied that he was uncertain as to the sailing but thought a boat was leaving about October 11. He consulted Mr. Ives who was not informed of the sailings of the Fabre Line from Constantinople for New York. (Two members of Mouhtar's future staff in Washington have told Mr. Crosby and Mr. Ives that the Ambassador would not leave before November.) . . .

After my interview with Tewfik Rushdi Bey, I returned with Ives to the Embassy and after changing from silk hat and cutaway back to traveling clothes, I left by the Anatolian Express at 7.30 for Constantinople as there was no purpose in remaining at Angora until my letters of credence have been presented. . . .

Saturday, September 24 [1927]

. . . Djevad Bey [Turkish Minister to Greece] called on me this morning and we renewed our old friendship of former years dating originally from St. Petersburg, where we were both young Secretaries, and later from Berne, where we were both Ministers. In the course of an extensive conversation I said that I had seen an announcement in the press that Djevad might go to Moscow as Ambassador and I inquired whether it would be indiscreet of me to ask whether this were true. Djevad replied that, for the present, no decision had been taken but intimated that he was being considered for the post. He said that he had wanted to go to Washington and would probably have been appointed if the matter could have been left a little longer in abeyance. Admiral Bristol, however, had urged Tewfik Rushdi Bey to expedite the appointment of an Ambassador in view of my own appointment and as Djevad was occupied with other matters at that particular moment it had not been found possible to appoint him. He said that Mouhtar Bey would make a splendid representative. I said that I realized this but was only sorry that he did not speak English and hoped that he would be able to learn it as it seemed to me very important that he should be able to establish personal contacts with businessmen and others throughout the United

States who seldom knew French. I said that Turkey was not always understood in our country by our public, as little had been done to counteract the old impressions of Armenian massacres and the Abdul Hamid regime [1876–1909]. I felt it important that Turkey's recent development and achievements and her program for the future should be made known as clearly as possible to the American people. Djevad Bey said that Bédy Bey, who had been appointed Counselor of Embassy at Washington, would undoubtedly learn English very quickly because he was young and enthusiastic and immensely keen to go to America.

After some further talk about Constantinople, my visit to Angora, etc., Djevad said that he had recently been with the "Gazi" and on the strength of our old friendship he wanted to take the liberty of a frank talk with me. He was good enough to say that I had a very favorable press in Turkey; that the Government and public were pleased with my appointment; that they were delighted to have relations renewed with the United States, and particularly to have me come as the first American ambassador to renew these relations. . . . He said, therefore, that I had a most favorable *terrain* upon which to build; that I enjoyed the sympathy and confidence of the Turkish Government and that, although Admiral Bristol had been dearly loved here, I might count on even greater success. He then said, speaking very frankly, that there were various unfriendly elements among the foreign and American colonies who were likely to stir up trouble and would probably try to enlist my sympathy in their designs. He did not know their names but they were chiefly members of religious societies who were fanatics and intolerant of anything Turkish. As an example, he said that a few months ago, the head of one of these societies had delivered an address at an American college here in which he had characterized everything Turkish as thoroughly bad and had predicted that the present regime could not possibly last. He had told the students that England was their real friend and would support them through thick and thin and that therefore all their sympathies should be with that country. If this had been said by an Englishman, it could have been put down simply as English propaganda but coming from an American it was rather surprising. Djevad said that he himself had two nieces at this college who had heard this address. They had not mentioned it to him but when he inquired they said it was quite true, but had merely laughed at it as a joke. Djevad pointed out, however, that this sort of thing could do great harm and perhaps explained the attitude of the Turkish Government towards some of these societies. I interrupted to say that the account of this address surprised me very much as I could not believe that the President of the college could have tolerated anything of that kind. Djevad said that the President was probably unaware of what was happening.

Djevad then said that Turkey was doing something that had practically never been done before, by attempting to clean her house overnight and undertake developments which generally were the process of years. If he had been told two years ago what Turkey was going to accomplish during this period, he would have laughed at it as impossible and idiotic. The accomplishment had been achieved none the less. They were going ahead so fast that they were sure to make mistakes now and then but there was not the slightest doubt that they would follow the straight road and ultimately arrive at their aim. He spoke at length about their financial situation; how they had balanced their budget; how they were rapidly building railways and making other improvements without having to resort to foreign loans. If Turkey could be left in peace for the next few years, her economic development would surprise the world, but she must count on the sympathy and tolerance of the outside world if she were to do it.

I said that I fully concurred in all that Djevad had said, that I had studied Turkey's recent developments with keenest interest and that my complete sympathy could be counted upon. I said that I was here for two purposes: to support American legitimate interests; and, to develop and strengthen to the uttermost the friendly relations between our two countries. I then said that I greatly appreciated Djevad Bey's friendly talk on the basis of our old personal friendship. He said that he would be entirely at my disposal, should I have occasion to turn to him, during the few weeks of his stay in Constantinople. . . .

Monday, September 26 [1927]

. . . Before closing this batch of diary, which will go out by the pouch on Wednesday, September 28th, provided the courier turns up on time, I mention three present *causes célèbres.*

(1) A few days before our arrival a band of communists were found to have taken a room directly next to the Tokatlian Hotel on the Grande rue de Pera and to have stocked it with bombs and other arms, evidently with a view to assassinating the Gazi on one of his visits to the hotel. The police broke in and were met by a fusillade which killed three of them. The members of the band who were not killed were arrested and an intensive search is now being made for others. They were Armenians, apparently financed from Russia as tracts proving their connection with the Third International were found. I have wondered whether they could have had any connection also with the Armenian societies in New York. They are known as the Altounian Band. The papers have of course suppressed the true nature of their activities and have stated that their purpose was to rob the Yildiz Kiosk Casino which was supposed to have taken in substantial receipts.

(2) The Yildiz Kiosk Casino has been running all summer with baccarat, trente-et-quarante and other gambling tables and has been frequented by High Turkish officials, diplomats and others. Just before our arrival it was raided, its manager, Serra, arrested and all those found there were called to appear in court, including the Counselor of the Persian Embassy and a high official of the Italian Embassy. The alleged reason of the raid was that the Casino had undertaken not to allow Turkish officials to play there and had failed in this undertaking. But Turkish officials have played there regularly and I imagine the Gazi found it inconsistent with his program of reform, a wise decision. It is said that Serra cleaned up $500,000

in the past year but has borrowed heavily on the credit of future receipts and will probably go to the wall financially.

(3) A Turk of influential family fell in love with a Jewish girl and pursued her for several months against her will. Recently he heard that she had become engaged to another man; he met her on the main street just below our Embassy and stabbed her to death. Immediate steps were taken to save him from punishment by declaring him insane and he was sent to an asylum. At the girl's funeral some of the Jews made a demonstration against the judicial authorities and were arrested. Another prominent Jew named Pardo wrote a letter to Ismet Pasha asking for justice against the murderer. Shortly thereafter he was arrested too. The papers were full of it at the time of our arrival. Now Ismet Pasha has published a letter which he wrote to the judicial authorities, saying that he had never seen the original letter from Pardo, which had been dealt with in his office and forwarded direct to the Ministry of Justice, but wished to say that he knew Pardo when he taught French years ago in the army training school and that he was an estimable character and could do no wrong. As a result of this letter Pardo was acquitted at his trial and the other Jews have now been acquitted too. Ismet is given great praise for his fairness and what looked at one moment like stern anti-Jewish measures on the part of the judicial authorities has ended with loud cries of the splendid magnanimity of the Government. But meanwhile the murderer is no nearer trial.[13]

One more word. In this diary I shall doubtless often criticize the Turkish Government, just as I often criticize our own Government at home. Every Government makes mistakes or is guilty of injudicious decisions. On the whole, a new Government, dealing with the immense problems which the Turkish Government faces, endeavoring in a few years to clean her house and effect radical changes and developments which generally have taken other nations generations to accomplish,

[13] Osman Ratib, the murderer, was legally judged insane in April, 1928, and committed to an asylum.

ought to be expected to make more mistakes than a long-established Government. So my criticisms, such as they may be, will be made with this thought always in mind. I have the greatest admiration for what the Turkish Government has already accomplished, the way it has taken hold of an almost insurmountable problem and already, contrary to many predictions, shown itself potentially capable of solving it. In watching the further development of her destiny, my sympathy will be solidly with Turkey in her larger aims, even if particular measures or decisions call forth my impatience or open wrath. An intense nationalism is essential to her success, for with internal forces openly permitted to pull in every direction, I doubt if any country in Turkey's position today could hope to survive. So we must bear with her chauvinistic frame of mind so long as our own reasonable interests are not interfered with, and our criticisms should be tempered, as they will be, with a hearty regard for the larger aims of the Turkish Republic. . . .

Conversation   October 1, 1927
    M. Joseph Wierusz-Kowalski, the Polish Minister to Turkey
    The Polish Minister, Mr. Kowalski, was good enough to call, by appointment without awaiting presentation of my letters to the President, and we had a thoroughly interesting talk. Kowalski was a Russian-Pole and having worked for Polish autonomy, he was obliged to leave Russia and became a professor in the University of Freiburg in Switzerland, where he had spent several years. . . .
    Mr. Kowalski said that he had great sympathy for Ismet Pasha and thought him a very fine type of man and an able administrator. Tewfik Rushdi Bey, he said, was an entirely different type and very pro-Soviet. He said, however, that Tewfik Rushdi was a devoted servant of the President and that the President was far from being pro-Soviet in his sentiments. Having received aid from Soviet Russia during the Greek War, the Gazi naturally felt a certain amount of gratitude to that country and was anxious to live in friendly relations with her but on the distinct understanding that Soviet Russia would

indulge in no propaganda whatever within Turkey. The first signs of communistic propaganda in Turkey had been stamped out ruthlessly by hanging those responsible and it was certain, the Minister said, that no further activity of that kind would be tolerated.

The Minister said that he considered Mustafa Kemal Pasha a really great man with fine sentiments who was accustomed to speak his thoughts in a perfectly straightforward manner and his mind worked in a thoroughly direct way. After the Great War [in 1919] he had been sent to Erzerum to disarm the Turkish troops there but he told the British frankly that, while he had been sent to disarm the troops, he had not the slightest intention of doing so, but would do just the contrary.

Naturally, the President was obliged to be a despot because Turkey could not be compared to democratic countries such as Switzerland and other European countries. The Turks were not yet ready to govern themselves and without despotism the country would fall to pieces. Most of the trouble came from the Minorities in Constantinople. The real Turk was a very fine sort of person. The Minister said that he had recently talked with a Polish engineer who had been building a railroad in the interior and had told him that he found the Turks, in the interior, hard working, patriotic, and devoted to the Gazi and scrupulously honest. He said that one could leave one's money around anywhere in perfect safety as theft was nonexistent.

The Minister said that . . . a knowledge of Russian was very useful here as many officers spoke only Turkish and Russian. The Persian Ambassador spoke Russian. The Minister said that he had recently negotiated a treaty with the Afghanistan Minister in that language. We spoke a little Russian together and it may be useful for me to try to brush mine up.

I told the Minister, before he left, that I should welcome co-operating with him and I hoped that we might, from time to time, exchange information particularly concerning Soviet Russia, to which he heartily agreed. . . .

Angora, Saturday, October 8 [1927]

. . . Angora was not so attractive as the day of my first visit as the air was full of dust. I remained in the Embassy all day, getting unpacked and settled, until 6 o'clock when I went to the Anatolian Club with Ives in order to meet Mouhtar Bey, the appointed Ambassador to the United States, by appointment, on neutral territory. He apparently did not wish to call on me. He is distinguished looking — slightly resembles Alexandre Cretzianu [First Secretary of the Rumanian Legation in Berne], gray-white hair, waxed moustache, well dressed, speaks good French but not a word of English. I found him agreeable but rather stiff — much "Excellence" and "Monsieur l'Ambassadeur." We had tea and talked for half an hour. Ives tells me that he thaws out after the first interview. The talk was general. He appeared to realize that the Lausanne Treaty might not be resubmitted to the Senate and in that case, he said, new conventions would of course be negotiated. He seemed to me reserved but undoubtedly intelligent. . . .

The Foreign Office has requested that three changes be made in the speech which I am to make to the President: two references to my residing near the Turkish Government are to be changed to residing near His Excellency the President and a reference to my hope for the President's "co-operation" is to be altered to "support." They are very protocolaire but I have no objections to the changes and will make them. Also they want me to alter the address on President Coolidge's letter of credence from "Mustafa Kemal Pasha" to "Gazi Mustafa Kemal," a title conferred on him by law. Of course I can't break the great seal of the United States but will make the change on the envelope and they can return the letter for correction after it has been opened by them, if they wish. Naturally I could not alter President Coolidge's letter, but the address is another matter; a man has a right to be called by his correct name.

Sunday, October 9 [1927]

Clear day, lovely colors. We walked up to an old temple on

which the will of Augustus is written on the walls in Latin
and Greek. Also saw the old Roman column, the exact origin
of which is said to be unknown. Almost every old column in the
town has a great stork's nest built on it. The patchwork clothes
of some of the inhabitants of Angora are extraordinarily picturesque, as well as the groups at the few fountains where a
thin stream of water issues, waiting patiently with their big
tin cans for their turn to fill them. The tiles on some of these
fountains are really beautiful. Also the process of shaving on
the public streets is amusing. A man had his entire beard
shaved off by a friend in front of the Embassy today while we
watched the operation from the windows with amusement.
They were equally amused when Ives went out to photograph
them. The little herds of donkeys carrying baskets and generally driven by some bearded patriarch riding on the tiniest
of them so that his feet almost touch the ground cause me no
end of amusement. There is plenty of interest in Angora. . . .
Safvety Zia Bey, Chief of Protocol, called on me after I had
met him in the hall of the Foreign Office. Shevki Bey, the
former Undersecretary, came to tea and stayed long. . . .

Conversation   October 12, 1927

Gazi Mustafa Kemal, President of the Turkish Republic

Safvety Zia Bey, Director-General of Protocol, called for me
at the Embassy at 2.45 P.M., and we drove, in full evening dress,
followed by the staff, in automobiles to the President's house
in Tchan-Kaya. Alighting from the automobiles some distance
from the house, we passed a guard of honor, drawn up at attention, and a brass band, which made a commendable, if not
an entirely effectual, attempt to render the "Star Spangled
Banner." At the entrance of the house we were received by
Tewfik Bey, the President's Secretary, an aide-de-camp, and
other officials.

I was shortly ushered into the President's room and found
him standing in front of his desk, with Tewfik Rushdi Bey on
his right, Safvety Zia Bey, Tewfik Bey, and the aide-de-camp
on the left.

The protocol prescribed three separate bows on entering, at given points. I carried out these directions to the letter, taking my place in the middle of the rug opposite to the President, and then read my speech in English, which Safvety Zia Bey had kindly characterized as a masterpiece. . . . Tewfik Rushdi Bey then translated my speech into Turkish. Afterwards, the President read his own reply in Turkish in a very low voice, as he is apparently suffering from a bad cold. Tewfik Rushdi Bey then translated the President's speech into French.

Having presented my letter of credence, and shaking hands with the President, we entered into informal conversation, he speaking in Turkish, which the Minister for Foreign Affairs interpreted to me, while I replied in French, which the Gazi understood without interpretation.

He first asked me whether I had ever been in Turkey before, to which I replied that I had been here twenty-two years ago for three or four days only, and as a visitor, not officially. The President asked how I came to visit Turkey. I replied that being *en poste* at Cairo I had made a short trip through the Near East to familiarize myself with this part of the world.

The Gazi then asked whether I noticed any change since my former visit. I said that I noticed great changes, great progress and development, and that I was particularly interested in the progress and development of Angora. The President asked my impressions of Angora. I said that, quite apart from its great historical interest the place itself had much charm and beauty and the surroundings reminded me of the western part of our own country, where I had spent some of the happiest days of my life. The President inquired if our house in Angora was satisfactory. I replied that it was very comfortable.

The President then invited me to present my staff, and they were requested by Safvety Zia Bey to enter. I introduced them in turn, Mr. Belin, First Secretary; Mr. Ives, First Secretary; Colonel Smith, Military Attaché; and Mr. Patterson, Second Secretary. The President said a few words to them to the effect that he hoped to see them often, and we then took our leave.

Coffee and cigarettes were served in the adjoining room, while I talked for a moment with Tewfik Bey and other members of the staff, and we then returned to the Embassy, accompanied by Safvety Zia Bey, where champagne was served.

The American flag was hung from the Embassy during the ceremony. . . .

I called on Tewfik Rushdi Bey shortly after the presentation of my letters to the President, and I expressed my thanks to him for having kindly interpreted at the ceremony. The Minister replied that he was glad to welcome me officially as American Ambassador to Turkey. He was good enough to say that an excellent impression had been made on the Gazi, who seemed more pleased than he had ever seen him before, especially by my speech, and the Gazi was not easy to please. I said to the Minister that the President had made a profound impression on me and that I was particularly impressed with the strength and determination of his face. He had the face of a man who could overcome all difficulties in reaching his goal.

I then asked the Minister whether the Ambassadors would be expected to attend the opening of the meeting of the People's Party on Saturday, October 15, to which the Minister replied in the affirmative. I said that I would remain in Angora to attend the opening meeting, but that I expected to return to Constantinople that night, as I had many things to attend to there. The Minister seemed disappointed at this, as he said he wished to give a dinner for me, but did not know whether he could arrange it before Saturday. I said that I expected to return to Angora with my family a day or two before the national holiday, on October 29.[14] The Minister said that that would be very satisfactory, as he would like to include Mrs. Grew in the dinner, and would, therefore, put it off until my return. . . .

After presenting my letters to the Gazi I called by appointment on Ismet Pasha, who received me in the Cabinet room of the Presidency, which is at the same time the Ministry of Finance. Ismet greeted me with great warmth and we sat alone and talked in French without an interpreter. He was good

14 On October 29, 1923, the Turkish Republic had been established.

enough to say that I looked younger than ever, and I said that I could not see that he had aged, although I realized the heavy responsibilities he was carrying. As a matter of fact, I was surprised not to find him more aged; although his hair is a little grayer and he has put on a little weight, he has really not changed much since Lausanne and he has the same pleasant smile and twinkling of the eyes.

Our conversation was of a general nature. Ismet talked about Turkey's endeavors and said she was in the position of the owner of a house in disrepair. He could not rent it until he had repaired it, and owing to very limited funds repairs were going slowly, and meanwhile no rent came in. However, he said that construction was proceeding apace. I referred especially to the building of railroads, in which I knew he was particularly interested.

We talked about the failure of our Treaty in the Senate and I explained that it had lacked only six votes and that a two-thirds majority was necessary under our law. Ismet enquired whether it would be resubmitted to the Senate. I said that would depend upon whether the President should find a changed point of view and believed that the adverse vote could be overcome. We could not tell until the Senate met in December. Ismet said that in any case our relations were well established for the time being. I replied that my Government had greatly appreciated the attitude of the Turkish Government in the matter and that my appointment as Ambassador had resulted.

The talk was very cordial indeed. I think Ismet has grown a good deal deafer since Lausanne, and it is not always certain how much he hears and how much he misses. Before leaving I said that I hoped to be able to have access to him when matters of importance between our two Governments arose, especially as we understood each other so well. . . .

Saturday, October 15 [1927]

. . . The meeting of the People's Party opened in the building of the Grand National Assembly at 10 o'clock. There is only one party in the Assembly. They tried allowing an Opposition, but when the tactics of the Opposition took the form of plotted assassinations and revolution, it was quite naturally not tolerated further. They hanged the leaders in Smyrna and got down to a single Government party. Thus the candidates for the Assembly were chosen by the Government and duly elected, many of them representing districts which they had never seen. Thus the meeting of the People's Party today was largely a meeting of elected Deputies — some 300 of them. The meeting has long been heralded because the President is taking this opportunity of reading his speech of 1200 pages tracing the history of Turkey since 1919. Dramatic revelations are to be made and the achievements of the Turkish Republic brought out in detail. The speech is being translated into French, English, German and Italian and published by a firm in Leipzig.[15] Its reading will, it is estimated, occupy six days, and it will surely be a mighty interesting document.

Ives and I arrived at 9.40, in morning coats and top hats, at the Assembly building and were shown upstairs to the diplomatic box, a small loge accommodating ten chairs, but the second row of chairs was taken out to give more standing room. There were present the Polish Minister, Kowalski; the Czechoslovak Minister, Miloš Kobr; the Afghan, Persian, Bulgarian, Albanian, Hungarian and Swedish Chargés d'Affaires; the Greek Minister, M. Tsamados; Rulli of the Italian Embassy; Robert Hadow of the British Embassy; Lev Kameneff, the Soviet Ambassador in Rome and his wife, to whom I was introduced; and finally came Comrade Souritz, the Soviet Ambassador to Turkey and Dean of the Diplomatic Corps. Safvety Zia Bey, who was chaperoning his flock of diplomats to their seats, told me in a dramatic whisper that he was coming and asked me what he should do. I said, "Introduce me, of course." We were duly introduced, shook hands and I surrendered my

15 See Turkey (1920–) Reisicümhur. 1923– , *A Speech delivered by Ghazi Mustapha Kemal, President of the Turkish Republic* (Leipzig: K. F. Koehler, 1929). The speech was delivered from October 15 to 20, and took thirty-six hours and thirty-three minutes in delivery.

seat on the right of the front row to him as a matter of common courtesy to an older man, moving down two places to make way also for Madame Kameneff who accompanied him — but Kameneff had to stand. Safvety Zia breathed relief at having avoided what he evidently feared might be an "incident."

Promptly at 10 o'clock the Gazi entered amid great applause, took his place in the Chair and opened the meeting.

After his brief opening speech he came down from the Chair and took a seat among the members on the floor, while Ismet Pasha took the Chair and held an election of officers which, as far as I could make out, was by lot. Then Mustafa Kemal ascended the tribune below Ismet Pasha and began to read his long speech. At first his voice sounded weak but it strengthened as he went on; it is high pitched and rather musical; he read well. When he came to quoting documents, he handed them to Rouschen Eshref Bey [Secretary of the National Assembly] to read. There was frequent applause.

About 11.15 there was a short adjournment. We went out in the foyer to smoke; Comrade Souritz joined me and we had a pleasant talk, first in French and then in German in which he seemed to be more at home. I shall avoid seeking him out, or calling him "Monsieur l'Ambassadeur," or leaving cards, or writing notes to him. For the rest, we can meet on a ground of common courtesy. This, at any rate, was Charles Evans Hughes' attitude. The colleagues chatted for a few moments and then the bells rang to resume the session. Just before we went in, Safvety Zia took me in to call on the President of the Assembly, Kiazim Pasha, and we had a short talk which Safvety Zia interpreted as Kiazim speaks no French.

Just as I was going to leave, Safvety Zia appeared and said that the Gazi had invited me to sit in his private box. Poor Mouhtar Bey, who was there, had to be routed out. And then Comrade Souritz also appeared and we sat there together, almost arm in arm, in full view of the entire Congress, the only two Ambassadors present! The situation amused me a lot.[16]

[16] On October 22, 1927, Mr. Grew wrote in his diary that "I spoke of having been invited to the Gazi's private box at the meeting of the People's Party and

Anyway, it left a couple of extra chairs in the diplomatic box for some poor colleagues who had been standing all the morning, and even now it was overcrowded. Good old Mouhtar Bey had scurried around to get me a text of the Gazi's speech; he finally routed out a résumé in Turkish but promised to find a French or German translation before I left. He is really very kindly and helpful, and pleasantly disposed.

The meeting again adjourned for lunch at 12.30 after the Gazi had dramatically shown the members a document which caused tremendous interest, but its purport was not clear, naturally, to me and I shall have to await the translated text. On going downstairs I ran into the Gazi coming up to his office and Ismet Pasha who stopped and greeted me warmly. Also saw and had a word with Rouschen Eshref Bey and Nousret Sadoullah Bey [Deputy in the National Assembly], both of whom were more than cordial. . . .

I left for Constantinople on the Express at 7.20 P.M., several of the colleagues coming down to see me off, which is still a custom in Angora. In the old days, meeting and seeing people off were the big events of the day. Those were the days, too, when most of the diplomats lived in railway cars. There is

of being joined there by Comrade Souritz, the Soviet Ambassador. Ives later discovered the inside story of this from Mouhtar Bey, to whom I had sent my regrets at having disturbed him when he was seated in the Gazi's box. Mouhtar Bey told Ives that he had not minded being disturbed at all and said that in fact it was due to him that I had been invited to occupy a seat in the President's loge. He went on to say with some feeling that he had been greatly annoyed by the action of Comrade Souritz who had made an issue of the seating arrangements . . . and insisted upon being given a seat in the loge occupied by the Turkish diplomatic officers. This attitude was of course wholly absurd; the diplomatic box is set aside for the Diplomatic Corps, and the President has a right to invite anyone he pleases to sit in his own box, whether official or not. However, Souritz' protest was allowed and he was invited to the President's box. I was then just on the point of leaving as I had made my *acte de présence* during the first session, the box was crowded and not understanding Turkish there was no point in remaining further. Several of the colleagues left at that time. But it was feared that it would appear as if Souritz was being given exceptional treatment, which might have been interpreted by those there as the reason for my departure, so I had also been invited to sit in the President's box, and they stopped me just in time! One has to watch one's step here."

still a long line of cars beside the station, all inhabited by families. . . .

Saturday, October 22 [1927]

. . . Now this is not history, but grim present fact. I have discovered, as a result of the washing of the outside of the Embassy, a coat of arms in marble under the apex of the roof over the terrace. The coat of arms is clearly that of the United States — the stars and stripes. But directly across it stands a British Lion rampant and the whole is surmounted by a crown! Ye gods, how did it get there? Was this a witticism of the architect — and why was it never discovered before? And what are we going to do about it? One thing is certain, I shall be mighty careful what American Senators I invite onto our terrace. Only shortsighted ones will be tolerated. For the present we shall have to regard it as a touching symbol of Anglo-American amity and I may suggest to Sir George Clerk [British Ambassador] that he reciprocate by placing an American Eagle — not rampant but screaming — over the Lion and the Unicorn. . . .

Angora, Thursday, October 27 [1927]

Arrived in Angora at 9.48 and were greeted by a brass band and a parade of troops, which Elsie was sure were in my honor but which, in fact, were there to greet Fevzi Pasha, Marshal of Turkey, Chief of Staff and head of the Army. Mouhtar Bey was there to meet us and I introduced him to the family. We drove to the Embassy in the usual whirl of dust and assorted our numerous family and staff as best we could. . . .

I returned the calls of the Egyptian and Hungarian Ministers by appointment and in the afternoon we all, including Anita, went to a tea at the Czechoslovak Legation to celebrate their national holiday. All Angora was there *en bloc,* including Ismet Pasha and Tewfik Rushdi Bey. It was a jam, but Alice and Anita had an opportunity to meet some of the Turks and the colleagues. . . .

Friday, October 28 [1927]

Census Day, at last. The streets deserted — not a soul but a few policemen and soldiers in sight, for nobody, without diplomatic passes, can go out until the guns announce that the census is completed. The papers have contained warnings for many weeks in advance. The effect in Constantinople can best be described by copying the following graphic letter received from Richardson, the Commercial Attaché, who with Crosby, who is ill, remained behind:

I am writing you this letter very informally to give you the account of an eyewitness of yesterday's census-taking. My experience was that of an average foreign citizen in Turkey, for I was in the same position as all other foreigners.

I awoke yesterday morning to an oppressive silence; there was no sound of people on the streets, of automobile horns, or of tramcars, and on looking out of the window I saw armed sailors patrolling the streets. A few daring people stood in their doorways but did not venture to cross their thresholds. I could plainly see the Old Bridge from Galata to Stamboul, which is usually black with people, but this morning was absolutely deserted.

As I was a virtual prisoner in the hotel I proceeded to the writing-room to write letters and to observe what I could. In the middle of the morning the census-taker arrived. He asked to see everybody in the hotel personally, and required that detailed blanks be filled out and passports be exhibited.

After the census-taker's departure, quiet reigned in the hotel. I occasionally looked out of the window, but there was nothing to see as the streets were completely deserted, except for frequent patrols of police and armed sailors that passed the hotel. I do not believe even if I had tried, that I could have gone the short distance to the American Embassy without being stopped by a patrol, as there was constant vigilance during the entire day.

I might remark in passing that all sorts of strange people in the hotel we had never seen before were smoked out of their rooms as the day progressed, and appeared in the halls and dining-room. By six o'clock in the afternoon everybody seemed to be getting very restless. Some of the people standing in the doorways became more adventurous and crossed their thresholds into the streets; but stepped back quickly on the approach of a patrol. I had a talk with a Turkish policeman, who was standing in front of the hotel, and used a Greek-speaking bell-boy as an interpreter. The policeman told me that everything was proceeding quietly without incident and held out hopes that the census would be finished by 10 o'clock. This news I passed on to the inhabitants of the hotel. The only other incident of the long afternoon was that I saw a cup of coffee passed out through a grilled window to one of the patrolling sailors, but on this day an event of this character assumed great importance.

At 10.15 P.M. the guns boomed, to announce that the census was finished and impatient people immediately emerged from every doorway and poured into the streets. I walked at once to the Grande Rue de Pera and within ten minutes the sidewalks were jammed with people, who overflowed into the streets. Taxis dashed through the crowds, moving picture theatres, cafés and restaurants opened, and stores raised their shutters. Within half an hour the whole city was buzzing with life. The populace walked up and down the streets like liberated prisoners. So ended the Turkish census day on October 28, 1927; the population having been imprisoned from 5 A.M. to 10.15 P.M., or 17 hours and 15 minutes. . . .

Saturday, October 29 [1927]

The Turkish National Holiday. At 2 we all went to the Assembly in full uniform (dress suits for us) for the reception by the Gazi and the military review. Alice and Anita were given seats in the diplomatic tribune directly next to that of the Gazi. At 2.30 each diplomatic mission was received separately by the Gazi in order of precedence; I made my little speech of felicitations, presented the staff and then went out to the tribunes where the five Ambassadors sat in a solemn row in the front seats — Souritz, Torikichi Obata [Japanese Ambassador], Emile Daeschner [French Ambassador], Sir George Clerk and myself. Daeschner and Clerk, heavy with gold embroidery and wearing the traditional diplomatic monocles, were decidedly distinguished, the picture being afforded an appropriate framework by the shining dress shirt bosoms of Comrade Souritz and myself. As Daeschner appeared on the scene there were cries of "Vive la France" and then as I followed, sort of as an afterthought somebody said, "Vive l'Amérique aussi."

Having completed his reception of officials, the Gazi walked past our tribune, followed by Ismet and Fevzi Pasha and the Cabinet and took his place, whereupon the parade began. Two or three regiments of infantry, cavalry and artillery filed by — fine-looking young soldiers, weather-beaten and erect — much better looking than the officers I thought, but the horses of the latter were splendid, all doing the goose step (the men not the horses). Then came boy scouts, girl scouts, athletic teams, red crescent detachments and finally representatives of the different trades of Angora — and a hard-looking crowd they were; even the droshkies and taxis were in line. Meanwhile various brass bands took turns in furnishing martial music opposite the reviewing stand, the martial music consisting in one Turkish march which was drilled into our ears until I feared it would never leave me in future. As each new band appeared we were all praying that it would choose another tune, but no such luck; groans went up from the diplomats as each succeeding band swung down the street towards us and we realized that they were playing the same old tune and would continue to play it until relieved by the next. The marine band was really good. . . .

At 8.30, the usual dinner hour in Turkey, we dined, Alice, Anita and I, with Daeschner at the French Embassy with George Filality, the Rumanian Minister and his daughter, the Kowalskis, Polish Minister, the Charles Brugères [Secretary of the French Embassy] . . . etc. The French Embassy was formerly a shop and the Ambassador has very cleverly arranged a combined dining room and salon, decorated with some beautiful tapestries.

And then the Ball. We arrived at about 10.45, were met at the door of the Evkaf Hotel (the ballroom of which had been opened for the occasion and very prettily decorated) by Noury Bey [secretary to Safvety Zia Bey] and escorted to the best table in the place, which Safvety Zia had very kindly reserved for us. They are certainly putting themselves out to be hospitable. The crowd was immense for all Angora was there, the ball being given in aid of the Turk Ojak about which more anon. The music was good and Anita danced steadily all the evening, but Alice and I did not dance. It seemed better not to do so.

The Gazi arrived soon after us and took his place on a dais at the end of the room, surrounded by the high officials. Alice and Anita were taken up and presented before anyone else (am told that Souritz glowered) and had a pleasant talk with him. Later I drew near and found an opportunity to pay my own respects. The Gazi has lost his voice again; the intense work of preparation for his great speech being over, he has again "relaxed." . . .

I met several Turkish officials and had good talk especially with Hamdoullah Soubhi Bey, head of the Turk Ojak, and Jussuf Aktshoura Bey, a Deputy and Professor of International Law. The former used to be Minister of Public Instruction and he told me that he was heartily in favor of our American Schools in Turkey. Also described to me the organization of the Turk Ojak which aims to form groups of young men throughout Turkey for the purpose of cultivating patriotic and nationalistic spirit and intellectual culture. It is essentially a domestic national propaganda organization, inspired by the People's Party, and already is said to include some 60,000 young men as members. I was also introduced to Nedjati Bey, the present Minister of Public Instruction, who will have the decision regarding the reopening of our schools. He barely acknowledged my presence and almost immediately turned away. This may have been (1) because he speaks nothing but Turkish, or (2) because he didn't understand who I was, or (3) because being opposed to all foreign schools in Turkey he didn't want to have any contact with me, or (4) because he was drunk. Judging from events later in the evening, I believe No. 4 may have been the case. . . .

Tuesday, November 1 [1927]

The Third National Assembly opened at 9.30. All the diplomatic chiefs of mission, accompanied by one secretary each, were present, the five Ambassadors (Souritz, Obata, Daeschner, Sir George Clerk and myself) being seated in the two boxes to the right and left of the Gazi's private box which was occupied by Fevzi Pasha (Marshal of the Army) and Mouhtar Bey. The other Ambassadors, Rudolf Nadolny, German, and Luca Orsini-Baroni, Italian, were absent from Angora. Madame Souritz was present with her husband during the morning, while Alice joined me in the afternoon.

The first hour and three quarters were occupied by the taking of the oath by each of the 288 Deputies present (there being 316 in all), who mounted the rostrum in turn and read the oath, pledging themselves to work for the principles of the Republic and for the people. Above the President's chair is a large inscription painted in Turkish saying that "Sovereignty is vested in the People." The oath-taking was interesting as it gave one an opportunity to see each individual deputy and I recognized many friends as they ascended the rostrum.

Then came the election of the officers of the Assembly, resulting in the re-election of Kiazim Pasha as President, Hassan Bey as one of the Vice Presidents and Rouschen Eshref Bey as one of the Secretaries. This will prevent the last-named from membership in the Foreign Affairs Committee, which I rather regret. Following this election came the election of the President of the Republic. Two silver urns were placed on the rostrum and each deputy deposited his vote therein as his name was called by Rouschen Eshref. . . . Then lots were drawn to choose eight tellers from the deputies, a table was placed on the floor and these eight, assisted by Rouschen Eshref, counted the votes. Kiazim Pasha made the startling announcement at 12.45: Gazi Mustafa Kemal had been unanimously elected President of the Turkish Republic for the next four years. Everyone arose and long applause followed.

We hurried home, lunched and changed into full dress for the afternoon ceremony which was to begin at 2. Alice joined me. The newly re-elected President appeared at 2.15, mounted to the Chair, took his oath of office and read his ten-minute speech. He expressed the unlimited thanks which he owed to the Turkish Nation and the Grand National Assembly for electing him President for the second time. He explained how the Republic had risen and developed — how independence, nationalism and victory had brought about the kind of State which Turkey wished to be, during the last four years. The Turkish Nation had been strengthened both internally and externally and it was a pleasure to know that the new Assembly started its work under these conditions. In the protection and interests of the nation, the Republic was always ready for defense as well as for foreign friendship. From the day on which Turkey entrusted her fate to the Grand National Assembly, she did away with darkness and created light and victory. The President trusted that the Third Grand National Assembly would bring about the realization of the progress for which the Turkish Nation was now fitted.

An amusing sidelight on the Gazi's entrance into the Assembly is that Alice, who was dreamily surveying the room and sort of drowsing, clapped most lustily as he ascended the tribune, perhaps instinctively wishing to dispel any impression that she had been dreaming. The next day the semiofficial *Milliyet* announced: "The hearty applause by Mrs. Grew from the Ambassadorial box while the Gazi was entering the Assembly is especially worthy of mention"!

At the conclusion of the presidential address, the Gazi received the Cabinet in the reception room and then the chiefs of diplomatic missions. We formed a circle, the President entered and passed down the line, stopping to receive a short speech of congratulations from each Ambassador, Minister and Chargé d'Affaires. As a rule on such occasions a single speech is made by the Doyen for the entire Diplomatic Corps, but as Comrade Souritz is Doyen and as he is not recognized officially by about a third of those present, he can hardly be said to represent the Diplomatic Corps. Afterwards we all presented our congratulations to Kiazim Pasha as well. . . .

Conversation   November 3, 1927
Tewfik Rushdi Bey, Minister for Foreign Affairs [17]

I called by appointment on Tewfik Rushdi Bey at three-thirty, and after thanking him for the most agreeable dinner which he and Mme. Tewfik Rushdi Bey had given for Mrs. Grew and myself last evening, I expressed my congratulations on his reappointment as Minister for Foreign Affairs. . . .

I then said that, as the Minister was no doubt aware, the American Senate would reconvene on December 6, next. At that time it might be possible to ascertain whether a change in the point of view toward our Lausanne Treaty had occurred and the President might then be in a position to decide whether it would be desirable to resubmit the Treaty or not. I could not venture at the present moment to predict what would be the outcome.

At that time, also, my own nomination as Ambassador to Turkey would be brought up for confirmation, as all nominations for Federal offices must be confirmed by our Senate. I said that there would undoubtedly be some opposition to my appointment on the part of certain Senators who opposed our Treaty, but that the leader of the opposition [James Gerard], while opposed to the Treaty, was a personal friend of mine and had assured me that he would not oppose the confirmation of my appointment, and that he thought there would be no difficulty in putting it through. I did not wish to be withdrawn from Turkey.

I said, however, that at that moment some Senator might say "Where is the Turkish Ambassador to the United States? Our own Ambassador arrived in Turkey in the middle of September, and now, three months later, no Turkish Ambassador has arrived in the United States." Obviously, this might cause an unfavorable reaction and I could not say what the result of such reaction might be. I said to the Minister that when I had arrived in Turkey he had told me that Mouhtar Bey would leave for the United States in a few days, probably before the

17 All talks with Tewfik Rushdi Bey were in French without an interpreter as he spoke that language fluently and accurately.

end of September, and that I had telegraphed this to my Government. The Ambassador's departure was then postponed until November 2, and I had again telegraphed to my Government. Somewhat later, his departure was again postponed until November 22, and I had cabled to my Government a third time. I was now much surprised and somewhat disappointed to learn from Mouhtar Bey himself that he did not expect to be able to sail until towards the middle of December.

The Minister showed distinct and, I believe, sincere concern at what I had said, and he immediately replied that he would instruct Mouhtar Bey to leave for the United States without further delay. He said he would take me into his confidence and tell me frankly the reason for his delay up to this point. It was purely a question of the Ambassador's personal comfort, as certain questions involving his allowance for a house and automobile could not be decided until the new Cabinet had been formed, and the Ambassador had been waiting for this decision. The Minister said that now that the new Cabinet had been formed, the matter could be disposed of very quickly; that Mouhtar Bey could leave at once and that he would be informed of the decision of the Cabinet en route. He thanked me for speaking to him so frankly and said that he fully appreciated the situation. I said I thought it very important that Mouhtar Bey sail by an American ship, as this would create a favorable impression in the United States, and that if he got off by the *Leviathan* on November 22, he could get to Washington in plenty of time before the opening of the Senate on December 6. . . .

The Minister said that so far as the ratification of our Treaty was concerned, it made no difference to him at all whether it were ratified or not. The reason for this attitude was that our Treaty was a little more favorable to us than any Treaty that Turkey had negotiated with any other country, and he intimated that in new negotiations we could not expect equally favorable terms, although the way he put it was "You could not expect to obtain a better treaty later." I said that I believed our Treaty was practically the same as that of the Allied

Powers. The Minister replied that it was more favorable to us than the other Treaties in two or three points, particularly in the consular clauses. I asked what points he had in mind, but he said he could not remember for the moment, although he had examined them previously. He said, in fact, that Turkey had been holding up some of her Treaties with other Powers until this question of the Treaty with the United States was finally settled, as these Powers were demanding the same advantages Turkey had given to us and the Turkish Government did not desire to give these advantages to other powers if they could avoid it. The Minister said that he was now speaking to me very frankly and confidentially, and not so much as Minister for Foreign Affairs as an "amateur des négotiations." He wished to assure me that our Lausanne Treaty was one of the most perfect Treaties which had ever been negotiated; that we had obtained these advantages because our Treaty was one of the first to be negotiated, and that while the Turkish Government was glad to have the Treaty as a symbol of friendship with a Great Power like the United States, and therefore considered its moral effect of great importance, nevertheless, from the technical point of view, they would be just as happy if it were never ratified. This, the Minister said, was the exact attitude of his Government.

I then took up with the Minister the question of the reopening of certain American schools which had been closed since the Great War, and read to him my informal *aide-mémoire* of November 3, supporting the application of the American Board for permission to reopen the schools at Aintab, Sivas and Caesarea, and especially the two schools at Talas and Marash without delay, for which the American staff were already there and waiting. I described to the Minister the various steps taken to obtain permission to reopen these schools, and the fact that, although both the Board of Education and the Foreign Office had expressed no objections, the Minister of Public Instruction had delayed since last March in giving a favorable decision.[18]

[18] The schools at Talas and Marash had been closed during the First World War. On May 1, 1925, the American Board of Commissioners for Foreign Mis-

Tewfik Rushdi Bey said that he was thoroughly familiar with the matter and he had taken the position that it was a subject which did not concern the Foreign Office at all, but lay entirely without the jurisdiction of the Ministry of Public Instruction, so that when consulted, the Foreign Office had merely replied that there was no objection so far as that Ministry was concerned. The question was not one for the Foreign Office to decide. Tewfik Rushdi Bey said that he would take the matter up immediately with Nedjati Bey in the Council of Ministers, which would meet next Wednesday (November 9), and that he would give it his personal support, although, in the last analysis, the matter would remain with Nedjati Bey himself. He said he hoped that at least some of these schools would be reopened, but he was not certain that all of them could be, as there were certain places where it was contrary to the policy of the Government to permit any Foreign schools at all. In any case, he would obtain a definite and concise answer, either in the affirmative or negative, in regard to all of these schools, so that the matter would not be longer left undecided. . . .

Wednesday, November 30 [1927]

Telegram from the Department announcing that Mouhtar Bey had arrived safely in Washington early yesterday morning and that Gerard had come out in the press with a blast to the effect that Mouhtar was responsible for the deaths of 30,000 Armenians and that our resumption of diplomatic relations and exchange of notes with Turkey were unconstitutional. It is at least a relief to know that Mouhtar has arrived in Washington, although if some fanatic Armenian is out to get him, he can probably do it there as easily as in New York. If anything happens to Mouhtar, Gerard will have a lot to answer for, at least to his own conscience. . . .[19]

sions had applied to the Turkish Government to reopen these and other institutions. After diplomatic relations between Turkey and the United States were resumed, another request was filed in March, 1927, to open certain schools. U.S. Department of State, *Papers Relating to the Foreign Relations of the United States, 1927* (Washington: Government Printing Office, 1942), III, 804–12.

[19] The protest lodged against the exchange of ambassadors between Turkey

Tuesday, December 6 [1927]

. . . As regards the Gerard outburst anent Mouhtar Bey's arrival in the United States and the press statements to the effect that Mouhtar was escorted from the *Leviathan* by a squad of armed motorcycle police, the Turkish press has been surprisingly temperate. Although Mouhtar must have arrived in New York on November 28, no comment appeared in the press here, save for the bare announcement of his arrival in Washington, until December 3, because little news reaches the Turkish press except through the European newspapers and these take three or four days to get here. On December 3 full accounts of the incident were published. However no editorial comment appeared until today, December 6, when the *République* carried a temperate article criticizing Turkey for not having taken steps to counteract the Armenian and Greek propaganda in the United States and stating that this propaganda was not in accord with the attitude of the American Government. . . .

Friday, December 9 [1927]

. . . Alice and I, with Mitzi, left for Angora by the express at 7.30. I am going there for three days to maintain contact with the Government and to talk over the Mouhtar-Gerard incident, with a view to assuaging the Turkish press, but shall take up no business of any kind. I don't want them to feel that every time I come to Angora it is for the purpose of asking for something, nor do I want them to feel that I am going to use my position to demand all sorts of rights for American scholastic

and the United States had been accompanied by rumors that plans had been laid to assassinate either Mr. Grew or Mouhtar Bey, or both. Mr. Gerard's attack on Mouhtar, timed to be published on the Ambassador's arrival in New York, had labeled him "the representative of a gang of ruffians who murdered since 1919 over a million Christians and expelled from their ancestral homes over two millions and who now hold in slavery multitudes of women and children." The Department of State took the precaution of having Mouhtar Bey met in New York and escorted to Washington under guard. On December 5, President Coolidge accepted the credentials of the new Ambassador, stating that Mouhtar had the confidence of the American Government and could expect to receive the co-operation of its officials at all times. See the *New York Times*, December 1, 1927, p. 10, and December 6, 1927, p. 28.

and philanthropic institutions in opposition to their own wishes. If they don't want American schools and other institutions, it is not for us to cram them down their throats; the days of the capitulations are over. . . .

Saturday, December 10 [1927]

. . . Tewfik Rushdi Bey received me by appointment at 7 P.M., our conversation lasting until 8. He greeted me cordially and, on my entering his office, sprinkled my hands with eau de cologne as an antiseptic against the cold from which he is suffering. . . .

I then said that I had been disgusted by Mr. Gerard's outburst against Mouhtar Bey on the latter's arrival in the United States and that I regarded the incident as most regrettable. However it must be realized that Gerard in no way represented or spoke for the Government and that, after all, it was the Government's point of view that counted. Mouhtar Bey had been received by the Government with great cordiality.

Tewfik Rushdi said that he cared only for the point of view of the American Government and that this outburst of a minority did not bother him at all. With the great American Government, one of the most powerful in the world, the Turkish Government was going to be friends and nothing could prevent that. The moral effect of this friendship was very great. He developed this theme at considerable length.

I then said that I regretted the publication in the *Milliyet* of the editorial by Yacoub Kadry Bey, not only on account of its disagreeable tone but because it was full of inaccuracies and misstatements. The Lausanne Treaty had not been rejected by our Senate twice as the author averred. I knew of no hostile demonstrations or street attacks against Mouhtar Bey having occurred. Yet this editorial gave the impression that he had been physically attacked and also that no police protection had been afforded. I thought that these false impressions ought to be removed.

Tewfik Rushdi Bey indicated that he entirely agreed with me; that he knew of no actual street demonstrations or physi-

cal attacks against Mouhtar; that he had not seen the editorial
before it was published; and that he would see that this sort
of thing did not happen again and that the misstatements were
corrected.

I then said to the Minister that I thought it would interest
him to see some of the comments of the more important American newspapers on the Mouhtar-Gerard incident and I read to
him extracts from the Philadelphia *Public Ledger*, the New
York *Herald Tribune* and the *New York World*, pointing out
that the last-named paper was a Democratic sheet and anti-Ad-
ministration. The Minister seemed much interested in these
American press comments (which had been cabled me by the
Department at my request) and said he would give them to the
press here, pointing out as a lesson to Turks how well the opposition press behaved in America. This remark amused me
considerably, but I let it pass without comment. I left with
him French translations of the three clippings mentioned
above, making it clear that I was doing so unofficially and on
my own personal initiative and that I did not wish the extracts
to appear in the Turkish press as coming from me. The Minister said that I could count on him never to place me in an
awkward position. I did not read or leave with him the article
from the Baltimore *Sun* as this contained controversial material
concerning Armenia. The first of the articles mentioned above
called the Gerard outburst "pitiably ridiculous"; the other
two said that the Government was entirely within its rights in
renewing diplomatic relations with Turkey. . . .

Friday, December 16 [1927]

. . . The press has taken a somewhat more friendly turn as
regards the Mouhtar-Gerard incident. Articles in the *Vakit*
and *Ikdam* refer to me as "a perfect gentleman" and an old
friend of the Turks, coupled with the intimation that nothing can go wrong while I am here. . . . The usually vitriolic
Agha Oglou Ahmed, writing in the *Milliyet* today, vents his
spleen on our treatment of the Negroes "who are torn to pieces
in the street and then burned," etc., but he acknowledges that

the American press comments (which Tewfik Rushdi Bey evidently turned over to the Turkish press) indicate disgust with Gerard's accusations and regards them as sufficient to satisfy Turkish public opinion. In sending the Turkish press comment to the Department I am saying:

The slurring comments in the Turkish press on American ignorance and fanaticism, the purchase of votes, savage treatment of the Negroes, the alleged burning alive of a German for having been heard to say "Prosit" during the war, et cetera, are to be deplored. They represent the editorial instinct of retaliation for the charges of responsibility for the Armenian massacres and for the injured prestige which is still felt as a result of the refusal of the Senate to ratify the Treaty of Lausanne, no less than the resentment occasioned by Mouhtar Bey's unfortunate reception in New York involving alleged street demonstrations against the Ambassador in that city. It seems probable that these comments were at least tacitly permitted if not actually inspired by the official Press Bureau, because similar international incidents, as for instance the *Aventino* case,[20] involving Italo-Turkish relations were passed over without editorial comment of any kind. I am informed that the publication of the article by Agha Oglou Ahmed Bey, following my conversation with the Minister for Foreign Affairs, was intended to counteract in a measure the caustic observations of his colleague, Yacoub Kadry Bey, although this "counteraction" might have been carried out with better grace.

From different sources I gather that a discussion of the Mouhtar-Gerard incident in the National Assembly is still possible. Tewfik Rushdi Bey intimated in a recent conversation that this might occur but that if statements criticizing the United States should be made, they would not reflect the opinion of, nor would they have been inspired by, the Turkish Administration. No such discussion in the Assembly has taken place up to the date of this despatch.

The general public appears to have taken very little interest

[20] An Italian vessel had rammed a Turkish vessel in Smyrna Harbor, resulting in the loss of Turkish lives.

in the matter and while many questions were asked in official circles in Angora, I believe that no undue importance has been attached by the public at large to the outburst of my erstwhile chief, Mr. Gerard. . . .

Saturday, January 14 [1928]

. . . The banquet for the Minister for Foreign Affairs, returning the one he gave us on our arrival, was an almost complete success. . . .

The dinner was for 8.30. The Tewfik Rushdis appeared at 9.15. We had borrowed a table and kitchen chairs from the local bar — nothing else was available — and managed to get 14 persons into our dining room very nicely. The table looked beautifully with some magnificent roses and violets which Patterson had ordered from Constantinople. He had also ordered caviar, live lobsters and filets and cream. Our Embassy had requested the Italian Ambassador to be good enough to bring up the live lobsters, but he thereupon decided to postpone his arrival by one day, thus missing a wedding in his own Embassy tomorrow morning. I thought he was more courageous. Neither the caviar nor the lobsters — although the latter were deliciously cooked — met with any favor from the Turks who hardly touched them, except Raghib Raif [Political Counselor of the Foreign Office].

As soon as we sat down to table, Tewfik Rushdi began to talk across the table to me in a loud voice, which effectually stopped all other conversation, and spent nearly the entire dinner in developing his political theories. His subordinates and Nousret Sadoullah looked utterly miserable and ashamed, but I was delighted, first because his theories are always interesting and second because it relieved me of the necessity of making kindergarten remarks to the ladies beside me. He began with China. Chiang Kai-shek, he said, was the coming man and would certainly win out. The Communists were practically down and out. Chang Tso-lin would eventually be driven into Manchuria; Chiang Kai-shek would take Peking and then consolidate Nationalist China. He, Tewfik Rushdi, had told him through the Turkish Chargé d'Affaires that he must not think of absorbing Manchuria, Mongolia or Turkestan into Nationalist China as these appendages would prove weakness rather than strength, just as Turkey today would not accept Iraq or Syria if they were given her because they were not populated by Turks. Manchuria was to all intents and purposes Japanese, Mongolia — Russian, Chinese Turkestan — Turkish. The rest of China could be consolidated on a Nationalist basis, just as Turkey had been. Turkey was infinitely stronger today than was the Ottoman Empire. He, Tewfik Rushdi Bey, proposed eventually to accredit his Ambassador in Tokyo to Chiang Kai-shek. Later, in speaking to me alone, he said that he would tell me something in confidence which was known only to the Gazi, Ismet Pasha and himself — namely that Chiang Kai-shek had originally planned to come to Angora with the present Nationalist delegation but had been prevented by the turn of events in China. He always waxes enthusiastic in speaking of Chiang Kai-shek.

Then he turned to Europe and the Balkans. He said: "Today the Balkan Question exists no longer; it has disappeared and has become the Mediterranean Question." The frontier of the Near East has changed; it no longer embraces Persia. The Near East includes the Balkans and Turkey and its frontier is the eastern frontier of Turkey. Persia, Russia, Iraq and Afghanistan compose the Middle East, and everything east of that is the Far East. Turkey is now a western power; the death of a peasant in the Balkans is of more importance to Turkey than the death of a king in Afghanistan. The question of the Straits is settled for all time, because they have been finally opened permanently, but Turkey will always be important to Europe on account of the Straits. A crazy man once suggested that the best way to settle the Straits Question was to fill up the Straits. I remarked that on the basis of the Minister's comments it would perhaps be well to fill up the Mediterranean too. Raghib Raif, who was enjoying his dinner, remarked from the end of the table that this would be highly undesirable because Angora would then get no lobsters. He then attacked his lobster as if it might be the last he would see. . . .

XXVI

Aiding The American Schools in Turkey
JANUARY – SEPTEMBER, 1928

In the old Ottoman Empire there were many foreign schools which had proved to be a powerful factor in influencing the development of the Near East. The system of Capitulations protected the foreign schools from Ottoman interference with their curriculum. Before the wars of 1912–22, in addition to such American institutions as the University at Beirut, the American College for Women and Robert College in Constantinople, and the International College at Smyrna, there were over five hundred American schools ranging from kindergarten to university level with over twenty-five thousand students in the Near East. In the Turkey of Atatürk, however, only a few of these schools of the old Empire remained.

Although no reference to the American and European schools was made in the Lausanne Treaty, Ismet Pasha had pledged in a letter to the Allied delegates that full privileges and immunities would be guaranteed to those schools which existed prior to October 30, 1918. The Nationalist Government did, however, exert close supervision over the foreign schools. Examinations and instructions were subject to inspection, Turkish subjects were made compulsory, and the Turkish staff was appointed to the foreign schools by the Government. Writing in 1926, Arnold J. Toynbee and Kenneth P. Kirkwood observed: "Toleration is shown by the Government so long as no definite religious teaching is carried on, no ideas contrary to the security of the Turkish national state are inculcated, and no subversive doctrines are taught. Where such conditions have been broken, whether advisedly or unintentionally, the Government has taken immediate and drastic steps, and has indi-

754

cated that the terms it lays down for foreign education must be strictly observed in the spirit as well as in the letter. In fact, the foreign institutions have been passing through a very difficult phase." [1]

Throughout Mr. Grew's five years in Turkey, the American schools remained a continuing problem and occupied a considerable amount of the Ambassador's time. The high regard which the American school authorities had for Mr. Grew's efforts is reflected in the following letter written by Fred Field Goodsell, Field Secretary of the Near East Mission of the American Board of Commissioners for Foreign Missions, to Secretary of State Henry L. Stimson on January 25, 1930: "I cannot leave this city without expressing to you my great admiration for our Ambassador, Honorable Joseph C. Grew, who has not only endeared himself to the American community in Turkey but has so ably carried forward the duties of his office. . . .

"Upon every occasion on which I have sought the judgment and counsel of Mr. Grew, he has been most generous and kind and wise. It seems to me that he incarnates the spirit of the finest men in the history of our American diplomatic service."

Sunday, January 22 [1928]

Miss Priscilla Ring [of the Associated Press] came to see me at 4 P.M. with a report that three Moslem girls in the American school at Brusa [2] had been converted to Christianity, that the Turkish authorities were conducting an investigation and that if proselytizing should be proved, the school would be closed. She asked me if I saw any reason why she should not cable the story to the Associated Press, as it had appeared in all the Turkish morning papers. Although realizing that every incident of this kind might have some conceivable effect on the consideration of the confirmation of my nomination in the Senate — as people like Senator King would doubtless make the most of it

[1] Arnold J. Toynbee and Kenneth P. Kirkwood, *Turkey* (London: Ernest Benn, 1926), p. 251.

[2] The school at Brusa, which was under the control of the American Board of Commissioners for Foreign Missions, was a high school for girls with an enrollment of 144 students.

— I raised no objections to the cablegram but suggested that she first consult Goodsell in order to learn his attitude. Her telegram was held up while Miss Ring saw Goodsell who said that he welcomed the investigation because the American Schools were scrupulously obeying the law against religious propaganda and he felt sure that the investigation would show this. He said that some of the girls in the school at Brusa greatly admired Miss Edith Sanderson, one of the teachers, and seeing her happiness and serenity had come to believe that Christianity must be a pretty good thing. Some of the other girls, from motives of jealousy, had stolen their diaries from under their mattresses, and had turned them over to the Turkish educational authorities, who had had them translated into Turkish and sent to the Ministry of Public Instruction in Angora. The investigation had resulted. I cabled the incident to the Department. Miss Ring fortunately included Goodsell's statement in her telegram.[3]

It seems to me highly probable that the school in Brusa will be closed as a result, especially with Nedjati Bey at the helm, as he will no doubt welcome the excuse. An editorial in the *Vakit* refers to the action of the teachers as one of "criminal treason to the Republic." The false rumor was started that the head mistress of this school was also the American Consul at Brusa and the *Vakit* venomously points out that when Consuls or even Ambassadors are guilty of criminal acts they must be punished. . . .

Tuesday, January 31 [1928]

Misfortunes seldom come singly. This has been a bad day. The morning papers reported the intention of the Ministry of Public Instruction to close the American school at Brusa and to prosecute those responsible for religious propaganda, given out in the form of an official communiqué. . . . This incident is only one more step towards the eventual closing of all the mission schools. The important thing now is to keep the colleges free from contamination. . . .

[3] See the *New York Times*, January 23, 1928, p. 5.

Golf with Belin . . . a Turkish cavalry officer appeared and announced that the Government had taken over half of our golf links and had turned it over to the cavalry for maneuvers and that we could play there no longer. The cavalry have steadily maneuvered on the links, even (by choice) on the putting greens. The club has just put a lot of money and work into improving the links and, having properly rented the whole property, had begun to fence it off with barbed wire. No doubt this gesture had enraged the cavalry who apparently got a court decree invalidating the lease. We shall see what can be done, but as the Army is supreme here — as it used to be in Germany — and as they would go out of their way to wreck the innocent sport of any foreigners — particularly a sport introduced by the British Army of Occupation — it looks rather black for the future of the game in Constantinople. The fact that they have boundless miles of open country to maneuver in, in almost every direction, apart from the comparatively limited stretch of the golf links, will probably not be taken into consideration. . . .

Miss Ring called on her return from Brusa and showed me a telegram which she was about to send to the Associated Press on the school incident.[4] In her telegram she made it clear that Christian propaganda had actually been going on in the school and that American opinion here condemned this propaganda as tending to jeopardize other American educational institutions. I suggested one or two changes and advised her to get into touch with Mr. Goodsell, Dr. Henry Schauffler [Acting President of Constantinople Woman's College] and Dr. George Huntington [Vice-President of Robert College] before despatching her message. She said that Miss Sanderson freely acknowledged that she had given informal Christian instruction to some of the girls at their request and Bibles as well, and that she accepted full responsibility for the incident. Miss Ring furthermore told me of an American who reported to her that some time ago he had called at the school and that Miss Sanderson had pointed out to him a group of girls who appeared to be

4 See *ibid.*, February 1, 1928, p. 4.

studying; she said in a triumphant manner that they were actually studying the Bible but that he must keep it quiet. . . .

Thursday, February 2 [1928]

Telegrams from the Department regarding the Brusa school
incident. . . .[5] The Department's attitude about the Brusa incident was considerate: it suggested immediate "official and
friendly contact to control and mitigate the situation" but
added that this was only a suggestion and that it left the han-
dling of the case to my judgment. My feeling is that the moment has not yet come for diplomatic intervention — and
friendly contact would inevitably be interpreted as intervention. The press would certainly know of my visit to Angora
and would assume that it was for the purpose of intervening;
I cannot be sure that in the present high tension Tewfik Rushdi Bey would agree to control the press — and access to Ismet Pasha is difficult and probably unwise just now. Better let
matters take their normal course for the moment. The charges
against the school, whatever we may think of them, have undoubtedly been sustained; our position is weak, and an intense
nationalistic feeling, which is at the bottom of it all, is hard
to cope with. In my opinion, the Government will ultimately
appreciate my having kept out of the row while it was at its
height and for this very reason will be more kindly disposed
when the time for action is ripe than if I had gone off at half
cock. I cabled the Department to this general effect. A nasty
article in the *Milliyet* today. . . .

Sunday, February 5 [1928]

. . . The first gleam of light in the darkness of the press campaign against the American schools appeared today in the shape
of an article by Falih Rifki Bey [Deputy in the National Assembly and journalist] which pointed out that, after all, the foreign

[5] See U.S. Department of State, *Papers Relating to the Foreign Relations of
the United States, 1928* (Washington: Government Printing Office, 1943), III,
964–81, for the correspondence between Mr. Grew and the Department regarding
the Brusa school incident.

schools were needed in Turkey until Turkey's school system should be perfected, and the budget wouldn't permit that as yet. It looks to me as if the word had gone forth from head-quarters that the time had come to let up on the press campaign, for Falih Rifki is in close touch with headquarters. I had expected this at just about this moment. . . .

Conversation   February 7, 1928
His Excellency Tewfik Rushdi Bey
MINISTER FOR FOREIGN AFFAIRS

I called on the Minister, by appointment, at 4.30 P.M., he arriving at the Foreign Office at 4.45. Although I had come to discuss the Brusa school incident, I had intended to take up two or three other cases first and to broach the school situation only incidentally. Tewfik Rushdi Bey, however, broached the subject immediately on his own initiative and said that it had caused him much regret and that he wished to have me know the considerations which had led the Turkish Government to take such drastic measures against the Brusa school. Speaking very confidentially, he said that Brusa is a fanatical community and the principal hotbed of opposition to the Government on religious grounds. They had resented the action of the Government in adopting a secular status and in cutting itself free from all religion.[6] In fact Brusa was the only district which had failed to elect the Government's candidate to the Assembly, but had instead elected its own candidate Noureddin Pasha. In

---

[6] The separation of church and state in Turkey was achieved by a series of laws and decrees, beginning with the laws of 1924 abolishing the Caliphate, suppressing the Seriat and the Ministries of Religious Affairs, and doing away with all Moslem religious schools. The following year the fez was outlawed, monastic orders abolished, convents and monasteries shut, and the number of persons who were permitted to wear Moslem ecclesiastical garb was limited. In 1926, the new civil code, modeled after the Swiss code, radically altered the laws concerning marriage, divorce, and inheritance. On April 10, 1928, the National Assembly finally amended the Constitution, removing the statement that Islam was the religion of the Turkish state. For the other steps taken by the Government in the process of secularization, see Webster, Donald K. *The Turkey of Atatürk* (Philadelphia: The American Academy of Political Science, 1939), pp. 126–29.

view of this situation it was necessary for the Government, merely as a matter of self-defense, to take extreme measures in this case of Christian proselytizing, for public opinion was much incensed and the Government therefore could not afford to overlook the case. The Minister said that when the public excitement had blown over, the American school at Brusa could probably be reopened. . . .

I went over the case in detail with the Minister and pointed out the entirely informal nature of the alleged Christian instruction in the Brusa school which had begun at the instance and request of certain Turkish pupils and that the instruction had been confined to answering their questions entirely outside of the school itself. I then explained to the Minister the unfortunate reaction which the incident was causing in the United States and the harm that could be done to Turco-American relations if the drastic attitude of the Turkish authorities and Turkish press should be permitted to continue. After considerable conversation along these lines, I said that I thought that something should be done to quiet the quite natural anxiety in the United States as to the outcome of the incident and I therefore asked the Minister if he would authorize me to inform my Government:

1. That the Minister would do everything in his power to stop the campaign in the Turkish press against American educational institutions;
2. That the Minister had assured me that the incident was regarded by the Turkish Government as a sporadic one and in no way compromised other American educational institutions in Turkey;
3. That prosecution of the teachers said to be responsible for the alleged Christian propaganda would not be permitted; and
4. That after a reasonable lapse of time, in order to satisfy public opinion, the Turkish Government would examine, with good will, the question of the reopening of the school at Brusa.

I also requested the Minister to authorize the Department of State to communicate these assurances to the American press, if the Department should consider it wise to do so in the interests of Turco-American relations.

The Minister said that he authorized me to communicate to the Department his assurances in the sense of points 1, 2, and 4, and to communicate this assurance to the American press if it should deem it best to do so. As for point 3, the Minister said, with the best will in the world, he could not control the action of the Turkish courts and that the matter would have to follow its normal course in that respect. He said that the Turkish courts were in every respect reliable and fair and would dispense unprejudiced justice. . . . The Minister did not know under what article of the Penal Code the teachers of the Brusa school would be charged, but as this was a first offense, he thought that if any conviction resulted, the penalty would probably not be more than a fine.

On my again urging the desirability of avoiding a trial and limiting the action of the Turkish Government to the already drastic step of closing the school, Tewfik Rushdi Bey suggested that Miss Sanderson might leave Turkey of her own free will as she was not under arrest. I replied that this suggestion surprised me as, in view of the announced intention of the Turkish authorities to prosecute her, her departure would have the appearance of fleeing from justice, and I could not advise her to place herself in such a position; furthermore Miss Sanderson might wish to return to Turkey later, which she presumably could not do if a conviction was standing against her. The Minister said if the penalty were only a fine, she could return to Turkey on paying the fine. I replied that a conviction and penalty, even in her absence, would have an equally unfortunate effect in the United States as if she had been present. Tewfik Rushdi Bey said that he would like to consult the Minister of Justice on this point and would let me know through Mr. Ives what the Minister thought about it. I made it quite clear to Tewfik Rushdi Bey that I could not approve of such procedure on the part of Miss Sanderson and that I did not think that either she or Mr. Goodsell would approve of it.

I then talked at considerable length regarding Mr. Goodsell's attitude towards the strict avoidance by American schools in Turkey of religious propaganda and his desire to carry out the regulations of the Turkish Government in perfect good faith and that the schools had full instructions to this effect. . . .

Before passing on to other subjects, I again urged the Minister to stop the press polemics against American schools which gave the impression to the public that all of our schools were compromised. I said that if a campaign against the schools were started, it would be easy enough to find incidents in almost every school, because there were always disgruntled teachers or pupils who were willing to testify against other teachers or against the schools themselves although their charges were generally without foundation. Tewfik Rushdi Bey said he could assure me again that there was no question of a general campaign against the schools and that he had already taken steps, particularly in Smyrna, to stop the propaganda against them. . . .

Tuesday, February 14 [1928]

. . . The first hearing in the proceedings against Miss Jeannie Jillson, Miss Sanderson and Miss Lucille Day, the teachers at Brusa, took place yesterday afternoon; some of the pupils were heard and an adjournment was then taken until March 5. Goodsell has not yet seen his lawyer but believes the adjournment was a clever move on his part in order to let public opinion quiet down.

The Guedik Pasha school was inspected with great rudeness on the part of the inspectors who made the pupils answer eight questions in writing. Miss Ethel Putney says that the attitude of the inspectors was "nasty." However, she was later called to the office of the inspector and congratulated on the excellent way in which her school is run, so all is well there.

The Merzifoun situation is worse. There the inspectors insisted on hauling down the American flag, which customarily flies together with the Turkish flag, and demanded that all school courses be given on Sundays, with half holidays on Mondays and Thursdays. Goodsell says that the Board will have to go to the bat on the Sunday issue and that if insisted upon, the Board will close all its schools and retire from Turkey. If that happens, I might as well withdraw too because I can't believe that the Senate, under those circumstances, would confirm my nomination. Unfortunately the inspectors found a Bible written in Turkish in the teachers' sitting room at Merzifoun; they said it was not accessible to the pupils, but why should they have a Turkish Bible for American teachers? . . .

Wednesday, February 15 [1928]

. . . On February 10, to my surprise, I received a telegram from Ives in Angora to the effect that the Minister had called him in and had told him that he, Tewfik Rushdi Bey, had gone too far in his interview with me and that the Cabinet would not consider the reopening of that school under any circumstances. He also said that he had documentary evidence against some of the other schools but that the Government would merely file this evidence and would continue to observe a benevolent attitude toward the American schools. On February 12 I had to cable this rectification to the Department, which was particularly distasteful and embarrassing to me as the Department had expressed its "gratification" at the results of my first interview. On February 15 I received a long cablegram from the Department telling me of the unfortunate effect which the incident was having in the United States, particularly in church circles and among women's organizations, and that it was furnishing the best sort of ammunition to the opponents of Turkey.[7] This telegram will be particularly useful

[7] The Department telegram of February 14 stated that the following points had been brought to the attention of the Turkish Ambassador in Washington: "(1) This incident furnishes the best kind of ammunition to Turkey's opponents in this country.

"(2) Trying in a Turkish court on a charge of carrying on Christian propaganda of three American women will do much to convince the American public of Turkey's still being fanatically Moslem.

"(3) This incident possesses tremendous value as news and will deeply impress all church circles and women's organizations.

"(4) Yesterday a Congressman, calling at the Department, showed three teleto me when I go to Angora on the 18th. In spite of Tewfik Rushdi Bey's promise to me to control the press, hostile articles are still appearing almost every day. . . .

Monday, February 20 [1928]

. . . We dined at the Polish Legation with Ennisse Bey and the Polish staff, proceeding to the Tewfik Rushdi ball at about 11. It was a brilliant affair, the Government, Assembly and Diplomatic Corps present. Fortunately the blizzard didn't interfere with the traffic. Last year, at Ismet Pasha's ball, the automobiles couldn't get near the house so that the guests had to walk through the snowdrifts; several ladies had their dancing shoes ruined and some, including Madame Tsamados, fell in the snow and couldn't get there at all.

I had a word with Ismet Pasha about the schools and made an appointment to see him tomorrow. The Gazi came about 12 and moved about, closely accompanied by Sir George and J. W. Collins [correspondent for the London *Times*] who didn't leave his side. The music and dancing were good, the buffet adequate (which in Turkey means a feast) and the champagne above criticism both in quality and amount. There were, I think, at least three separate champagne tables and all were crowded throughout the evening.

Sir George's innings terminated about 2 and mine began, for I then received word through Rouschen Eshref Bey that Mustafa Kemal wanted me to play poker with him. The bridge room, in which Alice, Filality and others were playing, was appropriated and we sat down five in number, the Gazi, two Turkish ladies, myself and, of all people, my dearly beloved Nedjati Bey, Minister of Public Instruction, whose fondness for American schools I may have mentioned in these pages. My dear colleagues looked on in serried rows, wondering, no doubt, why it is that American diplomacy always wins out. The

grams he had received about the trial of the three women missionaries. As these telegrams may well be the forerunner of many such messages, Congressional opinion cannot fail to be influenced by them." *Foreign Relations, 1928,* III, 972.

pack was stripped of all cards below the six, we bought and paid for our chips, and the game, with table stakes, was on; in other words, if you had 500 pounds in front of you, you could bet them all — and frequently did — and were frequently seen. I began with outrageous luck, winning pot after pot. Once when the Gazi had bet 500 pounds and I had raised him 500 and he had seen me, I laid down four tens to his full house. He leaned over and affectionately patted my cheek as he pushed over the pile of chips! After two or three hours I turned my hand over to Alice in order to seek some air. She continued the luck but was so ashamed when she again held four tens to the Gazi's full that she declared only three of them. On my returning, the Gazi said she played an excellent game. Little did he know how good a one. After that, my luck deserted me and I went down, down, down, holding never a hand. The Gazi, who had lost steadily, now began to win. Nedjati Bey, who played conservatively, lost steadily. During the last few hours it was quite clear that the Gazi was intended and expected to win. When I stayed out he always showed me his hand and he was playing a kind of poker not usually seen in the best circles — drawing two cards to a flush, failing to fill but still winning the pot because the others simply dropped. Breakfast was served at 7 or 8 in the morning, composed of tea, cold cheese sandwiches and champagne. In fact, champagne flowed merrily throughout. Alice retired about 5. The Gazi's particular pet, who had gazed at him in adoration throughout the evening, had long since retired to sleep under a fur coat on a couch nearby. At 9 A.M. the Gazi, having won all the money, declared a last round. On the last hand, the betting was in millions only, the bets being announced with great gusto. Rouschen Eshref, who was scorekeeper, then announced the results. Nedjati Bey had lost between 3000 and 4000 pounds, I was down 900. Only the Gazi won. He took a roll of bills from Rouschen Eshref and courteously handed back to each of us our exact losses. Thus a good time was had by all, nobody lost, nobody won — an eminently satisfactory poker party. Taylor and I left the house at 9.15 A.M., poor

Mesdames Tewfik Rushdi and Safvety Zia being still up to say good-night or good-morning or whatever was appropriate under the circumstances. Thus was I initiated into the inner circles of Angora society. Ives wrote me that two nights later the Gazi began a game of poker at the Club at 8 P.M. which continued until 1 P.M. the next day — seventeen hours. Ha, a man after my own heart. . . .

Conversation   February 21, 1928
His Excellency Ismet Pasha, Prime Minister

I called on Ismet Pasha by appointment and went over with him the American school situation. . . . I pointed out that a *beau geste* on the part of the Turkish Government at this moment would doubtless have a favorable effect in the United States and that some such gesture was necessary if the American public was to be convinced that the Turkish Government was holding no brief against the American schools as such but only against religious propaganda. Apart from my hope that the American teachers in Brusa would be acquitted, I said that immediate permission to reopen one or more American schools would undoubtedly be appreciated in the United States but, that if this permission were delayed for several weeks, the psychological effect would be lost. It ought to be done immediately.

Ismet Pasha listened sympathetically and said that after my talk with him last night at the Tewfik Rushdi Bey ball, he had immediately spoken both to Tewfik Rushdi Bey and Nedjati Bey and he thought that at least one school could be reopened but that the Ministry of Public Instruction must study the matter in order to ascertain the place or places where such schools were most needed. I replied that this study might well have been made earlier as the American Board had requested permission four months ago to reopen the schools at Talas and Marash for which staffs were ready and waiting. Ismet Pasha said that he would endeavor to expedite the matter and see that I was informed as soon as possible. . . .

We talked for some time of Turkey's economic developments especially with regard to railway construction which Ismet regarded as of primary importance. I told him of my admiration of all that had been done already.

We then discussed the situation in the Balkans and agreed that this was always the storm center of Europe. He agreed with me that Franco-Italian rivalry was perhaps the most important element of the situation.

Ismet Pasha confirmed to me that Turco-American relations could continue on their present basis until we are ready to negotiate new conventions.

The interview lasted for the better part of an hour and was of a particularly cordial nature.

Sunday, February 26 [1928]

I don't know whether it was my talk with Tewfik Rushdi Bey or my interview with Ismet Pasha or merely my benign smiles on Nedjati Bey across the poker table that did it, but this morning came a telegram from Ives saying that the Ministry of Public Instruction had authorized the reopening of the boys' school at Sivas and the addition of a vocational section to the school at Merzifoun. This is at least the *beau geste* that I asked for. Goodsell, to whom I immediately telephoned, was much gratified, although the American school building at Sivas has been leased to the Ministry of Public Health for five years. Nedjati Bey could hardly have been so puerile as to authorize something that he knew was impossible of fulfilment. I advised Goodsell to go to Angora and straighten this out. In the meantime I sent for Miss Ring and told her, so that we may at least have the advantage of publicity in the United States.[8] I dared not wait for, who knows, the debate on Turco-American relations may take place in the Senate tomorrow or any day. Miss Ring, at my suggestion, went to see Goodsell before drafting her telegram and then showed it to me; it seems admirable. . . .

8 See the *New York Times*, February 27, 1928, p. 2.

Wednesday, February 29 [1928]

The longer one lives in Turkey and deals with the Turks the more one realizes that you cannot judge by their faces nor their actions nor their words what is in their minds. Psychologically it is an interesting study if you can keep your patience and temper while pursuing the study. I have been analyzing my talks with Tewfik Rushdi Bey and this is what I find:

On September 22 he told me that Mouhtar Bey was to leave for Washington before the end of the month or by the first boat in October, although we now know that Mouhtar hadn't the slightest intention, even then, to leave before November.

On December 10 he promised me that he would have the Turkish press publish the complete text of President Coolidge's speech to Mouhtar Bey and also correct the erroneous statements made by Yacoub Kadry Bey concerning Mouhtar's arrival in the United States. Neither of these promises was kept.

On December 10 he told me definitely that Turkey would be represented at the meeting of the Preparatory Disarmament Commission at Geneva on March 15 and would at that time present a definite program. Later, on February 7, when I inquired about this, it developed that his own assistant who has to do with international conferences, Raghib Raif Bey, knew nothing about the matter and said that they had not even received an invitation.

On January 10 he told me that Chiang Kai-shek had greatly admired the work of Gazi Mustafa Kemal and, desiring to emulate his example in China, had sent a delegation of fourteen persons to Angora to study the Turkish system of Government; that this delegation was now at Port Said and would arrive in Angora before long. At the beginning of March nothing whatever concerning this delegation or its coming was known at the Foreign Office. It was said that Chiang Kai-shek had merely sent the Gazi his photograph.

On February 7 he suggested the advisability of Miss Sanderson leaving Turkey before her trial — in other words, fleeing from justice. Nothing could have had a worse effect on the school situation.

On February 7 he promised me to stop immediately the press

campaign against the American schools. It continued practically unabated for another ten days.

Several months ago he said that the reopening of the schools was dependent upon negotiations for the purchase by the Ministry of Public Instruction of some of our school property in Anatolia. I immediately requested an appointment for Goodsell to enter upon these desired negotiations, but no appointment has ever been given.

After our last interview on February 20 when I had asked the Turkish Government to make a *beau geste* by giving immediate permission to reopen one or more schools and so off-set in a measure the Brusa incident, Tewfik Rushdi Bey sent word to me that permission had been given to add a technical section to the school at Merzifoun and to reopen the Boys' School at Sivas. It now appears that the Ministry of Public Instruction had long ago, on its own initiative, *requested* a technical curriculum at Merzifoun, so that this authorization was no concession. As for the school at Sivas, that building has been leased to the Ministry of Public Health for five years, so that the school cannot in any case be reopened before 1930. Yet one of the conditions laid down for opening this school at Sivas is that it should open at the beginning of the next school term, in September 1928.

On the other side of the balance sheet I find the following facts:

When I finally impressed Tewfik Rushdi Bey with the importance of Mouhtar's immediate departure for the United States, he gave Mouhtar definite instructions to that effect within an hour.

He has been surprisingly frank with me regarding the Turkish attitude towards our treaty and on his own initiative he has stated, in concurrence with Ismet Pasha, that we could continue on our present basis until the American Government desired to undertake new negotiations. He granted a year's delay for the evacuation of the Russian refugees,[9] but I have no

---

[9] Refugees from the Soviet regime were ordered to leave Turkey in 1927, but

reason to believe that this decision was influenced by the American donations or by my representations. It was probably decided already.

He took a reasonable view of the Mouhtar Bey incident.

He did eventually quiet the press over the Brusa incident and stopped the provocative inspections, although these may have died a perfectly natural death, having run themselves out.

When he had told me that the Government would examine sympathetically the eventual reopening of the school at Brusa and later found that Nedjati Bey would not support him on that point, he did honestly inform me that he had exceeded his authority. This was an indication of trying to play fair, for there was no need of approaching that bridge until we came to it. The eventual "sympathetic examination" could have merely taken the course of other similar examinations.

My net impression is that Tewfik Rushdi Bey is a great theorist and a great talker, indiscreet, not very well informed of details. . . . Promises and assurances must always be taken with a grain, several grains, of salt. Naturally this causes me embarrassment with the Department: I report his promises and assurances and statements as given — later have to modify or reverse them. In most countries the Minister for Foreign Affairs speaks authoritatively and finally for the Government, unless he makes some reservation before committing himself; this is distinctly not the case with Tewfik Rushdi Bey: he commits himself and the Government and then reverses himself and the Government later or doesn't even bother to rectify his statements. A new kind of diplomacy for me. It is at least an interesting study.

As for the school authorization, I am inclined to believe that this represents Machiavellian tactics on the part of Nedjati Bey. I asked for a *beau geste* to quiet American public opinion. He

---

a year's delay was granted after many representations. The money contributed from the United States and the personal efforts by American citizens toward the facilitation of evacuation led to informal inquiries by Mr. Grew about this situation. See *Foreign Relations, 1928*, III, 981–88.

gave the *beau geste* — a gesture which cost him nothing because it is incapable of fulfilment. The gesture will presumably have had its favorable effect at home and to that extent may have been useful. The Department telegraphed me that the Brusa incident had tremendous news value; therefore this gesture should have news value too. But I haven't the slightest belief that Nedjati Bey intends to permit the reopening of any of our schools at all. . . . Goodsell wants me to make further representations. I will do no more at present. He must go to Angora himself and find out just what the situation is. He will probably go there and fail to get an appointment as last year. Nedjati Bey will stall him off somehow. I see no rosy prospect whatever for the schools. I have done my best and have met almost complete failure. Howland Shaw has been good enough to write that the first four months of my mission have been an unqualified success. Frankly I fail to see how — certainly not as regards our schools. . . .

Friday, March 23 [1928]
    . . . Another scholastic incident, this time in Constantinople College. The *Milliyet* attributed it to Robert College and alleged that a Greek student had torn up a map of Turkey in the face of the Turkish students. What actually happened, as reported to me by Miss Eleanor Burns — Dean at Constantinople Woman's College, is that two little tots of ten years or so, in the preparatory department of Constantinople College, punched holes in a map of Turkey hanging in the study hall and made some derogatory remarks about Turkey, which were promptly reported to the *Milliyet* by some Turkish students. The two guilty ones were Greek and Maltese. Both were immediately expelled. The police came to investigate, but it is hoped that the matter will end there. Expulsion was a pretty drastic punishment for the thoughtless action of two little kids of ten years of age, but it would have been unsafe for the College to have done less, so rampant is the chauvinistic feeling in the country just now. . . .

Good Friday, April 6 [1928]

... I was sitting at my desk when, at 5.15, two telegrams were handed in. The first words to be decoded were "The feelings of the Near Eastern Division are too. . . ." I took a turn around the room, wondering whether the next word was to spell condemnation or acquittal. It came out all right — "exuberant" — and I inwardly blessed good old Howland Shaw for thus breaking the news. Congratulations were proffered all around before proceeding with the telegrams and Betty Carp, who was waiting rather breathlessly at the foot of the stairs was duly enlightened and invited to join the gathering, as well as Anita and Elsie. Alice and Chuffy [Sheldon Crosby] were informed upstairs. Throwing modesty to the winds, I quote the telegrams received:

I am particularly pleased to inform you that the Senate today confirmed your nomination as Ambassador to Turkey. The President and I have appreciated the fine work which you have already done in Turkey under conditions unusually difficult for you personally. Your confirmation having now taken place I look forward with confidence to consolidation and development of American-Turkish relations.

KELLOGG

For the Ambassador from Shaw. The feelings of the Near Eastern Division are too exuberant to describe in a short telegram. We are too happy for words.

Apprends votre nomination approuvée Sénat. Présente avec réjouissance félicitation tout coeur. Hommages Madame Grew.

MOUHTAR. . . .[10]

10 Although Mr. Gerard and The American Committee Opposed to the Lausanne Treaty did not level an attack at the qualifications of Mr. Grew to serve as Ambassador to Turkey, their supporters both in and outside the Senate were able to exercise pressures which held up the confirmation of the appointment for almost eleven months after it had been made on May 19, 1927. The *New York Times* of April 8, 1928, reported that the "tangle over Mr. Grew's confirmation arises out of Senator King's prolonged opposition to the Lausanne treaty, negotiated by Mr. Grew. . . .

"The Grew nomination was approved by the Senate Foreign Relations Com-

Monday, April 30 [1928]

. . . I wired the Department that all three American teachers at Brusa were today convicted and condemned to three days imprisonment and a fine of three liras. The imprisonment to be served in their own residence. Their lawyer has appealed the case. . . . I also wired Patterson [Second Secretary, residing in Angora] as follows:

All three American teachers at Brusa have been convicted and condemned to three days' imprisonment. Of course this announcement will create a most unfortunate impression in the United States and will inevitably stir up renewed anti-Turkish propaganda. If the Minister for Foreign Affairs would now immediately carry out his promise given me on April nineteenth concerning the reopening of some American school other than the school at Sivas, which is impractical owing to the building at Sivas being leased to the Ministry of Public Health until 1930, and would authorize me to make an immediate announcement to the American Government and to the press through Miss Ring, I believe it could be so worded as to show the good will of the Turkish Government and that it would have a quieting influence on the situation. Such an announcement should be immediate to exert its best effect. The reopening of the school at Talas is most desirable.

You may discuss this matter informally with Ennisse Bey —

mittee on Wednesday, after having been held up since the beginning of the present session. Chairman Borah then agreed with Senator King that its consideration should go over until next week so that the Utah Senator might make a further study of the matter.

"When the Senate went into executive session Thursday both Senators Borah and King were absent and as matter of routine the nomination was confirmed. On subsequent protest of the Utah Senator the record of confirmation was kept confidential."

Although Senator Reed submitted a motion calling for reconsideration of the confirmation and Senator King submitted a resolution stating that Mr. Grew's appointment was "subversive of the harmonious relations which should exist between the Executive and legislative departments," the Senate on April 13, 1928, confirmed Mr. Grew's appointment as Ambassador to Turkey for the second time. U.S. Congress, *Congressional Record*, 70th Cong. 1st Sess., vol. LXIX, pt. 6 (Washington: Government Printing Office, 1928), pp. 602ŭ, 6142–43, 6386.

Under Secretary of State for Foreign Affairs — making it clear that you are doing so on your own initiative and not as a diplomatic *démarche* and that the suggestion for immediate action is your own. . . .

Conversation   May 2, 1928

Miss Priscilla Ring, Correspondent of the Associated Press

Miss Ring told me today that after the Judge had handed down the verdict against the teachers at Brusa, he had said to the lawyer that he was particularly sorry to have had to convict and sentence Miss Jillson but that he was obliged to do it. The lawyer's impression was that the Judge had either received direct instructions from Angora or else that he did not dare to place the Ministry of Public Instruction in a wrong position by acquitting any of the teachers. It is significant that Miss Jillson was not convicted on the ground that she had failed to keep in touch with affairs at the school and prevent all religious talks out of hours, but on the ground that she had observed silence before meals and that she had used books not approved by the authorities. Miss Ring thinks that the Court of Appeals at Eskishehr being away from the atmosphere of Brusa and examining the case purely on the merits of the evidence will probably acquit Miss Jillson at least.

Miss Ring said that the Judge had told the teachers that there would be no policeman stationed at the school while they were undergoing their three days imprisonment and that their word of honor to remain within the grounds during the three days would be sufficient. Miss Sanderson is entirely free to leave Turkey if she wishes even before serving her sentence, although, if the Court of Appeals should uphold the sentence and she should later return to Turkey, she would then have to serve the sentence.

Miss Ring said that the people of Brusa were now most friendly to the teachers and that the attitude of the public had changed from one of hostility to one of complete sympathy.

Constantinople, May 8, 1928

To Secretary of State Kellogg

Political sensationalism is the stock-in-trade of the average European diplomatist, for not only is it the element which chiefly lends zest to his profession, but by the very nature of things he must train himself to suspect the worst lest the worst happen and find him off guard. It is therefore not surprising that I find some of my colleagues inclined to ascribe increasing importance and strength to the undercurrent of opposition to the Government of the Turkish Republic which, while not permitted to show its head in print or public speech, is always present beneath the surface. Upon this phase of the political situation, I have the honor to submit to the Department such facts as are patent and such theories as arise therefrom.

First and foremost, the result of the trial of Ihsan Bey unquestionably constitutes a serious blow and loss of prestige to the Government in the person of Ismet Pasha, by whom the prosecution was instigated.[11] The charge of treason was not pressed, only the comparatively minor charges of abuse of power and neglect of duty having been sustained. Instead of being hanged, as was generally predicted at the commencement of the trial, Ihsan Bey received what must be regarded as the purely nominal sentence of two year's imprisonment. Conviction even on this score is said to have been obtained with difficulty, one-third of the Judges dissenting from the verdict which was finally rendered in obvious deference to the wishes of the Government.

The trial of Ihsan Bey, there can be no doubt, was primarily political. He was suspected, whether justly or not, of opposition to the Government. The charge of corruption . . . was largely or purely camouflage to obscure the real basis of the

[11] Ihsan Bey was impeached for signing a contract with a French company to repair the Turkish cruiser *Yavouz*, which had been damaged during the First World War. He had signed the contract without getting the approval of the National Assembly, when he was technically out of office, since the recent elections had made the appointment of a new Cabinet necessary. See the *New York Times,* December 27, 1927, p. 5, and January 29, 1928, III, p. 1.

prosecution. . . . The prosecution of Ali Djenani Bey [former Minister of Commerce] for alleged misuse of the cereals fund was instigated from sources said to be outside of the Government and got out of hand before the Gazi and Ismet Pasha, who are close friends of Ali Djenani Bey and did not desire the prosecution, could stop it.[12] There are no present indications of any intensive campaign against Government corruption and it is therefore hardly to be expected that the labors of the High Court will be progressively extended. As for Ihsan himself, the cheerful grin with which he heard his sentence pronounced was no doubt expressive of a feeling of victory rather than of defeat as a result of his trial.

That the political situation within the Turkish Republic is n. t as rosy as the Government would have the public believe is borne out by various indications, perhaps unimportant in themselves, but tending cumulatively to prove the point:

(1) Official assurances that the eastern vilayets, under the civil administration of Ibrahim Tali Bey [Inspector General], would be open to travel as soon as spring should render the roads passable, have not materialized. These districts are as hermetically sealed as ever.

(2) I am informed indirectly by a Turkish resident of Diarbekir (repeated through Mr. Alexander Waugh, the British Consul General) that when on the arrival of the new Civil Governor of the Eastern Vilayets, a deputation of local civilians was sent to Angora to express allegiance to the Government, they were met on their return by country peasants and sent into Diarbekir with their ears cut off and their noses slit as evidence of protest against the anti-Islamic measures adopted by the Government. The accuracy of this statement is of course open to doubt but the alleged incident is by no means impossible.

(3) I had occasion in January to talk with Mr. James Lyman, an American missionary from Marash, who said that the

---

[12] In May, 1928, Ali Djenani Bey was sentenced to one month in prison and ordered to pay back to the Government 173,000 Turkish pounds not properly accounted for. The prison sentence was suspended.

opposition to the Government, particularly owing to the abolition of the Caliphate, was continually growing and in that
part of the world more noticeable every day. When he had
recently called on the Prefect he had found him with a loaded
revolver on his desk and one in each of the top drawers at
his right and left hand, and the house completely surrounded
by armed guards who had not been present a few weeks previously.

(4) In my talk with Tewfik Rushdi Bey on February 7, he
acknowledged with frankness that the drastic measures adopted
against the American school in Brusa had been taken by the
Government in self-defense owing to the fact that Brusa was
a hotbed of fanaticism and of opposition to the Government.
In other words, local public opinion had to be assuaged and
the opposition deprived of a basis for anti-Government propaganda on religious grounds.

This leads us to a consideration of the recent disestablishment by the Grand National Assembly of Islam as the State
religion of Turkey, a logical sequence to the abolition of the
Caliphate, the Medressehs or ecclesiastical schools, Moslem
Courts, the Dervishes and the Tekkés, and the granting last
year of complete liberty of choice in religion to Turkish majors
by virtue of the adoption of the Swiss civil code. With the
progressive laicization of Law and Justice, the final step of
disestablishment was no doubt inevitable. Yet Islam was Turkey's civilization and, unlike genuinely Western states, such
as France, which have become Republics and have abolished
state religions, Turkey, divorced from Islam, has no inherent
civilization of her own as a basis for her future growth and
culture. All that she can do now is to imitate the West, and
whether she can achieve this imitation as effectively as did
Japan will depend first upon the strength, the wisdom and
the adaptability of her leaders and, secondly, upon the strength
and development of the undercurrent of opposition, based
largely upon religious fanaticism, with which her leaders may
have to cope. On the first point, one cannot blind one's self
to the fact — obvious to all who live in Angora — that the

present leaders are, with few exceptions, such as Fevzi Pasha, an atheistic group of men, some uncultured, some low-living and devoid of moral uprightness, but all imbued with a patriotic fervor for the consolidation and development of their country which may well maintain the material and political if not the spiritual progress of the nation. On the second point, the growth and strength of the opposition, there are differences of opinion which only time can prove to be right or wrong, but certain it is that the casting off of Islam, even more than the heavy taxation under which the people are suffering, has resulted in dissatisfaction among a probably large element of the public, particularly the Anatolian peasantry, which will provide the basis for such opposition as may in future be able to make itself felt.

There are therefore those among my colleagues who regard the Government's situation even now as precarious and who believe that a Cabinet crisis, with the enforced resignation of Ismet Pasha, was seriously threatened and narrowly averted as a result of the fiasco of the trial of Ihsan Bey. This school of thought foresees the crumbling of the edifice with the eventual passing of Gazi Mustafa Kemal who, in its opinion, is alone capable of holding the country together. On the other hand, there are those who minimize the strength and danger of the opposition and who consider that even if the Gazi should now disappear from the scene, Ismet, Fevzi and Kiazim, with the Army solidly at their backs, could and would control the situation as effectively as under the leadership of Mustafa Kemal.

While I share, in this respect, the views of the latter group, I realize clearly that all will depend upon the Army; if the Army chiefs remain faithful, all will be well; if dissension develops among the Generals, it is impossible to predict the outcome. It is said even now that such dissension exists. I shall endeavor to follow the situation as closely as is possible, although, with the muzzling of the press and the uncompromising measures of the Government against subversive speech and activities, even the best informed of my colleagues are more dependent on theory than on facts in gauging the strength and potentiality of the opposition which forms the subject of this despatch.

As regards the Gazi's health, there are no indications whatever that any of the sensational rumors which are continually being spread, doubtless from opposition sources, have any basis in fact. It was recently rumored and reported to me that the Gazi had been operated for the removal of a kidney, the alleged attendant circumstances, including the presence of three doctors, a Turk, an Armenian and a foreigner, being described in detail. Investigation showed that the operation was merely the treatment of an infected facial pimple which had been unsanitarily cut by the Gazi's barber. The Gazi is now leading a healthful life, riding daily, attending to his farm. . . . His group of intimates, who were, throughout winter, generally summoned between 7 and 9 in the evening for all-night gatherings, in which poker and duziko played a prominent part — summonses which not infrequently interfered at the last moment with diplomatic entertainments in the capital, guests being obliged to leave just before or even during dinners when the presidential telephone called them — are now found to be free throughout the evening, with obvious relief at this new found freedom. With Mustafa Kemal's superb constitution, hardened by long warfare and a military life, there seems to be no good reason to believe that he will not live for many years.

In any case, whatever the potentialities of future internal dissension and trouble, it is not surprising that the Turkish Government should be bending every effort to solidify Turkey's friendly relations with her neighbors and that the proposed nonaggression pacts with Italy and Greece,[13] the former

[13] On May 30, 1928, Mussolini and Suad Bey, Turkish representative in Rome, signed a five-year treaty binding both countries to neutrality in case of the conflict of either with a third country, and to arbitration of any disputes which should arise between them. On June 10, 1930, an accord of thirty-three articles was signed by Tewfik Rushdi Bey for Turkey and M. Polychroniadis for Greece. Disagreements over exchange of population, property settlements, and the citizenship of the nationals of one country in the other had long delayed the final agreement. See the *New York Times*, May 31, 1928, p. 8, and June 11, 1930, p. 13.

of which is now reported to be imminent and the latter in definite prospect, will be welcomed as enabling Turkey to concentrate all her efforts in dealing with domestic difficulties and as removing external cares in the event that serious internal trouble should develop. . . .

To Secretary of State Kellogg
Constantinople, May 8, 1928

. . . Looking back at the closing of the Brusa school and the prosecution of the teachers, one may well ask why all this fuss by a Government which was then on the point of complete laicization. Primarily, no doubt, Tewfik Rushdi Bey's frank explanation to me was sincere: the Government was obliged in self-defense to take drastic steps against alleged Christian propaganda in a locality which is well-known for its opposition to the Government on religious grounds — a fanatically Moslem community. Possibly if the incident had happened anywhere else than in Brusa, it might have been hushed up and passed over. But I doubt it. The incident represented to the Turks a matter of more far-reaching significance and importance than the mere interest of a few minor Turkish pupils in Christianity, with the possibility of ultimate conversion. The religious issue was subordinate and in itself of little consequence, but the interpretation of the religious issue as an anti-nationalistic tendency was of serious moment and called forth the Government's drastic action. The real explanation is perhaps best expressed in the three articles in the Turkish magazine *Hayat* of February 2, 9 and 16. . . . Cultural-nationalism was the underlying cause and determining factor. Christianity in itself is of little consequence to an irreligious Government; Christianity — even "unnamed Christianity" — as an educational influence held to be contrary to Turkish culture and Turkish nationalism, and therefore in effect essentially anti-Turkish, is quite a different matter. In the eyes of the Government and indeed of the Turkish people, the mere discussion of Christianity with minor Turkish pupils, even the application of so-called "unnamed Christianity," let alone attempted conversion, is the weaning away of impressionable youth from spiritual allegiance to the Turkish State. "The influence of the foreign school upon the naturally more sensitive and more romantic-spirited young girls," says Mehmed Emin Bey, "is more penetrating. The Sister, looking and talking like a Madonna, and the Miss, acting like Mary and named Mary, are attractive in such degree as easily to capture the soul of the young Turkish girl who is seeking an ideal and is made fancy-loving by her age. . . . The foreign school is a political influence over youth; it teaches history from foreign sources and from foreign view points. . . . In a word these schools are institutions which by their lessons, by their training turn Turkish youth away from the society to which they belong to another society and carry them toward a foreign ideal. . . . Another evil of foreign schools not less important than others is the fact that because of high rates they are institutions exclusively for the children of wealthy and high families. There is nothing so harmful for a democracy as class education. The education of the children of the wealthy classes in a different way from the general public is a sociological error whose result is very dangerous. . . . The educational ideals of some of those who belong to the high class can be turned exactly to these three points: a foreign language, piano, social manners. . . . The outer splendor of the foreign school is also one of the factors which attract parents. Even think of the effect on rich but simple parents of very immaculately dressed, very elegant man or woman teacher. . . . Look at the greatest leaders of the country. Has a single one studied a single hour in a foreign school? . . . Character is very much a matter of nationality. It takes shape only in a national environment. I stress the phrase both the good and the bad. Character cannot be brought in from outside, for it is not an external, a corporeal thing. The foreign school molds a character only according to foreign ideals; as for this character be it in a religious form or in a political form, it is harmful for the national Turkish ideals. . . . Should not the families who are giving their children to foreign schools think that they are by their own hands doing away with the probability that their children may become great Turks in the future?"

In such an issue, according to the Turks, there can be no compromise. Cultural-nationalism. That is quite clearly the underlying basis of the whole matter, reduced to its simplest terms.

An opposite theory which I have heard expressed is that there is a pronounced inclination on the part of those now in power in Turkey to adapt to Turkish uses the methods of instruction and general education which are in vogue in America and Northern Europe. The proponents of this theory believe that the trend towards these forms of instruction has been emphasized by the realization of the importance of Anglo-Saxon and Teutonic commercial enterprise and of Turkey's need of adopting modern methods of commercial instruction for the sake of the economic well-being of the country. It is said that Falih Rifki Bey (whose position as Deputy and journalist enables him to give wide currency to his views), as a result of his visit to Rio de Janeiro last year, has been particularly impressed by the character of American and British commercial enterprise in Brazil, as contrasted with the easy-going methods in vogue among the Latin natives of the country. In short, Turkey, according to this view, is veering from its admiration of Latin culture to emulate the culture of North America and Northwest Europe. Examples are cited in the increased interest in the study of the English language latterly manifested by certain prominent deputies, such as Safvet and Rouschen Eshref Beys. Whether this theory is well founded (as seems not unreasonable in view of Turkey's need for economic development and of the predominance of Anglo-Saxon and Teutonic peoples in that field of expansion) and whether it will have any effect upon the future of Anglo-Saxon schools in Turkey remains to be seen and cannot yet be accurately determined.

While in my opinion Nedjati Bey, the Minister of Public Instruction, a politician of the rougher sort with little culture and little claim to be regarded as an educationalist, is fundamentally opposed to foreign institutions in Turkey, I do not now interpret the Brusa case as a calculated step towards the imminent progressive closing of the foreign schools as a whole. Even Nedjati Bey cannot blind himself to the patent fact that, for the present at least, these schools are needed in Turkey and will be needed for some time to come. While progress is slowly being made in developing the educational system of the country, inadequate funds are available for the establishment of sufficient schools to care for all the nation's youth; trained teachers are inadequate to staff them. . . .

Tuesday, July 3 [1928]

I arose reluctantly from a bed of pain to attend the annual meeting of the missionaries of the Near East, some sixty of them, at the school at Scutari. Goodsell had asked me about ten days ago to come and I had provisionally accepted, but then, on thinking the matter over, it seemed to me that I had done my share by speaking at each of the school commencements and that it was unwise to associate myself too closely with all of their activities, as the Turks would soon come to the conclusion that I was conspiring with the missionaries, would lose confidence in me and would inevitably be less inclined to listen to my future representations in their interests. I felt it was far better for me to remain as much as possible in the background and thus be in a better position to help them when help should be required. I suppose, of course, that Goodsell intended to have me address the meeting as I had done in January, and there was nothing particular that I wanted to say at this juncture. Charles Allen [American Consul at Constantinople] strongly advised against my going; he said that the Turks would undoubtedly have detectives at the meeting and would report everything that I might say. So I asked Miss Carp to telephone to Goodsell that I could not come and that I would explain my point of view to him as soon as he could come to see me when the convention was over. I wanted him to know my position even although I could quite properly have pleaded illness.

Goodsell was furious at Miss Carp's message, said that Admiral Bristol had always attended these annual meetings and explained that all he wanted was for me to meet the missionaries informally at tea. That being the case, I decided to go rather than to engender ill-feeling.

As a matter of fact the tea, which Alice and I attended, was entirely informal and agreeable and I was glad to meet a great many of the missionaries from the interior of whom I had heard, notably Dr. Paul Nilson, Dr. William Nute, Harry Dwight's sister [Adelaide Dwight], etc. Goodsell was perfectly cordial, but I am convinced that unless I had taken the position which I did, he would have had me up before the whole crowd for a speech. He was much gratified at my talk with Tewfik Rushdi Bey concerning Talas. The convention had given one or two sessions to discussing the Brusa incident and had come to the conclusion that the net result of the affair and its influence were favorable rather than the reverse. I am inclined to think they are right.

In reading Oscar Straus' *Under Four Administrations* — published in Boston in 1922 — it is interesting to see that even in his day, back in the nineties (he was three times Minister or Ambassador here), the protection of the missionary schools was the outstanding feature of his work. The Turks closed our schools then just as they do now, and for the same reasons. Cheerful promises, interminable delays he experienced too. Turkish officialdom has not changed, much. . . .

Friday, July 20 [1928]

Just before dinner, Rouschen Eshref was called to the telephone and said that the Gazi had summoned him immediately, so that he could not stay to dinner. Alice and I both told him just what we thought of such arbitrariness, which would not be found in any other country, and that the diplomats were far from pleased with this practice of deputies upsetting dinner arrangements at the last minute. I said that the President of the United States would never expect a guest to break a dinner engagement at short notice.[14] Fortunately we knew Rouschen Eshref well enough to speak frankly and I welcomed the opportunity. He took our remarks perfectly well but said that Turkey was run by a small group of about a dozen men of which he was one, that the Gazi slept most of the day and that he generally desired to begin work in the evening; there was therefore no way of getting out of it when summoned. He thought that in this case the Gazi had something of importance for discussion, probably the adoption of the Latin alphabet.[15] Later he told me that they had dined at the palace at 10, begun work at midnight and left at 5 in the morning. He could perfectly well have dined with us and left immediately after dinner so far as the Gazi's work was concerned. But when the Gazi calls, nobody dares to plead other engagements. That is the crux of the matter. . . .

A friend of Ali Nour Bey's, a deputy, told him that the Gazi is suffering from serious kidney trouble and other ailments and that his health is very bad indeed. I believe that most of these rumors are exaggerated but do not wish to be caught napping if something happens and accordingly felt it

[14] Jay Pierrepont Moffat later commented on this statement in a letter to Mr. Grew. On September 13, 1928, Mr. Grew wrote in his diary: "Safvet and Falih Rifki were both on my black list for having given out of one of our dinners at Angora at the last minute without excuse, but when Pierrepont wrote me that the President of the United States frequently asks guests at the last moment and expects them to break other engagements to come (which I never knew or believed was the case), I decided that my position was unsound and the 'black list' was discarded. The inconvenience of having dinners disrupted at the last moment and sitting down with several vacant seats was annoying but unimportant; the only important question was the prestige of the Embassy and it did not seem to me that this prestige would be helped if the Turks saw us accept such treatment subserviently and without objection. On the other hand, it is certainly not desirable to cut off important contacts for a comparatively trivial matter in which no offense was intended and I am not sorry to see Safvet, Falih Rifki and others restored to favor, although Sir George will say that I have let him down completely."

[15] On November 3, 1928, the National Assembly passed a law which substituted the Latin alphabet for the one then in use. Change from the Turkish script to the Latin alphabet had begun, however, before the passage of this law. On June 26, 1928, a group of specialists on the new alphabet had first met, and the propaganda campaign for the change had begun about six weeks after this meeting. See Webster, op. cit., pp. 130–31.

wise, rather against my will, to send the following further despatch to the Department on this general subject:

As the Department is no doubt aware, there are few cities in the world where rumors and counterrumors are more rife than in Constantinople. This is inevitably the case in a country which muzzles its press, permits no opposition party in its legislative body and sternly suppresses free speech among the people. In this respect the situation in Turkey today is exactly similar to that which existed in many of the belligerent countries during the war; the public is fed through the press in large measure what the central Government wants the public to believe; disagreeable truths are either glossed over or are entirely suppressed; free speech and an articulate opposition are nonexistent. We know by experience the extent to which such a situation stimulates rumor.

Much of the rumor that comes to one's ears in Constantinople is purely idle gossip; some of it contains a modicum of truth; a small part of it is based upon actual fact. To separate the wheat from the chaff is not a simple task, but I believe it is my duty to keep the Department informed from time to time of the general trend of these rumors, for even where it is impossible to confirm them by investigation (as is generally the case), it is a fairly safe axiom that a great deal of smoke does not occur without some fire.

With reference to my despatch of May 8, I have the honor to report that from all accounts the momentarily abstemious life of the Gazi, reported in that despatch, was short-lived. The luxurious palace life in Constantinople cannot be conducive to asceticism. In any case, one now hears from every side that the President is drinking heavily, indulging in duziko all day and occasionally proceeding to a state of complete intoxication by nightfall. His companions are not of a high order for they include such rough minor elements in the political scene as Kilidj Ali, Redjeb Zuhdi, Hassan Djavid Bey and Djevad Abbas. Much of the Gazi's time is spent at Dolma Bagtché Palace where he resides, the daily official press bulletin generally announcing that His Excellency spent the entire day at his desk, engaged upon business of state. Occasionally he takes a trip up the Bosporus in the presidential steam-yacht late in the afternoon, stopping

at the Tokatlian Hotel in Therapia for "tea," but more frequently his visits are to the Beylerbey Palace on the Asiatic shore.
In recently applying for permission for some friends to visit the
Beylerbey Palace, I was informed very politely by the Prefect of
Constantinople that while he would ordinarily be delighted to
comply with my request, he dared not do so now as the Gazi had
a way of dropping in at that palace at odd moments without
warning. In connection with the Gazi's drinking, the recent reappointment of Tewfik Bey as Secretary of the Presidency while
still retaining his position as Ambassador at Moscow, may not
be without significance, as Tewfik Bey is known to be one of
the few people who exercises a steadying influence on the
Gazi. . . .

Monday, July 23 [1928]

Spent the morning at the chancery. There is little work
and few troubles, save the perennial school question. Goodsell
writes me from Marash that an official of the Ministry of Public Instruction at Angora read to him excerpts from an alleged
note from the Foreign Office saying that the "American Ministry of Public Instruction" desired to sell all of its school property in Anatolia and that I had so informed the Foreign Minister. Goodsell asked me if I could throw any light on this.
The only light I can throw on it is that the wish is father to
the thought and that the Turkish officials are trying to put
into my mouth the words which they would like to have me
say. I sent Goodsell the correspondence with Tewfik Rushdi
Bey and Ismet Pasha, so that he might know just what I had
done on behalf of the schools. If there should ever be future
criticism of the Embassy on the part of the missionaries at
home, the record of my conversations will speak for itself. . . .

Thursday, July 26 [1928]

In the morning Anita, Elsie, Mrs. Charles Wylie, Heather
Tompkins and I started to swim the Bosporus from the Selvi
Burnu (Asiatic) side. It was a perfect day but the current was
infinitely stronger than when we did it last year, so that it was
a continuous fight to make headway, especially as we drew near

to the European side. Mrs. Wylie had to quit after an hour
of swimming owing to a luncheon engagement. Anita and
Heather Tompkins finally succeeded, landing just below our
house. Elsie and I stuck together and were in the water, working hard, for an hour and a half but finally were swept below
our house at Yenikeuy and were being steadily carried down
toward the rapids at the point, although we were hardly a
hundred yards from the European shore. I began to appreciate
the feelings of the Channel swimmers who manage to get
within a few hundred yards of their goal and then have to give
up on account of the adverse current. We simply couldn't
fight through it, although Elsie showed splendid pluck, and
we had to give it up, especially when Shakir appeared with
peremptory orders from Alice who was watching us from our
balcony and saw that we were being carried farther away with
every stroke. Anyway, we had plenty of exercise and I had lost
all sensation in hands and feet. Incidentally a big swordfish
came up close beside me and after investigation decided not
to become familiar. However, I felt him nibble my foot. Alice
saw him through the glasses and was quite worried, but after
a few joyous leaps in the air, he departed. The American
Export Lines steamer *Half Moon* passed close to us and Kias-
sim, the sailor on the *Cuff Button,* our little collapsible boat
which was escorting us, waved the American flag. I asked Miss
Maher, who is going home on leave on the *Half Moon,* to tell
the Captain that the gentleman in mid-Bosporus whom he
had almost run down was the American Ambassador. . . .

Friday, August 17 [1928]
    . . . We all lunched at William Taylor's [Second Secretary
of the American Embassy at Constantinople] and then Alice
and I went on the barge to Souadié, beyond Moda on the
Marmora, for the summer games at the Y.M.C.A. camp, a long
run. Moda was gaily decorated and crowded with Turkish
warships and yachts for the annual regatta. I noticed that the
Gazi's large yacht, the *Ertogrul,* had her name newly painted
in Latin letters. The Latin numerals began to appear on the

new tramcars about a month ago. I saw the first Turkish ship with her name in Latin characters pass our house a few days ago. Rouschen Eshref tells me that they have daily classes to study the new alphabet at Dolma Bagtché always attended by the Gazi himself, and Rouschen's committee meets almost daily too. He believes that the change can be effected in from one to two years, much less than originally proposed. The French *Milliyet* is beginning to print Turkish articles with the new lettering, one nearly every day. Every effort is being made to stir up interest; in a recent speech the Gazi said that it was a scandal that about 80 per cent of the Turkish population should be illiterate and that every one must make it a patriotic duty to learn the new alphabet. . . .

Monday, August 20 [1928]

. . . Excellent news came from Goodsell at Talas. The Ministry of Education has finally authorized the reopening of the American school at Talas subject to five conditions which have been accepted by Mr. Nilson. These conditions relate chiefly to the teaching of certain subjects by Turkish teachers (Morals and Civics, Turkish Geography and Turkish, and Turkish Commercial Law); furthermore, the Vice Principal of the school must be a Turk. These conditions seem reasonable. I am very happy for this represents a distinct victory in a long-pending issue; I had a long memorandum ready to give to Tewfik Rushdi Bey this week, reminding him of his thrice repeated promise as yet unfulfilled, which I can now destroy — and, as a matter of fact, it is a great relief not to have to present it. He has come across nobly in his own good time, or Nedjati Bey's own good time, and once again the value of patience ("seldom found in woman and *never* found in man" — as Alice frequently remarks) is exemplified. I may add that slow hammering must accompany the patience. Goodsell kindly ascribes the result largely to my "thoughtful and well-timed efforts." This success, coupled with the still unofficial news of the winning of the appeal of the Brusa teachers at Eskishehr, removes from my mind a load that has sat upon it, like an undigested dinner, for many months. . . .

Saturday, September 8 [1928]

. . . Some of the deputies had criticized the method of applying the new alphabet. The Gazi called a large meeting of some three hundred officials at Dolma Bagtché, made the recalcitrant deputies get up on the platform and explain their criticisms and then sent word to them through Ismet Pasha that they had better come to heel. Thus is opposition stifled at birth and the revised Turkish language drawn up and dictated by one man. . . .

Thursday, September 13 [1928]

. . . To luncheon came Charles de Chambrun — French Ambassador, Safvet Bey, Secretary General of the People's Party, Falih Rifki Bey, General and Madame le Rond, our old friends of Paris whom we hadn't seen for nearly ten years, Princess Murat, Mrs. Jesse Elliott [wife of the American Military Attaché] and Mrs. Ives. . . .

Falih Rifki, who is President of the Committee for the new alphabet, and Safvet, who is in charge of spreading the work through the People's Party, were both full of their subject and both enthusiastic at the progress already made throughout the country. The girls say that in Stamboul they see the lowest types of people studying the primer. We are the first Embassy to use the Latin characters on our automobile tags; as soon as the Gazi's fiat went forth to the country, I promptly gave orders to have all the Embassy tags brightly painted: "U.S.A. –Amerika Sefâreti –359" or whatever the number, and took particular pleasure in pointing them out to Rouschen Eshref so that the Gazi might promptly learn of it. The other day we wrote our first customs declaration in the new letters; when the kavass presented it the customs official merely glanced at it and told him to take it away and come back with a Turkish translation, but on being informed that it *was* in Turkish, he reluctantly accepted it! The greater number of Turkish ships that pass our house on the Bosporus now have their names painted in huge Latin letters, even the shirkets — ferries. This is indeed a progressive country. They waste no time when a decision has once been reached in putting it into effect. The next step will be the adoption of Sunday instead of Friday as the day of rest and I should not be a bit surprised to see it go through at the next session of the Assembly.[16] As Safvet pointed out, it is a tremendous handicap to the financial and economic life of Turkey to have all foreign business cut off on practically three full days in the week, Thursday afternoon, Friday, Saturday afternoon and Sunday. That will be about the final step in the outward westernization of Turkey.

One step only will not be taken: there will be no attempt to transcribe the Koran into the new alphabet. That, I believe, would be a grave danger and, as Safvet remarked, there is no reason for doing it. The religious element in the country has been obliged to stand one shock after another, but to tamper with the Koran would probably be the hardest shock of all. . . .

Thursday, September 20 [1928]

. . . Goodsell and Luther Fowle [Treasurer of the Turkey Mission of the American Board] came to report the results of the retrial of the teachers at Brusa. Ali Haidar spoke for half an hour for the defense, after which the Judge merely asked two or three brief questions and announced that he would give his verdict next Wednesday. Goodsell received the impression that the Judge is a very second-rate man and fears that' he will be guided only by his own prestige rather than by the merits of the case. The Court of Appeals can send a case back for retrial only on points of procedure, but not on the ground that the original verdict was incompatible with the evidence. The grounds for retrial were: (1) the local Court had neglected to provide an official interpreter at every session of the trial; (2) the Court had not given the accused sufficient opportunity to object to the nature of some of the testimony of the witnesses for the prosecution; (3) in rendering its verdict the Court had ignored important arguments for the defense. Goodsell and the other Americans present believe that the Judge is strongly

16 Sunday was made the official weekly holiday on May 27, 1935.

inclined to assume an attitude of self-justification and to hold to his former verdict. The case would then be appealed again and, so far as I can gather, this process could continue *ad infinitum*.[17]

Goodsell is applying officially for permission to reopen the school at Brusa as he thinks it wise to have the application on record. He says that a great many of the parents have expressed to him their desire that the school be reopened as the Turkish lycée for girls, which Nedjati Bey promised to Brusa. He is inclined to doubt if the Cabinet had ever actually considered the matter or ruled that the Brusa school could under no circumstances be reopened, as Tewfik Rushdi Bey told me was the case. . . .

Friday, September 21 [1928]

. . . On my return from leave I expect to spend more time in Angora than heretofore, in order to establish more and closer contacts. Patterson goes to Angora tonight to reopen the Embassy there and to make his own farewells before departing on leave. Ives will go next week. Crosby's plans are to go to Angora with Kippy Tuck — S. Pinkney Tuck [assigned as First Secretary of the American Embassy at Constantinople], (who arrives on October 2) immediately after my departure and to remain there until my return, leaving Ives in charge of the Constantinople office. My intention is to make more of the Angora office during the winter months. Most of the Ambassadors, excepting the British and Japanese, are now coming to it. Crosby's intention to remain there as Chargé d'Affaires is on his own initiative, a good indication. . . .

I have now nearly finished Halidé Edib Hanum's book *The Turkish Ordeal*, of which Howland Shaw sent me an advance copy. It is a thoroughly *ex parte* statement of events from 1918 to 1923 and is excellent publicity for the Nationalist cause and their heroic deeds, painting the crimes of the British, Armenians and Greeks in most lurid colors. I should think that it

[17] On September 26 the Court confirmed its original conviction, and the case was again appealed.

might have a useful effect on American public opinion if it obtains any wide sale, for it dramatically describes the trials and tribulations and the ultimate triumph of the "underdog" with whom the generous-minded American usually sympathizes. . . .

Halidé has been enthusiastically loyal to the Nationalist cause but entirely frank in her uncomplimentary opinion of M.K., cleverly summed up in the last lines of her book:

> All through the ordeal for independence the Turkish people itself has honored Mustafa Kemal Pasha as its symbol. For this reason Mustafa Kemal Pasha will have a pedestal in the heart of every true Turk, even among those who have been irretrievably wronged by him.[18]

Thus is the Gazi "damned with faint praise." Lèse majesté is the unforgivable sin here. Nevertheless I think that Halidé, in her expressed opinion throughout the book, and in her articles in *Asia,* has attributed to the Gazi the very characteristics which have enabled him, and most great men, to accomplish great things. Force, will power, determination, arbitrariness, personal ambition, even ruthlessness, have been the attributes of many national heroes who would never have become national heroes without them. Perhaps Halidé has gone a bit far regarding his private life, but after all it is all true and M.K. is not the only strong man who has had to work off superfluous energy!

Results are what count, and if the G. had been less ruthless and more conciliatory to opposition, the whole show would long since have tumbled like a house of cards. The Nationalists will have to follow their autocratic and ultrachauvinistic policy for some time to come, until the present show has crystallized and a new generation has sprung up, and much as all the deification in the press and elsewhere rubs one the wrong way, it is certain that for this particular people and situation it is the

[18] Halidé Edib, *The Turkish Ordeal* (New York: The Century Co., 1928), p. 407.

only wise course to follow. No doubt the governing personnel has deteriorated from the high point of the "heroic age of nationalism," but I am not convinced that this deterioration is going to be progressively downhill by any means. I am personally optimistic as to the future of the country and shall try to remain in that frame of mind until there is more evidence than at present that reversion to type is inevitable. My job would be far less congenial if I felt that the show were doomed in advance. It is a great adventure and I want to see it succeed. . . .

Angora, Saturday, September 29 [1928]

I referred to the Foreign Minister's repeated promises that an American school should be reopened and explained the present situation regarding the school at Talas: that the Ministry of Education had informed Mr. Nilson that the school could be reopened under certain conditions and that Mr. Nilson had accepted those specific conditions, therefore believing that the matter was settled. On that understanding I had informed my Government of the Turkish permission and had, as the Minister would recollect, expressed my full appreciation at our last interview. But the permit had never come and when a representative of the Embassy had recently inquired of Noureddine Bey of the Ministry of Public Instruction, the latter had replied that the matter was before the Council of Education which was much occupied with the application of the new alphabet and that no action regarding the school could be expected until the alphabet problem was solved. Meanwhile the date for the semester was fast approaching. Tewfik Rushdi immediately telephoned to Nedjati Bey and had a long and apparently a somewhat heated discussion with him in Turkish, in which I caught a reference to Ismet Pasha. At the end of the conversation he said to me that Nedjati Bey had already informed the American Mission that they should get in touch with the Ministry. I replied that the American Mission had been in constant touch with the Ministry and that there was clearly some incomprehensible misunderstanding.

Within a few minutes the telephone rang again and after a short conversation in Turkish, Tewfik Rushdi informed me that Nedjati had called him up to say that he had not been *au courant* of the matter but had now learned of the situation and that the permit would be forthcoming without further delay. The mention of Ismet Pasha's name leads me to believe that it was my previous talk with him that had swung the matter. . . .

XXVII

Treaty Negotiations
1929

Aristide Briand, French Minister for Foreign Affairs, and Secretary of State Frank B. Kellogg negotiated the Pact of Paris pledging the two nations to solve disputes by pacific means and agreeing to renounce war as an instrument of national policy. The United States and France then invited fourteen major nations to join in the signing of the Pact on August 27, 1928. Soon after this signing, other nations of the world were also invited to join the Pact.

As early as April 10, 1928, the Foreign Minister of Turkey had expressed to Mr. Grew Turkey's willingness to adhere to such an international agreement. In a number of meetings thereafter Mr. Grew and the Minister for Foreign Affairs discussed the Pact. On December 12, 1928, Tewfik Rushdi Bey informed Mr. Grew that the Kellogg Pact would be ratified by the Assembly, as soon as it had been ratified by the United States Senate and that the Assembly would act as soon as it had word of the action by the Senate.

Constantinople, Thursday, January 17, 1929

. . . At 5.20 P.M. Jan. 16 the following telegram from the Department was received through Paris: "The Senate today, with only one dissenting vote, gave its advice and consent to the ratification, without reservations or conditions, of the General Pact for the Renunciation of War. Please inform Government to which you are accredited."

I promptly telegraphed the information to the Minister for Foreign Affairs and to Crosby in Angora. It now remains to be seen whether the Minister was sincere in his statement to me that he has everything lined up in the Assembly so that Turkey may be the first country to ratify after the United States. There is a session tomorrow, which accounts for my desire to receive the news officially from the Department as promptly as possible. I do not know how much Mouhtar Bey can be depended upon.

I cabled to the Secretary of State my personal congratulations and later received from him: "Many thanks for your kind message." . . .

Sunday, January 20 [1929]

The Turkish Grand National Assembly yesterday unanimously ratified the Kellogg Pact, Tewfik Rushdi Bey getting out of a sickbed especially to make the speech necessary to put it through and then returning to bed immediately thereafter. It looks as if he did wish to be the first to ratify after the United States and I imagine that he has succeeded. This ought to make a good impression at home and I asked Miss Ring and W. G. Tinckom-Fernandez [correspondent for the *New York Times*] to play it up. I telegraphed the news to the Department. The Department's circular of January 18, noon, through Paris, marked "RUSH, DOUBLE PRIORITY, FLASH," saying that the President had ratified the Treaty, was received here at 10.30 this morning, January 20, 46 hours after sending. Perhaps those stentorian words were used as a result of my message of the 17th, but they did little good as far as we are concerned. However, it made no difference, since the G.N.A. had already ratified without waiting for the President's signature. In telegraphing to the Minister for Foreign Affairs I had used the French words "Le Sénat a ratifié" because to have explained in French that it had merely given its advice and consent would not have been understood at all. Everyone knows that the President must sign the ratification of a treaty before it becomes law and as this, in the present case, was a foregone conclusion, I saw no reason to hold back the action of the G.N.A. by trying to put the formula "advice and consent" into French and thereby clouding the issue in the minds of the Turks. I feel rather proud that this promptness on the part of the

Turkish Government in ratifying the Kellogg Pact may be due, in some small measure, to my various talks with the Minister on the side lines. . . .

In 1830 the United States negotiated a Treaty of Commerce and Navigation with Turkey which was to govern relations in these areas between the two countries for almost the next century. However, the problems arising as an aftermath of the First World War and from the establishment of the Ataturk regime in Turkey made the negotiation of new treaties by the major Powers, including the United States, with Turkey imperative. On August 6, 1923, at Lausanne, Mr. Grew had concluded a Treaty to regulate general relations between the two countries, but this Treaty had been rejected by the Senate in January, 1927.

The equanimity with which the Turkish press received word of the rejection of the Lausanne Treaty reflected the fact that the defeat had not disturbed the Turkish Government. Tewfik Rushdi Bey often told Mr. Grew that relations between the two countries were extremely satisfactory. Milliyet, *a semi-official paper, indicated that the Government was not entirely unhappy with the rejection, because the Turco-American Treaty had given the United States more advantages than any of the Allies had secured.* Vakit *called attention to the lack of ill-feeling among Turkish official circles about the defeat, and* Aksam *credited the action of the Senate to American party politics.*[1]

In February, 1927, a modus vivendi *had been worked out by Admiral Bristol and Tewfik Rushdi Bey, under which normal diplomatic relations, broken during the war, were resumed. Commercial relations were also governed by a* modus vivendi *which had been arranged by Admiral Bristol, and extended by Mr. Grew in May, 1928. This was due to expire on April 10, 1929. In February, 1929, Mr. Grew took up the matter of extending this* modus vivendi *until a time when a*

[1] See Leland James Gordon, *Turkey, 1830–1930; an Economic Interpretation* (Philadelphia: University of Pennsylvania Press, 1932), pp. 211–12.

Treaty of Commerce could be negotiated between the two countries, replacing the Treaty of 1830 which for all practical purposes was inoperative.

Wednesday, February 13 [1929]

. . . Have been burning much midnight oil during the past week to prepare completely for my forthcoming interview with the Minister for Foreign Affairs concerning our commercial relations. No detail must be left to chance. The success or failure of my mission to Turkey may depend upon the result of this interview, and I haven't the slightest idea what the Minister's attitude is going to be. . . .

Angora, Sunday, February 17 [1929]

Had my interview with the Minister for Foreign Affairs at 5, of which the memorandum is appended. It was more successful than I had believed possible. Certainly the impression he conveyed, both by his manner and definite assurances, was that Turkey wishes to leave nothing undone to cultivate the friendship of the United States and to give us the best of everything that Turkey gives to other countries. Naturally there is every reason why he should take this position, but in these days of extreme nationalism and xenophobia one cannot always be certain that the Turkish Government will appreciate where its best interests lie. I believe that we have established a fair basis of confidence which, as Mr. Dwight Morrow [American Ambassador to Mexico, 1927–31] has so well exemplified, is essential before getting results. . . .

Conversation   Angora, February 17, 1929
His Excellency Dr. Tewfik Rushdi Bey, Minister for
Foreign Affairs

MULTILATERAL TREATY FOR THE RENUNCIATION OF WAR

After the usual amenities, I expressed my satisfaction at the prompt way in which Turkey had ratified the Kellogg Pact and I told the Minister also of the appreciation of my Government, of which I had already written him. Tewfik Rushdi Bey asked me what Mr. Kellogg thought of the action of the Soviet Government in making a regional agreement based on the Pact with Poland, Rumania, Estonia, etc. He said that Turkey had been approached first but had declined to join. However, circumstances might lead Turkey to change her mind. I replied that while I had received no direct information in the matter, I was aware that Mr. Kellogg regarded the General Pact as all-embracing, sufficient and effective for all nations and that therefore this regional agreement seemed to me superfluous. . . .

"With regard to our commercial relations, I should like to make the following observations, in order to explain to Your Excellency exactly the point of view of my Government.

"Expiration of Commercial Modus Vivendi

"The commercial *modus vivendi* between Turkey and the United States will expire on April 10, 1929. I understand that according to the provisions of the Law of April 10, 1927, no commercial *modus vivendi* can be extended for more than two years from that date.

"Desirability of Unbroken Commercial Relations

"Your Excellency has been good enough to tell me in previous conversations that the Turkish Government desires no interruption in the present commercial relations between Turkey and the United States, and that a way could be found to tide over any interim until a commercial treaty can be negotiated. His Excellency Ismet Pasha has confirmed this statement to me. The Government of the United States of America shares this view. You informed me that if there were any legal difficulties, you would request the Grand National Assembly to remove these difficulties. . . .

"It is my earnest desire to see the commercial relations between our two countries eventually solidified in a formal Treaty of Commerce. . . .

"To assure equality of treatment for American commerce and for American citizens my Government has adopted a uniform commercial treaty policy with regard to all nations, which is based upon mutual, unconditional most favored nation treatment. We now have commercial agreements with a large number of countries based on this policy. . . ."

THE MINISTER'S REPLY

Tewfik Rushdi Bey, in reply to my foregoing statement, said that he saw not the slightest difficulty in coming to an arrangement satisfactory to the United States. It was, as a matter of fact, out of regard for the United States that he had proposed to negotiate with us among the first of the Nations. He thought that they would begin with Italy and then with us. He did not approve of European sectionalism, and therefore wished to include the United States among the first of the countries with which Turkey would negotiate.

As he saw the matter, he thought that our respective policies were practically identical. The Turkish Government was quite willing to give us unconditional most favored nation treatment under all circumstances, and nothing that might happen could alter this intention. . . .

The Minister thought that we had two tariffs, a conventional tariff and a preferential tariff for bargaining, and seemed surprised when I told him that we had but one single tariff list for all countries. . . . He said, "Who knows, perhaps the Grand National Assembly will adopt a single list in our own tariff." He said that the new Turkish tariff law would undoubtedly be passed before April 10, probably before April 1, and that it would contain an article providing for *modi vivendi* with the various nations until January 1, 1930, which would give ample time for the negotiation and ratification of treaties. These *modi vivendi* would extend up to the end of August on the basis of the old tariff when the Allied commercial convention of Lausanne expires, and after the end of August on the basis of the new tariff. I pointed out that with unconditional most favored nation treatment there would be no alteration in the terms of the *modi vivendi,* no matter what tariff was in effect in Turkey. The Minister assented.

I asked the Minister what he would do to preserve our own commercial relations in case, by any unexpected emergency, the new tariff law should not be passed before April 10. He replied that in that case, which he thought extremely unlikely, he would have a special law passed by the Grand National Assembly which would permit the continuance of our *modus vivendi* for a few months beyond April 10th, until the final law should be passed. I asked if I might inform my Government definitely to this effect. The Minister replied in the affirmative.

In view of the turn taken by the conversation, I thought it best to say nothing at this point about the possible difficulty of getting a treaty ratified by the Senate or of the risk of anti-Turkish agitation in the United States, leaving the matter for further consultation with the Department.[2]

The Minister went on to say that the new Turkish tariff would be a very reasonable one, and in any case infinitely lower than that of the United States, which he thought, with the exception of one other country, had the highest tariff in the world. Turkey would be about halfway up the scale. They were simply putting their tariff back to approximately where it was at the time of the Lausanne treaty. . . .

Wednesday, February 27 [1929]

Pouch day and a busy one. We sent a considerable number of reports which I believe the Department will find of interest and which represent a great deal of work, including despatches on the reliability of the last Turkish census . . . the personal

[2] Secretary of State Kellogg had advised Mr. Grew on December 26, 1928, that while "the opposition in this country to the American-Turkish Treaty of August 6, 1923, which led to its rejection by the Senate has doubtless decreased and will eventually disappear, it is believed that, with a view to avoiding any action that might encourage further anti-Turkish agitation in the United States and thus perhaps compromise the growing sentiments of friendliness toward Turkey, it would be preferable to postpone for the time being the negotiations of a further formal treaty with Turkey. In any event, it would probably not be possible to secure the consent of the Senate to the ratification of a treaty with Turkey until sometime after the expiration of our present commercial *modus vivendi*." *Foreign Relations, 1928*, III, 962.

prestige, private life and habits of the Gazi, comment of Ismail Haki Bey on religious reforms in Turkey, the Latin characters . . . commercial relations between Turkey and the United States, the salaries of Turkish officials, political conditions in Turkey, a thorough post report for Constantinople, present situation of the Russian refugees, etc., etc.

With regard to the salaries of Turkish officials, after quoting figures to indicate their total inadequacy, the despatch continues:

What then has been the result? Members of the American Embassy at Angora, who have had frequent opportunities to talk with American businessmen seeking contracts and concessions in Turkey, are forced to the conviction that a good deal of graft, and a certain amount of corruption, play a part in the lives of a considerable number of Government officials in the capital. An explanation offered for this state of affairs has been that the Turkish Government has found it necessary to employ, in administrative capacities, a number of persons who occupied such positions during the former regime and who inherited its evil traditions. This, however, is not the case. Monsieur Jacquart, the Director-General of Statistics for the Turkish Government, who visited as many as 22 of the principal Vilayets of Turkey in connection with the 1927 census, stated that in only four of the 22 districts visited, did he meet officials who held responsible positions previous to the days of the Republic. It is certain that in Angora there are practically no such officials in office today. An exception may possibly be found amongst the few members of the Republican Diplomatic Service stationed abroad.

The tendency, therefore, to accept bribes is due to the pitifully inadequate salaries which the Government officials of Turkey receive today. On such salaries they can barely live or support their families; and it is perhaps natural that they should seek to supplement their revenues by whatever means present themselves.

The ill results of the underpayment of these officials are apparent in other forms. It has been said that the younger officials find it very difficult to marry on their salaries; furthermore, they are, in many cases, so undernourished that they are incapable of sustained work, mentally or physically. Again, it is said that the classes of educated Turks, from which the Government should be in a position to draw its officials, are unwilling or reluctant to advise their sons to enter the Government service. There is yet another curious mental phase of the situation which shows itself in the difficulties which individuals and corporations encounter in the capital in obtaining pecuniary satisfaction in accordance with the terms of a bona fide contract from the various Governmental Departments. Men who are hopelessly underpaid and yet who have it in their power, by the stroke of a pen, to allocate considerable sums of money to other people, develop a curious dog-in-the-manger inclination to frustrate and hinder — by "red tape" or the invoking of regulations — the normal transaction of business. Cases have been brought to the Embassy's attention in Angora which show this curious attitude very clearly. It is known that on several occasions the refusal by a subordinate employee in the Ministry of Finance to affix his signature to an order, already countersigned by the Minister and Under Secretary, has held up for months the payment of sums which were admittedly due an individual and a firm by the Turkish Government. Furthermore, this state of affairs is by no means restricted to contacts between Ministries and foreign firms and individuals, but is encountered in interdepartmental relations.

The above is a black picture of the situation, but, in all justice, the present state of affairs presents an extremely dark aspect. It is true that when incidents of wholesale graft occur on too large a scale, such as the Ihsan Bey case . . . the Gazi steps in and summary punishment is dealt out to the offenders. There follows a wave of official integrity, which, if encountered by a newcomer, might give the impression that Turkish Government officials are above reproach. When such affairs have blown over, however, the Turkish Government official returns to his hopes of graft. A remark, made very late at night, by a Turkish official, seems to sum up the situation more than adequately. He is reported to have said, "How could we *live* without these kind foreign concession hunters?" . . .

Wednesday, March 6 [1929]

. . . The Court of Cassation yesterday confirmed the sentence of a fine of three liras and confinement for three days on Miss

Sanderson and Miss Day of the American School in Brusa, although both have left Turkey. It is not clear whether the sentence on Miss Jillson has also been confirmed. She has been living in the school ever since it closed, hoping against hope that it might be reopened. If her acquittal can be obtained, I shall make another attempt to get the school reopened, although the reopening of the school at Talas was clearly given us as a *quid pro quo* for the closing of the Brusa school. Brugère tells me that Tewfik Rushdi Bey said to him recently, when he was pressing some issue with regard to the French schools: "Mr. Grew respects our sovereignty and never makes protests with regard to our treatment of the American schools." I laughed and told Brugère that the Minister's memory was short, for I had made the most emphatic protests and representations on behalf of our American schools, time and again, and not without success. However, there is something in the method pursued, as I have carefully avoided making formal representations and have invariably labeled my remarks as "informal" and as an appeal rather than as a demand. It helped the Turks to save their face and brings results far more effectively than pugnacity. . . .

Tuesday, April 2 [1929]

. . . On returning from the dance after midnight, I found a telegram from the Embassy in Angora which gave me great concern. Our arrangements for a new commercial *modus vivendi*, the texts for the exchange of notes and the proposal eventually to negotiate a brief and simple commercial convention, had all been settled and approved both by the Department and by Tewfik Rushdi Bey. There only remained the actual exchange of notes before April 10. Now came a telegram from Malik Bey (Patterson having come down for the visit of the *Raleigh*) [3] saying that the Foreign Office had altered in its note the phrase "pending the conclusion and going into

[3] The U.S.S. *Raleigh* with Vice Admiral John Dayton, commander of American Naval Forces, Europe, aboard, visited in Turkish waters from March 27 until April 4.

effect of a Commercial Convention" to "pending the conclusion and going into effect of a Convention of Commerce and Navigation" and that it desired the same change to be made in our note. At first sight, this looked very much like an eleventh-hour attempt to hold us up on the Commercial Treaty as they had held us up in the Arbitration Treaty [4] in order to kill the Treaty of 1830 for good and all. The Treaty of 1830 was a "Treaty of Commerce and Navigation." That treaty is, of course, dead as a doornail for all practical purposes, but the Senate does not, or did not, wish to think so, and I have interpreted the wish of the Department for a brief and simple Treaty of Commerce, eliminating all controversial questions, to be based upon a desire to negotiate and submit to the Senate no instrument to which it could possibly take exception on the ground that it impaired American rights already possessed through the Treaty of 1830. A new treaty of commerce and navigation would undoubtedly cancel certain old capitulatory rights, the fiction of which the Senate seems desirous of preserving (in alcohol).

I doubted very much if the Minister himself was trying to play a game of duplicity with me, for if this were his intention it would involve a complete breach of faith on his part, after our definite and categorical understanding. But I was not so sure of the experts in the Foreign Office who might readily persuade the Minister to insist on the alteration either to conform to the new law, or else to conform to the notes which were to be exchanged with other Powers, and then, when our negotiations began, to maintain that we were pledged to negotiate a treaty of commerce and of navigation both. There seemed

[4] After the Pact of Paris had been ratified, the United States attempted to negotiate with nations outside the Americas treaties of arbitration and conciliation. In 1928 Mr. Grew made efforts to complete a bilateral arbitration treaty with Turkey, but he soon became involved in difficulties over the interpretation of the phraseology of the proposed treaty. The Turks desired to add to or alter the treaty, so as to make it "impossible for the United States to invoke at any time either treaty in connection with any question pertaining to the Armenians." By May 15, 1949, the United States had negotiated such arbitration treaties with twenty-eight countries, among which Turkey was still not numbered. See *Foreign Relations, 1928*, III, 946, and Samuel Flagg Bemis, *A Diplomatic History of the United States* (3d ed.; New York: Henry Holt & Co., 1950), pp. 721–22.

to me only one thing to do and that was to go immediately to Angora, in spite of the Admiral's farewell dinner and Anita's prospective departure for Berne, in order to have the matter out with the Minister.

I drafted a telegram to the Department, which went off at 2 A.M.,[5] stating that I believed the proposed alteration might be for the purpose of conforming to the text of the new law which I should have before me shortly. But in the morning the text was received from Angora and I found therein no mention of treaties of "Commerce and Navigation." Thereupon I sent another telegram to the Department saying that Gillespie and I both believed the alteration was probably inserted in order to conform to the texts of the notes to be exchanged with other Powers, in order to limit the scope of their forthcoming negotiations to treaties of commerce and navigation only, omitting consular clauses. I added that it didn't seem to me that the inclusion of the new phrase committed us to anything, any more than the allusion in our last *modus vivendi* to "pending the ratification of the Treaty of Lausanne" committed us to ratify that Treaty, and that in view of the Minister's clear understanding with me that we were going to negotiate a brief and simple Treaty of Commerce only, I hoped the Department would not risk jeopardizing our commercial relations by insisting upon the elimination of the new phrase. If an issue should have to be made of the matter, I feared that the experts might persuade the Minister to hold up our new *modus vivendi*. In spite of my recommendations, I greatly feared that the Department would insist upon the elimination of the phrase and that a fight might develop with the Turkish experts (who had doubtless thrown the monkey wrench into our negotiations for a Treaty of Arbitration) which might really knock our new *modus vivendi* on the head. On the other hand, if the Department should regard the new phrase as binding, I certainly did not want to sign something which could later leave

[5] See U.S. Department of State, *Papers Relating to the Foreign Relations of the United States, 1929* (Washington: Government Printing Office, 1944), III, 820.

us open to a charge of bad faith. I was very much worried indeed. . . .

Angora, Thursday, April 4 [1929]

The good old Department came across in fine style. I was greeted soon after our arrival at the capital by a telegram saying that the Department saw no fundamental objection to the alteration in the texts of the notes, but that, if I saw anything to be gained thereby, I might, in my discretion, point out to the Minister the exact nature of our understanding which had been noted by my Government, and that I presumed that the proposed alteration was merely to convenience the Turkish Government. Clearly, the Department saw the disadvantage of making an issue of the matter and agreed with me that the new phrase committed us to nothing, in view of my understanding with the Minister himself. I breathed a sigh of profound relief. . . .

At 4 I had my interview with the Minister. . . . It went smoothly as a marriage bell. I got the Minister orally on record a third time as to our definite understanding and also to the effect that the proposed change in the texts of the notes did not modify that understanding in any way. But I am not at all convinced that the Minister knew what I was talking about; he merely assented to everything I said. I am more than ever inclined to believe that the experts made the change, perhaps entirely without his knowledge. However, that is not our responsibility. If I had pinned the Minister down to eliminate the phrase, he would undoubtedly have consulted his experts, with the risk, to us, of knocking our whole agreement on the head. The matter is now in proper shape and can peacefully rest until our negotiations begin, when, if I am not much mistaken, the experts will submit a provisional draft of a complete treaty of commerce and navigation and will have to be enlightened as to the precise understanding between the Minister and myself. We shall see. It is a hazardous pursuit to deal with a Minister for Foreign Affairs so vague and so lavish in general promises as Tewfik Rushdi. The Department sized him up perfectly in a single phrase — "The well-known propensity of the Minister for Foreign Affairs to promise more than he can deliver." In the meantime, however, we shall have concluded our *modus* and shall have a whole year for any wrangling with the experts, if wrangling there is to be.[6]

All this may have been a tempest in a teapot; I might have spared myself two abominable nights in the train, incidentally catching my first cold of the winter, and the expense of a couple of hundred dollars to the Government in tickets and telegrams over three short words "and of navigation." But I still think the issue was too important to ignore.

I left on the Conventional, there being no vacant places on the Express, at 7.30. . . .

Tuesday, April 9 [1929]

Was greeted in the morning by Patterson's telegrams announcing that he had exchanged our notes for the new commercial *modus vivendi* yesterday afternoon at 4.15 with Fuat Simavi Bey, Chief of the Commercial Section of the Foreign Office, and that instructions would immediately be telegraphed to the customs authorities throughout Turkey. Just as I was giving vent to my sighs of profound relief and relishing the good news (for one is always anxious in this country until an agreement is signed and sealed), the text of Tewfik Rushdi Bey's note arrived by mail, together with a letter from Patterson pointing out that several alterations had been made in the text at the last moment, quite contrary to the Minister's understanding with me, but that as the changes had appeared to Patterson to be mere details of phraseology and to make no material difference in meaning, he had gone ahead with the exchange, while orally observing to Simavi that the text of the note was not what I had agreed to. After examining these alterations, I agree with Patterson that they are not material and I approve of his action in not holding up the *modus*. I only

6 The exchange of notes of April 8, 1929, had extended the commercial *modus vivendi* between the United States and Turkey for one year from the date of April 11, 1929. *Ibid.*, p. 820.

hope that the Department will be able to concur. . . . Probably
much of the trouble that we encounter in this respect is due to
the lack of adequate contact between the Minister and his experts; they seem to be in awe of him and to have the greatest
disinclination to seek access to him. He, on the other hand,
seems to leave all details to his experts, and I don't believe that
half the time he gives them any definite indication of his oral
undertakings with foreign representatives. I doubt if he was
even aware, when he signed the note, that these changes had
been made, or, if aware of them, that he realized what an un-
statesmanlike trick he was playing in foisting them upon me at
the last moment before our *modus* expires. Perhaps I am too
optimistic about his intentions; perhaps he is really Machiavellian or considers himself a wily poker player. Someday I shall
probably find out. But for the present I believe him to be
merely a vague and voluble but well-meaning theorist to whom
details and precision mean nothing. His experts, on the other
hand, would no doubt be capable of any maneuver which they
thought would bring some advantage. Nothing can be done
now until the Minister's return from Geneva, but if the Department is unwilling to accept the changes of phraseology . . .
I shall make the first big row with Tewfik Rushdi since my arrival in Turkey. . . .[7]

Wednesday, June 19 — Wednesday, July 3 [1929]

. . . The press reports that General Charles G. Dawes [Ameri-
can Ambassador to Great Britain] not only refused to wear
knee-breeches to Court in London but has stated that the Embassy will henceforth be dry as he sees no reason to alter his
American habits when coming abroad. It doesn't seem to occur
to him that when foreigners come to the United States we like
them to conform to our own customs and that such a thing as
international courtesy exists. Canuti, Reuter's correspondent,

---

[7] The Department of State agreed that the alterations were not serious and
stated: "The Department fully appreciates the difficulties which attended the
negotiations preceding the present exchange of notes and has noted with satisfaction the skillful manner in which this matter was handled." *Ibid.*

temporarily representing Miss Ring during her absence, received an order from the Associated Press in London to ascertain whether this Embassy was going dry likewise. I replied in French, as he knows no English, "L'Ambassade Américaine en Turquie n'a pas encore envisagé la question de régime." I thought it unwise to refuse to reply and still more unwise to say that the Embassy was under the instructions of its Government, because that would probably have resulted in some correspondent saying to the Secretary of State, "How about it?" with particular reference to my answer. I should like to have talked for half an hour on the subject and to have told the correspondent just why this Embassy hadn't the slightest intention of going dry, but discretion is the better part of valor.

If public opinion ever forces our Government to take the matter up, I hope it will at least consider the Finnish compromise which provides that its Legations abroad may serve drinks on "international occasions" only — that is, when any foreigner is present. Nadolny told me that his Finnish colleague in Stockholm loved his drinks and served them perpetually on the ground that his household was perpetually international, he having married a Swedish wife. . . .

Wednesday, July 3 — Wednesday, July 17 [1929]
         . . . Estimate of Situation

In summing up the general situation of American educational and philanthropic institutions in Turkey and the attitude of the present Turkish Government towards them, I am of the opinion that the past year has brought about a marked change for the better. Nevertheless I still await further concrete results before jumping to the conclusion that there has been any radical change of heart and policy on the part of the Turkish Administration. . . .

The attitude of the authorities at Angora conveys an impression of friendliness and helpfulness rather than an impression of obstruction which was so obvious a year ago. Only time will show whether this new-found friendly attitude is a policy carefully planned for the purpose of misleading our institutions into a feeling of false security. I am not of the opinion that this is the case, for if obstruction were planned, it is highly improbable that the authorities in the Ministry of Public Instruction would have talked to Mr. Fowle in the constructive manner of their recent conversations. It seems to me far more likely that there has been a change, or at least a modification of attitude, and that this change or modification is due to the following considerations:

(1) The removal by death of Nedjati Bey [Minister of Public Instruction] whose lack of culture and whose fanatical nationalism rendered him constitutionally and fundamentally hostile to foreign educational and philanthropic activities in Turkey.

(2) A growing realization that the Turkish educational program must for a long time to come be handicapped by lack of funds and trained teachers, and that, within bounds and proper control, the foreign colleges and schools are an asset of great value in carrying out this program.

(3) The tendency to regard nationalism rather than religion as the unifying principle of Turkish thought and action resulting in a corresponding tendency towards religious tolerance on the part of the authorities as contrasted with the fanatical intolerance of a year ago. The following incident, which I have checked up and found to be correctly reported, is significant in this connection:

The Scottish Mission School in Constantinople recently received directions from its principals in Scotland stating that the school was supported and maintained essentially as a religious institution and instructing the director to inform the Turkish authorities that unless the pupils were allowed to attend daily prayer and the reading of the scriptures, the school would be closed. After some negotiation the Turkish educational authorities acceded orally to the demand. This was communicated to the principals in Scotland who replied that they wished to avoid further misunderstandings and friction such as frequently had occurred in the past and they therefore insisted upon receiving the foregoing assurance from the Turkish authorities in writing, failing which the school would be closed. To the surprise of the British Embassy, the Turks acceded to this further demand in a letter addressed by Said Bey, Assistant Director of Education, and therefore representing, in Constantinople, the Ministry of Public Instruction to the Scottish Mission School confirming the permission already orally granted to give instruction and hold ceremonials of a religious nature in the case of non-Moslem pupils. This privilege was also extended to all schools by a circular of April 24, 1929. . . .

(4) A gradual but clearly perceptible diminution of the fanatical chauvinism which, considering the circumstances of the founding of the Turkish Republic, was a perfectly logical phase of the first few years of its existence. The basis of this chauvinism was a marked inferiority complex, induced by fear of foreign aggression, suspicion of foreign influences and uncertainty as to domestic security. While these elements have not been wholly dispersed, they have greatly moderated. The results of Turkey's negotiations with her neighbors during the past year or two have for the time being set at rest any immediate fear of armed aggression. While suspicion of subversive foreign influences will always be present, there is now a greater feeling of confidence that they can be controlled. Similar confidence as to domestic security is on the upward curve, of which an indication, trivial but significant, perhaps is to be found in the recent order permitting non-Moslems to visit Brusa where religious unrest has hitherto been a cause of suspicion and concern to the Turkish Government. In other words, the wind is clearly blowing in the direction of increased self-confidence, the inferiority complex is moderating, and proportionately with this development a new psychological outlook is created which is automatically reflected in a more tolerant attitude of the Government towards foreign educational and philanthropic institutions in Turkey.

The proof of the accuracy of this theory will be established only as concrete results are forthcoming.

In closing this report it is desirable to add that since coming to Turkey my efforts on behalf of our educational and philanthropic institutions have been confined to friendly and informal representations, for with every desire to support and aid them I have felt, and I believe rightly, that anything savoring of an official demand would promptly have defeated its own purpose. I have encouraged the American representatives of these various institutions to make their own efforts with the Turkish authorities in the first instance and have taken part myself only when some impasse appeared to have been reached. In this policy I have had the full approval and support of Dr. Caleb Gates [president of Robert College], Luther Fowle and others concerned, whose sane and practical outlook and methods and whose limitless patience in the face of many discouragements it is a pleasure to record. If anything can accomplish constructive results it will be this attitude on their part, for my experience with the Turk convinces me that the two qualities essential to success in dealing with him are first courtesy and second patience, and I would add to these a studious avoidance, in dealing with the higher officials, of any word or gesture reminiscent of the capitulatory regime. . . .

August 15 to 26 [1929] Black Sea Trip [8]

We had long wanted to see something of Turkey outside of Constantinople, the Bosporus, Brusa and Angora, particularly the Black Sea littoral, for our imagination had been whetted by the ships passing up and down the Bosporus, trying to picture their ports of destination, and furthermore the desirability of learning something of conditions in Turkey at firsthand was obvious. The thought of a ten-day cruise with congenial companions in probably fine weather was especially attractive. I had mentioned our plan to the British Ambassador earlier in the summer and he at once proposed joining us. So the party grew, and . . . we started eleven strong, including Sir George Clerk, Colonel Harold Woods [British Commercial Secretary],

[8] The Washington *Star*, August 16, 1929, said of this trip: "Rarely has a foreign diplomatic representative made such a tour of Anatolia, and Mr. Grew's trip is considered to emphasize the increasing importance of Asiatic Turkey. It is believed it will act as a stimulus to Commerce between Turkey and the United States, as he will investigate the trade possibilities of the region."

Colonel and Mrs. Elliott and Duncan Elliott, A. H. Reid [of the Ottoman Bank], Mavroudi [an Hellenic Turk], Alice, Anita, Elsie and I, ably supported by the American and British kavasses Hassan and Ihsan, Mitzi and the faithful Joseph, Sir George's Czechoslovak valet. We had a scare at the last moment that Anita might not be able to come, as she developed a high fever in the afternoon and of course this would have meant that the whole family would have given up the trip. But Dr. Hajisava, who went out to Yenikeuy to see her, reported that it seemed to be merely a touch of sun or "summer fever" and allowed her to go. The poor child was however very ill during the first week of the trip and was able to be up and to go ashore only on the last two or three days.

The cruise was a great, I might say a complete, success had it not been for Anita's illness. The scenery surpassed in beauty and interest anything that I had imagined. Certainly the country from the Bosporus to Rizeh might well be called the Riviera of Turkey and from Kerassoun on, it surpasses in beauty and grandeur anything that the French Riviera has to offer. Add to this delightful scenery the interest of seeing port after port, each different from the last, and the produce for which they are famous — the coal of Zonguldak, the tobacco of Samsoun, the nuts of Kerassoun — add to all this the thoroughly romantic experience of passing over the first étape of the old Persian caravan route, of descending the very valley where Xenophon's soldiers, returning after the Anabasis, suddenly caught sight of the sea and shouted "Thalata, thalata!" as they rushed down the slopes, of skirting the shores of ancient Bithynia, Cappadocia and Pontus and of visiting the country of the Amazons and the homes of Diogenes and Miletus and Mithradates, and it will be evident that we returned from the cruise with indelible impressions, a modicum of historical knowledge and much valuable information of a specific nature.

As for comfort, the *Izmir* of the Turkish Séiri Séfaine, with its all-Turkish officers and crew, might have been our private yacht. Nothing was left undone for our convenience. Both food and service were beyond praise, quite as good as on the average Atlantic liner. The Captain placed his private deck behind the bridge at our disposal, and there, in complete privacy, with comfortable chairs and tables, we read or played cards or watched the moving panorama, in clear sunshine by day and moonlight by night, with a calm and smiling sea throughout. Indeed it was difficult to picture the fearful storms that lash the Black Sea coast in winter, so that sometimes for weeks no ship can establish contact with the shore, for there are no real ports offering security from the north wind except at Sinope. For several days after Samsoun there were few passengers, so that all our meals were served at a big table on deck, always with a refreshing breeze to blow the heat away. We had our own meal times, at 1 and 8, while the other passengers . . . lunched and dined at 12 and 7, and thus we were alone. Whenever we wished to swim, which we did almost daily on rising at 7 and again in the evening on returning from a hot day ashore, the Captain's private caique was instantly at our disposal with its handsome, well setup crew. Ship's stewards always accompanied us on our picnics and brought the lunch. In effect, we visited these lovely places to all intents and purposes on a private yacht.

It seemed to me too that there was none of the red tape of minor officialdom which one meets so often in Constantinople. We used no papers or permits anywhere. Perhaps this was because I had written to Tewfik Rushdi Bey of our plans and, as a result, the Minister of the Interior had telegraphed to the authorities of the places at which we called, instructing them to facilitate our visit in every way. We were generally met by a delegation of welcome, presents of fruit or nuts or eggs were frequently sent us, cars were at our disposal ashore, police guards of honor were drawn up as we disembarked, and nothing whatever was left undone to help us. It is probably the first time that any Ambassador, much less two Ambassadors at the same time, have visited these ports under the Turkish Republic and this fact seems to be appreciated. The Stars and Stripes and the Union Jack fly side by side from the yard arm of the *Izmir* and are lowered or raised, with nautical precision, as one or both of us leave the ship or return on board. Whatever the protocol may be, we called on every Vali [governor] along the way, at Samsoun, Zonguldak, Kerassoun, Trebizond and Rizeh, and in two cases on the Prefects, and our calls were meticulously returned on shipboard. My opinion of the courtesy, hospitality and kindliness of the Turks has been enhanced.

August 15

We sailed, or were due to sail, at 8 P.M., but at that hour the ship was still far from loaded as several large lighters of watermelons and iron rails lay alongside discharging their cargo. The representative of the Line was most polite: he did not apologize for the delay, obviously due to the incomplete loading of the cargo but said to me that as we were about to dine at 8, the Captain, desiring to please us in every way, had postponed sailing until we should finish dining so that we should not lose a moment of the beauties of the Bosporus by moonlight! Thus the Turk. As a matter of fact, we did not get off until 10.30, nearly two hours after finishing dinner, when the last melon (save for two which we saw the boatman surreptitiously kick under the seats for baksheesh) had been thrown on board. The moonlight trip up the Bosporus was quite marvelous.

Zonguldak, August 16

A pretty town, the center of the coal region, of allegedly 15,000 inhabitants. It is built in a little valley and extends up the green slopes of hills on either side, while the central valley runs inland to the base of other wooded hills beyond — a refreshing spot, not at all the kind of place that one associates with the coal industry. There is no real port — only a short breakwater over which enormous waves dash in the winter storms, making anchorage impossible. A Séiri Séfaine ship was wrecked there last winter. But the town is dependent upon the sea for there is no railroad except for the short lines to the various coal mines. Last year they exported 1,200,000 tons of coal; this year they expect to reach a million and a half and next year two millions. The French Compagnie Française d'Heraclée is the largest organization, turning out approximately 700,000 tons of the whole output. Most of their mines are at Heraclea, famous in history, a little way down the coast. There is also an Italian company and the rest are Turkish. Those of the miners who are natives of the local vilayet, so the Vali informed me, work in shifts of fifteen days and then return for fifteen days to the cultivation of their crops so that these shall not suffer by their absence. They were all at work on Friday.

As the Ministry of the Interior had telegraphed to the Vali of our arrival, we were met by a deputation including the Prefect, the Chief of Police and the Director General of Mines, Memet Refik Bey. The last named, who at one time replaced Professor L. A. Scipio in the Engineering School at Robert College during the latter's absence on leave, and has two sons there, took us over the place, showing us first the School of Mines (of 70 pupils — three of the professors being Belgian) — a fine building, very light and airy as Refik's hobby is big windows and he is having them installed, in spite of the opposition of the architects, in several new buildings which are being constructed — and then to one of the smaller mine pits, belonging to a Turkish family named Suleiman. We examined the plant but did not descend into the mine for sartorial reasons.

As the Vali, Akin Bey, had signified that he would welcome our visit, we waived technical objections of protocol and called at his house. He is quite a young man — the youngest of all the Governors. . . . He speaks fair French but still the conversation could not have been termed brilliant.

In the afternoon the Captain got out his smart caique as well as that of the engine-room staff, each with three husky oarsmen, and took several of us to a delightful beach where we had a most refreshing swim after a hot day. The surrounding country was lovely, with high thickly wooded hills rising abruptly from the shore, interspersed with trim little beaches. What a country to develop as a summer resort!

Before sailing at 7 the Vali came on board to return our call and joined us all at tea. The French Consul also came to call on Sir George and said that the French were having a more and more difficult time with their mining, because as soon as a foreign company begins to make profits, it is looked at with suspicion by the Turkish authorities and one obstruction after another is put in its way. He said that they were obliged to accept three pupils of the graduating class of the Turkish School of Mines every year but that the last thing they let them do was to go into the mines lest they ruin them by ignorance. All these men did was to supervise the payrolls of the workmen and squeeze as much out of their hard-earned salaries as they could manage. A miner in Turkey is paid from 40 to 80 cents a day, according to his ability — about 10 per cent or less of the wages of a miner in the United States.

A delightful evening as we sailed slowly along the lovely shore in the moonlight while our portable Gramophone discoursed sweet music. Our impressions of Zonguldak were of the best. . . .

Sinope

Arrived at about 3.30 P.M. and went ashore after tea, with the American and British kavasses, the agent of the Séiri Séfaine and a policeman, as well as the Third Officer of the *Izmir,* a young cousin of Madame Ratib Bey, as guide. Sinope is an intensely interesting town. It is built across the narrow neck of a promontory. The north water front is conspicuous for the immense ruins of an old Genoese fortification, the high wall being still in fairly good condition, and as one passes through the town one walks up a broad avenue paved with great smooth stones which must be of immense age; it seemed to me to have a Roman look about it, reminding me of Pompeii and the Appian Way, but it may come down even from the old Greek days of Miletus. It was here that Diogenes lived about 400 B.C. Sir George was busily looking for the old tub but failed to locate it. Indeed, Sinope has an historic past of great interest. It was once the capital of Pontus and the outlet for the trade of

Mesopotamia and the Euphrates. Xerxes and his ten thousand
embarked here for home. Mithradates held out long against
the Roman advance but was finally overcome. Going back still
further, it was here that the Amazons lived — or at least somewhere in this general stretch of country. What a history could
be written of all that Sinope has seen! But now, from the commercial point of view, it is dead.

We climbed the Genoese walls, visited the old mosque, had
coffee in front of a Turkish coffee house, which looked on a
big square with an old fountain in the center and many picturesque types of old Turks sitting at their coffee or passing by,
and then we repaired to the prison where the work of the
prisoners in mother-of-pearl set in wood is especially renowned.
The workshops were empty as the prisoners had been locked
up for the night in buildings surrounding the courtyard where
hundreds of them were watching us through the bars, although
several of the workmen, presumably privileged, were allowed
to sell us their wares. We bought a great quantity, feeling that
every lira spent was a charity as it meant a few more cigarettes
or a little more food for the men, and the work, including
cigarette cases, backgammon boards, wooden shoes, etc., worked
with inlaid mother-of-pearl, was well worth the trivial prices
charged.

Before returning to the ship we inspected the Belgian match
factory which failed owing to the fact that it was built on sand
and the buildings are subsiding. Small but dangerous cracks
are to be seen in the enormous chimney of the boiler house.
The machines are new and of the best types, many of them
American, and the buildings seem, at first sight, to be brand
new and in perfect condition. The caretaker told us that an
American company had taken it over, but I know nothing of
this; however, the place is closed and deserted. . . .

Samsoun, August 18

Arrived early in the morning and arose for a delicious swim
with Elsie at 6.30 although we had not retired till nearly 4 A.M.
owing to the marvelous moonlight as we steamed along the

coast — and other things. Went ashore about 9 and called on Currin of the Gary Tobacco Company and on the director of the local branch of the Ottoman Bank with Reid. After the usual cup of Turkish coffee at Currin's office, he and Flannigan, of the American Tobacco Company, took us in automobiles first to one of the big tobacco workshops and then out into the country to see it growing on its native heath, for of course Samsoun is the center of the Turkish tobacco crop and all our American cigarettes are practically made up of it. Downstairs in the shop was a room packed with babies and little tots of a few years old, sitting in tiers with their feet through the bars, the children of the women who were working upstairs, parked here during work hours. Upstairs, two big lofts were filled with a couple of hundred women in each, sorting out the tobacco leaves according to quality. We saw how the leaves, after sortment, were emptied into bins and then pressed for shipment on another floor below. It was all most interesting. Samsoun has the appearance of a thoroughly modern town, quite the antithesis of Sinope. The former is alive and wide-awake; the latter commercially dead but with an atmosphere of great age which renders it far more picturesque and attractive. . . .

Rizeh, August 20 and 21

The loveliest place of all and the most hospitable although the poorest, having to depend for their support partially upon their richer neighbor the Vilayet of Trebizond. The Vali sent us his motor launch to take us ashore, together with the imposing Chief of Police, a guide and an interpreter, lent us his car, as there are only three automobiles in the whole town and in fact did everything possible for our convenience. Sir George and I called on him on the first afternoon and he told us the details of the disaster in June when a cloudburst which lasted for four hours caused the mountain streams and rivers to swell, in some places forming dams and then breaking through and roaring down on field and dwelling. The coast now extends some two hundred yards further out owing to the great deposits of sediment carried down by the floods. A few people were drowned here at Rizeh but the great loss of life occurred at Off, a near-by port. Bridges were carried away, houses destroyed. We saw the river bed down which the main torrent had rushed and the remains of the bridges. An old mill, two hundred years old, was uprooted with its four inhabitants and lost. Had the cloudburst lasted a few moments longer, the whole town would probably have been destroyed.

The climate of Rizeh is very damp; there is much rain and angry storm clouds hung over the mountain peaks during our stay in port. It is said that they are always present. Several of us took a walk in the afternoon of our arrival to an old fishing village in a pouring tropical rain. The luxuriance of the vegetation astonished me; it was almost junglelike and took me back to the East; the cornstalks grew to six feet and more in height and orange groves were frequent along our way. That walk was the most delightful of our entire trip. At the end of it we sat for a while among some of the old fishermen and then climbed from the beach into the launch by a precarious plank while the launch rolled in the heavy waves.

The Vilayet of Rizeh has long been overrun with brigands until the present Vali was appointed three months ago to deal with the situation. He was given two thousand soldiers who placed themselves along the boundary of the Vilayet and then gradually hemmed the brigands in, capturing the leaders to the number of 37. The last leader is said to be now surrounded and his arrest is expected shortly. I was told in Trebizond that several of these leaders escaped from jail after their arrest and are again infesting the countryside but it is difficult to learn the truth. These bands of brigands were especially dangerous because, to be admitted a member of a band, one had to have committed murder in order that his life might be forfeit to the Government and so that if captured he would not give away the names of his associates. Many committed murder merely to join a band and for long they have terrorized the country.

The inhabitants of Rizeh are not Lazes as one would be led to suppose on account of its proximity to the borders of

Lazistan but rather descendants of the Genoese and the Pontine Greeks. The women are treated as beasts of burden, carrying enormous loads and often their babies to boot, while their husbands walk unencumbered before them. These women wear blankets or shawls of red and blue stripes over their heads and quickly draw them over their mouths and turn their backs as men pass by. We met one woman carrying a heavy load of wood on her back, another with an old woman in a chair, a third with planks. The men are warlike but when not on a vendetta they loaf about, sip their coffee and smoke their nargiles while their women cultivate the fields alone.

The Department of Agriculture has been busy laying out a nursery garden high up above the town with the object of educating the people in modern methods of forestry and market gardening. We were taken over it, after a hot climb up the hillside, were given coffee, cold spring water and cigarettes by the director and then shown the tea planting, nursery orange and mandarin trees and beautiful flowers. The same Department encourages the manufacture of cane chairs which are woven from the stalks of the maize and we ordered a dozen or so to be sent us for use in our garden at Yenikeuy.

Rizeh is said to be rich in copper and manganese but little or nothing has been done to exploit its mineral wealth. With capital, energy and expert assistance and the business elements of which Turkey has deprived herself she might well become a wealthy country.

After bazaring, we returned to the ship, laden with purchases, received the Vali's call and sailed on our return voyage for home, deeply, very deeply impressed with the beauties of Rizeh and its genuine hospitality. . . .

Trebizond, August 22

A simply glorious day. We began it with a refreshing swim at 7 A.M. after I had routed out the swimmers from profound slumber, and at 9 Sir George and I went ashore to call on the Vali. He is said to be 65 years old but looks not more than 55, and, as usual, his French was so sketchy that the conversation was in Turkish, the British Consul interpreting. He told us that trade from Trebizond to Erzerum and the transit trade into Persia were greater than before the war but this information was denied by another high official (whose name had better be withheld) who said in confidence that, on the contrary, trade was nearly stagnant. With the monopolics on sugar, matches and other commodities requiring a customs deposit which could not be refunded until the goods were exported, the transit trade into Persia had suffered severely and most of it was now routed through Russia. This official, while his views may be prejudiced with a tinge of "ancien régime," maintains that the present regime is headed for certain disaster, not only because of the hopeless economic situation but also because the Gazi has little personal following in the Black Sea regions, which is probably symptomatic of the rest of Turkey, and dissension in the army is steadily increasing. There is much criticism that all available money has thus far been spent on strategic railways instead of for irrigation and other economic betterments. This is perfectly true, but it must be remembered that the Government's first and most vital problem is to create means to enable it to throw troops into any quarter immediately if national domestic security is to be maintained, and that once this is accomplished, more funds for economic development will be available. Already there are signs that this point has nearly been reached. I am informed that the projected plan of extending the railway from Argana to Diarbekr has been abandoned. This decision may have been taken to satisfy public opinion but it at least indicates that the Government is fully alive to the necessity of early economic reconstruction. But the official of whom I speak is thoroughly pessimistic as to the future. He acknowledges, however, that nothing better than the present regime is in sight.

After our call on the Vali, the others, with the exception of Alice and Anita, came ashore and we started in four automobiles, accompanied by the British Consul and Mrs. William Matthews, two kavasses and the faithful Joseph guarding the lunch, for the high pass over the mountains into Armenia, the

Zigana Pass, 6600 feet high, 68 kilometers from Trebizond. The road led from the lovely port of Trebizond, with its long beach, its old caiques drawn up on the shore, its houses thickly banked on the rising slope and behind it the big hill of Boz Tepe, which reminded me much of the Gurten behind Berne, steadily up into the mountains, passing through many villages, each with its camel han, in some of which we saw camel caravans resting through the hot day until the cool of night should enable them to continue their journey. It was this valley through which Xenophon marched at the end of the Anabasis and it was these very slopes down which the tired soldiers leapt with joy and camped on the promontory beside Trebizond before embarking for home. The road, which is very, very old, but reconstructed by a French company in 1912 and later improved by the Russians during their occupation in 1915, is decidedly good as a whole. It leads through scenery which can hardly be outdone for beauty even in beautiful Switzerland, although much of it reminded me of the valley leading up to Adelboden. The imprint of Greece is ever present, not only in the fact that Greek is still spoken by the majority of the inhabitants, although the Turks are doing their best to stamp it out, but in the presence of innumerable Greek churches and monasteries, now deserted, some of them, like the famous monastery of Petra, built into the face of sheer cliffs in impregnable positions, others quite tiny as if exemplifying literally the scripture "When two or three are gathered together. . . . " Lazes are in evidence, too, with their unusual headcoverings, tall, slim and handsome, although the actual borders of Lazistan are farther to the east. The women, once one leaves the city and its suburbs, are invariably veiled or, if not, they pull their brightly colored scarfs across their mouths and turn their backs as we pass. Perhaps the most unusual and amusing object that we passed on our ascent into the mountains was a very small donkey carrying on its very small back some bags of grain surmounted by a shawl surmounted by a calf and the whole surmounted by an open umbrella! Down in the valley the growth was almost junglelike in its luxuriance, hazel nut trees, olive trees, tobacco and corn, immense stalks six feet in height in places. Corn, in fact, seems to be the principal staple of native consumption and it is grown on every available patch on the hillsides up to several thousand feet.

The last part of the way was steep and curvy, very curvy. Our chauffeur, who was an excellent chauffeur, wanted us to appreciate his dexterity and whenever a particularly sharp curve appeared ahead he promptly put on a burst of speed and took the curve at full tilt, invariably on the extreme outside of the road so that we might fully appreciate the beauties of the yawning precipices, sometimes of great depth, immediately beneath us. As we had passed four or five big camions coming down from the pass while we ascended, I found myself trying to calculate just where the body would be found if we happened to meet one of them on one of those curves. Sir George, in his car, apparently had the same experience because, on our return from the top of the pass, he complained of lack of exercise and insisted on walking four full kilometers, which included most of the most "precipicy" curves. I also needed exercise and accompanied him, very gladly.

There was another element of interest in the fact that brigands are still abroad in this part of the country, a considerable number having recently escaped from jail in Rizeh, and holdups have occurred on this road within a few days. However, the Government had clearly taken precautions for we continually met soldiers, both mounted and on foot, with guns unslung. The whole road was being patrolled for our visit.

The top of the pass was magnificent. No other word can describe it. We had left the tree line and were up among the open crags with patches of snow in evidence. Suddenly there burst upon us, as we topped the pass, a scene of great splendor — immediately below was the road winding dizzily down into the valley and beyond it tier upon tier and chain upon chain of great mountains, cloud-capped, magnificent — the subranges of the Caucasus, in fact Armenia itself. That scene alone has justified our journey.

We picnicked on a grassy slope lower down among the trees

and then descended as we had come and took tea with the hospitable Matthews at the British Consulate on their charming terrace. I did not wait for the Vali, who was also invited and came later, but went with Elsie and Reid to see the ancient Genoese walls of the city, drove to a prominence for a last view of Trebizond and then returned to the ship where we had a delicious swim, as usual, before dinner. Two thousand sheep were being loaded on board so that we did not sail till 10. . . .

Buyukdere, August 26

Entered the Bosporus at 8.30 A.M. and anchored at Buyukdere for quarantine examination at 9. Made our farewells and left on the *Heather* which had come out to meet us with Miss Carp and Patterson. The Barge had also come out to meet us but the engine exploded in a mass of flames just as it reached Buyukdere, the crew, Vincent and Kim escaped in a caique, Noltsch, the engineer, being somewhat badly burned on the hands; a firepump was sent out from shore but just as the flames were extinguished the old Barge sank to her final resting place beneath the waves. Vale! I hate to see the old tub go but am thankful that it did not happen when Alice and the girls were on board, or in the middle of the Bosporus instead of in port with caiques near by. Otherwise there might well have been loss of life. I am having a full investigation made into the cause of the disaster. . . .

The *Izmir* passed our house half an hour after we arrived and saluted us with three blasts of her horn. Elsie put out a Rizeh scarf on the parapet of our balcony and we all waved farewell.

Thus ends an unforgettable voyage — one of the most interesting and agreeable that we have ever made. My conclusions regarding the economic, social and political situation on the Turkish Black Sea littoral based upon our observations and the data which we were able to gather will follow in this diary later, but it is questionable whether my eventual report to the Department will be of any great value. We shall see. Out of the 80 photographs which I took, about half are very good and the rest mediocre or poor; I find that I overexposed most of them, particularly the distant scenes, for it is difficult to estimate the great amount of extra light that interposes itself between the lens and a distant object. Have written letters of appreciation to Tewfik Rushdi Bey, Shukri Kaya Bey [Minister of the Interior] and Sadoullah Bey, Director General of the Séiri Séfaine. As for the Captain, Sir George and I are giving him a silver cigarette box engraved with our respective national coats of arms and an appreciative inscription.

To Secretary of State Stimson, September 6, 1929
. . . My general impressions may be summed up as follows:
Economic

This magnificent country, rich in historical association, scenic beauty, fertile soil, plantations, orchards, forests, mines, could become a veritable treasure-house to the Turkish Republic were it properly developed. But apart from the limited output of coal from Zonguldak, tobacco from Samsoun and nuts from Kerassoun and Trebizond, the Turkish Black Sea littoral is from the economic point of view relatively stagnant. This stagnation is due to a variety of causes.

First and foremost is the sparseness and indolence of the population. Never thickly settled, this countryside since the elimination of the Greeks, who formed a not inconsiderable part of the population, now gives the visitor the impression of being almost destitute of inhabitants and even in the towns there seems to be little doubt, from information obtained from reliable foreign residents, that the figures of the last census are greatly overdrawn. . . . They subsist on the barest margin of nourishment, their main staple being corn which is grown in great profusion, the cornstalks in this most fertile country often reaching six or seven feet in height but with a single ear for each stalk; nor does the Government offer incentive to greater industry, for individual wealth is immediately taxed out of all proportion to its value to the peasant. Owing to lack of communications he has been accustomed throughout history to produce only enough for his immediate needs and sees no good

reason to develop his output. Only in the coal mines of Zonguldak, where the peasants alternate in shifts of fifteen days between the mines and the cultivation of their crops, earning a
pittance of from forty to eighty cents a day in the mines, in the
tobacco fields of Samsoun and in the nut woods of Kerassoun
do the inhabitants, spurred largely by foreign incentive, appear
to make an effort towards the development of industry and
commerce. But even this effort remains unsupported by the
Government. A campaign by the Government to eliminate in-
sects and parasites would at a small cost probably double the
revenue in a few years, but the step remains untaken. This
year the nut crop of Kerassoun has been a failure. This is
ascribed to Allah's will and the weather, but with more scientific methods and more intelligent care, there appears to be
no good reason why the loss should not have been greatly reduced. In the Zonguldak coal mines, the largest exploiter of
which is a French Company, the French Consul states that as
soon as profits are made the Government becomes suspicious
and places one obstruction after another in their way.

Another element contributing to the lack of ambition of the
inhabitants in the countryside about Trebizond and Rizeh is
undoubtedly the presence, until recently, of bands of brigands
who for years have preyed upon the population. . . .

Only in Samsoun is a degree of prosperity obvious. Here,
owing to the presence of the foreign tobacco companies (representatives of the Gary Tobacco Company, the Alston Tobacco
Company and the American Tobacco Company reside in Samsoun and make their purchases and shipments on the spot),
the gradual opening up of the new Samsoun-Sivas railway and
the ability and energy of the Vali, Kiazim Pasha, is there evidence of successful business activity. Money is said to be abundant and a new water supply provided by a Viennese firm has
been installed but has not yet begun to function until payment
by the municipality has been made.

Manganese and copper exist in the country from Kerassoun
to Rizeh but these are now unexploited. British prospectors
have attempted to develop the mining of manganese in times

past without profit. Until better communications are opened up and foreign initiative and capital welcomed and supported, the potentialities of mine development in this region will remain an unknown quantity.

Oranges and mandarins are grown in the almost tropical soil about Rizeh but, although large in size, they are dry, acrid and generally poor specimens of fruit. With scientific study there seems to be no reason why this fruit crop could not be greatly improved and the industry developed.

This leads us to the important question of communications. Only second to the sparseness . . . of the population, in gauging the comparative economic stagnation of the country, is the almost total lack of railway facilities. There is no riparian railway whatever to link up the various ports, save for the short narrow-gauge lines connecting Zonguldak with its few outlying coal mines and a short private line of thirty kilometers connecting Samsoun with the rich vegetable district of Tcharshamba. This latter line has proved a financial failure owing to the competition of camion traffic along the shore road which is here in good condition. The only railway into the interior is that from Samsoun which now extends to Zileh but within two years is to be completed to Sivas. A Swedish group is constructing another railway from Filios near Eraclea, the coal center near Zonguldak, towards Angora, but on this line less than seventy kilometers have been completed.

The roads, such as exist, are in a deplorable state of disrepair and I observed no work being done upon them save for a few repairs on the road from Inebolu leading into the interior. The shore road connecting Kerassoun, Trebizond and Rizeh is at present impassable owing to the recent floods which carried away most or all of the bridges, the replacement of which will doubtless be a long and expensive task. The road connecting Kerassoun with Sivas and Malatia in the interior is in bad condition and no camion traffic passes over it. Only the highway connecting Trebizond with Erzerum, leading into Armenia and Persia, the old Persian camel caravan route, which was rebuilt by a French company in 1912 and improved by the Russians during their occupation in 1915, is in good repair as far as the divide and fit for the passage of camions of which I observed five in the course of one day between Trebizond and the Zigana Pass leading down into Armenia. . . .

This entire littoral, from the Bosporus to Rizeh, is devoid of adequate ports, with the exception of Sinope, so that in the winter gales which habitually rage in the Black Sea, ships are frequently unable to establish contact with the shore for weeks at a time. Yet in the absence of sufficient roads and railways, ships are the principal means of exportation. Apart from the Turkish coastwise traffic, there is a French and an Italian service and occasionally a ship of the American Export Lines calls at Samsoun for consignments of tobacco.

To sum up, the Turkish Black Sea littoral, owing to its richly fertile soil, its forests and its mines, has great potentialities for economic development, but before this can proceed to any great extent money must be available for the construction of roads and railways, the Government must adopt a policy of incentive, while foreign initiative . . . must be welcomed and supported.
Social

The social reforms of the Republic appear to have made little headway in this region. The fez, of course, has gone — for the wearing of the fez is now a hanging matter. The Latin characters have been accepted simply because it is a great deal easier for the illiterate peasant to learn to read them than it was for him to master the old script, but to what extent illiteracy is really being overcome is a question no foreign observer can accurately answer for some time to come. In matters of religion and women, no change is evident. Probably in no part of Turkey is religious fanaticism more rife than here. The women, almost without exception, save in the larger towns, are veiled or wear a shawl over their heads which they rapidly draw over their faces and turn their backs when a man passes. Only at night are they permitted to bathe on the beaches which abound in this region. They do the work in the fields and carry the burdens, often loaded down like pack animals, while their menfolk walk unencumbered in advance. No progress whatever in this respect is to be seen.

Political

Of course the various Valis upon whom I called, while frank enough as to the deplorable economic situation, painted the political outlook in rosy colors. But between the lines one could read the contrary. . . . There is criticism that too much available money has thus far been spent on strategic railways instead of for irrigation and other economic betterments and that the Government has thought only of measures to keep itself in the saddle rather than of the welfare of the people. Such expressions of opinion on the part of a Turk, particularly a Turkish official under the present Government, are rare for whatever the Turkish public may think they seldom dare express such views to a foreigner. Nevertheless, the official in question acknowledged that much as he deplored the present regime he could see no possibility of a better one.

In closing this despatch I must give full credit to the Turkish officials and others with whom I came in contact during this visit for their genuine courtesy, kindliness and hospitality. There seemed to be none of the chauvinism nor the petty pomposity of minor officialdom which is ever to be met with in Constantinople. The Turk on his genuinely native heath is a far simpler and more approachable person than in the midst of the political complexities of the former capital.

September 8 [1929]

First plenary session with the Turkish Treaty Delegation at 3 o'clock. Numan Rifat [Undersecretary of State for Foreign Affairs] and Mustafa Cherif were both absent, so the Turkish Delegation was composed of Zekai Bey [Deputy of Diarbekr], Soubhi Zia Bey [technical adviser] and Shevket Bey [Chief of the First Section of the Foreign Office]. It was conducted with all formality, Zekai always addressing me as "Monsieur le Président" and I addressing him likewise. Two Turkish stenographers took notes but I made it clear that all my statements were *"ad referendum."* We went through the whole text in three hours, the Turkish objections being mainly on matters of form and phraseology and the necessity of complying with

Turkish legislation, much misunderstanding occurring through the difficulty of translating the English text literally into French. I had marked our French text, which served as a basis for the negotiations "non-guarantie." The Turks are to draw up a counterdraft and give it to us tomorrow, based on our discussions. . . .

September 10 [1929]

. . . A second plenary session with the Turkish Treaty Delegation resulted in smoothing out several more of the Turkish objections to our text. I encountered particular difficulty in explaining satisfactorily our desire to exclude police and revenue laws from most favored nation treatment but finally succeeded. The Turks are more reasonable than I had expected and if they can be made to understand the reasons for a given provision they are generally inclined to accept it. . . .

September 14 — October 1 [1929]

. . . The long awaited telegram in reply to mine of September 11th regarding the first stage of the treaty negotiations came on the afternoon of September 22nd.[9] I spent the evening in town discussing it with Gillespie and left on the evening of the 23rd for Angora, accompanied by Crosby and Gillespie, and Goldstein, Gillespie's clerk. There we remained for eight days, until October 1st. The Turks accepted most of the Department's views regarding the commercial articles but were very obstinate regarding navigation.[10] They made many exceptions

[9] See *Foreign Relations, 1929*, III, 830–32.

[10] Although Mr. Grew had reached an understanding with Tewfik Rushdi Bey that negotiations were only to concern a simple commercial convention, the Turks had later evidenced a desire to extend the most favored nation treatment not only to customs matters but also to navigation. In answer to Mr. Grew's inquiries about the willingness of the United States to consider such an extension, the Department of State on August 6, 1929, sent a telegram stating that although the "suggestion of the competent Turkish authorities is contrary to the verbal understanding previously arrived at between you and the Turkish Minister for Foreign Affairs regarding the scope of the treaty to be negotiated, the Department has, after a careful study of the situation, decided to accommodate the Turkish Government in this matter and encloses here-

to national treatment and declined to grant most favored nation treatment to those exceptions on the ground that most favored nation treatment in matters respecting the Turkish flag smacked of the capitulations. They would not even mention national and most favored nation treatment in the same breath. They said that Western countries could afford to give this but that if Turkey were to do it, it would place her in a category with those oriental countries where capitulations still exist by implying that national treatment could sometimes be less favorable than most favored nation treatment. In the protocol to the British treaty they had agreed that national treatment implied treatment at least as favorable as most favored nation treatment, but they begged us not to insist on such a provision. They said that the British, by insisting, had again proved their unsympathetic attitude towards the Turkish Republic and its reasonable susceptibilities. The French had not insisted and no such provision was in their treaty. I reported these views to the Department and recommended against insisting upon this provision. The Department accepted my recommendation.[11] The Senate, of course, may put this in as a reservation but it seems to me better for the Senate to do it than for us to do so. The Turks have continually said that so long as they possess the friendship of the Government of the United States they care very little what the Senate does on political grounds. . . .

There followed some disagreeable conferences, in one of which Zekai Bey, the President of the Turkish Delegation, became very petulant, asked for several new provisions in the treaty not hitherto mentioned and vowed that he would not sign a treaty in English anyway as he didn't know what he was signing. . . . Half of the difficulty of our negotiations was that the treaty had to be negotiated in French (although to be signed only in English and Turkish) because Zekai knows no English and it was complicated to find exactly the right translation to

with for your consideration and presentation at an appropriate time a short draft treaty of commerce and navigation which this Government would be pleased to negotiate with the Government of Turkey." *Ibid.*, p. 821.

11 *Ibid.*, p. 835.

express our precise meaning. Things did not look any too rosy on the night of September 29.

In treaty negotiations, just as in bridge and poker, the first thing to do is to size up your cards. That is where Lord Curzon failed so signally at the Conference of Lausanne. In our present negotiations the United States is in the most favorable position of any country and holds the four most important cards in the pack:

(1) Turkey exports vastly more commodities to us than we do to her.

(2) Turkey wants reputable American companies and American capital to interest themselves in her public works and she knows that she cannot interest them until our relations are regularized by treaties.

(3) Turkey fully realizes the moral prestige which a treaty with the United States will give her and therefore she wants such a treaty ratified.

(4) Finally, Turkey understands the danger of another rebuff in the United States Senate and does not want to jeopardize the treaty's ratification by insisting upon unreasonable provisions with us. Although as a negotiator she is inclined to be a great deal more difficult to deal with than most countries owing to her recollections of the capitulatory regime.

This being the case, I resolved to stand pat and to offer no compromises knowing that they would give in eventually. . . . I refused to consider a modifying phrase in connection with "regulations of a sanitary character intended to protect human, animal or plant life," knowing that the Department of Agriculture would never consent to be bound by any such modification. Finally I enumerated the concessions that we had already made, said that the treaty as it now stood had been approved word for word by my Government and that if Zekai insisted upon the change of a single word or a single comma, this would reopen the negotiations to several new proposals on our part with what eventual result it would be impossible to foresee. This turned the trick as I had expected and after arguing for about an hour he said, "All right, we will sign tomorrow."

At this point, when the negotiations were completed and we had agreed upon the text, it seemed to me highly desirable to make a drive for a provision in the minutes according most favored nation treatment to cover the exceptions to national treatment in navigation. This had not been given either to the French or the British and the Department had not asked for it after the Turks refused to accept the Department's original text. But I felt that it would be very helpful to have something of the kind ready in case the Senate should be inclined to make a reservation. Therefore I put it up to Zekai on political rather than on technical grounds. To save their face, Gillespie and I had worked out a formula which without mentioning "most favored nation treatment" amounted to exactly the same thing, namely a statement by the Turkish Delegation that it was their understanding that the exceptions to national treatment in navigation would be applied to our respective vessels in a way "not discriminatory in favor of a third country," which understanding I would confirm. Zekai called in Soubhi Zia and they discussed the formula in Turkish for nearly an hour at the end of which he agreed to accept it. I had fully intended to take the point up to Tewfik Rushdi if he refused but was glad not to have to do so. We got rid of the statement in the minutes protecting Turkish monopolies and secured the inclusion of a declaration making it clear that the cabotage law would not prevent our vessels from discharging and taking on both passengers and cargo in Turkey if coming from or bound to a foreign port. The British had this in their protocol. This concluded the negotiations in which I believe we obtained as favorable provisions as was possible — rather more favorable than either the French or the British.[12] Zekai said that they would have been willing to conclude such a treaty with no other Power. Practically all of our conferences were informal and there was no initialing of paragraphs or anything of that kind, and no stenographers were present except at the opening plenary session. Once a point had been orally ac-

[12] See *ibid.*, pp. 838–42, for the full text of the Treaty, which was signed at Angora on October 1, 1929.

cepted, no matter how informally, we simply put it aside and it appeared in the final text. In fact, after the first plenary session the negotiations developed into a series of informal conversations which made them much simpler and more agreeable and both sides were able to talk much more openly and freely than if the discussions had been formal.

Fortunately, before our negotiations began, I had been able to obtain a copy of the final French treaty and a copy of the initialed British treaty, from de Chambrun and Sir George, which were very helpful. I had sent both to Washington so that the Department could get an idea of the frame of mind of the Turks. These were given to no other colleague.

October 1 [1929]

A cold, windy, rainy day. We were suddenly informed that the Gazi had decided to return immediately to Angora and would arrive at eleven o'clock and we were asked to be at the station at 10.30. I went down with Crosby and Gillespie at 10.45 only to find that the special train would not arrive until after 12. The entire Government was at the station, all in top hats, and the entire Diplomatic Corps although the only chiefs of mission were the Russian Ambassador, the Polish Minister and myself. The press photographers were busy and one of them took a picture of Tewfik Rushdi Bey between the American and Soviet Ambassadors. This would make quite a hit if published in America under the caption "Turkish Minister for Foreign Affairs establishes entente cordiale between the United States and Soviet Russia." . . .

The Gazi arrived at 12.08 and was helped down from his car; he looked haggard and worn and much aged since I first saw him two years ago. He went along the line shaking hands and disappeared in the crowd. The Government had been working feverishly, night and day, to complete the widening of the road between the Grand National Assembly and the Angora Palace Hotel before the Gazi's return and the papers had spoken of the erection of ten triumphal arches. The road was very nearly ready and makes a fine impression as one comes up from the station. Buildings have been springing up like mushrooms these last two years so that the old town is already taking on the appearance of an up to date city. Some of them, particularly the Agricultural Bank, are very fine and imposing. As for the triumphal arches, it seems fortunate that the city was spared that foolish expense through the Gazi's sudden change of plans. . . .

XXVIII

Political Developments

1930

Friday, January 31 [1930]

. . . With reference to my despatches of December 18 and 20, respectively, concerning the Russo-Turkish Protocol of December 17 1929,[1] I have the honor to inform the Department that such information and comment as have subsequently reached me tend to confirm my original opinion as to the general circumstances and intended scope and purpose of this instrument, namely that while in itself it cannot be regarded as a political alliance in the usual sense of the term, it was concluded as a sort of mutual insurance policy to lay at rest, for the time being, certain apprehensions that have existed, rightly or wrongly, on both sides of the frontier. The initiative in the matter appears to have been taken by Soviet Russia.

Russia's apprehensions may be said to have been twofold: first, an increasing anxiety as to the westward drift of Turkey's political interests and tendencies, this anxiety having been brought to a head by the cordiality attending the reception in Turkey of the British Mediterranean fleet in the month of October; second, the lively fear of an eventual Turco-Polish-Rumanian *bloc* aimed specifically against Russia.

On the Turkish side, the apprehensions were perhaps less distinctly defined, although Russia's political relations with Persia and Afghanistan and the perennial danger to be feared through the incitement by Russia of the Kurdish elements in

[1] On December 17, 1929, Turkish and Russian plenipotentiaries signed a protocol extending for two years the Turco-Russian Treaty of Friendship and Neutrality signed in Paris on December 17, 1925. See *Foreign Relations, 1929*, III, 842–45.

Persia may have been uppermost in the minds of the Turkish Government. Then, too, Turkey realized quite clearly that until her political relations with the various countries to the west are finally placed upon a solid basis, she cannot afford to risk a breach of friendship with Russia which might, in time of stress, deprive her of essential moral and material aid and leave her eastern frontier a cause of anxiety. Russia's aid during the Turkish revolution has not been forgotten. Therefore, Turkey has merely undertaken not to do something which, for the three-year period of the agreement, she would in no case consider doing — namely, to enter a political entanglement with any third country. Through such an insurance policy she has everything to gain and, in her opinion, nothing to lose.

I furthermore have reason to believe — and this belief has been confirmed to me by the German Commercial Attaché — that a special inducement was held out to Turkey by Karakhan — the Russian plenipotentiary — in the shape of an advancement of two million Turkish pounds to be reimbursed to the Soviets in cotton and other commodities and that a further advance in the same amount under the same or similar conditions has been provisionally arranged for the future. In agreeing to these advances the Soviet Government had in mind not only the negotiation of the Protocol but also the eventual negotiation of a new commercial treaty, in the hope that they may thus obtain such terms as they desire. The present penury of the Turkish Government would seem to lend color to the probable accuracy of this report.

To amplify my first report of the circumstances surrounding the conclusion of the Protocol, it is well to hark back to the signature of the original Turco-Soviet Treaty of Neutrality signed at Paris on December 17, 1925. This occurred the day after a decision unfavorable to Turkey in the Mosul controversy had been handed down by the League of Nations [2] and the

2 On December 16, 1925, a decision was handed down by the Council of the League of Nations regarding the disputed boundary between Iraq and Turkey. The Brussels Line which was fixed by the Council was not considered by Turkey to be a satisfactory settlement of the matter.

treaty was no doubt prompted on Turkey's part as much by the unfavorable decision of the League as by the fear that the new Labor Government in England might develop an Anglo-Soviet rapprochement to Turkey's detriment. But today the situation has altered; Turkey's relations with Europe are on a far sounder basis and the element of anxiety has passed to Soviet Russia. The Anglo-Soviet rupture of diplomatic relations following the fall of the former Labor Government in England caused the Soviets to fear the effect of British influence in Turkey and although new hopes were nursed by Russia upon the return to power of the Labor Government last year, it was soon seen that England's interest did not lie in close relations with the Soviet Government. Hence, in an endeavor to prevent Turkey from being brought under the influence either of England, or of France in the latter's Eastern European policy in Poland and the Balkans, or of the Western Powers interested in China and opposed to the Soviet policy and aims in that country, the Soviets took steps to eliminate these potential dangers.

It now appears that in spite of Tewfik Rushdi Bey's statement to me that he had extended the invitation to Karakhan — as he probably did do — the actual initiative for the visit to Angora at that particular moment originated with the Soviet Government, and it seems more than likely that the friendly October visit of the British fleet to Turkish waters was an important factor in motivating the visit. On this point all observers appear to agree. The necessity of considering the renewal of the Turco-Russian Treaty of December 17, 1925, at that particular date furnished an obvious excuse for the visit. It is generally believed that Karakhan hoped to take away with him a still more binding agreement than he actually secured and the present attitude of the Turkish Minister for Foreign Affairs conveys the impression that he is vastly relieved to have escaped so easily from an embarrassing situation. It will be remembered that the Gazi suddenly and unexpectedly departed from the capital for Yalova, his pet resort on the Gulf of Ismid, together with Shukri Kaya Bey and several of his cronies, shortly before Karakhan's visit and that he returned to Angora only just in time to receive the Soviet representative in audience. Rumor at that time was rife that the Gazi had little desire to meet this agent of a regime which, indirectly, had threatened the Gazi's own personal safety and that his well-known Western leanings furthermore contributed to his distaste for Karakhan's company, a distaste moreover which was no doubt accentuated by the fact of Karakhan's Armenian origin. However that may be, there is little doubt that political expediency led the Gazi to change his mind and to repair to the capital in time to receive the Soviet envoy before his departure. To state the matter frankly, Turkey knows on which side her bread is buttered and while she will tolerate no Soviet propaganda within her gates, she realizes full well that her interests lie in co-operation rather than in discord with her relatively powerful neighbor.

With regard to the alleged danger of the formation of a Turco-Polish-Rumanian political *bloc* aimed against Russia, my German colleague is of the opinion that such a combination, prior to the conclusion of the recent Turco-Russian Protocol, was an actual and practical possibility and that Russia acted just in time to stave off developments in that direction. My own opinion, which is shared by my British colleague, is that such a movement on the part of Turkey was not and never has been in serious view.

To sum up, the Turco-Russian Protocol was concluded as a mutual insurance policy for the purpose of keeping Turkey out of potential political mischief in the west and Russia in the east. While it may be regarded as a temporary political entanglement, it is in no respect an actual alliance, its aim being merely to prevent either party from concluding full or quasi-alliances with other powers for the time being. It cannot in any way affect Turco-American relations or interfere with any of the types of treaties which the United States might be disposed to negotiate with the Turkish Republic now or in future. . . .

Wednesday, February 19 [1930]

Great news! A telegram from the Department told us that

the Senate had yesterday given its advice and consent to the ratification of our Treaty of Commerce and Navigation without amendment. That's fine, a really important hurdle passed, and it smooths the road for other treaties in due course. I am greatly relieved for although I did not think it would be defeated there was at least ground for anxiety until the matter was *fait accompli*. I immediately telegraphed the good news to Tewfik Rushdi and Zekai and Patterson. . . .

Sunday, February 23 [1930]

. . . The longer I live in Turkey the more I realize what an immense and nefarious part "baksheesh" and personal pique play in the life of the country. The baksheesh question is continually coming to my attention: contracts are given or withheld, Government favors are granted or refused, favorable or unfavorable reports are turned in according to the rake-off accorded by the interested parties to the subordinate officials responsible. The other day an indirect message was brought to me from an official in the Defterdarat [Finance Ministry] that he had been charged with the duty of examining the books of foreign educational and philanthropic institutions with a view to levying the tax on donations and that the Government's action with regard to our American institutions would depend greatly on the nature of his report. I know what that message meant but he will not get a piastre from any American source, come what may. In this respect, American interests, particularly American business interests in Turkey, are under a handicap in competing with foreign interests because, while the foreigner will often, perhaps generally, oil the wheels liberally with baksheesh and thus purchase favor, few Americans will do so. They are absolutely right but it sometimes means the difference between success and failure.

As for personal pique, it must be acknowledged that this element has played and still plays a far more important part in Turkish politics than does political conviction. Ever since the beginning of the nationalist struggle in Anatolia, dissensions between the leaders have been based probably in the majority of cases on personal considerations rather than upon any fundamental political disagreement. The illustration of this is readily to be seen in the co-operation between politically heterogeneous elements on the one hand and dissension between politically homogeneous elements on the other. Although in the earlier days of the Republic the dissenting group were supposed to be conservatives, they were really no more conservative than many of those who rallied around the Gazi were progressive. The main political issue at that time was parliamentarianism vs. dictatorship but certainly the groups were not divided on that issue alone. It is difficult, for instance, to classify people like Fethi, Hamdoullah Soubhi, Nousret Sadoullah, Edib Servet [Deputy in the National Assembly] and others in the same hard-boiled political school of thought as the Ali Beys of the Tribunal of Independence, Nedjati, etc., yet these people have all managed to pull together while many others of the former type broke and departed. I do not know Halidé Hanum or her precise political ideals but certainly the impression one gets from her book is that personal pique played an important role in determining her position. It seems to me that the personal relations of the prominent actors in the earlier scenes of the Republic counted for far more than their respective political convictions — the steadily growing power of one group and the resulting neglect of others, with all the complications of conflicting ambitions, injured pride and rivalry. It is a topic worth debating.

As for the situation today, I doubt if it has much changed in that respect and I am inclined to believe that the Gazi encourages rather than discourages personal animosities within the circle of his satellites and advisers on the ground that a wise balance can best be secured by playing one off against another. It is merely the old, old Turkish game of Abdul Hamid and his predecessors; the leopard does not change his spots so easily. Pugilistic encounters have occurred only recently between Nuri and Falih Rifki and between Redjeb Zuhdi and Vasif [Deputies in the National Assembly]. One day not long ago, it is said, Nuri Bey, Deputy from Kutaiah and an intimate of the Gazi, privately approached the Cabinet with the request that the installation of central-heating systems in public buildings and schools be awarded to a company which he was representing. It appears that this request was rejected at the instance of Ismet Pasha as it was incompatible with the rule of awarding the contract to the lowest bidder. Nuri Bey was furious and, according to reports, began a private campaign against the Premier by criticizing his economic policy with particular reference to railway construction which he characterized as stupid and liable to lead the country to economic ruin. It is not known how far Nuri succeeded in estranging the Gazi and Ismet Pasha but this, I believe, was at the bottom of one of the recent perennial rumors of Ismet's pending resignation. Of course all these rumors must be discounted but there is generally some fire to account for so much smoke. I am inclined to believe that the Gazi watches these encounters with secret glee, feeling that his own security depends more upon dissension than harmony among his followers. And the rumored episode of Nuri Bey's heating apparatus is so typical that I give it full credit. Meanwhile Ismet Pasha pursues his way serenely amidst "a sea of troubles," reaping the fruits of some of his economic errors but not bothering very much, I imagine, about those who yap around his feet. . . .

Wednesday, March 12 [1930]

. . . The following are a few observations on the work of this mission in particular and of the services in general:

Method

The system and the methods at this mission must necessarily be different from those at any other mission because the Embassy is divided into two separate parts during eight months of the year. Periodical interchanges of secretaries between Constantinople and Angora prevent continuity, so that it is impractical to assign specific fields of work to certain individuals exclusively. Every secretary must be kept so far as possible *au courant* of every subject so that any secretary may be competent to take charge of the office in Angora at any moment. Therefore certain studies or the preparation of certain despatches must be assigned more or less indiscriminately as need arises, in order to balance the work as evenly as possible.

Few despatches are written in Angora, although I encourage the preparation of rough drafts there. The senior secretary keeps a daily diary of all information, conversations and developments and sends it periodically to Constantinople where much of the material is incorporated or used in the despatches prepared here.

The ideal arrangement would be a counselor and one secretary in Angora and two secretaries in Constantinople from October till June, but this would seldom work out in practice owing to transfers, leaves of absence, illnesses, etc., and I can get along well enough with but one secretary here. Experience has shown that out of a staff of four, the full complement is seldom available. Leaves of absence should in principle be granted so far as possible only during the summer, but *force majeure* often intervenes.

As regards the advantage of regular staff meetings, different chiefs have different opinions and methods. Admiral Bristol held them daily from 12 to 1 o'clock but I found them a great waste of time and abolished them. In fact, they tended, after an exchange of information which nearly everyone knew already, to develop into mere gossiping parties. I find it much more practical to consult the members of the staff individually, and collectively only when some point of policy is at issue. The members of the staff themselves are kept fully *au courant* by seeing every incoming document and a copy of every outgoing document before it is filed. Furthermore, every secretary who picks up information in a conversation or otherwise is asked to embody it in a written memorandum which is seen by all. I am continually consulting the Commercial Attaché, the Military Attaché and the Consul but almost always alone. In my experience the best work can be done two by two and that is the only principle on which I personally can do it. In all of this work, the training of young secretaries is a responsibility which no chief should shirk. Out of fourteen chiefs I can remember but one who really went out of his way to teach me the game and he was a littérateur who loved correcting English. The average official is not disposed to think out loud with his subordinates and to seek their reactions and advice before forming his own judgment, but that is the best way to help them and, incidentally, to help himself. My own training, such as it is, has come about more by observing the mistakes of various chiefs and the results thereof than by any constructive assistance on their part. This sounds rather bitter but in most cases it was true.

So much for method.

Despatch Writing — Quantity

On this subject there are two schools of thought. The consular system tends to compute the matter on the basis of the old conundrum: "If a hen-and-a-half lays an egg-and-a-half in a day-and-a-half," etc., on which basis a mission with four secretaries would be expected to write four times as many despatches as a mission with one secretary. But I have always found this theory of quantitative output unsound and fallacious. The Department doesn't need and ought not to want junk, yet an appalling amount of junk is turned in nevertheless. I once knew a secretary in a small mission where there was little work to do who used to turn in two or three dozen despatches every week, but when I arrived as Minister and investigated, I found that about 90 per cent of his despatches were merely paraphrases of local press articles. His industry was no doubt praiseworthy and the Department was duly impressed by it for it has since brought him to high rank, but I fear I dampened his ardor at that time by suggesting other more productive outlets for his fertility than filling the Department's archives with junk. Man power is a sacred asset which should not be squandered.

My feeling is that there is a great deal too much despatch writing in the Service and that much superfluous and ineffective labor is performed merely to create the impression in the Department that one is busy and industrious. The net result of a large proportion of the despatches turned in, I fully believe, is merely to overwhelm the already overburdened departmental officials and file clerks.

In the preparation of despatches the following general rules would seem to me to be fair guides:

(1) A general report on the press should be turned in by every pouch, briefly surveying the whole field of developments as published by all sections of the press, together with brief comments or interpretations when desirable, as well as summaries of significant editorial opinion. (This duty is effectively and admirably performed here by the Consul whose long experience in Turkey qualifies him to do it better than anybody in the Embassy.)

(2) Despatches should be written·on developments or events of outstanding importance or significance, with interpretation and, when possible, prognostication. In long-drawn cases, such as the Turco-Greek controversy over the exchange of populations and abandoned property, it would be much better to await the final outcome and then to summarize the case with its results instead of reporting the bickering details by every pouch.

(3) Despatches should be written on developments or events bearing directly or indirectly on American interests.

(4) Reports should be turned in on matters on which individuals, companies or other organizations in the United States might be likely to turn to the Department for information or statistics. This, of course, is a very broad qualification and should be determined by common sense and imagination. It should not be overdone because the Department can call by cable for desired information at any moment.

(5) Significant conversations with statesmen, diplomatic colleagues and others should be reported.

(6) General surveys or studies should be prepared from time to time on various phases of the life of the country to which the mission is accredited — political, economic, financial, social, etc., in order to give the Department a general picture of conditions.

It may be held that these categories pretty well cover the entire potential field of despatch writing, but I differ on that point. A great many despatches are turned in, even from this mission, which cannot be considered to fall under any of the foregoing headings. Briefly summarized, these categories would include only a weekly or fortnightly survey of the press, a series of studies of the life of the country and, in the meantime, the reporting only of matters of outstanding significance or of special interest to the United States. They should and would be amply sufficient to enable the home Government to formulate its policies or to call, by cable or mail, for further reports on particular subjects when desired.

To depart for a moment on a tangent, one Under Secretary of State sent out an historic circular instruction to all missions directing them to send to the Department complete information regarding the countries in which they were located covering every possible subject from a, astronomy, to z, zoology. No possible subject or topic was omitted from the printed tome distributed to the missions and having reported on these subjects, the missions were to keep them up to date. A wonderful Bureau of World Information was established in the Department under Prentiss Gilbert with a wonderful card catalogue, so that any inquiry from any source on any subject could in future be immediately and completely answered. The theory was magnificent. But in practice the Bureau began to swell until Gilbert had some forty or more hardly spared departmental clerks collating the information which dribbled in from a few of the more conscientious missions abroad. The less conscientious frankly rebelled. I watched the thing for a year and then sent out another circular instruction quite simply but definitely cancelling the former one and dispersed Gilbert and his potential army — which would surely have eventually assumed the proportions of that of Xerxes — among the other divisions and bureaus of the Department where every man or woman was sorely needed. The missions sent up a sigh of relief and the World's Almanac venture was dead as a doornail from which status, let us hope, it may never recover. So much for quantitative output.

Despatch Writing — Quality, Form

How well I know from my own experience in the Department how one blesses the writer of "readable" despatches and how one damns those who present a subject like a suet pudding. Charles Hart's reports from Tirana as Minister to Albania were like beams of sunshine. Lewis Einstein, Minister to Czechoslovakia, could say in two pages what others said in fifteen, leaving the reader quite groggy. The fact is that some men have the knack of writing well in matters of construction, rhetoric, style, consolidation and general readableness, while others haven't and they'll never get it. But, after all, they're not writing themes for school and there are so many other duties and functions in the Service besides despatch writing that I venture to hold a brief for the man who, while lacking literary ability, nevertheless makes up for that handicap in many other useful ways. I cannot undertake to remodel every despatch that comes across my desk and while correcting the more glaring errors can only give advice for future drafting.

Furthermore, at a mission where the pouch mail leaves only once a fortnight, there is often a natural tendency to crowd a despatch through at the last moment rather than to hold it over for two weeks. In cases where we are following some line such as the recent financial developments, it is important to wait until the last moment until all available information is in — from the press, from Angora and from other sources — in other words, until pouch day — before setting about to draft the despatch at all. Then the rough drafts come to me with a rush and the result is obvious. These are at least up to date even if they lack well-rounded drafting. This applies quite as much to my own despatches as to those of my secretaries and I often wish that they could be redrafted the next day.

Substance

In this country, more than at any post at which I have served, the facts necessary to present a subject adequately are often not available and no amount of industry can elicit them. In Turkey, the borderline between fact, fiction and rumor and gossip is often untraceable. I often deplore the lack of thoroughness of some of our despatches, but it is frequently beyond my power, or anybody's power, to make them more thorough. The Department presumably wants facts and opinions based on facts and a few guesses, but it ought not to want opinion based only on rumors of which there are always a plethora in Turkey.

As to contacts, it is possible that my own and those of my staff are not so broad as they might be. The Turkish professors, doctors, businessmen and so forth might be cultivated, the minority leaders might be oftener approached, the old religious elements might more frequently be consulted. A great many interesting views might be turned in to the Department as a result. But I venture to believe that while such material might be academically very interesting — as interesting in some cases, let us say, as the articles in *Foreign Affairs* — I doubt very much indeed if they would shed a great deal of light upon the practical matters which the Department needs to know in order to direct the policy of the United States Government towards Turkey and the Near East. Patterson has made some flights in this direction, but I frankly doubt whether the returns justified the efforts. However, this is a question of opinion. Howland Shaw, when he comes, will be a solid rock of strength in this respect and I daresay that with his exceptional background and interests and contacts he will delve into many matters which the present staff have only very superficially studied.[3]

Concrete Results

The foregoing applies principally to desk-work but I cannot feel that desk-work — apart from keeping the home Government adequately informed — is the most important of a mission's activities or the best criterion of its usefulness. It is not desk-work to develop good international relations nor to protect and promote the specific interests of the home Government and of its citizens. It has not been due to desk-work that we have managed, I believe, to build up a position for our Embassy second in prestige to no other mission in Turkey and to obtain probably the maximum results possible under

[3] Howland Shaw, former Chief of the Division of Near Eastern Affairs, was assigned as Counselor of the Embassy at Istanbul on March 14, 1930.

the present chauvinistic regime; to establish relations with our diplomatic colleagues and prominent bankers whereby they are willing to talk to us in the utmost frankness, to tell us in detail of their various negotiations and to give us in confidence the texts of treaties and other agreements long before they come into the hands of other missions; and to gain the frequently expressed satisfaction of the local American business, educational and missionary interests with our co-operation and support.

So for the present I think we may profitably continue along the general road that we have tried to follow, without any radical alterations in policy or method.

Conversation   Ankara, April 8, 1930

His Excellency Tewfik Rushdi Bey, Minister for Foreign Affairs
. . TAX ON DONATIONS AND BEQUESTS

I said that I now wished to appeal to the Minister's sympathy and help in a matter which I considered of prime importance. Ever since coming to Turkey, I had consistently avoided making official representations on behalf of our American educational and philanthropical institutions because, regardless of rights conferred by Treaties, letters or any other agreements, I knew that these institutions could not continue to exist without the good will of the Turkish Government since whatever their juridical standing the Turkish Government — if they were not welcome in Turkey — could force them out through mere administrative regulations. I said that I had advised the Presidents and Directors of these institutions so far as possible to maintain their own contacts with and to make their own representations to the Turkish Government and that only when they arrived at some impasse would I consent to use my informal good offices.

The Minister said that he was fully aware of this attitude on my part which had distinctly commended itself to the Turkish Government and that this had contributed to the fact that our American institutions were more welcome in Turkey than the institutions of any other foreign Power. There were two elements, said the Minister, which the Government could not tolerate in foreign institutions on Turkish soil; one was religious propaganda and the other foreign political propaganda. A year and a half from now (when the Lausanne Establishment Convention expires) measures would undoubtedly be taken against many of these foreign institutions . . . where religious propaganda was the main purpose of their existence. These measures, however, would distinctly not apply to our American institutions, which, the Minister was aware, were studiously endeavoring to meet the views of the Turkish Government in the kind of instruction given to their pupils.

I then explained to the Minister the point at issue, namely, that the local financial officials in Istanbul [4] had called upon the Constantinople Woman's College to pay taxes amounting to Turkish Ltqs. 109,000 by applying the tax on donations and bequests to the regular income received by that institution from its parent organization in the United States to cover its maintenance and annual deficit. I said that I did not see how the law could possibly be interpreted to apply to these funds and, in fact, some of the officials of the Defterdarat in Istanbul had taken this view, but others had taken a contrary view and had imposed their will by demanding the payment of the tax. I then advanced in detail the arguments. . . . I said that the matter was really of the utmost seriousness, because if the present policy should be followed and should be applied to all of our colleges and schools I had been advised by the Presidents and Directors thereof that it would definitely drive them from the country because they could not continue to exist under such a heavy burden of taxation, nor would the American public be willing to continue to subscribe funds, of which approximately one-third would have to be used for the payment of these taxes. I said that I had marked my letters to the Minister "Privée" because I did not wish to regard my representations as official and formal, but I thought that in the interests of the Turkish Government, no less than American in-

[4] The name Constantinople was officially changed to Istanbul in 1930.

terests, the Minister should be made fully cognizant of the situation before it was too late. I said that there was a distinctly political angle to the matter, as the driving out of these institutions would have a deplorable effect on American public opinion and the relations of the two countries. I said that the matter was extremely urgent because the college might be required to pay this money within a very few days and that I proposed to bring up the matter in my interview with Ismet Pasha tomorrow, and I asked the Minister's permission to lay before the Prime Minister copies of the letters which I had addressed to Tewfik Rushdi Bey.

The Minister listened sympathetically to my statement and said that he perfectly remembered my previous letter of December 24 last, which he had passed on to the Minister of Finance. He would now have a talk immediately with the Minister of Finance and he also entirely approved of my laying the case before the Prime Minister and of submitting to him copies of the letters in question. He replied that he quite agreed with me that these institutions could not be expected to pay taxes amounting to one-third of their income, and he also agreed that the tax on gifts and bequests did not appear to him to apply to such funds. He said, however, that the Ministry of Finance was faced with the technical and juridical aspects of the question involved in the interpretation of the law. In any case he would do his best. . . .

Conversation   Ankara, April 9, 1930
    His Excellency Ismet Pasha, Prime Minister

I called by appointment on Ismet Pasha at six o'clock and laid before him in detail the question of the imposition on Constantinople Woman's College of the tax on gifts and bequests in much the same terms as I had presented the matter to Tewfik Rushdi Bey yesterday. The Prime Minister listened with attention and then said that he was fully *au courant* of the matter as the Minister for Foreign Affairs had told him of our talk and that this morning they had had a conference on the subject with the Minister of Finance and the Minister of

Public Instruction. Ismet Pasha said that the whole difficulty lay in the danger of discrimination in case the law should be interpreted in a manner favorable to our institutions and in a manner unfavorable to other institutions, including Turkish organizations such as the Red Crescent, etc., which had to pay the same tax. The Minister of Finance held that the law does apply to the funds received by the colleges and schools from America, while the Minister of Public Instruction holds that it does not so apply. Ismet Pasha said that the matter must come up before the Council of State, where the Minister of Finance will probably uphold his point of view while the Minister of Public Instruction will fight for his point of view and that he, the Prime Minister, will carefully watch the matter and see that no injustice is done. He said this with a twinkle in his eye, which gave me the distinct impression that a decision favorable to our institutions would probably be handed down.

I asked Ismet Pasha whether in the meantime it would not be possible to instruct the financial officials in Istanbul not to press the matter, and I said that I understood that even in a Defterdarat there were two schools of opinion as regards the propriety of claiming this tax from our institutions. I further pointed out that a decision by the Council of State might involve much delay and that it was important for our colleges and schools to know just where they stood so that they could make their arrangements for the next academic year. Ismet Pasha replied that instructions would be given to the officials in Istanbul to hold off for the time being and that he would do his best to secure a prompt ruling by the Council of State. . . . He added that our American colleges and schools are much appreciated and needed in Turkey and that every effort would be made to avoid placing them in a position which would necessitate their withdrawing from the country. I talked with him at some length concerning the policy of our institutions and my own attitude toward them in their relations with the Turkish Government, all of which appeared to meet with Ismet Pasha's approval. . . .

Mr. Grew was in the United States on a leave of absence from late April, 1930, until his return to Istanbul on July 6, 1930. While in New York City he delivered a speech over Radio Station WOR on June 12, 1930, about the American Hospital of Istanbul. One of the members of the American community in Turkey wrote Mr. Grew in 1930: "Our hospital is indebted to you for many an indispensable push."

My Friends of the Radio Audience:

I have come a long way from my post in Constantinople, which is now called Istanbul, to help forward a work which is very close indeed to my heart. . . . A wave of educational enthusiasm is sweeping through the country and even the farmers who till their land during the day attend night schools to master the new alphabet. Within the city of Istanbul, cooperating with the Turks in their formidable task, there are many institutions, both educational and philanthropic, which for generations have been centers of American culture, American scholarship and American ideals. Robert College, one of the foremost academic institutions in the East, looks down from a high bluff above the Bosporus and sheds its lamp of learning not only through the Turkish Republic but the entire Near East as well. Upon another hill beside it stands the Constantinople Woman's College — likewise an American institution, while many American schools carry on their constructive work within the city and far into the center of Anatolia.

Tonight I wish to say merely a word concerning one of these organizations, which in some respects is the most important of them all, for it spreads the torch of healing, of modern medical knowledge and of scientific nursing throughout this part of the world, and acts as a leaven of modern medical science and methods through the many people with whom it comes in contact. This is the American Hospital of Istanbul. Its doors are open to the people of every race and every creed — to Moslem and Christian, to Turk or Jew, Armenian, Bulgarian or Greek — whoever may have need of its aid. And those who cannot pay are treated free. Dr. Lorrin A. Shepard, its director, is at once a brilliant surgeon and physician and a most able administrator. Its Nurses' Training School accepts young Turkish or other Near Eastern girls for a three years scientific course of medicine and nursing and sends them out to other institutions in that part of the world to spread their knowledge and to raise the standards in a part of the globe where the advantages of modern nursing methods are as yet but little understood. But above all, it is a tremendous boon to American citizens whose work entails living in this distant country, and especially to American visitors who, like yourselves, may have occasion to visit the Near East on some winter cruise and require medical or surgical aid when far from home. Only the other day, the life of a young American girl — daughter of a prominent American woman — was saved by prompt operation in this American Hospital. I know of many such cases. Maternity cases are an important element of the Hospital's work, and on the shelves of a small room one can at any time see a dozen or more baskets containing each a precious newborn babe which has been ushered into the world under the same sanitary conditions as obtain here in the great cities of the United States.

The United States is a charitable country. Year after year American men and women give testimony to their altruistic desire to help in distant parts of the world. I have lived in many countries, have seen many peoples, and have known many conditions of life. Often have I come across the practical results of America's philanthropy, but in no country have I known of a more noble, helpful and effective institution than the American Hospital in Istanbul. But our present building is cramped. We have not sufficient space or material to carry on the work adequately. Nor have we sufficient funds to insure the future even of the present establishment. It cannot continue a hand-to-mouth existence. The American community in Turkey has done its best, heartily and liberally. But that community is not a wealthy one. The Hospital must close its doors unless adequate help is forthcoming from home. So today a committee of public-spirited men and women has been set up in New York at a meeting held at noon under the active patronage of Admiral Mark L. Bristol, American High Commissioner in Turkey for eight years, who himself assisted at the Hospital's birth and who gave it his wholehearted support during his entire sojourn in Turkey. This committee hopes to solve the problem of funds. Ever since I succeeded Admiral Bristol in Turkey in 1927, three years ago, I have realized — more every day, I think — the benefits of his work, and I have helped to push forward what he began. Many millions of dollars are spent annually in charity and, while charity begins at home, the American people have never held that it should end at home.

Thank you sincerely for the opportunity to lay before you this matter of import in which every American citizen may well be directly or indirectly interested.

Monday, July 14 [1930] Istanbul
The Council of State has handed down its decision regarding the levying of the donations tax on the school at Erenkeuy, ruling unanimously that the law cannot be interpreted as covering the money received by the school in a current account from its parent organization. So far as we can now see, this decision must apply in equal force to the colleges and all the schools, which is an immense satisfaction as it removes what was unquestionably my outstanding diplomatic problem and a problem which has caused a great deal of anxiety. Certain comment let drop by the officials indicates that it was my representations to Ismet Pasha that turned the trick. The Ministry of Finance can obtain another ruling if it can submit further evidence or advance further reasons for its position, and it may try to do so in the case of the other institutions, but for the present, at least, this may be regarded as a major victory and I doubt very much if the verdict can be shaken. . . .

Wednesday, August 6 [1930]
. . . The interest of watching the ships passing up and down the Bosporus never palls; I still write down the names of every

The American Embassy, Tokyo — the Chancery

The American Embassy, Tokyo — the Residence

The Author speaking at a dinner of the America-Japan Society. The third on the Author's right is former Prime Minister Koki Hirota, executed as a war criminal. The naval officer at the right is Admiral Osumi, Minister of the Navy

At the graves of the five American sailors of Commodore Perry's expedition (left to right): Debuchi, Chief Priest, Mrs. Grew, the Author, Dickover, Admiral Nomura, Mrs. Dickover, Commander Mizuno, Count Kabayama

Mr. and Mrs. Grew with their granddaughters, Alice and
Lilla Lyon, in Tokyo

THE GAIMUSHO
TOKIO

May 14, '41.

Dear Mr. Ambassador,

I have given a short
order at once to attend the matter
your Excellency brought to my
knowledge this afternoon & also to prepare a brief of the case so that I
may be ready to take it up
with the Finance Minister immediately.

I am wondering, to be frank,
why you appeared so disturbed when
I referred to the American attitude & decision, before your Excellency's

departure; it all sounds
now somewhat strange to an
that I misused a word (!) of
course I was not speaking in
my own language & you must
make some allowance for my
reasonably wishing to hesitate in
choosing words, particularly when I
speak off-hand.) Of course,
I didn't mean to say in-
decency, no! I wanted to
say indiscretion. What I
wished to say (& that was an
frank statement) was to warn
into regard of having a grave

Letter of "explanation" from Yosuke Matsuoka, Japanese Foreign Minister

Mr. and Mrs. Grew placing sasaki branches before the shrine to Townsend Harris, first American Minister to Japan, on the 80th anniversary of the arrival of Commodore Perry's "Black Ships" at Shimoda

Unveiling of a plaque to the memory of Townsend Harris. The speaker is Prince Tokugawa, President of the America-Japan Society. The old gentleman with the white beard, second from the left, front row, is Baron Masuda, who as a boy swam out against Perry's ships with a knife in his teeth. He later became Townsend Harris' office boy

The Author and William Turner of the American Embassy in
Tokyo, on the repatriation ship *Gripsholm*, 1942

The Dumbarton Oaks Conference, 1944. Left to right: Charles
E. Bohlen, Leo Pasvolsky, Secretary of State Edward Stettinius,
Mr. Grew

new one and record its funnel with colored pencils, so that not only are most of the lines now familiar but many of the ships themselves are old friends and recognizable at first sight without the aid of the glasses to read the names, although the new Zeiss glasses are a tremendous boon when necessary. It is a harmless hobby, much like that of stamp collecting, but it is also instructive for it gives one a pretty good idea of the shipping traffic with Russia, Bulgaria and Rumania, the preponderant flags, tonnage, new types of ships, etc. Although the relative tonnage during my first two summers was clearly (1) Italian, (2) Greek and (3) British, it seems to me that Greece has outstripped Italy this year; the former has an amazing number of small tramps perpetually moving into the Black Sea and back. The largest number of passing ships observed in one day is 25, but this does not include the "ships that pass in the night" or while I am away from my post of observation, for which one might add 25 per cent or more. The American Export Lines send a ship into the Black Sea about three times a month. The newest and largest, the *Exilona,* is fitted out to carry forty cabin passengers. There must be some old New England shipping blood in my veins for ships have thrilled me since childhood. . . .

In the afternoon Gillespie dropped in to tell me confidentially that two of his Turkish friends, one of them a Deputy, had told him that the Gazi was unwilling longer to shoulder the responsibility for the mistakes of the Government, that he was therefore going to resign from the People's Party and remain aloof from any party, that he would shortly summon Fethi Bey [Ambassador to France] to stand for election to the Assembly and to form a new Party to be known as the Liberal Party, which would, in effect, become the Party of Opposition, and that the old exiled liberals such as Rauf Bey, Dr. Adnan Bey, Halidé Hanum, etc., would be welcomed back to Turkey.[5]

---

[5] Rauf Bey, former Prime Minister, Dr. Adnan Bey, former Minister of Public Education, and his wife, Halidé Edib Hanum, writer and pioneer in the Turkish women's movement, were forced to leave Turkey after the Kurdish revolt of 1925. At that time many who opposed openly, or who were suspected of secretly

This was a momentous statement, and if true, will require very careful thought and discussion in the Embassy in order to diagnose correctly the sudden change in orientation and to determine whether it is merely a maneuver to get rid of Ismet or a bona fide departure from the dictatorship to a genuine attempt at normal republican two-party government. The statement presages the biggest political development that has taken place since I came to Turkey and whatever may be behind it, it is of course of the utmost interest. . . .

Monday, August 11 [1930]
. . . Of course the new political bombshell fills our thoughts and calls for considerable mental acrobatics in trying to reach an accurate diagnosis of its precise purport and what lies behind it. This morning we had a staff meeting and discussed it for an hour. I prepared a draft despatch which Howland Shaw didn't like, and then he prepared a counterdraft which I didn't like; today I sat down at 5 and wrote till 11, the resulting redraft incorporating, more or less, the views of all of us. Shaw had a hack at it in the morning and here it is in its final form:

Istanbul, August 11, 1930
A political development of importance has taken place in this country of sudden and surprising changes: Fethi Bey has resigned as Ambassador to France and in a letter to the Gazi, now published but written, allegedly, a month and a half ago, has announced his intention of forming a Party, to constitute in effect the Party of Opposition. In his letter Fethi Bey charges the Government with having followed an unsound policy in financial and economic matters, to which he partially attributed the present economic depression in the country, and he criticizes also the administration of justice as well as the conduct of foreign affairs. In summing up, he ascribes this ad-

opposing, the Kemalist regime were banished. In 1927, following the plot against the life of the Gazi, Rauf and Dr. Adnan who appeared to be implicated in the plot were sentenced to imprisonment by the Revolutionary Tribunal, although they were still out of the country. Dagobert von Mikusch, *Mustapha Kemal* (Garden City: Doubleday, Doran & Co., 1931), pp. 364–65, 372.

verse state of affairs in Turkey to the fact that the Grand National Assembly is composed of but one party, the members of which abstain from free discussion in the Assembly and from healthy criticism of their own Cabinet, with the result that the Government has become quasi nonresponsible. The remedy he finds in the creation of a Party of Opposition with complete freedom of political discussion both in the Assembly and in the press.

In acknowledging the receipt of this letter, the Gazi gives his full approval to Fethi Bey's proposal, welcomes the new party about to be formed and expresses his conviction that its creation for the purpose of stimulating free discussion of national affairs is in line with the fundamental principles of the Republic.

The birth of the new Party has been attended by all the éclat worthy of the occasion; the Gazi has been photographed with Fethi Bey at a ball at the former's summer residence in Yalova; Fethi Bey and Ismet Pasha have appeared together in public and the latter has publicly welcomed his old "comrade" into the political arena while expressing his conviction that the Government and the People's Party will be able fully to justify their policy and measures when the time comes to discuss them in the Assembly, as well as registering a certain lack of enthusiasm for opposition parties — at least of the past; the tempestuous editor of the *Yarin* has telegraphed his congratulations to Fethi Bey and the latter has replied with the statement that he is already at work on his program. The *Yarin* has, however, not waited for the completion of Fethi Bey's labors but has already published the program and also the names of some sixty deputies who, it is said, will join the new Party. The list includes persons of such widely differing political ideals as to suggest a negative rather than a positive bond of union. Even more important events may take place in the next few months. Fethi Bey, it is said, will succeed Ismet Pasha as Prime Minister and the Gazi will resign from the People's Party and confine his political authority to keeping the peace between the two Parties.

These happenings give rise to a flood of conjectures of intense interest — and conjectures they must remain until further facts and further evidence are available to justify a sure diagnosis of the situation and all that lies behind it. One asks one's self: how much of it can be ascribed to the development of a political ideal, how much to a purely opportunist political maneuver to get rid of Ismet and the present Government? By what machinery will the new Party be formed, how will its members be chosen, and what proportion of the present deputies will join it; by what ingenious procedure will Fethi Bey eventually become Prime Minister and form his own Cabinet if Ismet, who is a fighter by nature, should decline to yield? And finally arises the inevitable question: to what extent is the whole matter "window dressing," to what extent will normal party government really succeed the dictatorship of the past five years, and fair and free discussion and criticism both in the Assembly and in the press be tolerated by those in power?

So far as the political ideal is concerned, it must be acknowledged that an eventual two-party system has for some time existed in the minds of certain Turkish leaders as an ultimate goal to be attained when conditions should justify the step. According to this view the Gazi has been keenly aware of the anomalous character of Turkish political life since 1925 and has been eagerly awaiting the moment when Turkey's position at home and abroad would permit a closer approximation to the ways of western democracy and parliamentary practice. There is good reason to believe that the two-party system was being discussed by the Gazi with certain of his more trusted friends as long ago as 1928, and it must be admitted that the creation of an Opposition Party by fiat of the Gazi is quite in line with the manner of bringing other reforms into effect — and incidentally quite different from the unwelcome spontaneity attending the foundation of the Progressive Party in 1924.[6]

6 The Progressive Party had been composed of "Young Turk" politicians, royalists, intellectuals, members of religious orders, and the *Entente Libérale*. It had formed around such men as Rauf Bey, Refet Pasha, Dr. Adnan Bey, and Kiazim Qara Bekir Pasha as an opposition party to the People's Party of which

It may also be argued that, certainly during the past year, criticism in the press of government policy and measures has been tolerated — not completely, it is true — but still to a far greater degree than was the case during the earlier years of the dictatorship. The general tendency has been toward greater liberty of speech and it therefore may be held that the creation of an Opposition Party is the outcome of this tendency and a development of Turkey's aspirations towards westernization.

On the other hand more realistic explanations of the step are not wanting. Things have not been going any too well in Turkey recently, chiefly because of the economic depression for which the Government's policies are blamed; too much building of strategic railways, too many foreign purchases, too chauvinistic an attitude toward foreign loans, too little attention paid to agricultural development. Dissatisfaction with the Government, so far as public opinion exists in Turkey at all, has been rife, and on top of this the revival of the Kurdish troubles has brought vividly to the attention of Turkey's leaders the existence of an Achilles' heel the future consequences of which are difficult to foresee. Incidentally, it is worth noting that while the Kurdish revolt of 1925 brought about the fall of Fethi Bey because he refused to adopt a general policy of repression in order to put down the revolt, the better organized Kurdish uprising of 1930 coincides with the return of Fethi Bey to a position of importance and leadership in the domestic policy of the country.[7] In short, the present is not a

the Gazi was the head. Although Atatürk at first evidenced willingness to allow an opposition party, the growing strength of the Progressives and their suspected connection with a Kurdish revolt in 1925 led to attempts to suppress the party and intimidate its leaders. The Cabinet of Fethi Bey who had been sympathetic to the Progressives fell, and Fethi was sent to Paris as Ambassador. See Arnold J. Toynbee and Kenneth P. Kirkwood, *Turkey* (London: Ernest Benn, 1926), pp. 193–95.

[7] The Kurds were numerically the largest of the non-Turkish peoples remaining within Turkey in 1925. They held not only a hostility toward their Turkish rulers but also had developed a sense of nationality. The Treaty of Sèvres had granted the Kurds autonomy and independence, but the failure of the treaty to obtain ratification had disappointed the national hopes of the Kurds. In this situation of discontent it was not difficult for a Dervish-Sheik to

time when the rulers of Turkey can rejoice in the responsibility which is theirs and theirs alone. It is a time when one likes "to pass the buck," but as things are organized in Turkey, responsibility is highly centralized. The Gazi, it is generally admitted, is very sensitive to anything that threatens his personal prestige and he is said to be getting tired of being blamed for everything that goes wrong. If such is the case, how entirely natural to have recourse to a new party, especially when the new party could so easily pave the way for a new Prime Minister and Cabinet. The Turkish dictatorship is an admirable system from the point of view of the dictator when things are going well, but in times of stress and strain the responsibility of the dictator is too directly and obviously involved and such success as is achieved is more likely to redound to the advantage and prestige of the Prime Minister than to his superior. There has been much talk of disagreement between the Gazi and Ismet Pasha, of the Gazi's desire for a change and of Ismet's determination not to yield his office, for Ismet, as I have said, is a fighter by nature and no weakling.

In consideration of all of these facts and circumstances, therefore, the view most commonly held by those diplomatic colleagues and others with whom I have talked is that the new developments represent a twofold purpose: (1) the creation of a "safety valve" by which Fethi Bey and the Liberal Party will help to ease the strain and burden of criticism to which the

arouse the Kurds, who had been outraged by the steps against the Moslem religion taken by the Turkish Government. An insurrection broke out in February, 1925, the arrest of several Kurds for sedition serving as an immediate pretext to open the revolt. By April the insurrection had been put down, after severe military action in the eastern vilayets, where the Kurds and their sympathizers were strongest. *Ibid.,* pp. 263–68. In June, 1930, Kurds living in Persia crossed over into Turkish territory joining with Kurds in Turkey in the raiding of Turkish villages. By the end of July the Kurdish forces were said to number 15,000. The Turkish army encountered difficulty in suppressing the revolt, because the retreating Kurds fled across the Persian border, only to rearm and return. Turkey came to an agreement with Persia about exchanging territory which facilitated the settlement of the matter. See the *New York Times,* June 21, 1930, p. 6; July 26, 1930, p. 4; December 3, 1930, p. 13.

Gazi feels he is now subjected, and (2) the eventual dethrone-
ment of Ismet Pasha, whose strength cannot be altogether pleasing to Mustafa Kemal, by means of a large political maneuver
the very nature of which prevents Ismet from combating it,
at least at its inception.

In addition to these points, the comment has been made that
Fethi Bey is well and favorably known in French banking circles
and should Turkey desire a loan from France, or a modification
of the Ottoman Debt Settlement, his presence at Ankara [8]
whether as Party leader or Prime Minister could not fail to be
opportune.

The foregoing appraisal, so far as the facts and evidence now
available permit any appraisal, appears to me and to my staff to
be sound, but further developments must be awaited before
the actual working out of the new system and its results can
be intelligently predicted. . . .

Saturday, August 30 [1930]
    . . . From all accounts the new Party is having some difficulty
in organizing and only 13 Deputies have so far publicly transferred their allegiance. It is said that the People's Party is very
busy reorganizing itself and that all members have been asked
to define their position; if they are against the Government
they must leave the Party at once, otherwise they will be expected to remain permanently. I have heard, however, that the
new Party will be gratuitously accorded seventy seats in the
Assembly pending the elections and I have very little doubt, if
this is true, that seventy Deputies will find themselves tapped
on the back much as if they were being tapped for Bones or
Keys and that few if any will dare to disobey the summons.
Meanwhile the press is daily becoming more of an arena for
political warfare and mutual recriminations are rapidly becoming the order of the day. Exception has been taken by
Ismet's supporters to Fethi's declarations about the right of
minorities to take part in parliamentary and municipal elec-

[8] The name of the Turkish capital was changed from Angora to Ankara in
1930.

tions. It is also pointed out that the new Party is providing a rallying ground for all sorts of discontented and disgruntled politicians and that such a nucleus cannot form a satisfactory basis for a really strong progressive party. The Minister of Justice has also entered the lists by warmly defending the present judicial system, adding that the People's Party owes explanations to no one, not even to Allah. Fethi Bey answered this speech, said to have been made while the Minister was drunk, cleverly pointing out several absurdly illogical arguments therein, to which Mahmud Essad replied in a lofty tone completely ignoring Fethi's telling points. Turkey's political life is going to be great fun this year because the high-flown praise of Government which monotonously filled the press up to a few months ago (when the *Yarin* began its first attacks) is now giving place to political criticism, discussion and bickering. Whether this is to be a healthy or an unhealthy departure it is too soon to predict. Ordinarily it would serve as a useful balance wheel on the Government, but in Turkey's present stage of political development it is very questionable whether she is ready for, and can assimilate, an active opposition. . . .

Friday, September 5 [1930]

. . . Smyrna has broken completely loose on Fethi Bey's arrival and received him like a conquering hero, having at last an opportunity to manifest its disapproval of the Government's policy and measures; the offices and printing press of the local sheet of the People's Party, and *Anadolou,* were stormed and damaged, one person was killed, many injured and 300 arrested according to the press reports. The *Milliyet's* explanation of the affair, that it was due entirely to vagrants, communists and criminals and that it had no political significance whatever, is even more puerile than the usual Turkish press explanations. One high official states that the reports are grossly exaggerated and that apart from 300 arrests no incident whatever occurred! This situation must at least give pause to those who maintain that Fethi and his new Party can muster no strength in the country. Alexander Helm [British Consul] and I agreed

that we are distinctly in a minority among the colleagues in
believing that Fethi is going to succeed and that Ismet is going
to go, sooner or later, for the whole thing is the Gazi's initiative
and the Gazi's battle and the Gazi is not accustomed to losing
battles. He is, in large measure, staking his reputation on it
and he must be aware that if Fethi fails it will amount to his
own personal failure. But as Ismet is just as obstinate a fighter
as the Gazi, it is going to be one of the most lovely scraps ever
staged. Meanwhile the Smyrna incident is probably significant. . . .

Thursday, September 11 [1930]

A request from Yunus Nady [editor of *République*] for the
Gazi's guidance in the present confused state of politics in Turkey has brought forth an open letter from the Gazi stating
categorically that he has no intention of resigning from the
People's Party to which he is bound by historical tradition
and that although he will preserve strict neutrality while Chief
of State, he will return to work for the old Party as soon as he
quits office. In the meantime he deplores the recent incidents
in Smyrna. The editor of *Son Posta*, a liberal sheet, has been
arrested and is to be tried for publishing comments of an
inciting nature, in response to which the editor of *Anadolou*,
the Government sheet in Smyrna, has likewise been arrested at
the instance of Fethi Bey. So much for the alleged freedom
of the press. The situation is as bewildering as it well could
be and to prophesy results at the present moment is a hazardous
undertaking; one guess is as good as another. The chief thing
to bear in mind is that developments in Turkey should seldom
be taken at their face value and that intrigue behind the
scenes is steadily in progress. The meeting of the Assembly
will probably give us something more concrete to go on. . . .

To Secretary of State Stimson, September 24, 1930

The leaders of Turkey were taken by surprise by the warmth
of the reception accorded to Fethi Bey at Smyrna. The local
authorities lost their heads. Mahmud Essad Bey, the much

hated Minister of Justice, probably helped them in this respect. He was at Smyrna at the time and doubtless the local authorities wanted to show what they could do for the People's Party. Certainly the crowd was tactlessly handled by the Police and much of the trouble came from that fact. But the higher-ups, including even the Gazi, inclined to the view that there was too much enthusiasm for the new Party and that a bit of cooling off would do no harm. Kiazim Pasha, the President of the Assembly, was sent to Smyrna. He brought Fethi and Mahmud Essad together and made the necessary arrangements for them to embrace each other at the cemetery before and after the funeral of the boy who was killed during the disturbances; an article of the Smyrna *Hizmet* having been considered offensive to the Republic, the editor was arrested as was also the responsible editor of the Istanbul *Son Posta* which had reproduced the offending article. But far more important, the Gazi spoke — twice. Through the Agence d'Anatolie he declared he was not on the side of the new Party and in an open letter he affirmed the historical connection between himself and the People's Party. The words were intrinsically not especially significant, but the circumstances under which they were given to the public lent to them great force. They meant in effect: "A second party is an excellent thing, but be careful."

Fethi's speech at Smyrna on September 7, was colorless as a speech but as an occasion it was a huge success. A vast crowd was on hand and enthusiasm was at fever pitch. It made no difference that Fethi was hoarse and had frequently to utilize Nuri Bey as loud speaker; it made no difference that the speech afforded little or no evidence of a concrete program.

Fethi's brief visits to Balikesir and Manisa were likewise marked by great public enthusiasm. A small boy made a speech at one of the stations and set forth the grievances of the peasantry, the backbone of Turkey. "Fethi," said this small boy, "the future of the peasantry is the future of your Party."

The Grand National Assembly was summoned to meet in a special session on September 22, ostensibly to pass legislation which has become urgently necessary because of the marked surplus of foreign exchange at the present time. Other items to be included in the agenda seem to be: a defense of his policy by Ismet Pasha, with or without a vote of confidence, and Fethi Bey's election as Deputy. There is also talk of dissolution and new elections. The meeting of the Assembly coincides with the resignation of the Minister of Justice. Other changes in the Cabinet are imminent. It seems certain that the Ismet Pasha Cabinet will resign in order to permit the Prime Minister to reconstruct his Cabinet and then at once ask for a vote of confidence from the Assembly.

It is now possible to explain, at least in part, the establishment of the new Party. I am confident that this explanation is to be sought in a combination of factors rather than in any one particular factor. I suspect that the Gazi has gradually come to look upon the single party system as a sign of Turkey's inferiority in comparison with Europe and the West. American and European writers have in recent years devoted much space to the Turkish dictatorship which has often been described as Western in form but Oriental in fact. These descriptions have been brought to the Gazi's attention and he has not been pleased. Doubtless Fethi Bey with his admiration for French political institutions has played an important role as the interpreter of Western and particularly of French opinion in this connection. It should never be forgotten that the Turkish leaders have an almost juvenile respect for what is done in other countries, a great sensitiveness to any suggestion that they are not European and an astonishing power of imitating the external.

So much for the first factor which has led to the formation of the Opposition Party. More practical considerations, however, have played a part and among these I should place first a recognition that the single-party system when the Chief of State is head of the Party has serious disadvantages from the point of view of practical politics, for instance; responsibility is inconveniently centralized — and obvious. It is clear that one effect of the formation of a second party has been to disengage the responsibility of the Gazi and to convert the Turkish political game into a struggle between Ismet and Fethi. In dealing with popular discontent, the two-party system has undeniable advantages.

I have no illusions as to the difficulties which confront an Opposition Party in Turkey. Because of the political immaturity of the Turkish people and the personalization of political issues, the Opposition Party attracts all sorts of people for all sorts of reasons. The Opposition therefore tends to be discredited by its more extreme members or if it ever comes to power its heterogeneous character makes the carrying out and even the formulation of a specific program exceedingly difficult. I have some doubts as to Fethi Bey's ability to cope with these difficulties, but the support of the Gazi may make up for certain deficiencies in leadership.

The Government of Ismet Pasha had gotten itself into a rundown condition. Certain members of the Cabinet were notoriously incompetent; there was a good deal of inefficiency and unquestionably some corruption. The creation of the Opposition Party is being made the occasion for readjusting and rejuvenating the People's Party and may, if wise and restrained leadership is forthcoming, become an instrument for the political education of Turkey.

Monday, September 29 [1930]

Gillespie, who has returned from Ankara, gives an interesting description of the opening of the Assembly — on September 24 — which he attended in person. The Gazi sat in his private box watching the tilting between the Government and the Opposition from the tribune — beaming when a telling point was scored, frowning when a point was awkwardly handled. Gillespie says it reminded him of nothing so much as of a proud father watching his sons competing in two opposing debating teams. He says that the Gazi looks better than he has ever seen him, probably as a result of the summer rest at Yalova, and that now he is working day and night with Ismet, Fethi and the other Deputies and can be seen through the windows of his room in the Assembly after adjournment, holding conferences with one group after another, always standing, till far into the night. The whole outlook of the Assembly has changed and whereas formerly the measures of the Government were accepted and voted in an automatic and apathetic fashion, now everyone is full of zest, important points are freely debated, constructive criticism formulated and a real parliamentary atmosphere prevails.

The new Cabinet is a great deal stronger than the old one and it begins to look as if radicalism in Turkey had run its course.[9] The four new Ministers are all solid, conservative, efficient men, and they immeasurably raise the whole tone of the Government. Government measures will I believe in future be far less arbitrary and chauvinistic than heretofore. If Fethi will keep his opposition on an equally high and constructive plane and not let it descend to radicalism and demagogy, the future of parliamentarism in Turkey and indeed the whole outlook for the country will look bright. Having talked with a great many people and having observed their obvious sincerity and keen interest in the new move, Gillespie is now ready to confirm my original theory that the step was merely another move in the normal development of the Gazi's political idealism, taken at the psychological moment. As Dr. Refik said to him: "Two years ago this step would have been impossible; we had to wait until the country was in order and had assimilated the reforms already put into effect; that time has now come and we are ready to go ahead on a normal parliamentary basis." . . .

Angora, Monday, October 27 [1930]

An historic day — the visit of a Prime Minister of Greece to the capital of Turkey; the signing of treaties;[10] the placing

[9] The new Cabinet consisted of Ismet Pasha as President of the Council; Tewfik Rushdi Bey, Minister for Foreign Affairs; Abdul Halik Bey, Minister of National Defense; * Yusuf Kemal Bey, Minister of Justice; Saradjoglou Shukri Bey, Minister of Finance; * Zekai Bey, Minister of Public Works; * Mustafa Cherif Bey, Minister of National Economy; Refik Bey, Minister of Hygiene; * Essad Bey, Minister of Public Instruction; and Shukri Kaya Bey, Minister of Interior. The asterisks denote new ministers.

[10] The Greco-Turkish Treaty of Friendship, Neutrality, Conciliation, and Arbitration was signed at Ankara by Venizelos and Ismet on October 30, 1930.

of the seal of friendship on the relations of the two countries after four centuries of intermittent warfare. Mr. and Mrs. Venizelos and Mr. and Mrs. Michalacopoulos, Minister for Foreign Affairs, arrived by special train at 9.30. Greek flags are flying and there is an inscription of welcome in Greek, KALOS IRTHATE, hung across the street from the station so that the visitors must pass under it. It is hard to believe that one is really in Ankara. Finding myself for the first time Acting Dean of the Diplomatic Corps, in the absence of the Russian, German and British Ambassadors, and with no senior officer to consult, I hung out our flag for the occasion. The Italians and Poles followed suit but not the others. . . .

In the evening we attended the ball given at the Ankara Palace in honor of Mr. Venizelos. The last time I had seen him was the night I spent in going back and forth between him and Ismet Pasha trying, as a disinterested neutral and with the approval of the Allies, to prevent the two countries from breaking and going to war over the reparations question. For three solid months I sat in the next seat to him at the conference table. He still wears the same old black cap but looks no older than in 1923. These balls are useful as they afford occasions for many conversations with members of the Cabinet and others whom one ordinarily sees but seldom. Had an excellent talk with Essad Bey, the new Minister of Education, about our colleges and schools which he seems to regard with favor. Had a perfectly splendid "Blue Danube" waltz with Anita with the old Vienna step — fine music, lots of room and an admirable floor. She got into it at once and danced it magnificently which resulted in many compliments from high quarters. . . .

To Secretary of State·Stimson, December 3, 1930

Fethi Bey dissolved his party on November 17. . . .

The atmosphere of the days preceding the death of the new party was ominous. Fethi had interpellated the Minister of the Interior on alleged forcible and fraudulent practices carried on by or in behalf of the People's Party in the course of the recent municipal elections. Fethi's speech was not good — he read too much. And some of his facts couldn't stand up under fire. The fire became very hot. Ali Bey, who appears to be a kindly old gentleman but who was President of the Tribunal of Independence which functioned at Smyrna and Ankara in 1927, in the course of a blistering speech pointed to Fethi Bey and said: "There is the man who is responsible for Mudros," and then turning to Ismet Pasha, "and there is the man who is responsible for Mudania." [11] Of course, when Ali Bey begins to indulge in personal remarks the atmosphere created is anything but reassuring. In fact, people begin to think and talk in whispers about the setting up of tripods or gallows. Following these ostensibly parliamentary proceedings, Fethi met with his followers and then participated in a bewildering series of talks with the Gazi, Ismet Pasha, Kiazim Pasha and others. The upshot of the whole business was the dissolution of the Party. The next night Fethi left for Istanbul with Agha Oglou Ahmed. I happened to be at the station. Fethi looked cheerfully out of the compartment window and once in a while somebody stepped up and shook hands and exchanged a few words. They were not numerous, however, and the words they spoke were few. Agha Oglou Ahmed, Fethi's Chief Lieutenant and formerly a member of the Russian Duma, surrounded by newspapermen on the platform, was voluble in explaining what had happened, but finally he clambered heavily on board; the whistle blew and the train pulled out. It was Fethi's second exit from Ankara. The first took place in 1925, and the Tri-

[11] The Armistice of Mudros, signed October 30, 1918, between Turkey and the Allies, had been completed at a time when the Turkish forces were anxious to abandon a seemingly hopeless fight, and when the Turkish people were exhausted. Its terms were severe and humilating to the Turks. Fethi Bey had been Minister of Interior in the Cabinet of Ismet Pasha, under whom the Armistice of Mudros had been concluded. The Armistice of Mudania had been signed by Ismet Pasha on October 11, 1922, after the forces of the Nationalists had successfully met those of the Allies, particularly those of Greece. It represented an Allied surrender to the Nationalists. H. W. V. Temperley (ed.), *A History of the Peace Conference of Paris* (London: Hodder & Stoughton, 1920–24), I, 135–36. Toynbee and Kirkwood, *op. cit.,* pp. 57–58, 108–10.

bunal of Independence followed.[12] His latest exit was less dramatic; in fact, it was mournful, the failure was patent.

Why has Turkey once more failed in trying to practice a little democracy? A failure it is — a serious one — more serious than 1925–1926, since then one could make out a more convincing case for strong arm methods than now. Many people are blaming Fethi. He's weak, they say; won't work, won't dig down and get the facts. He should never have gone to Smyrna; he shouldn't even have set up a party organization throughout the country; he should have come quietly to the Assembly and criticized the Government there. Perhaps he took his role of leader of the opposition too seriously and without a sufficiently clear understanding of the difficulties — and dangers — of leading an opposition in Turkey. Given the great political immaturity of Turkey, I think these statements are sound, but before the events of Smyrna their soundness was not generally recognized. The Gazi, Fethi, even Ismet didn't know the state of opinion in Turkey, had no idea apparently of the strength of the resentment which was gathering momentum underneath. Fethi had been dreaming about Turkish parliamentary life while gazing upon the Chamber of Deputies at Paris; the Gazi had been carrying on monologues on the ancient history of the Turks until all hours of the night at Tchan-Kaya with a group of sycophants. Ismet had been carrying the load of the railroads — but I suspect he never really believed in the new party. Smyrna was the beginning of the end. The Gazi was worried. Having given Fethi to understand that he would take an attitude at least of benevolent neutrality towards the new party he now affirmed his close and historical connection with the People's Party and with-

12 Fethi Bey, the Prime Minister, was forced to resign in March, 1925, as the result of a vote of censure by the Assembly for his failure to take more active measures to suppress the Kurdish revolt which had broken out earlier in that year. The Tribunals of Independence which had first been set up in December, 1923, were re-established. These Tribunals meted out stern justice, as a sort of "political inquisition." All Dervish monasteries were closed by their order, and repressive measures taken against some of the newspapers of Constantinople and the provinces. See *ibid.*, pp. 188–89, 269–70.

drew his financial and moral support from the new Party. With such a cue most of the press began a virulent, and at times highly personal, campaign against Fethi and his Party. Then came the disorders incidental to the municipal elections; they took a nasty turn and the police couldn't handle the situation. The new Party had become a clinical thermometer for taking the political temperature of the country and there could be no doubt of the fever which it registered. The Gazi became even more worried and Fethi did not seem to be doing anything convincing in the Assembly; his speeches had no punch; Agha Oglou speaks Turkish with a Tartar accent which makes it hard to understand him; the other ten deputies of the Liberal Party simply did nothing except sit in one place together. The final break, I am told, came over the question of the direct 'election of Deputies. Fethi wanted it — the Gazi didn't. There is also talk that Fevzi Pasha at the last came out against Fethi — perhaps because of disagreement between the Opposition Party and General Staff on the value of railroads.

But something has been gained; the Gazi is going to learn at firsthand about Turkey and the People's Party is being reformed and may be divided into right, center and left groups. The very night the new Party collapsed the Gazi started on a tour of study through Anatolia which, it is said, will last two months. To date he has visited Kayseri, Sivas, Tokat, Trebizond, Amasya, Samsoun and Istanbul. He has been talking with the peasants, and the school children and with everybody else. He wants to learn their grievances. The younger generation is suspected of communistic leanings — more than suspected. I have been assured that 75 per cent of the students of Istanbul University have communistic leanings. The younger generation must be brought back to the straight and narrow path of nationalism. The chief of the opposition can't go about Anatolia without starting riots and having in short order to do away with his party; but the Gazi can travel wherever he wants. Perhaps after all it's not so much self-education as a plain old-fashioned campaign tour. . . .

XXIX

The End of the Mission to Turkey
1931 – 1932

Monday, January 5 [1931]

. . . An hour's interesting talk after dinner with Muzaffer Bey, Istanbul Director of Education, who has direct oversight over our colleges and schools. Not at all satisfied with the situation at Constantinople College. Believes our schools in Turkey useful for secondary but not for primary education. The practice of religion must be and is absolutely free in the country for any creed or faith but outside, not inside, the schools; it must be absolutely apart from education. I observed that Turkey must be pinning her faith on the coming generation, the youth of today, who are growing up in the ideals of the Republic. He replied, "No, not on the coming generation; we are pinning our faith on the next generation but one; the youth of today gets half its education and idealism from the school and half, the larger half, from the home. Today the home is still of the old regime, reactionary and unable to grasp the new movements. Therefore the coming generation will not be wholly imbued with the modern ideals and new conceptions of the nation. But in the next generation but one there will be no more reactionary home influences to contend with. That is the generation on which we are pinning our faith for the future." Muzaffer also spoke at length of his desire for American contacts and his hope that Turkish professors can visit the United States from time to time and lecture there and profit by their educational experiences on their return to Turkey. The only handicap is the long journey and the expense which few Turks can afford. I gather that he favors a departure from Latin culture and a trend towards the development of American culture in Turkey. . . .

To Secretary of State Stimson
Istanbul, January 27, 1931

The incident which took place at Menemen in the Izmir vilayet [formerly Smyrna] on December 23, 1930, was briefly characterized in the Embassy's telegram of December 31, 7 P.M. Reports which have filtered in from various sources now make it possible to gauge the importance of this manifestation of reaction and to present what I believe to be an accurate estimate of its consequences.

As far as the conflicting accounts can be reconciled, the events at Menemen were probably as follows: Early in the morning of December 23 a band of six or seven armed fanatics belonging to the Nakhshbendi sect and led by one Dervish Mehmet arrived in the public square of Menemen. After a preparatory period of fasting and prayer they had walked from Manisa, preaching in the intervening towns to such of the faithful as would listen. It is reported that their utterances were seditious; they advocated the return of the Seriat or Holy Law, the wearing of the veil and the fez, the readoption of the Arabic script — in fine, they were preaching against the very reforms of which the Republic is most proud.

Menemen is a small town, some twelve miles north of Izmir. Facing on its public square is the mosque, the Government offices and some shops. It was here that the band of pilgrims, who are alleged to have been crazed by drugs and fasting, started a demonstration of some sort. If some witnesses are to be believed, the dervishes were wildly prophesying the overthrow of the Republic by the militant forces of Islam of which they were the leaders; Abdul Hamid's son would be reinstated as Caliph; the great army of the faithful which was now surrounding Menemen would march on Ankara and from there set out to conquer the world; those who opposed them would be destroyed. Attracted by the noise, a crowd of the curious formed a circle about the demonstrators. It has not been possible to learn with any certainty whether the attitude of this crowd was sympathetic to the dervishes or merely passive, but it is supposed that the dormant fanaticism of the crowd was aroused by the inflammatory exhortations of the agitators.

At this juncture a young reserve officer, Koublay Bey, appeared upon the scene. Reports vary as to whether he had been sent there with a detachment of troops or whether he merely happened to be crossing the square. At all events he approached the agitators alone and, apparently relying on the prestige of his uniform for protection, started an argument with Dervish Mehmet and tried to disperse the crowd. It is the consensus of informed opinion that he acted, rashly and most unwisely. He was shot, allegedly by Dervish Mehmet. A night watchman then shot Dervish Mehmet and was in turn shot down. The Government papers insist that Koublay's head was sawed off and carried about on a pike, and that the fanatical dervishes and their acolytes drank his blood; but there is reason to doubt the authenticity of these reports. By this time the military authorities had been notified and a squad of gendarmes with a machine gun made its appearance; in the firing that then took place three dervishes were killed and another fled. The crowd dispersed and the incident was over.

The Government was not slow to react to the situation thus created. An intensive press campaign was immediately inaugurated, fulminating against the reactionaries who had attempted to "overthrow" the Government. Many arrests were made in various localities, principally in the Izmir region. Ismet Pasha read a report on the situation to the Grand National Assembly on January 2, 1931. . . . Martial law was established in the *Kazas* of Manisa, Menemen and Balikesir and a court-martial with almost plenary powers began its hearings on January 15. More than 100 persons are facing the court-martial, 15 or 20 of whom are *hodjas* (Moslem clergy); a second group are now being rounded up for trial by the same court; they may not be represented by counsel. The crime they are generally charged with is exciting the population to sedition, which is punishable under Article 149 of the Penal Code by at least fifteen years hard labor. The specific charges range from the murder of a Government official to the concealment of fezzes. Five officers and 20 soldiers are also up for court-martial on the charge of insubordination. This seems almost to be a confirmation of the generally accepted rumor that the soldiers called upon to suppress the riot refused to fire upon the crowd. Moreover, the mosques have been placed under special surveillance; all sermons must be submitted for approval before delivery and extemporaneous utterances from the pulpit are forbidden.

While there is evidence that the manifestation at Menemen was directed against the Government and was therefore seditious in character, nevertheless the incident was not in itself of great importance. Why, then, did the Government establish martial law and suspend ordinary justice in the Izmir region? While I cannot be sure that I have found the answer to this important question, there are strong grounds for my belief that what follows is substantially sound.

Dissatisfaction with existing economic and political conditions was rife throughout Turkey when Fethi Bey visited Izmir in September, 1930. The Department remembers the great demonstration, surpassing in size and intensity anyone's wildest predictions, which took place upon his arrival in that port. The occurrences in and near Izmir during the four or five days of Fethi Bey's presence plainly showed a real discontent with the Government of the People's Party. There were instances of resistance to the forces of law and order, and the reason that more serious trouble did not occur was apparently due to the presence of mind of a local police captain. Malcontents from all classes of society saw in an Opposition Party a rebuke to the Government; they believed that by joining it their grievances would be redressed. Many of the members of the closed *tekkés* [Dervish convents] joined, either formally or informally, with the Liberal Party, the intentions and purpose of which they misrepresented to themselves.

The Government at Ankara was disturbed by this manifestation of dissatisfaction. It had been taken completely off its guard. After the tumult had quieted down upon Fethi Bey's departure from the Izmir district, it became necessary to discover how widespread was the disaffection which had taken concrete form in the Izmir demonstrations, and to devise ways and means for preventing any further manifestation of this latent discontent. The Gazi made an extensive trip of observation through Anatolia and Thrace and had planned to visit Izmir. At the same time, a thorough reorganization of the People's Party was undertaken. If I am right in my conclusions, this reorganization will develop the People's Party into a politico-educational organism based on Fascist principles; Fascism translated into Turkish will equal a new "Kemalism." . . .

Then came the Menemen incident. This time the Government was prepared and determined to turn the event to its own advantage. Here was a golden opportunity to reaffirm the prestige of the Government which had suffered (perhaps more than we realized) from the Fethi campaign. Drastic measures were taken at once in the very locality where discontent had manifested itself most clearly. As a concomitant to the suppression of a reactionary religious movement of sedition, the malcontents who held subversive political doctrines would be taught a salutory lesson; the principles of the Republic would be taught afresh; the solidity of the Government and the People's Party would be reaffirmed. At the same time reactionism, especially that clerical reactionism which combats the progressive and Westernizing policies of the Government, would be smitten hip and thigh. The Menemen disturbances provided the suitable occasion for the accomplishment of all these correlated objectives.

To Western ears the word martial law has an ominous sound. It suggests organized revolution or very serious rioting. But in the Near East governments are willing to use small disorders as pretexts for suspending the ordinary rights and privileges of the citizenry. Thus the murder of a junior officer by a fanatical mob is ample pretext for the establishment of martial law and justice.

It was expected by many that the Government would resort to the same extreme measures which characterized the suppression of the Kurdish revolt in 1925. But the Menemen incident had nothing like the importance of the sinister Kurdish uprising; thus, less severe measures could be adopted with safety. Although a military regime was clapped upon three districts, the whole country was not subjected to repressive legislation such as the 1925 Law on the Consolidation of Public Order. It is understood that many influential Deputies, evoking that Law, at first favored the re-establishment of the Tribunals of Independence; but the less Draconian councils of Ismet Pasha finally prevailed and more legalistic methods of repression are being pursued.

In this connection, a word must be said of the tone of the press in reporting this incident. The promptitude and unanimity with which the press took up the subject, the lurid manner in which it was reported, the implication that the Government must act harshly to save the Republic — all show that the campaign was directed by the same mentality which dealt with the Kurdish revolt in 1925. But after Ismet Pasha's speech to the Assembly on January 2, as shown above, more temperate measures than those advocated in the press were adopted. The press was then used to awaken public enthusiasm for the dead "hero" Koublay and, by inference, to exhort the youth of Turkey, particularly the youth in the Army, to blind loyalty to the Republic.

In contrast to the privately expressed opinion in Ankara that Koublay was conspicuously foolhardy, the Government has officially laid great stress upon his heroism. Public demonstrations have been organized in his honor in most Turkish cities. He is held up by the press as an inspiration to Turkish youth. But the public remains apathetic. So far as one can judge, there is no particular enthusiasm over this young officer who was a school teacher; indeed, the whole Menemen incident has aroused but little public interest.

The Government and the Army, however, are very much interested. The Gazi is reported to be distinctly worried over the implications of this riot, for although he must have been aware of the popular discontent throughout the country he now sees more clearly that the reforms sponsored by his Government have not penetrated into the minds of the mass of the people. He cannot but realize that the Republic is not popular and that its aims are generally misunderstood or mistrusted. Out of this incident, unimportant in itself, may develop an educational campaign to try to inculcate upon the Turkish population the aims and purpose of the Republican Government.

For between the Government and the people a wide gulf is fixed. The military bureaucracy that rules from Ankara is not in touch with the masses. Government is imposed from above, and is regarded by the average Turk as one of the necessary evils of life. The political, social, educational and religious reforms which have been the chief achievement of the Republic have received but very limited endorsement from the people. It results that practically the only Turks who are not at least passive reactionaries are those few who are of the governing class; the vast majority of the population has always been reactionary. Indeed, no systematic efforts have been made to translate these reforms, which have merely been legislated, into the hearts and lives of the people. Therefore, that the Government has not been successful in leavening the mass with liberal principles makes it all the more remarkable that instances of active reactionism, such as the Kurdish and Menemen demonstrations, have not been multiplied. It can only be explained by the docility and apathetic fatalism of the average Turk.

To summarize: Reactionism which is endemic throughout Turkey became active in the Izmir region. A localized disturbance has served the Government's purpose in affording an opportunity (1) for chastening the discontented and reactionary elements in the Izmir region who have actively opposed the Government and its reform policies, (2) for reaffirming the solidity and power of the Government, (3) for arousing the enthusiasm of the youth for the Republic, (4) for spreading the gospel of progress along Western lines and instilling the lessons which the Republican Government must inculcate in its people if it is not eventually to be overwhelmed by the forces of reaction. It remains to be seen whether the lesson of Menemen will have a salutory effect upon the Ankara governors in their relations with and attitude toward the governed.

Wednesday, February 4 [1931]

Twenty-seven wretched persons were hanged early this morning at Menemen. It was difficult to sleep for the vision of those horrible tripods insisted on intruding itself, involving, as they do, death by slow strangulation. Added to that I have just been reading Edwin Dwinger's terrible book *Die Armee hinter Stacheldraht* — published in Jena in 1929 — the true story of a young German prisoner of war in Russia, and also the firsthand accounts published in the London *Times* of the forced labor in the Soviet prison lumber camps. All these things have depressed us beyond measure. The world is like Dr. Jekyll and Mr. Hyde. We see its suave, smiling, highly civilized side; we deal daily with men on a basis of mutual courtesy, friendliness, considerateness. Yet a few altered circumstances and many of those men, most perhaps, would be capable of unimagined cruelties. The war proved this, if we didn't know it before. . . . What a world! What a Jekyll and Hyde business life is! . . .

Conversation   Ankara, February 16, 1931
    His Excellency Tewfik Rushdi Bey, Minister for
                    Foreign Affairs

NARCOTICS

. . . The Minister said that he was particularly glad to inform me that largely as a result of our representations concerning the clandestine traffic in narcotics emanating from Turkey the Cabinet had decided immediately to seal up the three factories producing opium derivatives as well as all stocks of the manufactured product now on hand and henceforth to allow no such products to issue from the factories until the manufacturers have submitted documentary proof of destination and Government permits issued. The Minister stated his

conviction that this system, which is to be controlled by reliable Government agents stationed in each factory, will effectively put an end to the contraband traffic and will preclude any such narcotics from reaching the United States in
future. The Turkish Government realized the force of our
representations immediately but desired to delay action until
the Opium Commission at Geneva had adjourned and the press
campaign against Turkey had ceased.[1]

The Minister furthermore informed me that he was going
to request the League of Nations to furnish him with a list of
names of persons in Turkey believed to be engaged in the
clandestine traffic in narcotics and that the Government after
appropriate investigation will expel these people permanently
from the country. He also said that a state monopoly of the
manufacture of opium derivatives had been decided upon and
will go into effect within a few months as soon as the necessary arrangements can be made.

I expressed due appreciation of these steps on the part of
the Turkish Government and said I felt sure that they would
be much appreciated by my own Government. I said that in
my own country, as well as in Turkey, contraband traffic of
various kinds was a fruitful source of revenue to a good many
people of various stations in life, which sometimes included
officials, and I wondered whether this element might render
difficult the complete control of the entire output of the factories. The Minister replied that he was well aware that many
Turkish officials, including officers of the police and others,
obtained a rake-off from this clandestine traffic and that the
Government had this element distinctly in view in taking the
steps now proposed. He said that the control would be so

[1] The League of Nation's Advisory Committee on Traffic in Opium and Other
Dangerous Drugs had met in Geneva for its Fourteenth Session from January
9 to February 7, 1931. Turkey was in this period the most important world
producer of the opium used in the manufacture of morphine. In 1930, Turkey,
for the first time, sent a representative to an international conference dealing
with questions of the control of narcotics. The foreign press had been severe
in its attacks upon Turkey for her lack of co-operation in regard to the reduction and control of opium production. See L. E. S. Eisenlohr, *International
Narcotics Control* (London: George Allen & Unwin Ltd., 1934), pp. 250–54.

strict that there would not be the slightest possibility of a single centigram of drugs escaping from the factories without the issuance of official permits based upon documentary proof of destination and that if there were any doubt in the mind of the Turkish Government as to the propriety of the shipments the Embassy or Legation of the country of destination would be consulted before the issuance of permit. He said that the Cabinet had come to its decision at its last meeting and that the factories would be sealed up either today or tomorrow. Turkey had at once realized the seriousness of the situation when it was brought to her attention but the Government did not wish to act under fire and had therefore waited until the Commission at Geneva had adjourned and the press campaign against Turkey had abated. He said he would convey to Ismet Pasha my expressions of appreciation, which he thought would please him very much in view of the great responsibility which he was taking in putting these new measures into effect. . . .

To Secretary of State Stimson [No date]

Menemen was more a symptom than an event and as such suggests the desirability of trying to get at the underlying sequence of the last dozen years of Turkish history.

There was the heroic period when nationalism meant primarily an armed struggle against Greeks and Allies, and Westernization was well in the background. That period began in May, 1919, with the landing of the Greeks at Smyrna and ended with the signature of the Lausanne Treaty in the summer of 1923. Differences of opinion were for practical purposes held in suspense by the stimulus of war. The abolition of the Sultanate was an act dictated by immediate considerations of self-defense rather than a political act.

But after the Lausanne Conference the picture changes. The Republic was proclaimed. The political impossibility of maintaining a Caliph at Istanbul became clear. He was thrown out; the medresses were abolished; the desire for ruthless reform became apparent but the kind of Government best suited for this purpose had not yet been evolved. The Caliph left

in March, 1924. The Progressive Party — essentially a conservative party — came into existence in October, 1924. There
followed a brief period of indecision — the three months of
the Fethi Bey Ministry.

The fall of Fethi Bey in February, 1925, the voting of the
Law of the Maintenance of Order and the rebirth of the Tribunals of Independence represent a conscious decision in favor
of dictatorship. At the same time the Westernization program
became a more explicit and a more clearly formulated policy.
The trials at Izmir and at Ankara in 1927 [2] are the high water-
mark of the dictatorship. Opposition was reduced to silence
and ruthlessness ruled.

The Government was right when it decided to put the reforms into effect by strong arm methods. Turkey being what
Turkey is, that was the only way they could be put into effect.
The method of gradual reform advocated by the Progressives
was theoretically admirable but practically impossible. But
while the Government was right it paid a price for being right.
It ostracized from its service a number of men of ability and
independence and its policy of ruthlessness inevitably attracted
a type of individual who is not unknown in Turkish history:
the man who carried out orders 100 per cent but who is a
sycophant and therefore a potential grafter.

In any revolution a time comes when a positive phase must
succeed the negative or destructive phase. The timing of the
transition is a nice problem of statesmanship. In the case of
Turkey the timing has been bungled — hence Menemen.

---

[2] In 1927, a plot was discovered against the life of Ataturk. The attempt to
assassinate him, which was to have been made during his visit to Smyrna, was
planned by one of the Deputies of the National Assembly, Sia Hurshid Bey. In
the course of the investigation in Smyrna the names of other persons apparently
implicated in the plot were brought forward, among them those of many of the
leaders of the suppressed Progressive Party. As many of the accused as could be
found and arrested were brought to trial in Smyrna. Fifteen men were condemned to death. A month later another trial followed in Angora, and others
accused of participating in the plot were given the death penalty. Among these
was Djavid Bey, former Minister of Finance, and Dr. Nazim Bey, one of the
men who had founded the Committee of Union and Progress. Dagobert von
Mikusch, *Mustapha Kemal* (Garden City: Doubleday, Doran & Co., 1931), pp.
371–73.

The results of the dictatorship were not long in making themselves felt. There came a period of complacency. The brutality of the Tribunals of Independence had produced a passivity which Ankara mistook for acquiescence in its reforms. The new Ankara — the city, with its fine new buildings and its self-sufficiency, its isolation from the rest of the country — was a daily and powerful invitation to complacency. The Gazi spent hours at his farm, educated his numerous daughters and harangued till all hours of the night groups of sleepy and semi-intoxicated Cabinet Ministers and Deputies, who assured him that he was quite right in his view that the Hittites were really Turks. The Gazi began to write the history of the ancient Turks and forgot the modern Anatolian peasant. The general acceptance of the reforms was taken for granted; the drive behind them slowed down.

There is a certain irony in the fact that the Gazi himself unwittingly brought the era of complacency tumbling down in ruins. Last summer he approved, if he did not urge, the founding of Fethi's Opposition Party. Why? Perhaps it was something as naive as this: there are a lot of modern buildings in Ankara; Turkey is therefore a modern country; modern countries have Opposition Parties; Turkey must have an Opposition Party. It was the inferiority complex which explains so much in Turkey.

Fethi made a mistake; as a result of his contact with the West he acted as a Western leader of an Opposition would act. He organized his party; he went about the country, he made speeches and he made speeches where they would count: Izmir, for instance. The Gazi was ignorant of Turkey because he lived at Ankara and Fethi was ignorant of Turkey because he had lived in Paris. Fethi's reception at Izmir was the most significant event in Turkey since the hanging of Djavid. The second marked the zenith of the dictatorship; the first the initial crack. It disorganized the whole show. Complacency came to an abrupt end and uncertainty followed.

In spite of his genuinely Western attitude, Fethi had enough sense to realize what was going on. He abolished his party. Less than two months later came Menemen. Intrinsically

Menemen has no importance: a few people were killed, one of them apparently under circumstances of brutality. But as a symptom Menemen is of incalculable importance. It means that Westernization hasn't penetrated; that while the Ministry of Public Instruction at Ankara may sit at the feet of Professor John Dewey and talk about Teachers College at Columbia and Bergson and Durkheim and all the rest, Sheik Essat, leader of the reactionary Nakhshbendi sect, has the inside track. It is impressive to visit the Bacteriological Institute at Ankara and see Zeiss binocular microscopes and all the centrifuges that Paris manufacturers can produce, but *muskas* (amulets) are being used in all the villages around Ankara itself and a catalogue of *muskas* is at present of more practical value than a catalogue of Zeiss microscopes.

Should one be pessimistic? Not necessarily. Turkey has learned a lot since August, 1930 — chiefly that Westernization cannot be decreed from Ankara and that it is not quite so simple and completely materialistic a thing as was at first imagined. Ankara isn't at all sure as to just what it wants to teach, but in view of the success of Sheik Essat it is perfectly certain that something must be taught and taught in a hurry. But how? That is the question that is now agitating Ankara. Will it be mass education with Russia and Italy as examples or will it be an attempt to educate individuals in the path of responsibility, initiative and the other qualities that have distinguished Anglo-Saxon countries? I fear the former. I hope for the latter. At any rate momentous thoughts and actions are in the air.

Monday, July 27, to Monday, August 10 [1931]

The best thing about diplomatic life, as I have often said before in these pages, is that one never knows when some event or development of prime importance is going to occur. We pursue the even tenor of our way for weeks or months and then, often suddenly and unexpectedly, something breaks, pleasantly or unpleasantly, and we find ourselves in the midst of a maelstrom of hectic activity, working day and night, rushing telegrams, drafting press communiqués and speeches, dashing from place to place, doing useful work. This is the spice of the Foreign Service and it has just come to us again, this time literally, not merely metaphorically, out of a clear sky. A tremendous fortnight, vivid, constructive, never to be forgotten. An event has occurred which has done more to consolidate the affections of Turkey for the United States than could have been accomplished by years of careful diplomacy.

On the 28th, it being a Turkish holiday, we all went with Reid on the *Izond* to Yalova to show the place to Alice. . . . Alas, her impressions were not happy ones for we had chosen a sweltering day and Yalova, sct like a cup between the hills, seemed to have absorbed all the heat in creation. We showed her the springs and the baths and tried to walk her to the Nightingale's Nest in the woods, but she came to the end of her rope long before reaching there and we quickly made tracks for the sea in order to escape from that veritable oven. Incidentally we saw the Gazi on the terrace of his house; he stood up and bowed and later sent me a message that he was distressed at not being able to receive us but that being in pyjamas and seeing ladies in our party he thought discretion the better part of valor. The best part of that day was the two swims we had, one before luncheon on the fine beach at Yalova town on the sea and the other at Chamliman at Halki on our way homewards, and then the grand sunset immediately followed by the rising of a tremendous full moon over the bay and lighthouse of Moda, one of those scenes, unbelievably beautiful, which will fasten this lovely place in our minds forever. . . .

We dined at home with the Woods, Reid, etc., on July 29, and at that moment Anita and I decided to go to the aviation field at Yechilkeuy on the chance that Russell Boardman and John Polando, the American aviators who had taken off from New York at 6 A.M. (American time, 1 P.M. our time) yesterday for a nonstop flight to Istanbul, might succeed in their exploit. The Department had advised us of their departure and a rumor had come that they had crossed the Atlantic and were seen over Valentia, Ireland, early this morning. This rumor proved later to be unfounded but accepting it as possible, we calculated that the plane might arrive at Yechil-keuy at any time after 3 A.M. and we didn't want to be caught napping. Eugene Hinkle [Third Secretary] and Miss Carp asked to join us. As a matter of fact, when we arrived on the field at 3, the plane was still over France and still had ten hours of flight ahead, all of which we spent on the field. The early part of the evening was pleasantly spent at the Greek Legation and rowing in the magnificent full moonlight and then we drove into town and over the terrible road that leads past San Stephano to Yechilkeuy.

My impressions of those ten memorable hours coincide pretty well with Anita's, except that there is a certain difference between 22 and 51 in point of staying power. . . . As for our giving up the vigil at 10 A.M. and returning to town, I can only thank the particular deity who gave me the "hunch" to turn back to the field with the firm resolve to wait either till they came or for definite news that they were not coming. Howland Shaw had telephoned a rumor that Boardman and Polando had come down at Hendon in England; this was erroneous as it referred to Pangborn and Herndon who are attempting a flight around the world, but it was enough to start us homewards.[3] Twice I stopped the car to discuss the situation with Anita; she said: "Dad, I'm with you, but you've got to make the decision"; the first time we kept on, the second time, after driving for half an hour and being on the outskirts of the city, I said to her: "If this flight does materialize, it will be one of the biggest events in the history of aviation and we can't afford to run the least risk of missing it; let's go back" — and we did. Thank heaven for that. All the other

3 Clyde E. Pangborn and Hugh Herndon, Jr. took off from Floyd Bennett Field for a flight around the world seventeen minutes after Boardman and Polando had left. Although they were disappointed in their hopes of bettering the round-the-world record of Wiley Post, they succeeded in setting a new record in their nonstop flight from Tokyo to Wenatchee, Washington, on October 4 and 5, 1931. See the *New York Times*, July 29, 1931, p. 1, and October 6, 1931, p. 1.

Americans gave it up — P. E. King [tobacco merchant], Franklin Bell [of the Gary Tobacco Company] and others. Only a handful of newspaper correspondents stayed — Miss Ring, J. W. Kernick [correspondent of the *New York Times*], etc., but they too were getting restive. The Vali, the local Kaimakam and their staffs turned up just before luncheon, went away again and got back barely in time to greet the fliers on their arrival.

The appearance of the *Cape Cod* and its landing were probably the most thrilling moments of our lives. A good many planes, military and civil, had arrived during the morning, so that the appearance of one more in the sky led me merely to get out my glasses in leisurely fashion. And then I saw that she was yellow and black and we all began to shout. A prettier landing was never seen. I was the first to reach the plane as it taxied in and to grasp Polando by the hand. Both he and Boardman were shaking their hands in token of success just before they landed. I asked at once: "Was it non-stop?" Polando answered "Yes." That was all I wanted to know just then. They got out, gingerly, untangling their stiffened joints; Boardman could barely stand and wobbled on the field; they could scarcely hear us and Polando said to Boardman, "Do you think we'll ever get rid of this deafness?" to which Boardman replied, "Oh, that will pass." I introduced them to the Vali and then we all went to the buffet prepared in the military office and toasted them in champagne. Bits of the story came out: they hadn't even seen the Atlantic Ocean, so thick were the clouds; only one momentary glimpse of the green countryside of Ireland through a hole in the clouds; a copy of Tuesday's *New York Times* dropped on the field at Le Bourget which they hoped would be picked up (it was); fierce rainstorms after leaving Paris; impossible to get over the Balkan mountains owing to clouds so they had to follow the Danube, low, down, missing the surrounding cliffs by less than fifty feet and swaying dangerously in the air currents so that at one moment they were absolutely on end and didn't think they would get through; another precarious moment when the gasoline ran dry in one tank and they had to shift while the motor actually stopped although the propeller continued to revolve and they soon got the second tank working. They were terribly tired so I soon rescued them and took them into town in the Buick (how proud Nadji and Abduraman were!) and to the Embassy where I introduced the staff and then the photographers got to work on the front steps. Then I took them to the Pera Palace Hotel and turned them over to the Turkish Aviation League whose guests they are to be.

At this moment there occurred what was perhaps the most dramatic incident of all. A French aviation squadron, as I have said, is here on one of those carefully staged propaganda tours for which the French are past masters; it is said that they want to sell planes to the Turkish Government. Coste,[4] the hero and holder of the distance record, is their principal card and they are playing him for all he is worth. Just at this moment, spontaneously, sportively, uncommercially, two quiet, unassuming Yankees drop from the skies in their *Cape Cod*, beat Coste's own record, take Turkey by storm, demonstrate the efficiency of the Wright Whirlwind Motor and the Bellanca plane, take the wind out of the Frenchmen's sails and completely ruin their carefully planned propaganda. I take these two gentle disreputable-looking specimens into the Pera Palace Hotel and who do we run into but the entire French delegation, nattily dressed in their immaculate white duck uniforms, covered with decorations. I introduce my compatriots to Coste and General Goys and the other Frenchmen who, of course, run up with outward chivalry but, I fear, with inner chagrin. What a moment! We are all photographed together. Gillespie, who is helping the American company to sell its planes to the Turkish Government, literally chortles with joy. And the next day in an interview, General Goys, while paying tribute to Boardman and Polando, remarks that the alleged new record cannot be accepted until it has been officially proven! That is the only outward sign of their discomfiture.

[4] Dieudonné Coste and Maurice Bellonte held the previous distance record of 4912 miles for their nonstop flight from France to China.

De Chambrun sends me a delightfully worded card: "Hearty congratulations for the wonderful success of America's aviators. I am happy with you." But how bitter must be his disappointment. Nadolny telephones to express his congratulations; Sir George Clerk calls to do the same. Both are simply delighted at the discomfiture of the Frenchmen.

But Boardman and Polando are all in. The officials of the Aviation League order shirts, collars, socks, ties, razors, toothbrushes (their only clothes were a couple of suits which had been brought along carefully carried on hangers in the fuselage to preserve the crease!) while we pilot our noble aviators to their rooms and see them safely in bed. I do not doubt that they could readily sleep "the horologe a double set" if they could be spared so long from the Turkish officials and public who are now frantically eager to do them honor. We shall protect them to the extent of our ability but they are going to have to face the music now. I told them a little of what they must expect and added that they had brought it on themselves. They have never been out of the United States before! And they are fortunately ideal representatives of America for such a job. Boardman, serious, quiet, thoughtful, slow-spoken; Polando, a little wiry fox terrier from Lynn, loquacious, full of humor, tremendously appreciative; both of them modest, not a word of self-praise, no blowing whatsoever. We've always said, with Herrick, "Thank God for Lindbergh." I can now add: "Thank God for Boardman and Polando." . . .

Friday, July 31 [1931]
. . . Telegrams from the Governor of Massachusetts and Mayor Curley [of Boston, of course]. Shaw brings them out on the *Halberg* to lunch with us quietly at Yenikeuy; Sir George invites himself and makes a great hit with Polando who thinks him a "fine gentleman" — probably the first Englishman of that type he's ever seen. Clerk draws him out and meets his humorous sallies with equally humorous replies which delight our fox terrier. . . .

Saturday, August 1 [1931]

Miracle of miracles, the Gazi has sent word that he wishes to receive our noble aviators at Yalova. Foreigners of great distinction, Admirals, Generals, Ministers of State, are often denied access to that sacred sanctum even when audiences are requested in the official capital, and at the best they are kept waiting for days, but these two American boys are immediately summoned so that the great Gazi may promptly do them honor. At 2.15 we write in the Gazi's book at Dolma Bagtché Palace and at 2.30 set out for Yalova on the Gazi's own private yacht, the *Sakarya,* together with the Vali and a numerous group of officials, Turkish newspaper correspondents and press photographers, Boardman, Polando, Shaw and myself. I am glad to see that Miss Ring has been included, ill though she is, while Kernick, of the *New York Times,* Walton [correspondent of the *Christian Science Monitor*] and others have to charter a launch of their own. We reach Yalova at 4.30 where an official deputation and a great crowd receive the aviators with immense enthusiasm, cheers and handclapping. The usually stolid Turkish public has been stirred out of its lethargy; indeed I have never seen such spontaneous enthusiasm. We drive to the Casino at Yalova Springs and there are received by Ismet Pasha, Tewfik Rushdi Bey and a large group of high Turkish officials, to whom I present my compatriots. Ismet Pasha makes a charming speech, part of which is very kindly directed at me personally as a friend of Turkey, though I feel very much like keeping out of the picture where these heroic youngsters are concerned, and he pins on their coats the highest decoration of the Turkish Aviation League in diamonds, possessed by only four other foreigners, including Mrs. Lindbergh on behalf of her son and a Russian who once flew over the Black Sea. As Ismet said, the American youths had made the Black Sea look like a pond. I have to answer Ismet's speech extemporaneously on the spot, in French, no easy task. Then we drink champagne, Boardman and Ismet Pasha choose partners and dance, while Tewfik Rushdi takes me aside and reads me the speech which the Gazi is going to make in ten minutes and to which I must reply. We drive to the Gazi's house and are shown by Tewfik Rushdi Bey into his sanctum where I introduce Boardman and Polando. The Gazi seats himself behind his desk, the aviators on the sofa opposite, with the Minister for Foreign Affairs, Tewfik Bey and the military aide, Shaw and myself in a half circle. The Gazi makes his speech without notes in Turkish, Tewfik Rushdi translates into French and Shaw into English — a very warm and splendid welcome. They tell me that the Gazi has been unable to think or speak of any other subject since the aviators arrived. Then I make my reply on behalf of Boardman and Polando, again extemporaneously, for we had not anticipated speeches. The Gazi begins to ask questions about the flight which I put into English, and translate into French Boardman's answers. He is tactful and complimentary to Turkey. Finally the Gazi remarks that he doesn't want to take up too much of their time and prevent their seeing Yalova, so the audience breaks up and we all, including the Gazi, go on to the terrace to be photographed. That ends the visit. As we start homewards, Ismet comes with springy step across the garden from his house to say good-bye with that charming, magnetic smile of his and he waves to us until we are out of sight. I know of few men with so attractive a personality, of any nation. He made a great hit especially with Polando who never misses a trick. Yalova, fortunately, is at its best, cool and green and refreshing. . . .

Wednesday, August 5 [1931]

The other day I sent a telegram to the Department telling of the Gazi's cordial reception of the aviators, the conferring of the aviation medals on them, etc., and inquiring whether President Hoover could not send them some sort of a telegram of congratulations on their flight as I believed it would be much appreciated here. But meanwhile the Gazi himself sent a most cordial telegram to President Hoover on his own initiative, as follows:

The American heroes have filled the entire Turkish nation with joy. The cheerfulness and determination which I personally noticed in these intrepid youths after their marvellous feat has brought me the conviction that the great victory which they have won for humanity is for them only a beginning.

It gives me great pleasure to congratulate through your illustrious self that great nation which has produced these noble heroes.

To which the President replied to the Gazi:

I wish to express my sincere appreciation of the courtesies which you have shown the American fliers Boardman and Polando following their successful flight from New York to Istanbul.

This telegram, I fear, must have been drafted in the Department on one of those long, hot, nerve-racking days when imagination is at its lowest ebb, for it is far from adequate as a reply to the Gazi's unusually expansive message. Furthermore it appears that the Turkish translation of it made in Yalova made it sound even less cordial. At any rate, the Gazi was distinctly irritated, and before giving both telegrams out to the press, he sent his secretary, Tewfik Bey, into town to see Shaw and to ask whether this telegram was actually in reply to the Gazi's. Shaw found from the dates that this must probably be the case, for the Gazi's message was sent on Saturday, August 1, and this was dated Monday afternoon, August 3, and as the Gazi's telegram was, we are informed, sent in English, there would have been no delay in translating. However, Shaw was able to tell Tewfik Bey that the words "sincere appreciation" were, in English, saying "a mouthful" and he promised to give to Tewfik Bey an accurate Turkish translation. I am sorry that the Department couldn't have helped our hand by making the President's telegram at least as long and as cordial as the Gazi's. These little things count enormously here and it's a pity that anything should mar the extraordinarily fine feeling engendered by the Boardman-Polando flight, which President Hoover's telegram distinctly appears to have done. . . .

Thursday, August 6 [1931]

I was made very happy this morning by a telegram from

the Department saying that a very cordial message had been received by the President from the Gazi *after* the despatch of the President's message of August 3rd and adding that while it was not considered necessary that this message be acknowledged by the President, I was authorized to make clear to the Turks that Mr. Hoover was not in receipt of the Gazi's message when the former's message was sent. There must have been some hitch, perhaps in departmental routing, to account for the delay in the receipt of the Gazi's telegram, or perhaps the Gazi did not send it on the date he said he did. Anyway this makes things much simpler here and I instructed Shaw to call at once on Tewfik Bey at Dolma Bagtché to explain the situation. Shaw demurred as he thought that Tewfik Bey would at once inquire whether the President was not going to reply to the Gazi's telegram. I said, "In that case, ask him whether the Gazi is going to reply to the President's telegram." That is exactly what happened; Tewfik saw the point at once and said that he would at once explain the situation to the Gazi and that the matter was now entirely in order, especially as Shaw told him that I myself would communicate through the Minister for Foreign Affairs the President's appreciation of the Gazi's cordial message. Therefore, in order to lay. completely at rest the Gazi's irritation, I sent a polite telegram to Tewfik Rushdi Bey in Ankara, based on the Department's authorization, that I might "on an appropriate occasion refer to it (the Gazi's message) with appreciation." This authorization I interpreted somewhat broadly perhaps, but it seemed absolutely essential to leave no cloud on the present happy horizon. I understood perfectly the Gazi's irritation: In a moment of expansiveness, called forth by his personal enthusiasm over the exploit of the American aviators and the fact that they chose Turkey as their goal ... [he] sends a message to President Hoover couched in terms absolutely unprecedented for their warmth and cordiality; in reply (as he thinks) he receives a telegram from President Hoover, pleasant enough but distinctly curt in comparison with his own telegram. Quite naturally he feels that he "slopped over" and is being told so by Mr. Hoover. Therefore we must leave nothing undone to relieve him of this feeling for it would be a misfortune to let any incident impair the remarkably good feeling engendered by the flight. . . .

Sunday, August 9 [1931]

Last evening the aviators made up their minds to start this morning for Genoa or Marseilles, in order to ship their plane thence to New York by the American Export Lines steamer *Excalibur,* instead of proceeding around the world via Calcutta and Tokyo. The weather reports from India were not seriously unfavorable but various considerations led them to give up this further flight. I believe that Polando was probably the restraining influence for the strain on his nerves by the long flight had been great and he must have realized that the strain on the motor of the *Cape Cod* was equally great. Perhaps, also, the hope of the Turks that they would rest on their laurels and be satisfied with their one great achievement, a hope which we have all tried to impress on them, may have influenced their wise decision which will be most pleasing to their Turkish hosts.

At any rate, we were up at 2.30 and on the field at Yechil-keuy, the whole family and the whole Embassy staff, at a little after 4 just as dawn was breaking. The assistant Vali, Fazli Bey, and a great crowd of representatives of the Turkish Army and Aviation League, as well as many Americans, a company of aviation cadets and a band of music, were also on hand. Indeed the Aviation League had made plans to run special trains to the field to bring out a large proportion of Istanbul's population, in order to give the aviators a royal send-off, but these plans fell through owing to the short notice given them of the aviator's intention to start this morning. Anyway, the send-off was royal enough. An hour or so was spent packing things in the plane (I climbed half in to examine the artificial horizon and other instruments and was astonished to see how little space the men had had to move about in and stretch their legs during their long flight); then good-byes were said; an exchange of informal speeches between Fazli Bey and Boardman; the latter motored out to the take-off to survey the rather rough field; on returning he said good-bye to Alice, the girls and myself, climbed into the plane, and off they went at 5.45 A.M., soon after the sun had risen, soaring into the air after a very short run. In a minute or two they had made their height and then came sweeping back and down in a graceful swoop over the crowd to wave good-bye. I watched the *Cape Cod* until she was a mere speck in the distance, much moved, as I imagine everybody was who witnessed that great ending of a great interlude, especially those few of us who had likewise witnessed the arrival. As time is measured by events, it seems that months have passed since that dramatic landing ten days ago. The day's work is going to seem rather unusually trivial for some time to come. . . .

As for Boardman and Polando, the beneficial effects of the flight on Turco-American relations and on our work here are incalculable, and in the absence of adverse incidents or developments they should be permanent.[5] Of course I realize, always, that Turkey is a very small spot for the United States on the political map of the world, but my job is to consider it a large and important spot and to act and think accordingly, until, in the wisdom of my superiors, I am sent to a more important spot — or to the ash heap. From that point of view my enthusiasm over the events of the past ten days is perhaps understandable. . . .

Tuesday, August 18 [1931]

Anita accomplished her big swim today from the Black Sea to the Sea of Marmora, covering the entire length of the Bosporus in the astonishing time of exactly five hours, the distance being thirty and a half kilometers or nineteen miles.

---

[5] The press of Turkey had given wide and favorable coverage to the flight of the two Americans. In reporting the departure of the fliers on August 10, the Turkish *République* opined that prayers of all the population would accompany the daring fliers on their return voyage, and the *Journal d'Orient* of the same date stated that a measure of Turkish joy and happiness had flown away with the *Cape Cod*.

Only a perfect combination of wind and current conditions and great skill on the part of Noltsch, German shipbuilder from Stenia, who directed the swim, in choosing the most favorable possible course, can account for such fast time, for although Anita maintains a steady and rhythmic pace with her powerful breast stroke, she does not use the crawl or attempt speed. Yet four miles an hour is just about as fast as a man can walk, and this is about what she was doing. The time is especially significant of the conditions obtaining today when one considers that she took five and a half hours last year to get to Rumeli Hissar, about two-thirds of the whole course.

Anita has had the firm intention all summer to accomplish this swim sooner or later, for she didn't like the headlines in a certain American newspaper last year: "Girl fails in swim," but the difficulty was to find good conditions on a day when neither of us had to go to town and such days this summer have been comparatively few. We decided last Sunday to start at 11 o'clock in the morning, which we thought would get Anita down into the lower reaches of the Bosporus towards the evening calm, for both of us figured on about eight hours for the swim, but Sunday proved far too windy and we then thought a start at dawn would be better and set today for the attempt. I didn't do much sleeping last night, being up every half-hour or so to watch the conditions. These looked anything but favorable for instead of the usual dead calm at night a steady wind blew all night long. We dressed at 3.15, had a little hot breakfast and started out in the launch soon after 3.30, towing Diamandi — the caïquejee — in the caïque. Noltsch shook his head at certain ominous clouds in the usually clear sky and the steady wind blowing at this early hour and feared that it would get steadily stronger, but we all knew that a north wind blowing all night would materially help the currents and that if the waves didn't get too fierce later on, the conditions might be ideal. At best Anita could try a training swim and stop whenever it seemed best, to try again tomorrow or Thursday.

Noltsch and Chaban both wanted her to take the water opposite the signal station at Buyuk Liman, but while that is the official entrance to the Bosporus it is not the geographic entrance, so we kept on to a line between the Rumeli Phanar light on the European coast and the Anatolie Phanar light on the Asiatic side, well into the Black Sea, so that there could be no possible question as to Anita's swimming from sea to sea. She dove overboard at exactly 4.50 A.M., well greased from head to foot with automobile grease, and it took her 45 minutes to reach Buyuk Liman which gave me many questioning doubts as to whether I had been justified in adding that considerable distance to her swim merely through overconscientiousness. In the end we were both glad that we had done so.

The start was very agreeable and propitious. The water was not too cold, the north wind not too strong. There was a deep swell in the Black Sea, but she soon got out of that and there were no waves slapping into her face as with the south wind last year. Dawn was just breaking; the shadowy forms of the first morning flock of ships from the Black Sea passed us and then the sun rose from behind a bank of clouds, fiery and golden, giving Anita much joy. I was in the caïque with the portable gramophone and the hot chocolate and in fact stayed there, playing almost steadily, for over four hours until relieved by Elsie and Mrs. Wylie towards the end of the course. A white flag on a long pole warned passing ships not to interfere, while the launch, which followed closely behind, had hoisted two black spheres as a signal "unable to maneuver" and a red flag to say "keep off." A dozen or more big ships passed us during the swim and many shirkets, the officers of some of the ships waving as they went by (two of them saw both start and finish) but only one Greek tramp caused us any anxiety. She bore straight down on us until fairly close before shifting her course, as much as to say "You're impeding traffic." The gramophone was a great asset; unfortunately Anita's favorite tune which encouraged her so much last year, "I'm following you" and others carefully selected in advance were left at home by mistake, but Pagliacci and two or three others filled the bill finely and stimulated Anita throughout the swim. I fed her twice with hot chocolate in a big china mug which she could hold with ease while treading water. She also wore a vizored cap which prevented the bad sunburn on her forehead which stayed with her all last summer. She enjoyed every minute of the swim, said she was neither cold nor tired and her morale was kept up splendidly by the amazing speed of the currents. For the first two hours her times were exactly to the minute the same as last year, but then she got into the better currents and in certain stretches where last year she had had to fight every foot of the way, this year she was carried on in half or a third of the time. Last year it took her 30 minutes from our house to the dock at Yenikeuy; this year 10 minutes. . . . In fact, Anita did not have an uneasy moment during the entire swim. She was swept so fast past Scutari, through the port of Istanbul and past Leander's Tower that we were all amazed and let her continue well into the Marmora to a line between Seraglio Point and the big barracks at Haidar Pasha. As it was now 9.50, exactly five hours since she took to the water, I gave the signal to stop and climb aboard; she had accomplished her purpose in splendid style and we all, including the crew, applauded lustily. She came aboard beaming, very happy and apparently not a bit tired. She said that the whole swim from start to finish had been delightful. So far as we know this is the first time that that particular swim has been accomplished. I suppose that Richard Halliburton will now be on her trail.

After it was all over I landed at Dolma Bagtché, and although unshaven, hatless and tieless I went to the Embassy to keep a long-made promise to inform the newspaper correspondents of the swim when it should have taken place. It also seemed fair to Anita that the rankling headlines of last year "Girl fails in swim" should be properly rectified. The correspondents, both Turkish and foreign, were keen as mustard to get the whole story with details, for the world fortunately seems glad to pause now and then in its consideration of politics and finance to enjoy the lighter side of life as expressed in athletic prowess; the establishment of a record is always good news and, besides, there is something romantic about the Bosporus which appeals to the public imagination. So I let them have it all and off they scurried to spread it to the waiting world.

On the way out to Yenikeuy I stopped at Stenia, where our boats are moored, and gave substantial presents to each of the captains, the Russian engineer, to each member of the crew and to Diamandi, to celebrate the exploit and their decidedly interested part in it. Indeed, they were all very keen about the swim and very proud of its result.

This afternoon Anita played tennis!

The next day congratulatory telegrams came in from many different sources, from the Perrys, Ranny [Randolph Grew], the Archibald Browns in New York, from George Carey in Paris and from the Kleists in Germany, indicating that the publicity has been pretty widespread. Flowers, letters and cards also poured in. The Turkish papers carried it in headlines with many complimentary remarks. In fact, our Mr. Shaw was called from bed by a correspondent who asked permission to borrow for publication "the photograph of Miss Grew in his apartment." Shaw said he possessed no photograph of Miss Grew, to which the correspondent replied that he had merely "taken a chance!" . . .[6]

The last treaty that Mr. Grew negotiated with the Turkish Government while serving there as Ambassador was a Treaty of Establishment and Residence. There had been a number of

[6] Many of the newspapers of the United States carried the Associated or United Press despatches recounting the story of the swim. See, for instance, the *New York Times,* August 19, 1931, p. 1. The papers emphasized the difficulty of the swim due to the length and the water currents. Their accounts were worded in a complimentary manner about the endurance and ability of Miss Grew in completing such a swim for the first time. She was said to have accomplished a feat which even the ancient Greeks never dared credit to their heroes, and the *London Evening Standard* of August 19, 1931, wrote that she had "taken the shine out of Europa." Mr. Grew has written: "For two or three years Anita's swim was listed in the *World's Almanac* together with those who had swum the English Channel. Even today people occasionally say: 'Oh, it was your daughter who swam the Hellespont,' not realizing that the Hellespont is several hundred miles from the Bosporus and only about three miles across, slightly different from the nineteen miles of the length of the Bosporus! I suppose a father's pride is pardonable."

meetings prior to the one chronicled here. See U.S. Department of State, Papers Relating to the Foreign Relations of the United States, 1930 (Washington: Government Printing Office, 1945), III, 852–72, and U.S. Department of State, Papers Relating to the Foreign Relations of the United States, 1931 (Washington: Government Printing Office, 1946), III, 1037–44. On October 28, 1931, Mr. Grew wrote in his diary: "It is a profound satisfaction to have our Treaty relations with Turkey now pretty well established, provided the Senate ratifies this last one, and I can't see how it can refuse to do so." The Treaty was ratified on May 12, 1932.

Ankara, Thursday, August 27 [1931]

. . . The situation on August 27 was therefore this: I had sent to the Foreign Office a text for the treaty containing a new preamble which the Turks had never seen; the Foreign Office had apparently accepted this revised text because they sent me a Turkish translation of it exactly as it stood. This had surprised me not a little, as I had not thought that the new text would get by Zekai Bey so easily. Therefore I was not wholly surprised when Zekai, on reading the English and Turkish texts which I had brought with me, immediately bridled and said that he had never seen either of these texts. What had happened is that the Foreign Office had simply submitted my text to its translation bureau in a purely routine way without consulting Zekai Bey, the actual negotiator, at all. He became very angry and it was obvious that unless I took a firm stand the negotiations would be entirely reopened. Besides, I wanted if possible to maintain the preamble preferred by the Department. So I had to become equally angry and told Zekai that the Minister for Foreign Affairs himself had approved of the final text and translation; that the negotiations were closed; that I had no intention of remaining in Ankara to reopen them and proposed to leave at 7, and that if the Treaty were not initialed before then, there would probably be no treaty at all. Zekai promptly calmed down and after carefully studying the Turkish translation made in the Foreign Office, he asked merely that two expressions be changed as they did not give the sense intended. I telephoned down to Allen and read to him the changes proposed to which he said there were no objections whatever as they were practically synonymous with the phrases used by the Foreign Office and merely clarified them. I therefore accepted them. Zekai then wanted a French text to be initialed too, in case of future disagreements over the English and Turkish texts. He said they had done this with the Germans. I said that I could not do this and that it had not been done in the case of our Treaty of Commerce and Navigation. It had been understood that there would be only English and Turkish texts. He then wanted to make several other alterations in the Turkish text but I refused point-blank. This discussion had lasted nearly two hours and it was nearly 1 o'clock before he finally gave in and agreed to initial at 5, after the texts had been copied on treaty paper and bound in final form. . . .

At 5 I returned to the Treaty Delegation, but the texts were not yet ready and they were not actually initialed until 6.15, leaving me just time to catch my train. With the initialing, which was done at the big green conference table in all solemnity (the Turks clearly regarding it as tantamount to signature), Zekai became once more entirely friendly; he said he was sorry that they would have to postpone giving me the usual "treaty dinner" owing to my departure but ice cream, cake and coffee were served and I managed to consume enough to fulfill the courtesies. We congratulated each other on the happy termination of our negotiations and he came down to the station to see me off, with the Treaty in my pocket. . . .

Tuesday, October 20 [1931]

. . . These nuances of diplomacy, I fear, sometimes escape me — guileless as I am. For instance, I suggested October 28 as the date for signing our Treaty simply because I am arriving in Ankara on that day and we were instructed to sign about the end of October. To my surprise, when I saw Tewfik Rushdi a day or two later, he said that he couldn't thank me enough for my delicate compliment to Turkey by suggesting the signing of the Treaty on the day before the National Holiday, so that the press announcement on the 29th would constitute a magnificent birthday present to the entire Turkish nation! I seem somehow to blunder into masterpieces of diplomacy. . . .

To Secretary of State Stimson
Istanbul, November 11, 1931

Mr. Litvinoff [Soviet Commissar for Foreign Affairs] has come and gone. His long-heralded visit to Ankara took place from October 27 to 30 including, appropriately, the celebration of the Turkish National Holiday on October 29, with all the usual concomitant festivities and functions. There is no interest or significance either in the program of these functions or in the saccharine interviews and communiqués in the press which differed in no respect from the emanations customary and expected on such occasions. From the latter it can be conclusively accepted that "the auspicious visit has served still further to consolidate the friendly relations so happily existing between the two countries."

What are of interest and significance are the reasons for the visit at this particular moment and the practical results thereof. It is true that the Treaty of Amity and Neutrality between Turkey and Russia was renewed for a period of five years, together with its various protocols including the Naval Protocol signed at Ankara on March 7, 1931, but the signing of these documents did not in itself presumably demand the presence in Ankara of the People's Commissar for Foreign Affairs of the Union of Socialist Soviet Republics. More significant is the fact that the visit was timed to follow closely on the return of Ismet Pasha and Tewfik Rushdi Bey from their visits to Athens and Budapest, and still more closely on the heels of the Balkan Conference which had just terminated its session in Istanbul; [7] the delegates to that meeting had almost to be

[7] Two hundred delegates from six Balkan states met in Istanbul from October 20 through the early part of November, 1931, to discuss questions such as inter-Balkan communications, the marketing of products, and a compact for arbitration and nonaggression. Little progress was made toward concluding a compact because of the minorities problem. *New York Times*, October 21, 1931, p. 13, and November 15, 1931, III, p. 3.

hustled out of Ankara, after their one day's visit, before the arrival of Mr. Litvinoff.

As usual, rumor concerning the purpose of the visit was rife. Most of the newspapers were fulsome, but the *Son Posta* was inquisitive. It was mooted abroad that Turkey was to negotiate for a solution of the Bessarabian question between Russia and Rumania; that she was to bring about a rapprochement between Russia and Bulgaria; that Russia disapproved of Turkey's injection into Balkan affairs; that Russia was apprehensive lest Turkey ally herself with western capitalists by turning to the West for economic assistance, the mission of Saradjoglou Shukri Bey to the United States being freely mentioned in this connection.[8] But the rumor principally emphasized (and officially denied) was that Mr. Litvinoff desired to insert an article in the renewed Turco-Russian treaty which would effectively prevent Turkey from joining the League of Nations without Soviet approval and that in this he failed.

That Turkey's Western leanings, her rapprochement with Italy, Greece and Bulgaria, the possibility of closer relations with Rumania and the probability of her eventual entrance into the League of Nations are causing apprehension in the minds of the Soviet leaders there seems to be little doubt. In spite of the often declared gratitude of Turkey for the help of Russia during the former's struggle for independence, and despite the well-known pro-Soviet leanings of Tewfik Rushdi Bey and his almost fraternal relations with Comrade Souritz, the Soviet Ambassador in Ankara, suspicions as to Turkey's wholehearted fidelity cannot be wholly absent from the Soviet mind. Mr. Litvinoff's choice of date for his visit may well have been made with every intention of offsetting at the psychological moment the strong magnetism of the West, or at least of maintaining a proper balance between Turkey's Western flirta-

[8] On October 7, 1931, Saradjoglou Shukri Bey, former Minister of Finance, left Turkey for the United States. The threefold purpose of his mission was to make contacts, to obtain a loan of from fifty to one hundred million dollars for public works and bank credits, and to interest American concerns in developing the cotton industry in Turkey.

tions and her fundamental loyalty to her powerful Eastern friend. He cannot have forgotten that the Russians stubbornly refused to grant to Turkish citizens in Russia the points in regard to inheritance which Turkey had requested; that Russia had insisted upon the establishment in Turkey of commercial offices in not only the three principal cities of Istanbul, Izmir and Ankara, but in numerous other cities as well; that commercial controversy between the two countries has been rife; and that Turkey vigorously suppresses communist propaganda within her borders. Keen observers found that while every proper mark of courtesy attended Mr. Litvinoff's visit, his reception in Ankara was unenthusiastic.

I asked Tewfik Rushdi Bey what he could tell me about the results of the visit. His reply was precise and clear-cut: far from disapproving of Turkey's eventual membership in the League, Mr. Litvinoff had taken the position that to have Turkey in the League would be an asset to Soviet Russia (a champion, presumably, at the council table); and that with respect to Turkey's relations with the Balkan countries and the West any pact that might eventually be evolved in the interest of peace would find favor with the Soviet Government. It is difficult to see how the Minister could have told me anything else.

We are informed that Ismet Pasha is to go to Moscow next month to return the visit of the Soviet Commissar but this rumor has not as yet been confirmed. . . .

Tuesday, January 5 [1932]

. . . Dinner at the Japanese Embassy for Tewfik Rushdi Bey who has just arrived from Ankàra en route for Teheran. Alice was hostess. T.R., with whom I had a long talk after dinner, was lyric about Saradjoglou's visit to the United States and his reception there. He felt he had laid a good basis for future business, especially in connection with the textile industry, and the point which pleased the Turks most of all was Shukri's report that American statistics fully bore out the Turkish policy and contention that railroads were used far more than roads for the carrying of merchandise. I think he quoted some such

figure as only 3 per cent traffic over the roads as compared with
the railroads as carriers in the United States. I don't know
what the proportion is but at any rate the point is clearly
proven to the satisfaction of the Turks as a result of Shukri's
report. T.R. told me that tomorrow there would appear in
Akcham an article which he himself had inspired, over the
signature of Nejmeddine Sadik, supporting the attitude of the
United States against the cancellation of debts, on the ground
that any sacrifice in working out the economic rehabilitation
of the world should be borne by the nations proportionately
and should not be saddled on America alone as certain nations
were trying to do. Good. T.R. was not drinking but he was
expansive enough to say to Alice at dinner that the Government didn't care a hang whether we lived in Ankara or Constantinople so long as we stayed in Turkey, that the Turks
couldn't possibly get along without my friendship and counsel
and a lot of other talk which isn't worth putting down on
paper. But it's the first time, I imagine, that any member of
the Government has ever placed the stamp of approval on a
diplomat's living away from the capital. . . .

Monday, January 18 [1932]

Was greeted this morning by a telegram from Pierrepont saying "Peter sends Grandfather heartiest congratulations," and
one from the Perrys: "Double congratulations." The cry "It's
a boy" quickly rang through the house, and so joyful was I at
the news that the dual implication of the telegrams never occurred to me until Alice called it to my attention. Peter
would have been fully justified in congratulating me on his
own birth — and as for the Perrys' telegram, my first thought
was "Twins"! However, after the first flurry of excitement was
over we did a little Sherlock Holmes work and deduced that
something else must have occurred of interest to the family
apart from the transcendent occurrence of the birth of our
first grandson. So "now it can be told" that on November 4th
I received a letter from Bill Castle saying that he wanted me
to go to Japan to succeed Cameron Forbes who was resigning

and would I object to his proposing my name when the time should be ripe. I spent a few hours thinking it over in Ankara, but there was really only one reply to send, and so the same afternoon I cabled him that I realized the great opportunity, was deeply appreciative of his confidence and would accept if the appointment should come. Nothing further was heard of the matter until January 13th when a second telegram came from Bill in answer to a letter I had written him about leave of absence, saying that the President would probably send me to Japan and that I should be prepared to receive instructions to that effect before going on leave. The thing seemed to be shaping up, but having heard nothing definite I cabled Pierrepont to ask the precise reasons for his *other* congratulations, and he replied that press despatches from Tokyo indicated that my agrément as Ambassador to Japan had been asked for. The same evening, before Pierrepont's reply came, the Agence d'Anatolie telegrams carried a message from Washington stating that I "had been appointed" to succeed Forbes, and the next morning the announcement was in all the papers here and we began to receive congratulatory telegrams from America and from all over Europe.

Of the two events, Peter easily occupied first place in our thoughts because it was easy and most agreeable to adjust ourselves to that, while anything but easy to adjust ourselves to the thought of leaving Turkey, where we have been so unusually happy, and to trek across the world to a post of unusual difficulty. I feel quite humble that the post is to be entrusted to me but keen enough to take over what seems to be the opportunity of a lifetime. But there's no good in trying to analyze our feelings now. Alice is pretty depressed at the thought of leaving her beloved Constantinople, but she fully recognizes the importance of the new job and on the whole is immensely pleased that it should have come to us. I say "us" advisedly, for in our job a wife is fully half the team, often the better half, and I do not for a moment delude myself by thinking that I could ever have pulled the boat to this point upstream alone. . . .

Monday, February 22 [1932] George Washington
Bicentennial

A long and difficult but inspiring day. First the exercises at
Constantinople Woman's College at 11.30, then luncheon at
the College, then the exercises at Robert College at 2.15, followed by a reception at the Embassy. For this, invitations had
been issued to all the principal Turks and diplomats and it was
also announced in the press that all Americans would be welcome. We had the portrait of Washington, which had been
sent out by the Bicentennial Commission, framed and hung on
the stairs surrounded by laurel wreaths, while a huge American
flag hung over the banisters. The text of my address . . . took a
lot of work to prepare it but I am very glad to have had the
opportunity to get to know Washington better. . . .

The only other amusing incident of the day was afforded by
the British Ambassador. On the evening of our dance, Clerk
asked me smilingly if I really expected him to come to our
George Washington reception, and when I said that of course
we would be deeply honored by his presence, he said: "Well, I
suppose I've got to come to show that there's no hard feeling."
He came, all dressed up in morning coat and top hat, shook
hands with Alice, shook hands with me, sought out and shook
hands with Anita, and then accompanied by his single retainer
Christopher Bramwell [Second Secretary of the British Em-
bassy], he departed within about 60 seconds of his arrival. . . .
The other diplomatic chiefs of mission all came and stayed
throughout the reception and incidentally, had a bully good
time as the dancing was good and the champagne excellent.
The Vali was also present. Meanwhile, the Father of our
Country looked on benevolently from his imposing frame of
laurel wreaths and I feel sure must have approved of the genuine feeling with which, throughout the day, we had all sought
to honor his memory. . . .

Thursday, February 25 [1932]
. . . At 2.30 the civil wedding at the **Pera Municipality.**[9] Our

[9] Anita Grew married Robert McCalla English. Before coming to Constanti-

own regulations require that weddings in the Embassy shall
be held in accordance with the local laws, so the civil wedding
was necessary in any case, but the Vali has taken it as a friendly
gesture on my part and is making much of it, so there is no
good in relieving him of that idea.[10] As the Vali indicated that
he would like to be invited to be one of the witnesses, we did
so and Anita asked the British Ambassador, who is very fond
of her, to be the other, the witnesses in Turkish weddings being
almost more important than the couple themselves. We had
the staff of the Embassy there in gala clothes; the bride and
groom were seated at a table with the Vali and Sir George
seated at each end while Sedat Bey, the Kaimakam of Pera,
performed the ceremony. He asked each if he or she wished
to marry the other; after affirmative replies they signed the
contract which was then signed by the witnesses, and then Sedat
Bey made a pleasant little speech in Turkish, which was translated into English by an interpreter, giving the newly married
couple some useful advice with regard to their mutual spiritual
relations — very touchingly and appropriately done, I thought.
It was a decidedly dignified little ceremony. Afterwards the
Vali [Muhiddin] sent Anita two carpets as a wedding present
and an enormous floral piece, accompanied by the following
rather touching letter:

> I have been very deeply impressed by the noble gesture of
> Your Excellency in having the marriage of your honorable
> daughter celebrated according to the laws of this country.
> The sincere interest and sympathy you have displayed and
> your noble feelings towards the Turks and Turkey have always

nople as Vice Consul, he had been Vice Consul at Algiers, a post to which he
had at first been assigned as clerk, after his graduation from Harvard in 1926.
In 1931 he was sent to Bangkok as Third Secretary and Vice Consul. This was
followed by assignments to Budapest, Paris, and Ottawa. In 1940, he became
Consul at Wellington, New Zealand, holding also the rank of Second Secretary.
Posts as Consul at Edmonton, Ottawa, and Hamilton in Canada, and at Cebu
in the Philippine Islands followed. Mr. English subsequently resigned from the
Service.

[10] The religious wedding was performed by Dr. Caleb Gates, President of
Robert College. — J. C. G.

been immensely appreciated by every one of us and it is hardly necessary for me to reiterate here the great esteem of all those who have had the good fortune of meeting Your Excellency.

Allow me to say only that this country has seen in the celebration of the marriage, with all the formalities as for Turkish citizens, not only a mark of friendship going far beyond the mere courtesy and deep into our hearts, but also an evidence of Your Excellency's most precious sympathy with Turkey's efforts to modernize her institutions.

I particularly wish to convey to you with my personal thanks those of the Municipality which considers itself greatly honored to have had the privilege of registering the happy event of today.

In my own name, and in that of the City of Istanbul, I take the liberty of congratulating Your Excellency and Mrs. Grew and of expressing our heartiest wishes for the happiness and prosperity of the new-married.

I beg Your Excellency on behalf of this City to kindly transmit to the bridal pair the two carpets of local manufacture that the City is taking the liberty of presenting as a souvenir of this happy day. . . .[11]

Conversation   Ankara, February 29, 1932
His Excellency Shukri Kaya Bey
Acting Minister for Foreign Affairs

TRANSFER TO JAPAN

I called on the Acting Minister for Foreign Affairs and said that it was my sad duty to inform him officially of my transfer from Turkey to Japan, telling him of my deep regrets at leaving this country where we had been happier than at any previous post and where we had made friends whom we would never forget. The Minister was good enough to say some pleasant things which need not be recorded. . . .

NARCOTICS

I said to the Minister that it seemed to me that the relations between Turkey and the United States were at present on an

11 This, I believe, was the first diplomatic wedding to be performed according to Turkish law since the Capitulations. — J. C. G.

excellent basis; that I had interpreted my duties here not only to explain my own country to Turkey but also to explain modern Turkey to the United States, and I believed that much of the former animosity to Turkey shown by certain elements in my country had now very largely disappeared. Shukri Kaya Bey said that the Turkish Government was well aware of this change in view of reports from Mouhtar Bey at Washington and from Saradjoglou Shukri Bey after his recent visit to America. This altered situation caused the greatest satisfaction. I then observed that there was still one unfortunate element which could exert an adverse effect on these relations; namely, the continued clandestine traffic in narcotics from Turkey to the United States, and I hoped that the Turkish Government in the interest of both countries would leave nothing undone to put a complete and permanent end to this traffic.

The Minister said that he quite appreciated the situation which I had described; that Ismet Pasha was deeply concerned about it and that Dr. Refik Bey was quite fanatical on the subject. It was the intention of the Turkish Government to "Etatise" the production of narcotics; that the Government was unanimously determined to stop this smuggling, and he was sure that in spite of the great difficulties involved they would eventually be successful.

LEAVE-TAKING

After taking formal leave of Shukri Kaya Bey, I said goodbye to Kemal Aziz Bey and then called on Numan Bey, the Undersecretary, for the same purpose. Munir Sureyya Bey, Chief of Protocol, was ill but I asked Numan Bey to tell him that I had called. Personal calls on other members of the Government are to be made within the next few days.

Ankara, Thursday, March 3 [1932]

A busy day — our last in Ankara. My calls included the Afghan Ambassador (who begged me to arrange to have his country recognized by the United States by a treaty of friendship which, he said, could be negotiated in London or here or anywhere), Tahy [the Hungarian Minister], Kobr [the Czechoslovakian Minister], Brandao [the Brazilian Minister], Nagy Pasha, Nousret Sadoullah, Djemil [Dean of the International Law Institute at Ankara] and Halil [teacher at the University of Stamboul] Beys. We lunched at the Polish Embassy, where Olszowski [the Polish Ambassador] had placed the flag on the table at half-mast in honor of our departure. During luncheon Madame O. asked me who my successor would be; I replied that the matter was not decided, when Shukri Kaya, who was on her other side, leaned forward and said: "Oh yes it is; I telephoned to the Gazi last night and he said that if Mr. Grew recommended the appointment, the agrément should be given immediately." I never have recommended the appointment, but the giving of the agrément in two days is gratifying; it took about three weeks to get mine in Japan.[12] I asked Shukri Kaya if the matter was definitely settled and if I could cable Washington that the agrément had been given, to which he replied in the affirmative. But I have particularly requested that no publicity be given to the appointment here until it is announced from the White House; we mustn't have the same leak that occurred in Tokyo and caused me a lot of embarrassment until the appointment was officially announced some three weeks later.

Then we all went to the special concert given for us by the Gazi's orchestra. I have never in my life seen such hospitality as the Turks have shown us. The other night Elsie admired an oil painting of the Ankara citadel in Shukri Kaya's house; the next day it came to her with his good wishes. Ismet Pasha's secretary gave her a lesson in backgammon the other night and the next day around comes a beautiful new backgammon board with Ismet's compliments. Elsie remarked quite casually to Safvet that she was disappointed never to have had a chance to hear the Gazi's orchestra; the next day we were informed that a special concert had been arranged and we were asked to choose the program and bring any friends we wished. We

[12] Charles Hitchcock Sherrill succeeded Mr. Grew.

asked for Tschaikovsky's Fifth Symphony, because it will always remind us of Turkey and the Bosporus. Zeki Bey [conductor of the Gazi's orchestra] received us; they played beautifully, and afterwards Zeki's son played a couple of solos. Edib Servet was also there, and we brought Madame Olszowska and the Sigurd Bentzons [Norwegian Minister].

A few friends came to tea and then we went to the station. Perhaps I had better let Howland and Eugene tell of the send-off; it was very moving; Ismet and Kiazim and their wives, Shukri Kaya and a lot of other Turkish friends and officials and most of the colleagues were there. Ismet, Alice said, was weeping when he said good-bye to her. It sounds perhaps rather fulsome to record these things, but there are a lot of unpleasant things in life and it is human nature to want to remember the pleasant ones. . . .[13]

Address of the Ambassador on the Occasion
of the Farewell Luncheon Given for
Him and for Mrs. Grew

Istanbul, March 11, 1932

. . . As for Turco-American relations in general, I believe that any American Ambassador to this country, would see a steady strengthening and improvement in that direction. How can it be otherwise? Turkey knows not only that America is one of her best customers but also, and of immeasurably greater importance, one of her most disinterested friends. We have shown that fact constantly in many concrete ways and we are prepared to continue to show it. We have no political row to hoe in Turkey; there is no *arrière pensée* whatever in the practical friendship that we wish to show. The American institutions which have grown up here are aiming to make their respective contribution to the specific needs of the Turkish

[13] The Turkish press was warm in its praise of Mr. Grew's work in Turkey. The *Hakimiyete Milliye*, for instance, stated on March 2: "While bidding him farewell we feel the profound sorrow which one experiences when parting from a real friend. . . . We have reserved a warm place in our heart where Mr. Grew will forever remain. With respect we salute him and bid him farewell."

Republic. Their presence in Turkey is a powerful and practical demonstration of the disinterested friendship America bears the new Republic.

As for Turkey herself, I consider it a great privilege to have been able to watch, during these intensely important five years of development of a young Republic, the progressive unfolding of a novel scene. To anyone who sat for six months at the conference table at Lausanne not yet ten years ago — a conference replete with international hatreds, replete with international dynamite, with moments when the nations hung literally on the brink of further war — the practical and eminently successful working out of a new policy of international friendship to take the place of the old policy of international bickering, suspicion and enmity, has been one of the most inspiring experiences in history. Certainly few events in history have ever equalled in dramatic significance that memorable first visit of Venizelos to Ankara a little over a year ago — the genuinely cordial reception of a former bitter enemy, the welcoming arch with its words of welcome in Greek surrounded by Greek flags, the hospitable banquets and speeches — and then Ismet Pasha's return visit to Athens under exactly similar circumstances — the burying of the hatchet after centuries of open or latent hostility. Could any finer example of courageous and farsighted statesmanship be given to the world than this splendid triumph of these two men? Tewfik Rushdi Bey has continually said to me since my arrival in Turkey: "Our foreign policy is simple and direct; we seek friendship with all, alliance or *groupement* with none." Five years ago Turkey was surrounded by potential enemies; today she is surrounded by trusted friends. Is not the working out of this enlightened policy a worthy object lesson to the nations?

As for Turkey's internal problems, they are many and difficult; but the achievements of the past justify optimism for the future; much has been accomplished, much will be accomplished; and with the intensely virile will to succeed, I confidently believe in the future of the Turkish Republic. . . .

March 6–12 [1932]

... The last few days of our stay in Turkey were full of work and very full of emotion. It is a hard wrench to pull ourselves away — from a place where we have been happier than in any previous one and from friends that we love. The farewell luncheon of the American colony was very difficult and very beautiful. Alice wept and thereby apparently endeared herself to the Americans for all time. The next day I was requested to attend a meeting of the entire staff with all kavasses and servants at which Howland made a moving speech and presented me with a magnificent cigar box on behalf of all of them. That last night we dined alone in Howland Shaw's apartment with only Gene Hinkle and Burton Berry [Vice Consul]. Of course "Der kleine Garde-offizier" was duly played. It has become the farewell song of our little group.

The page of Sunday, March 13, on my calendar has only three large exclamation marks placed there by Carpie [Miss Carp], but this being the day of departure, the quotation at the top from Stevenson was peculiarly significant:

> When we look into the long avenue of the future, and see the good there is for each of us to do, we realize after all what a beautiful thing it is to work.

We sailed at 10 on the *Italia* formerly of the Sitmar Line, now of the Lloyd Triestino. Practically all our friends were there to see us off, the Turks, the colleagues, the Americans, 108 of them. There were tears. Fortunately the day was lovely. Nearly everyone stayed on the dock until we were out of sight and as we rounded Seraglio (how well I remembered the point where Anita completed her great swim) our last glimpse of the Bosporus and the Port, Galata and Pera and Scutari, the Seraglio itself, and finally the Islands rising like precious stones from their brilliant blue setting, was sublimely beautiful and we took away with us something that can never fade. Few more beautiful spots exist on earth, and with the intimate associations of the past five years it all has a meaning for us which no mere traveler can ever visualize or fathom.

The press was very fine. One paper reported our leaving with the headlines "Departure of a Great Friend of Turkey." Ismet and Shukri Kaya replied by radio to my farewell messages in warmest terms.

Thus ends our mission to Turkey.

PART FIVE

The Rising Sun in the Pacific

1932–1941

*I*T WAS a decade of aggression. Japan seized Manchuria in
1931. In 1933 Germany began to rearm under Hitler. Two
years later Italy invaded Ethiopia. The next year Hitler tore
up the Treaty of Locarno and fortified the Rhineland. In
1937 Japan again attacked China, and the following year Hitler
occupied Austria and dismembered Czechoslovakia. Early in
1939, Germany destroyed the independence of Czechoslovakia
and took Memel, while Mussolini invaded Albania. Then on
September 1, 1939, Hitler invaded Poland, and the world soon
was at war.

"The first battles in the Second World War were fought in
remote Manchuria," Professors Harley F. MacNair and Donald
F. Lach have written. "Shaken by the whirlwind of Japanese
expansion, the structure of peace was thereafter buffeted
mercilessly until the horrors of aggression and war were ultimately visited upon most of the civilized world." [1]

Japan, of course, had begun to build an Asiatic empire long
before 1931. By defeating China in 1894–95, Japan acquired
Formosa and the Pescadores Islands. Japan's defeat of Russia
in 1905 resulted in her acquisition of southern Sakhalin. Japan
also obtained the lease of the Liaotung peninsula and control
of the railroad from Port Arthur to Changchun. Five years
later Japan annexed Korea.

During World War I Japan seized all former German possessions in the Pacific north of the Equator. At the Paris Peace

[1] Harley Farnsworth MacNair and Donald F. Lach, *Modern Far Eastern International Relations* (New York: D. Van Nostrand Co., Inc., 1950), p. 347.

Conference, these islands were mandated to Japan. Japan's effort to control China was checked, however, when Japan was unable to exact the "Twenty-One Demands" on China. Had these demands, first proposed in 1915, been secured China would have been reduced to the status of a protectorate.

The decade of the nineteen-twenties found the civilian elements in control of Japanese policy. The Japanese Diet refused to appropriate funds for the Japanese Army's intervention in Siberia, and the Army had to withdraw. Japanese leaders agreed to the naval limitations of the Washington Peace Conference and signed the Kellogg-Briand Pact to outlaw war. Japanese militarists, however, seeing their control being weakened and their hopes of conquest disappearing, provoked the attack on Manchuria in 1931 to reassert their power both in domestic and foreign affairs.

As Samuel Eliot Morison has written: "Japan was the only important nation in the world in the twentieth century which combined modern industrial power and a first-class military establishment with religious and social ideas inherited from the primitive ages of mankind, which exalted the military profession and regarded war and conquest as the highest good. True, the country possessed an intellectual elite who had accepted the Christian ethic if not the Christian religion, and attempted to guide the Japanese nation into the ways of peace; but those Western ideals vaguely comprehended under the term 'democracy' had made so little dent on the people at large that they were swept away by a self-conscious and active group of military extremists." [2]

After the aggression in Manchuria, Japanese militarists consolidated their power during 1932 by assassinating the Prime Minister. Four years later in the February Mutiny Army extremists assassinated Admiral Saito, Lord Keeper of the Privy Seal; General Watanabe, the Inspector General of Military Education; Takahashi, the Finance Minister; and failed in their attempts to kill the Prime Minister and Count Makino,

---

[2] Samuel Eliot Morison, *History of United States Naval Operations in World War II*, vol. III, *The Rising Sun in the Pacific, 1931–April 1942* (Boston: Little Brown & Co. and Atlantic Monthly Press, 1948), p. 5.

an elder statesman. After this wave of assassination moderate statesmen had a rapidly declining influence on the course of Japanese affairs.

In addition to the powerful hold which the military had over so many Japanese, the structure of the Japanese Government provided for by the Constitution of 1889 made it easier for the military to impose their will on the civilian leaders. The portfolios of defense in the Japanese Cabinet were held by Army and Navy professionals who were not under the control of the premier and his civilian colleagues. In fact the military was able, by indirect means, to bring the downfall of many cabinets. Although the premier and the foreign minister might adopt one line of diplomacy, the military, by such incidents as those in Manchuria in 1931 and North China in 1937, were able to short circuit the civilian policy.

Another important aspect of the Japanese political structure was the role of the Emperor or the "imperial principle." One Japanese professor of law at the Tokyo Imperial University glowingly said of a rescript issued by an emperor: "The Imperial Rescript on Education . . . is the foundation and principle of the moral activity of the Japanese. Why? Because it is an imperial rescript. . . . There can be no reason or argument whatever about it. . . . The Emperor is the vital center of the Japanese nation. His is the personality upon whom all Japanese depend. This is the essence of our nationality and the foundation of our morality. In this manner did the Imperial Ancestors establish the nation, and through this idea has the country passed from one Imperial rule to another, and will pass for ever. Our nationality is centered in one person, and it is our duty to develop and fulfill our destiny by observing our duty to the Throne, ultimately attaining the highest pinnacle of morality. We profess our faith, neither doubting nor fearing, and enjoy in it that perfect peace of mind which is the sum of happiness. Sacrificing ourselves, both in mind and body, with joy for the imperial idea, we promote it and obey it. This is the backbone of Japanese morality and the foundation of the national spirit.

"Thus the Imperial Rescript is above all criticism. The

standard of justice and injustice, of right and wrong, is to be fixed by the imperial will. . . . The Imperial Rescript embodies truth, righteousness, wisdom, and all the virtues. All religions defer and yield pride of place to it. Philosophy holds good only when it is in conformity with the imperial will. If the Emperor should say, 'Go to the left,' we should be to the left. If he should say, 'Go to the right,' we should go to the right. That is the way and doctrine of the Japanese. We have but to obey, without doubt or demur; and we should do so, not because the saints and sages of old so taught us, not because the learned have shown us that it is reasonable so to do, but because it is an imperial rescript. It is an imperial rescript — it claims our obedience." [3]

Summing up the factors that helped to explain Japanese tactics in the recent past, Professor Harley F. MacNair concluded: "[It] may be stated that the Japanese were living under feudal conditions and government until well past the middle of the nineteenth century. At the time, therefore, in which it became desirable for the Japanese to change from isolation to participation in the life of the family of nations, they were reasonably well qualified to make a start because of the administration and the discipline under which they had lived for centuries. They were accustomed to obey arbitrary commands issued by both local and national authorities. They were motivated by a strong sense of nationalism and by a highly developed spirit of patriotism and emperor-adulation. They were consumed, moreover, by a zealous determination to save their country from Western aggression and to develop it into a world power by any and all methods. They would, if necessary, stoop — and they have, indeed, on more than one occasion, stooped — to conquer." [4]

Ambassador Grew's mission to Japan from 1932 to 1942

[3] An article of Shinkichi Uyesugi quoted by Kenneth Colegrove, "The Japanese Emperor," *The American Political Science Review*, August, 1932, p. 647.

[4] Harley Farnsworth MacNair, *The Real Conflict between China and Japan* (Chicago: The University of Chicago Press, 1938), pp. 171–72.

came in the midst of the re-emergence of the military extremists and the decline in influence of the civilian leaders of the decade before. Mr. Grew's records of his Japanese Mission are voluminous. His diary over these years is rich and rewarding. Extracts from the diary have already been published in Ten Years in Japan, published in New York in 1944. In addition to his diary, letters, and copies of his despatches to Washington, Mr. Grew has a particularly unique and valuable document in his manuscript collection. During spare hours in 1941, he wrote a history of his mission in Japan. This history was based on his diary, his letters, his despatches and on his memory. Mr. Grew's history of his mission was written while the events he was describing were still fresh in his mind. It also was written before the events of the last turbulent months of 1941 distracted his attention and altered his focus on the recent past.

The history of his mission follows in Chapters XXX, XXXI, and XXXII. It has been presented in almost its entirety. The editor has deleted only material that duplicated earlier passages or that threw no particular light on Japanese-American relations. The form which has been used for Chinese and Japanese names has been that set by Mr. Grew in his diary. When Mr. Grew wrote this history, he footnoted the various despatches mentioned in the text using the asterisk as his symbol. Whenever the editor has added to Mr. Grew's own footnotes it has been done by placing brackets around the additional material. Whenever the editor has added his own footnotes, these are distinguishable from Mr. Grew's by the use of numerals as the symbol.

XXX

Relations Between the United States and Japan
1932 – 1935

To Cordell Hull, September 21, 1940

Much water has gone over the falls in the history of American-Japanese relations during the eight years since the beginning of the present mission to Japan on June 6, 1932,[1] and when that history comes to be written, it will show a fluctuating curve in those relations, with periods of marked friendliness interspersed between periods of intense antagonism in the attitude of Japan towards the United States, but with a general worsening tendency. Indeed, in the present era of world power politics and rampant militarism, no other trend could have been expected. Once Japan, as one of the so-called "have not" countries, had determined to achieve by force what she was convinced could not be achieved by orderly processes and peaceful methods, a progressive clashing with American policy, with the rights and legitimate interests of the United States, and with the ideals and international principles for which America stands, was inevitable. Diplomacy might retard but could not stem the tide of aggression. Japan, alas, has become one of the predatory Powers, frankly and unashamedly opportunist, having submerged all sense of international morality, seeking to profit at every turn by the weakness of others. While I earnestly hope that the final chapter of my work in Japan will not have to be characterized, as was Sir Nevile Henderson's work in Berlin, as the *Failure of a Mission*, nevertheless, as matters stand today, the odds will presumably have been

[1] The date upon which Mr. Grew arrived in Japan.

too great ever to qualify it as a mission of constructive success. Its main purpose has been and probably will continue to be to endeavor, while aiming steadily to support and protect American interests in the Far East, to keep the boat of American-Japanese relations from rocking dangerously. The degree to which either of these aims can effectively be achieved is under present conditions limited.

The occasion of this 5000th despatch is respectfully taken to survey the trends of those relations during the past eight years, in the full realization that such a survey is likely to be of more interest to the historians than of any current value to the Department. This survey does not purport to be in any respect a complete chronicle. Its aim is rather to bring out the highlights in the Embassy's activities and correspondence with Washington during the period under consideration, touching briefly upon such events and developments as have had a direct or indirect influence on American-Japanese relations or have been of outstanding importance in the history of Japan, as well as to furnish future students with full references to pertinent telegrams on any given subject. For more extensive contemporary comment and data, the Embassy's mail despatches, which are mentioned only in outstanding cases, should also be consulted. Unless otherwise specified, all references in the footnotes are to telegrams from the Embassy to the Department of State.

1932

BACKGROUND OF THE SEIZURE OF MANCHURIA

The historical background and the precise factors in the Far Eastern situation which led to the seizure of Manchuria by the Japanese Army in the autumn of 1931 and the setting up of the puppet state of "Manchukuo" in 1932, are open to debate. The Lytton Commission aimed at a purely objective approach, but owing to divergent political interests among its members, compromises in the formulation of its report were inevitable and its final presentation as a fact-finding body cannot be said to have comprised the whole truth.[2] I myself have been favorably impressed, so far as background is concerned, with the presentation in Professor A. Whitney Griswold's book *The Far Eastern Policy of the United States* — published in New York in 1938 — but special importance should in my opinion be attached to the verdict of the Honorable John V. A. Mac-Murray, former Minister to China and generally recognized as an expert authority on Far Eastern affairs, who in 1935 submitted to the Department a memorandum in which the following significant passage occurs:

Patient efforts of Japan for nearly ten years tried to preserve the letter and spirit of the Washington Treaties in the face of Chinese intransigence and the selfishness of the signatory powers, each country aiming to advance its own interest at the expense of collective security. Treaties with Japan were unilaterally abrogated. Japan forces had then done in good faith only what had been forced upon them to do in fulfillment of their mission to protect the lives and property of their nationals. The effect of our own attitude was to condone the high-handed behaviour of the Chinese and to encourage them to a course of further recalcitrance. The Chinese had been wilful in their scorn of their legal obligations, reckless in their resort to violence for the accomplishment of their ends, and provocative in their methods. Though timid when there was any prospect that the force to which they resorted would be met by force, they were alert to take a hectoring attitude at any sign of weakness in their opponents, and cynically inclined to construe as weakness any yielding to their demands.

The policy of co-operation among the Powers, which might well have averted the catastrophe of subjugation by Japan, was no longer available. It was wounded in the house of its friends — scorned by the Chinese and ignored by the British and ourselves,

2 The Lytton Commission of the League of Nations spent six months making an intensive firsthand study of the Sino-Japanese dispute. The final report of the Commission was submitted to China and Japan and the members of the League on October 1, 1932. See League of Nations, *Appeal by the Chinese Government, Report of the Commission of Enquiry*, Geneva, October 1, 1932, and MacNair and Lach, *op. cit.*, pp. 376–85, for a discussion of the report.

until it became a hissing and a byword with a Japanese nation persuaded to the belief that it could depend only on its own strong arm to vindicate its rightful legal position in eastern Asia.

COMMENCEMENT OF MISSION TO JAPAN

Whatever may have been the merits of the case for Japan and of the incentive which led to the seizure of Manchuria, the methods adopted to achieve her ends placed her, legally [3] and logically, out of Court so far as the United States was concerned, and it was at the height of the bitterness and anti-American sentiment aroused by the position taken by the United States in the controversy over Manchuria that the present mission to Japan commenced. Most of the so-called welcoming functions given on my arrival afforded opportunities for my hosts to express their views and feelings, sometimes in highly discourteous terms, on the subject of alleged American arrogance and obtrusion into affairs which did not concern the United States, and little was done to temper the antagonism of the Japanese public, incited by the press and the inflammatory utterances of such officials as the spokesman of the Foreign Office, Mr. Toshio Shiratori [Director of the Bureau of Information and Intelligence]. These attacks converged on Secretary of State Stimson, who was held responsible for the American attitude.[4]

From July until December, 1932, the general atmosphere

[3] For a discussion of the legal situation in regard to the upheaval in the Far East, see Quincy Wright, *The Existing Legal Situation as It Relates to the Conflict in the Far East* (I.P.R. Inquiry Series; New York: Institute of Pacific Relations, 1939).

[4] Secretary of State Stimson on January 7, 1932, despatched identic notes to China and Japan stating that the United States "cannot admit the legality of any situation *de facto* nor does it intend to recognize any treaty or agreement entered into between those Governments, or agents thereof, which may impair the treaty rights of the United States or its citizens in China, including those which relate to the sovereignty, the independence, or the territorial and administrative integrity of the Republic of China, or to the international policy relative to China, commonly known as the open door policy; and that it does not intend to recognize any situation, treaty or agreement which may be brought about by means contrary to the covenants and obligations of the Pact

and the developing situation in Japan were described, apart from our telegrams and despatches, in a series of official letters to Secretary Stimson which are presumably on file in the Department.[5] Copies at least are in the official files of this Embassy. In October of that year, two conversations were reported as significant. In one conversation Prince Chichibu, the Emperor's brother, asked point blank whether it was true that the United States was preparing for war with Japan. The other comprised certain comments by Mr. Yenji Takeda, Secretary of the America-Japan Society,[6] which are given in résumé as follows:

Mr. Takeda states that, when the Army first started on its

of Paris of August 27, 1928, to which Treaty both China and Japan, as well as the United States, are parties." U.S. Department of State, *Papers Relating to the Foreign Relations of the United States, Japan: 1931–1941* (Washington: Government Printing Office, 1943), I, 76.

5 In a diary entry of December 20, 1932, Mr. Grew wrote concerning his correspondence between the Department of State and the Embassy: "Our whole system of intelligence should be vastly strengthened, and it should be systematic, not haphazard. . . .

"There ought also to be constant and prompt comment by the Department on the Embassy's work and actions. For the first four months here I hadn't the slightest idea whether our despatches were considered useful. Then came a bully critique commenting on all that had been written. But those critiques ought to come by every pouch, promptly and when the Department can piece out the Embassy's information by intelligence from other sources, it ought to give the Embassy the advantage of all the background it can. I don't yet know, and probably never shall know, what the Department thought of my representations and general action in the National City Bank case, or what it thought of my Osaka speech, or of the general tone I have used in speeches here, and a lot of other things. . . .

"Indeed, I have had to formulate my own policy ever since coming to Japan. The President [Hoover] said that the Japanese must get out of Manchuria but that in no circumstances must we, have war. The Secretary said that the Japanese must get out of Manchuria, even more emphatically, but he didn't touch on the other aspect of the case. So, according to those instructions, I came out here to get the Japanese out of Manchuria. Those are the only instructions that were given me. Nothing was said about trying to develop more friendly relations whether the Japanese got out of Manchuria or not. After five months here I told the Secretary what I thought our policy ought to be and Mr. Stimson replied that I had diagnosed his attitude correctly. But during those five months, it has been all battledore and no shuttlecock."

6 See U.S. Department of State, *Foreign Relations of the United States, Diplomatic Papers 1932, The Far East* (Washington: Government Printing Office, 1948), IV, 717–18.

Manchurian adventure, the people of Japan looked doubtfully at the matter. Later, when the League and the United States started to condemn the Japanese for their actions, the people rallied behind the Army, like all members of a family will stand behind one member who is being attacked from outside. Just now they will not admit that the Army was wrong, but, just like a family, eventually they will admit that maybe the person who was attacked (Japan) was in the wrong. Any violent move against Japan now will strengthen this family feeling and keep the Army in power, but if everyone stays quiet for a while, feeling will arise against the Army and maybe the Shidehara diplomacy [7] will return. Nations are like people; they do not like to be disliked.

The Army is trying very hard to keep in power, and they are trying to keep the people aroused. The National City Bank affair was for the purpose of advertising the Army. They are trying to show the people that they are necessary to the country. That was one of the reasons why they started the Manchurian affair. There was a feeling in Japan that the country had to have an economic outlet, but also the Army felt that it would lose all influence if it did not do something for the good of the country. If disarmament was successful, the Army would not amount to anything in the future, so they had to act to save their position.

The Japanese people are very nervous. They are like a boy who has hit another boy and is looking around fearfully, expecting someone to punish them. They will be nervous until after the League meets to discuss the Manchurian affair.

The Japanese Army's operations are really aimed at Russia — not at present, but at some time in the future. Japan is afraid of Bolshevism and feels that it must drive Bolshevism out of Asia.

THE NATIONAL CITY BANK INCIDENT

One significant incident during this period was the absurd campaign against the National City Bank, which was described

[7] Baron Kijuro Shidehara was Japanese Minister for Foreign Affairs from 1924–27 and again from July 2, 1929, to December 11, 1931. "Shidehara diplomacy" could best be described as a policy of economic retrenchment at home and peace and conciliation abroad.

to Secretary Stimson in my letter of September 10, as follows:

> Another rather nasty case has just occurred. The National City Bank of New York instructed its branches throughout the Far East — in China, Manila, and Singapore quite as much as in Japan — to forward photographs of the business sections of their respective cities in order to indicate the modern building progress in those cities. In Osaka the Japanese gendarmes suddenly directed the Bank to stop taking these photographs and shortly thereafter the Japanese press, not only in Osaka but throughout the entire country, carried sensational headlines and many columns of print charging the Bank with taking these photographs (although in strict accordance with law and police regulations) for the purpose of furnishing the United States Government with plans for bombing these districts in case of war. The matter on the face of it was ludicrous because these precise photographs can be bought in the open shops and the Yokohama Chamber of Commerce had recently circulated in the United States a pamphlet containing similar photographs for purposes of business propaganda. The action of the Bank was distinctly in the interests of the Japanese themselves. The authorities have taken no steps, in spite of my urgent request, to right, by a public statement, the heavy wrong done to the prestige of the National City Bank throughout Japan. The poison has worked its course, at least one Japanese member of the Bank's staff has resigned, threatening letters and delegations of patriotic societies calling for wholesale resignations are being received, and the Bank's business will inevitably suffer as a result. I am in touch with the local manager and am to see Count Yasuya Uchida — Minister for Foreign Affairs — to discuss the matter this afternoon. I give this incident merely to indicate the extent which this anti-American press campaign has reached.[8]

The public flurry over this incident, however, duly ran its course and the incident was closed with the publication in at least two prominent Japanese newspapers of the Department's press release conveying the statement of the Foreign Office holding the bank blameless and its motives free from suspicion.

[8] See *Foreign Relations, 1932, The Far East,* IV, 241.

ANTI-AMERICAN PROPAGANDA

The spy scare nevertheless continued, and anti-American propaganda, fanned by the Foreign Office and the military, was steadily intensified. The United States was accused, by following a "dog-in-the-manger" policy, of obstructing Japan's expansion in the Far East; the specious arguments advanced by the Government in a puerile endeavor to prove that Japan had not violated the provisions of the Nine Power Treaty were accepted even by the intellectual classes, and every effort was made to persuade the public that the United States, especially with the Atlantic Fleet of the American Navy temporarily retained in the Pacific Ocean, was a potential and warlike enemy. Mr. Shiratori, the vitriolic spokesman of the Foreign Office, when asked if he actually believed there would be war, replied: "Certainly not. Do you think that we would be attacking Secretary Stimson as we have been doing if we thought that there was any danger of war?" The main purposes of this propaganda were believed by the Embassy to be (1) to maintain the existing war fever for the purpose of obtaining as much money as possible for the Army, and (2) to keep the people in a defiant, warlike frame of mind while the Manchurian crisis lasted.[9]

9 On November 28, 1932, Mr. Grew stated in his diary that "the hostility in Japan towards the United States is temporarily quiescent. . . . This noticeable amelioration in the bitterness displayed last spring and summer is due to three factors: (1) nothing has recently been said or done to excite hostility. (2) When Japan recognized 'Manchukuo' the public felt that from the Japanese point of view the main issue between the two countries had been finally settled by that step and this gave them a sense of complacent satisfaction. (3) The at least temporary improvement in industrial conditions is an important psychological factor. While there is open dissatisfaction with the heavy drains on the budget, social conditions are a good deal easier than they were during the summer and a spirit of optimism prevails which was lacking a few weeks ago. . . . Nevertheless latent hostility towards the United States is always present and any provocation would fan it into flame. War with the United States, however, is unthinkable if only because Japan's purse is empty and her hands are full. This is the best guarantee of peace."

JAPAN'S RECOGNITION OF "MANCHUKUO"

On September 3 the following confidential appraisal was sent to the Secretary of State:

(Paraphrase)

Adverting to my letter to you of August 13, the certainty that Japan intends to go through with the venture in Manchuria regardless of whatever foreign opposition develops cannot too strongly be impressed upon the Department. Only superior physical force can now stop this movement, and what gives added strength to the Japanese determination is the fact that the elements which now control policy are convinced of the justice of their cause. They believe that their whole course of action in Manchuria is one of self-defense and of supreme and vital national interest, and they are determined if necessary to fight to support their action, difficult as it is to believe that the obviously false premise of self-determination for Manchuria can be given honest credence by the conservative statesmen. Military preparations steadily continue. While an unfavorable report is awaited from the Lytton Commission and while it is realized that action may be taken by the League of Nations, it is the United States that is regarded as their principal obstacle. Just now there is very little talk of friction with Soviet Russia.

My observations and information from many sources have confirmed with increasing assurance the foregoing opinions. After studying the situation from all angles, no approach is apparent by which Japanese intransigence could be modified or overcome. In the course of time it is possible that internal economic pressure added to moral pressure from without may compel the Japanese to modify their policy, but there is no doubt that for the present the openly conflicting policies and principles of the United States and Japan must be squarely faced.*

Japan recognized "Manchukuo" on September 14.[10]

* Telegram No. 224, September 3, noon. [*Foreign Relations, Japan: 1931–41,* I, 102.]

[10] Japan recognized Manchukuo on September 15, 1932. See *Foreign Relations, 1932, The Far East,* IV, 253–54.

Shortly before Japan withdrew its delegation from the League of Nations, the following analysis of the situation was presented:

(Paraphrase)
Outwardly self-assured, the Japanese are inwardly hypersensitive. Having been misled by chauvinistic propaganda, they feel that the world is against them, and they do not understand why. Predominant public opinion has tied the hands of the saner thinkers in the country, but they nevertheless realize that the Manchurian venture has led the country into a serious muddle. That any concessions can or will be made at Geneva which would prevent Japan's recognition of "Manchukuo" or which would result in withdrawal, is out of the question. Serious domestic disturbances would probably ensue and the Government would undoubtedly be overturned if any radical concessions were made to foreign opinion at present.

Under these circumstances I continue to believe that a restrained course is the best and the only profitable one to follow. By refusing to recognize "Manchukuo," since effective enforcement is impossible, the determination of the nations to uphold the sanctity of the peace treaties can at present best be given expression. Coercive measures would merely serve to weld Japan more firmly together in opposition and we had therefore best acknowledge to the world that the most effective way of serving the cause of peace, which is the principal issue at stake, is to proceed by gradual rather than by immediate attempts to solve the problem. If anything can modify the Government's policy in the long run it is more likely to spring from the difficulty and overburdening expense of pacifying and organizing "Manchukuo" than from any overt foreign opposition. The time factor is therefore important.*

This hypothesis, alas, was not destined to eventuate.

As of pertinent interest during this period, reference is made to the speeches of Viscount Kikujiro Ishii [former Minister

* Telegram No. 275, November 28, 8 P.M. [ibid., pp. 372–73. In this instance and hereinafter the ibid. appearing in brackets refers to the preceding bracketed footnote.]

for Foreign Affairs] and of Prince Iyesato Tokugawa at the first dinner of the America-Japan Society after my arrival * [11] and a speech by the undersigned before the Japan-America Society in Osaka.† [12]

1933
THE SINGER SEWING MACHINE COMPANY INCIDENT

Almost at the start of the new year Japanese-American relations were aggravated by an attack on January 18 of some two hundred workmen on the Singer Sewing Machine Company's offices in Yokohama, the controversy having arisen from a

---

* Telegram No. 163, June 22, 2 P.M.

[11] On June 21, 1932, Mr. Grew commented in his diary on the speeches made that day before the America-Japan Society: "Prince Tokugawa made a perfectly bully welcoming speech. Then Viscount Ishii got up and read his speech. Some think he had his cue from the Government, others that he simply wanted to get some favorable publicity in Japan. I had been given a copy only shortly before the dinner and had had no time to analyze it, but my reaction was that while the tone of it was distinctly inflammatory, we could hardly take exception to the substance; it warned us from opposing Japan's expansion in Manchuria but acknowledged that we were justified in desiring the maintenance of peace and the respect of the peace treaties (which certainly include the Nine Power Treaty) and confirmed the Japanese policy of preserving the open door, equal opportunity in China and the absence of any territorial ambition in any land. He intimated that America had no right to interfere in the eastern hemisphere while good Prince Tokugawa said that Japan's problems were everybody's problems. . . . Some, at least, of the Japanese and all of the Americans whose comments were later reported to me thought Ishii's speech in very bad taste on such an occasion."

† Telegram No. 272, November 22, midnight.

[12] Mr. Grew spoke in Osaka, a commercial center of Japan, on November 22, 1932. He discussed the success of American-Japanese business enterprises and the way in which these joint efforts had contributed to a feeling of good will between the two countries. He expressed the hope that advances toward the goal of world peace could be made as successfully as advances had been made in the field of business. The American people were devoted, he said, to the ideal of peace and were interested in financial and economic prosperity as a corollary of permanent peace. Although he felt the two countries disagreed at times on the means to achieve world peace, Japan and the United States were united in devotion to the ideal. He assured the Japanese that the "peace policy of the United States, far from being contrary to the real interests of Japan, is precisely in accord with those interests."

strike in which the employees of the Company had refused to join. The interior of the building was almost completely demolished with an estimated loss of several hundred thousand dollars in contracts destroyed while two Japanese employees were reported as seriously injured. Although the Yokohama police had been fully warned through the Embassy's repeated representations to the Foreign Office in Tokyo that such an attack was brewing, it appears that the police did not appear on the scene until the damage had been done. A few days later it was reported that a thousand members of the Japanese Federation of Labor planned to attack the American Consulate, but whether the police actually prevented the attack or merely wished to give the appearance that they were now on the job, it did not eventuate. The Singer Sewing Machine Company dispute, after giving rise to much inflammatory comment in the Japanese press, was finally settled on February 8, the American company having made no concessions with respect to the objects for which the agitation and strike were first started, but it was ominously symptomatic of the antiforeign, and especially anti-American, feeling in the country. This incident, and that of the National City Bank, are here described in detail because they loomed large in Japan at the time of their occurrence.* 13

JAPAN SECEDES FROM THE LEAGUE OF NATIONS

In February 14 the Japanese Government decided to secede from the League of Nations after Mr. Yosuke Matsuoka [Japanese Chief Delegate, League of Nations Council and Assembly], with his delegation, had previously withdrawn from the meeting which was deliberating Japan's invasion of "Manchukuo," formal notice of withdrawal from the League being sent to

---

* (See in this connection despatch from the Embassy to the Department, No. 364, April 21, 1933.) [U.S. Department of State, *Foreign Relations of the United States, 1933, The Far East* (Washington: Government Printing Office, 1949), III, 700–702.]

13 See also *ibid.*, pp. 716–17.

14 On February 20 the Cabinet voted to withdraw from the League of Nations.

Geneva on March 27. Shortly before that final step was taken, an analysis of the Far Eastern situation was sent in confidence to the Secretary of State along the following lines:

(Paraphrase)

Preparation to burn her most important bridges with the outside world was indicated by the Cabinet's decision to secede from the League of Nations, involving a basic defeat for the moderate elements in Japan and the complete supremacy of the military. There is now no question of bluff in Japan's attitude. Her determination to be independent of and to disregard western interference with what she conceives to be her own vital interests has been demonstrated by her action in forestalling or succeeding by a *fait accompli* every important step taken by the League. Rather than surrender to moral or other pressure from the West, the military, and the public through military propaganda, are fully prepared to fight, and that determination is strengthened not modified by the moral obloquy of the rest of the world. Further assassinations if not internal revolution would almost certainly follow any inclination on the part of the Government to compromise.

The following factors play their part in an appraisal of the present temper of the nation: (*a*) the determination of the Army to brook no interference whatever in maintaining its prestige; (*b*) the fact that no backward step is permitted on account of the essential importance of saving face; (*c*) the belief that Manchuria represents Japan's "lifeline," a belief which has been carefully nurtured through propaganda; (*d*) the failure of the Chinese to fulfill their treaty obligations, coupled with the former chaotic conditions in Manchuria, has given rise to long-strained exasperation; (*e*) the fact that future financial difficulties arising out of the huge expenditures in the Manchurian campaign are completely disregarded by the Army; and (*f*) the fundamental failure of the Japanese people to understand the sanctity of contractual obligations when such obligations conflict with what they conceive to be their own interests.

The Japanese drive into Jehol will probably be carried out without going south of the Great Wall, even although the campaign will thereby be rendered more costly and difficult, but if the League of Nations should apply active sanctions, Japan would very likely reply by occupying North China, including seizure of the Peking-Tientsin Railway, an act which of course constitutes the greatest potential danger by bringing foreign interests into direct conflict with Japan.

Finally we must accept the fact that the Army and a large section of the public have been led by propaganda to believe that eventual war with the United States, or with Soviet Russia, or with both, is inevitable; that the military possess complete arrogance and self-confidence; that the Navy is becoming more bellicose and that both military and naval machines are rapidly being strengthened and are in a high state of efficiency; and that in the present temper of the country any serious incident tending to inflame public opinion might lead Japan to radical action without counting the cost.*

MOBILIZATION OF NATIONAL RESOURCES

The Ides of March brought what was perhaps the first clear indication of the movement to mobilize the resources of the nation, a movement in which foreign industry and commerce in Japan were to be circumscribed and restricted with ever-increasing intensity: commercial motor trucks began to be requisitioned while the Standard Oil Company and the Rising Sun Petroleum Company (Shell) were directed to submit figures of their imports during the past calendar year and their prospective imports for three months ahead, the first time that such an order had ever been received by the American company.†

As of perhaps greater personal than official import it may be here chronicled that President Franklin D. Roosevelt decided not to accept the resignation which I had, according to tradition, sent him on December 5, 1932, and expressed the desire that I should continue as Ambassador to Japan.‡

---

* Telegram No. 45, February 23, 1 P.M. [*Ibid.*, pp. 195–96.]

† Telegram No. 59, March 13, 8 P.M.

‡ Telegram No. 28, March 22, 6 P.M. (from the Department).

HOPES FOR A REORIENTATION OF JAPAN'S POLICY

In the middle of April there were reverberations as to the impending fall of Viscount Makoto Saito's [Prime Minister] Government, which brought from me the following further analysis of the situation:

(Paraphrase)

Political predictions under present circumstances in Japan are unwise but the reports in the press heralding an early fall of the Cabinet are probably premature. In all likelihood the Government will not last very much longer, but Prince Saionji, the Genro, does not wish it to relinquish power immediately. According to one influential Japanese, Japan does not yet know just how to get out of the serious rut she is now in, and until some way is found, a new Cabinet is not desired. When a new Government does come in, however, its course in international affairs will be along more conciliatory lines. Moderate views in Japan feel that the nation must extricate itself from the deplorable international position into which it has been brought by the policy of the present Government and must pursue a new course. Throughout Japanese history the country has passed through cycles of anti-foreign chauvinism which have always been followed, as in the Meiji era, by periods of international co-operation. These moderate elements confidently predict a similar movement in the present case and they hold that even the Army is now ready to modify its attitude.

I have heard similar statements for many months past but there seems to be more assurance and conviction about these present reports than formerly. Indeed, I happen to know that their source is Prince Saionji. The moderates have been waiting for a long time for some sort of foothold, and it may be that Japan's decision to leave the League of Nations, by which the nation is placed in an unenviable position before the world, will give them that fulcrum.

Now that Manchuria has been completely and effectively occupied one cannot foresee just what form a new conciliatory policy would take, but the pendulum is held to have swung about as far toward chauvinistic nationalism as it is likely to go and instead of a continuance of defiant isolation, the future trend is expected to be in the direction of international conciliation.

The foregoing hopes and views are merely set forth as those held by the moderate elements in the country and for the present they are reported more as worthy of attentive consideration than as reliable prophecy. Until concrete evidence is forthcoming I personally consider that it is idle to predict a change of orientation in foreign policy as long as the nation's affairs are dominated, as they are at present, by the military.*

The Open Door in Manchuria

During this period we received continual assurances from official quarters that the principle of the Open Door in "Manchukuo" would be upheld, and when Mr. Tokuzu Komai, a Privy Councilor of "Manchukuo," announced in May that this principle would apply only to those countries which recognized "Manchukuo's" independence, the Vice Foreign Minister, Mr. Hachiro Arita, authorized me on May 3 officially to inform my Government that Mr. Komai had spoken without authority and that the principle of the Open Door in that country would be strictly maintained. . . .

Control of Petroleum Resources

In May foreign oil interests in Japan were given another indication of the handwriting on the wall when the Ministry of Commerce and Industry drew up and announced plans for licensing the importation and refining of oil under which the operation of the oil trade and industry could, if it should become necessary, pass exclusively into the hands of Japanese companies. Plans were also contemplated for securing crude oil from sources other than British or American. In order that the foreign companies might determine their own plans in advance, the American, British and Netherlands diplomatic representatives approached the Japanese Government and infor-

* Telegram No. 80, April 15, 11 A.M. [*Ibid.*, pp. 275–76.]

mally expressed the hope that their respective companies might be given some indication as to the future outlook for their business.*

MR. ARITA AND MR. SHIGEMITSU

On or about May 16, Mr. Arita, allegedly being in disagreement with the more chauvinistic elements in the Foreign Office, resigned as Vice Foreign Minister and was succeeded by Mr. Mamoru Shigemitsu, formerly Minister to China.

IMPROVEMENT IN JAPANESE ATTITUDE TOWARD THE UNITED STATES

In June an improvement in the attitude of Japan toward the United States began to appear. A number of factors contributed to this improvement, including a recent outburst against the British on account of the abrogation of the Indian Trade Agreement,[15] and, as is well-known, the Japanese seldom set out to stimulate anti-American and anti-British sentiment simultaneously, the last thing they wish being to drive the two countries together through common troubles. The desired appropriations had been secured by the Army, the situation in China was less acute while Japan's withdrawal from the League of Nations had been carried out without a clash with Western nations. This improved attitude toward the United States was indicated by the prominent and favorable comment in the press accorded to several events which a few months ago would probably have received less favorable attention: (1) public ap-

* Telegram No. 94, May 8, 11 A.M. [*Ibid.*, pp. 732–34.]

15 On April 1, 1933, the Indian Government notified Japan that in six months it would terminate the Indo-Japanese Trade Agreement of 1904. Japanese cotton goods in 1932 had supplied 48 per cent of the imports of this nature into India, a fact which the manufacturers of both India and England had viewed with alarm. Negotiations were opened on September 23, 1933, between Japan and India. An Agreement was reached whereby a 50 per cent tariff was placed upon Japanese textiles entering India, and Japan arranged to purchase from India a certain amount of raw cotton. M. Epstein (ed.), *The Annual Register . . . 1933* (New Series; London: Longmans, Green & Co., 1934), p. 278.

preciation of Viscount Ishii's reportedly cordial reception by the President [on May 24–27] and the general belief that the President had listened sympathetically to Viscount Ishii's exposition of Japan's problems; the public was beginning to feel that the United States was, after all, not fundamentally hostile to Japan and to Japan's allegedly vital interest; (2) the unqualified success of the visit to Japan [from June 2–14] on the flagship *Houston* of Admiral Montgomery Taylor, Commander in Chief of the United States Asiatic Fleet; the Admiral was most cordially welcomed in Tokyo, partly owing to the general appreciation of his helpful co-operation with Admiral Kichisaburo Nomura [Commander of the Japanese Third Squadron in the Yangtze area in 1932] in restricting last year's troubles in Shanghai; [16] (3) the favorable impression created on high Japanese officials by the brief visit [on June 5–6] of the new Governor General, Frank Murphy, of the Philippine Islands; (4) the wide publicity given to the visit of Bishop James DeWolfe Perry [Presiding Bishop of the American Episcopal Church], descendant of Commodore Perry, and his pilgrimage to the Perry monument at Uraga [on June 1]; (5) the opening [on June 5] of St. Luke's International Medical Center, built largely by American funds, in presence of the Emperor's brother Prince Takamatsu and a distinguished Japanese representation. The Japanese press had given prominence to these various factors and they had appealed to the public imagination.* A further hopeful factor was the removal from the Foreign Office and appointment as Minister to Sweden of Mr. Shiratori, properly regarded by Americans as the "enfant terrible" of the Gaimusho [Foreign Office], and his replacement by Mr. Eiji Amau. It was understood that Mr. Arita had refused to continue to be associated

16 On January 29, 1932, Japanese marines landed in Shanghai, beginning hostilities which lasted until March 4. On May 5 an agreement was reached providing for the immobilization of Chinese forces outside of Shanghai and the confinement of Japanese troops within specified portions of the International Settlement.

* Telegram No. 114, June 8, 11 A.M. [*Ibid.*, pp. 702–3.]

with Mr. Shiratori in the Foreign Office and that in order to eliminate the latter, the former had to be sacrificed.

JAPAN'S RELATIONS WITH SOVIET RUSSIA

In July evidence began to appear of a worsening of Japan's relations with Soviet Russia and a series of comparatively small incidents, such as continually occur on the border between Siberia and Manchuria and in the Japan Sea, began to be magnified in the press, indicating that for some reason an endeavor was being made to capitalize these incidents. The military may have been utilizing these incidents to stir up public opinion in order to ensure their obtaining their full defense budget for the coming fiscal year, or possibly the Army might have decided that the eventually inevitable clash with Soviet Russia had better take place before the Soviets became too powerful, time being on the side of the Soviets. We considered the fact that in order to maintain their present prestige the military might find it necessary to proceed with further imperialistic adventures, and we knew very well that a prime desideratum of the Army and Navy was eventual possession of Vladivostok and its air bases, which they have always regarded as a "dagger aimed at the heart of Japan." The working up of these incidents in the press bore close resemblance to the tactics used before the occupation of Manchuria. The Embassy doubted any imminent danger of war but believed that the situation had ominous potentialities and should be watched closely. Any attempt to appraise the situation was, as always, difficult owing to the headstrong policy of the Japanese military clique which cannot be gauged by occidental standards.*

HIROTA SUCCEEDS UCHIDA

On September 14 Count Uchida was succeeded as Foreign Minister by Mr. Koki Hirota, formerly Ambassador in Moscow, and soon indications emerged of an apparently genuine

* Telegram No. 127, July 18, noon. [*Ibid.*, pp. 372–73.]

desire on the part of the Government to improve relations with the United States — so far as they could be improved without in the slightest degree relinquishing Japan's stranglehold on Manchuria. In fact Mr. Hirota, at his initial reception of the diplomatic chiefs of mission, told me that his principal preoccupation while in office would be the development of better relations with the United States and that this, in fact, was the primary reason for his having accepted the appointment which had come to him as a complete surprise.* It was at least gratifying to begin dealings with a Minister who professed a friendly attitude and with whom one could discuss public affairs. With Count Uchida such discussion was impossible for he was tight-lipped and seldom vouchsafed any comment more than to say that he would take our periodic representations under advisement.

ETHICS OF THE JAPANESE PRESS

Furthermore, while the Foreign Office was under Count Uchida, I had restricted my visits to a minimum simply because every such visit was splashed widely in the press, often with sensational headlines and totally inaccurate versions of what took place at such meetings, stated as fact. When I explained this situation to the new Minister he arranged that I should meet him at his official residence instead of at the Gaimusho and for several years such meetings took place with a minimum of publicity until the newspaper correspondents learned that they had to cover both places. It was not until the totalitarian regime of Mr. Matsuoka [as Japanese Minister for Foreign Affairs] in 1940 that a censorship ban was placed on reporting all diplomatic calls at the Foreign Office and even in the spring of that year my series of conversations with his predecessor Mr. Arita had to be held at the private houses of mutual friends to avoid the intrusion of the press.

* Telegram No. 144, September 18, 4 P.M. (see also in this connection the Embassy's despatch to the Department No. 595, November 29, 1933). [*Ibid.*, p. 710.]

Indeed, my experience with the Japanese newspapermen, at least during the early years of my mission, was not a happy one. As in every walk of life there were high-principled men in that profession, but the average reporter was much more inclined to report what he thought the public would like to hear, or something of a sensational nature, than the truth. On my initial arrival in Yokohama in 1932 a large group of pressmen met me at quarantine and solicited an interview, which I courteously explained was impossible at least until after the presentation of my credentials and establishment of official contact with the Japanese Government, although in order to help them fill their assignments I talked at length about my pleasure on returning to Japan after twenty-nine years, of previous posts, and of family matters. The net result was that at least two of the most prominent and presumably reputable Japanese newspapers carried on the following morning statements attributed to me in quotation marks to the effect that Japanese-American relations were in a very bad state and that in my opinion any untoward incident at present would produce the gravest consequences.[17] Little sympathy was, however, met with among my new diplomatic colleagues who said that I had yet to learn a few things about the Japanese press.

In my first long talk with Mr. Hirota on October 3 I said that one of the chief factors militating against good relations between our two countries was the irresponsible utterances of the Japanese press which were often cabled to the American press and created in the minds of the American public a feeling of suspicion and distrust based on the belief that Japan was fundamentally hostile to the United States, and I appealed to him to control this handicap. The Minister replied that he especially desired to convey to the American public his own

[17] The evening edition of the Tokyo *Jiji* of June 6, 1932, stated that "the new Ambassador said in a mild and soft tone of voice that the situation is serious indeed," and *Nichi Nichi* of the same date quoted Mr. Grew as saying that it "is quite perplexing for me to discuss such current topics as the Manchurian question, the round-table conference, etc., at the moment. Both Japan and the United States are at present showing such a tension as to sting their nerves even by a slight touch of a tiny needle."

wish and policy to develop closer relations with the United States but he feared that he was misunderstood by the American press which had already characterized him as an ultra-nationalist * owing to his earlier association with Mitsuru Toyama [Japanese founder of the Black Dragon Society] and the group of chauvinists who surrounded that super-patriot, an association which would be helpful to him in conveying his own views to that faction.† A few days later, on October 12, an informal dinner was arranged at the Embassy at which the Minister met the principal American newspaper correspondents in Japan and chatted with them until late, a dinner which he himself later reciprocated. Helpful contacts were thus established.

Good Will Missions

During that first talk with Mr. Hirota I found him already thinking of sending a so-called Good Will mission to the United States, but at that time and always subsequently every effort was made to discourage such plans on the ground that far more could be accomplished by the individual contacts made by distinguished Japanese visitors to the United States (such, for instance, as Prince Tokugawa) than by formal missions. So far as I am aware, no constructive work was ever accomplished by such Japanese missions, and in the case of American missions of editors, teachers, lawyers, businessmen, hotel managers and other groups frequently brought for propaganda purposes to Japan at the expense of the Japanese Government, the Japanese conception of hospitality is such that more harm than good was frequently done. That hospitality invariably entails an ironclad program of a tour to spots of historic interest, including always a trip to "Manchukuo," with daily luncheons, receptions, banquets and formal speeches, and very

* Telegram No. 149, October 3, 2 P.M. [*Foreign Relations, Japan: 1931–41*, I, 123–24.]
† Telegram No. 156, October 11, noon. [*Foreign Relations, 1933, The Far East*, III, 710–11.]

little opportunity for informal contacts and investigations, with the result that the members of such groups have usually returned to Tokyo in an exhausted condition and not at all sure that their sympathies for Japan and the Japanese had been enhanced by their experiences. I have often told my Japanese friends of the unwisdom of these programs which tend to irk the average American in his dislike of regimentation and formality, but in vain. Habit and custom are too solidly intrenched to adapt Japanese plans to foreign inclinations. So far as I can remember the only visit of such an American group to Japan that could be called an unqualified success was that of the Garden Club of America in 1935, and that success was due to the fact that the visitors were received by Japanese of the highest culture and sensitive appreciation, often in their lovely gardens and private homes.

PROPOSED AMERICAN-JAPANESE TREATY OF ARBITRATION

At about this time trial balloons were going up to sound out opinion on both sides of the Pacific with regard to a proposal to start negotiations for an arbitration treaty between the United States and Japan. On his return from abroad, Viscount Ishii was reported to have expressed his belief that the negotiation of such a treaty would go a long way toward improving relations between the two countries. The time, however, was not propitious and the project was given no encouragement from the American side.*

CABINET DISAGREEMENT

In anticipation of the opening of the Diet in December, it now became apparent that a schism was growing within the Government with the War and Navy Ministers [Sadao Araki and Keisuke Okada] pressing for increased budgets while Mr. Hirota, the Minister for Foreign Affairs, and Mr. Korekiyo Takahashi, the Minister of Finance, strenuously opposed ex-

* Telegram No. 155, October 11, 11 A.M. [*Ibid.,* pp. 747–48.]

cessive military appropriations. The former group, caring little for foreign opinion and with little grasp of financial affairs, were ready to go to almost any lengths to ensure what they conceived to be the country's needs. The latter faction felt that the nation was at present in no danger and that it needed friendly relations and peace with foreign Powers and they held that ill will abroad, which would cost Japan more than the margin of safety was worth, would be created by excessive military expenditures. Viscount Saito might find himself unable to meet the Diet with his present Cabinet, and should Messrs. Hirota and Takahashi have their way, there would be grave danger of a coup d'état by dissatisfied military elements who saw their power waning.*

A little later there was evidence that a compromise between the two factions had been reached, to the effect that while the Army and Navy would get their money, on the basis of their technical needs for new equipment to keep abreast of the general advance in modern armament, the Foreign Minister was not to be embarrassed in the conduct of his office by measures and utterances tending to nullify his efforts to improve Japan's foreign relations. It was therefore expected that thenceforth there would be less bluster and truculence from the military respecting foreign affairs and it was thought that the outlook for a continuance of the Saito Government was brighter.†

AMERICAN RECOGNITION OF SOVIET RUSSIA

The United States recognized Soviet Russia on November 16, thereby creating a degree of anxiety in Japan. In October, while the American-Soviet negotiations were still incomplete, Mr. Saburo Kurusu, Chief of the Commercial Bureau of the Foreign Office, had said to Mr. Edwin Neville, Counselor of the American Embassy, that the step was regarded by the Japanese as a natural one and to be expected, but that one point was causing anxiety to the Foreign Office: Mr. Hirota had

* Telegram No. 156, October 11, noon. [*Ibid.*, pp. 710–11.]
† Telegram No. 164, October 23, 2 P.M. [*Ibid.*, pp. 440–41.]

been successful to a considerable extent in separating the discussions of the budget for the Army and Navy from foreign affairs, but the Foreign Office might have its work to do all over again if the Russians, through American recognition, were to believe that they would receive American support in their discussions with Japan, or if the Chinese were to believe that the United States would support Russia in the Far East. The press and public had up to the present remained quiet but a new situation might well be seized by certain elements in Japan to stir up trouble. For instance, the penultimate paragraph of President Kalinin's letter to President Roosevelt of October 17, referring to the "element of disquiet, complicating the process of consolidating world peace and encouraging forces tending to disturb that peace," might be falsely interpreted by the Russians and Chinese as applying to the Far Eastern situation.[18] Mr. Hirota had encountered great difficulty in persuading the military that there was no probability of a combination of the United States, Great Britain, Soviet Russia and China against Japan, and if now the American-Soviet negotiations were to afford grounds for suspicions to the contrary, outbursts might occur leading to renewed activity by the military which would nullify Mr. Hirota's progress in the recent discussions in the Cabinet. The foregoing was reported merely as a firsthand indication of the trend of the current thoughts of the Foreign Office.*

DISCRIMINATION AGAINST AMERICAN TRADE IN MANCHURIA

Occasion was taken in an interview with the Foreign Minister on October 27, when Mr. Hirota asked for suggestions for improving Japanese-American relations, to draw his attention to the unfortunate effects which would accrue from discriminations against American trade in Manchuria. The Minister hoped that American merchants would study the opportunities for business in "Manchukuo" as certain French business repre-

18 For the text of the letter see U.S. Department of State, *Press Releases,* October 21, 1933, p. 227.

* Telegram No. 166, October 24, 7 P.M.

sentatives were already doing. Mr. Hirota was extremely friendly.*

TRANSFER OF AMERICAN FLEET TO THE ATLANTIC OCEAN

The report of the transfer of our fleet from the Pacific to the Atlantic Ocean was given unusual publicity in Japan and was received with expressions of great satisfaction in the Japanese press, the move being interpreted as further evidence of the Administration's desire to improve American relations with Japan and as a friendly gesture to counteract the effect of the then impending recognition of Soviet Russia by the United States. The only dissenting voice was that of the Japanese Navy, which was reported as declaring, through an unidentified spokesman, that the transfer had no significance and that it was premature to conclude that the ill-feeling created over Manchuria could be removed by a mere transfer of the American fleet. Apparently the Navy feared the effect of this step on its budgetary demands. . . .†

HIROSHI SAITO CHOSEN AS AMBASSADOR TO THE UNITED STATES

On December 23 the Foreign Minister sent for me to announce the choice of Mr. Hiroshi Saito, formerly Minister to the Netherlands, as Japanese Ambassador to the United States to succeed Mr. Katsuji Debuchi,‡ regarded by the military as too much a follower of the so-called Shidehara diplomacy.

PROPOSED PROCLAMATION OF AN EMPEROR OF "MANCHUKUO"

At the same time Mr. Hirota took occasion to tell me in strict confidence and not as an official communication that within a few months a new dynasty would be founded in "Manchukuo" by proclaiming Pu Yi as Emperor. This step, said Mr. Hirota, would effectively offset the unfounded rumors that Japan

* Telegram No. 170, October 27, 5 P.M. [Ibid., p. 443.]
† Telegram No. 172, November 7, 3 P.M. [Ibid., p. 449.]
‡ Telegram No. 193, December 23, noon.

planned annexation and would assure the complete independence of "Manchukuo" within its present frontiers.*

1934

REVERBERATIONS FROM INACCURATE REPORTING OF A SPEECH

Apropos of a speech by an officer of the State Department [19] which was reported in Japan as saying, with reference to Far Eastern affairs, that "the nonrecognition of governments made by swords" was still the policy of the United States, the spokesman of the Foreign Office issued a strong statement criticizing a public revival of the much-contested Stimson doctrine at a time when the Japanese authorities were allegedly exerting their utmost efforts for the promotion of friendship between Japan and the United States. My view, as expressed to the Department, was that while I staunchly supported the Far Eastern policy of our Government, I believed that public reiteration of our determination not to recognize "Manchukuo" would tend to undo the constructive work which I had been carrying on, not without some favorable result, and that Hirota's efforts to carry out his prime policy of improving Japanese-American relations would thereby be rendered more difficult, a policy which in the long run might prove helpful to American interests if allowed to bear fruit. I felt especially that we needed every asset to meet the strain on our relations which would inevitably develop in the coming Naval Conference of 1935, and that when it became necessary further to reiterate our policy regarding "Manchukuo," it would cause less disturbance to our relations if communicated in diplomatic conversations rather than in public speeches. It was made clear that the foregoing considerations had to do exclusively with questions of procedure and not of principle.†

In reply to the foregoing telegram the Department informed

* (Ditto).

[19] On January 18, 1934, Dr. Stanley K. Hornbeck, Chief of the Division of Far Eastern Affairs, had spoken unofficially on foreign policy before a conference held in Washington.

† Telegram No. 12, January 22, 11 A.M.

the Embassy that the officer in question, who was speaking on the subject of "Principles of American Policy in Relation to the Far East," had made no such statement as was attributed to him.[20] The Department appreciated having my comments and suggestions as set forth in my telegram under reference and had had and would continue to have in mind the points which I had brought out, but neither action nor utterance could be formulated with a view exclusively to insuring none but pleasant reactions in Japan. I was authorized to inform Mr. Hirota that the spirit and the letter of the reported statement had evidently been subject to distortion either in the process of their being brought to light or in the consideration of them in the Foreign Office.*

I duly informed Mr. Hirota of the facts and was promised that Mr. Amau would make rectification in the press. The Tokyo correspondent of the Associated Press told me that the report of the speech came from the Associated Press in the United States to Rengo precisely as published here, and that the distortion therefore did not appear to have occurred in Japan.†

Mr. Amau's rectification of the report of the speech mentioned above was published prominently in all the important Japanese newspapers.‡

In reply to an interpellation in the Lower House of the Diet concerning the speech under reference, Mr. Hirota stated that the speech was not delivered in the official capacity of the

20 Dr. Hornbeck had said that "American Far Eastern policy has grown from, and is shaped by, the belief of the Americans that free States should remain free in the Orient and elsewhere, and that nations should live and let live with due respect for the rights and interests of one another. . . .

"I need only call attention to the fact that the formula of non-recognition has been employed by the American Government on several occasions, by several administrations and in connection not only with developments in the Far East but developments in Latin America. This formula gained world wide attention when it was invoked by the identic notes addressed by the American Government to the Chinese and Japanese Governments in connection with developments in Manchuria."

* Telegram from the Department No. 7, January 22, 6 P.M.
† Telegram No. 16, January 24, 11 A.M.
‡ Telegram No. 17, January 25, 11 A.M.

officer in question, who had stressed to his audience the point that he was speaking privately and not for the Administration or the State Department. Furthermore the version of the speech published in Japan had been distorted and the American Ambassador had corrected the mistake. The Foreign Minister wished the Members to understand the true situation.*

General Araki Resigns as Minister of War

Illness was given as the ostensible reason for the resignation as Minister of War of General Araki, who was succeeded by General Senjuro Hayashi. Various conjectures were advanced to account for this move, especially the hypothesis that the saner elements in the Government, and indeed the Emperor himself, realizing the dangerous position into which Japan was drifting, had taken advantage of the General's illness to remove a firebrand and an officer who stood as the symbol of a policy of military aggression. Furthermore, with Hirota's growing strength and general indignation at the size of the military budget, Araki's position in the Cabinet was believed to have become more and more isolated. Varying reports as to General Hayashi were current: On the one hand he was said to be of silent disposition and was reported to have stated that Army officers should abstain from politics; on the other hand he was characterized as self-willed, impetuous and capable of rapid decisions, as when he moved the troops from Korea to Manchuria on his own responsibility in 1931 [21] in spite of Baron Shidehara's protests, and that he was not conciliatory

* Telegram No. 19, January 26, 3 p.m.

[21] On September 21, 1931, while the Japanese Cabinet was still debating what action should be taken in regard to the crisis in Manchuria, an announcement was made from the headquarters of the garrison army in Chosen, where General Hayashi was commander in chief, that Japanese troops had left Chosen for Manchuria. This action had been taken by Hayashi on his own initiative. Premier Wakatsuki stated his dissatisfaction with Hayashi's action, for Foreign Minister Shidehara was actively trying to gain support for his policy of non-aggravation and containment of military operations to a small area. See Tatsuji Takeuchi, *War and Diplomacy in the Japanese Empire* (Chicago: The University of Chicago Press, 1935), p. 353.

and less prone than Araki to compromise. We felt that the coming debates in the Diet might afford enlightenment.*

Incidentally, on May 11, 1933, General Araki was reported in the press as having said *inter alia* in a speech before the National Defense Association in Kobe with reference to the United States and Soviet Russia: "Japan must defend herself against these wolves which are sharpening their fangs, and castaway cats showing their teeth for attack." As the speaker was then a member of the Cabinet I made official representations with regard to the reported utterance, but without effect save that several weeks later the Foreign Office informed me that General Araki, to whose notice my representations had been brought, had replied that he kept no notes of his speeches and could not accept responsibility for the way in which the press reported them.

CONSERVATION OF OIL

A further step towards oil conservation was taken when a Government bill was submitted to the Diet, with every probability of passing, which would place virtually complete control of oil importation and refining in the hands of a Government commission. The bill (*a*) required all importers and refiners of petroleum products to obtain annual licenses to operate and to conduct operations in accordance with Government instructions; (*b*) required importers and refiners to maintain minimum stocks to be kept at the disposal of the Government at current prices; and (*c*) authorized the Government to fix prices when deemed necessary in the public interest. Ostensibly designed to assure the Government a permanent supply of oil at reasonable prices for use in time of war, its effect upon American and other foreign oil companies in Japan would of course depend more upon the administration of the law than upon its specific provisions. The present Minister of Commerce and Industry [Kumakichi Nakajima] orally assured the Standard-Vacuum Oil Company that the purpose of the legis-

* Telegram No. 15, January 23, 5 P.M.

lation was more to protect than to jeopardize the business of the foreign oil companies, but this assurance would of course not be binding upon future administrations and it was obvious that with the passage of the bill the foreign companies could at any time be forced to abandon their business in Japan.* The bill was approved by the Diet toward the end of March.

Exchange of Good-Will Messages by Mr. Hirota and Mr. Hull

On February 21 the Japanese Ambassador in Washington, Mr. Saito, handed to Secretary Cordell Hull an informal and personal message from Mr. Hirota bearing upon friendship between Japan and the United States in which the Minister stated with all the emphasis at his command that "the Japanese nation makes it its basic principle to collaborate in peace and harmony with all nations and has no intention whatever to provoke and make trouble with any other Power." On March 3 Mr. Hull replied with appreciation and reciprocation of Mr. Hirota's cordial sentiments and set forth, for his part, the peaceful and friendly policy of the United States.† The texts of these messages were published in Washington and Tokyo on March 21 and are to be found in the press releases of the Department.[22]

The Amau Statement

On April 17 Mr. Amau, the spokesman of the Foreign Office, issued his famous statement [23] regarding the attitude of Japan

* Telegram No. 39, March 5, 2 P.M.
† Telegram from the State Department No. 25, March 3, 1 P.M. [*Foreign Relations, Japan: 1931–41*, I, 128–29.]

22 U.S. Department of State, *Press Releases*, March 24, 1934, pp. 160–62.

23 The statement of April 17 opened with the assertion of Japan's special position in relation to China, and Japan's mission and special responsibilities in East Asia. Amau went on to say that the order and unity of China must be achieved and the territorial integrity of that country preserved. "History shows that these can be attained through no other means than the awakening and the voluntary efforts of China herself. We oppose therefore any attempt on the part of China to avail herself of the influence of any other country in order to

toward the rendering of assistance to China by other countries, an utterance which was generally regarded in Tokyo and abroad as the most important pronouncement of Japanese policy toward China since the presentation of the Twenty-One Demands, the essential basis of the statement reflecting the view of the Japanese Government that it should be consulted by other Governments before they took any action in China.* The circumstances of the release of the statement were obscure. At first Mr. Amau characterized the announcement as "unofficial" but later said that it "could be considered as official." It seems that in a press conference on April 17 Mr. Amau was questioned regarding the reported opposition of Japan to assistance to China by other countries, and that he went to his files and produced a document in Japanese which appeared to be in the form of an instruction addressed to the Japanese Minister in China [Akira Ariyoshi]. Of this document he made a rough translation into English which he said was unofficial although asserting that the document had received the approval of the Foreign Minister, and later the same evening he issued to the Japanese press a statement in Japanese labeled "unofficial" which was translated and cabled all over the world.

Whether the Foreign Minister had actually approved both the statement and its issuance at that time is a point which, so

---

resist Japan: We also oppose any action taken by China, calculated to play one power against another. Any joint operations undertaken by foreign powers even in the name of technical or financial assistance at this particular moment after the Manchurian and Shanghai Incidents are bound to acquire political significance. Undertakings of such nature, if carried through to the end, must give rise to complications that might eventually necessitate discussion of problems like fixing spheres of influence or even international control or division of China, which would be the greatest possible misfortune for China and at the same time would have the most serious repercussion upon Japan and East Asia." Amau concluded that "supplying China with war planes, building aerodromes in China and detailing military instructors or military advisers to China or contracting a loan to provide funds for political uses, would obviously tend to alienate the friendly relations between Japan and China and other countries and to disturb peace and order in East Asia. Japan will oppose such projects. . . ." *Foreign Relations, Japan: 1931–41*, I, 224–25.

* Telegram No. 71, April 18, 5 P.M.
Despatch to Department No. 751, April 20, 1934.
[*Ibid.*, pp. 223–25.]

far as I am aware, has never been cleared up. Some informants reported that Mr. Hirota was angry and displeased at Mr. Amau's action on the ground that the statement ran counter to Mr. Hirota's conciliatory policy of cultivating better relations with China and other nations, and that the step had been taken by Mr. Amau to please the military in an effort to emulate Mr. Shiratori. Others believed that the Minister had taken this indirect method of registering the Government's views, being fearful of its effect abroad and desiring to maintain a position where he could deny that such a statement had ever officially been issued.*

On April 25, during my call on the Foreign Minister on another matter, Mr. Hirota on his own initiative said that he wished in confidence to clarify the Amau statement. He said that the statement had given the world a totally wrong impression of the policy of the Japanese Government and that the announcement had been released under pressure from newspaper correspondents entirely without his own knowledge or approval. The policy of the Government, he said, was in every respect to observe and support the provisions of the Nine Power Treaty and that Japan had not the slightest intention of interfering with the territorial or administrative integrity of China nor of opposing, by seeking special privilege, the bona fide trade of other countries with China. Owing to Japan's propinquity to China it was in Japan's interest that peaceful conditions should be maintained in that country, and those peaceful conditions had suffered interference through foreign activities, but this did not mean that there was any desire or intention on the part of Japan to seek a privileged position contrary to the provisions of the Nine Power Treaty, the signatories of which should enjoy equal responsibilities and equal rights. Owing to the fact that the ultranationalist elements in Japan were steadily pressing for a more aggressive foreign policy, the Minister said that his own position was not an easy one, but he was constantly endeavoring to develop the most friendly relations with other countries, particularly the United

* Telegram No. 72, April 20, 8 P.M.
   Telegram No. 73, April 21, 9 P.M.

States, in accordance with the precise policy of the Emperor with whom he was always in direct touch.

Mr. Hirota, in this conversation, then turned to Japan's relations with Soviet Russia. He said that the settlement of the sale of the Chinese Eastern Railway, for which negotiations would begin tomorrow — and he intended to leave nothing undone to bring those negotiations to a successful conclusion as soon as possible — would bring about an improvement of relations between Japan and China which the Minister wished to develop in every possible way. Mr. Hirota, being backed by the Emperor and having also the support of the Minister of War, would continue to fight for his policy even if it should mean his own assassination (and such a remark, be it said, was by no means a matter of heroics because few if any Foreign Ministers in recent times have been free of such a risk). His observations to me must therefore be regarded as confidential (and in view of the possible danger to the person of Mr. Hirota I urged most strongly that this confidence be respected by the Department) owing to his difficult position, but he earnestly desired that Mr. Amau's statement be understood perfectly by the Government of the United States which might rest assured that no action would be taken by Japan which would purposely provoke friction with other nations or would run counter to the letter or spirit of the Nine Power Treaty. I added, in reporting this conversation, that in spite of Mr. Hirota's somewhat halting command of English the foregoing was as accurate and close a report of his remarks as was possible and that in my opinion there could be no question as to the sincerity of his statement. I did, however, say to Mr. Hirota that the American Government and people were less likely to be impressed by statements of policy than by concrete evidence in the carrying out of policy.*

In this connection it should be noted that while many of my diplomatic colleagues scoffed at Mr. Hirota's alleged "sin-

---

* Telegram No. 75, April 25, 1 P.M. (Confidential for the Secretary).
  [*Ibid.*, pp. 227–28.]
  Department's telegram No. 55, April 24, 6 P.M.

cerity," my own opinion was that he genuinely meant what he said at the time he said it.

There followed an exchange of telegrams between the Department and the Embassy in which the former was evidently seeking to obtain an authoritative text of the Amau statement, but, as I replied, there was no authoritative text. The best text obtainable was the unofficial English translation of the unofficial oral statement made by the spokesman of the Foreign Office to the newspapermen. My final verdict, as communicated to the Department was that the Japanese text, as read by Mr. Amau to the press correspondents, was taken from an instruction approved by the Foreign Minister for communication to all Japanese diplomatic missions for their guidance but given out by the spokesman without the knowledge or consent of Mr. Hirota.*

On April 26 Mr. Hirota sent me in Japanese a document which represented the gist of what Mr. Amau "said or should have said" on April 20.† Two days later, the Department directed me to deliver to the Foreign Minister an *aide-mémoire* which was in effect a reply to the Amau statement.‡ This instruction was carried out within one hour and a half of the decoding of the Department's telegram, Mr. Hirota's only comment being that the whole affair had caused "great misunderstanding" and that he would reply to our *aide-mémoire* in due course.§ The Department expressed very much gratification at the promptness with which its instruction had been carried out.|| At the press conference at the Foreign Office the next day, Mr. Amau said that no·further statement by the Japanese Government would be issued and that he regarded the affair as "a closed incident."¶ In an interview with Mr. Wilfred Fleisher [editor of the *Japan Advertiser*] on May 1, the Vice

---

* Department's telegram No. 56, April 25, 1 P.M.
  Telegram No. 77, April 26, 5 P.M.
† Telegram No. 78, April 26, 9 P.M.
‡ Department's telegram No. 59, April 28, 7 P.M. [*Ibid.*, pp. 231–32.]
§ Telegram No. 83, April 29, 7 P.M. [*Ibid.*, p. 232.]
|| Department's telegram No. 60, April 30, 6 P.M.
¶ Telegram No. 84, April 30, 1 P.M.

Minister said that the American statement, which was published in full in Japan, was regarded as frank and friendly and was received in the same spirit in which it had been sent by Mr. Hull. The tone of the communication, he said, was entirely different from that previously used by Mr. Stimson; the Japanese Government welcomed it as affording it an opportunity to express its own views in the same friendly way and it would therefore be answered with the same traditional frankness.* On May 7 the British Chargé d'Affaires [Charles Dodds] was told by the Vice Minister that the Foreign Office was still undecided as to whether to reply to Mr. Hull's statement of policy, but that if a reply were made, it would merely be Mr. Hirota's statement of April 26 "on another piece of paper." † (No reply was made.) . . .

VISIT TO THE UNITED STATES OF PRINCE KONOYE

On May 5 I sent a personal telegram to Mr. William Phillips, then Under Secretary of State, informing him of the coming visit to the United States of Prince Fumimaro Konoye, President of the House of Peers and the highest noble in Japan, whose visit was ostensibly to attend the graduation of his son from Lawrenceville Academy but actually to familiarize himself with life and thought in the United States by way of preparation for his important political future. At that time it was even planned that he eventually would succeed Prince Saionji as Genro but in any case he would be highly influential, both in domestic and foreign affairs, as adviser to the Government and Throne. Prince Konoye was going on no official or unofficial mission but I felt it important that he should receive the happiest impressions of our country, and merely as my own thought I expressed the opinion that it would make a very fine impression if he could be given a degree by Harvard University. I said that Mr. Phillips would know best whether it was feasible or desirable to act on this suggestion.‡ Harvard did not give

* Telegram No. 86, May 1, 6 P.M.
† Telegram No. 91, May 7, 7 P.M.
‡ Telegram No. 89, May 5, noon.

him a degree but arrangements were later made by Mr. Thomas Lamont [banker and overseer of Harvard] and Mr. Jerome Greene [educational administrator] for Prince Konoye to attend the Harvard-Yale boat races at New London and to lunch on the *Corsair.**

IMPENDING FALL OF SAITO CABINET

Already in May there were indications of the early fall of the Cabinet. Hideo Kuroda, Vice Minister of Finance, and other officials of that Ministry had been arrested on charges of accepting bribes, and since Viscount Saito had taken office as a super-party man with the avowed purpose of eliminating corruption from the Government, hc was considered to have failed in that endeavor. The Cabinet furthermore had been weakened through successive resignations and it had lost prestige as lacking force and initiative. General Kazushige Ugaki [Governor General of Chosen] was mentioned as a possible successor.†

SAN SALVADOR RECOGNIZES "MANCHUKUO"

The Belgian Ambassador [Baron Albert de Bassompierre, Dean of the Diplomatic Corps] was informed by the Consul General of Salvador that his Government had recognized "Manchukuo" on March 3. It was not clear how the recognition was originally extended or why it had not sooner been given publicity, but it was announced in the Japanese press that the Consul General had now addressed a note to the "Manchukuo" Minister in Tokyo [W. S. Y. Tinge] informing him of the fact of recognition.[24] The Consul General thought that the step had been taken with a view to trade considerations, especially to increasing the sale of Salvadorean coffee to Japan. His instructions expressed the belief that the recognition might react unfavorably on the relations between the United States and

* Department's telegram No. 96, June 12, 4 P.M.
† Telegram No. 96, May 21, 4 P.M.
24 See Westel W. Willoughby, *The Sino-Japanese Controversy and the League of Nations* (Baltimore: The Johns Hopkins Press, 1935), pp. 534–35.

Salvador, or between the United States and Japan, and directed him to endeavor to allay any ill-feeling which might result.*

HYPOTHESIS OF AN ANGLO-JAPANESE RAPPROCHEMENT

In a strictly confidential telegram to the Secretary I cited six points as worthy of consideration in support of the theory that some sort of rapprochement between Great Britain and Japan might be under consideration on the basis of England's support in the coming Naval Conference of Japanese claims to naval parity in return for an agreement on policy in China.† [25]

DEATH OF ADMIRAL TOGO

Admiral Togo, hero of the Battle of Tsushima Straits in the Russo-Japanese War of 1905, died toward the end of May and was accorded a State funeral on June 5. A message of condolence was conveyed to the Foreign Minister from Mr. Hull; Admiral Frank Upham, Commander in Chief of the United States Asiatic Fleet, at my recommendation came from China in his flagship the *Augusta* and represented the United States Government at the funeral; while I represented the person of the President of the United States. . . .

LONDON NAVAL CONFERENCE

The Foreign Minister told me on May 30 that the Japanese Government welcomed the British proposal that bilateral preliminary conversations be held to determine the time, place and procedure of the coming naval conference, but that the Japa-

* Telegram No. 97, May 22, 7 p.m.
† Telegram No. 98, May 23, 3 p.m.
25 Throughout the nineteen-twenties certain elements of the Japanese navy had been restive under the restrictions imposed upon Japanese naval armaments in the Five Power Naval Treaty of 1922. The moderate groups within the Government resisted effectively this pressure for a change in the 5-5-3 ratio of 1922 until the thirties. Following the London Naval Conference of 1930, however, serious naval rivalry resumed, and Japan's policy in regard to naval affairs was shaped by military and reactionary groups in the Government. As the time approached for the naval conference of 1935 it became evident that Japan would demand fundamental changes from the naval program outlined in the previous treaties and conferences. See MacNair and Lach, *op. cit.*, pp. 429–30.

nese Navy was not yet ready to discuss technical questions. Mr. Hirota expected that such conversations would be held not only with the Americans and British but also with the French and Italians.*

VISIT OF THE PRESIDENT TO HAWAII

Press reports having intimated that the President desired to meet high officials from Japan during his forthcoming visit to Hawaii, the Department denied the reports and said that the President's trip was to be recreational, not political. The Foreign Office spokesman mentioned the matter in a noncommittal way, while Mr. Hirota made some semihumorous observations to the press that if invited to Honolulu he might accept. I characterized the story as a trial balloon and thought it best to let the reports die a natural death through inanition.†
The Department replied that the Japanese Embassy in Washington seemed to be overworking the procedure of "trial balloons," and since the stories of deep sea conferences of the President with Japanese officials apparently were persisting in the Japanese press, it was felt advisable for me to see the Foreign Minister and to point out that the cause of improving relations between the United States and Japan was harmed rather than helped by public statements and hints by responsible officials speculating or provoking speculation on future developments involving matters of high policy. I duly set forth these views to Mr. Hirota who said that he was taking steps to stop the local press speculations but that press despatches from the United States had tended to keep the story alive. Mr. Hirota assented when I expressed the opinion that the unreliable despatches which he had in mind came from Mr. Kiyoshi Kawakami [correspondent in Washington, D.C., for *Nichi Nichi*].‡

* Telegram No. 104, May 31, 10 A.M.
† Department's telegram No. 94, June 11, noon.
   Telegram No. 122, June 13, 5 P.M.
‡ Department's telegram No. 101, June 15, 8 P.M.
   Telegram No. 128, June 18, noon.

Preliminary Naval Conversations

A high Japanese naval officer gave in informal conversation the first authoritative information we had had touching upon the naval policy of Japan, which was briefly summarized as follows: no Japanese Government which agreed to the present 5-5-3 naval ratio could survive and no Japanese delegates who signed such a treaty could return to Japan and live; this had become a national issue in Japan and there would be no use in holding the conference if we were to insist on maintaining the present ratio; if parity with the United States and Great Britain were conceded in principle, it was not believed that Japan would build up to it; the conference should be purely naval and not political; Japan might propose that "Manchukuo" remain in its present status, unrecognized; Japan absolutely supported the Open Door policy and had no ambitions in the Philippines or on the continent of Asia; a naval agreement with the United States was regarded as of greater importance than an agreement with Great Britain because the British Empire was already looked upon as "an old man."

The preliminary naval conversations were held in London in October [26] and it soon became evident that the Japanese were unwilling to subscribe to the old ratio. They proposed that any agreement should be based on the principle of nonaggression and nonmenace and that the Powers should fix a common upper limit within which each Power might equip itself as it saw fit. An important appraisal of the Japanese attitude was conveyed to the Department in our 230, October 17, 3 P.M. The Japanese press began early to give the impression that the lack of harmony in the proceedings was due to American intransigence. On December 19 the Privy Council gave unanimous approval to the Government's decision to abrogate the Washington Naval Treaty, and notice of intention to abrogate the treaty on December 31, 1936, was conveyed to Secretary

---

[26] Preliminary conversations had also been held in June and July, 1934, by representatives of the United States and Great Britain.

Hull by the Japanese Ambassador in Washington on December 29.

Developments in connection with the conference are set forth in the correspondence listed below.* . . .[27]

THE PROPOSED OIL MONOPOLY IN MANCHURÍA AND THE JAPANESE PETROLEUM INDUSTRY LAW

The correspondence with regard to these two subjects became eventually so intertwined that it appears preferable to deal with them together because only through study of the voluminous exchange of telegrams between the Department and the Embassy can a fair comprehension of the various developments and the complicated negotiations be obtained.

* Telegram No. 132, June 22, 8 P.M.
Telegram No. 199, September 10, 3 P.M.
Telegram No. 200, September 11, noon.
Telegram No. 201, September 13, noon.
Telegram No. 202, September 17, noon.
Telegram No. 203, September 17, 2 P.M.
Telegram No. 204, September 18, noon. [*Ibid.*, pp. 253–54.]
Telegram No. 207, September 19, 4 P.M.
Telegram No. 230, October 17, 3 P.M.
Department's telegram No. 182, October 25, 7 P.M.
Telegram No. 239, October 31, 11 A.M.
Department's telegram No. 186, October 31, 9 P.M. [*Ibid.*, pp. 257–59.]
Telegram No. 240, November 1, 11 A.M.
Department's telegram No. 191, November 22, 5 P.M. [*Ibid.*, pp. 260–62.]
Telegram No. 263, November 29, 2 P.M.
Telegram No. 267, December 3, 1 P.M.
Telegram No. 268, December 4, 4 P.M.
Telegram No. 269, December 5, noon.
Department's telegram No. 202, December 10, 9 P.M.
Department's telegram No. 217, December 29, 4 P.M.
Department's telegram No. 218, December 29, 5 P.M. [*Ibid.*, pp. 275–76.]

[27] The preliminary conversations between Great Britain, Japan, and the United States were carried on from mid-October until December 19. On October 24 Admiral Yamamoto outlined the Japanese position and called upon the powers to fix a "common upper limit" to naval armaments. The British and American delegations were unwilling to agree to this principle. In a speech delivered on December 6, 1934, Norman H. Davis, the chief American representative, said that the "fundamental issue in the naval conversations now in progress is essentially as follows: Is the equilibrium that was established by the system

In July the American and British Ambassadors were directed to make similar representations to the Japanese Government concerning the reported intention of the Manchurian authorities to establish a petroleum producing, refining and selling monopoly in contravention of the provisions of the Nine Power Treaty [28] and in violation of the principle of the Open Door which Japan was committed to uphold and which it had declared that it would uphold. The Japanese Foreign Office replied that while the Japanese Government could not prevent the investment of Japanese capital in the Manchurian Oil Company and could not persuade the "Manchukuo" Government to abandon its plans for control of the oil industry, it understood that the Government of "Manchukuo" intended to respect the interests of foreign merchants in "Manchukuo" to the greatest possible extent in connection with the purchase and sale of petroleum. Direct negotiations between the inter-

worked out in the Washington treaties to be continued or is it to be upset. The American Government stands for continuance. The only alternative that has so far been suggested is that of a new naval agreement based on the principle of equality in naval armaments, a principle which if adopted and applied would not give equality of security." Since the representatives of the three countries were unable to reach an agreement about either the qualitative or quantitative limitations which should be placed on naval armaments, the conversations were suspended on December 19, 1934. A communiqué issued at the time of the adjournment stated that although "the three Governments represented in these conversations are in favour of a continuation of naval limitation with such reduction as can be agreed upon by all the Powers concerned, the principle and methods for achieving this in the future remain to be determined. Now that the respective views have been made known and fully discussed, the conversations have reached a stage when it is felt that there should be an adjournment in order that the delegates may resume personal contact with their Governments and the resulting situation can be fully analysed and further considered." See Merze Tate, *The United States and Armaments* (Cambridge: Harvard University Press, 1948), pp. 185–87, and *Foreign Relations, Japan: 1931–41*, I, 271, 273.

[28] In an Informal Memorandum from the American Embassy to the Japanese Minister for Foreign Affairs on July 7, 1934, the attention of the Japanese Government was called to Article III of the Nine Power Treaty of 1922. Article III stated: "With a view to applying more effectually the principles of the Open Door or equality of opportunity in China for the trade and industry of all nations, the Contracting Powers, other than China, agree that they will not seek, nor support their respective nationals in seeking —

"(a) any arrangement which might purport to establish in favour of their

ested merchants and the "Manchukuo" Government were recommended.

In August, having discussed the matter with my British colleague [Sir Robert Clive], I expressed the opinion with regard to the proposed oil monopoly in Manchuria that since the Japanese Government obviously did not intend to intervene with "Manchukuo" in support of American oil interests, further diplomatic representations in Tokyo would appear to be futile. We should not blind ourselves to the fact that an issue of great seriousness was at stake, involving our traditional policy and our future commercial interests in the Far East, and I suggested that we consider, in consultation with the British Government, the political expediency of placing a partial or total embargo on the export of certain crude oils to Japan. While reluctant to recommend any course of action which might exacerbate Japanese-American relations, I expressed the opinion that the policy of suppression of contentious issues should not be carried to a point where important American interests and policies might become seriously jeopardized. It seemed to me that it would be merely self-injury to continue to supply the Japanese and future Manchurian refineries with our best oil and thereby enable them to drive our long-established oil organizations out of Japan and Manchuria, rendering useless their installations and wiping out their investments.

Voluminous correspondence and many conferences with the representatives of the Standard Vacuum and Shell Companies both in Washington and Tokyo occurred as a result of the proposed Japanese Petroleum Industry Law. The Department held that the objections raised by the interested companies to certain provisions of the law seemed well-founded and our

interests any general superiority of rights with respect to commercial or economic development in any designated region of China;

"(b) any such monopoly or preference as would deprive the nationals of any other Power of the right of undertaking any legitimate trade or industry in China, or of participating with the Chinese Government, or with any local authority, in any category of public enterprise, or which by reason of its scope, duration or geographical extent is calculated to frustrate the practical application of the principle of equal opportunity." U.S. Department of State, *Papers Relating to the Foreign Relations of the United States, 1922* (Washington: Government Printing Office, 1938), I, 279.

Government was prepared to give sympathetic consideration to proposals for joint or concurrent action with the British and Dutch interests looking to an amelioration of the situation. Representations were made by the British, the Dutch and ourselves. In October I informed the Department that the oil situation in Japan and Manchuria appeared to be rapidly approaching a crisis. With regard to Manchuria, the Foreign Office spokesman said that as "Manchukuo" is an independent country, representations should be made to Hsinking but that if foreign countries claim that Manchuria is still a part of China they should protest to Nanking, adding that Japan does not consider that the Nine Power Treaty applies to "Manchukuo." * . . .

* Telegram No. 142, July 3, 6 P.M.
  Department's telegram No. 112, July 5, 6 P.M.
  Telegram No. 151, July 8, 1 P.M.
  Department's telegram No. 123, July 20, 5 P.M.
  Telegram No. 166, July 31, 6 P.M.
  Telegram No. 168, August 3, 6 P.M.
  Department's telegram No. 132, August 4, 12 noon.
  Telegram No. 170, August 6, 7 P.M.
  Telegram No. 174, August 8, 11 A.M.
  Telegram No. 182, August 30, 3 P.M.
  Telegram No. 184, August 22, 11 A.M.
  Telegram No. 185, August 23, 10 A.M.
  Telegram No. 189, August 24, 5 P.M.
  Department's telegram No. 149, August 29, 5 P.M.
  Telegram No. 191, August 31, 2 P.M.
  Department's telegram No. 151, August 31, 5 P.M.
  Telegram No. 196, September 5, 1 P.M.
  Telegram No. 205, September 19, 11 A.M.
  Department's telegram No. 162, September 21, 8 P.M.
  Telegram No. 213, September 25, 6 P.M.
  Telegram No. 222, October 10, noon.
  Telegram No. 232, October 22, 5 P.M.
  Telegram No. 236, October 26, 6 P.M.
  Department's telegram No. 183, October 26, 6 P.M.
  Telegram No. 238, October 29, 6 P.M.
  Department's telegram No. 184, October 31, 7 P.M.
  Telegram No. 241, November 1, 6 P.M.
  Telegram No. 242, November 2, 3 P.M.
  Telegram No. 243, November 5, 10 A.M.
  Department's telegram No. 187, November 5, 2 P.M.
  Telegram No. 244, November 6, 7 P.M.

Saito Cabinet Resigns; Admiral Okada
Appointed Prime Minister

The Saito Cabinet having resigned *en bloc* on July 3, Admiral Okada, former Minister of the Navy, was charged by the Emperor with the formation of a new Cabinet, which was completed and formally installed on July 8. Mr. Hirota, Foreign Minister, General Hayashi, War Minister, Admiral Mineo Osumi, Navy Minister, and Mr. Sadanobu Fujii, Finance Minister, retained their respective posts. The choice of Ministers

Telegram No. 245, November 6, 8 P.M.
Telegram No. 246, November 7, 10 A.M.
Telegram No. 248, November 7, noon.
Department's telegram No. 189, November 8, 6 P.M.
Telegram No. 249, November 8, 7 P.M.
Telegram No. 250, November 8, 9 P.M.
Telegram No. 251, November 13, 4 P.M.
Telegram No. 253, November 20, 6 P.M.
Telegram No. 254, November 22, 8 P.M.
Department's telegram No. 192, November 23, 4 P.M.
Department's telegram No. 193, November 23, 7 P.M.
Telegram No. 257, November 24, 10 A.M.
Telegram No. 258, November 24, 3 P.M.
Department's telegram No. 194, November 24, 3 P.M.
Telegram No. 259, November 24, 8 P.M.
Telegram No. 260, November 24, 11 P.M.
Telegram No. 262, November 27, 6 P.M.
Department's telegram No. 197, November 28, 5 P.M.
Department's telegram No. 198, November 28, 7 P.M.
Telegram No. 266, December 1, noon.
Telegram No. 271, December 8, 9 A.M.
Department's telegram No. 200, December 8, 5 P.M.
Department's telegram No. 201, December 10, 8 P.M.
Telegram No. 274, December 13, 2 P.M.
Telegram No. 275, December 13, 5 P.M.
Department's telegram No. 204, December 14, 8 P.M.
Telegram No. 276, December 15, noon.
Department's telegram No. 206, December 17, 5 P.M.
Department's telegram No. 210, December 20, 8 P.M.
Telegram No. 283, December 22, noon.
Department's telegram No. 215, December 24, 1 P.M.
Telegram No. 284, December 25, 7 P.M.
Telegram No. 285, December 27, 5 P.M.
Telegram No. 286, December 29, noon.
Telegram No. 287, December 29, 4 P.M.

was held to represent an outstanding victory for the moderate elements in Japan as opposed to the extremists.* . . .

INSULTING ARTICLE BY GENERAL TANAKA

On August 5 the *New York Times* carried an article by General Kunishige Tanaka, President of the Meirinkai, an organization of retired army and navy officers and other men of nationalistic leanings, attacking the United States and containing the word "insolent," which from the context might be held to apply to the President or to a series of American acts to which General Tanaka took exception. Under instructions I took the matter up informally with the Foreign Minister, who received our remonstrance sympathetically and expressed appreciation of the informal manner of our approach. Mr. Hirota said that General Tanaka would be "advised" by the Foreign Office, and the *Japan Advertiser* was officially censured for publishing the obnoxious phrase. No other paper in Japan appeared to have carried it.† [29]

OPPOSITION OF AMERICAN FARMERS TO JAPANESE FARMERS IN ARIZONA

Some farmers' organization near Phoenix, Arizona, announced that all Japanese living in that district must move out

* Telegram No. 141, July 3, 4 P.M.
  Telegram No. 144, July 4, 1 P.M.
  Telegram No. 146, July 5, 7 P.M.
  Telegram No. 147, July 6, 2 P.M.
  Telegram No. 153, July 9, 11 A.M.
† Department's telegram No. 134, August 6, 3 P.M.
  Telegram No. 173, August 7, 8 P.M.
  Department's telegram No. 136, August 8, 8 P.M.
  Telegram No. 181, August 18, 12 noon.
29 In a speech in which he discussed many aspects of the naval situation, General Tanaka included the following comments: "The American naval and war authorities are loudly proclaiming the necessity of vast naval and air forces. . . .

"With the co-operation of a private naval society, propaganda for replenishment of the navy has been spread. The Atlantic Fleet is being stationed once more in the Pacific.

within ten days. The American press indicated that the Japanese Government and press were more agitated than the situation warranted, and meanwhile the American authorities were doing everything possible to protect the Japanese. Under instructions I took the matter up with the Vice Foreign Minister and urged discouragement of sensational discussion. The Vice Minister promised co-operation and expressed appreciation of the Department's efforts. There was then no sensational comment in the Japanese press which had confined itself to a mere report of the facts, but a few weeks later a good deal of agitation arose in Japan growing out of exaggerated press reports.* [30]

AMBASSADOR AND MRS. GREW REPORTED MISSING AT SEA

On September 19 I left Tokyo with Mrs. Grew to visit our daughter, Mrs. Cecil Lyon,[31] in Peiping, returning to Tokyo on

"President Roosevelt has traveled to Hawaii and there inspected the Pearl Harbor base, which is regarded as the centre of American offensive operations in the Pacific, telling the world in loud tones its equipment is perfect.

"Such insolent behavior makes us most suspicious. It makes us think a major disturbance is purposely being encouraged in the calm Pacific." *New York Times,* August 5, 1934, p. 3.

* Department's telegram No. 143, August 23, 5 P.M.
  Telegram No. 190, August 24, 4 P.M.
  Telegram No. 221, October 8, 6 P.M.
  Department's telegram No. 176, October 9, 8 P.M.
  Telegram No. 272, December 10, 5 P.M.
  Department's telegram No. 203, December 11, 6 P.M.

30 Anti-Japanese feeling had arisen in Arizona, particularly in the Salt River Valley region. Here farmers held mass meetings, threatened to use "night riders," and threw crude bombs in efforts to eject certain Japanese owning and cultivating farm land in this area. Arizona authorities sought a solution for the problem by attempting to enforce the Alien Land Law which forbade Orientals who were not native Americans to own or lease agricultural land in Arizona. On March 16, 1936, the Arizona Supreme Court upheld the Alien Land Law, but the court ordered dismissal of complaints against five of the Japanese Salt River Valley farmers. *New York Times,* August 23, 1934, p. 12; October 31, 1934, p. 15; February 17, 1935, IV, p. 6; March 17, 1936, p. 4.

31 On October 7, 1933, Elsie Grew married Cecil Burton Lyon, who was at that time Third Secretary of the Tokyo Embassy. Mr. Lyon had entered the Foreign Service in 1930. He had been Vice Consul at Havana and Hong Kong before coming to Tokyo in 1933. Shortly after their marriage the Lyons moved to Peiping, where Mr. Lyon served as Third Secretary. Subsequently Mr. Lyon held posts at Santiago and Cairo and was Assistant Chief of the Division of

October 12. On our way through the Inland Sea we struck a typhoon and our ship, the *Fuso Maru,* had her wireless antenna blown away so that ours was the only Japanese ship not heard from, and Mr. Wilfrid Fleisher reported the fact to his paper in New York with an indication that concern was felt for our safety. The Department considerately inquired and was informed by Mr. Neville, Chargé d'Affaires, that our ship had been in no danger. Unfortunately Mr. Fleisher's telegram caused a good deal of misunderstanding among our friends at home, especially to our daughter, Mrs. English, who while passing down a street in Maine overheard a remark to the effect that her parents had both been lost at sea, and in the midst of reporting a baseball game a radio broadcaster in the East interrupted to announce the same news. Fortunately the true situation was known and announced a few hours later.* . . .

In connection with American-Japanese relations during the year 1934, reference is made to the following documents:

Department's instruction No. 539, June 18, 1934. [*Ibid.,* pp. 237–39.]

Embassy's despatch No. 855, June 23, 1934.

Embassy's despatch No. 912, August 4, 1934.

Embassy's despatch No. 970, September 14, 1934.

Embassy's despatch No. 1102, December 27, 1934 (important).[32]

West Coast Affairs, Chief of the Division of River Plate Affairs, and Special Assistant in the Office of the Assistant Secretary for Political Affairs. In 1948 Mr. Lyon was sent to Warsaw as First Secretary and Consul. On September 15, 1948, he became Counselor of the Warsaw Embassy.

* Department's telegram No. 163, September 21, 11 P.M.

Telegram No. 209, September 22, 8 P.M.

[32] This despatch concerned the importance of American naval preparedness in connection with the Far Eastern situation. In pursuing a "logical" policy in the Far East of maintaining and supporting the normal development of our legitimate rights and interests in the area, the United States, Mr. Grew thought, should not rely completely upon diplomacy but should give support to diplomatic methods through national preparedness.

Mr. Grew went on to say that it was always possible that the elements within the Army and Navy, which held expansionist ideas about Japan's role in the Far East might gain control of the Government. "There is a swashbuckling temper in the country, largely developed by military propaganda, which can lead

1935
AMERICAN-JAPANESE RELATIONS

During the year 1935 it was obvious that Mr. Hirota, the Minister for Foreign Affairs, was endeavoring to develop good relations with the United States so far as was possible in the face of the activities of the extremists and that he recognized the importance to Japan of such relations. On April 10 the Minister told me that he had recently announced that there would never be war while he was in office and that in this respect he was directly expressing the views of the Emperor. In July, in my final interview with him before my departure on leave of absence, he expressed the belief that our relations were good and were improving steadily, and he said that he was steadily directing his efforts along the general lines which he had mentioned to me when he first took office because he con-

Japan during the next few years, or in the next few generations, to any extremes unless the saner minds in the Government prove able to cope with it and to restrain the country from national suicide." The ability of the "saner" groups to control the extremists, Mr. Grew thought was problematical. "The idea that a great body of liberal thought lying just beneath the surface since 1931 would be sufficiently strong to emerge and assume control with a little foreign encouragement is thoroughly mistaken. The liberal thought is there, but it is inarticulate and largely impotent, and in all probability will remain so for some time to come."

In light of these considerations Mr. Grew felt that unless "we are prepared to subscribe to a 'Pax Japonica' in the Far East, with all that this movement, as conceived and interpreted by Japan, is bound to entail, we should rapidly build up our navy to treaty strength, and if and when the Washington Naval Treaty expires we should continue to maintain the present ratio with Japan regardless of cost, a peace-time insurance both to cover and to reduce the risk of war. . . .

"Theodore Roosevelt enunciated the policy 'Speak softly but carry a big stick.' If our diplomacy in the Far East is to achieve favorable results, and if we are to reduce the risk of an eventual war with Japan to a minimum, that is the only way to proceed. Such a war may be unthinkable, and so it is, but the spectre of it is always present and will be present for some time to come. It would be criminally short-sighted to discard it from our calculations, and the best possible way to avoid it is to be adequately prepared, for preparedness is a cold fact which even the chauvinists, the military, the patriots and the ultra-nationalists in Japan, for all their bluster concerning 'provocative measures' in the United States, can grasp and understand." The despatch is printed in full in Joseph C. Grew, *Ten Years in Japan* (New York: Simon & Schuster, 1944), pp. 145–52.

sidered good relations with the United States as more important to Japan than its relations with any other country.*

In March 1935, during a round of farewell dinners given
for Lieutenant Henri Smith-Hutton, departing Assistant Naval
Attaché, the younger Japanese naval officers were freely out-
spoken in stating that war with the United States was regarded
as a foregone conclusion because the United States was bound
to oppose certain definite policies of Japan in China and that
an inevitable conflict would result.

JAPANESE PETROLEUM INDUSTRY LAW

Conversations between special representatives of the American and British oil interests and Japanese officials began at the
Tokyo Club on January 9 in a conciliatory and pleasant atmosphere and continued over a considerable period. As the conversations progressed it became clear that the Japanese officials
seemed to recognize the necessity for some modification in the
oil regulations but they took the position that they could not
take action until after the sessions of the Diet owing to the risk
of internal political repercussions. In February the British Ambassador recommended that we make joint informal representations to the Foreign Office and this was done on February
19, the representations being favorably received, but little headway was made in the negotiations and the Japanese definitely
recommended suspension of the conversations until the Diet
had adjourned on March 22. The principal difficulty of the oil
companies lay in the Japanese demands that they maintain a
six-month supply of oil, which would mean expansion of their
plants, and the question arose whether the foreign companies
would not have to withdraw from Japan should no modification in the regulations be made. This was the last thing the
Japanese desired and when I talked the matter over with Mr.
Hirota he said that the subject was an acute question in the

---

* Telegram No. 144, September 18, 4 P.M., 1933.
  Telegram No. 149, October 3, 2 P.M., 1933.
  Telegram No. 154, July 18, 6 P.M., 1935.

Diet and had better be left in abeyance until after adjournment, but he added significantly: "You know we are absolutely dependent on American oil." The American and British representatives then left for Manila to return to Tokyo about April 1.

On April 13 a final meeting of representatives of the Standard-Vacuum Oil Company and the Rising Sun Petroleum Company with representatives of the Japanese Ministry of Commerce and Industry was held in Tokyo and an understanding was reached which would reduce the stock-keeping requirements to three months and would, among other concessions, sanction an increase in the quota allocations of oil to the foreign companies with a fair division between importers and refiners, as well as an increase in price if the present price should be shown to be unremunerative, and no discrimination between the companies was to be practiced. In any case, the foreign companies would not be obliged to sell at a loss. These concessions, which were known as the five-point plan, were accorded because the Japanese were faced with a definite break with the foreign oil companies, but the understanding was informal and not guaranteed, and it could not be published for fear of ultrapatriotic reaction which might defeat the plans of the Japanese authorities to ameliorate the requirements of the law. The status in which the matter was left was that as soon as the Japanese law had been altered, the foreign companies would then decide whether the expenditure on additional storage facilities to cover three months' stock-keeping was justified by the altered conditions.

In July we were informed that the Foreign Office was encountering opposition from some of the other Ministries to the proposed modification of the petroleum law but they hoped to be able to obtain a satisfactory solution before October by discreetly using the compelling argument that Japan was dependent on foreign oil.

In September the Foreign Office said that the six-month storage requirement would be postponed from October 1, 1935, to June 30, 1936, but that this was only a postponement, and

in spite of a plan for compensation, some of the other desiderata of the foreign companies were not met. This arrangement did not appear to comply with the April informal agreement. Unless we could properly invoke our Treaty of 1911 on
the ground that the storage requirements constituted a measure
of national defense, and therefore in contravention of the final
paragraph of Article I of the treaty, there appeared to be no
further step except for the American oil company either drasti-
cally to curtail its operations in Japan or to withdraw altogether.

Further official representations were recommended in November and more specifically in December; the British Ambassador brought up the subject incidentally in the course of a
conversation with the Foreign Minister on December 17. Further negotiations were to be carried on after the holidays in
January and thus the situation remained unsettled at the end of
the year.*

* For reference, telegrams:

To the Department			From the Department		
1, January	4,	5 P.M.	2, January	4,	6 P.M.
2,	7,	6 P.M.	3,	7,	7 P.M.
4,	8,	4 P.M.	4,	8,	5 P.M.
5,	10,	11 A.M.	10,	30,	6 P.M.
21,	31,	7 P.M.	20, February	15,	2 P.M.
28, February	8,	6 P.M.	23,	23,	1 P.M.
31,	15,	11 A.M.	29, March	1,	2 P.M.
34,	19,	6 P.M.	53,	30,	2 P.M.
41,	27,	6 P.M.	110, July	18,	4 P.M.
44, March	2,	2 P.M.	160, October	7,	noon.
76, April	8,	6 P.M.	176, November	14,	6 P.M.
82,	13,	6 P.M.	184,	27,	6 P.M.
83,	15,	3 P.M.	194, December	11,	6 P.M.
94, May	2,	5 P.M.	196,	12,	6 P.M.
952, July	18,	4 P.M.	198,	13,	11 A.M.
187, September	28,	noon.	199,	13,	7 P.M.
211, November	15,	5 P.M.			
224,	30,	6 P.M.			
238, December	11,	4 P.M.			
240,	13,	6 P.M.			
246,	19,	3 P.M.			
251,	26,	2 P.M.			
253,	28,	noon.			

MANCHURIAN OIL MONOPOLY

In February the British Embassy let it be known to the Foreign Office that while the foreign oil companies had not necessarily reached a final decision, it was understood that if the Manchurian authorities should carry out the monopoly scheme, the foreign companies, as a purely commercial proposition, could see no alternative to disposing of their investments in Manchuria. The foreign companies were opposed to supplying the monopoly with products which would be marketed and distributed by the monopoly alone. The replies of the Japanese Foreign Office to the representations made by the British and ourselves last November were received in March and April and were unconciliatory, taking the position that the Japanese Government could not agree to bear responsibility for the actions of "Manchukuo" and could not allow any contention based on a denial of the independence of "Manchukuo." Regulations in connection with the enforcement of the monopoly law were put into effect in Manchuria on April 10. On April 12 and 13 respectively the British Ambassador and I made formal representations to the Japanese Foreign Minister declining to accept the contentions of the Japanese Government and maintaining that the Manchurian monopoly was in contravention of the principle of the Open Door and of the fulfillment of treaty obligations which both the Japanese Government and the authorities in Manchuria had on numerous occasions declared that they would uphold. The ultimate responsibility for injury to American interests resulting from the creation and operation of the monopoly was placed squarely on the Japanese Government, and it was added that the creation of the monopoly and the part played therein by Japanese nationals would have a deplorable effect upon American public opinion. Sir Robert Clive said that the matter would probably be set forth in the House of Commons and that the correspondence would probably be published. For the first time Mr. Hirota said to me that the Japanese assurances with respect to the Open Door had been given on the understanding that "Manchukuo" would be recognized by other nations and that until the existence of "Manchukuo" were recognized "no dispute whatever could be entertained with regard to that country." After long discussion I said in conclusion that the American Government based its case on treaty commitments and past assurances. The Netherlands Minister [General Pabst] also received a reply in April to his representations of last December. He answered the reply on June 8, disagreeing with the views of the Japanese Government.

Negotiations then ensued with regard to the presentation of claims on behalf of the foreign companies for damages and for the loss of their business. The question of the sale to the monopoly of plants and equipment also arose.

Negotiations by the American and British consular officers in Manchuria were ineffective, and judging from a letter from Mr. Chuichi Ohashi [Japanese Consul General at Harbin] to Mr. Joseph Ballantine [American Consul General at Mukden] in December it became evident that the foreign companies could not expect anything more favorable than a partial settlement based exclusively on the physical value of the properties and without consideration of the principle of compensation for loss of business. It was therefore believed that the companies should proceed to the filing of claims.* . . .

* Telegrams

To the Department				
16, January	28, 5 P.M.	81,	11, 6 P.M.
27, February	8, 5 P.M.	87,	16, 7 P.M.
29,	9, 11 A.M.	89,	22, 10 A.M.
33,	18, 2 P.M.	90,	22, noon.
36,	21, 7 P.M.	91,	23, 5 P.M.
45, March	2, 3 P.M.		
59,	21, 1 P.M.	*From the Department*	
63,	25, 5 P.M.	44, March	22, 6 P.M.
65,	27, 7 P.M.	61, April	12, 6 P.M.
66,	28, 10 A.M.	62,	12, 8 P.M.
69,	29, 11 A.M.	65,	18, 6 P.M.
73, April	4, 4 P.M.	67,	24, 7 P.M.
75,	7, noon.	68,	26, 8 P.M.
77,	10, 7 P.M.	72, May	1, 10 A.M.
		73,	1, 11 A.M.

LONDON NAVAL DISARMAMENT CONFERENCE

So far as Japan was concerned, the London Naval Disarmament Conference, which opened on December 9, was a failure, Japan proving completely intransigent and standing squarely on the demand for a "common upper limit" of tonnage.[33] Japan's position was discussed in several despatches from the Embassy and also in the telegrams listed below.*

SINO-JAPANESE NEGOTIATIONS

During February reports were circulating with regard to possible Sino-Japanese negotiations on political, economic and financial matters, but basic difficulties appeared to block their inception and nothing came of the proposals. It was possible that the reports were based on the desire of the Kwantung Army to come to an understanding concerning Jehol with the local Chinese authorities. The reported intention of Mr.

75,	4, 2 P.M.	93, April	26, 5 P.M.
77,	8, 6 P.M.	103, May	11, 11 A.M.
204, December	30, 4 P.M.	124, June	8, 6 P.M.
		196, October	22, 5 P.M.
To the Department (cont.)		249, December	21, 11 A.M.

[33] Representatives of France, Great Britain, Italy, Japan and the United States met in London on December 9, 1935. The first item on the conference's agenda was the discussion of Japan's proposal of parity. None of the other delegations were willing to negotiate on the basis of the establishment of a "common upper limit." On January 15, 1936, Japan withdrew from the London meeting. An agreement was finally reached by France, Great Britain, and the United States on March 25, but the failure of Japan and Italy to adhere to the pact definitely marked the end of the period of effective limitation of naval armaments. Tate, *op. cit.,* pp. 188–96.

* To the Department		From the Department	
8, January	14, 6 P.M.	49, March	26, 7 P.M.
40, February	27, 5 P.M.	106, July	13, 4 P.M.
64, March	27, 6 P.M.	131, August	30, noon.
149, July	15, 6 P.M.	257, (to Shanghai)	
154,	18, 6 P.M.	October	4, 4 P.M.
203, November	5, 9 A.M.	174, November	4, 3 P.M.
204,	7, noon.		
231, December	6, 9 A.M.		
237,	11, 3 P.M.		

Hirota to proceed to China was denied. The Department found helpful the reports from Tokyo and Nanking on this subject and desired to be kept fully informed of developments, together with estimates of the situation. Developments of far-reaching importance seemed to be in process. It later became apparent that Mr. Hirota himself was in favor of a loan to China, in line with his wish to improve the general atmosphere of Sino-Japanese relations slowly and progressively, but that the chauvinist or military school of thought was opposed to it, and the businessmen and banks in Japan were likewise opposed to a loan in view of the absence of reliable security.* (See also "Crisis in North China.")

CRISIS IN NORTH CHINA

In January the Military Attaché [William Carey Crane] was informed that a small detachment from the Kwantung Army proposed to drive from Jehol certain so-called bandit troops said to be the remnants of Chang Hsueh-liang's forces. The move was characterized by the Japanese military authorities as of no importance and as having no other purpose than that stated. Later, reports began to circulate of demands under pressure by the Japanese Army to eliminate from the vicinity of Manchuria all supporters of the Young Marshal. [34] Opposi-

* Telegram No. 17, January 29, 6 P.M.
  Department's telegram No. 12, January 31, noon.
  Telegram No. 22, February 2, 11 A.M.
  Telegram No. 23, February 4, 7 P.M.
  Telegram No. 43, March 2, 1 P.M.
  Department's telegram No. 43, March 19, 7 P.M.
  Telegram No. 60, March 22, 6 P.M.
  Department's telegram No. 46, March 23, 2 P.M.
  Telegram No. 78, April 11, noon.

[34] After the violent death of his father, Chang Hsueh-liang, the Young Marshal, assumed rule in the Three Eastern Provinces of Manchuria. In December, 1928, Chang placed himself under allegiance to the Nanking Government, and the Nationalist flag was raised at Mukden. When the Japanese troops entered Manchuria, Chang and most of his forces were driven out by the Japanese. See Paul Hibbert Clyde, *The Far East* (New York: Prentice-Hall, Inc., 1948), pp. 616–17 and MacNair and Lach, *op. cit.*, pp. 312–15.

tion of the military to Mr. Hirota's policy of conciliation with China appeared to be growing, marking an increasing schism between the civil and military elements in the Government. Rumors of a desire to overthrow Chiang Kai-shek began to circulate in June. General Ho Ying-chin [Chinese Minister of War] was reported to have met the Japanese demands but troops were moved to various points in North China to ensure the carrying out of the promises. It was said that the local military authorities desired to create a buffer state in North China but had abandoned the idea because of the disapproval of the higher military authorities in Tokyo who desired only a peaceful North China with no political change. The report was current that the Japanese military, with the approval of the Japanese Government, had demanded that the Chinese Government should appoint no high officials in North China without Japanese approval. The British Ambassador, Sir Robert Clive, inquired of the Foreign Office, which ridiculed the reports and said that it was only the presence of anti-Japanese officials that had caused recent trouble and had led to the suggestion that only officials be appointed who were friendly to Japan. Sir Robert and I both felt it advisable to invoke the Nine Power Treaty only in the last resort. Mr. Litvinoff [People's Commissar for Foreign Affairs] told our Ambassador in Moscow [William C. Bullitt] that he was disturbed by the situation in North China and felt that action by the United States and Great Britain would turn public opinion in Japan against the Army. The Embassy disagreed with Mr. Litvinoff's opinion and believed that intervention at the present juncture would almost certainly tend to solidify public opinion in favor of the Army's actions rather than the reverse. On June 29 I reported that I had received direct word from the Prime Minister that he was determined that the difficulties in China should be settled by peaceful means and that there should be no major military operations; he believed himself to be fully in control of the situation. Informant expressed the opinion that the Premier, Admiral Okada, was in a stronger position than any Prime Minister in recent years, his ability and adroitness being evidenced by the fact that he was the only man then in high office who had supported the moderates at the London Naval Conference, the others having been sidetracked or eliminated. Okada was said to have the support of the Emperor.

In July — on the 16th — the relief of General Jinzaburo Mazaki from his post as Inspector General of Military Education caused Mr. Hirota to tell me that the incident was significant as indicating the Government's control of affairs and at the same time he thanked me in appreciative terms for the fact that during the North China crisis we had not asked him official questions which would have rendered more difficult his efforts to control the situation.

It was later reported by the Chinese Ambassador in Moscow, but not confirmed, that the Japanese Government had presented four demands to China, including recognition of "Manchukuo," a military alliance, an economic alliance, and cultural co-operation. Dr. W. W. Yen added that he had telegraphed to General Chiang Kai-shek that rather than accept the alleged Japanese demands it would be better to fight even if fighting meant suicide. Mr. Neville informed the Department that these alleged demands corresponded in general with the instructions said to have been given to Mr. Ariyoshi on his return to China last June but there was no indication that these desiderata were to be presented in the form of demands. Later Dr. Yen informed our Ambassador in Moscow that his Government felt impelled to accept the Japanese demands for full economic co-operation.* . . .

* To the Department					
10, January	19,	noon.	132,	18,	1 P.M.
17,	29,	6 P.M.	138,	24,	2 P.M.
115, May	31,	7 P.M.	141,	26,	5 P.M.
117, June	1,	6 P.M.	143,	29,	11 A.M.
119,	5,	8 P.M.	151, July	16,	4 P.M.
123,	8,	10 A.M.	161,	31,	6 P.M.
125,	10,	5 P.M.	209, November	13,	6 P.M.
128,	11,	6 P.M.	212,	20,	4 P.M.
129,	15,	1 P.M.	213,	21,	noon.
130,	15,	8 P.M.	214,	23,	4 P.M.
131,	17,	11 A.M.	216,	25,	6 P.M.
			219,	27,	1 P.M.

PROPOSED ARIZONA LAND LAW

In February the Japanese Ambassador in Washington called the attention of the Secretary of State to a bill pending before the Arizona State Legislature which would deny to aliens ineligible to citizenship the right to cultivate agricultural lands. The Department believed that such a law would be unconstitutional but feared that if it passed, similar legislation might be enacted in California and other states where there were large numbers of Japanese. The Department was endeavoring to secure withdrawal of the bill or to secure its modification, but asked me, in case I should feel obliged to discuss the matter with the Foreign Minister, to request him to regard as confidential the Department's efforts. I replied that I would discreetly use the information only if approached by the Minister. Owing to questions in the Diet I later approached the Foreign Minister, who assured me that he would avoid giving specifications, it having been pointed out to him that the intrusion of the Federal Government into State lawmaking was a very delicate matter.*

On March 22 we were informed that the Arizona State Legislature had adjourned and that the alien land bills had died on the calendar.† . . .

223,	28,	1 P.M.	191, December	5,	5 P.M.
From the Department					
12, February	1,	5 P.M.			
93, June	15,	4 P.M.	*To the Department (cont.)*		
94,	17,	6 P.M.			
95,	22,	3 P.M.	225, December	2,	noon.
115, July	29,	2 P.M.	226,	2,	5 P.M.
129, August	27,	5 P.M.	228,	4,	4 P.M.
177, November	19,	5 P.M.	232,	7,	noon.
178,	20,	4 P.M.	233,	7,	1 P.M.
179,	22,	5 P.M.	236,	10,	5 P.M.
185,	29.		239,	12,	11 A.M.
187,	30,	2 P.M.	245,	19,	11 A.M.

* Department's telegram No. 25, February 23, 3 P.M.
 Telegram No. 39, February 25, 11 A.M.
 Department's telegram No. 28, February 28, 6 P.M.
 Telegram No. 42, March 2, noon.
 † Department's telegram No. 45, March 22, 7 P.M.

SOVIET-MANCHURIAN FRONTIER INCIDENTS

Word came from our Embassy in Moscow in July that the succession of incidents on the Soviet-Manchurian border had caused apprehension in Moscow and the belief that Japan might be about to press for the sale of the northern half of Sakhalin Island and for the demilitarization of a frontier zone. This report was subsequently denied by Mr. Litvinoff who, however, said that the Japanese Government had proposed setting up a commission to regulate frontier difficulties. He was convinced that whatever a few militarists in Japan and Manchuria might desire, the Japanese Government did not wish for war. In this connection, certain facts and opinions were given us by the Soviet Ambassador in Tokyo [Constantin Youreneff] who saw no cause for alarm but realized the ever-existing danger that some frontier incident might flare into a conflagration which nobody could stop.* [35]

AMBASSADOR'S LEAVE OF ABSENCE

I sailed for the United States on leave of absence on July 19, arriving in Washington August 4 and returning to Tokyo on December 16. Mr. Neville was Chargé d'Affaires during my absence.†

* Department's telegram No. 100, July 3, 6 P.M.
Department's telegram No. 102, July 9, 6 P.M.
Telegram No. 146, July 9, noon.
Department's telegram No. 112, July 17, 7 P.M.

[35] Mr. Grew had a conversation with Soviet Ambassador Youreneff on July 17, 1935. In recording his general impressions of this talk Mr. Grew wrote in his diary: "The Ambassador said that while certain difficult questions were at issue between the two countries he was not at all anxious concerning the outcome because the Japanese did not want war and were not prepared for war. He thought the questions which I had to handle between Japan and the United States were much more difficult than his own questions and that the outlook for Japanese-American relations was much less favorable than that of Japanese-Soviet relations. He implied that he thought the future of relations between Japan and the United States was ominous."

† Telegram No. 156, July 20, 9 A.M.
Telegram No. 242, December 16, 5 P.M.

XXXI

Relations Between the United States and Japan
1936

The February 26 Incident

In the early morning of February 26 there occurred one of the most dramatic and tragic events in Japanese history, permanently known as "The February 26 Incident." The writer, having been personally and intimately in touch with the incident, its leading figures and its aftermath, here narrates the story in some detail.*

On the night of the 25th, Mrs. Grew and I had given at the Embassy a dinner for some 36 guests in honor of the Lord Keeper of the Privy Seal, former Prime Minister Viscount Admiral Saito and Viscountess Saito, and among our other guests were Admiral Kantaro Suzuki, Grand Chamberlain to the Emperor, as well as Viscount and Viscountess Ishii. Viscount Saito had told me that he had never seen a modern sound-film and in order to interest the old gentleman, for whom we had great affection, I had chosen Victor Herbert's film *Naughty Marietta* which was shown, with the playing of its romantic music, in our salon after dinner. Viscount Saito was clearly delighted, and instead of retiring at his usual early hour he remained through the film and even for supper afterwards. I saw him off at about half past eleven with every indication on his part of having thoroughly enjoyed the evening. In the light of afterevents it has always been a source of gratification that we had been able to afford Viscount Saito those last few hours of pleasure. Some five hours later he was assas-

---

* For the precise chronology of the incident, our despatch No. 1721 of March 6 should be consulted.

sinated at his home, and Admiral Suzuki was shot through the chest, a wound from which fortunately he recovered.

On the following morning I went to the Viscount's house to pay my respects, kneeling beside the body and burning incense according to Buddhist rites. His widow was there, kneeling at his head, with her arm in a sling because she also had been machine gunned in attempting to defend him. She lifted the sheet, showing a single bullet hole through the forehead, and said: "My husband would wish me to thank you for having given him such a happy last evening on earth." Such are the tragic moments of life which are ineffaceable from memory.

In the light of afterevents it is interesting to look back on our first telegram to the Department which was sent on February 26 at 10 A.M.:

> The military took partial possession of the Government and city early this morning and it is reported have assassinated several prominent men. It is impossible as yet to confirm anything. The news correspondents are not permitted to send telegrams or to telephone abroad.
>
> This telegram is being sent primarily as a test message, to ascertain if our code telegrams will be transmitted. Code room please acknowledge immediately upon receipt.

The February 26 Incident was carried out by a small group of extremist military officers, none higher than the rank of captain, who were dissatisfied with the restraining influence of the statesmen about the Emperor.[1] They had rehearsed their plans with soldiers who, when called out on the morning of the 26th, supposed that the usual routine practice was to be undertaken; surrounding each of the marked houses, the offi-

---

[1] For a discussion of the extreme military groups and their roots in Japanese life, see Hugh Borton, *Japan Since 1931, Its Political and Social Developments* (New York: Institute of Pacific Relations, 1940); Hugh Byas, *Government by Assassination* (New York: A. A. Knopf, 1942); Kenneth W. Colegrove, *Militarism in Japan* (Boston: World Peace Foundation, 1936); Hillis Lory, *Japan's Military Masters* (New York: The Viking Press, 1943); John M. Maki, *Japanese Militarism* (New York: A. A. Knopf, 1945); and O. Tanin and E. Yohan, *Militarism and Fascism in Japan* (New York: International Publishers, 1934).

cers entered and shot Viscount Saito, stabbed Finance Minister Takahashi to death, and shot Director of Military Education, General Jotaro Watanabe, and Admiral Suzuki. The first three were killed outright; Admiral Suzuki recovered. Entering the official residence of the Prime Minister the assassins mistook Admiral Okada's brother-in-law [Colonel Matsuo] for the Premier and shot him while the Admiral hid and escaped. Efforts to kill Prince Saionji and Count Shinken Makino [former Keeper of the Privy Seal] failed; both were in the country at the time; the former was apparently forewarned; the hotel in which the latter was staying was set on fire, Count Makino escaping by a rear exit and climbing a cliff where his heroic granddaughter, Kasuko, and his trained nurse spread their kimonos about him for concealment. The officers assigned to the assassination of Count Makino were either killed or wounded by his guard, and it is believed that the soldiers, although recognizing Count Makino on the cliff, refused to shoot.

Following the assassinations, the insurgents took refuge in the official residence of the Prime Minister and the Sanno Hotel, having failed in their intentions to capture strategic government buildings; martial law was declared and loyal troops with tanks took up positions in the vicinity of the British and German Embassies with the intention of attacking the insurgents to whom an ultimatum to surrender had been sent. As the American Embassy was in direct line with the projected line of fire, a General Staff officer called on me and asked us to evacuate to a place of safety which had been arranged, but I declined the offer with thanks, while warning all members of the staff and their families not to expose themselves needlessly. This decision was based on the belief that our evacuation would cause undue alarm among the American community in Tokyo. We felt that the Embassy cellars offered adequate protection in case of necessity and several families in adjacent houses came to our residence for the ensuing critical days and nights when we scarcely slept. During that entire period the flag of the insurgents continued to fly from the Prime Minister's residence.

The atmosphere throughout the night of the 28th and the morning of the 29th was tense and every indication pointed to the imminence of combat, but during the course of the morning of the 29th a relaxation of this tense atmosphere became noticeable. The Government was exerting patience and making every effort, through radio broadcasts and by dropping leaflets from airplanes, to persuade the revolutionaries to disband without resorting to armed attack, and it is significant that the leaflets were addressed only to insurgent soldiers and not to the insurgent officers, the soldiers being asked to reconsider their position and ordered to obey the Emperor's command to return to their barracks; otherwise they would be treated as revolutionists and shot. From the windows of the chancery we could see small groups of soldiers continually emerging, and at 4 o'clock in the afternoon of the 29th it was announced that all of the revolting troops had surrendered and that normal conditions would be restored at 4.10.

During the whole period of the revolt it was difficult to sort out the wheat from the chaff in the great volume of reports and rumors that reached us. Indeed, it was not until the evening of the 29th that Baron Gonsuke Hayashi, former Grand Master of Ceremonies, returned from the Palace and told me that Prime Minister Okada, whom everyone believed dead, was alive and uninjured. It appeared that his brother-in-law, who somewhat resembled him, had been killed by mistake and that the Premier had escaped and had remained undercover since the night of the 25th. He suddenly announced himself to the Emperor, whereupon Home Minister Fumio Goto, appointed Acting Premier, withdrew from the premiership which was resumed by Okada. Few more dramatic incidents have ever occurred in history, and during the crisis there were outstanding cases of heroism which need not be recorded here but which deserve their place among the great examples of heroic behavior of all time.

On March 1 official announcement was made that one of the insurgent officers had committed hara-kiri (although the public had rather expected all to do so) and that the others had been dismissed in disgrace from the army. Their dismissal without trial was believed to indicate a more drastic policy than had hitherto been followed in dealing with incidents of that character. Indeed, several of the insurgent officers were later condemned and shot, perhaps the first occasion in recent times of the execution of military officers. Our first reaction to the circumstances of the four days of the revolt was that it might well cause a revulsion of feeling against the military and that the final results might be salutary.

On the 29th I telegraphed the Secretary, for use in his press conference:

> Excellent order has been maintained in Tokyo throughout the recent incident and no injury or molestation of American citizens has been reported to the Embassy, except the inconveniences necessarily caused by the precautionary measures of the authorities.

And on March 2 a letter was sent to the Foreign Minister requesting him to convey to the competent authorities my sincere appreciation of the thoroughness of the measures taken by various departments to ensure the safety of ourselves and the personnel and property of the Embassy during the uprising. The situation was admirably handled.

On the same day the Protocol Bureau of the Foreign Office conveyed to us the following message from the Home Office:

> Although the mutineers have surrendered, the Home Office cannot say that everything is quiet; peace has been partially but not completely restored. The Home Office is still anxious about the safety of the American, Soviet Russian and British Ambassadors, Counselors, Military and Naval Attachés (excluding Assistant Military and Naval Attachés). The Home Office must assume responsibility for anything that might happen to these persons and would consequently like to detail a plainclothes man to each of the officials in question to sit beside their chauffeurs when they drive about the city.

A meeting with the British Ambassador and myself was requested by the Soviet Ambassador who said that he had informed his Government that this step by the Japanese police was clearly taken for the purpose of keeping closer watch on our movements and was unjustified as a precautionary measure. Sir Robert Clive and I agreed with Mr. Youreneff at least to the extent that the proposed surveillance should not become permanent and that we would request that the guards be removed as soon as practicable, and certainly when the period of martial law came to an end. It was reported that a few of the revolting officers were still at large and this might account for the anxiety of the police. I did not feel in a position to appraise the necessity of the step as a measure of protection, but I told Washington that since our movements were known and at all times reported, I believed that the measure, if taken only for the purpose of watching our movements, was futile. . . .

On March 7 our Military Attaché, Lieutenant Colonel Crane, was told personally and not officially by an officer of the General Staff that the incident of February 26 had been planned and executed by officers forming the radical fringe of the nationalistic group to which all officers belong. Noncommissioned officers and men knew nothing of the officers' real purpose as they were told merely that they were to take part in a night maneuver. This was the same small group of radicals which was responsible for the "May 15th Incident" [2] and all subsequent incidents of that character. It was said that three of the officers had committed suicide and that more suicides were expected later when opportunity was afforded, but so far as was subsequently known, no such further opportunity ever was afforded, the guilty insurgents having been immediately arrested. Several senior members of the Supreme Military Council, including Generals Araki and Mazaki, assumed responsibility for the incident and retired.

With regard to the peaceful methods employed by the authorities in securing the capitulation of the insurgents, it was

[2] On May 15, 1932, Premier Ki Inukai had been assassinated.

explained that to arrest them outright would have involved fighting in the heart of Tokyo and might have resulted in the destruction of buildings and loss of life among the civilian population; that the use of force against insurgents was contrary to Japanese custom; that no Japanese Army officer would order the Emperor's soldiers to fire on other soldiers of the Emperor; that the fighting, if it had taken place, would have been too close to the Emperor's Palace; and that, in any case, there was considerable sympathy among the people for the motives which animated the misguided young men and that consequently a certain amount of consideration had to be shown them or the Army would find itself possessed of a group of martyrs which must be avoided at almost any cost. This attitude, did not, however, prevent the subsequent executions.

It may here be recorded that the work of the Embassy staff during the rebellion was past all praise, the members having scouted through the city, at considerable risk to themselves, in order to observe developments and to obtain information which was promptly relayed to me for repetition to Washington, and during the final critical night we all sat up together in the Embassy residence. Especially gratifying to all of us was a most considerate message sent us by Mr. Hull on the 28th:

> I appreciate very much the high sense of official responsibility and duty which you and your staff are displaying during the present emergency situation; also the timely and helpful telegrams which you are sending the Department. I realize that the information contained in these telegrams has been difficult to obtain. We have complete reliance upon the soundness of your judgment in deciding whether or not the personnel of the Embassy should be temporarily transferred to a place removed from the danger zone. You will of course keep in mind that we should not wish that the Embassy staff be exposed unnecessarily to danger. . . .

To which I replied:

> The Staff and I sincerely appreciate your message. Members of the staff and their families living in the danger zone are stay-

ing with us in the residence which is still heavily guarded with troops, outposts and sandbag barricades below the chancery, also three detectives and two soldiers within. I believe that the only danger is from flying bullets and that in case of necessity the basements of the residence and chancery will afford the best possible protection.

On July 7 the War Office announced that of nineteen officers, seventy-five noncommissioned officers, nineteen privates and ten civilians indicted and tried for complicity in the incident, the following sentences had been given: thirteen officers and four civilians to death; five officers to life imprisonment; one officer, seventeen noncommissioned officers and six civilians to imprisonment from two to fifteen years; twenty-seven noncommissioned officers and three privates to imprisonment from eighteen months to two years with suspended sentences. The judgment stated that the sentences to death and to life imprisonment were pronounced upon certain officers because they had employed the Imperial Army without Imperial sanction. Thus it was not for murder that they were punished. Some of the noncommissioned officers and privates were found to have participated knowingly in the incident while others were acquitted because they had only obeyed the orders of their superior officers. Thirteen officers and two civilians were executed by shooting on July 12. The Press generally approved the executions and no disturbances were reported.

Martial Law in Tokyo was repealed on July 18.

In August the War Office announced that the Army court-martial had sentenced six other military officers to varying terms of imprisonment, from life in one case to four years, for their connection with the February 26 Incident.

Incidentally, Mrs. Grew has constantly remained in touch with Viscountess Saito and has sent her flowers annually on the anniversary of her husband's death.

Our contemporary reports on the incident and subsequent analyses are listed below.*

* To the Department		
36, February	26, 10 A.M.	37,	26, noon.
	38,	26, 7 P.M.

Trial and Execution of Lieutenant Colonel Aizawa

The trial of Lieutenant Colonel Saburo Aizawa for the assassination of Major General Nagata, Director of the Military Affairs Bureau of the War Ministry, on August 12, 1935, resulted in Aizawa's conviction and execution on July 3. The

39,	26, 11 P.M.	25,	26, 5 P.M.
40,	27, noon.	27,	28, noon.
41,	27, 1 P.M.	28, March	3, 5 P.M.
43,	27, 11 P.M.		
44,	28, noon.		
45,	28, 6 P.M.	*To the Department (cont.)*	
46,	28, midnight.		
47,	29, 11 A.M.		
48,	29, 1 P.M.	57,	4, 1 P.M.
49,	29, 4 P.M.	63,	7, 9 P.M.
50,	29, 6 P.M.	66,	9, 11 P.M.
51,	29, 7 P.M.	136, June	23, 6 P.M.
52, March	1, 6 P.M.	140,	24, 7 P.M.
54,	2, 5 P.M.	149, July	7, noon.
55,	3, 6 P.M.	154,	13, 2 P.M.
From the Department		158,	18, 11 A.M.
24, February	26, 11 A.M.	165, August	1, 11 A.M.

Despatches from the Embassy

No.	1718, March 6:	Analysis of the causes leading to the Incident.
	1719, March 6:	Messages of Condolence, et cetera.
	1721, March 6:	Chronicle of events during the uprising.
	1735, March 19:	Analysis of the measure of success achieved by the insurgents.
	1746, March 20:	Trial of Lieutenant Colonel Aizawa and its connection with the February 26 Incident.
	1784, April 17:	Aftermath of the February 26 Incident.
	1821, May 12:	Second trial and death sentence of Lieutenant Colonel Aizawa.
	1826, May 13:	Speech delivered in the Diet by Mr. Takao Saito on May 7.
	1833, May 14:	Aftermath of the February 26 Incident.
	1900, June 12:	Further developments in the situation created by the February 26 Incident.
	1935, July 8:	Aftermath of the February 26 Incident. (Trial and sentences.)
	1952, July 22:	Aftermath of the February 26 Incident. (Execution of officers and civilians implicated.)
	1955, July 23:	Political consequences of the Incident.
	2044, September 18:	Aftermath of the February 26 Incident.

political implications of the case were discussed in several despatches from the Embassy, not recorded here.* ³

RECONSTRUCTION OF CABINET; HIROTA SUCCEEDS OKADA

Soon after the February 26 Incident, conferences began for the purpose of forming a new Cabinet and I was confidentially informed by the Vice Minister that the primary and fundamental consideration under discussion was to choose a Government that would not only maintain but would constructively improve Japan's foreign relations.† Early rumors pointed to Prince Konoye as the next Prime Minister, but it was soon reported that after consultation with the Genro, Prince Saionji, Prince Konoye had declined.‡ Mr. Hirota was then chosen. Mr. Kurahei Yuasa was appointed Lord Keeper of the Privy Seal and Mr. Tsuneo Matsudaira Imperial Household Minister.§ In the new Cabinet, owing to the Army's disapproval of Mr. Shigeru Yoshida [Ambassador at London] Mr. Hirota continued temporarily as Foreign Minister, while General Juichi Terauchi became War Minister, Admiral Osami Nagano Navy Minister, and Mr. Eiichi Baba Minister of Finance.|| In an analysis of the new Cabinet the Embassy re-

---

* Telegram No. 145, July 1, 10 P.M.
  Telegram No. 147, July 3, 1 P.M.
³ On July 16, 1935, General Mazaki, a member of the Kodoha, a radical, direct action military faction, was dismissed from his post of Inspector General of Military Education. His removal represented a victory of the Control Faction, another military group, over the Kodoha. Major General Tetsujan Nagata, a leader of the Control Faction, was held responsible by members of the Kodoha for the dismissal of Mazaki. On August 12, 1935, Lieutenant Colonel Aizawa, a sympathizer with the movement for national reconstruction and a friend of Mazaki, cut down Nagata with his sword. Chitoshi Yanaga, *Japan Since Perry* (New York: McGraw-Hill Book Co., 1949), pp. 512–15.
† Telegram No. 53, March 2, noon.
  Telegram No. 56, March 4, noon.
‡ Telegram No. 58, March 4, 6 P.M.
  Telegram No. 59, March 4, 10 P.M.
§ Telegram No. 60, March 5, 6 P.M.
  Telegram No. 61, March 6, 9 P.M.
|| Telegram No. 65, March 9, 10 P.M.

ported that as long as Mr. Hirota was in control, the tendency of the new Government would be to tranquillize Japan's foreign relations but that only time would show whether he was sufficiently strong to curb the dangerous tendencies of the Army in China and Manchuria.*

AMERICAN-JAPANESE RELATIONS

On February 1 the Tokyo *Nichi Nichi* published an article to the effect that as a result of conversations between the Japanese Ambassador in Washington and the Secretary of State, and between the American Ambassador in Tokyo and Mr. Hirota, the following principles had been established: (*a*) there are no American-Japanese problems insoluble by diplomatic means, and (*b*) both countries should refrain from irritating speech and actions. The article then alleged that steps were being taken for the conclusion of an American-Japanese political agreement based on the principle of the division of the Pacific into American and Japanese spheres of activity and including the spirit of the Hull-Hirota messages of 1934. The article further intimated that this political agreement might lead to a bilateral naval disarmament agreement. On the same day the *Jiji* published a short article alleging that Mr. Hirota was working toward a tripartite agreement between the United States, Great Britain and Japan whereby each country would undertake the maintenance of peace in its particular sphere, the United States in the Americas, Great Britain in Europe and Japan in the Far East, the tripartite agreement to replace the peace machinery of the League of Nations. The Embassy believed that these articles, as they appeared simultaneously, might in effect be trial balloons put out by the Foreign Office.†
The American press reported these stories as affirming that comprehensive political negotiations between Messrs. Hull and Saito, and Hirota and Grew, were taking place. Interrogated by press correspondents, the Secretary of State said that

* Telegram No. 66, March 9, 11 P.M.
† Telegram No. 21, February 1, 11 A.M.

there were no new developments in relations between the United States and countries of the Far East, and officers of the Department had informally explained to correspondents that there had been held numerous conferences with regard to particular questions of trade but no conferences on political matters had been held or suggested.*

On February 10 Senator Key Pittman, Chairman of the Foreign Relations Committee of the Senate, delivered a speech in the Senate charging that Japan was closing the Open Door in China.[4] Secretary Hull replied to questions in press conference to the effect that while Senator Pittman occupied an important position in the legislative branch of the Government, there had been no consultation or collaboration between the Senator and himself, and there was therefore no reason for comment from Mr. Hull. The Japanese press was restrained, attributing the speech to the Senator's anti-Japanese attitude and his desire to get himself before the public in election year, while official quarters evidently desired to minimize the importance of the utterance.† The Senator desired to receive a complete set of Japanese newspaper clippings commenting on his speech.‡

With the reconstruction of the Cabinet after the February 26 Incident the new Prime Minister, Mr. Hirota, received me

* Department's telegram No. 16, February 1, 1 P.M. [*Foreign Relations, Japan: 1931–41*, I, 241.]

4 Concerning the "Open Door" Senator Pittman said: "The door of China is to be closed to us, even if war is necessary to accomplish it; this in spite of the fact that Japan, in reply to the mild inquiry of the British Foreign Minister, promised to maintain the open door to Manchuria.

"Well, there is no open door in Manchuria — to us! American bankers, importers, and businessmen have been run out of Manchuria and replaced by Japanese. Our educators and missionaries will not long be able to remain. But if the so-called law of necessity, pleaded by every conqueror, justifies the breaking of the solemn promises contained in the treaties to which I have referred, why should Japan worry about breaking a promise to maintain the open door in China?" U.S. Congress, *Congressional Record*, 74th Cong., 2d Sess., vol. 80, pt. 2 (Washington: Government Printing Office, 1936), p. 1705.

† Department's telegram No. 19, February 10, 7 P.M.

Telegram No. 26, February 12, 5 P.M.

‡ Department's telegram No. 21, February 13, 5 P.M.

on March 13 and said that there would be no change in his former policy as Foreign Minister, that owing to his present position as head of the Government that policy would now always prevail, that the Cabinet unanimously supported that policy and that he would soon choose a new Foreign Minister equally in sympathy with that policy. The "positive diplomacy" mentioned in the press applied only to Soviet Russia and to China and simply meant the speeding up of the policy already enunciated. Mr. Hirota said that the principle of the Open Door in China would not be injured by Japan and that the only possible way in which foreign interests might be affected by Japan's policy would be by her relinquishment in due course of her extraterritorial rights in China. He saw no serious problems between the United States and Japan.

I took occasion on my own initiative to speak to the Prime Minister of the difficulties encountered by the Government in Washington arising from the increasing flow of cheap Japanese goods into the American market; the pressure on our Government from domestic industrial interests was becoming increasingly heavy and it might be necessary eventually to appeal to him to place greater restrictions on the exportation of this class of goods to the United States.* A somewhat similar conversation took place with the new Foreign Minister, Mr. Arita, on April 17.† . . .

As pertinent to the subject of American-Japanese relations and as significant in the light of developments in those relations during the past four years, despatch No. 2000, of August 22, 1936, entitled "The Importance of Naval Preparedness in connection with Future Developments in the Far East," is quoted in full:

As of possible interest to the Department I have the honor to transmit herewith two articles from, respectively, *The Japan Advertiser* of July 30 and *The Japan Times and Mail* of August 16, reporting press interviews with Mr. Frederick Moore, Ameri-

* Telegram No. 74, March 13, 7 P.M.
† Telegram No. 86, April 17, 10 A.M.

can journalist and formerly foreign counselor to the Japanese Foreign Office, who is at present revisiting Japan.[5]

It will be noted that Mr. Moore's statements to the press concerning the attitude of the American Government and public towards the Far East are summed up in the phrase in the final paragraph of the second interview: "As I see it, therefore, Japan is free to do what she likes in the Far East. . . . " supplemented by the thought, implied by the substance of the whole interview, "so far as the American Government and people are concerned."

Much of Mr. Moore's argument can no doubt be accepted as accurate and sound. The great majority of the American people today are probably less interested in the Far East in general, and in the welfare of China in particular, and less inclined, if not actually adverse, to the taking of positive steps by the United States to protect either China herself or aggressively to support American interests in China than they have been in times past. So far as the Embassy is aware, the majority of the American public today, in the face of developments in China similar in nature to those which occurred in Manchuria in the autumn of 1931 and the winter of 1932, would probably deprecate if not openly oppose positive action on the part of our Government if such action should exceed the mere technical steps necessary to register our legal position on the basis of treaty rights.

Mr. Moore however tends to forget American history. It is conceded that the trend of American public opinion today is more firmly than ever opposed to foreign entanglements and to policies or measures which might conceivably lead the United States into eventual war.[6] Indeed, our people, since the founding of our nation, have been opposed in principle to political commitments abroad and to war as an instrument of national policy. If latterly there has been a change in that respect, more intensely emphasizing our revulsion against the thought of war, it is only one of degree. Although we have been ready enough in times past to fight for important principles, we are not and never have been fundamentally a warlike people. Nevertheless we are without question one of the most inflammable people in the world.

---

[5] See Frederick Moore, *With Japan's Leaders* (New York: Charles Scribner's Sons, 1942).

[6] President Roosevelt signed the Neutrality Act on August 31, 1935.

The Spanish War was a concrete and vivid illustration of this axiom. Neither President McKinley nor the American public nor Congress desired war with Spain — until the blowing up of the *Maine*. With that incident the public overnight became war-conscious and war-determined, unmanageably so. Even after our Minister in Madrid had brought his negotiations with the Spanish Government to a point where a peaceful and acceptable solution of the Cuban situation appeared to be definitely in view — indeed, after the Spanish Government had actually capitulated to our demands — American public opinion became uncontrollable and forced the hands of the President and Congress, against their wishes and better judgment, to declare war.[7] In the World War, President Wilson in 1916 was re-elected on the primary basis of the slogan "He kept us out of war," yet in little more than a year, owing to the results of Germany's ruthless submarine warfare, his hand was forced by public clamor for hostilities.[8] These incidents are historic lessons in the psychology of the American people which should not be forgotten.

By all means, let us continue to follow the enlightened policy of the Good Neighbor; let us do everything in our power "to seek peace and ensue it" by carrying out our foreign policy with broad vision and tolerant statesmanship, endeavoring to understand the problems of other nations and aiming to shape our policy with the long future in view rather than to be stampeded by current issues; let us sedulously avoid provocative actions or gestures or petty international irritations which may tend unnecessarily to exacerbate the feelings of foreign governments and peoples. But let us not forget that, as our own history has repeatedly and undeniably demonstrated, unforeseen incidents can at any moment inflame the entire American nation, and an inflamed nation is stronger than laws or policies or governments themselves. It is all very well for Mr. Moore to say that Japan is

[7] For a discussion of the events leading to American entrance into the Spanish-American War, see Walter Millis, *The Martial Spirit* (Boston: Houghton Mifflin Co., 1931), and Julius W. Pratt, *Expansionists of 1898* (Baltimore: The John Hopkins Press, 1936).

[8] For a discussion of America's entrance into the First World War, see Charles Seymour, *American Neutrality 1914–1917* (London: Oxford University Press, 1935), and Charles Tansill, *America Goes to War* (Boston: Little, Brown & Co., 1938).

free to do what she likes in the Far East, even to the extent of breaking treaty commitments and of interfering with American vested rights and legitimate interests — up to a certain point. But we should always "remember the Maine." A moment may come when the bounds of international irresponsibility will be overstepped, when the tolerance and patience of the American people will be subjected to too great a strain. Such a point might be reached by a long series of injuries, an accumulation of indignities, or it might be reached by one single incident. To hold that the time has passed when such a contingency could occur is to ignore history and fundamentally to misjudge the psychology of the American people.

Therefore, once again, and after the experience of more than four years in Japan and a fairly comprehensive understanding of the basic strains and stresses that sway the Japanese Government and people, I unhesitatingly urge adequate naval preparedness on the part of our country to meet at any moment, now and in future, unforeseen developments in the Far East which might lead us, contrary to all calculations and policies, into war with Japan. I see no reason to alter in the slightest degree the recommendations conveyed in my despatch No. 1102 of December 27, 1934.[9] The present lull in Japanese expansionist measures is, and in the very nature of things can be, but temporary. Nothing is with certainty predictable in the Far East except that the inherent urge towards Japanese expansion is uncontrollable and will continue. The movement will no doubt proceed in cycles of varying intensity; there will be temporary lulls probably succeeded by sudden strokes as has happened in the past. The movement will be primarily economic but economic penetration will almost inevitably lead to eventual political or military domination. Whether this movement continues in the direction of China or turns towards the Philippines, the Dutch East Indies and the southern seas, or both, American interests will sooner or later be injured by the juggernaut, perhaps gradually, as in Manchuria, or perhaps more suddenly elsewhere. The risk of inflammable incidents will always exist. The inherent temper of the American people, regardless of trends of thought or cycles of policy, is fundamentally unalterable. What happened in 1898

9 *Supra*, p. 974, n. 32.

and 1917 can happen again. Therefore we should not be too much lulled into a sense of security by our isolationist propensities and our proclivities towards neutrality and peace. We should remember our own history and the capacity of our people for uncontrollable inflammability in the face of cumulative or sudden and sporadic injury. To speak softly but to carry a big stick is as sound a doctrine to follow now as it ever has been in the history of the United States.

In this general connection reference is respectfully made to an article published in the *United States Naval Institute Proceedings*, April, 1936, Vol. 62, No. 398, entitled "The Navy and the Diplomatic Frontier." [10] It is well worth reading.

SINO-JAPANESE RELATIONS

During the progress of the London Naval Conference, Sir Robert Craigie, Assistant Under Secretary of State, told Mr. Norman Davis, chairman of the American delegation, in strict confidence, that the Japanese were then engaged in negotiating a nonaggression pact with Chiang Kai-shek on the latter's initiative and that the proposal was favored by the Japanese Foreign Office but was opposed by the Japanese military group on the ground that such a pact would put an end to their operations in China. Sir Robert felt that such a political agreement would be a necessary prelude to a naval agreement and that if a nonaggression pact were accepted by Chiang Kai-shek it would automatically solve the Manchurian question. Furthermore, it could lead to a nonaggression pact applying to the Pacific area between Japan, China, the United States and Great Britain which would maintain the *status quo* and would give to Japan justification for entering a naval agreement. Mr. Davis doubted the feasibility of endeavoring at that time to reach any political agreement which would raise very serious questions then regarded as insoluble.[11] The Department asked for

[10] The article was written by Lieutenant Commander Frank S. M. Harris.

[11] For a report of the American delegation to the London Naval Conference and conference documents, see U.S. Department of State, *The London Naval Conference 1935*, Conference Series No. 24 (Washington: Government Printing Office, 1936).

the Embassy's comments and pertinent information.* The Embassy replied that a meeting in Nanking to discuss the Sino-Japanese situation had been proposed some ten days ago, according to reports, by the Chinese Chargé d'Affaires in Tokyo, but that the Japanese Foreign Office, before acceding, desired a list of points to be discussed. It was said that Mr. Yakichiro Suma, Consul General in Nanking, and Mr. Ariyoshi, Minister to China, were to proceed to Tokyo for consultation about January 20. My own comments on Sir Robert Craigie's proposal to Mr. Davis were substantially as follows: The military program of the Japanese Army in China had not been proceeding successfully, the effort to include the five provinces in an autonomy movement, the immediate Japanese military objective, having failed.[12] Indeed, the military had been taken by surprise by the determination and solidarity of a movement by professors and students in Japan opposing the policy of the Army, and while the importance of the movement had allegedly been discounted, nevertheless it had caused embarrassment. The military, however, were determined eventually to dominate North China. They did not at that time visualize military occupation because this would weaken their defensive power in Manchuria against Soviet Russia and would greatly increase expenses, but they believed that through a nonaggression pact with Chiang Kai-shek, the *status quo* in Manchuria would be accepted by the Chinese and provision might be made for one or two Japanese military advisers in Hopei. The foregoing

* Department's telegram No. 2, January 7, 7 P.M.

12 After the Tangku truce in May, 1933, the Japanese embarked upon a program of penetration into northern China. The Japanese hoped to attain a favored position in these Chinese provinces by encouraging and creating "autonomy" movements within the northern areas. On November 24, 1935, Yin Ju-keng, who was a Japanese collaborator, announced that an anti-Communist Government had been formed in the demilitarized East Hopei zone. Yin urged the ,creation in the five provinces of Hopei, Chahar, Suiyuan, Shantung, and Shansi likewise of such autonomous governments. There was no immediate answer from the five provinces to Yin's message, although on December 11 the establishment of a semi-independent Hopei-Chahar Political Council was agreed to by the Chinese Government. Harley F. MacNair and Donald F. Lach, *Modern Far Eastern International Relations* (New York: D. Van Nostrand Co., Inc., 1950), pp. 416–22.

thoughts were, however, pure conjecture based on recent developments, and I was skeptical as to the possibility of such a non-aggression pact eventuating. However, if such a pact should be concluded, it would presumably render obsolete the whole treaty structure in the relation of the Powers to China. In such an eventuality we should shape our own policy with the long future rather than the past and immediate present in mind, aiming to secure the most effective guarantees with regard to our relations with Japan in particular and the safeguarding of our interests in the Far East in general. The time was obviously coming when our whole future policy and outlook in the Far East must be reconsidered, and even if such a reconsideration might, as Mr. Davis had opined, raise apparently insoluble questions, I was inclined to feel that the alleged insolubility of those questions was predicated more on the difficulty of adjusting ourselves to new conditions and facts, however unwelcome those conditions and facts might be, than upon insuperable obstacles. If Chiang Kai-shek should enter into such an agreement as Sir Robert Craigie believed to be "probable in the near future," it would appear that those conditions and facts suggested above would definitely have materialized. If then the present naval *status quo* could be secured through bilateral pacts between the United States, Great Britain and Japan, based on the fundamental principles already subscribed to in the Kellogg-Briand Pact, I felt that the suggestion should not be turned aside without most careful consideration.*

Towards the end of January Sir Robert Clive, the British Ambassador, inquired of the Foreign Minister whether there was truth in press reports that China's recognition of "Manchukuo" would be one of the three Japanese conditions for a Sino-Japanese rapprochement, to which Mr. Hirota replied in the negative. He appreciated the fact that under present circumstances China could not possibly extend such recognition, but he hoped that this might eventually come about through a gradual development of the situation. He also hoped that China would cease to refer to "Manchukuo" as "a puppet

* Telegram No. 7, January 9, 6 P.M.

state" and would enter more fully into factual relations involving customs, posts, et cetera. Sir Robert Clive took that occasion to say to the Minister that in his opinion the alleged autonomous government in East Hopei was a farce and that Yin Jukeng was a notorious scalawag, but Mr. Hirota made no comment.*

In my initial talk with the new Prime Minister after the reconstruction of the Cabinet following the February 26 Incident, Mr. Hirota said that the three points already enunciated [13] would form the basis for negotiations with China and that the Chinese Government had already accepted these points in principle, namely:

(a) Cessation by China of anti-Japanese activity and propaganda.
(b) Recognition by China of the existence of "Manchukuo" and regularization of factual relations such as communications, customs, transit, et cetera. This need not imply *de jure* recognition.
(c) Sino-Japanese co-operation to combat the spread of communism.

The Prime Minister also said that Japan would not injure the principle of the Open Door.†

Late in April Mr. Suma, then Japanese Consul General in Nanking, informed the British Commercial Counselor, G. B. Sansom, in connection with the smuggling situation, that this was a political and not an economic issue; that pending Chinese acceptance of Japanese views the Japanese Government would

* Telegram No. 19, January 30, noon.
[13] On October 28, 1935, Hirota had presented the three principles of Japan's new China policy to the Chinese Ambassador. Professor Hsü Shu-hsi in *The North China Problem* (Shanghai: Kelly & Walsh, Limited, 1937), p. 82, has written that summed up "the three Hirota principles meant practically this: that China shall recognize the *fait accompli* in Manchuria, Jehol, Hopei and Chahar, forsake the world, and make common cause with Japan against Soviet Russia."
† Telegram No. 74, March 13, 7 P.M.

do nothing to improve the situation;[14] that the determination of the Japanese Army to proceed with a firm hand in China had been consolidated and strengthened by the February 26 Incident; that until the five northern provinces had become completely independent of Nanking the situation could not be stabilized; and that the efforts of China to strengthen armaments was an absurd and dangerous move because any incident could lead to open conflict.   In a subsequent interview with newspapermen on returning to Japan Mr. Suma was reported to have stated that he had told Chiang Kai-shek that "China must now choose between interdependence with Japan or war with Japan." Other versions of Mr. Suma's statement in the vernacular press quoted him as saying that "the future course of the Chiang Government must be either to rely upon Japan or to open hostilities against Japan." *

In June the Military Attaché was informed at the War Department that the movement of troops for the reinforcement of the North China garrison had been completed and that the garrison now had a strength of slightly under 5000 men of all branches of the Army.†

Press reports of an alleged agreement whereby the United States would furnish financial and other aid to China in the form of a credit to finance the purchase of munitions were accompanied by an indication that the Foreign Office was opposed to economic assistance to China by any of the Powers and that an inquiry would be made of the Nanking Government concerning the details of the alleged agreement.   The Department replied that American assistance in the unification of the Chinese currency and revenues consisted of advice only,

14 Smugglers in Hopei and Shantung sent silver from China to Japan, increasing the difficulties in the Chinese financial system. A dope ring sold narcotics in China south of the wall. Japanese military and consular officials protected these smugglers in their illegal operations, and Japanese naval pressure kept the seaport towns of the two provinces open for smuggling. These smuggling activities also cut deeply into cherished markets of the Western powers. MacNair and Lach, *op. cit.*, p. 419.

* Telegram No. 117, May 30, 1 P.M.

† Telegram No. 139, June 24, 6 P.M.

and that the other items in the story were without basis. The story was regarded by the Department as having been planted for political purposes and to elicit information.*

In September, incidents at Chengtu and Pakhoi [15] gave rise to reports that the Japanese Army and Navy desired to use them as an excuse for demanding a fundamental settlement of Sino-Japanese issues and to weaken Chiang Kai-shek, but the Foreign Office evidently desired a "fair settlement" and believed that the incidents would blow over, intimating that the agitation in the local press was inspired by military influences.† Later there were indications that the moderate counsel, which had seemed to prevail after the first excitement over the incidents had died down, had met with renewed pressure from the proponents of a strong policy toward China.‡ The Japanese military continued to bring pressure to bear on the Foreign Office to make strong demands on China,§ while press reports indicated that four demands on China were being considered: (1) organization of a completely autonomous regime in the five northern provinces; (2) perfection of communications between Japan and China; (3) reduction of the Chinese import tariff; and (4) employment of as many Japanese advisers as possible. These reported demands were in addition to those relating to eradication of anti-Japanese activities. The Embassy did not, however, feel that the Japanese Government would push matters with China to a critical point at that time. It was of interest, in connection with the Pakhoi incident, that

* Telegram No. 160, July 21, 1 P.M.

  Department's telegram No. 96, July 21, 5 P.M.

[15] At Chengtu on August 24, 1936, two Japanese journalists were killed and two other Japanese visitors in the city were injured, when a group of about forty Chinese, who were returning from a mass meeting protesting the reopening of the Japanese consulate at Chengtu, attacked the four Japanese at a local inn. On September 3, 1936, a Japanese storekeeper was killed by anti-Japanese demonstrators at Pakhoi. New York Times, August 26, 1936, p. 1; September 10, 1936, p. 13.

† Telegram No. 176, September 2, 11 A.M.

‡ Telegram No. 182, September 11, 5 P.M.

  Telegram No. 186, September 15, 5 P.M.

§ Telegram No. 188, September 17, 6 P.M.

according to the Embassy's information the French Ambassador [Albert Kammerer] had reminded the Japanese Foreign Minister of the Declaration of 1897 concerning nonalienation of the island of Hainan.* [16] A further incident at Shanghai, involving Japanese marines, led to an immediate strengthening of Japanese naval forces in China and a marked increase in local tension.† [17] It was also reported that the failure of the negotiations at Nanking to make progress, owing to a lack of appreciation of the present situation on the part of the Chinese Government, had caused dissatisfaction in Japanese circles and that the Foreign Minister had impressed upon the Chinese Ambassador [Hsu Shih-ying] the urgency of Chiang Kai-shek's return to Nanking to be personally present at the important negotiations.‡

At a press conference with foreign correspondents on September 28 conducted personally by the Foreign Minister, Mr. Arita said that China was at the crossroads and declared that the Japanese Government was then in the course of deciding what steps it must take to protect its nationals. The Minister's statement was notable for its firmness and comprehensiveness in enumerating outstanding issues and for his refusal to define or to limit the scope of the negotiations desired by China.§

* Telegram No. 190, September 22, 3 P.M.

[16] The Tsung-li Yamen sent Gerard, the French Minister to China, a declaration in regard to the nonalienation of Hainan. In this China stated that the island would never be alienated or ceded to any foreign power. See William Woodville Rockhill (ed.), *Treaties and Conventions With or Concerning China and Korea, 1894–1904* (Washington: Government Printing Office, 1904), p. 173.

† Telegram No. 192, September 24, 6 P.M.

Telegram No. 193, September 25, 6 P.M.

[17] On September 21, 1936, it was announced that the Japanese fleet in Chinese waters was being reinforced in order to provide better protection for Japanese living in Hankow and Shanghai. Chinese gunmen shot three Japanese sailors on September 24, and the Hongkew district of Shanghai was immediately occupied by Japanese marines. On the following day, however, Japanese forces in the International Settlement were reduced, and the marines were withdrawn from the larger part of Chinese territory. *New York Times*, September 22, 1936, p. 1; September 24, 1936, p. 1; September 26, 1936, p. 9.

‡ Telegram No. 194, September 26, 11 A.M.

§ Telegram No. 197, September 28, 7 P.M.

Telegram No. 198, September 29, 6 P.M.

An inquiry from the Department as to the truth of press reports that the War Minister might resign owing to rejection by the Cabinet of extensive administrative reforms advocated by the Army and Navy brought from the Embassy the opinion that the proposals for administrative reform, while they would play a prominent part in political issues in the coming months in Japan, would probably have no significant influence on Japanese policy in China, and there was no present indication that the Cabinet would resign on the basis of that issue.*

At the end of September the question arose as to whether anything might be gained by an approach to the Japanese Government by the American and British Embassies with a view to counseling moderation, but Mr. Erle Dickover, then Chargé d'Affaires, felt that such an approach would only serve to stiffen Japanese determination, especially if publicity resulted. The Foreign Minister had told Sir Robert Clive that Japan's demands on China were not unconditional and after some hesitation he had denied that the demands included detachment of the five northern provinces, involving separate currency and separate customs administrations. It was thought advisable, however, to let the Japanese Government know, through informal conversations, that the American Government was watching the situation constantly and with interest.† The Foreign Office characterized as malicious propaganda, aimed at alienating Japan and China, a Reuters' despatch reporting that the Japanese demands included the right to station troops along the Yangtze, the right to edit Chinese school texts, and autonomy for the five northern provinces, and said that it was sending the Director of the Asiatic Bureau to Nanking immediately in order to convey to Ambassador Shigeru Kawagoe [Japanese Ambassador to China] the intentions of the Government.‡

---

* Department's telegram No. 125, September 30, 6 P.M.
  Telegram No. 199, October 1, 9 P.M.
† Department's telegram No. 126, September 30, 7 P.M.
  Telegram No. 200, October 1, 10 P.M.
‡ Telegram No. 202, October 2, 7 P.M.

On October 3 Mr. Joseph Ballantine [First Secretary of the American Embassy] saw the Vice Minister [Mr. Shigemitsu] at the latter's request, and the Vice Minister later had a talk with Mr. Dickover in the hospital in which assurances were given that the present discussions with China were in no respect like the Twenty-One Demands and that Japan had no intention of using force to obtain her desiderata. He said that the only demand upon which Japan would insist was the suppression of anti-Japanese propaganda because the resulting agitation raised the danger of grave incidents. Other matters were to be discussed in a friendly way and were subject to negotiation and designed to promote more normal and healthy relations between the two countries. The Embassy believed that in spite of the alarming attitude of Japanese representatives in China, the Government had full command of the situation and was directing its efforts towards objectives less sweeping than those reported abroad.* The Embassy was then directed by the Department to convey to the Vice Minister an oral statement with regard to the American Government's interest in the situation and its desire to be kept informed of developments, which was done. The Foreign Office was reported to have told the press that the British Government had made no representations with regard to affairs in China but that the Ambassador had inquired as to the situation on his own initiative and had been informed thereof, as well as the American Embassy.†

The local press continued to take a strong stand in connection with the demands on China but this was believed by the Embassy to be due to official inspiration aimed at impressing the Chinese Government with Japan's seriousness, and that the concerted stiffening in tone of the press did not justify the

* Department's telegram No. 127, October 2, 9 P.M.
  Telegram No. 203, October 3, 7 P.M. [*Ibid.*, pp. 245–46.]
  Telegram No. 204, October 4, 1 P.M.
† Department's telegram No. 128, October 4, 2 P.M. [*Ibid.*, p. 246.]
  Telegram No. 206, October 6, 3 P.M.
  Telegram No. 208, October 9, 4 P.M.
  Telegram No. 217, October 22, noon.

assumption that a change in Japan's policy was imminent.* A few days later, however, a somewhat altered tone in the press conveyed the impression that in view of the increasingly unfavorable effect of Chinese tactics upon Japan's position, Japan was approaching the point of preparing to close with China on the best terms obtainable, provided that its minimum conditions were met.† Towards the middle of November the press reported a meeting of representatives of the Foreign, War and Navy Offices to discuss Ambassador Kawagoe's report of his interview with Chang Chun on the 10th and indicated that owing to a sudden hedging of the Chinese Government on points already conceded, the outlook for a satisfactory outcome of the negotiations had now become unfavorable.[18] No decisions, however, appear to have been reached.‡

For nearly a month the Sino-Japanese negotiations appeared to be in eclipse, or at least were overshadowed by the conclusion of the Anti-Comintern Pact between Japan and Germany,[19] but on December 5 the press reported that at a conference on the previous day between the Foreign, Navy and War Ministers it was decided to disrupt for the time being the

* Telegram No. 218, October 23, 1 P.M.
  Department's telegram No. 136, October 24, 2 P.M.
  Telegram No. 219, October 24, 11 A.M.
  Telegram No. 220, October 25, noon.
† Telegram No. 221, October 27, 1 P.M.
  Telegram No. 222, October 28, 1 P.M.
  Telegram No. 224, November 5, 3 P.M.
[18] Eight conferences were held by Ambassador Kawagoe and Chang Chun, Chinese Foreign Minister, in September, 1936, in the course of which the Japanese Ambassador tried to convince the Foreign Minister to accept Hirota's principles. The Chinese nation, however, was so aroused by Japanese activities in China, that the Kuomintang would not have been able to accept Japan's new China policy, even if it had wished to do so. MacNair and Lach, *op. cit.,* p. 422.
‡ Telegram No. 234, November 14, 11 A.M.
[19] The Anti-Comintern Pact was signed on November 25, 1936. It provided for consultation in regard to defense measures, co-operation in the measures taken, and an interchange of information about Communist activities. A secret addendum was added to the effect that the Pact was not only to be considered as directed against the Comintern but was also a political and military treaty aimed against the Soviet Union.

negotiations with China for the general readjustment of Sino-Japanese relations but to present to China a demand in the nature of an ultimatum for the realization of the four points upon which basic agreement was alleged previously to have been reached, namely, (a) opening of air services between Japan and China, (b) reduction of Chinese tariff rates, (c) employment of Japanese advisers by China, and (d) control of anti-Japanese Koreans in China. The press furthermore stated that unless a definite answer were given by Nanking, the Japanese Government would take measures for self-defense. The *Hochi* averred that the abandonment by Japan for the time being of the North China and anti-Communist issues constituted a serious diplomatic defeat for Japan and might cause the Diet in its next session to attack the Hirota Cabinet whose fate would then be uncertain.*

The Japanese landed 800 marines in Tsingtao.† [20]

Failure of the Sino-Japanese negotiations and the loss of face involved were believed by the Embassy to be the underlying cause of the weakening of the Hirota Cabinet.‡

In the middle of December, Sir Robert Clive told me that Mr. Eden had strongly advised the Nanking Government not to overplay its hand, having everything to gain by making such unessential concessions as would save Japan's face. The Japanese Cabinet was in a precarious position owing to the unfavorable reaction to the agreement with Germany, the consequent holding up of the fisheries treaty with Soviet Russia, and the failure of the negotiations with China. Nevertheless if China should prove completely intransigent to all overtures, Japanese

* Telegram No. 252, December 5, 6 P.M.

† Telegram No. 254, December 8, 6 P.M.

[20] In Tsingtao two weeks of labor unrest were climaxed in the decision taken by the Japanese owners of the textile mills there to lockout 23,000 workers. To protect the Japanese owners in their decision, Japanese marines were landed in Tsingtao on the morning of December 2, taking up strategic positions in the city. The textile mills soon resumed full operation, and on December 23, 1936, the last detachment of Japanese marines left the city. *New York Times*, December 3, 1936, p. 15; December 24, 1936, p. 7.

‡ Telegram No. 255, December 9, 9 P.M.

public opinion would tend to become unified and solidified in favor of stronger measures. We were told that Moscow had made similar representations in Nanking. I had a long talk with the Chinese Ambassador, deriving the impression from his manner and from what he said that China was at present "feeling its oats" and was very likely to overplay its hand in resisting the overtures of Japan. We were furthermore informed that the Japanese military had for the present abandoned all hope of separating North China from Nanking. This telegram was drafted prior to the receipt of news of the reported rebellion of Chang Hsueh-liang and his kidnapping of Chiang Kai-shek.* On the 19th I was informed by the British Ambassador of a suggestion by Mr. Eden that civil war in China might be avoided if the Powers could arrange by concerted action for the safe evacuation of Chang Hsueh-liang by air to Tientsin or Shanghai in return for his releasing Chiang Kai-shek. The Department instructed Ambassador Nelson T. Johnson [American Ambassador to China] to discuss with his British colleague any possible means of avoiding tragedy and political complications in connection with the Sian situation, proceeding cautiously in the attempt to save lives.† (Chiang Kai-shek was subsequently released.) 21

* Telegram No. 258, December 14, noon.
† Telegram No. 263, December 19, noon.
  Department's telegram No. 161, December 19, 3 P.M.
  Department's telegram No. 162, December 21, noon.
21 In October, 1935, Chiang Kai-shek made the decision to send troops under command of General Chang Hsueh-liang to Sian in order to blockade the Communist forces of the border area. After General Chang's arrival in Sian he was won over to the idea then widely popular in China of forming a "united front" with the Communists against Japanese aggression. Chang and his troops almost ceased military operations against the Communists in Sian. In December, 1936, Chiang Kai-shek went to Sian in order to see that hostilities against the Communists were renewed by Chang and his troops. On December 12, 1936, some of Chang's men stormed the house where Chiang Kai-shek was staying and took him into custody. After negotiations with the Nanking government the Generalissimo was allowed to return to Nanking on Christmas Day, 1936. It is probable that Chiang Kai-shek promised to give serious consideration to the idea of the "united front," which Chang and his troops supported. MacNair and Lach, op. cit., pp. 408–13.

LONDON NAVAL CONFERENCE
AND SUBSEQUENT NAVAL DEVELOPMENTS

Mr. Norman Davis, chairman of the American delegation to the London Naval Conference, informed the Department that in view of most important developments then taking place, it would be very helpful if I would keep the delegation fully advised of the situation in Japan, especially with regard to conflicting views between the Japanese Navy and the Foreign Office.* 22

The Embassy reported that owing to differences in views between the Navy and the Foreign Office, the situation in Tokyo was as usual shrouded in fog. These differences related not so much to general objectives as to tactics and methods. In demanding parity, the Japanese Navy had the American Navy chiefly in view but it had failed to foresee the complications which this attitude would create in Europe. The Japanese had burned their bridges, and since a reconsideration of the parity issue was now out of the question, we must now expect to see

---

* Department's telegram No. 6, January 11, 4 P.M.

22 About the London Conference Toshikazu Kase has written: "I attended this conference as a member of our delegation. It was led by Admiral Nagano, representing the Navy, and Ambassador Nagai, representing the Foreign Office. Soon after our arrival at London the delegation split into two groups. That led, by Nagano insisted on immediately walking out of the conference. The other, under Nagai, tried to obtain a compromise and to avoid a break. I supported Nagai, but his position became impossible in view of the chauvinism of the public in Japan.

"Frankly speaking, the theory of our proposed 'common upper limit' was rather obscure. At the Palladium, a vaudeville theater in London, a number called 'The Japanese Proposal' was presented. A black curtain slowly descended on the empty stage with the announcement, 'Ladies and Gentlemen, the Japanese proposal!' And when it fell to me to explain the formula of a 'common upper limit' to the foreign press I did not know what to say. But I collected as many cans as possible of the cigarette known as 5-5-5 and had them put out in the press room of our delegation's headquarters. When I was questioned about our proposal, I referred the journalists to the label 5-5-5 on those cans. There was an outburst of laughter. But in spite of the most genial cooperation between our delegation and the press, misunderstanding increased as the conference went on." *Journey to the Missouri*, ed. David Nelson Rowe (New Haven: Yale University Press, 1950), p. 32.

the Foreign Office exploring some alternative of a political nature. We were informed that final instructions to Admiral Nagano [Chairman of the Japanese delegation] in London had been drafted in a six-hour conference between the Navy and the Foreign Office and had been approved by the Cabinet on January 9, and that while the Navy was prepared to break up the Conference by withdrawal, the Foreign Office had been able to secure authority for continuance in order to avoid blame for a complete rupture. The latter, while finally closing the chapter of the parity issue, would like to see some new program involving political agreements set in motion.*

On January 11 Mr. Hirota personally and definitely confirmed to me the fact that he had been successful in his controversy with the Navy over the question of withdrawal from the Conference, and that while Admiral Nagano might return to Tokyo he hoped and expected that Ambassador Matsuzo Nagai [Japanese Ambassador to France and member of the delegation] would remain in London.† The delegation, however, did withdraw, leaving Ambassador Nagai only as an observer. The Japanese press, which usually on such occasions indulges in bitterness and recriminations in unrestrained language, was restrained in its comments, obviously under official inspiration, and there were faint but apparent signs of a growing apprehension as to the possible effect on Japan of a resulting closer Anglo-American understanding, of an increased isolation and of a naval construction race. Somewhat in the manner of whistling in the dark, the press reassured the public that there was little danger of "Britain or the United States challenging us to a naval building contest," basing its opinion largely on the assumption that public opinion in those two countries would not tolerate such a contest in the face of Japan's protestations of "nonmenace and nonaggression." The press also pointed out that the importance of the possible fortification of the present unfortified areas in the Pacific was over-

* Telegram No. 9, January 12, 7 P.M. [*Ibid.*, pp. 290–91.]
  Telegram No. 10, January 13, 6 P.M.
† Telegram No. 11, January 13, 11 P.M.

estimated and actually presented no problem to Japan's national defense.*

In May we reported that the Navy Minister had been quoted in the press as having stated in the Budget Committee of the Diet that he hoped for another naval conference and that a naval treaty satisfactory to all could be concluded in order to avoid the agitation for naval building caused by a no-treaty status. The question of fortifications in the Pacific was also discussed, according to reports, and apprehension was expressed as to the cost that might be incurred if a race should develop in the construction of fortifications and ships. The press also reported proposals by the Japanese Ambassador in London, Mr. Yoshida, for averting an Anglo-Japanese naval race.† In June the Japanese Cabinet approved a recommendation by the Foreign and Navy Ministers to refuse the British invitation to adhere to the London Three-Power Naval Treaty.[23] The press gave two reasons: (1) having withdrawn from the London Naval Conference because its demands for quantitative restriction and offensive arms abolition were rejected, Japan saw no reason now to participate in an agreement reached after its withdrawal; (2) the London Treaty made no quantitative restrictions, was based primarily on a program of exchanging building information, and was therefore of little assistance to Japan.‡

In August the Department informed me that I would soon be consulted by the British Ambassador with regard to an approach to the Japanese Government to ascertain the intentions of the Navy to limit guns to fourteen inches in caliber, it being felt that their refusal to adhere to the treaty necessarily in-

* Telegram No. 14, January 18, noon.
† Telegram No. 106, May 15, noon.
   Department's telegram No. 60, May 20, 6 P.M.
[23] The Naval Treaty signed by France, Great Britain, and the United States in 1936 sought to preserve general naval limitation and prevent naval armament competition. The Treaty provided for restrictions on the size of ships which could be built, limited the caliber of guns, and called for an interchange of information about naval construction plans. Merze Tate, *The United States and Armaments* (Cambridge: Harvard University Press, 1948), pp. 190–91. For specific provisions of the treaty, see *London Naval Treaty of 1936*, pp. 27–45.
‡ Telegram No. 138, June 24, 10 A.M.

THE RISING SUN IN THE PACIFIC

volved a refusal to accept qualitative stipulation concerning gun calibers. Sir Robert Clive discussed this subject with me towards the end of August. We felt that the only practical method of approach would be a point-blank inquiry although it was impossible to foresee whether a frank reply would be given. An indirect approach would be futile. There seemed to be no reason for haste in making the inquiry and I suggested that this might be left until my return from leave of absence in November, on the basis of direct conferences in Washington. We felt that the tremendous outlay already envisaged in the budget would seem to dictate economy, the Vice Navy Minister having said to our Naval Attaché [Harold Bemis] that the Japanese Navy had much to do but very little money to do it with. Nevertheless it was Japan who first adopted the sixteen-inch guns and *amour propre* is a powerful force in this country; there must exist a certain feeling of inferiority from the fact that whereas the United States and Great Britain together had the marked superiority of six ships with sixteen-inch guns, Japan had but two. The Vice Minister of the Navy had further-more said to our Naval Attaché that in view of the unsettled conditions in the world, especially in Europe, Japan could not consider entering any treaty for naval limitation for perhaps another ten years.*

Certain correspondence followed with regard to destroyer, gunboat and submarine tonnage,† and the question of bringing up to date and extending existing fortifications under the Washington Naval Treaty also arose.‡ The sixteen-inch gun

* Department's telegram No. 101, August 1, 3 P.M.
  Telegram No. 172, August 27, 11 A.M.
† Department's telegram No. 105, August 14, 6 P.M.
  Telegram No. 168, August 17, 5 P.M.
  Department's telegram No. 114, September 10, 1 P.M.
  Department's telegram No. 139, November 5, 4 P.M.
  Telegram No. 225, November 6, noon.
  Telegram No. 229, November 9, 5 P.M.
  Department's telegram No. 141, November 9, 6 P.M.
  Department's telegram No. 166, December 30, 2 P.M.
‡ Department's telegram No. 115, September 11, 6 P.M.
  Department's telegram No. 124, September 25, 6 P.M.

issue was further discussed, as well as the Japanese building program.*

On my return from leave of absence in November,[24] Sir Robert Clive said that he had suggested to his Government that an approach concerning the gun caliber question might be delayed until my arrival but that the British Government had felt that the matter should be taken up more promptly and he had then suggested that it be done in London through Ambassador Yoshida. This was done and the latter replied that he thought it unwise to take up the subject diplomatically with Tokyo because an impression of British pressure might thereby be conveyed and he recommended that the subject be discussed by the Admiralty with his Naval Attaché as a purely technical question. I suggested that if the Department approved this method of approach, it would be well to make it through our Naval Attaché who enjoyed friendly relations with the Navy Ministry here. An inquiry as to the situation had in the meantime come from the Department. In reply to my report, the Department said that Sir Robert Craigie in London was dealing directly with Ambassador Yoshida on the basis of a semiofficial assurance by the Japanese that they had no plans for the building of ships carrying guns larger than fourteen inches and that they would inform the British Government before altering such plans. The British requested a tolerant attitude on our part at least until the end of the year, and no action on our part before then was contemplated.†

Later indications were that the Japanese Navy was testing sixteen and even eighteen-inch guns. We discussed with the Department whether and when an approach should be made to inquire as to Japanese intentions.‡ Trial balloons were sent up to the effect that the Foreign Minister was studying the best

* Telegram No. 262, December 18, noon.
[24] Mr. Grew was on a leave of absence in the United States from August 28 until November 27.
† Telegram No. 174, August 29, 1 P.M.
‡ Department's telegram No. 151, December 2, 6 P.M.
  Telegram No. 249, December 3, 4 P.M.
  Department's telegram No. 157, December 10, 7 P.M.

diplomatic means of meeting the treatyless naval situation commencing on January 1, 1937.*

JAPANESE CONTROL OF AUTOMOBILE INDUSTRY

Representations were made by the Counselor of the Embassy, Mr. Neville, to the Vice Minister for Foreign Affairs, Mr. Shigemitsu, in January, with regard to the proposed Japanese law aimed to place the automobile manufacturing industry in Japan under a system of control through the issuance of licenses. Mr. Neville pointed out, in reply to the Vice Minister's observations that the Treaty of 1911 did not provide for rights of manufacture, that irrespective of such rights, assembly and manufacture under present-day practice were incidental to and necessary for the automobile trade and that not only would a limitation of the right to assemble motorcars under the same conditions as applied to Japanese firms seriously interfere with the American automobile trade but it would clearly contravene the terms of our treaty through discrimination.† The Department took the position that the indisputable right to manufacture on terms of complete equality with Japanese subjects was conferred on American citizens by the use of the word "manufactories" in Article I of the Treaty of 1911.‡ 25 The Foreign Office disagreed, on the ground that Article I applied to individuals, and that there would be no discrimination between Japanese subjects and foreigners resident in Japan in the operation of the proposed law. Companies or corporations were regulated by Article VII of the treaty with which the proposed provisions of law would not be inconsistent. The Foreign Office thought the project of law unwise but forces beyond its control were at work, and despite its dislike of the project, the

* Telegram No. 267, December 23, 8 P.M.
  Telegram No. 269, December 25, 1 P.M.

† Telegram No. 6, January 9, 11 A.M.

‡ Department's telegram No. 14, January 31, 11 A.M.

25 See U.S. Department of State, *Papers Relating to the Foreign Relations of the United States, 1911* (Washington: Government Printing Office, 1918), pp. 315–19.

Foreign Office was not in a position to state to other Departments that there was a treaty obligation which would stand in the way of the proposed legislation.* The Automobile Industry Law passed the Diet on May 23.†

IMPORTATION OF JAPANESE COTTON TEXTILES INTO THE UNITED STATES

On May 21 the Department telegraphed that for the past three weeks it had been discussing with the Japanese Embassy in Washington the terms of a proposed "gentlemen's agreement" with regard to imports into the United States of Japanese cotton piece goods, and that although an agreement had been reached as to the general terms of such an agreement, it had not been found possible to dispose of certain technical difficulties. Accordingly the President had on that day issued a proclamation increasing as recommended by the Tariff Commission the rates of duty on certain types of cotton textiles.‡ While this announcement was featured in the news columns of the Japanese press, there was at first very little editorial comment. The Japanese newspapers were occupied with discussion of retaliatory measures contemplated against Australia owing to the wool situation and what comment appeared in regard to the American tariff had none of the acrimonious tinge that characterized the attitude against Australia.§ [26]

Toward the end of the year plans were made for a cotton textile mission to visit Japan in January under Dr. Claudius

---

* Telegram No. 22, February 1, noon.
† Telegram No. 112, May 23, 7 P.M.
  Telegram No. 152, July 10, 5 P.M.
‡ Department's telegram No. 63, May 21, 6 P.M.
§ Telegram No. 113, May 25, 5 P.M.
[26] On May 23, 1936, changes were announced by the Minister in Charge of Trade Treaties in Australian overseas trade policy, and a new tariff schedule was issued by the Minister for Customs. The higher duties penalized Japanese textile exports to Australia. A settlement of the Australian and Japanese trade difficulties was reached on December 27, 1936. M. Epstein (ed.), *The Annual Register . . . 1936* (New Series; London: Longmans, Green & Co., 1937), pp. 141–42.

T. Murchison, President of the American Cotton Textile Institute.*

IMPORTATION OF JAPANESE COTTON TEXTILES
INTO THE PHILIPPINES

Owing to the rigid attitude of the Japanese authorities, the negotiations in Washington with a view to limiting the importation of Japanese cotton textiles into the Philippines, which had resulted in agreement for the purpose of laying the ground-work for a mutually satisfactory settlement of this troublesome question, had become imperiled, and all efforts in Washington to reach a reasonable and mutually satisfactory readjustment of the agreement had been blocked. There was no desire to transfer the general negotiations in this field from Washington to Tokyo and I was not asked to go into details, but the Department wished me to examine the matter with the authorities in Japan in the hope that the position of the Japanese Government in the future negotiations in Washington might become more constructive. This subject was discussed in two telegrams from the Department, one of them seven pages in length.† I took up the matter with the Foreign Minister who said that he was unfamiliar with the situation but that he would instruct Mr. Kurusu, Chief of the Bureau of Commercial Affairs, "to endeavor to conciliate." The Commercial Attaché [Frank S. Williams] and the First Secretary then went into the subject with Mr. Kurusu who made a counter-proposal.‡ The negotiations continued.§ The Department reiterated its desire to retain the main negotiations in Washington but said that in view of the advanced stage of our own negotiations with Mr. Kurusu on the present problem it was considered wise that the details of a final adjustment be

* Department's telegram No. 154, December 5, 3 P.M.
† Department's telegram No. 12, January 29, 6 P.M.
  Department's telegram No. 13, January 30, 6 P.M.
‡ Telegram No. 20, January 31, 8 P.M.
§ Department's telegram No. 15, January 31, 7 P.M.
  Telegram No. 23, February 3, 6 P.M.

arranged in Tokyo.* An arrangement was duly reached, consisting in a voluntary amicable adjustment by the Japanese exporters of cotton textiles, undertaken to meet the wishes of the American side, the Japanese Government most strongly urging that the American and Philippine Governments make every effort to control transshipments from Hong Kong. Such transshipments, it was said, had doubled the difficulties of the Japanese exporters because, in addition to their voluntary curtailment of shipments, they were obliged to meet the price competition of the transshipments from Hong Kong, thereby reducing their profits. The Japanese wished it to be understood that the rayon question had no connection with the cotton agreement.†

JAPANESE PETROLEUM INDUSTRY LAW

Official discussions with regard to the effect on the foreign oil companies of the Japanese Petroleum Industry Law were continued immediately after the New Year holidays, the issue having been further brought to the attention of the Vice Minister for Foreign Affairs on January 7. The Vice Minister said that there was no intention on the part of the Government to deprive the foreign companies of a fair economic return on their enterprise and that he would look into the matter to see what, if anything, could be done. Similar representations were made by the Netherlands Minister at about the same time.‡ The negotiations of representatives of the foreign companies with Mr. Kurusu, Chief of the Commercial Bureau of the Foreign Office, were also continued, the former receiving the impression that the Japanese authorities were sincerely trying to find some solution of the problem which would permit the foreign companies to continue in business in Japan, although any alteration of the stockholding obligation seemed highly

* Department's telegram No. 18, February 7, 6 P.M.
  Telegram No. 25, February 8, 8 P.M.
† Telegram No. 28, February 14, 7 P.M.
‡ Telegram No. 3, January 7, 1 P.M.

unlikely.* Later it was indicated that the law could not be altered and that the six-month storage provision must therefore stand but that there might be negotiated some modification with regard to the maximum quantity of oil to be stored, with a consequent reduction in quotas.†

The oil companies then agreed to explore the possibility of an arrangement under which the companies would undertake to carry fixed maximum quantities of oil, with indemnification and guarantees of future business and provided that Japanese capital would finance the stockholding. The Embassy abstained from participation in the ensuing conference on the ground that participation would imply official sanction of the proposed plan. While the Embassy at all times co-operated, we had never entered directly into the negotiations.‡ Mr. Kurusu expressed pessimism as to the outlook for an agreement.§ The Department authorized the Embassy, without participating in the negotiations, to inform the Japanese Government orally and informally that the oil interests desired to discuss a plan designed to meet the needs of both parties and to express the hope that a solution of the problem mutually satisfactory to all concerned would flow from the contemplated negotiations.|| In March the oil interests entered into negotiations with Mitsui in order to find some solution of their problem.¶

Toward the end of December the negotiations of the oil companies with the Japanese Government, after two years of unremitting effort, had reached an impasse and the Department was approached with a request for diplomatic assistance;

* Telegram No. 12, January 15, 11 A.M.
† Telegram No. 34, February 24, 8 P.M.
  Telegram No. 42, February 27, 4 P.M.
‡ Telegram No. 64, March 9, 5 P.M.
§ Telegram No. 73, March 13, 4 P.M.
|| Department's telegram No. 30, March 10, 2 P.M.
¶ Telegram No. 77, March 20, 8 P.M.
  Department's telegram No. 33, March 20, 6 P.M.
  Telegram No. 78, March 23, 7 P.M.
  Telegram No. 137, June 23, 7 P.M.
  Department's telegram No. 140, November 6, 3 P.M.

the Ministry of Commerce and Industry had failed to confirm in writing its previous oral undertakings in regard to the future security of the foreign oil interests in Japan, discrimination was being practiced, and no good faith shown. Sir Robert Clive and I were in agreement that the time had come for strong diplomatic representations and a request for a categorical statement of the intentions of the Japanese Government. If the Government did not intend to drive the foreign oil interests out of Japan we should ask for the written assurances desired by the companies. I believed the present moment to be psychologically favorable for such a step and recommended that the Acting Secretary should send for Ambassador Saito, as Mr. Eden intended to do with Ambassador Yoshida in London, and to have a frank and forceful talk with him along the lines suggested.* The Department concurred in our view that diplomatic representations should be made but felt that this could better be done in Tokyo, to the Prime Minister, and it doubted the wisdom of "strong representations" in a positive sense at that stage, estimating that such representations would not be effective. The Department envisaged merely an expression of anxiety and a request for a clear indication that the Japanese Government did not intend to drive out the foreign interests and a further request for assurances in writing sought by the foreign companies. It desired that the American and British action be approximately simultaneous and substantially identical in character.† At this time the press reported that the Japanese oil companies were "agitating" against any increase in quotas for the foreign oil companies and expected that the subject would become an issue during the coming session of the Diet. This indicated the situation with which the foreign oil companies were faced in Japan.‡

I discussed the Department's views with Sir Robert Clive who agreed to recommend to his Government that action be taken in Tokyo but we both felt that such action should be

* Telegram No. 259, December 14, 1 P.M.
† Department's telegram No. 160, December 17, 2 P.M.
‡ Telegram No. 261, December 17, 11 A.M.

taken at both ends of the line; former methods here had been ineffective and a new way of approach seemed to be indicated; we doubted the advisability of going to the Prime Minister over the head of the Foreign Minister as such procedure was not understood in Japan, although I might find an opportunity to discuss the matter informally with the Premier later. We felt that our representations should now be delayed until after the New Year holidays.* The local representatives of the oil companies, however, requested that we act at once,† and we proposed to make joint representations to the Foreign Minister on the 24th. Mr. Eden had already talked with Ambassador Yoshida in London. The Department approved of our proposed procedure but explained why it considered circumspection in the tone of our representations to be called for until the foreign companies were prepared to come to a definite decision as to their future action. The proposed action was taken by the British Ambassador and myself; the Minister said that he was unfamiliar with the subject but would study it and would reply as soon as possible; he received my representations and the reading of the *aide-mémoire* in a wholly friendly way. The Foreign Office threw a smoke screen about my representations in order to avoid publicity.‡

SOVIET-JAPANESE RELATIONS

The possibility of the outbreak of a conflict between Japan and Soviet Russia in the spring or summer of 1936 was in February creating a feeling of uneasiness in Soviet circles.§ In reply to this report from the Department, the Embassy sent a long analytical telegram indicating that under present circumstances the influences surrounding the Throne, the For-

* Telegram No. 264, December 19, 6 P.M.
† Telegram No. 265, December 22, 8 P.M.
‡ Telegram No. 266, December 23, 7 P.M.
    Department's telegram No. 164, December 23, 1 P.M.
    Telegram No. 268, December 24, 6 P.M.
    Telegram No. 269, December 25, 1 P.M.
§ Department's telegram No. 17, February 3, 5 P.M.

eign Minister, the majority of the business interests and, probably, the General Staff in Tokyo, would oppose war, although in the event of war in Europe we could not predict the result of the cleavage of opinion among Japanese leaders for and against a war with Russia. The chief danger lay in the risk of some grave border incident which might make it impossible to restrain the opposing armies, and some elements among the military held that Japan must attack this year because the increasing strength of the Soviet defenses rendered it a case of "now or never." * Toward the end of February, with reference to reports from Peiping of the movement of large bodies of Japanese troops to North Manchuria, Japanese army sources indicated that these reports might refer to local maneuvers and that no increase in the army in Manchuria was then contemplated. There were no indications in Tokyo that the Japanese military anticipated major operations in the near future.†

In my initial talk with the new Prime Minister after the reconstruction of the Cabinet following the February 26 Incident, Mr. Hirota said that the Army wished to establish defensive forces in Manchuria more nearly equalling those of Soviet Russia, but that war with Soviet Russia would be stupid because both parties would have everything to lose and nothing to gain, and he added that there would be no war while he was in office.‡

In June we were informed by the Soviet Embassy that in the course of a general discussion between the Prime Minister and the Soviet Ambassador prior to the latter's departure on leave of absence, the Premier had brought up the question of the large number of Soviet troops stationed on or near the Soviet — "Manchukuo" — Korean frontiers. Mr. Youreneff replied that a political rather than a military solution for this question might be found and he recalled the fact that in 1931 the Soviet Government had proposed a pact of nonaggression, but Mr. Hirota shrugged the suggestion aside with the comment

* Telegram No. 24, February 4, 5 P.M.
† Telegram No. 33, February 24, 7 P.M.
‡ Telegram No. 74, March 13, 7 P.M.

"We shall find some other way." The Counselor of the Soviet Embassy [Nicholas Rayvid] said to us that without a non-aggression pact the Soviets would not remove their troops from the frontier, and that in any case, while the troops might be moved farther away, there would be no demolition of border fortifications.* . . .

MR. ARITA BECOMES FOREIGN MINISTER
MR. HORINOUCHI SUCCEEDS
MR. SHIGEMITSU AS VICE MINISTER

Mr. Hachiro Arita, recently Ambassador to China and formerly Vice Minister for Foreign Affairs, was appointed Foreign Minister and took office on April 2.†

Mr. Shigemitsu was succeeded as Vice Minister for Foreign Affairs by Mr. Kensuke Horinouchi on April 10. . . .

SUGGESTED VISIT OF U.S.S. ALDEN TO
JAPANESE MANDATED ISLANDS

In June the Department brought up an interesting suggestion. For several years the Japanese Government had requested permission for the entry of two Japanese public vessels into harbors in the Aleutian Islands and Alaska not usually open to foreign commerce and such permission had been accorded. For some time there had existed an undercurrent of suspicion and speculation with regard to the possibility that the United States and Japan might be conducting harbor developments and fortification of the Pacific possessions of both countries. The American Government had raised no objection to Japanese public vessels visiting the closed harbors in Alaska, believing that such visits would serve to remove any suspicion that we might be carrying out such improvements as would violate the Washington Naval Treaty,[27] and we considered it unfortunate that

---

* Telegram No. 133, June 22, 6 P.M.
† Telegram No. 84, April 4, 11 A.M.
27 Article XIX of the Treaty signed at Washington on February 6, 1922,

Japan had not been similarly compliant in allowing us to visit the Japanese mandated islands and thus to remove such suspicion in the face of allegations that Japan was fortifying those islands in contravention of treaty obligations. As the U.S.S. *Alden* was shortly to proceed to the Asiatic station via Guam, it was felt that an invitation from Japan for her to visit the larger unopened ports of the Japanese mandated islands would have a highly beneficial effect on Japanese-American relations, and after several exchanges of views between the Department and the Embassy, I broached the matter informally and as on my own initiative to the Foreign Minister on July 8. In due course we were informed that the Foreign Office had consulted the Overseas Ministry and that probably other departments would also have to be consulted, but there the matter died and nothing further was heard of it. This, of course, was the Japanese method of politely saying no.*

Assuming that no prospect of favorable action existed, the Department in August informed us that a request from the Japanese Embassy in Washington for permission for the Japanese Government's training ship *Shintoku Maru* to enter a harbor in Hawaii not listed as a port of entry had been refused.†

In this general connection it may be said that a request for

stated that the "United States, the British Empire and Japan agree that the *status quo* at the time of the signing of the present Treaty, with regard to fortifications and naval bases, shall be maintained in their respective territories and possessions specified." *Foreign Relations, 1922*, I, 252–53, includes the list of the territories and possessions covered by this article and a further definition of what was meant by maintenance of the *status quo* in these areas.

* Department's telegram No. 75, June 13, 2 P.M. [*Ibid.*, pp. 307–8.]
Telegram No. 127, June 16, 9 A.M.
Department's telegram No. 79, June 18, 6 P.M.
Telegram No. 130, June 20, 11 A.M.
Department's telegram No. 83, June 25, noon.
Telegram No. 146, July 3, 11 A.M.
Telegram No. 150, July 8, 10 A.M. [*Ibid.*, p. 308.]
Telegram No. 153, July 13, 10 A.M.
Department's telegram No. 94, July 16, 6 P.M.
Telegram No. 163, July 28, 1 P.M. [*Ibid.*, p. 309.]
† Department's telegram No. 102, August 7, 7 P.M. [*Ibid.*]

permission for the United States transport *Gold Star* to visit Truk, Palau, and Saipan was refused by the Japanese Government.* This request was later renewed for a subsequent date, on the assumption that the initial refusal of the Japanese Government had been due to the fact that the dates originally indicated for the visit had been found to be inconvenient, and therefore other dates were proposed. In view of the numerous instances in which the Japanese Government had expressed its willingness for public vessels of the United States to visit any of the open ports of the Mandated Islands . . . the American Government assumed that there could be no objection to the proposed visits.† The Japanese Government replied that for various reasons it was unable to extend the desired permission and in connection with a similar request from the British Government, the British Embassy was informed that such a visit would be inconvenient for some time to come.‡

DIFFICULTIES OF AMERICAN CONSULS IN JAPAN IN OBTAINING COMMERCIAL INFORMATION

Japan's growing policy of industrial and commercial secrecy was becoming noticeable in 1936, and in July I suggested to the Department that on my next visit to the Foreign Minister I should draw his attention to the increasing difficulties placed in the way of our Consuls in obtaining commercial information customary in all countries, a situation which was steadily growing worse. The Minister had recently appealed to the prefectural governors to impose fewer restrictions on foreigners and to grant them greater courtesies and facilities, and I felt that an approach could properly be made on that basis. The Department approved.§

* Telegram No. 177, September 4, 10 A.M.
† Department's telegram No. 121, September 19, 3 P.M.
‡ Department's telegram No. 129, October 12, 5 P.M.
　Telegram No. 210, October 13, 3 P.M.
§ Telegram No. 146, July 3, 11 A.M.
　Department's telegram No. 88, July 6, noon.
　Telegram No. 151, July 8, 11 A.M.

Banning of May Issue of Current History

Having been requested by the Department to ascertain the facts in connection with the suppression in Japan of the May issue of *Current History*, we were informed by the local agent that in nearly every mail some foreign publication was banned and that this had been done in the case of the May number of that periodical. Inquiry indicated that the issue in question contained references to the February 26 Incident and that the action was apparently taken in accordance with law. The censor's office later stated that the issue had been banned owing to an article by Charles Hodges entitled "Japanese Enigma." * ... [28]

Mock Trial of the Japanese Emperor

In September the Japanese Embassy in Washington brought informally to the Department's attention the plans of a radical organization known as "American Friends of the Chinese People" to hold in New York on September 17 a mock trial of the Japanese Emperor for "crimes committed against China" and on September 18 an anti-Japanese demonstration. Neither the Federal nor the Municipal Government felt that it had any basis in law for intervention, and it was further felt that even informal action would not accomplish the desired result and would only be seized upon as a means of obtaining further publicity. The Embassy was authorized to express to the Foreign Office its personal view that it is a matter for regret whenever any incident arises calculated to give offense to a friendly nation. In the meantime every precaution was being taken by the authorities in New York to protect the persons and property of Japanese subjects against any threatened violence which might arise. Mr. Dickover talked with the Vice Minister who

* Department's telegram No. 95, July 16, 7 P.M.
  Telegram No. 157, July 17, 1 P.M.
  Telegram No. 162, July 27, 11 A.M.
  [28] Charles Hodges, "Japanese Enigma," *Current History*, May, 1936, pp. 105–11.

expressed his appreciation of the Department's interest in the matter and hoped that the story would not be cabled to the Japanese press in order to avoid arousing public feeling in Japan. Such action would also defeat the aims of the organization in New York which depended upon publicity for its existence.* . . .[29]

THE ANTI-COMINTERN PACT

In November an important diplomatic project having to do with Germany was being mooted by the Japanese Government and it was said that the matter would be submitted to the Privy Council, suggesting that an agreement requiring Imperial sanction was under consideration. Informed sources believed that any agreement which might be reached would not be in the nature of a military agreement or an alliance but would involve some joint declaration opposed to Communism, in other words, a declaration indicating that Japan was aligning herself with the Fascist nations.† At the same time the Department was informed by the Embassy in Rome that during a visit by Galeazzo Ciano [Italian Minister for Foreign Affairs] to Berlin a project was discussed to establish in Berlin a center for the purpose of combating Bolshevism and that Japan had been invited by Italy to participate.‡ Diplomatic circles in Tokyo understood that the Privy Council gave its formal approval to the German-Japanese agreement on November 16.§ The general terms and purport of the agreement were con-

* Department's telegram No. 119, September 16, 6 P.M.
  Telegram No. 187, September 17, 5 P.M.
  [29] On September 18, 1936, the Japanese Consulate in New York City was picketed by representatives of the American Friends of the Chinese People. *New York Times*, September 19, 1936, p. 6.
  † Telegram No. 231, November 11, 6 P.M.
  Telegram No. 232, November 13, 5 P.M.
  ‡ Department's telegram No. 144, November 13, 6 P.M.
  Telegram No. 235, November 18, noon.
  Department's telegram No. 146, November 19, 6 P.M.
  Telegram No. 236, November 19, 5 P.M.
  § Telegram No. 237, November 20, 5 P.M.

fidentially told to Mr. Dickover by the Vice Minister on November 23.* The text of the Anti-Comintern Pact was given to the Embassy and publicly announced on November 25.†

The Japanese Foreign Office appeared to be surprised at the unfavorable reaction both in Japan and abroad to the agreement with Germany and made every effort to minimize the effect by categorically denying the existence of a military understanding or any intention to participate in a Fascist bloc. Opposition to the agreement was reflected in the Japanese press and in talks with Japanese businessmen, members of the Diet and others who wished to strengthen Japan's relations with the United States and Great Britain and felt that the suspicion engendered by the agreement with Germany had been unfortunate in that respect. Mr. Arita described the agreement to me as in the nature of a police measure envisaging a standing mixed commission in Berlin for the exchange of information. He said that the pact was aimed against no country. In my talk with the Prime Minister, Mr. Hirota significantly said that the more the influence of the Comintern and communistic activities should spread abroad, the closer the relations between Japan and Germany would become. Most of my diplomatic colleagues were convinced that the pact involved a secret military agreement while the Soviet Ambassador went so far as to characterize it as only a façade to cover a secret agreement for concerted action in case of war with the U.S.S.R. He also regarded the pact as aimed at Great Britain and said he was certain that it involved an agreement or understanding for the division between Germany and Japan of various British overseas possessions as well as the Netherlands East Indies in the event of war; it was, in effect, he said, part and parcel of Japan's policy of southward advance and of Germany's need for colonies. Mr. Youreneff told me that indisputable evidence was in the possession of his Government of the existence of a military agreement and he said to Sir Robert Clive that at an

* Telegram No. 238, November 23, 6 P.M.
† Telegram No. 241, November 25, 7 P.M.

opportune moment this evidence might be published.[30] We understood that the negotiations had been conducted in Berlin by the Japanese Military Attaché, Major General Hiroshi Oshima, and that neither the Japanese Foreign Office nor the Japanese Ambassador in Berlin had taken any direct part. Major General Eugen Ott, the German Military Attaché in Tokyo, had just returned from Berlin and was studiously avoiding talks with other Military Attachés here.* . . .

[30] See *supra*, p. 1012, n. 19.

* Telegram No. 251, December 4, 1 P.M.

XXXII

The China Incident *

1937

THE SO-CALLED China Incident, which led to years of hostilities, broke out at the Marco Polo Bridge at Lukouchiao near Peiping on July 8, and here it should be noted that the connotation of the Japanese word for "incident," *Jihen*, is "altered situation," and it therefore has a broader significance than "incident." "Abnormal development" might be a better translation. Much later the English translation of the term was given as "The China Affair." [1]

Our first telegram went out on the afternoon of July 8:

We are informed by the Foreign Office that official Japanese re-

* Since from July 8, 1937, Japan's relations with the United States and other countries became inextricably bound up with the conflict in China, developments are hereinafter dealt with chronologically for ready reference under the above heading except in issues not directly related thereto.

[1] Professors MacNair and Lach have written: "With the outbreak of the 'China Incident' in July, 1937, Japan catapulted headlong into a constantly expanding and an increasingly disastrous war situation. From the beginning, the war in eastern Asia was advertised at home as a national crusade. The first Konoye cabinet concentrated its efforts upon 'spiritual mobilization.' *Kokutai* ('National Polity') and *Kodo* ('Imperial Way') became the catch words of the new Japanese spirit. In general, *Kokutai* and *Kodo* emphasized the close connection between the people and the imperial house. They stressed also the need for loyalty to the line of emperors 'unbroken for ages eternal,' and to the peculiar traditions and beliefs of Nippon. Although *Kodo* was not a new term, the 'imperial way' after 1937 was envisaged as the achievement of world peace and order through Japanese control over the 'backward' peoples of eastern Asia. Even labor organizations and certain radical groups were ultimately convinced of the sacred character of Japan's mission. Although internal dissent existed after 1937, the sceptical were mainly concerned over means rather than ends. Patriotic fervor and sincere conviction about the justice of the 'holy war' ran through all social classes." Harley F. MacNair and Donald F. Lach, *Modern Far Eastern International Relations* (New York: D. Van Nostrand Co., Inc., 1950), pp. 454–55.

ports from Peiping indicate that prospects are favorable for settlement of the brush which took place this morning near Peiping between Japanese and Chinese troops.[2] It was stated at the Foreign Office that "Our military people seem to believe that the firing by the Chinese troops which started the incident was not premeditated." *

On the following day we reported:

A newspaper extra issued early this morning states that according to reports from Peiping received at the War Office, mediation by the Mayor of Tientsin had resulted in an agreement whereby the Japanese forces would be withdrawn north of the Yungting River and the Chinese forces south of that river. However, later press despatches said that there had been a resumption of fighting this morning.

The Assistant Military Attaché of the Embassy, who has just returned from the War Office, was informed that the incident will not necessarily become an issue if the Chinese carry out their share of the agreement. The War Office reports of this morning's fighting indicate that press accounts received here are exaggerated.†

On July 12 the Foreign Office expressed to us optimism as

---

[2] The course of events of the night of July 7, 1937, when fighting broke out between a Japanese force on maneuvers near Wanping and a Chinese garrison in the area, is uncertain. Both sides have issued accounts of the incident. For the Japanese explanation see the "Foreign Office Spokesman's Statement of July 9, 1937, Concerning the Lukowkiao Incident," *Contemporary Japan*, September, 1937, pp. 351–52; the Chinese version of the event is given in H. G. W. Woodhead (ed.), *The China Year Book, 1938* (Shanghai: The North-China Daily News & Herald, Ltd., 1938), p. 353. Harold Quigley has written that of greater importance than the actual sequence of events near the Marco Polo Bridge was "the obvious fact that the Lukouchiao incident was in itself of slight importance and might readily have been settled as a local issue. It was not settled as such because the underlying attitude of the parties was that war was inevitable, while the commanders of the opposing forces on the ground were willing to try conclusions without further delay. . . .

"One cannot overemphasize the real issue revealed by the great concern on both sides — the political control of North China." *Far Eastern War 1937–1941* (Boston: World Peace Foundation, 1942), pp. 67–68.

* Telegram No. 185, July 8, 5 P.M. [*Foreign Relations, Japan: 1931–41*, I, 314–15.]

† Telegram No. 186, July 9, 1 P.M.

to a local settlement of the original clash and of the tense situation which arose from further fighting at Lungwangmiao on the night of July 10. The circumstances were described to us as follows:

> The situation resulting from the original Lukouchiao clash appeared to be clearly settled on the evening of July 9; hence the attacks by the Chinese at Lungwangmiao came as a complete surprise to the Japanese troops who were in the act of withdrawing from the river, and to the authorities in Japan; the situation today seems more hopeful than yesterday when the Japanese Government was considerably concerned; the War Office has decided "in principle" to despatch reinforcements to the Peiping area from Manchuria, Korea and Japan proper; however, these reinforcements will not be sent unless further clashes occur.
>
> The Foreign Office informant states that everything will now depend on whether a local agreement will be reached by the negotiators and respected by the Chinese troops and whether the Chinese military authorities will be able to restrain those elements of the 29th Army in which anti-Japanese feeling has been engendered by the Blue Shirts.[3] The informant stated further that the development which had caused most concern to his Government was the report that four divisions of the Chinese Army had been ordered by the Nanking Government to mobilize and to move northward; that the movement of these divisions and the flight of Chinese airplanes northward had been confirmed; that in the Foreign Office's belief the Chinese reinforcements from the south would not be moved into Hopei Province as long as any hope remained for a local settlement of the recent clashes.[*]

The same day, July 12, the Vice Minister for Foreign Affairs confirmed to us the news that an agreement providing for the withdrawal of Chinese and Japanese troops from the Yungting River had been signed by the local negotiators on the 11th, and he added that the higher officers of the Chinese 29th Army

[3] The "Blue Shirts" were the secret police of the Kuomintang.
[*] Telegram No. 189, July 12, noon.

would probably do their best to carry out the agreement, but he expressed doubt as to whether they would be able to control certain elements among the troops. Mr. Kuramatsu Kishi, private secretary to the Foreign Minister, stated that the clashes which occurred during the night of July 10 had resulted partly from the fact that both the Chinese and the Japanese soldiers had been ignorant of the exact terms of the oral agreements reached. He expressed the belief that now that the withdrawal agreement was in writing, there would be less likelihood of future clashes.* The same evening we were informed by the Foreign Office that further fighting had occurred that morning near Peiping. Although no casualties were said to have occurred among the Japanese forces during the latest engagement, the Foreign Office emphasized that the initiative in this case also had been taken by the Chinese, and that as the Chinese had breached the written agreement of settlement as well as the oral settlement, the Japanese military authorities were taking a serious view of the situation. Thus far I had refrained from making inquiries in person at the Foreign Office because it seemed wise to avoid giving the Japanese press occasion for misinterpreting the purpose of my visit. The Emperor that afternoon interrupted his summer stay at the seashore and returned to Tokyo. All efforts by the Military Attaché to interview liaison officers and others at the War Office had failed on the excuse that they were too busy.†

On July 13 I submitted the following analysis of the Japanese attitude with regard to China then obtaining. The unanimity of opinion was striking and there was no indication that this was a case of unwilling deference on the part of the Government to the initiative of the military. The Cabinet, which enjoyed high prestige, was wholly in command, and the steps recently taken by the Japanese Army in China had its full support. The press gave every indication of spontaneity in publishing wide expressions of approval of the stand of the Government on the incident of the Marco Polo Bridge.

* Telegram No. 190, July 12, 7 P.M. [Ibid., pp. 315–16.]
† Telegram No. 191, July 12, 8 P.M.

The Embassy had no intimation that a difference of views prevailed in the Foreign Office. The Government had taken
the precaution of ensuring the co-operation of leaders in the
Diet, the political parties, the press and in banking and business circles, and was gathering its forces to make effective
whatever decision might be reached, the preparation for such
further use of force in North China as might become necessary
being extensive and well co-ordinated. At no time during my
service in Japan had I observed indications of so strong and
unanimous a determination on the part of the Japanese Government to maintain Japan's position in North China even
if extensive hostilities should become necessary. Nevertheless
I believed it to be not impossible that the Government might
still be glad to find some way of avoiding general combat without loss of face, and I felt that we were not yet in possession
of sufficient evidence to justify the hypothesis that the incident
had been brought about either by the Japanese Government
or the Army in order to force a "showdown" in China.*

On the same day, conflicting reports as to further fighting
reached us, the Foreign Office announcing that there had been
a collision between two Chinese detachments on the west bank
of the Yungting River, each detachment supposing that the
other was Japanese. The Japanese Government still regarded
the incident as a local matter for negotiation with the Hopei-
Chahar Council but, according to the Foreign Office, the
Chinese Government had taken cognizance of the incident by
publicly denying the validity of the written agreement of settlement effected by the Japanese military authorities with the
Hopei-Chahar Council,[4] on the ground that such agreement

* Telegram No. 192, July 13, 5 P.M. [*Ibid.*, pp. 319–20.]

[4] Discussions between Japanese military leaders and Chinese authorities began
shortly after the occurrence of the incident at the Marco Polo Bridge. On
July 10 the Japanese presented terms to Peiping, and the following day an
official release from Nanking stated that an agreement had been reached. According to statements issued by the Japanese their terms, which included demands for an apology for the Lukouchiao Incident, for punishment of the
officers involved, for Chinese withdrawal from the area, and for suppression of
Communism and anti-Japanese movements, were all accepted by the Chinese.

could be effected only with the approval of the Chinese Government which had ordered a large body of troops to move toward the Peiping area. The unexpected return to Tokyo on July 12 of the Emperor, a meeting of the Imperial Princes and other similar recent events had been given prominent publicity and, in our opinion, had been arranged largely in the way of pageantry to encourage support by the Japanese people of the position taken by the Japanese Government, although there was little evidence that such encouragement was needed. On the other hand, there had been a conspicuous absence of the usual newspaper extras, tending to strengthen the impression that the Government was not striving to create an emotional condition which would prejudice the possibility of a settlement with the Chinese. Preparations were, however, being made to send additional troops to the scene of hostilities if and when required.*

On July 13 the British Chargé d'Affaires, Mr. James Dodds, told me that Mr. Eden had asked our Ambassador in London, Mr. Robert Bingham, whether the American Government would favorably consider combined Anglo-American démarche in Tokyo and Nanking. Mr. Dodds thought that the Japanese Government might still welcome some way of avoiding war if they could get out of it without loss of face, but he believed that Tokyo would resent any direct representations. A simul-

The Chinese, however, described the July 11 agreement as providing only for an ending of hostilities and a Chinese withdrawal from the area.

On July 12 General Sung Cheh-yuan, Chairman of the Hopei-Chahar Political Council, returned to Tientsin, and the Japanese tried to gain his support in carrying out the July 11 agreement. On July 18 General Sung met the Japanese Commander in Chief, General Katsuki, and Sung was said to have "virtually assented" to carrying out the provisions of July 11. The terms of the Sung-Katsuki agreement were approved by the Hopei-Chahar Council, and on July 22 were sent to Nanking where they were confirmed on July 24. Nanking considered that its approval of agreements reached between the Japanese and Chinese local authorities was necessary, and as early as July 12 Nanking had notified the Japanese that they would not accept the validity of such local agreements unless approved by the Central Government. Arnold J. Toynbee, *Survey of International Affairs, 1937* (London: Oxford University Press, 1938), I, 184–86.

* Telegram No. 193, July 13, 6 P.M.

taneous inquiry on the part of the British Government in both
Tokyo and Nanking as to whether it could in any way be of
help in the present contingency, however, might do no harm.
I saw no reason why the American Government should take
action.*

On the morning of July 12 the Japanese Ambassador in
Washington, at his own request, called on Mr. Hull and read
to him a statement concerning the outbreak of hostilities with
China. Mr. Hull, in reply, expressed his deep regret at the
incident, urged Japanese self-restraint and emphasized his approval of the statements, read by the Ambassador, to the effect
that Japan was doing its best to bring about a prompt settlement. The Secretary expressed the earnest hope that Japan,
through military operations, would not lose the opportunity
of materially contributing to the restoration of world peace
and stability, and he added that the preservation of peace in
every quarter of the world was of great interest to the American Government. The Chinese Chargé d'Affaires in Washington, who asked Mr. Hornbeck's advice, was told that the American Government could not advise, but the hope was expressed
that effective restraint would be exercised by both sides. An
official statement was issued by the Department expressing
the view that an armed conflict between China and Japan
would be a great blow to the cause of peace and world progress.
In reply to an inquiry from the British Government as to our
views and suggestions, Mr. Eden was told of the foregoing
steps and he expressed to the Japanese Ambassador in London
the concern of the British Government, while the French Government was reported to have expressed similar concern
through its representatives in both China and Japan.†

On July 14 I cabled to the State Department that the usual
battle of war propaganda had begun and was being intensively
organized; the daily radio broadcasts from Japan were to be
devoted entirely to news instead of entertainments. The Japanese boasted that their new short-wave equipment, the strong-

* Telegram No. 196, July 13, 9 P.M.
† Department's telegram No. 112, July 13, 2 P.M.

est in the Far East, would be used "in order to offset the Nanking absurdities" and in reply to Nanking's action in broadcasting "fabricated news throughout the world." *

Meanwhile the Chinese Government had asked the good offices of the American, British, French and Soviet Governments in connection with the hostilities. The French Government was agreeable in principle to urging moderation; the British Government, greatly disturbed at the news of Japanese troop movements and with the fear that a clash on a large scale might result if the situation should get out of hand, was prepared to urge restraint both in Tokyo and Nanking but believed that mediation could not usefully be attempted unless desired by both sides; the American Government in further conversations with the Chinese and Japanese representatives in Washington had urged at length the importance of preserving peace, and believed that co-operation with the British Government on parallel but independent lines would be preferable to joint or identical representations which might have an effect the reverse of that desired. An exchange of views and information between the American and British Governments was regarded as important. Resulting from the foregoing exchange of opinions, the British Government instructed its representatives in Nanking and Tokyo to urge restraint upon the Chinese and Japanese Governments, but the British representatives were to act independently and not jointly with the representatives of other countries.†

At this time the British Chargé d'Affaires in Tokyo, Mr. Dodds, who, incidentally, showed a spirit of close and helpful co-operation with me during the period of his chargéship, conveyed to his Government a recommendation that in certain eventualities he be directed to approach the Foreign Minister, Mr. Hirota, and to point out that if Japan should turn North China into a second Manchukuo, an improvement in Anglo-Japanese relations, so earnestly desired by the Minister, could not be expected to materialize. Mr. Eden, the British Foreign Secretary, approved the recommendation and instructed Mr.

* Telegram No. 197, July 14, 10 A.M.
† Department's telegram No. 115, July 14, 7 P.M.

Dodds to take this action without delay, but it appeared that the British Foreign Office had entirely overlooked the phrase "in certain eventualities" by which Mr. Dodds had intended to convey the meaning "as a last resort," and he therefore strongly advised against the action at that moment which, in his opinion, would produce no favorable results and would merely anger the Japanese Government. In the meantime a warning had been conveyed by Mr. Eden to Ambassador Yoshida in London that the expected Anglo-Japanese negotiations in London could not be expected to materialize if Japan should send further troops into China.

It was believed by foreign press correspondents in Tokyo that any offer of foreign mediation would be rejected by the Japanese Government on the ground that the China Incident was a matter for settlement by Japan and China directly and without foreign intervention. We set forth various reasons why, in the Embassy's opinion, the American Government should refrain from any offer of good offices at that time, pointing out especially the fact that the improvement in American-Japanese relations, which at that time had become better than they had been for a long while, had been made possible when the emphasis on American action in matters affecting Sino-Japanese relations had been transferred from (a) an endeavor to restrain Japan from the use of force to (b) the laying down of reservations respecting American rights in China. If organized hostilities in China should occur, we felt it advisable to continue the course which had been followed by the American Government during the past four years and to resort to protests against Japanese military action only when such protests could be made without aggravating the situation, or in case of the molestation of American citizens or property, or when an expression of American official opinion should be called for from humanitarian considerations. At that moment we felt that the situation had not sufficiently developed to justify recommendations for any other action which might helpfully be taken by the American Government.*

At this time the Military Attaché was informed by the Japa-

* Telegram No. 199, July 14, 5 P.M.

nese War Office that there was no intention of setting up any "independent country" in North China, and that the incident could be settled by faithful Chinese execution of the agreement already said to have been accepted by the Chinese 29th Army. A feeling of optimism was expressed by the Foreign Office, the prospects being thought favorable for the liquidation of the situation on the basis of the local agreement provisionally reached, and said to have been later repudiated by the Chinese. It was stated that future developments would depend on (a) whether the Blue Shirts would incite the 29th Army to further anti-Japanese activities, and (b) whether the Nanking Government would send troops north of Paoting, Hopei Province, in contravention of the Ho-Umezu Agreement of 1935.[5] It was emphatically stated that Japan would not allow Nanking Government troops to proceed north of that point.[*]

On the following day the Foreign Office informed us that negotiations at Peiping and Tientsin were in progress between the Japanese military and local Chinese authorities, but that it would still be premature to anticipate the character of the outcome of such negotiations. However, it was said that the release by the Chinese of several captured Japanese policemen and gendarmes had contributed something toward relieving the tenseness of the situation. In response to a question as to the basis of the negotiations, the Foreign Office informant stated that the only basis of discussion was the agreement of settlement said to have been signed by representatives of the Chinese local authorities and delivered to the Japanese on July 11.[6] He said further that if a settlement of the present disturbed situation could be reached, it might be possible that the Japanese Government would propose negotiations looking

[5] On July 6, 1935, General Ho Ying-chin, Chinese War Minister, accepted in writing the nine demands which had been submitted to him on June 9 by Lieutenant General Yoshijiro Umezu, commander of the Japanese garrison forces. See T. A. Bisson, *Japan in China* (New York: The Macmillan Co., 1938), pp. 54–57, for a discussion and the text of the agreement.

[*] Telegram No. 200, July 14, 6 P.M. [*Ibid.*, pp. 322–23.]

[6] *Supra*, p. 1039, n. 4.

toward a more permanent stabilization of conditions in North China, on which occasion it was not unlikely that economic matters would be discussed. He emphasized that the negotiations then in progress were designed to find a settlement of the military situation only.* . . .

The Foreign Office informant furthermore stated that Communist agitators were active in disseminating misinformation with regard to the concentration of both Chinese and Japanese troops, press accounts of large bodies of Chinese troops proceeding toward the north being greatly exaggerated while the reports current abroad of large Japanese troop movements were without valid foundation. He added that thus far no troops of the Chinese Central Government had proceeded north of the line laid down in the Ho-Umezu Agreement. Once again, the information furnished us by the Foreign Office was identical with that supplied the Military Attaché by the War Office.†

On the evening of July 15 it was announced in Tokyo that the Cabinet had decided to despatch to North China reinforcement of an undisclosed number of troops.‡

In the meantime Mr. Dodds, the British Chargé d'Affaires, came to the conclusion that in the light of his instructions he should see the Minister for Foreign Affairs and he therefore called on Mr. Hirota on the 14th, confining himself to a repetition of what Mr. Eden had said to Ambassador Yoshida in London to the effect that the present moment was not opportune for commencing conversations looking to an improvement in Anglo-Japanese relations. Mr. Hirota called Mr. Dodds' attention to the absence of propaganda in Japan. Mr. Dodds replied that he had already reported this fact to his Government.

On the 15th the British representatives in Tokyo and Nanking were instructed to counsel moderation on both sides. Mr. Dodds did not "counsel moderation" on the Japanese Government but he saw Mr. Horinouchi, the Vice Minister, and

* Telegram No. 201, July 15, 9 P.M. [*Ibid.,* p. 323.]
† Telegram No. 201, July 15, 9 P.M.
‡ Telegram No. 202, July 15, 10 P.M. [*Ibid.,* p. 324.]

said that the British Government was using such influence as it might possess at Nanking to persuade the Chinese Government to refrain from action which might complicate the situation in North China. If at any time, he added, the Japanese Government might care to make suggestions for British assistance in negotiations for a settlement, the British Government would be glad to consider such suggestions.

At the same time the French Ambassador in Tokyo [Charles Arsène-Henry] was authorized by his Government to make representations to the Japanese Government similar to such representations as might be made by his American and British colleagues, but the Ambassador was strongly opposed to any such step and decided for the moment to ignore his instructions, believing that the Japanese were anxious to avoid war and that they had neither premeditated nor begun the hostilities.*

On the 16th Mr. Yoshizawa, Chief of the American Bureau of the Foreign Office, gave to Mr. Dooman the following personal and unofficial appraisal of the situation.

1. The agreement signed and given to the Japanese on July 11 had not as yet been disavowed by either the Hopei-Chahar authorities or the 29th Chinese Army, and while the carrying out of the terms of the agreement would take some time, the 29th Army had taken no overt action which might suggest that the agreement was to be disavowed.

2. Nevertheless the decision of the Japanese Government on the 15th to send reinforcements to ensure the safety of the Japanese forces in the Peiping area had been taken as a direct result of the steady development of Chinese plans to mobilize and to concentrate their forces in North China.

3. Two separate issues had developed out of the incident of the Marco Polo Bridge: (a) settlement of the hostilities between Japanese forces and the Chinese 29th Army, and (b) the question as to whether the Chinese would abide by the terms of the Ho-Umezu Agreement. The 29th Army, Mr.

---

* Telegram No. 203, July 15, 11 P.M.

Yoshizawa said, was composed of conflicting elements but he believed that the peace faction was in the ascendancy.

4. Three possible developments might occur if the Chinese forces should cross the Ho-Umezu line: (a) with the friendly co-operation or even with the possible support of the Chinese 29th Army the Japanese forces might move against the Central Chinese forces; (b) such a movement might take place with the 29th Army remaining neutral; (c) the Japanese forces might have to deal with both the 29th Army and the Central forces at the same time. Of these possibilities Mr. Yoshizawa thought that (b) was the most probable.

At that time an officer of the War Office expressed the opinion that there was a 50-50 chance of a peaceful settlement. He emphasized the fact that no economic or political questions were involved in the agreement of July 11. In the meantime there were ample indications that the Japanese were preparing to use the force necessary to compel execution of that agreement if not carried out voluntarily.*

At press conference on the 16th the Secretary of State made the following statement:

I have been receiving from many sources inquiries and suggestions arising out of disturbed situation in various parts of the world.

Unquestionably there are in a number of regions tensions and strains which on their face involve only countries that are near neighbors but which in ultimate analysis are of inevitable concern to the whole world. Any situation in which armed hostilities are in progress or are threatened is a situation wherein rights and interests of all nations either are or may be seriously affected. There can be no serious hostilities anywhere in the world which will not one way or another affect interests or rights or obligations of this country. I therefore feel warranted in making — in fact, I feel it a duty to make — a statement of this Government's position in regard to international problems and situations with respect to which this country feels deep concern.

This country constantly and consistently advocates mainte-

* Telegram No. 205, July 16, 6 P.M. [*Ibid.*, pp. 324–25.]

nance of peace. We advocate national and international self-restraint. We advocate abstinence by all nations from use of force in pursuit of policy and further interference in the internal affairs of other nations. We advocate adjustment of problems in international relations by processes of peaceful negotiation and agreement. We advocate faithful observance of international agreements. Upholding the principle of the sanctity of treaties, we believe in modification of provisions of treaties, when need therefor arises, by orderly processes carried out in a spirit of mutual helpfulness and accommodation. We believe in respect by all nations for the rights of others and performance by all nations of established obligations. We stand for revitalizing and strengthening of international law. We advocate steps toward promotion of economic security and stability the world over. We advocate lowering or removing of excessive barriers in international trade. We seek effective equality of commercial opportunity and we urge upon all nations application of the principle of equality of treatment. We believe in limitation and reduction of armament. Realizing the necessity for maintaining armed forces adequate for national security, we are prepared to reduce or to increase our own armed forces in proportion to reductions or increases made by other countries. We avoid entering into alliances or entangling commitments but we believe in co-operative effort by peaceful and practicable means in support of the principles hereinbefore stated.* [7]

The Japanese press carried an extensive summary of the Secretary's foregoing statement, based on a Domei report, and the *Japan Advertiser* printed the statement *in toto*. No com-

* Department's telegram No. 116, July 16, 7 P.M. [*Ibid.*, pp. 325-26.]

[7] Of this statement Mr. Grew wrote in his diary on July 17: "Mr. Hull has made an admirable public statement in Washington: It is perfectly balanced; it accuses nobody; mentions no names, but it leaves no doubt as to our policy towards the maintenance of peace, the sanctity of treaties and the orderly modification thereof, respect for international law, American economic policy, disarmament and co-operation without entangling alliances. Whether it helps the situation or not, it is a great deal wiser than direct representations which not only would not help but would harm by engendering irritation. The Japanese won't like it because they will know it is directed at them, but the form of the statement absolutely precludes their taking umbrage."

ment by Japanese officials or by the press had come to the attention of the Embassy up to the 19th, except an editorial in the *Nichi Nichi* on July 18, incidentally citing the Secretary's statement, asserting that Japanese rights in the present North China incident rested solely on the Boxer treaty and that Japan was persistently refusing to aggravate the incident, and advising the Japanese Government to continue on its course. A press ban dated July 14 forbade the publication of any item calculated to oppose war or to give the impression that Japanese policy was aggressive.

In view of the announcement of the commencement of troop movements from Japan to China, and also in view of the Vice Minister's favorable reaction to his representations on the 15th, the British Chargé d'Affaires again called on Mr. Horinouchi on the 16th and made to him the following oral statement:

> The Japanese Government must of course be the judge of what measures are necessary for the security of their troops in North China. It is hoped that the representations being made at Nanking by His Majesty's Ambassador will succeed in persuading the Chinese Government to take no action which might make the situation more difficult. The Chinese may, however, be unwilling to listen to his representations if they are able to show that large reinforcements are being sent to the Japanese garrison in North China.
>
> The sole object of His Majesty's Government is to do all they can to ensure the maintenance of peace between the two Powers with which Great Britain is always anxious to remain on the· best terms.

Mr. Dodds, without instructions from his Government, thereupon orally communicated to the Vice Minister the contents of a telegram from the British Ambassador in Nanking which had been received just as the former was leaving for the Foreign Office. The substance of this highly important message follows:

> Chiang Kai-shek, with whom the Foreign Minister at Nanking has been in direct touch, states that he has no intention what-

ever of commencing hostilities, and he has stated in the most categorical terms that all movements of Chinese troops have been solely for self-defense and have occurred as a result of troop movements by Japan.

If similar action is taken by the Japanese Government, *the Chinese Government is ready to cease all troop movements in the affected area and to withdraw its troops to their position prior to the outbreak of the incident.*

The Chinese Minister for Foreign Affairs attaches the utmost importance to avoidance of aggravating the situation, and *he proposes,* as a preliminary measure, *that on July 17 all movements of troops on both sides shall cease.* (Underlining by J. C. G.)

Thereafter, arrangements could be made to restore the previous positions.

This would constitute a Gentlemen's Agreement under which no attempt would be made to take advantage of this intervening period, and the proposal would be conditional on the understanding that neither side should in the meantime attempt to occupy strategically important positions.

After having communicated the foregoing proposal, Mr. Dodds inquired as to Mr. Horinouchi's reaction, but no comment was made by the Vice Minister, nor did Mr. Horinouchi comment when Mr. Dodds pointed out the seriousness of the situation, the fact that in order to prevent hostilities time was a vital factor, and that this was a moment for control to be exerted by the statesmen, not the soldiers.

This very important communication, which was never acted upon, should not be overlooked in history, for had the Japanese desired to avoid the spread of hostilities a clear opportunity to do so was here presented. Mr. Dodds, in view of the importance of the time factor, courageously acted without instructions from his Government. He was somewhat apprehensive lest his action meet with disapproval in London as bordering on mediation, but he had consulted me before acting and I had expressed the personal view that he could not well assume the heavy responsibility of failing to act. Subsequently the

British Government approved of his action and, in fact, in the meantime had instructed him to take precisely the action which he did take. He, however, passed a somewhat anxious three days.

Mr. Dodds was informed by the French Ambassador that unless categorically directed by his Government to do so, he was still determined to take no step.*

From the Embassy's records it is not clear whether the British Government, in approving the action of Mr. Dodds set forth above, had altered its views or whether it had merely decided that Mr. Dodds' action was not of a mediatory character. In any event, the British Foreign Minister informed the British Ambassador in Nanking, in reply to his telegram communicating the message of the Chinese Minister for Foreign Affairs, that unless requested by both sides the British Government desired to abstain from offering mediation, and the view was expressed that since Chinese diplomatic channels were still open, the proposal of the Chinese Foreign Minister for a cessation of all troop movements on July 17 could appropriately be communicated to the Japanese Government direct.†

On the 17th we reported that at a conference which the Prime Minister had held the previous night with the War and Navy Ministers, continued on the following day with the added presence of the Foreign and Finance Ministers, it was decided that direct negotiations should be opened with the Chinese Central Government for which purpose Ambassador Kawagoe had been directed to proceed immediately to Nanking.‡

On the following day, July 18, the Vice Minister for Foreign Affairs told the British Chargé d'Affaires, who had gone to see him for further conversation, that Japanese troops had gone forward to China only from Manchuria and Korea; that every effort was being made by the Japanese to hasten a local settlement; that the Japanese terms for settlement included

* Telegram No. 206, July 16, 7 P.M.
† Telegram No. 207, July 17, 3 P.M.
‡ Telegram No. 208, July 17, 7 P.M.

no political demands; that Mr. Horinouchi could give assurances that the military would not demand more than the Government in Tokyo authorized, and that in general the situation looked brighter.

With regard to the proposal for a cessation of all troop movements, which Mr. Dodds had communicated on July 16, the Vice Minister said that the Japanese Government was not prepared to act as this was a matter for consideration by the local authorities. Mr. Horinouchi added that this proposal had been received from no other source. (Once again, history should take note of the importance of this reply.)

In the same conversation the Vice Minister asked Mr. Dodds "what the British Government had asked other governments to do and what they had replied." Mr. Dodds answered that no approach had been made to the French or Soviet or any other government except the United States, and that the American Government, when it was suggested that the American representatives in Nanking and Tokyo should co-operate with the British representatives along the lines of Mr. Dodds' various talks with Mr. Horinouchi, had not seen fit to act accordingly.

In the meantime the British Ambassador in Nanking had learned from Mr. W. H. Donald [Australian Adviser to the Chiangs] that General Chiang Kai-shek was planning to issue a proclamation calling for general resistance against Japan and that the British Ambassador was strongly urging against such a course. The Ambassador had informed Mr. Dodds that an early local settlement was most desirable because the Generalissimo would be eliminated from the picture if he failed to resist the Japanese demands.

Mr. Eden, said Mr. Dodds, was being pressed to announce that the proposed Anglo-Japanese conversations had been definitely cancelled and was planning to make another statement to the House of Commons.

On the 19th the German Counselor of Embassy [Dr. W. Noebel] asked Mr. Dodds what steps he had taken in Tokyo but the latter declined to reply.*

* Telegram No. 209, July 19, 4 P.M.

On the 19th we were informed by Mr. Yoshizawa of the Foreign Office that the Chinese 29th Army had not proposed to the Japanese military any alteration in the terms of the so-called agreement of July 11 and that General Sung Cheh-yuan, as the ranking officer of the 29th Army, had tendered an apology to the Japanese commander in fulfillment of one of the terms of that agreement. He also stated that the Japanese were on the alert to see whether the other terms would be carried out, but that complete fulfillment would necessarily take some time. It was his estimate that prospects were favorable for a peaceful settlement of the "local situation" in the Peiping area, but he stressed that the Japanese military would not consider the situation to have been liquidated until the 29th Army had completely fulfilled the terms of the above-mentioned agreement. He had no comment to make with regard to the Japanese representations at Nanking.

The Naval Attaché was informed at the Navy Department that thus far no troop reinforcements had been sent to North China from Japan proper, but that beginning on the 19th two vessels would leave Japan daily, one to Fusan and one to Taku, carrying ammunition supply units; that no landing force had been sent to China to reinforce the landing force already there; and that no vessels had been sent to reinforce the China squadron.

The Military Attaché called at the War Office and he also was informed that no reinforcements had been sent as yet from Japan to North China. The liaison officer in the War Office stated that no accurate information was available with regard to the size of the Chinese forces south of Paoting and north of the Lunghai railway, but it was believed that such units did not exceed five divisions, and that the main forces of the Nanking Government were still well south of that railway. The Military Attaché received the definite impression that the War Office did not believe that the movement of Chinese troops toward the Peiping area had sufficiently progressed to constitute an imminent threat to the safety of the Japanese troops in North China.*

* Telegram No. 211, July 19, 6 P.M.

The Chinese reply to the Japanese representations at Nan-king was sensationally displayed in the Japanese papers on the 20th.[8] The only editorial comment on the reply was that of the *Nichi Nichi* which contended that the reply left Japan no choice but "to cross the Rubicon." Other editorial opinion was obviously written before the reply was received here and agreed that a serious state of affairs would arise if the Chinese reply were unsatisfactory.

A statement issued to the papers late on the 19th by the Foreign Office charged the Chinese Government with seeking to befog the issue, which the Japanese contended was only whether or not the Chinese Government would continue to obstruct implementation of the local agreement reached by the Japanese on July 11 with the Hopei-Chahar authorities. The Japanese authorities in China were reported to have expressed strong dissatisfaction over the reply.

At the War Office on the 20th for the first time pessimism was expressed to the Military Attaché over the situation, this sentiment having been created by the character of the Chinese response. We learned at the Foreign Office that the Chinese reply was regarded as not responsive to the Japanese representations, so much so that the Japanese Counselor at Nanking [Shinrokuro Hidaka] had arranged to have a further interview with the Chinese Minister for Foreign Affairs [Wang Chung-hui] to obtain clarification of several of the points stressed by the Chinese note. Our informant at the Foreign Office stated that, although final opinion with regard to the Chinese note would have to await reports of this interview, the note was believed to be reflective of a desire by the Chinese

8 On July 19 a "last warning" from Tokyo had been delivered to the Chinese Minister of War, in which the Japanese stated that action would be taken to meet the appearance of Chinese troops or airplanes in Hopei. Nanking replied to the effect that "the arrival of Japanese reinforcements in North China necessitated measures of self-defence, but that China desired to avoid any aggravation of the situation; it was proposed that a date should be fixed for the cessation of military movements on both sides and for the withdrawal of forces to the positions occupied before the 8th July, and it was suggested that the two Governments should immediately enter into negotiations for a settlement through regular diplomatic channels." Toynbee, *op. cit.*, I, 186.

Government to avoid termination of discussions between the two governments.

The Foreign Office informant stated that one development on the 19th which might influence future developments adversely was the fact that the Ho-Umezu line had been crossed by several Chinese contingents. The situation in North China, however, was holding out greater prospects of favorable settlement, by reason of the fact that in further fulfillment of the reported July 11 agreement, Chinese troops were being withdrawn from Peiping. If it were not for the fact that the 37th Division were getting out of hand it could be said that the situation in the Pciping area was developing satisfactorily.

Other than military action, the alternatives open to Japan seemed to be to renew the discussions at Nanking or to allow matters to drift until there was introduced into the situatioṇ some factor which could not be foreseen. It was apparent that no responsible expression of opinion with regard to the future attitude or action of the Japanese Government could be obtained.

The foreign editor of an important Japanese paper stated to a member of my staff that, notwithstanding sensational treatment by the Japanese press of the Chinese note, editorial boards were privately of the opinion that the Chinese Government did not intend its reply to be construed as final rejection of Japanese representations. He regarded General Chiang's proclamation issued on the 19th [9] as intended principally for

[9] In a statement made on July 19 at Kuling the Generalissimo had discussed the Lukouchiao incident and the evidence that the Japanese were using it as a pretext to gain control in North China. "If," he said, "we allow Lukouchiao to be occupied by others by force then the result will be that Peiping . . . would then become a second Mukden. . . . If Peiping could become a second Mukden what is there to prevent Nanking from becoming a second Peiping? . . .

"If we allow one more inch of our territory to be lost or sovereign rights to be encroached upon, then we shall be guilty of committing an unpardonable crime against our Chinese race. . . .

"The following four points clearly show what is our stand in the issue:

"First, any kind of settlement must not infringe the territorial integrity or sovereign rights of China.

"Second, the status of the Hopei-Chahar Council was fixed by the central government and we will not allow any illegal alteration.

Chinese consumption, and that, while firm in tone, it was so drafted as to be capable of interpretation by Japan as a conciliatory statement.

In appraising the chances of a general war I felt that we should bear in mind the fact that the Chinese had proposed a settlement by diplomatic negotiation and had offered the Japanese an armistice and there could be no doubt that if the Japanese Government could accept that proposal its case before the world would be improved. On the other hand such acceptance would be hard to reconcile with the Government's previous contention that the matter was purely a local issue.

We had to remember also that the possibility of action by the Soviets in case of war could hardly be ignored in the calculations of the Japanese Government, and a report that Soviet forces had again attacked on the Manchurian frontier had brought another factor into the picture.*

At the termination of an emergency meeting of the Cabinet on the night of July 20, its third meeting that day, the following statement was issued:

> An agreement to settle the North China Incident locally was concluded at 11 o'clock on the evening of July 11, but among the Chinese regiments were some who impeded enforcement of the agreement and lawlessly fired on the Japanese, disturbing peace and order.
>
> Moreover, as there could be seen no sincerity at all on the part of the Chinese to enforce the terms of the agreement, the Imperial Government has decided, in accordance with its already fixed policy, to take self-defense steps adequate for surveillance of the Chinese in enforcement of the agreement.†

"Third, we will not agree to the removal by outside pressure of those local officials appointed by the central government such as the chairman of the Hopei-Chahar Council.

"Fourth, we will not allow any restriction to be placed on the positions of the Twenty-ninth Army.

"The four points constitute the minimum conditions for possible bases of negotiation for any nation, no matter how weak." *New York Times,* July 20, 1937, p. 16.

* Telegram No. 213, July 20, 5 ·P.M.

† Telegram No. 214, July 2 ˋ, midnight. [*Ibid.,* p. 330.]

On July 21 the Japanese Ambassador in Washington called on Mr. Hull at the latter's request in order to discuss the situation arising out of the China Incident and was told that the American Government continued to be seriously concerned with the Far Eastern situation and desired constantly to receive the latest and best information thereon from the Ambassador. Mr. Saito spoke of the clash near the Marco Polo Bridge and said that the Japanese, who had used only artillery, desired to avoid general hostilities by localizing the controversy. He still hoped that this result could be accomplished.

The Ambassador was then informed by the Secretary that, as of course Mr. Saito must be aware, the United States could not fail to be greatly interested and concerned when two nations comprising five hundred million people were engaged in a controversy involving the imminent danger of general hostilities. In the light of that situation and of the intense desire of the United States for peace everywhere in the world Mr. Hull had been undertaking to confer from time to time with both the Japanese and Chinese Ambassadors concerning present and prospective developments, and that in an earnest effort to contribute to the cause of peace and to the avoidance of hostilities in the Far East he had approached each of the two Governments in a spirit of impartiality and of genuine friendliness. Points which the Secretary had referred to in previous conversations with the Ambassador were re-emphasized and an earnest appeal from every possible standpoint to both Governments for peace was added, with an expression of opinion that irreparable harm to all governments involved would result from a war which, in the present unsettled condition of world affairs, would prove disastrous to all phases of human progress and welfare. Mr. Hull repeated the beneficent purposes and the great objective of the program adopted at Buenos Aires, including the eight-point "Pillars of Peace" proposed in his address in that capital,[10] and he emphasized the

10 On December 5, 1936, at Buenos Aires Mr. Hull had delivered a speech before the conference of representatives from American Republics. In *The Memoirs of Cordell Hull* (New York: The Macmillan Co., 1948), I, 498, he has

fact that world stabilization and the whole program of improving world relationships would now be jeopardized by general hostilities. A few days ago the Secretary had given out a statement based on that address, emphasizing to all nations and all governments the basic points of the Buenos Aires program, and he was gradually bringing that statement to the attention of foreign governments in the hope that it would meet with favorable expressions of their views, approving and supporting the principles therein stated. Mr. Hull said that he was glad to hand to the Ambassador, for the Japanese Government, a copy of that statement, adding that if the Government of Japan should join in carrying forward that great program, the American Government would be greatly pleased.

Mr. Hull then repeated that the American Government was ready and glad at any moment to say or to do anything short of actual mediation, which of course would require the prior agreement of both parties, which in any way whatever might conduce toward a settlement of the Sino-Japanese controversy. The Secretary made clear the fact that he was making no offer and was suggesting no particular method to be followed but was inviting voluntary suggestions from the Japanese or the Chinese Governments. The Ambassador said that he fully understood Mr. Hull's intention.

summarized this program for keeping peace:

"(1) Peoples must be educated for peace. Each nation must make itself safe for peace.

"(2) Frequent conferences between representatives of nations, and intercourse between their peoples, are essential.

"(3) The consummation of the five well-known peace agreements will provide adequate peace machinery. . . .

"(4) In the event of war in this hemisphere, there should be a common policy of neutrality.

"(5) The nations should adopt commercial policies to bring each that prosperity upon which enduring peace is founded.

"(6) Practical international cooperation is essential to restore many indispensable relationships between nations and prevent the demoralization with which national character and conduct are threatened.

" (7) International law should be reestablished, revitalized, and strengthened. Armies and navies are no permanent substitute for its great principles.

"(8) Faithful observance of undertakings between nations is the foundation of international order, and rests upon moral law, the highest of all law."

The Secretary furthermore said to Mr. Saito that he desired that his point of view be clearly understood and that he would like to inform the American Ambassadors in Tokyo and Nanking of the conversations held in Washington so that they could report what he had said, just as the two Ambassadors in Washington would similarly report to their respective Governments. Mr. Hull said the same thing to the Chinese Ambassador [Dr. Wang] indicating the great solicitude of the United States for peace. I was instructed to call on the Foreign Minister in Tokyo and to read to him the foregoing statement so that the Minister might be clearly informed of what the Secretary had said to the Japanese Ambassador in Washington, adding that the same things had been said to the Chinese Ambassador to the United States.*

On the previous evening the British Ambassador in Washington [Sir Ronald Lindsay], under instructions, had suggested to our Government a joint Anglo-American approach to the Japanese and Chinese Governments, asking them to agree to issue instructions for the suspension of all further movements of troops and further to agree to an effort by the American and British Governments to end the present deadlock by advancing proposals to that end. The British Ambassador was informed on the following day of the desire of the American Government to co-operate; that the courses of action hitherto followed by the two Governments were believed to have been co-operative and it was suggested that the importance of maintaining stability should again be urged on both the Japanese and Chinese Governments by the American and British Governments, each in its own way. In accordance with this suggestion, Mr. Hull on the 21st again urged upon the Japanese and the Chinese Ambassadors that self-restraint be exercised by both their countries; he furthermore emphasized the calamity to the world which would arise from hostilities, and once again he invited suggestions for any appropriate assistance which might be rendered by the Government of the United States towards reaching a solution of the controversy. The British Ambassador was

* Department's telegram No. 122, July 21, 6 P.M.

informed that these representations would be brought by Mr. Johnson and Mr. Grew to the respective attention of the Chinese and Japanese Governments.*

In the meantime, on July 21, the British Chargé d'Affaires in Tokyo showed me a telegram from his Government reporting Mr. Eden's conversation with Ambassador Bingham in which the former had proposed to Mr. Hull that as a last resort and to meet what Mr. Eden regarded as a very serious situation the two Governments should extend to both Nanking and Tokyo an offer of mediation. I expressed to Mr. Dodds the opinion, in which he concurred, that neither the Chinese nor the Japanese Government wanted war and that both sides were trying to find some way of avoiding it, but I still doubted if an offer of mediation would be either welcomed or accepted by the Japanese Government. I told Mr. Dodds of the various steps that had been taken in Washington by Mr. Hull.[11]

The Japanese Minister of War, through his private secretary, told the British Military Attaché that Chiang Kai-shek's difficult position was fully recognized but that in the opinion of the Japanese Government, Nanking intended nothing beyond "a war of words." He added that the nearer the Chinese troops approached the area of fighting the more unreliable they became, and while the trouble might possibly expand, this was

---

* Department's telegram No. 123, July 21, 7 P.M.

11 Mr. Hull has written in his *Memoirs*, I, 538: "To joint action I had three real objections. One was that it would create the impression in Tokyo that the major Western nations were bringing pressure to bear on Japan. This would only accentuate the crisis; the Japanese military could use it to strengthen their own position and to inflame the populace against us. The second was that, if there was to be any joint action, it should be by all the nations having an interest in the Far East, or, better still, by all the peaceful nations of the world, and not merely by two or three. The third was that anything resembling joint action with Britain inevitably aroused the fears and animosity of the isolationist elements in the United States.

"Moreover, I seriously doubted whether any joint action, unless it embraced a real show of force, backed by an intention to use force if necessary, would be of any avail. And I was certain that neither Great Britain, distracted by developments in Europe, nor the United States, unprepared psychologically and militarily, had any thought of employing force."

not believed to be probable. The evidence indicated a belief on the part of the Japanese that Nanking was bluffing.

On that day, the 21st, Mr. Dodds read to the Vice Minister the following excerpt from a telegram just received from the British Ambassador at Nanking, indicating that the Ambassador took a very serious view of the situation:

I feel I must emphasize the extreme seriousness of the present situation.

It is quite clear that Chiang Kai-shek still desires a peaceful solution but that anything amounting to complete surrender to the present Japanese demands would bring about his fall. A member of the Chinese General Staff (Major-General Chu) informed the Military Attaché today that it was no longer a question of settling the Lukouchiao incident but of loss or retention of two Chinese provinces (Hopei and Chahar). Position of the Central Government is that they are willing to negotiate with Japan through diplomatic channels on the present dispute in all its aspects and have offered arbitration and other method of settlement but that they cannot commit themselves to blind acceptance of some local settlement which will destroy their position in the North once and for all.

If the Japanese Government imagine that there is any element of bluff in the Chinese attitude they are making a great mistake.

The Chinese Government feel there is a point beyond which public opinion will not allow them to go in the direction of compliance with the Japanese demands.

If the Japanese Government insist on settlement with the local authorities in North China to the exclusion of the Central Government they must realize that war will be inevitable.

Mr. Dodds made it clear that in reading the foregoing statement he was acting without instructions and on his own initiative but that he could not take the responsibility of failing to convey what might be information of vital importance. The Vice Minister listened without comment and merely expressed his thanks for the communication.*

* Telegram No. 216, July 21, 5 P.M.

According to a reliable and well-informed source (Colonel Ott, German Military Attaché, later German Ambassador to Japan), Prince Konoye's illness was real and not feigned, and if the present situation in North China should continue difficult or should worsen, Konoye would probably resign and be succeeded as Prime Minister by General Gen Sugiyama [Minister of the Department of Army]. Colonel Ott confirmed the estimate of our Military Attaché that up to date the Japanese mobilization had been only partial as it had affected only some and not all divisions and had only somewhat increased the strength of units without raising them to war strength. He also confirmed the estimate of our Military Attaché that only part of a division (probably a reinforced brigade from the 6th Division) and some transport and communications troops had gone to North China from Japan proper; that about one division had gone from Chosen and that about one reinforced brigade had gone from the Jehol garrison of the Kwantung Army. It was believed by the informant that in addition to the above, one division of the Kwantung Army had gone. The situation in North China was characterized by Colonel Ott as "negotiations progressing with armed intervention."

The same informant agreed with Mr. William H. Chamberlin [newspaperman and author] that owing to the internal effects of the recent purge,[12] Soviet Russia would extend no military help to China. The Chinese themselves were thought to have only five or six divisions and judging from their movements and dispositions it was not believed that they then intended seriously to fight Japan. It was also believed that Japan wished to avoid war but was prepared to use force to ensure the carrying out of the agreement of July 11, at the same time affording sufficient support to General Sung Cheh-yuan to en-

[12] Shortly after the assassination of Sergei Kirov, an intimate of Stalin, on December 1, 1934, a series of treason trials began in the Soviet Union. This bloody purge continued until March, 1938. During the period of over three years some of the men who had figured most prominently in Soviet history were tried and executed. Zinoviev, Kamenev, Karakhan, Marshal Tukhachevsky, Rykov, Bukharin, and scores of lesser people were killed, while others committed suicide or disappeared.

courage him to resist Nanking in advancing toward practical independence from the Central Government.*

By a Japanese officer who had been fairly cordial and informative our Military Attaché was told that according to a conversation between an officer of the American State Department and Mr. Yakichiro Suma, Counselor of the Japanese Embassy in Washington, the United States was pro-Chinese and did not understand the situation in North China.[13] (This, incidentally, appears to have been one of the first recorded instances where a Japanese official charged the United States with "failure to understand," a shibboleth continually expressed during the next several years.) † . . .

In contrast to an apparent temporary standstill in the solution of the incident, Japanese military preparations were steadily advancing, and men leaving their home towns for military service had for several days been a common sight at railway stations. Practically all the foreign firms known to the Embassy reported that some of their employees had been called to military service, particularly to the motor transport service. Requisitioning of automobiles and trucks had been widespread.

Japanese immigration authorities at Yokohama had instructed the steamship companies that passengers for China must board vessels at least three hours before sailing in order to allow time for examination. Japanese authorities had also required the steamship companies to show copies of manifests of all cargoes destined for the Philippines and China, the latter requirement apparently being similar to the requirement of

---

* Telegram No. 217, July 21, 6 P.M.

13 Mr. Grew commented in his diary on July 21: "An officer of the Military Affairs Bureau of the War Ministry told Carey Crane that Suma's conversation with Hornbeck yesterday revealed our pro-Chinese attitude and the fact that we don't understand the situation in North China at all. That is precisely the impression which would inevitably be created by the carefully balanced observations which Hornbeck undoubtedly would have made to Suma. It reminds me of the naive remark made by the Japanese delegation in the Dutch-Japanese shipping conference: 'How can we compromise when you refuse to accept our views?'"

† Telegram No. 219, July 21, 8 P.M.

paragraph q of article 149 of the United States Customs Regulations.[14]

Messrs. Mitsui had expressed a desire to buy, on behalf of the Kwantung Army, Hsinking, all the gasoline that the Standard Oil Company would deliver immediately at Dairen in plain tins packed in roped boxes, according to confidential information supplied by the company manager in Yokohama who had telegraphed to New York for instructions. On July 13 the ship *Lise* had discharged at Dairen one million one hundred thousand gallons of aviation gasoline which the American Consul reported had been sold by the Texas Company to the Manchukuo monopoly. He also reported that tenders for an additional million and a quarter gallons were refused by the other companies.*

In accordance with the Department's instructions of July 21 I called on the Foreign Minister on the 22nd and thereafter cabled the following report of the conversation:

1. I carried out your instructions at 5.30 this afternoon immediately after your telegram had been decoded.

2. The Minister for Foreign Affairs said that he fully understands your message which he had not yet received from Saito, and your views. He will not however reply "for a few days" because the situation in North China is steadily improving and he is more optimistic than heretofore as to a satisfactory settlement of the controversy. He states that practical evidence of his optimism is given by the fact that all troop movements from Japan to China have been stopped for the present.

---

14 Paragraph "q" of Article 149 of the Customs Regulations states that the "master of a vessel with foreign cargo shall furnish the comptroller of customs at the first port of arrival in the United States with a copy of the manifest of the entire cargo. When subsequent calls are made at ports within the same comptroller district, whether or not for discharge of cargo, the master shall furnish the comptroller for said district with a report on customs Form 3253, in lieu of copy of manifest." U.S. Bureau of Customs, *Customs Regulations of the United States. . . . Edition of 1931* (Washington: Government Printing Office. 1932), pp. 125–26.

* Telegram No. 220, July 21, 9 P.M.

3. The whole situation he says depends on the carrying out of the agreement drawn up on July 11 and signed on July 19 by General Chang [Mayor of Tientsin] representing General Sung. The main difficulty is that the Nanking Government will not recognize this agreement and is actively obstructing a settlement. Hirota does not ask that Nanking recognize the agreement but only that it shall withhold obstruction. He is at present working along those lines and says he already sees signs of a more favorable attitude on the part of Nanking.

4. Confidential. The Minister said that General Sung desires the precise terms of the above-mentioned agreement to be kept confidential for the present. Hirota however read to me a rough translation from the Japanese text as follows:

a. Apology.

b. Punishment of the Chinese captain responsible for the outbreak of hostilities at the Marco Polo Bridge and the censuring of the Army commander.

c. Assurances for the future which comprise voluntary retirement of Chinese officials in North China who obstruct Sino-Japanese co-operation; expulsion of communist elements from that district; control of the Blue Shirts and other organizations hostile to Japan; control of education in the schools; cessation of anti-Japanese propaganda.

d. Withdrawal of the 37th Division from Peiping.

5. The Minister pointed out that no political demands are involved in this agreement and that headway is already being made toward carrying out its terms.

6. The Minister said that in view of the great sensitiveness of the Japanese press at the present moment he will answer any questions from newspapermen regarding the purpose of my call to the effect that I had come to inquire with regard to the present situation.* . . .

A brief period of marking time then appeared to intervene because no telegrams went forward from the Embassy for five days. On the 27th the Foreign Minister made a speech in the Diet [15] which we were informed had been cabled to the Japa-

* Telegram No. 223, July 22, 7 P.M. [*Ibid.,* pp. 333–34.]

[15] See "Address of Mr. Koki Hirota, Minister for Foreign Affairs, at the

nese Embassy in Washington for distribution, and on the same day an official statement was released by the Cabinet reaffirming the intention of the Japanese Government to take measures to maintain communications between Peiping and the sea and to protect nationals in that area. The statement declared that the Japanese Government had no territorial designs and that it would take every precaution to protect the rights in that area of other Powers. The statement concluded with an expression of hope that the Chinese Government would take measures to restrict the scope of the current difficulties, in order that a satisfactory solution might be found as soon as possible. While the content of the foregoing statement was uncompromising, we believed that it had been issued at that time with a view to facilitating compliance of the 29th Army with the terms of an ultimatum delivered by the Japanese commander in the Peiping area [General Katsuki].[16] It appeared that the Japanese commander had himself taken the initiative in issuing the ultimatum, which was due to expire on the 28th but the statement of the Cabinet indicated that if the ultimatum should expire without compliance by the Chinese with its terms, the Japanese commander would probably be given full authorization to act.

At the same time we had evidence of extensive troop movements in various parts of the country in southwest Japan and that among these moving troops there appeared to be a greater proportion of men from combat units than had been observed in the past. These movements appeared to be more of a preparatory or precautionary nature than as part of a general mobilization, but in spite of the difficulty of obtaining factual

Seventy-First (Extraordinary) Session of the Diet, on July 27, 1937," *Contemporary Japan*, September, 1937, pp. 357–59.

16 An ultimatum had been addressed to General Sung by the Japanese Garrison Headquarters on July 26, calling upon the Chinese to withdraw the 37th Division stationed near Lukouchiao to Changhsintien before noon on July 27 and the 37th Division in Peiping west of Yungtingho before noon on July 28. If the Chinese failed to meet these demands the ultimatum stated that "the Japanese Army must, to its greatest regret, take its own decisive measures." Bisson, *op. cit.*, pp. 25–26.

information we had the impression from all sides of an approaching crisis.* [17]

With regard to the suggestion made by General Chiang Kai-shek on July 25 to the American, British and French Ambassadors in Nanking, the first reaction of the British Chargé d'Affaires in Tokyo was that by exaggerating the Japanese menace the Generalissimo was trying merely to save face. In Tokyo there was little evidence of any effort to stir up war fever and Mr. Dodds felt that Chiang's purpose might be to saddle the three Powers approached by him with the odium of making representations to the Japanese Government. If the Chinese should fail to comply with their signed agreement there was danger of the Japanese military exceeding their instructions. Mr. Dodds felt that Japan had a fixed policy to dominate North China by successive stages, and the Chinese of course must determine at what point to offer serious resistance. Nevertheless it was believed unlikely that the Japanese intended the combat stage to intervene immediately. Mr. Dodds was unwilling, in the absence of further evidence, to recommend to his Government compliance with the Generalissimo's request of the Powers that they should urge the Japanese Government against making further demands. The Vice Minister had twice informed him that the Japanese military would stay within their instructions and if the Powers should ask Japan to make no further demands, Mr. Dodds believed that the Japanese Government would retort that it had no intention of doing so. Nevertheless if the Chinese failed to carry out their signed

* Telegram No. 226, July 27, 7 p.m.

[17] After a period during the third week in July when a peaceful settlement and a localization of the conflict still seemed a possibility, the situation was further complicated by the occurrence of new incidents involving Japanese and Chinese troops. On July 25 Japanese infantry and Chinese soldiers of the Thirty-Eighth Division engaged in fighting at Langfang. In Peiping on July 26 troops of the two countries battled at the southwest gate of the city. This was followed by a general assault of the Japanese military forces upon Chinese positions near Peiping, Langfang, and Fengtai. The Twenty-Ninth Army was quickly defeated, and one scholar has written that the "repulse of the Twenty-Ninth Army from the environs of Peiping marked the beginning of general Sino-Japanese hostilities." Toynbee, *op. cit.*, I, 188–93.

agreement, the situation would of course be radically altered. I agreed with Mr. Dodds and so informed the Department. "Co-operative action by the United States and Great Britain along lines more vigorous than had hitherto been attempted" or in fact any diplomatic representations by the Powers would, in my opinion, produce no favorable results.*

On July 28 the following instructions were received telegraphically from the Department:

> Department is informed from London that British Embassy at Peiping states that the senior commandant has been informed by the Japanese liaison officer that the Japanese intend to launch regardless of whether the withdrawal of 37th division is proceeding satisfactorily a general attack against all Chinese forces both within and without the city of Peiping.
>
> Please confer immediately with the British Embassy and in your discretion take action on lines parallel with the British Embassy's action toward dissuading Japanese authorities from proceeding with any plan for military operations which would be likely to endanger lives of American nationals. You may use as a part basis for such action the fact of the presence of large numbers of American nationals in Peiping, rights of the country along with other countries under the Boxer Protocol and assurances given by the Japanese Government during the present crisis, especially an assurance given this Government in writing when the Japanese Ambassador on July 12 called on me and gave me a memorandum from the Japanese Government numbered paragraph six of which concludes: "In any case the Japanese Government is prepared to give full consideration to the rights and interests of the Powers in China." The Department has sent a similar telegram to the Embassy at Peiping with the request that Peiping report immediately to the Department and repeat its telegram to you.
>
> Report by telegraph and repeat your telegram to Peiping.†

These instructions were carried out and the following reports submitted:

* Telegram No. 227, July 27, 9 P.M.
† Department's telegram No. 128, July 27, 1 P.M.

1. A telegram reporting the result of my call on the Minister for Foreign Affairs in compliance with Department's 128, July 27, 1 P.M., will follow shortly.

2. The Vice Minister for Foreign Affairs has just called me up on the telephone and, at Hirota's request, has read to me the substance of a report just received from the commander of the Japanese forces in North China to the following effect:

A Japanese officer called this morning on the Mayor of Peiping and stated that complete withdrawal of Chinese troops from the walled city would not be required by noon today, but that such withdrawal would be expected to begin and be completed "in due course"; measures are being taken to safeguard the interests in Peiping of other foreign Powers. The statement added that the Japanese troops within the walls of Peiping would not attack unless challenged.*

and:

1. The British Chargé d'Affaires and I saw the Minister for Foreign Affairs separately this morning. I carried out your instructions fully and with emphasis. . . .

The Minister for Foreign Affairs stated to me categorically that it is not true that the Japanese intend to launch a general attack against all Chinese forces both within and without the city of Peiping regardless of whether the withdrawal of the 37th Division is proceeding satisfactorily. He said that over two weeks' warning had been given to the Chinese troops to withdraw from Peiping on the basis of the agreement of July 11 and that since this warning had not been acted upon, it had finally become necessary to set a time limit at noon today and that a Japanese attack would be carried out only if withdrawal of the 37th Division has not already taken place. He said he had no news today as to whether this withdrawal had been effected. The Minister appeared to ignore the sporadic Japanese attacks already reported from Peiping.

The Minister gave me explicit assurances that every effort would be made to protect the lives and property of American and other foreign nationals and the rights and interests of the United States and other Powers in the affected area and he has

* Telegram No. 229, July 28, 4 P.M.

confidence in General Katsuki, who the Minister says has complete control of his troops. The Minister added, however, that the Japanese Consulate in Peiping had informed other foreign consuls that Japanese subjects in outlying districts had been advised to concentrate in the Legation Quarter in Peiping. The Minister thought that similar steps would therefore have been taken by the other foreign consuls with respect to their own nationals. . . .

In making these representations I had placed the emphasis on the avoidance of hostilities *per se* because the Department's instructions had precisely specified that I was authorized to dissuade the Japanese authorities from carrying out any plan of military operations which might jeopardize the interest and rights of the Powers in China or which might endanger American lives. . . . With regard to the general situation I expressed to the Secretary the view of Mr. Dodds and myself, after most careful thought, that whatever results might accrue from the repeated representations in Washington, London and Tokyo by the American and British Governments, no step had been omitted which might have served to avert the current crisis. As matters had worked out we felt that the crisis was inevitable. Nevertheless I had seen many crises overcome in the Far East and from the angle of Tokyo I could not conclude that it was yet too late to avoid general war or that the situation was without hope of improvement.* . . .

Ever since July 12 the Secretary had repeatedly urged both the Chinese and Japanese Governments to keep the peace and to avoid hostilities, but beginning with July 27 (Washington date) [18] the Department had been anxious about an attack on and in Peiping, and he had no hesitation in urging against such an attack. . . . The Secretary wished to avoid gestures of interference or protests which might be futile but he was neverthe-

* Telegram No. 230, July 28, 5 P.M. [*Ibid.,* pp. 337–38.]

[18] There is a difference in time of fourteen hours between Tokyo and Washington. In relation to the base meridian at Greenwich, Washington time is five hours slow and Tokyo time is nine hours fast. When it is noon in Washington, it is 2 A.M. of the next day in Tokyo, or when it is noon in Tokyo, it is 10 P.M. of the previous day in Washington.

less inclined to take such fully warranted action as might conduce toward peace or toward calling attention to American rights and interests and toward safeguarding American lives. He added that in view of the radio bulletin service, which we were now to receive, the Department would probably send us few and sketchy reports of its press conferences.* . . .

In the meantime the Department had reported to us on July 27 a conversation with the Counselor of the Japanese Embassy in Washington, as follows:

Department's 128, July 27, 1 P.M.

Counselor of Japanese Embassy called at the Department this morning, gave miscellaneous information about recent clashes, stated that the Japanese Government had ordered reinforcements to be sent from Japan proper to China, said that the Chinese were in various ways aggravating the situation and that his Government was continuing to exercise self-restraint.

The Counselor inquired whether the Department had any important news. He was told that we had received a report for which we could not vouch but which had the appearance of authority to the effect that the Japanese forces were contemplating launching a general attack against Chinese forces both in and around Peiping; that we felt that such an attack if made would be attended with great hazards jeopardizing lives of noncombatant population among whom were a considerable number of foreigners most especially of concern to us more than seven hundred Americans; that such action endangering or destroying foreign lives would procure an unfavorable reaction throughout the world; that it would be taking place on Chinese soil and in a region where the Treaty Powers including Japan have special and common rights and obligations. Mention was made to him of the Japanese Government's assurance that it is prepared to give full consideration to the rights and interests of the Powers in China. He was told that the lives of our nationals are with us a very important interest and that we wanted to ask that the Japanese Government give most serious consideration to all the implication and possibilities which might flow from such action if taken. Also in repetition that we were not charging or

* Department's telegram No. 133, July 29, 9 P.M.

affirming intent but that if such action is even in contemplation it seemed to us better to ask this before it happens.*

On the 28th the Foreign Minister made in the Diet the following statement:

The fact is that before the situation in North China arose conversations between Japan and Great Britain with regard to Far Eastern questions had made substantial progress. However, even though methods were to be devised for the rendering of assistance to China by Japan and Great Britain, such methods would be entirely inapplicable in the existing circumstances, and due to the deplorable situation which has arisen the conversations have terminated for the time being.

The papers yesterday evening took notice of the calls which Dodds and I made yesterday on the Minister for Foreign Affairs, and although the purposes of Dodds' visit were discussed at some length from a conjectural point of view, the purpose of my visit was merely stated to be to convey the earnest hope that hostilities in North China would be avoided.

This morning the Japanese papers closely examine the attitude shown by Great Britain toward the present Sino-Japanese crisis, and certain facts are stressed, as follows: (a) the British Government through Dodds has offered to the Japanese Government its good offices as mediator; (b) Eden stated in the House of Commons that the situation in North China was not a matter for local discussion but one to be settled by negotiations between the Japanese and Chinese Governments; and (c) the House of Commons was informed that the Anglo-Japanese conversations had been suspended. The conclusion is drawn that the British Government is seeking a favorable opportunity to intervene in any military action which may be taken by Japan and that it is building up for this purpose a close association between Great Britain, United States, Soviet Union and France. Several papers charge Great Britain with hostility and bad faith toward Japan.

In connection with the foregoing statement we referred to our telegram No. 206, July 16, 7 P.M., and pointed out that only

* Department's telegram No. 130, July 27, 7 P.M.

now had the Foreign Office disclosed to the press in Japan the substance of the message from Chiang Kai-shek which had been communicated to Mr. Horinouchi by Mr. Dodds on July 16.*

On July 29 we sent to the Department the following report:

The objectives of the current Japanese military operations, as explained in committees in the Diet, and to foreign military attachés by the War Office, are as follows:

a. Japanese operations, including use of bombing by aircraft, are intended to disperse concentrations of the Chinese 29th Army at Peiping and Tientsin, driving the 29th Army to the southwest of the Yungting River, and to clear the area between the two cities of hostile Chinese forces. These operations are progressing favorably and should be completed shortly, perhaps by the end of next week.

b. A path has been left open from Peiping to the west and northwest for the peaceful withdrawal of Chinese units still in Peiping.

c. After the completion of current operations no further military action is contemplated unless the Central Chinese troops, now concentrated along and north of the Lunghai railway, should proceed toward the north. . . .

It is not yet known what naval steps are being taken by Japan. The Naval Attaché was told at the Navy Department this morning that, notwithstanding press reports to the contrary, no additional warships have been sent to China since the situation began to develop on July 7.

There should be added to previous assurances of this character an assurance given to Byas by official of the Foreign Office that no planes or heavy guns will be used by the Japanese military to effect entrance into the walled city of Peiping.

In order to protect our sources of military information, this telegram has not been repeated to Nanking.

As for the situation in Shantung, our Military Attaché was informed by the War Office that all was quiet and that the fighting around Tientsin was unimportant. As for the situation

* Telegram No. 232, July 29, 4 P.M.

around Peiping, it seemed unlikely that the Chinese 29th Army would be reinforced and it was believed that the ousting of that army would settle matters.*

With reference to the Embassy's telegram No. 230 — of July 28 — we reported on the 29th that the British Chargé d'Affaires had on the previous day informed his Government that in his interview with the Foreign Minister Mr. Hirota had said that decisions for military operations in North China now lay with the commander of the Japanese troops in that area. Mr. Eden thereupon instructed Mr. Dodds again to call on the Minister and to say to him that he was greatly perturbed by this observation which appeared contrary to Mr. Hirota's statement in the Diet to the general effect that Japan did not want war with China. As Mr. Hirota could not receive him, Mr. Dodds called on the Vice Minister and left with him a letter for Mr. Hirota carrying out his instructions.

The French Ambassador had received instructions to take action "analogous" to that taken by Mr. Dodds but he saw no purpose in entering a plea for peace when hostilities had already started and he had not yet decided to act.†

On June 10 a despatch had gone forward applying for leave of absence with permission to visit the United States but on July 30 I cabled: "Obviously I have abandoned plans to take leave of absence at present." The Secretary considerately replied: "I regret necessity abandonment your plan for leave. I appreciate and thank you for your splendid reporting and commenting." This telegram was of course most gratifying and encouraging to the members of the staff of the Embassy who had done admirable work during this intense period.‡

On the 30th we reported:

In a press conference this morning Tatsuo Kawai, the Foreign Office spokesman, asserted that the Japanese Army has conquered Peking and that the military phase is over. In response

* Telegram No. 233, July 29, 5 P.M.
† Telegram No. 234, July 29, 6 P.M.
‡ Telegram No. 236, July 30, 11 A.M.

to questions he mentioned as entirely possible a movement by the inhabitants of the Peking-Tientsin area for the establishment of some peace preservation organization which might lead to a movement for autonomy. He referred to Manchuria following the 1931 incident and said that many movements for autonomy spontaneously sprang up among the inhabitants, which movements the Japanese finally came to assist because of Chinese inexperience in government. Kawai stated that in a similar way Japanese authorities in the Peking-Tientsin area probably will be approached and that they perhaps will have to help.* . . .

Meanwhile we were informed by the Department that the suggestions advanced to our Ambassador in London on July 28 had been renewed and the following possible action was proposed for consideration: good offices to be offered both to Japan and China by the American and British Governments, first in providing neutral ground for a meeting of plenipotentiaries, and second in helping to smooth out difficulties in the negotiations; if then both the Japanese and Chinese were in agreement in principle that the controversy should be solved by negotiation, the Japanese would be urged to send no more troops into Hopei and the Chinese Central Government would similarly be urged to send no further troops north, subsequent troop movements to be discussed by the negotiators; it would of course be made clear that such an approach constituted merely an offer of good offices and in no sense intervention. It was agreed by Ambassador Bingham and Sir Robert Vansittart [Permanent Under Secretary of State for Foreign Affairs] in London that before action were taken the American and British diplomatic representatives in Tokyo should be asked their opinion as to the probable reception by the Japanese Government of such an offer. My comments were requested.†

In reply I reported, as already stated, that we saw no evidence of enthusiasm for war with China either in the Japanese Government or among the Japanese people, but this of course did

* Telegram No. 237, July 30, 7 P.M.
† Department's telegram No. 138, August 5, noon.

not include the military machine. The prevailing feeling seemed to be that Chinese hostility toward Japan had brought about the present situation, and that if the action of the Chinese should indicate a Chinese desire for war, the Japanese people would support whatever military or other steps might be determined by the Japanese Government. Nevertheless, both the Government and people in Japan would still prefer to avoid general hostilities. A powerful argument for peace was presented by the four hundred million yen budget for military expenses on the continent accompanied by the certainty of steadily increasing costs in the event of an extensive campaign.

On the one hand, Japan insisted that China must take the initiative for either peace or war. On the other hand, in view of the virtual elimination of Chinese civil and military authority in the Peiping area it seemed to us very improbable that China would take an initiative for peace, although I naturally deferred to any contrary opinion on the part of Ambassador Johnson in Nanking, and unless the Chinese forces should stop their forward movement into Hopei and their reported continued concentrations, a general clash appeared unavoidable.

It nevertheless seemed to me of the utmost importance that the United States should leave no stone unturned to avoid general hostilities and I therefore could not conscientiously recommend against a final effort on the part of the American and British Governments, making it perfectly clear that the proposed step was in no sense intervention and was merely an offer of good offices on the practical basis suggested by the British Government. Acceptance by Tokyo we felt was improbable but not necessarily impossible. The method and manner of approach would be important and every effort should be made to avoid publicity. . . .

So far as concerned the probable reception of such a proposal in Tokyo, I thought that the best way of forestalling open resentment would be the confidential and exploratory approach suggested. When on my own responsibility and initiative I had asked Mr. Hirota a few hours before the drafting of the present telegram to let me know if at any moment I could be of help, he had shown no resentment whatever. It would be appropriate to phrase the proposed Anglo-American offer in such a way as to indicate that these channels were open both to the Japanese and the Chinese Governments, if needed, either now or later.

Emphasizing the foregoing views I repeated that it was highly desirable to avoid publicity and also that an exploratory, semi-informal and confidential talk with Mr. Hirota would be more likely to avoid possible resentment and to bring favorable results than would a formal "diplomatic démarche." In spite of my previously expressed opinion that nothing had been left undone by the American Government toward the maintenance of peace, I said to Mr. Hull that at this most pregnant and critical period in Far Eastern affairs I should like to feel that history would regard as exhaustive, unstintedly helpful and impartially correct the record of American action.*

On the same day, before sending the foregoing telegram, I had called on the Foreign Minister and we reported the conversation as follows:

1. Last night the press bureau of the Foreign Office informally issued a statement concerning the reports that a considerable number of Americans are planning to offer their services as aviators to the Chinese Army. The statement could be read as implying that the American Government is responsible for not deterring these aviators and that this may reflect on the good relations between the United States and Japan. The statement also invoked our Neutrality Act.

2. I therefore called this morning on the Minister for Foreign Affairs telling him that I had come on my own initiative and not under instructions and that I was making no formal representations, but that since he himself had recently spoken to me of the present sensitiveness of the Japanese press and the importance of avoiding undesirable comment and speculation I desired to bring this statement to his attention. The statement had not been published in this morning's Japanese newspapers but I

* Telegram No. 250, August 6, 9 P.M.

said I hoped it would not appear in the afternoon press. I told the Minister that, as he must well know, the American Government will do everything in its legal power to discourage or deter Americans from fighting in foreign armies. I also pointed out that the Neutrality Act is a domestic matter and that its interpretation by foreigners is difficult.

3. The Minister seemed much upset and immediately telephoned to the chief of the press bureau who informed him that the statement had thus far been given only to one correspondent, Byas of the *New York Times*. Hirota promised me that it would not be permitted to appear in the Japanese press and he thanked me for bringing the matter to his attention.

4. I believe that my step was justified because of its possibly restraining influence on future Foreign Office press comment concerning the United States.*

In the course of the same informal conversation Mr. Hirota recalled his statement to me some time ago that Japan did not desire war with China and that there would be no more fighting if only the Chinese Central Government troops which had come up to Hopei Province would withdraw. Thereupon, on my own responsibility and initiative, I expressed the hope that he would not fail to let me know if he ever saw any way in which I might be of help in the present situation. This informal statement involved no official commitment of any kind but showed the Minister that a channel was open through which he could without embarrassment informally explore the ground if our good offices should ever be desired.† . . .

On the following day — August 7 — Mr. Dodds informed his Government that the Foreign Minister had already made it clear in the Diet that he would reject any attempt at mediation. Good offices had already been tendered by the British Government but Mr. Dodds saw no harm in making a further offer along the lines of London's suggestion. Nevertheless he believed that there would be violent and unfavorable reaction in Japan if the Japanese Government were given any cause to

---

* Telegram No. 247, August 6, 4 P.M. [*Ibid.*, pp. 338–39.]
† Telegram No. 248, August 6, 5 P.M.

believe that such a new offer was being made primarily in the interest of China. The people in Japan were not in a mood to consider peace proposals in view of the reported massacre at Tungchow,[19] and while war with China was looked upon with distaste by intelligent Japanese, nevertheless the military had no conception of the dangers into which their course might lead and they regarded the present moment as opportune to proceed with their expansionist plans. Mr. Dodds, however, believed that there was some basis for hope that the proposed Anglo-American step might have a favorable effect and he was reporting to London my own views and recommendations.*

In replying to my 250, 251 — of August 6 — and 252 — of August 7 — the Department cabled its authorization, when my British colleague should also be authorized and prepared to take action along similar lines at a reasonably early moment, to approach the Foreign Minister in the way suggested. The approaches were to be made in an oral, exploratory, semi-informal and confidential manner and separately, not jointly. It was felt that if the approaches were in the first instance made to the Japanese Government alone, there was greater likelihood that unfortunate publicity might be avoided and that the approaches might accomplish favorable results. Mr. Johnson in Nanking was therefore instructed to take no similar action for the moment.†

In reply to our 247 — of August 6 — the Department telegraphed:

American press has carried account of statement made on August 6 by Hirota to the Diet to the effect that the American

[19] When the main body of Japanese troops stationed at Tungchow left the city to pursue fleeing Chinese forces, the *Paoantui*, composed of troops of which the basic elements were Chinese renegades, mutinied on July 29 against the remaining Japanese garrison. Twenty of the Japanese garrison and eleven members of the Japanese Military Mission were killed. Two hundred and fifty of the Japanese and Korean residents of the city were also slaughtered. Bisson, *op. cit.*, pp. 29–31.

* Telegram No. 252, August 7, 2 P.M.

† Department's telegram No. 140, August 7, 3 P.M.

Government was carefully guarding against reported attempts by Chinese to enlist American aviators.

The Department feels that your prompt initiative has served effectively to dispose of reports which might have been a source of harm to relations between the United States and Japan.

Your statement and Hirota's subsequent statement accord with the facts. You may in your discretion so inform Hirota.*

With reference to the Department's 140 — of August 7 — affirmative instructions were received by the British Chargé d'Affaires on August 10 and I therefore, on the same afternoon, called on the Foreign Minister at his residence and conveyed to him the offer of good offices on the part of the United States, based on the two points brought out in the Department's 138 — of August 5. The offer was received by Mr. Hirota in an entirely friendly way. He informed me, however, that through a meeting on the previous day between the Japanese Ambassador, Mr. Kawagoe, and the Chief of the Asiatic Bureau of the Chinese Foreign Office, Mr. Kao, an opening for direct negotiations had already been found, Mr. Kao having thereafter immediately left for Nanking to present to Chiang Kai-shek the Japanese plan for a settlement of the trouble. Mr. Hirota expressed the opinion that war might be avoided if Chiang Kai-shek would respond with some counterproposal upon which negotiations might be based, but in view of the situation, which he described as critical, general hostilities could be avoided only by a prompt and favorable reply from the Generalissimo. The most effective help the American Government could render, said the Minister, would be to persuade Chiang Kai-shek to return an early and favorable answer.

The Japanese "plan," the general nature of which Mr. Hirota appeared reluctant to divulge, included *inter alia* provisions for "good relations" with Manchuria and for doing away with all anti-Japanese activities in China. I was particularly requested by the Minister to regard as strictly confidential

* Department's telegram No. 141, August 7, 4 P.M.

the Kawagoe-Kao conversations which were unknown to the press.* . . .

On August 11 the British Chargé d'Affaires called on the Minister for Foreign Affairs and presented the offer* of good offices on behalf of his Government. A *pro memoria* which Mr. Dodds left with him, setting forth the two points previously mentioned, was read very slowly and with obvious care by Mr. Hirota who, after a long pause (estimated by Mr. Dodds to have lasted at least five minutes) replied that later it might perhaps be possible for the Japanese Government to avail itself of the offer. My own talk with the Minister was not mentioned but Mr. Hirota made to Mr. Dodds practically the same statement that he had made to me on the previous day, also in confidence. In subsequent conversation Mr. Dodds drew the impression that the Minister, while still expressing optimism of a favorable outcome, seemed to be somewhat less sure that Chiang Kai-shek would not fight. Mr. Hirota believed that in spite of reluctance on the part of the higher Chinese officers to go to war, the younger Chinese officers were eager for it, and he realized that the Generalissimo was in a very difficult position. In reporting this conversation to his Government Mr. Dodds expressed the view that our démarche had been well worthwhile.†

With regard to the military and naval situation, we reported the following information imparted to us by Japanese officials: (1) the Japanese Government had made compulsory the evacuation of Japanese nationals from the Yangtze valley and only about one hundred persons, chiefly officials, now remained; (2) the Hankow landing force and all Japanese gunboats on the Yangtze had been withdrawn to Shanghai; (3) in case of necessity the Japanese landing force in Shanghai would be strengthened and arrangements to that end had been made; (4) there had been organized a new naval unit, to be known as the southern squadron, which would operate in the waters of South China; (5) military reinforcements, the number and

* Telegram No. 254, August 10, 7 P.M. [*Ibid.*, pp. 339–41.]
† Telegram No. 256, August 11, 3 P.M.

whereabouts of which were not known to us, had been sent into North China and possibly into Manchuria. The Japanese military authorities regarded Chinese troop movements and distribution as "threatening" but unless the Chinese troops advanced, the Japanese Army would not attack. In the event that the efforts for peace should prove futile, we concluded from the foregoing information that preparations by the Japanese had been completed to act without delay.* . . .

A meeting of four Ministers (Foreign, War, Navy and Finance) was held on August 12 to consider the serious situation at Shanghai.[20] This was followed by an emergency Cabinet meeting on the morning of the 13th resulting in the issuance of a statement which would be reported in the American press.

According to the Senior Aide to the Minister of the Navy, Vice Admiral Kiyoshi Hasegawa, in command of the Third Squadron at Shanghai, had recommended on the 12th that a final effort be made to bring about a peaceful settlement. The Japanese naval landing forces then in Shanghai numbered only 3,000 and they were faced with the task of protecting 30,000 Japanese nationals now concentrated in the Japanese concession. Against the Japanese at that time were 10,000 of the Chinese 88th Division in Chapei and 20,000 to 30,000 of Central forces to the eastward of Chapei in the direction of Woosung. On the 12th the 88th Division had crossed the Nanking-Woosung railroad and the Japanese landing force had taken up defensive positions along North Szechuan Road facing the Chinese.

At the same time the Senior Aide told our Naval Attaché that at a meeting of consular officials at Shanghai on the 12th

---

* Telegram No. 257, August 11, 5 P.M.

20 On August 13 fighting broke out between Japanese and Chinese forces at Shanghai. The outbreak was preceded by a period of tension which had been occasioned, in part, by the shooting of two members of the Japanese Naval Landing Party and a Chinese sentry at Hungjao on August 9, and by the general unrest following the arrival of reinforcements for the Chinese troops in the area and of additional Japanese naval ships at the Whangpoo River. Toynbee, *op. cit.,* I, 204–13.

it was reported that the attitude of the United States was "very fair and just" while the attitude of the British, French and other consular officers was "different."

Our Naval Attaché at that time believed that there was a desire on the part of the Japanese to avoid aggravating the situation and that no further troops or vessels by way of reinforcements would probably be sent to Shanghai; part of the Third Squadron had already left that port.

The War Department, however, felt that the disposition of Chinese troops in North China was threatening the safety of the Japanese forces. Once again General Umezu stated that the Japanese would not attack unless the Chinese forces should advance, but several recent "counterattacks" against alleged "attacks" indicated the determination of the Japanese to bring about a definite settlement of the North China situation by enforcing fulfillment of the various military agreements already concluded.*

Although this study deals with developments essentially from the Tokyo point of view, it becomes necessary at this point, in order to explain action taken in Tokyo with regard to the protection of Shanghai, to quote three telegrams from Ambassador Johnson in Nanking to the Department, as follows:

1. Mr. Tuan, Secretary to the Minister for Foreign Affairs, called this morning and read to me a statement. The following is a reproduction made from notes taken from the original document which he could not leave as he was under instructions to read it also to British and French Ambassadors:

2. "The Chinese military authorities in formulating their general defensive plan, entertain no intention of launching an attack on the Japanese forces now stationed in Shanghai. It is our sincere wish that peace could be maintained in and around that city. While, however, the Chinese defensive forces will refrain from attacking the Japanese forces in Shanghai under the present circumstances the situation would be entirely altered if the Japanese on their side should choose to break the peace either by opening an attack, which would immediately meet with re-

* Telegram No. 262, August 13, 6 P.M.

sistance, or by unjustifiably sending any more armed forces to Shanghai. In the latter event, the Chinese defensive forces for strategic reasons cannot permit the Japanese to consolidate their positions from which they might direct assaults on the Chinese forces, but will take the first opportunity to prevent them from disturbing peace and order in Shanghai.

"We recall with regret that in 1932 the Settlement authorities should have permitted the Japanese marines and troops to use the Settlement as a base of operations for attacks on the Chinese army. We hope that the powers concerned profiting by their past experience will now take such effective steps as will prevent the Japanese armed forces in Shanghai using any part of the Settlement as a base of operations or a place of retreat in their clash with the Chinese defensive forces. Should such a contingency arise, the Chinese defensive forces would be compelled to take such necessary measures against the Japanese combatants in the Settlement as will deprive them of their fighting strength. In such a case it would be clear that responsibility for all the consequences does not rest with China." * . . .

My 389, August 8, 10 A.M.

My British colleague has just called and we have discussed Chinese communication preparatory to a meeting with our French, German and Italian colleagues tomorrow at 11 A.M. We propose to discuss with them a joint communication to the Japanese Embassy using the following text:

"In the midst of the general uneasiness occasioned by recent events in North China, we have been feeling increasing anxiety for the safety of our nationals and the welfare of the immense foreign commercial and shipping interests in Shanghai and its vicinity. You will agree that it would be deplorable if hostilities should unfortunately occur in that region precipitating eventually a chain of events which would gravely endanger foreign life and property.

"In an oral communication thc Chinese authorities have already announced to the American, French and British Embassies their desire to avoid all hostilities in the Shanghai region. We now address ourselves to Your Excellency in the hope that the

* Nanking's telegram No. 389, August 8, 10 A.M.

Japanese authorities concerned may be willing to give indication of a corresponding desire on their side to avoid any action which might lead to an increase in the tension, or to armed clashes with the Chinese forces in that area."

This text as it now stands avoids any commitment on our part as to the attitude of the Chinese and asks an expression from the Japanese of their desire to avoid hostilities at Shanghai. We feel, however, that this communication should be backed up by our Governments by representations at Tokyo urging the Japanese not to use Shanghai as a base of military operations against the Chinese.* . . .

Department's 132, August 7, 2 P.M. and my 390, August 8, 1 P.M.

1. The telegrams in reference crossed in transmission. The same five Ambassadors at conference August 9, 11 A.M. unanimously accepted the draft communication to the Japanese Embassy given in my August 8, 1 P.M. and also approved a draft of a corresponding communication to the Chinese Minister for Foreign Affairs. The second draft uses the same opening paragraph and then reads:

"In an oral communication addressed to some of the Ambassadors most interested there has been indicated the desire of the Chinese authorities to avoid all hostilities in the Shanghai region. Basing our action on this communication the undersigned diplomatic representatives are addressing a communication to His Excellency the Japanese Ambassador, expressing the hope that the Japanese authorities concerned may be willing to give indication of a similar desire on their side to avoid any action which might lead to an increase in the tension, or to armed clashes with the Japanese forces in that area.

"We are confident in the belief that the Chinese Government will do all in its power to carry out effectively the plan of excluding the Shanghai area from the scope of any possible hostilities and we should welcome any additional assurance to that effect which Your Excellency may feel able to give."

2. My colleagues are ready at once to sign these communica-

* Nanking's telegram No. 390, August 8, 1 P.M.

tions as a preliminary to any further steps to obviate hostilities in the Shanghai area which the interested Powers may later decide to take in Tokyo or Nanking. . . .*

On August 9 the Department informed us that with certain textual changes to be considered by the diplomatic representatives concerned it had authorized Nanking to sign the two communications as drafted.[21] At the same time I also was authorized to approach the Japanese Government orally along the lines set forth in the final paragraph of Nanking's 390 — of August 8 — provided that similar action should be taken, separately and not jointly, by my concerned colleagues in Tokyo.† In reply to the foregoing instruction I reported on the 13th that the two communications as signed and delivered in Nanking concerning the protection of Shanghai had reached me and that the attitude of my colleagues in Tokyo was as follows: the German and Italian Ambassadors [Dr. Herbert von Dirksen and Giacinto Auriti] had not yet received instructions but would advise me if and when such instructions came; the French Ambassador was authorized to support such action as might be taken by our British colleague and myself, and in that event he would do so although personally disapproving such action because he felt that it was then too late to influence Japanese action in Shanghai; mandatory instructions were received on that morning by the British Chargé d'Affaires to urge the Japanese Government not to land further forces in Shanghai and not to use that city as a base for hostilities. Mr. Dodds had therefore immediately called on the Vice Minister and had brought up these points incidentally while indicating that the main purpose of his call had been to inquire about

* Nanking's telegram No. 394, August 9, 1 P.M.

21 In his *Memoirs,* I, 539–40, Mr. Hull has written that on August 11, "we joined with the British, German, French, and Italian diplomats at Tokyo and Nanking in seeking to eliminate hostilities in the Shanghai area. Shanghai was a city of 3,000,000 people and had largely been built by foreigners. Major military operations there would be most destructive, and we did not see any occasion for them."

† Department's telegram No. 142, August 9, 7 P.M.

the situation. Mr. Horinouchi said in reply that it was the desire of the Japanese to avoid hostilities and that the Japanese forces would withdraw to their original positions provided that the Chinese should do the same, and that some of the Japanese forces would withdraw from Shanghai entirely. The interested Ambassadors in Nanking were to be informed to that effect by Mr. Hidaka. While the critical situation in Shanghai was most deeply appreciated by myself, I reluctantly shared the opinion of the majority of my colleagues in Tokyo that representations by us in Tokyo would exert no preventative effect and that unless such a step were taken with great care, even though taken separately, an antiforeign outburst in the Japanese press, tending to aggravate the already intense feeling aroused by the assassination of a Japanese naval officer in Shanghai, might well be provoked. On the same day, in fact, the Japanese Cabinet had determined to take all necessary measures in order that Japanese lives and property in Shanghai might be protected. Nevertheless, if my interested colleagues should eventually take action, I was prepared with careful discretion to carry out the Department's authorization.*

On the same day, with reference to the foregoing telegram, I reported to the Department as follows:

1. The Vice Minister for Foreign Affairs asked me to meet him at the Tokyo Club late this evening and gave me the text of the statement the sense of which Hidaka has been instructed to communicate today to the five ambassadors in Nanking in reply to their communication of August 11. In case any error should have occurred in communicating this message, the Vice Minister expressed the hope that I would cable the precise text to Washington. The text follows in section two.

2. The Vice Minister said that the situation in Shanghai is dangerous because Chinese troops have been sniping at the Japanese landing forces who have naturally returned the fire. The Japanese, he said, earnestly wish to avoid hostilities. He expressed the hope that the ambassadors in Nanking would ar-

* Telegram No. 263, August 13, 7 P.M.

range through their consular representatives in Shanghai for the Chinese troops to withdraw "to an arranged point" whereupon the Japanese forces would likewise withdraw to their original position. I asked the Vice Minister if this was a request for mediation. He replied "Yes, local mediation."

3. I took the opportunity of this unsolicited interview to say to the Vice Minister that I desired to support earnestly and to urge the importance of the representations made by the five ambassadors in Nanking to the Japanese Embassy to the effect that the Japanese would not use Shanghai as a base for hostilities and that they would not land further forces. The Vice Minister made no further comment except to thank me for having consistently had in mind the avoidance of undesirable publicity in the various steps which I have taken here.

4. The Vice Minister told me that he was communicating also to the other concerned ambassadors the instructions sent to Hidaka.

(Section Two.)

"(1) Since the Japanese Government desire most earnestly the safety of the lives and property of the Japanese and foreign residents in Shanghai, they sincerely hope that hostilities will be avoided in and around Shanghai.

"(2) It is, however, necessary that the Chinese regular troops and the equally armed peace preservation corps which have been concentrated in the neighborhood of the International Settlement constituting a grave menace to the Japanese should be withdrawn at least to a point out of the fighting range and their military works around the International Settlement abolished, as the first step toward the ultimate securing of a faithful execution by the Chinese of the Agreement of May 1932 [22] regarding the cessation of hostilities around Shanghai.

"(3) The Japanese naval landing party are under a strict order to act with the utmost patience and have, therefore, no intention whatsoever of embarking, without provocation, upon aggressive action against the Chinese troops or the peace preservation corps. The Japanese Government are prepared to restore the naval

[22] For the text of this agreement and comment on the situation in Shanghai in 1932, see Arnold J. Toynbee, *Survey of International Affairs, 1932* (London: Oxford University Press, 1933), pp. 510–13.

landing party to their original position when the Chinese accede to the condition above set forth. (Furthermore, when the Chinese have faithfully carried out the Agreement mentioned above, the strength of the naval landing party will also be restored to the normal footing.)

"(4) The Japanese Government, therefore, earnestly hope that the Powers concerned will use all available means to expedite the withdrawal of the Chinese troops and the similarly equipped peace preservation corps from the neighborhood of the International Settlement with a view to saving Shanghai from the imminent danger of an armed conflict."

In this connection I expressed in the same telegram the opinion that nothing further could now helpfully be done at the Tokyo end of the line.*

On August 14 we informed the Department that under instructions from Berlin there would be no participation in any collective démarche by the German Embassy in Tokyo.† As for the French Ambassador, he felt that the statement made by the Vice Minister on the previous day rendered superfluous any action on his part, and therefore, when summoned to the interview with Mr. Horinouchi, he failed to take that occasion to support the representations of the five ambassadors in Nanking.‡

The situation in Shanghai continued critical, and on the 14th we cabled to Washington:

1. With respect to the press reports of the naval bombardment yesterday at Shanghai a naval informant stated to the Naval Attaché that as several Japanese Yangtze River gunboats were leaving for a downriver rendezvous yesterday afternoon they were fired on from shore a few miles below Shanghai. The fire was returned and the ships proceeded downriver.

2. As regards blocking of the Whangpoo: Two Chinese steamers and several large junks were sunk by the Chinese above the

---

* Telegram No. 264, August 13, 11 P.M. [*Ibid.*, pp. 344–45.]
† Telegram No. 265, August 14, 2 P.M.
‡ Telegram No. 268, August 14, 5 P.M.

naval anchorage apparently to prevent Japanese gunboats proceeding up river to capture Chinese gunboats undergoing overhaul at the Shanghai-Whangpoo dockyard.

3. Informant further stated that five hundred additional men were landed last night from the *Idzumo* (flagship) and other Japanese ships to reinforce the naval landing force, bringing the number of the latter up to 3,500. As all of the landing force is on the front line, there are no reserves which makes the tactical situation precarious. The use of guns from the ships present to support or cover the landing force would be most dangerous to the civilian population and property as it would be necessary to fire over the Settlement.

4. Naval Attaché from the statements made by informant today and yesterday (Embassy's 262, August 13, 6 P.M.) is of the opinion that the Cabinet decided at the meeting this morning to send Army troops to Shanghai.

5. The Chief Secretary of the Cabinet after the Cabinet meeting this morning told press representatives that the Cabinet had determined "to take concrete measures." No other statement was made and the Chief Secretary's words are interpreted by many to mean that military reinforcements will be sent to Shanghai.*

The British Chargé d'Affaires had meanwhile called once again on Mr. Hirota, as instructed by London, and had presented a further communication, whose text is set forth below, with respect to the action of the Japanese forces in Shanghai. Mr. Dodds, however, took the responsibility of considerably toning down the text which, as received from his Government, had included such strong terms as "glaring" and "preposterous." Mr. Dodds furthermore wrote to the French Ambassador and myself to express the hope that we would support his representations, but while at first he had considered approaching the four interested ambassadors he finally decided to omit the German and Italian. The French Ambassador told me that his reply to Mr. Dodds would state that while it was his opinion that the proposed step came too late to prove effective he would nevertheless refer the matter to his Government for instruc-

---

* Telegram No. 266, August 14, 3 P.M.

tions which, incidentally, he believed would be negative. I
myself informed Mr. Dodds that unless specifically directed by
my Government I was not prepared to take further action. Mr.
Dodds' communication — on August 14 — to Mr. Hirota was
as follows:

> I have this morning received a most immediate telegram from
> my Government regarding the reports which have reached them
> of fighting in the Hongkew district of Shanghai.
>
> His Majesty's Ambassador at Nanking and I are instructed
> to impress upon the Governments to which we are accredited
> once more in the strongest terms the importance of avoiding
> hostilities in Shanghai. Both the Japanese and Chinese Govern-
> ments are under the strongest moral obligation to refrain from
> any action likely to lead, whether through their own immediate
> fault or that of the other party, to such hostilities and to the
> incalculable danger which will ensue to the many thousands of
> foreigners in no way concerned. Not only contact between the
> troops of the opposing parties but their presence in that area
> must be recognized as constituting a naked flame in a powder
> magazine and the responsibility cannot be avoided by argu-
> ment as to who started firing or what technical right exists to
> have troops on the spot. Both sides will be responsible for the
> disastrous results which cannot humanly speaking be avoided
> if their present attitude is maintained. To the impartial on-
> looker that attitude is the one most certainly leading to the very
> trouble which each side profess to wish to avoid. No word can
> alter this fact and His Majesty's Government must appeal to
> both the Japanese and Chinese Governments with the utmost
> insistence to make their deeds conform to their assurances. I am
> instructed to point out to Your Excellency that His Majesty's
> Government find it difficult to reconcile the assurances of Your
> Excellency's Government that they are most anxious not to im-
> peril Shanghai with the measure recently taken because two
> members of their landing party have been killed far outside the
> city boundary. I am to appeal to Your Excellency for the sake
> of the good name of Japan and in the interests of humanity to
> undertake that every effort will be made to avoid not only a
> recurrence of such incidents but exaggerated measures if and
> when they do occur and in general such disposition and use of

their forces. Under this heading certainly comes the use of the
International Settlement as a base in any form such as would lead
to Chinese counter measures. It is to be hoped that Your Excellency's Government will, on the contrary, take every possible
measure to prove to the Chinese that serious action is not intended at Shanghai.* . . .

In the meantime several telegrams had come from the Department. One telegram to Nanking, which was to be repeated
to Peiping, Tientsin, Shanghai and Tsingtao, for the guidance
of our military officers in those posts, merely as expository of
existing instructions, emphasized the fact that the presence of
American forces in China was for the purpose of protecting
American lives and property and in no respect for offensive
action or for coercing the Chinese or any other foreign governments. These forces were not in occupation of enemy territory
or defending American territory; they were in no sense ex-
peditionary forces, and while they were expected to protect
lives, and secondarily to protect property, they were not expected to hold positions regardless of hazards. While they
would be expected to repel threatened incursions of mobs or of
disorganized or unauthorized soldiery, they would not be expected to hold positions against foreign armed forces acting on
high authority in operations of occupation. If situations should
arise calling for the evacuation of American nationals, our
forces would be expected to facilitate and to assist such evacuation. The officers of the various agencies of our Government
were expected to act in close co-operation in accordance with
their own best judgment in any situation with which they
might find themselves confronted.† 23

* Telegram No. 269, August 14, 6 P.M.
† Department's telegram to Nanking, No. 138, August 10, noon.
23 In regard to the American troops in China Mr. Hull wrote: "On August 16,
1937, Admiral Yarnell, in command of the United States Asiatic Fleet, requested
that 1,200 marines at San Diego be sent to Shanghai, and the President and I
agreed they should go. Simultaneously, we began receiving widespread demands from American citizens and organizations to withdraw all armed forces
and all Americans from China. We had about 2,500 marines and infantrymen in
China by virtue of our treaties with China giving us the right to station them

With reference to our telegram No. 256 — of August 11 — the Department, on the 13th, repeated for our strictly confidential information its 145, August 12, 9 P.M., to Nanking, substantially as follows. The Department believed that no useful purpose would be served by an approach to the Chinese Government at that time in view of the fact that the Japanese Minister for Foreign Affairs, according to our 254 — of August 10 — had not accepted our offer of good offices. Nevertheless the Department was of the opinion that it might possibly be helpful if Ambassador Johnson were to take action along the lines suggested in our 254 and he was accordingly authorized to do so if and when his British colleague was prepared to act similarly. Reference might be made to press reports of Sino-Japanese conversations and the Chinese Foreign Minister might be asked if these reports were true. The Ambassador would then stress our Government's hope for a peaceful outcome and would speak of our efforts since the beginning of the incident in counseling circumspection on both sides; he was to make it clear that our Government did not wish to become involved or to be committed on the merits of any particular proposal, but if any proposals should be set forth by either the Chinese or Japanese Government for settling the dispute, a reply should be returned which would leave the door open to negotiations. If asked whether we proposed to make a similar approach to the Japanese Government, Mr. Johnson was authorized to say that he understood that we expected to do so. In the meantime the British Ambassador in Nanking had likewise been instructed by his Govern-

there to protect Americans. For the same purpose we also had a small fleet of gunboats on the Yangtze River by virtue of a treaty with China signed in 1858.

"I outlined our attitude at a press conference on August 17, saying that we found ourselves in between two extreme views: 'One is the view of extreme internationalism, which rests upon the idea of political commitments. We keep entirely away from that in our thoughts and views and policies, just as we seek, on the other hand, to keep entirely away from the extreme nationalists who would tell all Americans that they must stay here at home and that, if they went abroad anywhere for any purpose — tourist, urgent business, or otherwise — and trouble overtook them and violence threatened, they must not expect any protection from their government.' " Hull, *op. cit.*, I, 540.

ment to urge Chiang Kai-shek to "keep the door open" as originally suggested in our 254.*

On the same day Mr. Hull, in conversation with the Japanese Ambassador in Washington, had emphatically pointed out that terrific hazards for all concerned would be involved if Sino-Japanese hostilities should break out in Shanghai, and that if that city should be made an arena of combat, the world would consider both sides responsible regardless of arguments as to who had begun the trouble or who was at fault and regardless of technicalities and debate over rights. The British Ambassador in Washington had been advised of this conversation and had been told that Ambassador Johnson in Nanking had been directed to express to his colleagues the opinion that avoidance of aggravating the situation in Shanghai should be urged upon the Chinese authorities.†

On the 14th the Department informed us that the Counselor of the Japanese Embassy in Washington had called on the Chief of the Far Eastern Division and had embarked upon a narration of developments in Shanghai, by way of information, laying on the Chinese the entire blame for the situation. Dr. Hornbeck repeated to him what the Secretary had said to Ambassador Saito on the previous day as we had been informed in the Department's 146 and had emphasized the fact that the military situation in Shanghai was one in which, according to our Government's opinion, neither party could properly repudiate responsibility because the Chinese and Japanese had both contributed to its making. This view coincided with that of the British Government as expressed by Mr. Dodds to the Japanese Foreign Office according to our 269 — of August 14. Incidentally the Department felt not at all certain that the Japanese Embassy in Washington was reporting fully to its Government. Only if one or both parties to the dispute should withdraw their armed forces from Shanghai did it appear to the Department that dangerous and destructive military operations could be averted.

* Department's telegram No. 145, August 13, 7 P.M.
† Department's telegram No. 146, August 13, midnight.

In consideration of the foregoing facts the Department felt that without making a special occasion it would be well for me to lay before the Foreign Minister at the first possible opportunity what Mr. Hull and Dr. Hornbeck had said to the Japanese Ambassador and Counselor in Washington and to add that it would be physically easier for the Japanese to withdraw than for the Chinese, in spite of the psychological difficulties for both sides. I was furthermore authorized to say that we had urged the Chinese to withdraw their forces, but the proposed representations and their form were left to my discretion.*

In accordance with the foregoing instructions I took immediate action and reported to the Department as follows:

Department's 146, August 13, midnight, and 149, August 14, 10 P.M.

1. This afternoon I called on the Minister for Foreign Affairs at his residence and handed to him an informal note the text of which is set forth in paragraph 8 of this telegram.

2. The situation today at Shanghai is such that, whatever the contributory causes, the Japanese Government is now confronted equally with neutral governments with the problem of protecting the lives of great numbers of their nationals at Shanghai.24 Even if neutral governments were prepared to assume by delegation responsibility for protection of Japanese nationals, it is not to be expected in the present state of affairs that the Japanese Government would be willing to delegate such responsibility. The Chinese bombings have of course rendered the situation infinitely more difficult and the probability of any Japanese initiative towards withdrawal seems hardly to be expected.

3. Nevertheless, realizing the profoundly grave aspects of the

---

* Department's telegram No. 149, August 14, 10 P.M.

24 Mr. Grew wrote in his diary on August 29, 1937: "The bombing in Shanghai on August 14 was one of the most horrible episodes in modern times. The bombs fell indiscriminately, hitting the Cathay and Palace Hotels and killing hundreds of Chinese civilians gathered on the Bund and elsewhere. Bob Reischauer, the son of an American missionary, was fatally injured at the entrance to the Cathay and other Americans may have been killed or injured. I wrote to Dr. and Mrs. Reischauer in Karuizawa. Subsequently we received the most heartrending firsthand accounts from refugees."

present situation, I availed myself of the authorization granted me in the last paragraph of Department's 149. My note was formulated in such language as would, in our opinion, hold out some perhaps slender prospect of a solution.

4. In my conversation with the Minister I spoke to him of your grave concern over the safety of American nationals in Shanghai and of your feeling that the only way of now avoiding more serious destruction and possible loss of life was for the withdrawal of one or both combatants. I also told him of what had been done in Nanking. I then read to him my informal note pausing to render completely clear and to emphasize each separate point.

5. The Minister listened carefully and courteously and then said that he knew of the approach by the foreign consuls to the Japanese but he had not heard of their approach to the Chinese. He deeply regretted the loss of American life. He said that the Japanese Consulate General had been bombed today and that two persons therein had been seriously injured. He mentioned the Japanese decision to send reinforcements. I asked him whether these reinforcements could not be withheld until adequate time had been afforded for consideration and action on the proposals of the consuls and urged the great importance of such delay. The Minister said that these decisions now lay exclusively in the hands of Admiral Hasegawa.

6. The Minister referred to his previous comment concerning the Kawagoe-Kao conversation and to Kao's promise to return to Shanghai with Nanking's reply. Hirota added significantly that Kao had not returned.

7. The Minister said that Hidaka and other Japanese Embassy officials in Nanking had requested the American Navy for transportation to some safe spot. He emphasized the fact that this departure does not constitute a breach of diplomatic relations and that Hidaka will probably eventually go to Shanghai to join Kawagoe.

8. Following is the text of my informal note:

"The initiation at Shanghai of hostilities between armed Japanese and Chinese forces has given rise on the part of my Government, which had looked forward with lively hope to a speedy adjustment of matters at issue between the Governments of Japan and of China, to a feeling of alarm over the safety of the lives and property of its nationals residing in Shanghai. I make no reference on this occasion to the broader issues over which controversy has arisen between two powers with which the United States has long maintained ties of friendship: I now refer to the incalculable hazards to which combat operations at Shanghai between Japanese and Chinese forces are subjecting American nationals along with other nationals in no way involved in the creation of the military situation now existing in that area.

"My colleague in Nanking has expressed to the Chinese Minister for Foreign Affairs the hope that some means may be found whereby the two Governments may get together and bring about a cessation of hostilities in the neighborhood of Shanghai, a hope which I earnestly share. My Government has urged upon the Chinese that their forces should be withdrawn. The important issue at the present moment is not a question of determining the initial responsibility for the outbreak, but there can be no doubt that if the Shanghai region continues to be made the theatre of battle, neither side can divest itself of responsibility.

"There now appears to be but one hope of averting further destructive and dangerous military operations at Shanghai, and that lies in the withdrawal by one or both sides of its armed forces from Shanghai and from the environs of that city. The dangers imposed upon noncombatants of all nations and upon their property are so great that my Government feels warranted in entertaining the confident hope that the Japanese Government will contribute toward restoration of conditions of peace in and around Shanghai by giving speedy and favorable consideration to plans, of which Your Excellency is no doubt aware, calculated to bring about cessation of hostilities in the concerned area, that have been formulated by representatives at Shanghai of the interested powers." *

In reply to the foregoing message, Mr. Hull telegraphed on the 17th: "I heartily approve your action and excellent note. If not already done please inform your British and in your discretion French colleagues." † I replied: "Thank you sin-

* Telegram No. 272, August 16, 6 P.M. [*Ibid.*, pp. 347–49.]
† Department's telegram No. 150, August 17, 3 P.M. [*Ibid.*, p. 349.]

cerely. Copy of our note was handed to my British colleague August 16 and was sent to my French colleague August 17." *

On the 16th we reported as follows certain statements made to our Naval Attaché by the Japanese Navy Department:

> Japanese Government is considering a plan to stop shipment of armament (munitions of war) to China without becoming involved in complications with other governments. The purpose of such a move was stated to be "to avoid prolonging the existing situation." He inquired whether American ships were carrying such to China now. He did not appear conversant with the recent ruling of the Japanese Government whereby manifests of cargo of Dollar Line ships arriving at Yokohama from the United States were to be presented to local authorities irrespective of whether the cargo was destined for China or the Philippines.

On the same day the British Chargé d'Affaires presented to the Vice Foreign Minister the following *pro memoria:*

> 1. The situation that has arisen at Shanghai must be considered as ultimately due to the presence of the Japanese landing party there. The best practical contribution which the Japanese Government can make to a solution of it would be to withdraw their landing party. His Majesty's Government are urging the Chinese Government to guarantee that there will be no attack on the Japanese quarter and to dispose their forces so as to remove apprehension of any attack.
>
> 2. Arrangements are being made to evacuate a large number of British nationals from Shanghai and His Majesty's Government count upon the Japanese Government to enable this to be done.
>
> 3. The greatest and most immediate danger to the lives and property of noncombatants in the International Settlement arises from the presence of the *Idzumo* adjacent to the Settlement wharves and without prejudice to other aspects of the situation, the best practical demonstration that the Japanese Government could give of their expressed desire to avert danger to foreign life

* Telegram No. 275, August 18, 10 A.M.

and property would be the removal of the *Idzumo* to some more distant station.

His Majesty's Government are at the same time urging upon the Chinese Government in the most insistent manner possible that they should refrain from any repetitions of bombing raids.*

On the 18th our Naval Attaché had another talk with the Senior Aide to the Navy Minister, reported as follows:

1. When asked as to plan for stoppage of munitions to China Senior Aide stated that it was his opinion that the Japanese Government would evolve some such plan. It might be advisable to make this point clear to Washington as the Embassy telegram was to the effect that the Japanese Government was considering the plan. However, I believe that the Government is actually considering the plan. The British Naval Attaché [Captain Henry Rawlings] mentioned the matter to me yesterday, having obtained intimation of it from the same source.

2. Naval landing force reinforcements were landed in Shanghai yesterday and this morning (less than 500). Army reinforcements had not been sent up "to the present moment." Inferentially Army reinforcements are due soon. All operations — air, land and sea — up to now have been by naval forces under the command of Vice Admiral Hasegawa. . . .

5. Situation in Tsingtao is becoming threatening. The Customs Guards which the Japanese claim are Central Forces in disguise are closing in on Tsingtao. Two Japanese cruisers, *Tatsuta* and *Tenryu,* are there under command of Rear Admiral Shimomura, formerly Naval Attaché at Washington in 1930–32. So far no landing force units have been put ashore from them in order not to aggravate the situation.

6. When asked what the War Minister meant by the statements quoted in press today "abandonment of policy of nonexpansion adopted at outbreak of North China Incident" and "unanimous support for Government's future drastic policy towards China," it was explained as follows: "In order to avoid a prolonged struggle and repeat the calamity now in Spain,[25] a solution to

* Telegram No. 274, August 16, 8 P.M.

25 The Spanish Civil War had begun on July 18, 1936, with the revolt of army chiefs in Spanish Morocco.

this situation must, in the shortest possible time, be reached by every means possible." Asked if this meant the striking of a telling blow, the answer was in the affirmative.* . . .

Further British action was reported on the 18th:

1. The British Chargé d'Affaires under instructions from his Government today presented to the Vice Minister for Foreign Affairs the following *pro memoria*:

"If both the Chinese and Japanese Governments will agree to withdraw their forces including men-of-war from the Shanghai area and will both agree that the protection of Japanese nationals in the International Settlement and on the extra-Settlement roads should be entrusted to foreign authorities, His Majesty's Government in the United Kingdom will be prepared to undertake this responsibility if other powers will join with them in doing so.

"In putting forward this proposal His Majesty's Government are actuated solely by the desire to keep the International Settlement free from hostilities and the commitments contemplated would be of a temporary nature to hold good during the continuance of the crisis."

2. The Vice Minister replied that this was a very important communication but (a) that he doubted the ability of the concerned powers with the forces at their disposal at Shanghai to ensure the safety of Japanese nationals and (b) that the Japanese Government might find it difficult to accept in face of Chinese aggressive tactics at Shanghai. The Vice Minister said that Japanese reinforcements were ready to start from Japan but had not yet started. Dodds pointed out that if the British proposal could be accepted and put into effect it would become unnecessary for these reinforcements to sail. Favorable reaction from the Vice Minister was not forthcoming. Dodds inquired if the Japanese proposed to extend aggressive tactics to South China as well as in North China. The Vice Minister replied definitely in the negative. Dodds said that this was at least the fourth or fifth time that his Government had taken steps in Tokyo in an effort to bring about peace. The Vice Minister refrained from comment. . . .

* Telegram No. 277, August 18, 4 P.M.

4. The Vice Minister said that the Japanese war vessel *Idzumo* had moved downstream and away from the settlement wharves.*

On the same day the following letter was received by me from the Foreign Minister:

August 18, 1937.
My dear Ambassador:
On behalf of my Government, I wish to express my sincere appreciation for the kind assistance which the representatives of your country in China have so generously extended to Mr. S. Hidaka, Counselor, and other members of our Embassy in Nanking who thanks to their good offices have safely journeyed to Tsingtao arriving there early in the morning of the 18th. I am truly grateful for this help which is being keenly appreciated by our people as a token of your cordial friendship toward this country. I beg Your Excellency to be good enough to convey my deep gratitude to His Excellency Nelson T. Johnson and the staff of the American Embassy and Consulates in China. I am, my dear Ambassador, with cordial regards, Sincerely yours,
K. HIROTA.† . . .

On the same day — August 19 — the Vice Foreign Minister informed the British Chargé d'Affaires that Japan would not accept the British proposal for Chinese-Japanese withdrawal of forces in and around Shanghai on condition that foreign Powers would assume responsibility for the safety of Japanese nationals in the International Settlement and on the extra-Settlement roads because (1) foreign forces would not be adequate; (2) it was Japan's duty to protect her own nationals; and (3) the Chinese were entirely to blame for the existing situation. Mr. Dodds, however, obtained assurances that this refusal was only provisional and might be reconsidered. He believed, in fact, that a reconsideration of their refusal to accept the British proposal was not unlikely because the Japanese realized that they were "in a jam" in Shanghai. In the mean-

* Telegram No. 279, August 18, 6 P.M.
† Telegram No. 280, August 18, 9 P.M.

time the French Ambassador had informed the Japanese Government that if the Powers should undertake to protect Japanese nationals in the International Settlement, France would extend the same protection to Japanese in the French Concession.*

With reference to our 279 — of August 18 — the Department informed us:

> In reply to an *aide-mémoire* from the British Embassy of August 18 setting forth the British Government's proposal under reference and inquiring whether the American Government would be prepared to accept with the British Government joint responsibility in carrying out the proposal, the Department has handed the British Embassy a memorandum stating that shortly after receipt of this inquiry the Government received a telegram from the American Ambassador at Tokyo to the effect that the British Chargé at Tokyo had presented to the Japanese Vice Minister for Foreign Affairs the British Government's proposal and that the reaction of the Vice Minister to the proposal was of a character which could only be construed as unfavorable; that there had subsequently appeared no indication of an affirmative interest on the part of the Japanese Government in this proposal; and that in the light of this evidence it appeared to this Government that the question of the possible assumption of a joint responsibility such as is envisaged in the British Government's proposal has already been disposed of, adversely, by the attitude of the Japanese Government in regard to the proposal; and, further, that toward avoiding any possible misunderstanding, it should not be expected that this Government would look favorably upon any project envisaging military or police responsibilities beyond those which relate to the existing missions of its armed forces now present in China.† . . .

The long series of Japanese bombings of American missions in China began early, as witness the following:

> Reference Gauss's telegram of August 19, 2 P.M., regarding bombing by Japanese planes of American mission at Nantung-

---

* Telegram No. 283, August 19, 11 P.M.
† Department's telegram No. 154, August 19, 10 P.M.

chow. Senior Aide to Navy Minister called Assistant Naval Attaché to his office this noon to express regret and to give his assurances that it had not been deliberate, but probably due to bad weather (visibility) and indistinct bombing objectives. He asked for detailed list of places where Americans and American interests were centered in order that Japanese aircraft units might be given orders to take precautions. Such a list as furnished by Consul General [Clarence E. Gauss] and supplied by us this morning to the Foreign Office was given him.* . . .

The following information was gained by the Military Attaché through an interview with the Secretary of the Minister of War on the 20th:

(a) Although Japanese troops were ready and prepared to go to Shanghai, no units had yet left.

(b) The War and Navy Departments have been under great pressure from rightist organizations to take some decisive action at Shanghai, but the sending of large reinforcements has been delayed in the hope that they might not be necessary.

(c) The Secretary of the Minister of War gave as his "personal opinion" that a peaceful solution of the situation in Shanghai is improbable due to the pressure on both Chinese and Japanese Governments of public opinion.

(d) As regards the British proposal for the complete withdrawal of both Chinese and Japanese forces, the Secretary of the Minister of War thought it entirely unacceptable as it would be very humiliating to Japan to entrust the safeguarding of its nationals to troops of other countries.

(e) He said that he thought the only solution agreeable to Japan would be a return to the situation prescribed in the truce agreement of 1932, the violation of which by the Chinese was responsible for the present Shanghai incident. Due to the large numbers of Chinese troops in the Shanghai area, to the comparatively poor control over them by the Central Government and the pressure of Chinese public opinion, he thought it would be very difficult for the Nanking Government to arrange for a withdrawal of its troops from the area prescribed in the 1932 truce agreement.

* Telegram No. 285, August 20, 4 P.M.

(f) The situation in North China remains comparatively quiet with the reinforcements of Chinese concentrations limited to that near Nankow.

Referring to paragraph (b) above, it was uniformly explained to us by well-informed Japanese officers that owing to the necessarily prolonged dispersion of the forces involved and owing also to the expense and difficulty of extensive operations in the Shanghai area there was reluctance to send any units to Shanghai. It was the opinion of our Military Attaché that the primary objection on the part of the Army to the sending of troops to Shanghai was based on the fact that such units would be held there for an uncertain period at a time when the Army's chief objective was the settlement of the situation in North China, and that during the accomplishment of that objective all available forces would be needed for protection against any possible interference on the part of the Soviet Union.*

On the 21st the following informal note and enclosure were received from the Foreign Minister and were reported to the Department with reference to the Embassy's 272 — of August 16 — and 279 — of August 18:

> August 20, 1937.
> With reference to Your Excellency's note of August 16th, I wish to inform you that on the 18th instant, Mr. J. L. Dodds, British Chargé d'Affaires, called upon the Vice Minister Mr. Horinouchi and made a proposal to the effect that if both the Chinese and Japanese Government will agree to withdraw their forces including men-of-war from the Shanghai area and will agree also to entrust to foreign authorities the protection of Japanese nationals in the International Settlement and on the extra-Settlement roads, the British Government will be prepared to undertake this responsibility provided other powers cooperate.
> In reply, Mr. Horinouchi handed a note on the 19th to Mr. Dodds a copy of which I am enclosing herewith for Your Excellency's reference, in the hope that this, being an exposition

* Telegram No. 288, August 20, 7 P.M.

of our views regarding the situation, will be considered sufficient to serve as an answer to your note. For, under the circumstances now prevailing in and around Shanghai, this is the only possible reply we can make at this juncture, although we do not, of course, fail to appreciate the spirit which has actuated the Government of the United States to approach the Japanese Government with a view to keeping the International Settlement free from hostilities. . . .

Enclosure.

"1. The Japanese Government, earnestly desiring to protect the lives and property of foreigners as well as Japanese in and around Shanghai, have done everything possible to keep those areas from the disasters of hostilities. For instance, Ambassador Kawagoe, in reply to the letter dated August 11th, signed by the Ambassadors of Germany, the United States of America, France, Great Britain and Italy, stated, as Your Excellency must be aware, to the following effect:

" '(1) That the Japanese marines have been given a strict order to act with utmost patience and that Japan has not the slightest intention of taking aggressive action, without provocation, against the Chinese troops or Peace Preservation Corps.

" '(2) That if the Chinese withdraw their troops and the Peace Preservation Corps which, disregarding the Agreement for the Cessation of Hostilities concluded at Shanghai in 1932, have been massed near the International Settlement menacing the Japanese, and also abolish their military works in the neighborhood of the Settlement, we are prepared to restore our marines to their original positions.'

"Furthermore, our Government were giving their unfavorable consideration to the concrete proposal made to our Consul General Okamoto by the British, American and French Consuls General at Shanghai — on August 13. Notwithstanding such peaceful attitude on the part of the Japanese Government, the Chinese have not only failed to cease their aggression on the Settlement but even went the length of launching attacks upon our Consulate General and warships bombing them from the air on the 14th when our Government had just received a cable report concerning the said proposal from the above-mentioned Consuls General. This naturally compelled our forces to resort to self-defense.

"2. We believe that the authorities of the Powers on the spot are fully aware of the fact that the present Sino-Japanese hostilities in Shanghai have been caused by China which, by violating the Agreement of 1932, moved its regular troops into the district forbidden by the said Agreement, and by increasing the number and armaments of the Peace Preservation Corps took the offensive to provoke the Japanese marines.

"Therefore, we trust that Your Excellency will understand that the hostilities will cease as soon as the Chinese troops are evacuated to the districts outside the agreed area and the Peace Preservation Corps are withdrawn from the front lines; and that Japan is not in a position to consider the withdrawal of her forces whose continued presence in the Settlement and the harbor in their present strength does not constitute a cause of further hostilities, since their sole purpose from the outset has been to protect our nationals and they have been maintaining a purely defensive position, having no intention of advancing into the Chinese-inhabited area.

"However, Japan with her numerous nationals in the Settlement is as greatly solicitous as other Powers of the safety of the lives and property of Japanese and foreigners in that Settlement, and earnestly desires that hostilities will cease as soon as possible through the evacuation of the Chinese regulars and the Peace Preservation Corps which are similarly armed and are indulging in hostilities against the Japanese, to the areas outside the districts of the Agreement. For this reason, the Japanese Government sincerely hope that the Powers concerned, especially those that have assisted in the negotiations concerning the Agreement for the Cessation of Hostilities of 1932, will exert their influence upon China toward the realization of these aims." *

With reference to our foregoing telegram and to previous correspondence we were informed by the Department that the British Embassy in Washington had brought to the Department an *aide-mémoire* in which hope was again expressed by the British Government "that the United States Government will be able to declare their readiness to co-operate" in the project under reference. On the 21st the Department handed

* Telegram No. 289, August 21, 9 A.M. [*Ibid.*, pp. 353–55.]

to the British Ambassador a memorandum, the substantial part of which said:

> As stated in the Department's memorandum of August 19, it appeared to this Government at that time that the question of a possible assumption of a joint responsibility such as is envisaged in the British Government's proposal had already been disposed of, adversely, by the attitude of the Japanese Government in regard to the proposal. All information available, including press reports received from American official sources, tends conclusively to confirm that information.

The evidence upon which the Department's opinion was based was shown to the British Ambassador, including several of the telegrams from our Embassy, and in all friendliness it was made clear that the Government of the United States deplored the publicity given to this matter by the British Government, conveying the implication that since the British and French Governments were already in agreement, it depended on a favorable reply from the Government of the United States as to whether the British project would be carried out. The American Government expressed the hope that in future there would be no further publicity and no further charge would be laid at the door of the American Government that the failure of this project had resulted from an attitude of nonco-operation by the United States because of not having supported that project.*

On the same day the Department, in a rush telegram, repeated to us Nanking's 485, August 21, 1 P.M., to be communicated by me to my British, French, German and Italian colleagues, as follows:

> "Ambassadors of Germany, Great Britain, France, and Italy in Nanking decided to ask through me their respective colleagues in Tokyo to inform Japanese Government that Japanese airplanes have twice dropped bombs inside the walls of Nanking, causing apprehension for the safety of their staffs, archives, and

---

* Department's telegram No. 157, August 21, 9 P.M.

of themselves. They believe that in order to relieve this anxiety on the part of the representatives of friendly Powers, whose duty requires their presence in Nanking, Japanese Government may desire to instruct Japanese bombers to avoid operations in the area outlined by a line from the Hansimen gate to the circle (hsin-chiehkou), thence to Peichiko (meteorological observatory), continue the line to the wall, and follow the wall north to the point on the Yangtze located at the railway ferry. The area to the north and west of the line including the Yangtze and Hsiakwan, from that point upstream to a point near Hansimen gate, to be immune from attack. This line would include Yangtze River between city and Pukou where foreign naval and merchant vessels are anchored.

"Communications between Nanking and Tokyo now consume two days. In view of this it is requested that the Department repeat this message to Tokyo for action."

The Department approves of your associating yourself with the diplomatic representatives mentioned in making appropriate representations to the Japanese Government in accordance with the foregoing.* . . .

With regard to a shell which hit the United States flag ship *Augusta* in Shanghai we cabled the following report: [26]

1. An official of the Foreign Office called under instruction this morning at the Embassy to express regret over the casualties incurred by members of the crew of the *Augusta* now at Shanghai. The official stated that the Foreign Office had received no official report from Shanghai but that according to press reports the casualties were caused by a shell fired by the Chinese; that the Foreign Office is mindful, however, that the incident would not have arisen had there been no hostilities between the Japanese and Chinese forces; and that the Foreign Office desires to express its sincere regrets for the loss of life and the injury incurred by members of the American Navy.

2. We informed the official that we appreciate the action of

* Department's telegram No. 158, August 21, 10 P.M.

[26] An American sailor was killed and eighteen others were injured when the cruiser, *Augusta*, was hit by a "shell or aerial bomb" while lying anchored in the Whangpoo River on August 20. *New York Times*, August 21, 1937, p. 1.

the Foreign Office in instructing the official to call, and that the Department would be duly informed.* . . .

Reverting to the Department's telegram No. 158 — of August 21 — we reported on the 23rd:

Message received late Sunday evening. Endeavors to establish contact with my four colleagues failed. Owing to urgency of message this Embassy communicated it informally to the Foreign Office immediately. This was not done in the form of representations but merely the communication of advance information pending associated action.

I shall in due course report whether the other four representatives act.† . . .

Reverting to the question of bombings, we referred on August 23rd to our 294 — of August 21, paragraph 3 — and reported:

August 20 the Embassy delivered to the Foreign Office copy of the list of places of residence of American missionaries contained in Shanghai's August 19, 3 P.M. Today the Foreign Office orally stated that, after consultation with the Navy Department, the following reply is made:

"Desiring as Japan does to avoid harm to Americans or American property the Japanese Navy has issued orders to that effect, and the list received from the American Embassy has been transmitted to the Japanese officers in command. The Navy hopes that American properties will be conspicuously marked. The Navy suggests that Americans be advised to evacuate such properties as may become occupied by Chinese forces. It is also the hope of the Navy that the American authorities will continuously feel free to convey any additional information about such properties, which might add to the effectiveness of Japan's desire to keep American interests unharmed." ‡ . . .

* Telegram No. 290, August 21, 10 A.M.
† Telegram No. 295, August 23, 10 A.M.
‡ Telegram No. 299, August 23, 5 P.M. [*Ibid.*, pp. 488–89.]

With reference to the Department's 158 — of August 21 — and to the Embassy's 295 — of August 23 — the following urgent telegram was despatched to the Department on the 23rd:

1. I have today made oral representations to the Vice Minister in support of the recommendation of the five ambassadors at Nanking contained in Nanking's 485, August 21, 1 P.M., to instruct Japanese bombers to avoid operations in a specified area of Nanking.

2. My Italian and British colleagues have today done likewise. The German and French Embassies state that they have supported or will support the recommendation.

3. Acting upon the advance information supplied by this Embassy last night (our 295, August 23, 10 A.M., paragraph one), the Foreign Office last night submitted the recommendation to the Navy Department and has now informed the Embassy (by memorandum in English to be considered as oral reply) as follows:

"1. It is the earnest desire of the Japanese Government to safeguard the Embassies of Germany, Great Britain, France, Italy, and America in Nanking, and the warships and merchant vessels belonging to these Powers anchored there. The Japanese Government have already, on their own initiative, instructed the authorities concerned to use utmost caution in order to ensure as far as possible under the circumstances, the safety of these Embassies and ships, and they want to inform the Ambassadors of the Powers concerned that the Japanese authorities are acting in conformity with these instructions.

"2. The Japanese Government understand that the proposed area is one which embraces the sites of the Embassies above-mentioned and the mooring points of the men-of-war and merchant vessels of the Powers. In this area, however, there are various Chinese military works and a number of establishments connected with military operation as well as Chinese warships and fortresses. The Japanese Government desire to warn the Powers in advance that in case the Chinese should make use of them for any hostile or provocative acts, they might be forced to take necessary measures to cope with it.

"3. Even in the above-mentioned circumstances, the Japanese Government would try as much as possible to avoid inflicting damage upon the Embassies, etc. of the Powers concerned. They request, therefore, that the Powers will, as a precautionary measure, mark plainly their Embassies, warships and merchant vessels so that these may be easily identified from the air. August 23rd, 1937." *

On the same day — August 23 — the Secretary of State issued to the press a statement reading as follows:

At his press conference on August 17, the Secretary of State announced that, one, legislative action to make available funds for purposes of emergency relief necessitated by the situation in the Far East had been asked and that, two, this Government had given orders for a regiment of marines to prepare to proceed to Shanghai. The Secretary then discussed at some length the principle of policy on which this Government was proceeding.

The situation at Shanghai is in many respects unique. Shanghai is a great cosmopolitan center, with a population of over three million, a port which has been developed by the nationals of many countries, at which there have prevailed mutually advantageous contacts of all types and varieties between and among the Chinese and people of almost all other countries of the world. At Shanghai, there exists a multiplicity of rights and interests which are of inevitable concern to many countries, including the United States.

In the present situation, the American Government is engaged in facilitating in every way possible an orderly and safe removal of American citizens from areas where there is special danger. Further it is the policy of the American Government to afford its nationals appropriate protection, primarily against mobs or other uncontrolled elements. For that purpose it has for many years maintained small detachments of armed forces in China, and for that purpose it is sending the present small reinforcement. These armed forces there have no mission of aggression. It is their function to be of assistance toward maintenance of order and security. It has been the desire and the intention of

* Telegram No. 302, August 23, 9 P.M. [*Ibid.*, pp. 489–90.]

the American Government to remove these forces when performance of their function of protection is no longer called for, and such remains its desire and expectation.

The issues and problems which are of concern to this Government in the present situation in the Pacific area go far beyond merely the immediate question of protection of the nationals and interests of the United States. The conditions which prevail in that area are intimately connected with and have a direct and fundamental relationship to the general principles of policy to which attention was called in the statement of July 16, which statement has evoked expressions of approval from more than fifty governments. This Government is firmly of the opinion that the principles summarized in that statement should effectively govern international relationships.

When there unfortunately arises in any part of the world the threat or the existence of serious hostilities, the matter is of concern to all nations. Without attempting to pass judgment regarding the merits of the controversy, we appeal to the parties to refrain from resort to war. We urge that they settle their differences in accordance with principles which in the opinion not alone of our people but of most peoples of the world should govern in international relationships. We consider applicable throughout the world, in the Pacific area as elsewhere, the principles set forth in the statement of July 16. That statement of principles is comprehensive and basic. It embraces the principles embodied in many treaties, including the Washington Conference treaties and the Kellogg-Briand Pact of Paris.

From the beginning of the present controversy in the Far East, we have been urging upon both the Chinese and the Japanese Governments the importance of refraining from hostilities and of maintaining peace. We have been participating constantly in consultation with interested governments directed toward peaceful adjustment. This Government does not believe in political alliances or entanglements, nor does it believe in extreme isolation. It does believe in international cooperation for the purpose of seeking through pacific methods the achievement of those objectives set forth in the statement of July 16. In the light of our well-defined attitude and policies, and within the range thereof, this Government is giving most solicitous attention to every phase of the Far Eastern situation, toward safeguarding the lives and welfare of our people and making effective the policies — especially the policy of peace — in which this country believes and to which it is committed.

This Government is endeavoring to see kept alive, strengthened and revitalized, in regard to the Pacific area and to all the world, these fundamental principles.* . . .

Nanking's 497, August 23, 4 P.M., was repeated for communication by me to my German, British, French and Italian colleagues as follows:

1. At meeting of five interested Ambassadors this morning we decided to send following collective letter to the Minister for Foreign Affairs:

"Information received from apparently reliable sources is to the effect that the Chinese and the Japanese Government authorities in Tsingtao are endeavoring to solve present differences between them in such a way as to avoid the outbreak of hostilities at that port.

"There are in Tsingtao many hundreds, if not some thousands, of nationals of countries not concerned in the controversy between China and Japan and the undersigned Ambassadors earnestly request that the Chinese Government promote in all possible ways arrangements whereby there may be assurance that fighting may be avoided in Tsingtao and in its vicinity between the military forces of China and Japan. An early indication of the view taken by the Chinese Government toward this idea will be heartily welcomed by the undersigned Ambassadors."

2. My German, British, French and Italian colleagues asked that I transmit the contents of the collective letter to the American Ambassador in Tokyo and ask him to communicate them to the respective Embassies, it being our hope that they will all urge the Japanese authorities to take energetic measures in Tsingtao to avoid opening of hostilities.

3. Because of delay in telegraphic communication with Tokyo I request that the Department cable this request to Grew.

4. Naval report to the Commander in Chief dated August 23

* Department's telegram No. 161, August 23, 7 P.M. [*Ibid.*, pp. 355–57.]

states that the tension at Tsingtao is at such high pitch only a slight spark would be necessary to start serious trouble.*

On the 25th I reported to the Department that the Vice Minister for Foreign Affairs, in conversation on August 23 with the British Chargé d'Affaires, had inquired why the British proposal for neutralization of Shanghai had not been supported by the United States as it had been by the French Government, to which Mr. Dodds replied that while the inquiry should properly be addressed to the American Ambassador he understood that a belief that the Japanese Government had already rejected the proposal had determined the American attitude. This circumstance, which otherwise might appear of trivial importance, was reported by me because it indicated, among other similar circumstances, how minutely our acts and attitude with regard to China and Japan were scrutinized by the Japanese Government and how closely the Japanese Government noted and appreciated the restraint exercised by the American Government and its consideration of all factors in the situation.† . . .

Meanwhile apprehension as to American intentions arising from the Secretary's statement of August 23 had been reflected in editorial comment in the Japanese press of which a brief summary follows:

Hochi: If British and American peace declarations are directed specifically at Japan, Japan can only reject them. The Secretary of State's demand for avoidance of hostilities at Shanghai is not so antagonistic as Mr. Stimson's declarations but it clings to legalistic concepts and reveals serious misunderstanding. It fails to recognize that the Shanghai difficulties are too complex to submit to international discussion or diplomatic solution.

Nichi Nichi: The Secretary of State advises Japan to settle her difficulties by peaceful means; but why give Japan that advice? No one wishes for peace more than Japan, which must pay a terrific bill for hostilities. Japan has patiently exhausted all possibility

* Department's telegram No. 166, August 24, 7 P.M.
† Telegram No. 312, August 25, 1 P.M.

of peaceful settlement. President Wilson with regard to Mexico defined the entry of troops into a backward nation not as war but as a punitive expedition; atrocities by Chinese against Japanese give Japan the same justification. The United States and other countries must understand that special conditions prevail in the case of a backward country such as China.

Tokyo Asahi: Shares the views of the *Nichi Nichi* and adds that the important point with regard to the Secretary of State's peace views is whether China will modify its attitude. Comment in the United States in opposition to invocation of the neutrality act has emphasized that invocation would be unfavorable to China. The editorial expresses the hope that these arguments will be laid aside and the act be made a contribution toward peace in the Far East.* . . .

Perhaps the most important analysis and recommendation sent during these early months of the "China Incident" was cabled "Confidential for the Secretary" on the 27th, in paraphrase as follows:

"Following a conference on August 23 between the British Prime Minister, Mr. Eden and Lord Halifax, recent press despatches from London had stated that renewed efforts would be made by the British Government to persuade the Government of the United States to take part in a "joint declaration" with regard to the situation in the Far East. Much speculation as to the nature of such a proposed declaration was going on in Japan and the general belief was that the declaration would be of a vigorous character. In this connection and on the basis of extensive experience in Japan on the part of my staff and myself I respectfully ventured to submit to Mr. Hull some of our basic views with regard to the hostilities in China in the hope that these views might prove helpful in the formulation of future policy and action by the United States.

"First of all, we felt that it was not now of great practical importance to determine the question of premeditation and of the immediate responsibility for the outbreak of the conflict upon which divergent opinions existed. These points, in fact, had probably not yet been established.

* Telegram No. 318, August 26, 8 P.M.

"We must remember that the seeds of the present conflict had been sown long ago, and the important consideration was that regardless of dates or of provocative acts the clash was eventually inevitable. We believed that at first it was the hope of the Japanese to restrict the affair at the Marco Polo Bridge to a local incident but regardless of the wishes and intentions of the Chinese and Japanese Governments the situation had rapidly developed out of control and neither side could now avoid a settlement of the anomalous position of Japan in North China.

"The Manchurian conflict had left Japan with an eventual choice of two alternatives, either to prepare for an eventual retreat from Manchuria or to establish complete control in North China. Thus the present conflict was an inevitable corollary of the Manchurian affair, and no doubt could ever have existed as to the choice of the two alternatives resulting therefrom. The efforts of Japan during the past four years to attain her objectives by political maneuvering and gradually rather than by open combat had failed, whereupon eventual hostilities had become unavoidable and the only question was whether and to what extent the conflict could be circumscribed. Localization of the conflict, we believed, would have been welcomed by the Japanese Government, but any such hope was soon shattered either through uncontrollable circumstances or by the ineptitude of Japanese tactics in Shanghai and elsewhere. Once general hostilities had begun, there could be no question as to the determination of the Japanese Government to see them through, solidly supported by the Japanese public.

"It would of course be premature to venture prognostication as to the eventual outcome of the conflict. In Japan there existed complete confidence in an overwhelming military victory within a very few months, their mechanized forces and planes being regarded as certain to attain their objectives. The Japanese seemed unable to pause to consider that even after the possible destruction of the Chinese armies and repeated military victories, only then might the real war begin. (These were prophetic words!) We doubted whether the Japanese allowed the possible effects of almost unlimited guerrilla warfare to enter into their calculations, or of the immense financial drains which would progressively deplete the Japanese exchequer and gradually wipe out Japan's industrial and commercial stake in China. We felt that the Japanese were unable to estimate the long-range outlook as opposed to the immediate prospective or to visualize the risks involved. Herein, we believed, Japan was embarking upon important hazards which in the end might conceivably result in shearing the Japanese nation of much of its power and world prestige.

"We were in entire agreement with Ambassador Johnson's view that China could not afford to decline to meet the challenge of Japan and that no step should be taken by the United States towards urging China to sacrifice her sovereign rights in order to purchase peace. We furthermore believed that no good effect would accrue from any effort on the part of the United States, by expressing disapproval on moral or legalistic grounds, to thwart the development of Japan's policy in China. Japan's attitude of friendship towards the United States, which was daily being developed through the tactics and the method and manner of procedure on the part of our Government in the present conflict, would soon become obliterated if we were to persist in efforts to obstruct Japanese policy.

"In the present situation we felt that the basic objectives of the United States should be: (1) the avoidance of involvement; (2) the protection to the uttermost of American lives, property and right; (3) the maintenance of our traditional friendship with both combatants while preserving complete neutrality.

"A special effort to solidify our relations with Japan would be needed in connection with the last point mentioned above. We believed that the Japanese, in a day and age when national egotism was rampant, were capable in large measure of gratitude for manifestations of good will, and that we could accomplish more by encouraging confidence in our friendship for both combatants and in our impartiality than by any other method. Our friendship and help at the time of the great earthquake in 1923 were still constantly remembered.[27] On the other hand they never have forgotten the Exclusion Clause of our Immigration Act of 1924 nor our attitude at the time of the Manchurian affair. Now the Japanese were already showing marked signs of appreciation as a result of the policy and methods which were being followed by the United States Government. No similar appreciation was being shown toward Great Britain.

"Approaching these considerations from a purely material standpoint, we believed that a practical asset to American interests was here involved and that in direct ratio to a continuance of that policy and those methods this asset would increase. The important opportunity which lay before us should not be lost. If Japan should retain confidence in our impartiality and good will, she would be more prone to heed our counsel if and when the time should come for an effort by the United States to bring an end to the conflict than if Japan should regard us with resentment and suspicion.

"To advocate the development of friendship with Japan at the expense of friendship with China was far from our intention. We wished merely to emphasize in connection with every step to be taken by our Government the importance of considering the points brought out in the present telegram. By appealing, either alone or in concert with other Powers, for the circumscription or the restraint of military operations in particular areas where foreign lives and property might be in danger, we felt that much might be achieved, but we felt at the same time that moral intervention which could be interpreted as partial to either combatant until a military victory on one side or the other or until a stalemate had been brought to pass would have no good effect."

I added that the foregoing telegram had the complete concurrence of my entire staff including the Military, Naval and Commercial Attachés. A penned footnote on the Embassy's

27 The earthquake of September 1, 1923, and the fires following it resulted in the loss of many lives and great damage to Japanese property. The people of the United States contributed money and supplies to relieve the sufferers.

copy of this telegram states: "In this connection reference should be made to my letter of September 15, 1937, to the Secretary of State (Mr. Hull); also to the Secretary's reply of October 16, 1937. J. C. G." * 28

The Secretary of State cabled us his appreciation of the comment and estimate given in the foregoing telegram.†

The Senior Aide to the Navy Minister stated to our Naval Attaché on the 27th:29

* Telegram No. 321, August 27, 4 p.m.

28 On September 15 Mr. Grew addressed a letter to Cordell Hull in which he further explicated the position of the Embassy toward the situation in the Far East. Mr. Hull acknowledged on October 16 the receipt of the letter from Tokyo, and, "I am sure," the Secretary asserted, "that your views and mine of the situation and of the general attitude and position which this Government has adopted and must maintain with regard to it are as nearly the same as can be possible, due consideration being given to the difference in the locations and the atmospheres in which you and I are respectively functioning."

Mr. Grew's letter to Hull stated that "the principal difference of views which might be held to emerge . . . would appear to lie in our recommended three guiding objectives in the present contingency (to avoid involvement, to protect American lives and rights and, while preserving neutrality, to maintain friendship with both combatants). You agree with the first and second but doubt if it is practicable to aim at the same time at solidifying our relations with either of the combatant nations. In expanding that thought you instruct me to overlook no opportunity to suggest to Japanese officialdom that Japan is destroying the world's good will and building up a long-time liability of suspicion, distrust, dislike, and potential ostracism.

"I also am of opinion that the third of the objectives is less important than the first and second, but I still think it ought to remain among them — never to take precedence over the avoiding of involvement or over protection, but nevertheless kept in mind, though more as method than as principle. . . .

"I share your views, and the views of the American public, of outrage at the Japanese program. . . . The American attitude can be and has been made abundantly clear to the Japanese Government. . . .

"In agreeing that the expression of clear disapproval of Japan's course is desirable, nevertheless I wish at this point respectfully to raise the following consideration. This is a country of a controlled press, and treacherous twisting of news and opinion is not only possible but is the practice. . . . Repeated American public statements critical of Japan's course would be fully warranted, but they would not deter the course of military developments and they would reach the Japanese public so colored and so contaminated by other matter that the Japanese people would see American unfriendliness without the warrant. . . ."

† Department's telegram No. 176, August 28, 3 p.m.

29 The Japanese Foreign Office issued a statement on August 26, 1937, concern-

"The Japanese people, perhaps more than most people, are capable of long-remembered gratitude for what they consider friendly attitudes on the part of other nations, and long-remembered resentment for unfriendly attitudes. Whatever we may think of the Japanese military machine, need we penalize our own future interests, and perhaps our own future helpfulness in working for peace, by creating among the Japanese people a renewed antagonism against the United States? . . .

"Our thought is by no means a question of what may be pleasing to the Japanese but rather a question of maintaining and developing what we conceive to be a situation of maximum future value to American interests. I have not for a single moment advocated that we should in any way or in any degree sacrifice American interests or purchase Japanese good will at the expense of abandoning any American policy or law or any treaty to which we are a party on any action demanded by American public opinion. I do not advocate and have not advocated our tying our hands in order not to displease Japan. I did express our opinion that any attempt to thwart Japan's course in China by manifestations of disapprobation on legal or moral grounds would have no favorable effect on the situation, but that is quite a different matter. I have already made it clear that I thoroughly and heartily concur in every action thus far taken by our Government in the present situation."

Question. What was meant when you stated "blockade aims principally at destroying the fighting power of the Chinese and will not unnecessarily seize Chinese vessels and confiscate the cargoes aboard them" and "Japanese will duly respect peaceful commerce being carried on by third powers and will never interfere with it"?

Answer. The purpose of the blockade is to prevent war sup-

---

ing the China Coast Blockade which said that in order to effect a speedy settlement of the "China Incident," "the Japanese naval authorities found it necessary to close to traffic of Chinese vessels the Chinese sea coast from 32° 4′ north latitude and 121° 44′ east longitude, to 23° 14′ north latitude and 116° 48′ east longitude, beginning at 6 P.M., August 25, 1937.

"The above measure is solely one of self-defence against the lawless acts of the Chinese, and applies only to Chinese vessels. It may be added that peaceful commerce carried on by third Powers will be fully respected, the Japanese navy having no intention of interfering with it." *China Year Book 1938*, p. 365.

plies getting to the Chinese forces. As no war exists Japan will not interfere with the commerce of any nation other than China. Interference with Chinese trade only to the extent of confiscating war supplies on Chinese ships. By "peaceful commerce of third powers" is meant ordinary commerce which now might include cargo of a warlike nature.

A hypothetical question was asked as to what would happen to a Canadian Pacific or Dollar Line vessel bound for Shanghai with war material known to be destined for Chinese forces. The answer was "no interference would be made with that vessel." When asked as to the "status of Chinese vessels owned wholly or in part by third party" the answer was "war supplies if on board would be confiscated, vessel and remainder of cargo would be subsequently freed." * . . .

On the 27th the Department cabled that in view of the importance of the Embassy's having the benefit of as broad a picture as possible of the Sino-Japanese situation, it was considered desirable that an officer from the Embassy be detailed for a period of three weeks or less to visit certain points in China, including Shanghai and Nanking. Mr. Joseph McGurk [First Secretary] was chosen for this mission.† . . .

With reference to the Department's 177 — of August 28 — we reported on 31st:

1. On August 28 the French Ambassador sent his Counselor [Frederic Knobel] to the Foreign Office in connection with the "China blockade" announcement (1) to make "serious reservations" concerning the attitude of the French Government and (2) to inquire as to the interpretation of the term "peaceful commerce" mentioned in the announcement. The Vice Minister professed entire ignorance of the announcement by the Navy which gave the Ambassador the impression that the step had been taken without consulting the Foreign Office. Horinouchi said he would investigate and reply.

2. Yesterday the Vice Minister handed to the French Ambassador as an "oral" reply the following text:

* Telegram No. 322, August 27, 7 P.M.
† Department's telegram No. 172, August 27, 5 P.M.

"(1) The closing of the traffic applies, as clearly stated in the declaration made on the 25th instant by Admiral Hasegawa, only to Chinese vessels and does not apply to the vessels of third Powers. Consequently, arms and ammunitions carried on board the latter ships do not come within the scope of the present measures. However, since the above-mentioned declaration was issued, there have been Chinese ships flying foreign flags in order to evade the application of the declaration, and the Japanese Government are faced with the necessity of inspecting the suspected ships in order to identify their nationality. The Japanese Government, of course, do not want to create unnecessary misunderstanding with the ships of third Powers and, so, they would find it convenient to have advance notice of the ships entering the prescribed area, as to their names, their captains, and the matters concerning the capital invested in them.

"(2) As you are aware the Japanese Government have made it clear, in their statement of August 26, that in the face of the present situation they were forced to adopt this measure with a view to prompting China's reconsideration and bringing about a speedy settlement. Under the present circumstances, if large quantities of arms and ammunitions were to be supplied to China from abroad, it would only strengthen both morally and materially her antagonism toward Japan, and thereby prolong and intensify the present conflict. The Japanese Government, therefore, hope that the Governments of the third Powers concerned will appreciate the delicate situation, and refrain, as much as possible, from doing anything which is likely to encourage China in this direction.

"(3) The present declaration, as stated above, does not apply in the case of the ships of third Powers, and the Japanese Government do not, for the present, contemplate taking any action to prevent the importation of arms and ammunitions into China by foreign vessels. But in view of the fact that such importation of war supplies is bound to increase Chinese opposition against Japan, future developments may compel the Japanese Government to devise more effective and suitable measures to stop all importation of arms and ammunitions into China. August 30, 1937."

3. Any inquiry from us would probably draw forth an identic reply. Therefore if instructions from the Department to take

action should cross this telegram I shall nevertheless delay action until this telegram has been received and acknowledged by the Department.* . . .

On the same day — August 31 — we were informed that the British Embassy in Washington had addressed to the Department on August 31 an *aide-mémoire* asking whether the American Government would consider requesting me to endeavor, in concert with my British colleague, to elicit from the Japanese Government a precise statement with regard to the measures against shipping on the coast of China which that Government intended to take.

In reply, the British Embassy in Washington was informed of the opinion of the American Government that within its own limits the statement already made by the Japanese Government seemed to be sufficiently precise. The statements of the Japanese Government reported in our 322 — of August 27 — and 329 — of August 31 — that the Japanese Government had no intention of interfering with merchant vessels other than Chinese were referred to, and the view was expressed by the Department that a request for a more precise statement of intention would not in any likelihood alter Japanese plans. In the light of the statements already made by the Japanese Government it was felt that such an approach at that time would be neither advisable nor helpful.† . . . In connection with Mr. Hirota's observation that he would bring my representations to the War and Navy Ministries I expressed to the Department my fear that in the face of the Army and Navy under present circumstances the Foreign Office was practically without influence or authority.‡ . . .

An important telegram, in reply to my 321 — of August 27, came from Mr. Hull under date of September 2, of which the following is a paraphrase:[30]

* Telegram No. 329, August 31, 2 P.M.
† Department's telegram No. 185, August 31, 8 P.M.
‡ Telegram No. 335, September 1, 8 P.M.
[30] About this cable Mr. Hull has written in his *Memoirs*, I, 541: "As Japan continued to pour troops into China and enlarge the area of conflict, I sent a

"Having before him the Embassy's views and appraisal of the situation the Secretary expressed the hope that in order to appreciate and understand the position of the Administration it would be helpful to us to know its present thoughts with regard to policy and methods and to have an outline of the reaction of our Government to developments in the Far East.

"The policy of our Government during recent years had been based in part on the belief that encouragement of efforts on the part of both China and Japan to work toward genuine co-operation with each other and with the rest of the world would be advantageous, but little room for hope that such an attitude would develop in the near future now remained in view of the situation produced by the new conflict.

"The complete lack of responsiveness to our suggestions and the suggestions of other Governments which had been patiently and quietly offered to the Japanese military forces, that reasonable consideration should be given by them to the interests, rights, safety and susceptibilities *inter alia* of countries and individuals not participants in the hostilities, and the methods being used by those forces, had created doubt as to whether any real value was attached by those in actual control of Japan's actions and policies to the friendship of other nations or to the efforts of the Government of the United States and other Governments to cultivate confidence, good will and general stability.

"In the current crisis it had been the effort of the American Government to follow a course of complete impartiality. It was furthermore realized in Washington that the conflict was not likely to be brought to an end merely by manifestations of disapprobation on legal or moral grounds. On the other hand our Government must constantly bear in mind in shaping its course not only the possible effect of its measures on Japan or China or both, but also the wishes and attitude of the American people and the principles in which our nation believes. We must look beyond immediate and particular objectives to general and ultimate objectives.

strong cable on September 2 to Ambassador Grew so that he could communicate its substance to the Japanese Foreign Office."

"In his statement of July 16 Mr. Hull had made clear the principles by which our Government was guided; more than fifty nations had expressed themselves in favor of those principles, and in his further statement of August 23 the Secretary had clearly indicated that we considered those principles as applicable to the area of the Pacific Ocean. For a well-ordered existence of and in the society of nations our Government believed those principles to be fundamental, yet the course being pursued by Japan was directly in conflict with many of those principles, and in their present courses neither China nor Japan was acting in accordance therewith.

"It was gratifying to Mr. Hull to know that the Japanese appreciated the fact that the course followed by the United States had indicated our wish to be impartial and fair. Nevertheless the maintenance of unqualified good will toward us by either Japan or China or both could not be our primary solicitude. Our first consideration must be the general policies and broad interests of the United States and the protection of American citizens, and we must be guided by public opinion in the United States, by treaties and laws and other controlling factors. The Secretary agreed with our view that among our basic objectives should be included: (a) the avoidance of involvement, and (b) the protection of American lives, rights and property.

"It appeared to Mr. Hull doubtful if we could follow those objectives and at the same time expect to pursue the third objective which we had suggested, namely, the maintenance of our traditional friendship with both Japan and China while preserving complete neutrality, and he therefore did not feel that the cementing of our relations with either of the combatant nations should be a definite objective. The courses being followed by both countries, especially by Japan, had aroused our opposition. It was our desire to be a good neighbor to both the combatants and we had no wish to injure either of them, but, on the other hand, we could not allow our decisions to be obstructed by special solicitude for the avoidance of any course which might be displeasing to China or Japan or to both.

"We did not desire Japan to receive or to entertain any impression that we condoned in any sense whatsoever the course which that country was pursuing, or that we viewed that course with any less apprehension or any less disapproval than did the British Government.

"The strategy of the combatants, especially of the Japanese military forces, had outraged public opinion in the United States which had become increasingly critical of the Japanese. This divergence from hopes of impartiality in popular sentiment and thought had become intensified by the events of the previous week, especially by the statement of the Japanese Prime Minister that little or no importance should be attached to the representations of foreign Powers, and by the circumstances of the shooting of the British Ambassador to China. This sentiment had of course been somewhat offset by interference in the bombing of the *President Hoover*.[31]

"The Secretary said that he had no intention of threatening or of calling names in addressing either of the combatant Governments and he expressed his hearty approval of the tactful and dignified manner in which this Embassy was conducting its approaches to the Japanese authorities. He, however, wished the Japanese Government fully to understand that the present manifestation of the foreign policy of Japan and the methods which were being followed by the Japanese military in pursuit thereof were regarded by the American Government with complete disapproval. The Secretary felt that we should take every possible occasion to impress upon the Japanese authorities the importance which we attached to the principles set forth in his statement of July 16 as well as the signif-

---

[31] On August 26 Japanese aviators machine gunned the cars carrying Sir Hughe Knatchbull Hugessen and other members of the staff of the British Embassy from Nanking to Shanghai. The British Ambassador was wounded in the attack. The Dollar Line ship, *President Hoover*, was bombed by Chinese planes near the mouth of the Yangtze River on August 30. The Chinese Government offered formal apology, financial reparation for personal and property damage, and assumed responsibility for the incident. M. Epstein (ed.), *Annual Register . . . 1937* (London: Longmans, Green & Co., 1938), pp. 72, 269, and *New York Times*, August 31, 1937, p. 1; September 1, 1937, pp. 1, 2.

icance of his statement of August 23. He felt that we should suggest to the Japanese that they were destroying the world's good will by their policy and that the Japanese nation was laying up for itself among the nations a liability of popular antipathy, distrust, suspicion and possible ostracism which could only be removed by many years of benevolent efforts.

"The record of the efforts on behalf of peace and in support of principles which had been made by the American Government at the time of the invasion of Manchuria had been in no respect repudiated by the present Administration. While trying in the existing crisis to dissuade the present combatants from commencing and continuing hostilities, we had not offered to mediate, and Mr. Hull was not at all sure that our Government would desire to undertake the role and the responsibilities of a mediator. It was not his wish, at least at the present time, to encourage either of the combatants to believe or to expect that recourse might be had to our Government to serve as a friendly broker whenever it might suit their convenience, particularly in view of their rejection of our many current suggestions that they exercise restraint. If the combatants desired American good will and any form of impartial assistance, the Secretary wished them to realize that now was the time for them to manifest, through consideration of our essential solicitudes and legitimate interests, their appreciation of our policies and methods." * . . .

On September 6 the Department cabled "Triple Priority, for the Ambassador" requesting that I cable my appraisal of the speeches made at the convocation of the Diet relating to the question as to whether a state of war with China existed and what I felt would probably be the reaction in Japan and the results in this country if the United States Government should issue a proclamation by which the initial provision of the neutrality resolution of May 1, 1937, or more, would be put into effect.[32] My comment was also asked, if I should feel

* Department's telegram No. 187, September 2, 2 P.M. [*Ibid.*, pp. 361–64.]
[32] The Neutrality Act provided, in part, that whenever "the President shall find that there exists a state of war between, or among, two or more foreign

in a position to offer it, as to whether such action at that moment would be desirable.* . . .

Adverting to the Department's 192 I telegraphed "Confidential for the Secretary" a report of which the following was the substance:

"1. *My appraisal of the bearing upon the question of the existence of a state of war of the speeches delivered on the convocation of the Diet.*

" (a) The determination of the Japanese Government to continue to employ its armed forces until it had achieved certain objectives of a political nature in China was revealed by allusions with which the speeches were liberally interspersed. The Prime Minister had made pertinent statements indicating Japan's determination to administer 'a decisive blow to China' and he had used the expression 'to administer a thoroughgoing blow to the Chinese Army so that it may completely lose its will to fight,' while the Minister for Foreign Affairs had uttered the phrases 'calamitous hostilities' and 'force of arms.' The intention of the Japanese Army to crush the military forces of China had also been expressed by the Minister of War. When it was considered that there were believed to be at least 150,000 Japanese troops in China proper, the foregoing utterances left no room for doubt that the existence of a *de facto* state of war had been given formal recognition by the Japanese Government.

"(b) At the same time the Minister of Finance had made clear in his address that plans had been made by the Government to reorganize the country's industrial, commercial and financial systems on a prolonged war basis and under wartime control.

states, the President shall proclaim such fact, and it shall thereafter be unlawful to export, or attempt to export, or cause to be exported, arms, ammunition, or implements of war from any place in the United States to any belligerent state, named in the proclamation, or to any neutral state for transshipment to, or for the use of, any such belligerent state." For the text of the Act, see U.S. Congress, Senate, *Neutrality*, Document No. 40 (Washington: Government Printing Office, 1937). The Neutrality Act was not invoked in the Sino-Japanese conflict.

* Department's telegram No. 192, September 6, 5 P.M.

"2. *Appraisal of the probable reaction in Japan if the United States Government should by proclamation put into force the initial provision or more of the Neutrality Resolution of May 1, 1937.*

"(a) The predominant reaction would probably be favorable, although the Government and public opinion might possibly see in such a step a mark of American disapproval of the policy and actions of Japan toward China, especially since war had not been declared by either combatant. Such a step would in all probability be interpreted in Japan as indicating the intention of the American Government to conform its policy towards developments in the Far East with its policy toward similar situations elsewhere. The Japanese would also no doubt see in such a step a further indication of the intention of the United States not to intervene in the conflict.

"3. *Appraisal of the effects on Japan of such a proclamation.*

"(a) From a practical viewpoint it was not believed that such a move would materially affect Japan, possibly excepting the fact that the supply of aircraft which were being imported from the United States as models would be lost, and this effect might become more serious if the war were prolonged.

"4. *Comments.*

"While the Japanese Government had declared its intention to avoid interfering with peaceful commerce, nevertheless the supply of arms to China might have to be prevented by more drastic measures, as indicated by the Government (reference Embassy's 329 — of August 31 — and 341 — of September 4). Furthermore the serious risk would always be present, even if the foregoing circumstances should not arise, of Japanese naval action, whether premeditated or not, which might interfere with the sovereign rights of the United States. It was my belief that the risks incidental to the hostilities, interruption of transportation facilities in China, high war-risk insurance and other factors were rapidly diminishing the prospects of carrying on peaceful American trade. I also believed that the advantages derived by the United States from the sale of arms and munitions to China, which was steadily diminishing in volume, was not commensurate with the attendant risks involved in such commerce. I believed that neutrality action by the United States was advisable immediately, in view of the American desire to avoid involvement in the current hostilities." * . . .

On the 10th — of September — I informed the Department of a conversation with a prominent member of the House of Peers [Count Kabayama] with whom I was on terms of personal friendship and with whom I was in the habit of holding periodic talks. This gentleman alluded to the marked swing toward friendship with the United States of public opinion in Japan, even on the part of the Army, and he said that Japan was coming to regard the United States, especially since the consummation of the anti-Comintern pact and its results, "as the only real friend left." He spoke of the Japanese Government as weak, with Messrs. Hirota and Baba the only strong characters among the civilian members, but Mr. Hirota, as Foreign Minister, was not prone to taking initiative, while Mr. Baba, as Minister of Finance, was interested only in home affairs. Developments in China, he said, had proceeded very much farther and more rapidly than even the Army had intended.

I took the opportunity of this conversation to speak to my Japanese friend in the sense of the final paragraph of Mr. Hull's 187 — of September 2 — and I emphasized that Japan's present policy and course were arousing in the United States a strong trend of adverse feeling. I was told by my informant that similar information had been imparted recently to the Export and Import Committee of the House of Peers by a member thereof.

At the same time I spoke of reports in the local press to the effect that it was the intention of the Japanese Government to send a so-called good will mission to the United States in order to explain the viewpoint of Japan and I said that speaking unofficially and personally I knew that it would be in-

* Telegram No. 354, September 7, 4 P.M.

advisable to take such a step at the present time. My collocutor said that he would let this "important view" be known in the proper direction.* . . .

On September 12 we telegraphed to the Department in a "rush" message, with reference to our 302 — of August 23:

1. The following communication has just been received from the British Ambassador:

"British Embassy, Tokyo. 12th September, 1937.
"My dear Ambassador and Colleague:

"I have been instructed by my Government to make an enquiry of the Japanese Government on a point arising out of their oral reply made when the Representatives of the United States of America, France, Germany, Italy and Great Britain approached them on the 23rd August last with a proposal for a safety zone at Nanking.

"The enquiry arises out of the Japanese Government's request to the Powers to mark their merchant vessels plainly so that they may be easily identified from the air in anticipation of possible raids by Japanese bombers. I am instructed to point out to the Japanese Government that, if there is no war, an attack on merchant ships would be illegal. If there is a war, the position under international law is that no merchant ship, whether enemy or neutral, may be attacked unless she fails to comply with a lawful request to stop in order that she may be visited and her identity established or unless she thereafter resists lawful capture. In any case it is only permissible to use such force as is absolutely necessary to ensure compliance. Nor is it permissible to sink the vessel (if at all) unless the crew has been first placed in safety except when such sinking has been rendered inevitable by the conduct of the merchant ship herself in offering resistance and when no less use of force will suffice. Aircraft are in no way exempt from these rules and must refrain from action against merchant ships unless they can comply with them.

"In bringing these considerations to the notice of the Japanese Government, I am to remind them of the submarine protocol which in common with other Governments they signed last year and inform them that, in the view of my Government, indiscrim-

* Telegram No. 360, September 10, 2 P.M.

inate attack from the air which does not comply with the above rules is as illegal as in the case of submarines.

"My Government would be compelled to take a very serious view of any such attacks on British merchant vessels, and I am therefore instructed to ask for an explanation and a clarification of the Japanese Government's request in so far as it relates to merchant vessels.

"I am proposing to wait until tomorrow (13th September) before carrying out these instructions in view of the possibility of your receiving instructions from your Government to take parallel action, in which case may I ask you to be so good as to inform me accordingly?

"Believe me, my dear Ambassador and Colleague, Yours very sincerely, R. L. CRAIGIE." [33]

2. Please instruct whether I shall take parallel action.* . . .

On the 14th we telegraphed, urgently and with reference to our 363:

The British Ambassador yesterday called on the Vice Minister for Foreign Affairs and presented a memorandum covering his instructions concerning the marking of merchant vessels. The Vice Minister replied that while he took no exception to the Ambassador's raising these points of international law, nevertheless the action appeared superfluous because the Japanese forces had no intention of attacking neutral merchant ships whether marked or not. The Japanese Government had recommended plain marking merely to make assurance doubly sure and in order that the Japanese planes might give such ships a particularly wide berth and so that possible accidents might be avoided. The Vice Minister said that the Foreign Office would reply to the Ambassador's memorandum within a few days.

In this connection I added that Sir Robert Craigie had told me that he had informed not only me but also our French, German and Italian colleagues of his instructions and that they

[33] Sir Robert Craigie, the newly appointed British Ambassador to Japan, had presented his credentials on September 11.

* Telegram No. 363, September 12, noon.

were referring the matter to their respective Governments. Sir Robert, however, regarded his Government's instructions as "using a sledge hammer to drive a tack." I questioned whether, in view of the foregoing information, the Department would regard action on my part as necessary and I said that even if affirmative instructions should come in the meantime, I would nevertheless not act until a reply to my present telegram was received.*

On the same date — September 14 — we were confidentially informed by the Department of a telegram received from our Chargé d'Affaires in London, dated the 13th, reporting that the British Foreign Office had asked him to call and had told him of the action of the British and French Governments warning the Japanese Government that serious difficulties with third Powers would inevitably be caused if and when various islands should be occupied by Japanese forces. A general wish was expressed by the Foreign Office to learn what if any action in this matter the American Government proposed to take.

In this connection it was suggested by the Department that in my discretion I might informally approach the Japanese Foreign Office and refer to reports that the Chinese meteorological station on Pratas Reef [in the South China Sea] had been dismantled by the Japanese. The valuable services rendered by this station to shipping in that area might be mentioned and the dangers caused to shipping by the dismantling of the station could be pointed out. The intentions of the Japanese Government with regard to Pratas Reef could be asked. At the same time I was authorized to refer to Japanese official statements that no territorial ambitions in China were held by the Japanese Government and to call attention to the fact that Pratas Reef was far removed from the scene of the China conflict. It would be appropriate to express confidence that the Japanese Government had no intention to alienate Pratas Reef and other Chinese territory. I was instructed, however, to consult my British and French colleagues before acting and to keep the Department fully informed.† . . .

* Telegram No. 368, September 14, noon.
† Department's telegram No. 206, September 14, 7 p.m.

Noon editions of the Japanese newspapers on September 15 carried as feature news the report of action by the President prohibiting American Government-owned vessels from carrying arms, ammunition or implements of war to Japan or China. There was as yet no comment in the press but the Embassy stated that it would follow the matter and report.* [34] . . .

In the meantime the Department cabled us on the 15th, with reference to our 363 — of September 12 — and 368 — of September 14, as follows:

The British Chargé d'Affaires at Washington on September 11 handed an officer of the Department an *aide-mémoire* similar in substance to the communication quoted in your No. 363. Inquiry was made in the *aide-mémoire* whether this Government would be prepared to instruct the American Ambassador at Tokyo to take parallel action in the matter.

While this Government is in hearty accord with the desire of the British Government to keep alive in the Far Eastern area the principles of international law with regard to maritime commerce and desires to continue the course of collaboration which it has pursued since the beginning of the Far Eastern crisis the Department is of the opinion that the taking by this Government at this time of action parallel to that taken by the British in this matter would be inopportune especially in view of the reply of the Vice Minister for Foreign Affairs as reported in your 368 that the Japanese forces have no intention of attacking merchant ships of third Powers whether marked or not. The Department is replying to the British Embassy in the sense of the foregoing.† . . .

* Telegram No. 369, September 15, 1 P.M.

[34] The Presidential Statement on transportation of arms and munitions to China or Japan by merchant vessels was issued on September 14, 1937. It stated: "Merchant vessels owned by the Government of the United States will not hereafter, until further notice, be permitted to transport to China or Japan any of the arms, ammunition, or implements of war which were listed in the President's Proclamation of May 1, 1937.

"Any other merchant vessels, flying the American flag, which attempt to transport any of the listed articles to China or Japan will, until further notice, do so at their own risk.

"The question of applying the Neutrality Act remains in *statu quo*, the Government policy remaining on a 24-hour basis." Franklin D. Roosevelt, *The Public Papers and Addresses of Franklin D. Roosevelt*, 1937 vol., VI, *The Constitution Prevails* (New York: The Macmillan Co., 1941), p. 354.

† Department's telegram No. 208, September 15, 1 P.M.

Only the two leading Japanese papers commented editorially on the order of the President with regard to shipment of arms and munitions to China and Japan. Excerpts were as follows:

1. *Asahi.* After outlining course of American neutrality legislation, the editorial refers to the case of the *Wichita*[35] and states "It is clear that the President's order reveals determination to prevent the United States from becoming involved in the conflict. We feel that from the point of view of peace in the Far East and of relations between Japan and the United States, it was a clear-sighted and wise measure. Ignoring for the moment the argument that the embargo will not materially hurt Japan while it will adversely affect China to a substantial degree, the point to be emphasized is the basic purpose of the embargo. . . . We place a favorable interpretation on the President's action. It indicates the folly of the efforts of China at Geneva and elsewhere to secure the assistance of the United States." [36]

[35] The *Wichita*, owned by the American Pioneer Line and operated for the account of the Maritime Commission, was en route to China at the time of the Presidential Statement of September 14. The ship, which had left Baltimore with a cargo of nineteen Bellanca planes for China, was stopped at San Pedro, California, where the planes, two cases of revolvers, and two cases of cartridges were unloaded on September 16. *New York Times,* September 15, 1937, p. 1; September 17, 1937, p. 4; October 28, 1937, p. 4.

[36] On September 12, 1937, a letter was addressed by the Chinese Government to the Secretary-General of the League of Nations asking the League "to take cognizance of the fact that Japan has invaded China and is continuing the invasion with all her army, navy and air force." Four days later the Council of the League approved a proposal of the President that the Secretary-General take the steps necessary to bring about the meeting of the Far-East Advisory Committee as soon as possible. The Third Session of the Far-East Advisory Committee was held at Geneva from September 21 to October 5, 1937. Leland Harrison, American Minister to Switzerland, participated in the meetings of the Advisory Committee. On September 28 Cordell Hull cabled instructions to Harrison. "We outlined the steps we had already taken: direct appeals to Japan and China to stop fighting; offer of good offices; repeated protests to Japan against aerial bombing of noncombatants. I said we had been approached on several occasions by certain other governments with suggestions for 'joint action.' 'In general,' I commented, 'it is felt that spontaneous separate action on parallel lines, should two or more governments feel moved thereto anywhere, indicates more strongly serious feeling regarding matters under consideration and is more likely effectively to serve to attain the objectives sought than would inspired joint action.'

" 'It is felt,' I concluded, 'that the United States Government, in action taken

2. *Nichi Nichi.* ". . . We assume that the motive of the American Government in taking the new measure was to prevent the United States from being drawn into the conflict. Since the very beginning of the conflict the American Government has adhered firmly to an independent and calm attitude, and it has earnestly and intelligently endeavored to avoid becoming embroiled. Even so recently as September 11 the President stressed to press representatives the importance of the American Government not becoming involved, while the injunction given to American citizens in China to withdraw also evidences adherence to a policy of noninvolvement, which is after all a reflection of American public opinion. . . . The embargo may also be regarded as recognition in principle of that desire of the American people which has found expression in the Neutrality Act. As pointed out by the President, the embargo is not an invocation of the Neutrality Act, but when associated with the warning to private shipowners that they carry munitions to Japan at their own risk it reveals how earnestly and effectively the policy of noninvolvement will be pursued." * . . .

Referring to Embassy's 335 — of September 1 — concerning bombing operations in Nanking and elsewhere in China, the Foreign Office delivered to us a reply of which the following is a translation:

Aide-Mémoire.

His Excellency the American Ambassador, in an *aide-mémoire* of September 1st, 1937, conveyed the request of the American Government for the discontinuance of such bombing operations over Nanking of Japanese forces as might result in the destruc-

thus far, has gone further in making efforts calculated to strengthen general principles of world peace and world security and in indicating toward disregard of them disapprobation and disapproval than any other government or group of nations has gone. Therefore, it is felt that other nations might now well direct their efforts to go as far as or farther than the United States thus far has gone along these lines.'" Hull, *op. cit.*, I, 543–44. See League of Nations, *Official Journal, Special Supplement No. 177: Sino-Japanese Conflict* (Geneva, 1937), for an account of the work and reports of the Far-East Advisory Committee and Subcommittee and other documents in regard to League action at this time.

* Telegram No. 876, September 16, 4 P.M.

tion of property of non-military character and in the wounding and death of civilians, and also for their abstinence from attacks upon defenceless cities, hospitals, trains, motorcars, et cetera, with a view to preventing danger to the American citizens who are still scattered in the interior of China.

As His Excellency is aware, Nanking is the pivotal base wherein are planned and originated all Chinese hostile operations against the Japanese forces. In view of the fact that the city is defended by many forts, is possessed of numerous other military organs and establishments in and around it, it is quite proper that against these the Japanese should carry out bombing operations. It should be stated definitely that the objectives of their bombing are limited, from the standpoint of humanity, strictly to those military organs and establishments, and absolutely in no instance non-military property and civilians are ever made the direct objectives of attacks. That, in spite of all such caution exercised on our part, noncombatants should sometimes be made victims of the hostilities and suffer unforeseen disasters in respect of their lives and property, is also regretted deeply by the Japanese Government. That, however, has been an inevitable concomitant of hostile operations in all ages. In order to ensure, as far as possible, the safety of noncombatants in the present case, it is believed that, in parallel to the caution exercised by the Japanese as above stated, the Chinese on their part should take appropriate measures, such as the evacuation of noncombatants from the neighborhood of their military organs and establishments.

The Japanese Government, as has repeatedly been made known, are most solicitous for the security of the lives and property of the nationals of third countries, including American citizens, in China, and are prepared to do whatever lies in their power to facilitate their withdrawal to places of safety and to afford protection to their property. And they wish to assure Your Excellency that nothing is farther from the thought of the Japanese forces than to make attacks, such as are referred to in the American *aide-mémoire*, upon defenceless cities, hospitals, trains and motorcars, which are not used by the Chinese for military purposes. September 15th, 1937.*

* Telegram No. 379, September 16, 7 P.M.

The Department instructed us to address a note to the Japanese Government as from the Government of the United States as follows:

Since the beginning of the present fighting in China the American Government has received reports of attacks by Japanese armed forces in China upon American nationals and their property including attacks upon American humanitarian and philanthropic establishments and upon the persons and property of noncombatants generally.

The American Government desires in particular to bring to the attention of the Japanese Government a recent attack on September 12 by Japanese planes on an American missionary hospital in South China located at Waichow, Kwangtung Province. Information in the possession of the American Government indicates that three Japanese planes flew low three times over the mission compound where two large American flags were flying; that each time the planes dropped bombs all of which exploded seriously injuring personnel of the hospital as well as damaging the hospital and the residence, that there were no antiaircraft guns at Waichow, and that the mission itself is two miles distant from any Chinese military encampment.

Attack upon noncombatants is prohibited both by long accepted principles and by established rules of international law. Also attack upon humanitarian establishments especially those which are lawfully under the flags of countries in no way party to military operations have no warrant in any system of law or of humane conduct. The American Government therefore is impelled in fulfillment of its obligations toward its nationals and on behalf of those fundamental principles of law and of morality which relate to the immunity of noncombatants and humanitarian establishments emphatically to voice objection to such attacks and to urge upon the Japanese Government which this Government cannot believe approves of such disregard of principles that effective steps be taken toward averting any further such attacks.* . . .

With reference to the Department's 206, we reported:

* Department's telegram No. 210, September 16, 5 P.M.

1. Pratas Reef.

Both my British and French colleagues have approached the Japanese Government, either through the Foreign Office or the Navy Ministry, with regard to the reported dismantling of the meteorological station on the reef and both are satisfied with Japanese assurances that the services of the station will be shortly resumed by Japanese authorities.

Neither my British nor French colleague at present proposes to protest the occupation of the reef on the ground of illegality of such occupation.

2. Hainan.

My French colleague called on the Minister for Foreign Affairs on September 13 and referring to representations made just a year ago by his predecessor at a time when Japanese warships were gathered in ports of the island expressed the hope that the current presence of Japanese warships in that vicinity would in no way result in altering the territorial status of the island because France is interested in the maintenance of the status quo. Hirota professed to know nothing about the matter and has not yet replied to the French Ambassador's *note verbale,* but in the meantime the French Naval Attaché has been informed by naval authorities that the Japanese warships are there for the purpose of controlling the blockade of Chinese ports.

My British colleague has been awaiting the Japanese Government's official reply to the French Ambassador before acting himself but he will probably do so shortly in any case and will inform me of the result. He has been instructed to emphasize that occupation of Hainan or of Paracel Islands would be illegal and that British Government would take a serious view of such occupation, if effected. The French Ambassador says that Paracel Islands are too far from the zone of hostilities to justify mentioning them but that in any case they are claimed by France and that Japanese occupation would be a very serious matter.* . . .

On the following day — September 19 — I was instructed in a rush telegram to make immediate representations concerning the safety of American citizens and the American Embassy at Nanking, and to advise my interested colleagues of the step, having in mind the Department's 215 — of September 18 — and Shanghai's 728 which read as follows:

* Telegram No. 385, September 18, noon.

The Japanese Consul General has just handed me the following translation of a statement by the Commander in Chief of the Japanese Third Fleet with the request that it be communicated to you for the information of our nationals and with the further request that you communicate it to other foreign Embassies and Legations at Nanking: "It being the objective of the Japanese operations to bring the present state of hostilities to an early conclusion by terminating hostile action of the Chinese forces, and Nanking being the principal base of the Chinese military operations, the Japanese naval air force may, after twelve o'clock noon of September 21, 1937, have to resort to such offensive measures as bombing and otherwise upon the Chinese forces as well as all establishments pertaining to their military and activities, in and around the city of Nanking.

It needs no reiteration that the safety or the lives and property of nationals of friendly powers will be taken into full consideration during the projected offensive. In view, however, of the possibility of such nationals becoming dangerously involved in the Sino-Japanese hostilities in spite of all precautions the Commander in Chief of the Third Fleet, Imperial Japanese Navy, is constrained to earnestly advise such officials and residents as are now living in and around Nanking to take adequate measures for voluntarily moving into areas of greater safety. The foreign warships as well as those who propose to avoid the danger on the Yangtse Kiang are advised to moor upstream from Hsiasan Shan.* . . .

With reference to the Department's 217 — of September 19 — I went on the 20th to see the Foreign Minister and brought up the announced plans of the Japanese naval forces to bomb Nanking, making the most emphatic and earnest representations and pointing out that if such operations were carried out they would inevitably involve grave danger to noncombatants, including foreign diplomatic establishments and their personnel. If some accident should occur while such operations were being carried out the effect on American public opinion would be serious, and on this point I dwelt at length, calling the

* Department's 217, September 19, 2 P.M.

attention of the Minister to the already mounting feeling against Japan in the world at large and in the United States and the fact that by her policy and the course she was pursuing Japan was laying up for herself a liability of popular antipathy, distrust, suspicion and potential ostracism among the peoples of the world. In the most earnest manner I said that Mr. Hirota himself was responsible for Japan's foreign relations and that the duty devolved on him of restraining the armed forces of Japan from a course by which the world's good will was rapidly being lost. My statement and appeal, in their force and directness, left nothing whatever to the imagination.

The Foreign Minister, while making no effort to counter my observations, listened with gravity. The same afternoon, he said, orders had been issued to the naval command in China by the Japanese Government that noncombatants and foreign diplomatic establishments in Nanking were to be scrupulously avoided in any bombing operations over that city. It was his understanding that the bombing reported in that evening's newspapers was not important and had not occurred near the diplomatic buildings. Mr. Hirota volunteered the view that the Navy's warning of the commencement of operations on the following day was "too short."

It was my purpose in this talk with Mr. Hirota to bring home to him with maximum effect the fact that alleged accidents in the course of bombing operations in Nanking and elsewhere in China would have most serious repercussions in the United States. Unfortunately we must reluctantly come to the conclusion that very little influence was possessed by the civil Government in Japan in restraining the military and naval forces from reaching their objectives, and the grave risks involved in their present course of action could not be avoided even by the strongest representations.

The telegram, of which the foregoing is a paraphrase, was as usual repeated to Shanghai for communication to the Commander in Chief of our Asiatic Fleet [H. E. Yarnell] and to Ambassador Johnson in Nanking.*

* Telegram No. 395, September 20, 8 P.M.

Referring to our 392 — of September 20, we cabled to the Department the full text, in translation, of the Foreign Minister's note concerning the bombing of Waichow, as follows:

I have the honor to acknowledge receipt of Your Excellency's note of September 17, in which Your Excellency refers to the bombing, on the 12th of September, by Japanese military aircraft, of the compound of the hospital operated by an American missionary organization at Waichow, Kwangtung Province, and in which Your Excellency urges that effective steps be taken in the matter by the Imperial Government.

The Imperial Government, being especially solicitous toward noncombatants and humanitarian establishments, had issued strict orders to officials in the field, and an occurrence such as the bombing under reference had not been considered possible. However, an investigation has been made of the bombing of the hospital located in Waichow, to which Your Excellency refers, and the facts have been ascertained to be as follows:

Japanese military aircraft set out with the object of bombing Chinese military establishments; they became convinced that the single-storey black roofed building, located on the river bank at the northeast corner of the city of Waichow and having two poles resembling those used for wireless, was in fact a wireless station and barracks thereto adjoining, and they bombed it. At the time of the bombing, the American flag, which Your Excellency mentioned, was not at all distinguishable from the air.

It has become clear that the present incident was entirely due to an error and the Imperial Government accordingly expresses sincere regret.

The Imperial Government will endeavor to the utmost to prevent recurrence of acts of this character, and, in view of the present case, it has issued strict orders in the foregoing sense to each service in the field. At the same time, I assure Your Excellency that the Imperial Government are prepared to give full consideration to the question of damages to the above-mentioned hospital and to the personnel thereof.*

On the 20th the Acting Secretary of State, Mr. R. Walton

* Telegram No. 397, September 20, 10 P.M.

Moore, acknowledged the receipt of my telegram No. 395 — of September 20 — and informed me that on the same afternoon he had requested the Japanese Ambassador in Washington to call and had told him of the deep anxiety of our Government arising from the expressed plans of the Japanese Navy to bomb Nanking. The Ambassador was told that insufficient time had been given for adequate measures for the protection of the American Embassy and other American property to be taken by the American Ambassador and other American citizens in that city. This shortness of time between the announcement and the action was most regrettable. The Ambassador was informed of our Government's grave concern not only at the danger to the American Embassy and American citizens in Nanking but also with regard to the unfortunate reactions in the United States if large parts of Nanking should be destroyed by bombing and if noncombatants should be killed or injured; widespread and hostile repercussions would occur in our country as a result of a Japanese attack whether the destruction arising out of such attack should be accidental or premeditated. The Japanese Ambassador was furthermore informed of my representations on this subject to Mr. Hirota.

Mr. Saito told Mr. Moore that he had been telegraphically informed of my talk with the Minister for Foreign Affairs and that Mr. Hirota had said to me that in any bombing operations over Nanking noncombatants and the foreign diplomatic buildings were to be avoided and only Chinese military establishments attacked. Mr. Moore pointed out to the Ambassador the great importance of postponing the bombardment and of restricting its area. The Ambassador undertook to inform his Government of the concern of the American Government in the matter.

At the same time, in reply to an inquiry by the Department, our Embassy in London had reported that the British Ambassador in Tokyo had been directed to make similar representations, and I was requested to advise my British colleague of Mr. Moore's talk with Ambassador Saito and of my own conversation with the Foreign Minister.*

* Department's telegram No. 219, September 20, 7 P.M.

On the same day, with further reference to the proposed attack on Nanking, Ambassador Johnson had informed the Department as follows:

> I have come aboard *Luzon* and *Guam* with entire commissioned staff with exception of John Paxton [Second Secretary of the American Embassy at Nanking] who volunteered and with my approval is remaining to maintain contact with Chinese authorities. I shall keep in touch with Paxton by telephone from Wuhu from which place I can reach Nanking in two hours. About seventeen American citizens including press, doctors and nurses remain in Nanking. Would appreciate if you will inform Tokyo Paxton's presence on Embassy premises location of which should be well-known to members Japanese Embassy at Shanghai who can inform commander of Japanese forces.*

Furthermore, with reference to my 395 — of September 20 — and the Department's 217 — of September 19, I was directed in a rush telegram to present the following note to the Minister for Foreign Affairs as soon as possible and to report urgently by cable when this had been done:

> The American Government refers to the statement by the Commander in Chief of the Japanese Third Fleet which was handed to the American Consul General at Shanghai on September 19 announcing the project of the Japanese naval air force, after twelve o'clock noon of September 21, 1937, to resort to bombing and other measures of offense in and around the city of Nanking, and warning the officials and nationals of third Powers living there "to take adequate measures for voluntary moving into areas of greater safety."
>
> The American Government objects both to such jeopardizing of the lives of its nationals and of noncombatants generally and to the suggestion that its officials and nationals now residing in and around Nanking should withdraw from the areas in which they are lawfully carrying on their legitimate activities.
>
> Immediately upon being informed of the announcement under reference, the American Government gave instructions to the American Ambassador at Tokyo to express to the Japanese

* Department's telegram No. 220, September 20, 10 P.M.

Government this Government's concern; and that instruction was carried out. On the same day, the concern of this Government was expressed by the Acting Secretary of State to the Japanese Ambassador in Washington.

This Government holds the view that any general bombing of an extensive area wherein there resides a large populace engaged in peaceful pursuits is unwarranted and contrary to principles of law and of humanity. Moreover, in the present instance time limit allowed for withdrawal is inadequate, and, in view of the wide area over which Japanese bombing operations have prevailed, there can be no assurance that even in areas to which American nationals and noncombatants might withdraw they would be secure.

Notwithstanding the report that assurance that "the safety of the lives and property of nationals of friendly Powers will be taken into full consideration during the projected offensive," this Government is constrained to observe that experience has shown that, when and where aerial bombing operations are engaged in, no amount of solicitude on the part of the authorities responsible therefor is effective toward insuring the safety of any persons or any property within the area of such operations.

Reports of bombing operations by Japanese planes at and around Nanking both before and since the issuance of the announcement under reference indicate that these operations almost invariably result in extensive destruction of noncombatant life and nonmilitary establishments.

In view of the fact that Nanking is the seat of government in China and that there the American Ambassador and other agencies of the American Government carry on their essential functions, the American Government strongly objects to the creation of a situation in consequence of which the American Ambassador and other agencies of this Government are confronted with the alternative of abandoning their establishments or being exposed to grave hazards.

In the light of the assurances repeatedly given by the Japanese Government that the objectives of Japanese military are limited strictly to Chinese military agencies and establishments and that the Japanese Government has no intention of making nonmilitary property and noncombatants the direct objects of attack, and of the Japanese Government's expression of its desire to respect the embassies, warships and merchant vessels of the Powers at Nanking, the American Government cannot believe that the intimation that the whole Nanking area may be subjected to bombing operations represents the considered intent of the Japanese Government.

The American Goverment, therefore, reserving all rights on its own behalf and on behalf of American nationals in respect to damages which might result from Japanese military operations in the Nanking area, expresses the earnest hope that further bombing in and around the city of Nanking will be avoided.* . . .

On September 21st the Japanese reply to the British representations concerning the machine gunning of the British Ambassador in China was received by the British Embassy in Tokyo. Sir Robert Craigie told me that he considered the reply as satisfactory as could be expected, both in tone and substance, but that he did not yet know what would be the attitude of his Government. He felt that the Japanese authorities had made a genuine effort to get at the truth of the affair. While it had not been definitely determined that a Japanese plane was in the exact neighborhood of the Ambassador's car at the time of the attack, nevertheless the fact that bombing operations had been carried out at the same hour only a few miles distant had led the Japanese Government to express its sincere regret over the incident.†

With reference to the bombing of Nanking and to the Department's 221 — of September 21 — we reported that our note had been delivered to the Minister for Foreign Affairs at 5.30 that afternoon.‡ . . .

On September 25th we reported:

1. The *Japan Advertiser* this morning carries two despatches from Washington discussing American attitude with regard to the bombing of Nanking. The first is marked International News Service and states that American public opinion criticizes

* Department's telegram No. 221, September 21, 6 P.M.
† Telegram No. 402, September 22, 2 P.M.
‡ Telegram No. 403, September 22, 6 P.M.

the note to the Japanese Government as "weak-kneed," and that the Secretary is considering the sending of a second note. The second is a Domei despatch and suggests in effect that a "sharply worded note" was sent to Japan to offset the effect on American public opinion of the Administration's statement warning American citizens in China that they remain there at their own risk and of the withdrawal of Johnson from Nanking.

2. The vernacular press carries no despatch on American attitude, except for a brief Washington despatch in the *Asahi* reporting that the American Government maintains a cautious attitude toward a suggestion from Geneva that there be held a conference of the Pacific Region Powers.

3. We have now available practically no source of telegraphic information with regard to trends of American public opinion. We would, therefore, appreciate receiving from time to time from the Department brief telegrams on that subject. . . .

4. We have received nothing from Johnson describing the effects of the bombing at Nanking and the press reports here have been brief and vague.* . . . [37]

---

* Telegram No. 409, September 25, 11 A.M.

[37] In September Mr. Grew made the following entry in his diary: "There is something strange in living in a country engaged in a major war when so few outward signs exist in one's daily life to bring it to one's attention. In fact, apart from the war news in the newspapers, there is nothing to show that war is going on save the constant movement of troops on the railways and individual officers and soldiers being seen off at every railway station on practically every train. Crowds of friends, and sometimes crowds of school children or nurses, wave flags and shout 'Banzai!' as the trains pull out, but never a tear is shed. During the first few weeks of the war departing soldiers dashed cheering and singing through the streets of Tokyo with their families and friends in great trucks, decorated with flags and everyone, especially the soldiers, evidently full of *sake*, but so many fatal accidents occurred as a result of these wild careers that they were finally stopped by the authorities, and now the final processions take place only on foot. As for the newspapers they contain the daily reports of an unbroken series of victories for the Japanese, including skirmishes, battles, the shooting down of Chinese planes, the bombing of cities and the taking of towns. Japanese planes are never, or practically never, lost, while Chinese planes are shot down or destroyed on the ground by the score, almost daily. The Chinese losses are tremendous; the Japanese insignificant. For instance, today's paper says in reporting an engagement in the Shanghai sector: 'Six Japanese soldiers were killed and three wounded. It is estimated by Japanese that 500 Chinese were killed.' This goes on daily *ad nauseam,* but having lived through three years of war in Berlin we are perfectly

Japanese intentions with regard to Hainan Island first came into the picture when the French Ambassador on September 25th sought assurances that there was no intention to occupy that island. We made the following report:

> The French Ambassador informed me today that when he went to see the Vice Minister for Foreign Affairs yesterday afternoon regarding the reported bombing by the Japanese Navy of Hainan the Ambassador sought assurances that there was no intention to occupy the island. He said that the Vice Minister was noncommittal and was disposed to give no reply until the Ambassador informed him that the War and Navy Departments had that morning given explicit assurances respectively to the French Military and Naval Attachés that the island would not be occupied, whereupon the Vice Minister hastened to corroborate the fact and to give his assurances in addition.
>
> The French Ambassador related this incident to me as what he termed another example of the fact that the Foreign Office is uninformed as to decisions made by the military.* . . .

The general reaction of the American press toward the situation arising from the Sino-Japanese conflict was reported to us by the Department at this time, referring particularly to paragraph 3 of our 409 — of September 25:

used to it. Here in Tokyo we receive no reliable news of the fighting and cannot visualize the results save by what the Military Attaché can piece out on his wall maps from the names of towns reported captured. We know nothing whatever as to respective losses. Incoming newspapers from China are heavily censored. One lady told me the other day that she had just received through the open mails a large batch of her papers from Shanghai, neatly folded and apparently in perfect order, but when she opened the package she found that every bit of news with the exception of the advertisements had been cut out. But probably the news published in China is just as one-sided as that published here, for such is war. But meanwhile our life goes on just the same, and so far as our Japanese friends and the public are concerned they are apparently just as carefree and cheerful as ever. They, at least the public, visualize nothing but early and overwhelming victory. It takes more than a few months of war, as we well remember in Berlin, to register on the people's spirits and expressions. And one sees plenty of Chinese around, shopkeepers and servants; there is apparently no animosity against them — probably only a scornful sort of sympathy."

* Telegram No. 413, September 25, 2 P.M.

An Associated Press report today states in part that "The United States Government clung warily yesterday to a middle course amid conflicting demands that it invoke the Neutrality Act in the Chinese-Japanese conflict and that it refrain from doing so.

"Vigorously advocating imposition of the law are six recognized peace societies which contend that the alternative is eventual American involvement in the undeclared war. They have made repeated pleas to President Roosevelt that he apply the statute.

"Opposing such action are numerous groups in this country and China which argue that the invocation of the law would weaken China and strengthen Japan with consequent damage to American interests and prestige in the Far East."

Japan's actions in air bombardments of nonmilitary objectives in China have aroused widespread denunciation in the American press. *Philadelphia Inquirer* observes that "with yesterday's ruthless bombardment of Nanking from the skies, Japan virtually served notice of her withdrawal from the family of civilized nations and her utmost contempt for their humanitarian protests." After referring to the protests made by the American and other Governments against these air attacks the *Inquirer* concludes "This exhibition of Japanese war making at its worst should not and will not alter the resolve of the American people to keep out of war." *New York Times* after dwelling upon the lasting hatred among the Chinese people which Japan's brutal measures will produce notes "Every bomb that falls on Nanking or Canton destroys something of what remains in the western world of friendliness and admiration for the present rulers of Japan." *Christian Science Monitor* declares that "Consultation becomes more and more imperative as Japan's methods of warfare in China violate ever more blatantly all legal and humanitarian precepts. The carrying of the war to helpless civilians, the destruction of homes and public buildings, and the shocking slaughter of noncombatant victims must be opposed by civilized people the world over. The removal of the American diplomatic staff from Nanking indicates no lessening of American interest in consultation to check terrorism in the Far East. It bespeaks an unwillingness however to risk American peace while such risk seems only to encourage postponement of definite international action." *Washington Post* referring to the American note on the bombing of Nanking and to Ambassador Johnson's temporary withdrawal from the Embassy premises observes "If the note to Japan has any meaning at all, it means that we are not prepared to stand by with folded hands while Japan not only makes a shambles out of China and of international law but recklessly destroys our own interests as well."

The foregoing comments are fairly typical of opinion upon this phase of the Chinese-Japanese conflict. There has been no editorial comment observed anywhere in the United States attempting to defend Japan's course of action in China.

The Department will endeavor to telegraph the Embassy from time to time summaries of significant press comment.* . . .

At this time — September 29 — we received from the Department a repetition of Geneva's telegram No. 9, September 28, 8 A.M., reporting a resolution by the League of Nations on the subject of aerial bombardment by Japanese forces of open towns in China, as follows:

At the meeting of the Advisory Committee last evening the chairman announced that Germany and Japan had refused the invitation to participate and Australia and China had accepted. Two further Chinese notes on bombing were communicated.

V. K. Wellington Koo [of China] in public meeting urged denunciation of aggression, aerial bombardment, violation of international law and treaty obligations. He referred to American and British statements against bombing noncombatants, denied that the Chinese had used gas and asked the committee to study measures which could be recommended under the League.

An immediate expression on bombing was therefore strongly proposed by Viscount Cranbourne [of England], fully seconded by Yvon Delbos [of France], and supported by Rickard Sandler, Sweden, and Litvinoff [of the Soviet Union]. The resolution as adopted was as follows: "The Advisory Committee, taking into urgent consideration the question of the aerial bombardment by Japanese aircraft of open towns in China, expresses its profound distress at the loss of life caused to innocent civilians, as a result

* Department's telegram No. 231, September 27, 6 P.M.

of such bombardments, and declares that no excuse can be made for such acts which have aroused horror and indignation throughout the world, and solemnly condemns them."

The chairman will forward the resolution to the President of the Assembly with a view to its adoption also by that body.

The Department's telegram repeating the above from Geneva continued:

The Department has today issued the following statement to the press:

"The Department of State has been informed by the American Minister to Switzerland of the text of the resolution adopted on September 27 by the Advisory Committee of the League of Nations on the subject of aerial bombardment by Japanese air forces of open towns in China.

"The American Government as has been set forth to the Japanese Government repeatedly and especially in this Government's note of September 22 holds the view that any general bombing of an extensive area wherein there resides a large populace engaged in peaceful pursuits is unwarranted and contrary to principles of law and of humanity." * . . .

With reference to our 403 we reported on September 29th the text of the Foreign Minister's reply to my note of September 22 concerning the bombing of Nanking which had that day been received from the Foreign Office:

I have the honor to inform Your Excellency that I have duly noted the contents of Your Excellency's note No. 780 of September 22 regarding the bombing of Nanking by Japanese forces.

As Your Excellency's Government is well aware, Nanking is exceptionally strongly fortified and it is the most important strategic base of military operations for the Chinese forces. The bombing of the military facilities and equipment located in and around the said city is a necessary and unavoidable measure for the attainment of the military objectives of the Japanese forces. It goes without saying that bombing operations by Japanese forces will be strictly confined to such scope, and will not be

* Department's telegram No. 234, September 28, 6 P.M. [Ibid., p. 506.]

aimed at noncombatants, as evidenced by the fact that warning was given even to Chinese noncombatants.

The frequently stated policy of the Imperial Japanese Government to respect as far as possible the rights and interests of third countries and the safety of the lives and property of the nationals thereof remains unaltered in the present bombing operations. The recent proposal of the Imperial Japanese Government that the officials, citizens, and vessels of Your Excellency's country take refuge was the result of the desire to avoid if possible the occurrence of injury to nationals of third countries, which might be unavoidable notwithstanding the greatest precautions which may be taken by the Japanese forces.

It is earnestly hoped that Your Excellency's Government will understand that the Imperial Japanese Government has desired the safety of the nationals of third countries in spite of the fact that the Japanese forces are restricted in their strategic movements by reason of the giving of advance warnings, and it is earnestly hoped that Your Excellency's Government, with full appreciation of the circumstances, will cooperate with the measures taken by the Imperial Japanese Government. Furthermore, the view of the Imperial Japanese Government with regard to damages sustained by nationals of third countries as a result of the present hostilities in China remains as stated in my note No. 102, Asia I, under date of August 31.* . . .

With regard to bombing operations in general we received on the 30th and cabled in translation to the Department a memorandum from the Foreign Office. In reporting the following text we suggested that the Department instruct Nanking whether or not the Department desired that the information desired by the Foreign Office be supplied:

Tokyo, September 29, 1937. No. 30. Memorandum.
With a view to cooperating with the Japanese forces in their desire not to cause damage to the property of nationals of third countries, especially to eleemosynary institutions, during attacks on military establishments and facilities, the Japanese Department of Foreign Affairs has the honor to express to the American

* Telegram No. 431, September 29, 8 P.M.

Embassy the hope that a list will be supplied, as soon and in as much detail as possible, indicating the location of the hospitals, churches, schools, and other eleemosynary establishments belonging to the United States and to nationals of the United States, preferably accompanied by maps and photographs.* . . .

On October 2 the Department informed us that Shanghai had telegraphed substantially as follows and thereupon instructed us with regard to representations concerning the use of the International Settlement at Shanghai by the Japanese as a military base: . . .

In a letter to me dated yesterday the Commander in Chief suggested that the time has arrived for definite representations either by the Ambassadors or their Governments concerning this matter. He points out that since the arrival of the Japanese Army on August 23rd the wharves of the Hongkew section have been the main base for unloading supplies and troops and evacuating wounded, that on September 23rd five transports landed 4,000 troops and that it is understood fifteen transports have used the docks in the past three days. He points to the fact that the Chinese authorities in replying to protests concerning danger to neutrals and their ships in the river stress the point that the Settlement is being used as a Japanese base.

The record shows that on the 15th the Consular Body caused oral representations to be made on the subject to the Japanese Consul General who replied that the Japanese naval landing party being stationed here for the protection of Japanese interests had the right to use portions of the Settlement for the landing of supplies and reinforcements the same as other foreign military units and that the landing party or any other Japanese armed force was or would be acting only in self-defense.

Neither the Council nor other authorities have requested or suggested further protests and I do not think that the Department would wish me to initiate them but the Department may wish to consider a protest at Tokyo. I understand from the Commander in Chief that he has brought the matter to the attention of the British Commander in Chief who has referred it to London.

* Telegram No. 435, September 30, 1 P.M. [*Ibid.*, p. 508.]

The Department's telegram to the Embassy continues:

On September 28 the Department repeated to London Shanghai's telegram of September 25 stating that the Department inclined to the view that representations would be warranted and asking our Embassy to consult with the British Foreign Office and endeavor to ascertain the views and proposed action if any of the British Government in the matter.

According to an *aide-mémoire* of October 1 from the British Embassy here the British Government has directed the British Ambassador at Tokyo to make representations against Japanese use of the International Settlement as a base of military operations. The British Ambassador is under instructions to consult with you prior to taking such action.

The Department desires that you after consultation with your British colleague make appropriate representations to the Japanese Government. The Department feels that your approach should be oral supported by an *aide-mémoire* or memorandum and suggests that you inform the Japanese Government (1) that your Government has since the initiation of hostilities at Shanghai viewed with concern the action of the Japanese armed forces in making use of portions of the International Settlement as a base for military operations against the Chinese; (2) that you understand that the Japanese Consul General at Shanghai replying to representations made by the senior consul at Shanghai acting on behalf of his interested colleagues stated that any Japanese armed force in the Settlement was or would be acting only in self-defense; (3) that in the opinion of your Government the present Japanese military operations at Shanghai — their extent, place and seeming objectives — cannot with warrant be construed as a means of defense of the Settlement; (4) that you are authoritatively informed that portions of the Settlement particularly the Hongkew section are being extensively and continuously used as a main base for debarking Japanese troops and unloading military supplies to be employed outside the Settlement in major operations against Chinese troops; (5) that your Government feels strongly that the Japanese military forces should refrain from use of the Settlement in any way as a base or channel for military operations of any character except such as are exclusively for the protection of and defense of the Settlement; (6) that the Settlement is an area in which by treaties and agreements a number of foreign countries including Japan and the United States and their nationals have common rights and interests; (7) that use by the Japanese military of portions of the Settlement as a base for major military operations which are being conducted outside the Settlement against Chinese troops is not in keeping with the spirit of those agreements; and (8) that such use unwarrantedly endangers the rights and interests of all other countries including the United States which possess in common those rights and interests.*

Replying to the foregoing telegram we reported on October 4:

1. I called today on the Vice Minister for Foreign Affairs and made oral representations leaving with him an *aide-mémoire* embodying all of the points in paragraph numbered four of the Department's telegram.

2. The Vice Minister's only comment was that the Chinese forces are endangering Japanese lives and property in the International Settlement by fire from Pootung and Chapei and that the Japanese have landed a very small number of troops in the Settlement, their principal forces having been disembarked elsewhere. The Foreign Office will reply to our representations in due course.

3. My British colleague will make similar representations to the Vice Minister this afternoon as he is instructed to act on the same day as myself.† . . .

With reference to our 360 — of September 10 — and our despatch No. 2592, September 17, 1937, we reported on the 5th:

In spite of the Embassy's informal efforts to discourage the sending to the United States of so-called good will envoys plans have now been made for four prominent Japanese to undertake such a mission. These are Shingoro Takaishi, editor of *Nichi Nichi;* Hitoshi Ashida, member of the Diet and editor of the *Japan Times,* Bunjiro Suzuki, prominent labor member of the

* Department's telegram No. 245, October 2, 3 P.M.
† Telegram No. 444, October 4, 2 P.M.

Diet; and Kojiro Matsukata, member of the well-known commercial family. Takaishi plans to sail by the *Empress of Japan*
October 8, the others by the *Tatsuta Maru* on October 14.

It is understood that among other unofficial envoys Viscount
Ishii will go to England and France, Admiral Takuo Godo,
former Minister of Commerce and Industry, to Germany, and
Baron Kishichiro Okura [Japanese businessman] to Italy.* [38] . . .

Adverting to the foregoing telegram I reported further that
one of the principal members of the unofficial group which
was planning to visit our country, Mr. Kojiro Matsukata, had
come to see me on October 5th to have a talk before sailing on
the 14th for the United States where he hoped to stay from
two to six months and to visit Washington, New York and
Chicago among other cities. He made clear the fact that he
proposed to go merely as a businessman seeking business contacts and not at all as a so-called good will envoy. Japan needed
several commodities including trucks, scrap iron and oil, particularly oil, he said, and the main purpose of his visit to the
United States was to obtain supplies of these materials.

In the course of our talk the complete change in sentiment
in Japan away from Great Britain and towards the United
States was touched upon by Mr. Matsukata who said that great
indignation against the former had been expressed to him in
recent conversations by a number of officials in Japan, especially by naval officers. These officials had noted that the representations made by the United States in connection with

* Telegram No. 448, October 5, 5 P.M.

[38] About the success of these good-will missions to the United States, Mr. Grew
wrote on November 4, 1937, in his diary: "The Japanese press reports that the
'good will envoys' sent to the United States are sadly disillusioned — as I
definitely predicted in the diary they would be. According to the press these
envoys are sighing: 'We have repeatedly explained the just and fair stand of
Japan in the "China Incident." We have explained that we are fighting solely
for the purpose of eliminating China's anti-Japanese activities, that is, for correcting the attitude of the Chinese leaders toward Japan, but not only the
American people in general but even those Americans belonging to the intellectual class appear to have completely failed to understand us.' Sad, sad. How
unenlightened we Americans are."

the hostilities in China had been reasonable and had taken Japanese susceptibilities into account, whereas a consistently offensive tone had been evident in representations made by the British Government. Hostility toward Japan, he said, had repeatedly been shown by British naval and diplomatic officers in China. In this connection Mr. Matsukata cited a number of instances such as the publicity given by the British to the charge by Chinese fishermen that their junks had been sunk by a Japanese submarine, the use by Chinese of docks in Shanghai belonging to the British in order to facilitate the mining of a Japanese warship, and finally the British note with regard to the wounding of their Ambassador in China whose hostility to Japan, he said, was well-known.

In the same vein Mr. Matsukata stressed the fact that an offer of good offices by the United States in the Sino-Japanese conflict would be heartily welcomed in Japan, whereas the same would not apply to a similar British offer. If the United States should decide to make such an offer, he repeatedly urged, it should be done alone and not as an Anglo-American *démarche*. Such an offer by the United States, he said he had good reason to believe, would be favorably received in Japan even if made immediately.

I warned Mr. Matsukata that public opinion in the United States would not be found hospitable to Japanese efforts to place on China the responsibility for the current warfare, that recent actions by Japan had rendered it very difficult for us to apply to Japan our policy of the good neighbor, and that in formulating its policy and action the Government of the United States must take public opinion into full consideration.

I said to the Department that a concerted attack by the Japanese press against the attitude of Britain and British policy had recently been evident and that we were then in the course of preparing a telegraphic report on this subject which would deal with the suggestion advanced by Mr. Matsukata in his conversation with me. At that particular moment we saw no useful purpose in any offer of good offices or mediation by the United States.* . . .

* Telegram No. 449, October 5, 6 P.M.

Referring to our 435 — of September 30 — with regard to Japanese attacks on American properties in China we were directed by the Department to reply to the Foreign Office substantially as follows:

In the light of the assurances repeatedly given by the Japanese Government that the objectives of Japanese military operations are limited to Chinese military agencies and establishments and that the Japanese Government has no intention of making nonmilitary property and noncombatants the objects of attack it is not perceived that there is need for the supplying of a list and the indicating of the locations of American properties with the possible exception of properties located in the immediate vicinity of Chinese military agencies and establishments.

Although it has been our procedure for the purpose of safeguarding and serving the American interests involved to inform both the Japanese Government and the Chinese authorities of the location of American establishments endangered by their proximity to places in the range of military operations when and so far as practicable, Japanese bombing operations have now been extended to a vast area and have been directed against objectives where it is often not apparent that any military purpose is thereby served. Consequently no reliable indication is afforded as to what places are likely to come next within the range of Japanese military operations. Furthermore American institutions generally so far as this Government has been informed have been adopting the practice of plainly displaying on their buildings clear nationality marking and the location of such buildings is usually described in published directories, maps, et cetera, which are doubtless available to the Japanese military authorities. It would thus appear to the American Government that the Japanese military authorities are in better position than are the American authorities to determine what American institutions will be endangered by virtue of their proximity to Japanese military objectives and to take adequate precautions accordingly.

In the event that Japanese authorities request information to supplement that which is already available in regard to a particular point where American property may be located near to a Chinese military establishment which the Japanese authorities contemplate attacking, the American authorities would be prepared as heretofore to give such information as may be practicable in regard to the location of American property and institutions. However, in giving any such information the American Government does so only for the purpose of protecting American life and property; it reserves entirely its declared attitude and position in regard to the hostilities in which Japanese and Chinese armed forces are engaged; and its reservation of rights in regard to destruction of American life or property which may arise thereafter will in no way be altered by the fact of its having given or not having given such information.*

Supplementing the foregoing telegram and with reference to our 431 — of September 29 — 435 — of September 30 — and 450 — of October 5 —. the Department informed us:

The publication of the text of the Japanese reply of September 29 to this Government's note of September 22 was followed by widespread comment in the press in this country to the effect that the reply was "unsatisfactory." [39] There was much comment, some of astonishment, some severely critical, and some expressive of perplexity on the expression of hope that this Government would "co-operate with the measures taken by the Imperial Japanese Government." We realize that Hirota's statement in that context related to measures which the Japanese wish to take to avoid endangering or destroying American lives and property. But many commentators failed accurately to grasp the intended application and dealt with this suggestion that we "co-operate" without reference to the limitation implicit in the context. Subsequently both in the memorandum reported in your 435, September 30, 1 P.M., and in the last paragraph of

* Department's telegram No. 250, October 5, 7 P.M. [*Ibid.*, pp. 509–10.]

[39] The *New York Times*, for instance, on September 30, 1937, p. 1, commented that the "note was so brief as to be almost perfunctory, if not routine. As such it was a disappointment to those who had been encouraged to believe, because of the lapse of a week in which Japan considered her reply, that it would contain a comprehensive statement of policy along moderate lines.

"It contributed no essentially new element to the situation and gave no intimation of a recession in policy in deference to world public opinion. . . .

"The unsatisfactory character of the reply at once posed the question of what further steps the United States might take."

Hirota's note reported in your 450, October 5, 7 P.M., the Foreign Office again solicits our "co-operation" in relation to procedure for the safeguarding of American lives and property.

The idea that we should or that we can co-operate with Japan in anything related to or connected with the carrying on of the hostilities to which Japan and China are parties is an idea entirely contrary to our whole attitude and policy in regard to those hostilities. Disapproving as we do of the military operations in their entirety we cannot take a step or make a contribution which implies assent on our part to such operations provided they do not endanger or destroy American lives and property. We must and we will do what we appropriately can toward causing American lives and property not to be endangered. But in so doing it should not be expected or be construed that we are "co-operating" with either of the parties engaged in military operations or that what we do is done in any sense for the purpose of facilitating the conducting by either party of such operations.

In view of the type of comment to which the Foreign Office use of this expression "co-operate" has given rise both in unofficial and in official circles we feel that you should bring this matter to Hirota's attention and make clear to Hirota that what this Government seeks and expects is not "co-operation" between the two countries in relations to any phase of military operations but that American lives and property shall not be endangered by and in consequence of any military operations. We appreciate the assurances and the apparently sincere effort of the Japanese Foreign Office to help toward avoiding endangering American lives and property but in our opinion it would be advisable to avoid use of the term "co-operate" in any context relating to or bearing upon the military operations.* . . .

On October 6 the Department cabled, with regard to the President's famous "quarantine" speech in Chicago:[40]

* Department's telegram No. 251, October 5, 8 P.M. [Ibid., pp. 510–11.]
[40] On October 5, President Roosevelt delivered his "Quarantine Speech" in Chicago Among other things he said: "The peace, the freedom and the security of ninety percent of the population of the world is being jeopardized by the remaining ten percent who are threatening a breakdown of all international order and law. Surely the ninety percent who want to live in peace under law

Inasmuch as the press here contains press comments emanating from Japan in regard to the President's address of October 5 at Chicago the Department assumes that the significant portions of the address have been published or arc available in Japan. The text of the address is contained in radio bulletin No. 232 of October 5 and the Department will not cable the text or the pertinent portions thereof to you unless you so request.*

To the foregoing telegram we replied on the 7th:

and in accordance with moral standards that have received almost universal acceptance through the centuries, can and must find some way to make their will prevail. . . .

"It seems to be unfortunately true that the epidemic of world lawlessness is spreading.

"When an epidemic of physical disease starts to spread, the community approves and joins in a quarantine of the patients in order to protect the health of the community against the spread of the disease." Roosevelt, *op. cit.*, p. 410.

Secretary Hull has written about the speech that the "reaction against the quarantine idea was quick and violent. As I saw it, this had the effect of setting back for at least six months our constant educational campaign intended to create and strengthen public opinion toward international cooperation. Those of us who had been carrying on this campaign, through speeches, statements, and actions wherever possible, had been working as actively as we could; but we were always careful not to go too far lest a serious attack by the isolationist element throw us farther back than we were before. If we proceeded gradually and did not excite undue opposition, our words and actions, although not so dynamic or far-reaching as we might wish, had more effect on the world at large than if we made startling statements or took precipitate action and then, because of the bitter reaction we aroused, presented the world with the spectacle of a nation divided against itself.

"Six of the major pacifist organizations issued a declaration that the President 'points the American people down the road that led to the World War.' The American Federation of Labor resolved: 'American labor does not wish to be involved in European or Asiatic wars.' Two Representatives, Fish and Tinkham, threatened to have the President impeached. A Philadelphia *Inquirer* telegraphic poll of Congress showed more than two to one against common action with the League toward the Far East. A campaign was launched to secure 25,000,000 signatures to a 'Keep America Out of War' petition.

"All this reaction, of course, received wide publicity and was dulcet to the ears of Hitler, Mussolini, and the Japanese war lords. It undoubtedly emboldened the aggressor countries, and caused the democracies of Europe to wonder if we could ever be with them in more than words. It was certainly followed by the bolder actions of Japan, culminating in the sinking of the United States gunboat *Panay* by Japanese planes two months later." Hull, *op. cit.*, I, 545–46.

* Department's telegram No. 253, October 6, 6 P.M.

Yesterday the Foreign Office spokesman released to the correspondents a statement on the President's address of October 5 at Chicago. Byas states that he has telegraphed the complete text to the *New York Times*. The spokesman asserted a right of all honest and industrious people to live anywhere in the pursuit of life, liberty, and happiness, referred to the doubling of the population of Japan in the past fifty years, and stated that the American Japanese Exclusion Law of 1924 is against the natural law of mankind and is greatly deplored by the Japanese. He said that if the "haves" refused to concede to the rightful demands of the "have nots" peace will be very difficult to maintain. He stated that in the present affair China has refused by force of arms the peaceful co-operation which Japan wants.

At the same time the spokesman released a statement referring to an editorial of the *New York Times* of October 4.[41] Byas says that he has also telegraphed this statement in full. The statement aims at showing that on the night of August 14 the lives of thirty thousand Japanese in Shanghai were imminently threatened by Chinese forces and that military action of Japan taken thereupon in Shanghai was consequently defensive.

Dooman was told at the Foreign Office this morning, and the statement is repeated in this afternoon's Japanese press, that the releases of the spokesman yesterday were made in the capacity of the chief of the Press Section, not as official statements by the

[41] In the *New York Times*, October 4, 1937, p. 20, an editorial entitled "Japan's Futile Words" was published stating that Japan's "present postulate of the causes of the conflict, their anger at the effectiveness of Chinese 'propaganda' abroad, their defiant refusal to consider any suggestions of mediation and their assurances that Japan seeks only fruitful 'cooperation' with China — these remonstrances cannot be expected to blind the rest of the world to the patent fact of Japan's guilt.

"We are now told that the slaughter in Shanghai was precipitated as 'part of a well-considered Chinese plan to attack and annihilate the Japanese.' So maintains the Foreign Office spokesman, without offering any proof and, needless to say, without reference to the flimsy pretexts for Japan's sudden concentration of forces in Shanghai and for its invasion a month earlier of North China. Japanese officials never showed more plainly their overestimation of the credulity of foreign opinion. . . .

"To frustrate Chinese unity under a Government independent of Japanese dictation — not to curb communism — Japan prosecutes relentless war against Chiang Kai-shek."

Foreign Office. He was also told that the Foreign Office has instructed Saito to so inform the Department.*

Further Japanese press comment on the President's address was reported by us:

1. The two principal Japanese papers this morning editorially discussed the President's address at Chicago.

a. The *Asahi*, referring to the traditional partiality of the American people to the underdog, states that it is natural that American sympathy should be largely with China, but it objects to the President's assuming without examination that the complaints of the party (China) which initiated the conflict are necessarily true. Although it shares the ideals of the President with regard to world peace, it declares that the facts upon which the President rests his statements need revision. The editorial concludes with the statement that the President's address, by stimulating the hopes of the weakening Chinese army, will only vainly protract the hostilities; and that if the United States intends to express its views with regard to the Far East, only by maintaining an attitude of neutrality will it qualify itself to be heard on that subject.

b. The *Nichi Nichi* states that it is reluctant to compare the President with the Archbishop of Canterbury, who has taken a leading part in fostering a movement prejudicial to good international relations.[42] The attitude of the Roosevelt Administration toward Far Eastern problems has thus far been fair and just, but the paper considers the address at Chicago to have been imprudent and lacking in the keen political insight which Mr. Roosevelt usually shows. It regrets that the President is unable

---

* Telegram No. 455, October 7, 4 P.M.

42 Cosmo Lang, the Archbishop of Canterbury, was chairman of a meeting in Albert Hall in London on October 5, at which eight thousand persons met to protest the deaths of civilians in the Sino-Japanese conflict. A resolution was adopted at that time stating: "It is resolved that this meeting record its horror at, and the emphatic condemnation of, the indiscriminate attacks upon civilian noncombatants by Japanese forces in China and urges the British Government to take the lead in securing such concerted action by economic measures or otherwise as may prevent their continuance." *New York Times,* October 6, 1937, p. 5.

to realize that the conflict was brought about by the policy of the Chinese Government of hostility toward Japan, as indicated by refusal to co-operate in the economic field with Japan and by threatening the lives and property of Japanese nationals in China.

2. The Department's announcement of October 6 with regard to violation by Japan of the Nine Power Treaty and Kellogg Pact was published this morning by the newspapers in extras and special editions. The only reaction in official Japanese circles thus far described in the press is attributed to the Foreign Office and is as follows:

"The Japanese Government has already made it clear that special consideration must be given to the application to the Far East of the principles set forth in Secretary of State Hull's recent declaration. It betrays an actual lack of knowledge to propose the application to the Far East of the Nine Power Treaty, which was concluded many years ago, and of the Kellogg Pact. Conditions having changed, these two treaties cannot be applied as a basis for regulating relations between Japan and China."

3. As indicating one line which may be followed by the press in discussing the Department's statement, it was privately stated at the Foreign Office this morning that as the American Government has in effect declared that Japan has resorted to war, it will be interesting to observe whether the American Government will continue to take the view, in relation to the Neutrality Act, that a state of war does not exist in the Far East.*

On October 6 the Department released to the press a statement which read as follows:

The Department of State has been informed by the American Minister to Switzerland of the text of the report adopted by the Advisory Committee of the League of Nations setting forth the Advisory Committee's examination of the facts of the present situation in China and the treaty obligations of Japan. The Minister has further informed the Department that this report was adopted and approved by the Assembly of the League of Nations today, October 6th.[43]

* Telegram No. 456, October 7, 5 P.M.

[43] The day after the "Quarantine Speech" the League of Nations Assembly

Since the beginning of the present controversy in the Far East, the Government of the United States has urged upon both the Chinese and the Japanese Governments that they refrain from hostilities, and has offered to be of assistance in an effort to find some means, acceptable to both parties to the conflict, of composing by pacific methods the situation in the Far East.

The Secretary of State in statements made public on July 16th and August 23rd made clear the position of the Government of the United States in regard to international problems and international relationships throughout the world and as applied specifically to the hostilities which are at present unfortunately going on between China and Japan. Among the principles which in the opinion of the Government of the United States should govern international relationships, if peace is to be maintained, are abstinence by all nations from the use of force in the pursuit of policy and from interference in the internal affairs of other nations; adjustment of problems in international relations by process of peaceful negotiation and agreement; respect by all nations for the rights of others and observance by all nations of established obligations; and the upholding of the principles of the sanctity of treaties.

On October 5th at Chicago the President elaborated these principles, emphasizing their importance, and in a discussion of the world situation pointed out that there can be no stability or peace either within nations or between nations except under laws and moral standards adhered to by all; that international anarchy destroys every foundation for peace; that it jeopardizes either the immediate or the future security of every nation, large or small; and that it is therefore of vital interest and concern to the people of the United States that respect of treaties and international morality be restored.

adopted two reports. The conclusion reached by the Subcommittee of the Far East Advisory Committee in the First Report was that "the military operations carried on by Japan against China by land, sea and air are out of all proportion to the incident that occasioned the conflict; that such action cannot possibly facilitate or promote the friendly co-operation between the two nations that Japanese statesmen have affirmed to be the aim of their policy; that it can be justified neither on the basis of existing legal instruments nor on that of the right of self-defence, and that it is in contravention of Japan's obligations under the Nine-Power Treaty of February 6th, 1922, and under the Pact of Paris of August 27th, 1928." League of Nations, *Sino-Japanese Conflict*, p. 42.

In the light of the unfolding developments in the Far East the Government of the United States has been forced to the conclusion that the action of Japan in China is inconsistent with the principles which should govern the relationships between nations and is contrary to the provisions of the Nine Power Treaty of February 6th, 1922, regarding principles and policies to be followed in matters concerning China, and to those of the Kellogg-Briand Convention of August 27, 1928. Thus the conclusions of this Government with respect to the foregoing are in general accord with those of the Assembly of the League of Nations.* . . .[44]

With reference to the Department's 254 — of October 6 — we reported:

1. The Department's announcement of October 6 on the Sino-Japanese conflict and press telegrams on that subject from Washington and from various European capitals are sensationally featured this morning in all papers. The attitude of the United States is the only subject of editorial comment.

2. Official comment, pending study of the situation, is cautious and reserved. However, first impression views in official

* Department's telegram No. 254, October 6, 7 P.M. [*Ibid.*, pp. 396–97.]

[44] On October 7, 1937, Mr. Grew wrote in his diary: "It was today that we heard of the Department's espousal of the action of the League of Nations, following the President's Chicago speech of October 5th. The shock to us all was great. However, I called in the entire staff and told them that no matter what we individually might think or feel about the new tack taken by our Government — which was in effect widely at variance with our own carefully considered recommendations — we must take the utmost care (and our wives as well) not to utter a word outside of the Embassy which could give the impression that we were out of sympathy with the Administration's action. The members of the staff, I think unanimously, felt so bitterly about this new development that I feared they would sputter about it outside and that my cautionary word was wise. . . .

"This was the day that I felt my carefully built castle tumbling about my ears and we all wandered about the chancery, depressed, gloomy and with not a smile in sight. That afternoon Alice, Elsie and I went to the cinema to see *Captains Courageous* and a review of the prize Walt Disney cartoons for the past five years — 'Trees and Flowers,' 'Three Little Pigs,' 'The Hare and the Tortoise,' 'The Country Mouse,' etc., all admirable. And then I sunk myself in *Gone with the Wind* — which is precisely the way I felt."

circles are: that the Nine Power Treaty is obsolete and the Kellogg Pact inapplicable to the Far East; that Japan will, if invited, refuse to attend the proposed Nine Power Treaty conference; [45] and that Japan will not acquiesce in any intervention between Japan and China. One paper reports that consideration is being given to denunciation by Japan of the Nine Power Treaty.

3 Editorials, although not violent in tone, clearly reveal that recent announcements of the American attitude have been a shock to Japanese opinion. They generally conform to a pattern somewhat as follows:

The League of Nations has consistently ignored actual conditions in the Far East, and, moved by Chinese propaganda, it has denounced Japan as a violator of the Nine Power and Kellogg Treaties. The United States had been taking an independent course of action which was impartial and just. However, it is now evident that the United States, in associating itself with the League in denouncing Japan as a treaty violator, is equally with the League unable to understand conditions in the Far East and must share with the League responsibility for aggravating the situation. The initiative in the present conflict was taken by China and the measures of force resorted to by Japan were necessary to protect its interests in China. It would not be in the interests of peace, either in the Far East or in the world at large, if Japan were to permit third parties to intervene.

4. It is understood that the Foreign Office will issue, probably tomorrow, a statement with regard to the League resolution and to the Department's announcement.* [46]

---

[45] Shortly after the League of Nations action on October 6, the Belgian Government invited the signatories of the Nine Power Treaty to attend a conference at Brussels. Japan refused to attend.

* Telegram No. 459, October 8, 6 P.M.

[46] In prefacing the section of his diary dated September 26 – October 10, 1937, Mr. Grew wrote: "I have no right, as a representative of the Government, to criticize the Government's policy and actions, but that doesn't make me feel any less sorry about the way things have turned. An architect who has spent five years slowly building what he hoped was going to be a solid and permanent edifice and has then seen that edifice suddenly crumble about his ears might feel similarly. Or a doctor who has worked hard over a patient and then has lost his case. Our country came to a fork in the road and, paradoxical as it may seem to a peace-loving nation, chose the road which leads not to peace

On the same day we repeated to the Department the following telegram sent by us to Shanghai:

> October 8, 7 P.M. Japanese Navy Department has confirmed through the Foreign Office offer communicated by Hasegawa to Yarnell to facilitate evacuation to Shanghai of Americans from Yangtze Valley either by water or by direct land route.*

In a rush telegram on the 9th we reported the text of the Foreign Office statement in reply to the declaration of the League of Nations:

> The League of Nations has declared that the actions now being taken by Japan in China are a violation of the Nine Power Treaty and the Treaty for the Renunciation of War, and the State Department of the United States has issued a statement to the same purport. However, these steps must be attributed to an unfortunate lack of understanding of the real circumstances as well as the true intentions of Japan, a state of affairs which the Japanese Government deem very regrettable.
>
> The present Sino-Japanese affair originated in the unwarranted attack made by Chinese forces on Japanese garrison troops

but potentially to war. Our primary and fundamental concept was to avoid involvement in the Far Eastern mess; we have chosen the road which might lead directly to involvement.

"If this sudden turnabout in policy could possibly help the situation either now or in future, if our branding of Japan as an aggressor and our appeal to the Nine Power Treaty and the Kellogg Pact and our support of the League of Nations, could serve to stop the fighting in China or limit its sphere or prevent similar aggression in the world in future, my accord with this step would be complete and wholehearted. But, alas, history and experience have shown that Real Politik and not ethereal idealism should govern our policy and our acts today. With Manchuria, Abyssinia and Spain written in big letters across the pages of history, how can we ignore the practical experience of those events and the hopelessness of deterring them *unless we are willing to fight?* Moral suasion is ineffective; economic or financial sanctions have been shown to be ineffective and dangerous to boot. Once again I fear that we shall crawl out on a limb — and be left there — to reap the odium and practical disadvantages of our course from which other countries will then hasten to profit. Such is internationalism today. Why, oh why, do we disregard the experience and facts of history which stare us in the face?"

* Telegram No. 460, October 8, 7 P.M.

legitimately stationed in North China under rights clearly recognized by treaty. The troop which was maneuvering at the time of the outbreak was a very small unit. The Japanese garrison force was then scattered in different parts, engaged in peacetime duties. After the outbreak of hostilities, Japan did everything in her power to reach a local settlement of the incident, even at the sacrifice of strategical advantages. These facts are sufficient to prove that the action of the Japanese force was by no means premeditated but simply defensive.

China is undoubtedly responsible for the spread of the affair to Shanghai and then to other points of Central China. She openly violated the Agreement for the Cessation of Hostilities concluded in 1932 by concentrating overwhelmingly numerous forces of more than forty thousand in the demilitarized zone and attempted to annihilate our Naval Landing Party, numbering but a scant three thousand, and our 30,000 nationals living in the Settlement, amongst whom were many women and children.

The subsequent development of the Japanese military action has been but the unavoidable consequence of the hostile operations of China, who, ignoring our policy of a local settlement and nonaggravation of the situation, moved and concentrated her large armies against us. The action which Japan is taking at the present time is a measure of defense to which she has been compelled to resort by the premeditated provocative acts of China.

What the Japanese Government seek today is merely the abandonment by China of her anti-Japanese policy and the establishment of the enduring peace in East Asia, through sincere cooperation between Japan and China. They have no territorial designs whatever.

In the light of these circumstances, it must be firmly declared that the present action of Japan in China contravenes none of the existing treaties which are in force.

The Chinese Government lending themselves to Communist intrigue, have brought about the present hostilities by their persistent and malicious anti-Japanese measures and their attempt to do away with the rights and vital interests of Japan in China by force of arms. It is they who should be deemed a violator of the spirit of the Treaty for the Renunciation of War — a menace to the peace of the world.* . . .

* Telegram No. 463, October 9, 2 P.M. [*Ibid.*, pp. 399–400.]

On October 13 the Belgian Ambassador in Tokyo informed me of his receipt on the day before of an informatory message from his Government to the effect that the Belgian Government was then considering an approach which had been made by the British Government, with the approval of the American Government, with regard to the proposed choice of Brussels for the conference of signatories of the Nine Power Treaty. On his own initiative Baron de Bassompierre had told the Vice Minister for Foreign Affairs of reports in the press on that subject and had inquired as to the attitude of the Japanese Government toward the calling of such a meeting and whether Japan would take part. The Vice Minister replied that the Japanese Government was not interested and that in any case the matter had not yet been given consideration in Tokyo because the Japanese Government had not been apprized of the proposal.

Sir Robert Craigie, without prior consultation with the Belgian Ambassador, had also discussed this subject with the Vice Minister who could see no good reason to hold such a meeting because the terms which Japan would eventually demand from China as a result of the current conflict would not in the slightest degree be affected thereby.

Baron de Bassompierre had informed his Government that no international action short of force could in any way change the course of developments in China, and since Belgium would thereby be futilely injuring its own interests in Japan he had strongly recommended that the proposed meeting in Brussels be not held.* . . .

On the same day the following rush telegram was received from the Secretary of State with regard to the proposed Brussels conference and with reference to our 470 — of October 13:

> We are considerably perturbed at the indications given by the Japanese Vice Minister both to Bassompierre and Craigie that the Japanese Government was disinterested in the proposed conference of the parties to the Nine Power Treaty and could not

* Telegram No. 470, October 13, 5 P.M.

see the purpose of holding such a meeting. I should be glad to have you call on the Minister for Foreign Affairs and impart orally that this Government is proceeding on the assumption that the Japanese Government will attend, believing as we do that the proposed conference will offer a useful opportunity for a reasoned and frank discussion of the difficulties both present and underlying of the situation with a view to seeking to arrive at a constructive solution by process of peaceful agreement.

If the time element is raised in conversation you should make it clear that in the opinion of this Government the meeting should be held in the immediate future.

The British Ambassador we understand is being instructed to make a somewhat similar *démarche*. You should await, before acting, information of his having received such instruction.*

My reply to the foregoing instructions concerning the Nine Power Treaty Conference was telegraphed on the 15th:

1. I precisely carried out the Department's instructions in an interview with the Minister for Foreign Affairs at four o'clock this afternoon. Hirota replied that no invitation to attend such a conference had yet been received by the Japanese Government and that therefore no decision had yet been reached but that "according to the present tendency within the Government such an invitation would be declined."

2. Having carried out my instructions I then said to the Minister that I would like to discuss the matter informally and I then elaborated in my own words the Department's views and brought out various arguments in favor of Japan's participation. The Minister informally replied that as the League of Nations had already formally taken the part of China against Japan such a conference would be useless and that far from providing a basis for an earlier termination of the hostilities it would in fact result in prolonging the hostilities by persuading China that with foreign support she can afford to continue the warfare. The Minister said that a discussion of terms for peace would be superfluous because he has been discussing these terms with Chiang Kai-shek during the past four years and that "in general" these

* Department's telegram No. 261, October 14, 5 P.M.

terms are embodied in his announced three points. The Minister said that the Sino-Soviet pact which he believes to contain unpublished clauses has rendered much more difficult an early solution of the difficulties.[47]

3. My British colleague is making similar representations today.* . . .

On the 16th I informed the Department that my British colleague had given me for my confidential information a copy of the memorandum which he had left with the Minister for Foreign Affairs on the previous day with regard to the Brussels Conference, as follows:

His Majesty's Government in the United Kingdom desire to emphasize that the proposed conference under the Nine Powers will, in the words of the League Assembly, have as its objective "to seek a method of putting an end to the conflict *by agreement*."

The present situation is causing His Majesty's Government grave and continuing anxiety and it is earnestly to be hoped that the Japanese Government will cooperate in this aim and will accept an invitation to the Conference.† . . .

With regard to the International Settlement at Shanghai and referring to our 444 — of October 4 — we cabled on the 20th the following text in translation of a memorandum in which the Foreign Office replied to our representations of October 4:

October 19, 1937.

Memorandum

The Japanese Foreign Office presents its compliments to the American Embassy and, having duly noted the proposal set forth in the *aide-mémoire* of October 4 from the Embassy of the United States in Tokyo with regard to the use by the Japanese

---

[47] China and the Soviet Union had signed a nonaggression pact on August 21, 1937, at Nanking. See *China Year Book 1938*, p. 373.

* Telegram No. 475, October 15, 5 P.M.

† Telegram No. 476, October 6, 10 A.M.

forces of the Shanghai International Settlement, has the honor to make the following reply:

Japan's present military operations at Shanghai had their origin in the fact that China massed quantities of troops around the Settlement and defied the Japanese landing force charged with protection of Japanese residents there. Thereafter China mobilized and rapidly brought up a large number of troops over a wide area in the rear of Shanghai, and assumed an antagonistic attitude against the greatly outnumbered Japanese forces. The Japanese army was therefore obliged to dispatch reinforcements for reasons of defense. The area of military operations has been necessarily enlarged. Because of the need of protecting the International Settlement and because of the inherent right to protect Japanese residents, the Japanese Government is of opinion exception cannot properly be taken to the action of the Japanese army in landing troops necessary for defense, and munitions of war, in the northern area of Shanghai, an area allotted to Japan for purposes of guarding, in order to carry on military operations against Chinese forces which constitute the menace.

Japan, as one Power in the International Settlement, has large rights and interests there, as have also other Powers. As a result of military operations against China, which assumed an unwarrantably provocative attitude in the present instance, Japan is now sustaining heavy sacrifices. In view of the fact that the Japanese Government is keenly alive to the safety and the rights and interests of nationals of other Powers, it is bending every effort to the protection of such rights and interests, and is consequently obliged to use part of the International Settlement in the present military operations.*

Referring to our 475 — of October 15 — we reported on the same day:

Yesterday the *Asahi,* one of the leading papers, editorially raised the question whether it would not be advantageous for Japan to attend the Nine Power Conference. It was stated that if the purpose of the conference is to sit in judgment on Japan, national honor must prevent Japan from attending, or if it is to

---

* Telegram No. 481, October 20, 4 P.M. [*Ibid.,* pp. 403–04.]

implement the policy of the League of Nations to help China, Japan should announce in no uncertain terms its intention not to appear. The editorial points out, however, that if the purpose of the conference is to study the causes of unrest in the Far East, an opportunity would be had for Japan to demonstrate that the Nine Power Treaty is obsolete, to prove that China has long pursued a policy of hostility toward Japan, and to cite examples of Chinese violations of treaties. It suggests that the course of wisdom would be for Japan to attend and "from inside the conference to bomb anti-Japanese feeling."

I added confidentially that on the previous evening a Japanese who enjoyed the best contacts in military and other official circles had said to us that the editorial set forth above represented a viewpoint which forward-looking and progressive leaders were strongly backing although he did not appear to hold out much hope that their arguments would be accepted. The Foreign Office spokesman now declined to commit himself on this subject although he had previously taken the position that Japan would not attend a Nine Power Conference.

On this subject our own opinions at that time were necessarily of a speculative nature. The Japanese military, we believed, were opposed to Japanese representation at the forthcoming conference even although the primary purpose of the conference might be to find some plan for a Far Eastern peace. Japan had as yet received no invitation to the conference, according to the Foreign Office, but it appeared probable that the Japanese Government would take part in some limited form provided that the terms of the invitation should make it possible for Japan to attend without prejudice to her national honor. One argument that appealed to the Japanese was that the conference would afford a sounding board for presenting Japan's case to the world. That the military would agree to unconditional Japanese representation, in view of their emphatic opposition to western intervention in East Asia, would appear to be unlikely; Japan's participation in discussing a peace plan would, in any event, probably be hedged about with rigid restrictions.*

* Telegram No. 482, October 20, 5 P.M.

With reference to our 475 we reported on the 20th that Reuter's correspondent in Japan had sent to his principals in London on October 12 his views as to the terms of peace which would be demanded by the Japanese extremists if they should be successful in crushing China, and he proposed from time to time to modify or supplement these terms according to new developments:

(1) China's recognition of Manchukuo.

(2) Japan, Manchukuo, North China and the Chinese Republic to form an economic bloc.

(3) An autonomous anti-communist state to be established in North China which would be under Japanese protection and whose taxes and customs revenues would be subject to Japanese control.

(4) Inner Mongolia would be incorporated into Manchukuo or else an autonomous anti-communist Inner Mongolia would be placed under the protection of an independent Manchukuo Empire.

(5) All national departments and prefectural governments would have Japanese advisers and the Inspector-General of Customs would be a Japanese national.

(6) China's tariffs would be revised with a view to promoting the exchange of China's raw materials for Japanese finished goods.

(7) A pro-Japanese statesman would be chosen to replace Chiang Kai-shek.

(8) China would be expected to join the anti-communist bloc.

(9) China's military forces would be limited to a Peace Preservation Corps and the entire country would be demilitarized.

(10) No military or commercial airplanes to be possessed by China.

(11) China's air services would be operated on a co-operative basis, Japan providing the planes and pilots while the aerodromes and ground staffs would be furnished by China.

(12) In the treaty ports on the coast, namely Shanghai, Foochow, Amoy, Swatow and Canton, Japan might require larger concessions including space for military aerodromes, while various coastal islands, already in Japan's possession, might be retained by Japan. These might include the islands lying off Haichow,

those in the estuary of the Yangtze, the Pratas and the islands lying off Wenchow, to be used as bases for bombing points in the interior if they should refuse to carry out the terms of peace or should manifest an anti-Japanese attitude. If such requirements were enforced, this would mean an indefinite continuation of semi-hostilities in South China and the Yangtze Valley, resulting in a general stoppage of trade.

(13) If Japan's policies in China were to be carried out successfully, the vital importance of controlling the guidance of public opinion and the dissemination of news would become obvious, and it was therefore probable that Japan would insist on a general control of China's broadcasting stations, wireless emissions and official news agency.

With reference to the foregoing points we expressed the opinion that with the exception of such apparently speculative items as those set forth in points 9 to 11 they represented a substantially accurate and intelligent appraisal of Mr. Hirota's "three points" when concretely interpreted.*

With further reference to the Brussels Conference the Department cabled on the 20th:

In an article by Fleisher [48] under Tokyo date line October 20 it is reported that Japanese officials are mystified over the fact that the Japanese Government has not yet been invited to participate in the Brussels conference and that the Belgian Ambassador told Fleisher on October 20 that he had as yet received no instructions from his Government to invite Japan to attend the conference.

Please report urgently on this matter making inquiry of Bassompierre but not of the Japanese authorities if you deem it advisable.†

Replying to the foregoing telegram we reported on the 21st:

1. My British colleague yesterday made renewed representations to the Minister for Foreign Affairs repeating the representa-

* Telegram No. 483, October 20, 6 P.M.
[48] The article appeared in the *New York Herald Tribune,* October 20, 1937, p. 10.
† Department's telegram No. 263, October 20, 11 A.M.

tions which he had made on October 15 in an endeavor to persuade the Japanese Government to participate in the Nine Power Conference at Brussels. He advanced the argument that the Japanese case had gone by default at Geneva and that Brussels would offer a further opportunity to present Japan's case which will be carefully considered by the assembled Powers who wished above all to be helpful towards arriving at a peaceful settlement of the Sino-Japanese hostilities. The Minister replied that since his last talk with the Ambassador he had consulted a great number of prominent people here and that the sentiment against participation in the conference especially among the leaders of the political parties was practically unanimous. However, as no invitation had yet been received no final decision had yet been reached.

2. I have just telephoned to the Belgian Ambassador who informs me that he received the invitation for the Japanese Government at 8 o'clock this morning and that he is just now starting for the Foreign Office to present it. Bassompierre mentioned the "unaccountable delay" in the receipt of the invitation.*

On the same general subject and with reference to our 482 — of October 20 — we telegraphed the same day:

The following is a summarized translation of an editorial entitled "Moderation of American Attitude" which appeared in this morning's *Asahi*:

"The statement originating in Hyde Park presumably reflects the final instructions given by the President to Mr. Davis.[49] In

* Telegram No. 484, October 21, 10 A.M.

[49] A statement by President Roosevelt on the Brussels Conference was issued on October 20, 1937. In it the President stated: "Mr. Davis is going to Brussels to represent this country at a meeting of the Signatories of the Nine Power Washington Treaty, in response to an invitation issued by the Belgian Government. The purpose of the conference is in conformity with the original pledge made by the parties to the Nine Power Treaty in 1922 to have full and frank exchange of views with regard to the Far Eastern situation.

"In the language of the invitation to which this Government is responding, the Powers will examine the situation in the Far East and study a peaceable means of hastening an end of the regrettable conflict which prevails there.

"As I said in my radio broadcast on the evening of October twelfth: 'The purpose of this conference will be to seek by agreement a solution of the

pointing out that the purposes of the Conference are to examine
the Far Eastern situation and to devise a peaceful solution, the
President is apparently endeavoring, by obscuring the fact that
the Conference rises out of the League resolution, to render more
easy participation by Japan. The statement may perhaps also be
construed as indicating that opposition within the United States
has made necessary a moderation of American attitude. In view
of the unfavorable domestic reaction to the disclosure by the
President's Chicago speech and the State Department's announcement of an extreme policy, that policy was modified by the President's radio address of October 12 and again by the recent statement. This is all to the good, as the less the Western Powers
interfere in the Far East the sooner will peace in the Far East
be reestablished." *

Still on the subject of the Nine Power Treaty Conference
and with reference to our 484 — of October 21 — we informed
the Department in strict confidence that Mr. Dooman had
been informed by Mr. Yoshizawa, Chief of the American
Bureau of the Foreign Office, on October 21 that a definite
decision had been reached, so far as the Foreign Office was
concerned, to decline the invitation to the Conference, but
that the reply would have to be submitted to the Cabinet for
approval. As long as the invitation did not make clear that
the Conference was not being called on the basis of the resolution of the League of Nations and the announcement of the
American Government of October 6, a favorable reply from
the Japanese Government was not to be expected.†

Also on the 22nd we cabled, with reference to the Embassy's
484:

present situation in China. In our efforts to find that solution, it is our purpose to cooperate with the other Signatories to this Treaty, including China
and Japan.'

"Mr. Davis, of course, will enter the conference without any commitments on
the part of this Government to other governments." Roosevelt, *op. cit.*, pp.
462–63.

* Telegram No. 485, October 21, 4 P.M.
† Telegram No. 487, October 22, 10 A.M.

My French colleague also made representations on October 20 urging the Japanese Government to participate in the Nine Power Conference. I gained the impression that he confined himself to a formal expression of hope on the part of the French Government that a favorable response would be given to an invitation to participate at Brussels, and that he did not advance any detailed arguments in favor of participating.

The Minister for Foreign Affairs made approximately the same reply as he made to me, namely, that as no invitation had been received the Japanese Government had not yet reached a decision but that "the pressure of public opinion in this country would probably require the Government to refuse." * . . .

As for the Nine Power Conference we reported on the same day — October 27:

The Japanese refusal of the invitation of the Belgian Government to the Nine Power Treaty Conference was approved by the Cabinet in its meeting this afternoon and by the Emperor at 5 o'clock. The Minister for Foreign Affairs handed copies of the reply to the British Ambassador at 6.10, to myself at 6.20 and the original to the Belgian Ambassador at 6.30. The Vice Minister is meanwhile informing the French, Italian and German Ambassadors. The note is to be released to the press at 7 o'clock.

In handing me the copy of the note Hirota gave me also a long explanatory statement in Japanese which he informs me will be made available to the Department by the Japanese Embassy in Washington.†

Following our 498 we cabled the text in translation of the reply of the Japanese Government, as follows:

The Japanese Government have the honour to acknowledge the receipt of the *Note Verbale* under the date of the 20th instant, by which the Royal Government, in accordance with the request of the Government of Great Britain, and with the approbation of the Government of the United States of America, pro-

* Telegram No. 488, October 22, 6 P.M.
† Telegram No. 498, October 27, 7 P.M.

pose to the Powers signatory to the Treaty of February 6, 1922, to meet at Brussels on the 30th of this month in order to examine, in conformity with the Article VII of the said treaty, the situation in the Far East and to study amicable means of hastening the end of the regrettable conflict which is taking place there.

The League of Nations, in the report adopted on the 6th of the month, has declared on the basis of the declarations of only one of the two parties that the military operations carried on by Japan in China are a violation of the Nine Power Treaty. The action of Japan in China is a measure of self-defense which she has been compelled to take in the face of China's violent anti-Japanese policy and practice, especially by her provocative acts appealing to force of arms; and consequently, it lies as has been declared already by the Imperial Government outside the purview of the Nine Power Treaty.

The Assembly of the League of Nations has even gone the length of assuring China of its moral support and of recommending to its members to abstain from any action that might weaken that country's power of resistance and add to its difficulties in the present conflict, and also to study how they might individually give aid to China. This is to take no account of the just intention of the Imperial Government, who propose to bring about a sincere cooperation between Japan and China, to assure enduring peace in East Asia, and to contribute thereby to the peace of the world. This is to take sides with one of the parties and to encourage its hostile disposition, but in no way to contribute to an early settlement.

The Royal Government make in their invitation no mention of the connection between the proposed Conference and the League of Nations. However, in view of the fact that in its resolution, the League of Nations has suggested a meeting of those of its members who are party to the Nine Power Treaty, and that the Government of the United States, who have acquiesced in the request of the Government of Great Britain for the convocation of the conference, have declared on October 6 their approval of the Resolution, the Imperial Government cannot but conclude that the convocation of the conference is linked to the Resolution of the League of Nations. Now the League of Nations, as mentioned above, has expressed its views casting reflection upon .the honour of Japan, and it has adopted a resolution which is incontestably unfriendly towards her. In these circumstances, the Imperial Government are constrained to believe that frank and full discussion to bring about a just, equitable and realistic solution of the conflict between Japan and China, can not be expected between the Powers concerned at the proposed Conference.

Moreover, the present Sino-Japanese conflict arising from the special situation of East Asia has a vital bearing upon the very existence of the two countries. The Imperial Government are firmly convinced that an attempt to seek a solution at a gathering of so many Powers whose interests in East Asia are of varying degrees, or who have practically no interests there at all, will only serve to complicate the situation still further and to put serious obstacles in the path of a just and proper solution.

For these reasons explained above, the Imperial Government regret their inability to accept the invitation of the Royal Government.

The present conflict has been caused by none other than the Chinese Government who for these many years have been engaged as a matter of national policy in disseminating anti-Japanese sentiment and encouraging anti-Japanese movements in China, and who, in collusion with the Communist elements, have menaced the peace of East Asia by their virulent agitations against Japan. Consequently, what is most urgently needed for a solution of the conflict is a realization on the part of the Chinese Government of the common responsibility of Japan and China respecting the stability of East Asia, a revision of their attitude, and a change of their policy to that of cooperation between the two countries. What Japan asks of the Powers is that they comprehend fully this need. Their cooperation based upon such comprehension can alone, she believes, contribute effectively toward the stabilization of East Asia.*

On the 28th we received from the Department telegraphic instructions to take the action which we had taken on our own initiative on the 27th urging the Japanese authorities in Shanghai to see that the lives of foreigners in Shanghai were protected from Japanese bombs and gunfire, a step which the

* Telegram No. 499, October 27, 8 P.M.

Department desired me to take at my discretion and after consultation with my interested colleagues.* The British Embassy made similar representations on the 28th.†

In this connection and with reference to the Embassy's telegram No. 481 — of October 20 — the Department cabled us on the 27th:

> According to an *aide-mémoire* of October 26 from the British Embassy the British Government has instructed the British Ambassador to make further representations in regard to the use of the International Settlement as a base for Japanese military operations.
>
> You are authorized after consultation with your British colleague to inform the Japanese Government that this Government continues to hold the views as set forth in our 245, October 2, 3 P.M. (Your *aide-mémoire* of October 4.)‡

Action in the sense of the foregoing telegram was taken by the British Embassy on the 27th and by us on the 28th.§ . . .

On the 29th the Department cabled:

> Under date of October 28 the Associated Press reports from Paris that a high Japanese source has disclosed what were said to be the minimum conditions on which Japan was willing to negotiate peace in China;[50] that the informant said that Japan was disposed to accept friendly conversations on peace in China and he suggested that the Brussels Conference might give several interested nations a mandate to sound out the Japanese and Chinese Governments on their minimum terms. According to the press the Japanese terms were said to be (1) temporary occupation by Japan of China's five northern provinces, (2) creation of a neutral zone about Shanghai, from which Chinese troops would be excluded and in which order would be maintained by an international police force of Japanese, American, British, French

---

* Department's telegram No. 269, October 27, 11 A.M.
† Telegram No. 500, October 28, 11 A.M.
‡ Department's telegram No. 270, October 27, 6 P.M.
§ Telegram No. 501, October 28, 5 P.M.
50 *New York Times,* October 29, 1937, p. 2.

and Italian troops. The terms were said to represent the views of Japanese diplomats in Europe and presumably also of the Tokyo Government although the view of the Japanese army leaders had not been ascertained. The significant point of the Japanese attitude, according to the report, was that Japan intended to keep its armies on a line to the south of China's five northern provinces for the purpose of preventing Russia from sending troops to China through Mongolia.

In connection with the foregoing the Department desired me to cable urgently (1) whether there was public knowledge in Japan of the making of this statement with its description of Japanese terms; (2) whether these terms represented the Japanese Government's attitude; and (3) my own comment with regard to the significance of the report from Paris.*

In reply to the foregoing telegram we reported on the 30th:

A Domei despatch from Paris, which was published by all papers yesterday evening, attributes to the Associated Press a report that there is a growing feeling that a conference inclusive of Powers with little or no interests in the Far East would serve no useful purpose, and that it would be advisable for the United States, Great Britain, France and Italy to endeavor jointly to mediate. The source of this suggestion is not indicated, except in another Domei despatch published in the *Japan Advertiser* reporting Yotaro Sugimura's [Japanese Ambassador to France] denial of having mentioned the word "armistice" in his interview with Associated Press correspondent or in any other conversation. Several of the papers state this morning that Japan desires direct negotiations with China without interposition of Third Powers, and that if the latter wish "to save the prestige of the Conference they should individually urge China to ask Japan for an armistice." They stress that there can be no change in Japan's stated attitude. Summary of editorials of the *New York Times* and *Herald Tribune* of October 28 cabled by Domei was also published this morning.[51]

* Department's telegram No. 272, October 29, 1 P.M.
[51] Both these editorials commented upon Japan's refusal to participate in the Brussels Conference. *New York Times*, October 28, 1937, p. 24, and *New York Herald Tribune*, October 28, 1937, p. 20.

By way of comment on the foregoing reports I said to the Department that up to that time the attitude of the Japanese Government regarding terms of peace had envisaged Mr. Hirota's "Three Points" and had been expressed to me only in the most general way.[52] Those three points, as the Department was well aware, unless or until they were explained with greater precision, were open to interpretations so broad as to leave completely nebulous the question of actual peace terms. I had once expressed to Mr. Hirota the hope that he would let me know if at any time I could be helpful in a personal way, and having in mind that remark it seemed to me that the best way of ascertaining the opinion of the Japanese Government in this question of peace terms would be for me to ask to see Mr. Hirota at his private residence in order to avoid publicity, to tell him that I had come without instructions and on my own initiative, and then to explore the situation. Without in any way committing or involving our Government I could lead up to the subject of the Brussels Conference, and this exploratory approach might reveal some closer indications of the present intentions of Japan. I said that of course I would take no such step until a reply should be received from the Department, but I believed it not impossible that such an opening to mobilize those elements in Japan which did not favor war to the bitter end might be welcomed by Mr. Hirota. In any case, in obtaining information on such important issues the use of "go-betweens" was liable to be unreliable and unsatisfactory. I added that we would continue carefully to follow developments.*

In reply to that telegram the Department left to my discretion the making of informal inquiries concerning the foregoing and other reports, especially as the Department wished to have as authoritative information as possible, and it was believed that during the coming days there might be frequent news reports and *ballons d'essais* concerning the attitude of Japan. So far as the latest report was concerned it was thought better by the Department that I make inquiry only when approaching

52 See *supra,* p. 1006.
* Telegram No. 503, October 30, 4 P.M.

the Foreign Office on some other matter than to make a separate and special approach.* . . .

With further reference to the Department's telegram No. 272 — of October 29 — the Department informed us of the receipt of a confidential telegram from Paris, dated the 29th, of which the purport was as follows:

The source of the Associated Press story quoting a high Japanese authority on Japan's attitude toward the China conflict was Mr. Joseph Sharkey of the Associated Press who had interviewed the Japanese Ambassador in Paris on the 28th. Inasmuch as Mr. Sharkey had been endeavoring to obtain the interview for the past fortnight, he was of the opinion that it had been prepared for him in advance and that it had the sanction of the Government in Tokyo. Mr. Sharkey was told by the Japanese Ambassador, furthermore, that a statement regarding Japan's position would be issued in Tokyo on the 29th.†

Adverting once again to the Department's 272, I told the Department in confidence on the 30th that I had been considering, together with my British and French colleagues, whether the Brussels Conference could be assisted by any recommendation which we might usefully make here in Tokyo. As a result of these talks Sir Robert Craigie and I had agreed to send to our respective Governments an identical telegram along the following lines, and it was my understanding that my French colleague was cabling to his Government similarly:

1. It is improbable that any offer of good offices or of collective mediation, however carefully phrased, would prove acceptable to the Japanese Government because an element of foreign pressure would be found by the Japanese to be implicit therein. Mediation by the United States and Great Britain would be even more unacceptable than mediation by a greater number of Powers, and Japan would resist to the last ditch any semblance of pressure by foreign nations.

2. Some day in the future, at an appropriate moment, an offer of good offices or of mediation by a single Power, prefer-

* Telegram No. 276, October 30, 7 P.M.
† Department's telegram No. 274, October 29, 4 P.M.

ably the United States or Great Britain, might be accepted by the Japanese, but that moment had not yet arrived. Such a moment might come if there were indications that the Government in Nanking were more ready to undertake negotiations than was then apparent or in the event of an important Japanese military victory of a more striking nature than the recent Japanese successes at Shanghai.

3. In order not to close the door to such eventual mediation, it seemed of particular importance that the Brussels Conference should avoid any further expressions of opinion on the responsibilities involved in the China conflict or on the origins thereof, and that it should adhere strictly to its mandate of endeavoring to promote peace by agreement. The chances of eventual successful mediation would increase in direct ratio to the degree of impartiality observed. As we regarded the situation from the angle of Tokyo, it seemed to us that the best procedure would lie in the appointment by the Conference of a small number of interested Powers to follow future developments closely and to be prepared, when warranted by the situation, to offer either mediation by one of their number in agreement with the others or mediation of a collective nature. Mediation might in effect be ruled out altogether if mediation by a single Power should unfortunately in practice be ruled out through some decision of the Conference.

4. The Conference should constantly bear in mind the possible effects on the internal situation in Japan of the proceedings in Brussels. Mr. Hirota's replacement by Mr. Matsuoka is said to be favored by the Army and Navy and constant rumors exist that the former's position is not too strong, and we must take into consideration the fact that such an eventuality would in all probability lead to even more ruthless methods in China and the eventual imposition of terms of a harsher character. Unfortunate results to American and British interests would accrue from the fall of Mr. Hirota, implying the retreat of the moderate elements in Japan.

5. The war spirit in Japan is noticeably growing.*

* Telegram No. 505, October 30, 7 P.M.

On October 31 the Department informed us confidentially of the receipt of a message from our Ambassador in London reporting that on October 30 he had been told by the Japanese Ambassador that the Japanese Foreign Office had informed the American and British Ambassadors in Tokyo of a desire on the part of the Japanese Government to terminate the conflict in China and would therefore be glad to discuss this subject with the American and British representatives. The Department in reply informed our Ambassador that neither in Tokyo nor in Washington had any such approach been made to us. Ambassador Yoshida furthermore suggested to Mr. Bingham that there might take place a meeting between a subcommittee of the Brussels Conference and Japanese representatives; such representatives would be all the more disposed to participate in such a meeting if the United States and Great Britain were represented thereon, and if any direct action by the plenary conference in the matter of definite findings could be preceded by a meeting of this subcommittee. In reply to a telephone inquiry from Ambassador Bingham, Mr. Eden said that the same statement had been made to him by the Japanese Ambassador on the preceding day. During this conversation between Mr. Yoshida and Mr. Bingham, the former said that public sentiment in Japan had turned against the military; that the people were influenced by the heavy taxation inseparable from the hostilities; that the Chinese resistance had been much stiffer than expected and that the conflict had already cost more than foreseen; the public felt that the Army and Navy had gone too far and the people wanted an end to the struggle. Japanese public opinion was being influenced by all of these factors and the people, together with the Government itself, wanted to stop the conflict as soon as feasible.

With regard to the foregoing report the Department said it would appreciate having my comment both on Mr. Yoshida's analysis of Japanese public opinion and on his specific suggestion.*

To the foregoing telegram I replied, in paraphrase, as follows:

* Department's telegram No. 277, October 31, 2 P.M.

"1. The statements of Ambassador Yoshida astonish me.

"2. Neither to me nor to any member of the Embassy staff has Mr. Hirota or any other responsible Japanese official given any indication whatever that it is the wish of the Japanese Government to discuss with American and British representatives the question of putting an end to the conflict in China.

"3. As occasion has offered we have reported opinion in the Japanese press reflecting, as accurately as we can appraise it, the attitude of the Japanese Government and public. An excerpt from an editorial in yesterday's *Asahi* is now added because that newspaper is not only the most moderate of Japanese press organs but is also probably the most influential:

> "The position of Japan is that it positively wants no armistice until China reconsiders its attitude and is prepared to liquidate its anti-Japanese policy. There is need for the concerned Powers to revise their knowledge on this point. Rumors to the effect that Japan desires an armistice derive from prejudiced intrigues which seek to succor China from the plight into which it has fallen, and the effort of the Powers toward peace which is based on these rumors is, so far as Japan is concerned, merely misplaced kindness.

"All evidence indicates that no substantial element of the population now holds any such opinion as that described by Mr. Yoshida, apart from 'big business,' the section of the public engaged in foreign trade, and that element does not dare to proclaim its views. No substantial increase in taxation, the weight of which would fall on the masses, has recently occurred; there are no considerable numbers of unemployed; sports continue; and while losses in China are minimized, the campaign is played up as an uninterrupted series of military victories. In view of these various considerations we must accept the *Asahi* editorial quoted above as fairly interpreting the national will, particularly since no manifestations of opposition occur to offset the daily reiteration of such expressions of public opinion.

"4. The suggestion that there take place an early meeting

of Japanese representatives with a subcommittee of the Brussels Conference seems to us in all probability to have originated with Mr. Yoshida himself rather than that it was conveyed under instructions from the Government in Tokyo. Mr. Yoshida, as the Department is well aware, is not in sympathy with the military, he has personal initiative, and his efforts to restore good Anglo-Japanese relations have been imaginative and active. That the Ambassador is trying on his own initiative to find some way out of the present difficulties is suggested by the foregoing facts. We cannot, however, entirely eliminate the possibility that he spoke with the knowledge of his Government. Japan's attendance at the Brussels Conference was advocated by some Japanese, and it is our understanding that this opinion is still being put forward, although Japan's subsequent refusal to attend the Conference has necessarily modified the form of such expressed views. In the light of all these considerations it is not impossible that through Mr. Yoshida some basis for an indirect contact with the Conference by Japan is being sought by the Japanese Government." * . . .

With regard to the Brussels Conference we telegraphed on November 5:

1. Japanese public opinion as reflected in newspaper editorials continues to be strongly hostile toward the Conference. Continued emphasis is placed on the Japanese view that (a) Japan's actions in China constitute measures of self-defense and are outside the purview of the Nine Power Treaty; (b) the present Conference arises out of the resolution of the League, and that it is the firm policy of the Japanese Government to have no political co-operation with the League, which in this case has recommended to all countries a policy of assisting China; (c) there is no likelihood of any just solution arising out of participation in the deliberations of the conference called at the initiative of the League.

2. The evening papers yesterday carried a story of the "informal opinion in official sources," presumably originating with the Foreign Office spokesman, on the suggestion reportedly being

* Telegram No. 507, November 1, 6 P.M.

discussed at Brussels to organize another conference comprising the five great European Powers and the United States, to which new conference Japan would be invited. "Informal opinion in official Japanese quarters" is that:

(*a*) The Sino-Japanese conflict can be settled only by direct negotiations between the two countries involved and the interposition of third countries will not be permitted.

(*b*) The participation of the Soviet Union in the Conference must necessarily react adversely upon any question of Japanese participation.

(*c*) However, if the Powers having interests in the Far East are able to appreciate Japan's position and should feel disposed to offer friendly mediation which would include urging China to reconsider its position, Japan might feel disposed to accept such offer.* . . .

With reference to the Embassy's 509 — of November 2 — on the subject of Imperial General Headquarters we reported on the 5th the following general tenor of a press report published that morning: (paraphrase)

1. The Navy, which has been taking a relatively conservative position, and the Army have in principle reached an agreement that the proposed Imperial General Headquarters should not be clothed with any political power. The establishment of these headquarters in the opinion of the Navy necessarily involves a declaration of war. The Army on the other hand feels that the prosecution of a long war requires the establishment of such headquarters, but it also feels that difficult trade problems and other international issues would be raised by a declaration of war. The general tendency, however, is toward a declaration of war although no decision will be reached until the military situation further unfolds in Shanghai where the answer to this question is to be found.

2. This project for the establishment of general headquarters with its various implications, the heavy concentration of troops in Mongolia and Manchuria, the continued agitation against Great Britain, and the forthcoming anti-communist pact with

* Telegram No. 520, November 5, noon.

Italy are obviously parts of a carefully formulated plan. We are studying this matter and hope shortly to be able to cable our appraisal.*

In reply to the foregoing report the Department informed us that our telegrams on this important subject were very much appreciated and that it hoped to receive at the earliest practicable moment our analysis and estimate of the situation, the Department being particularly interested in the likelihood of Japan's declaring war and, in the event of such a declaration, Japan's probable attitude toward the rights and interests of the United States and other third countries in and concerning China.†

Responsive to the above desire of the Department we reported on November 6 in paraphrase as follows:

1. We were given last night a copy of Mr. Hugh Byas' despatch of November 4 to the *New York Times* [53] in which the suggestion was set forth that American mediation might be welcomed by Japan. Mr. Byas' analysis of the significance of the project of establishing an Imperial General Headquarters as well as of the Italian pact and of various other factors is from the point of view of press reporting an able piece of writing, but it is our belief that the situation is still too obscure to justify, except with the greatest reserve, any sure estimate.

2. The conclusion which we have reached based on statements of Army and Navy officials and other information obtained by the Naval and Military Attachés on the trend of recent discussions of the Imperial Headquarters project is as follows:

(*a*) No final decision with regard to the establishment of these headquarters has yet been taken because

(*b*) although majority opinion desires that these headquarters should be exclusively an organ to coordinate and formulate naval and military functions and should be deprived of any powers in the political, financial or economic fields,

---

* Telegram No. 521, November 5, 2 P.M.
† Department's telegram No. 288, November 5, 2 P.M.
53 *New York Times*, November 4, 1937, pp. 1, 3.

(c) nevertheless the question as to whether the establishment of such headquarters would inevitably involve from both the practical and legal point of view a declaration of war has not yet been settled.

3. This Embassy and other foreign observers are unanimously of the opinion that the Japanese military now expect the conflict in China to last for a long time and there therefore has apparently been no serious divergence of opinion as to the need of establishing an Imperial Headquarters. So far as the scope of further implications in the project involving positive or negative action against other countries than China is concerned, however, foreign observers differ in their opinions and this last point is discussed hereinafter. As to the future conduct in the campaign in China, indications have come to us during the past three weeks of a divergence of thought within the Army. It is advocated by one school of thought that the military objectives should be limited to an advance to the Yellow River on the theory that to further extend the Japanese lines would create difficult supply problems, would impose undue hardship on the troops, and in general would require paying a disproportionately high price for tactical successes of relative unimportance and would at the same time seriously expose the Japanese west flank to Soviet Russia. It is, however, argued by the other school of thought that the situation can be fully liquidated only by the complete destruction of the Chinese Army. It therefore appears possible that the friction between these two schools of thought has developed to a degree where the device of having the Emperor issue the plans of operation has had to be resorted to.

4. With respect to point (b) above, it is stated by the Navy that the establishment of Imperial Headquarters, if it takes place, will involve organization only as an instrument of the armed service. While the Army holds that this question has not yet reached a decision, we learn from other sources, however, that the viewpoint of the Navy according to present indications will prevail.

5. Concerning point (c) it is held that the establishment of Imperial Headquarters can take place without running counter to the provisions of its organic ordinance in view of the fact that the Diet has officially recognized the China conflict as a "national emergency." In our opinion any declaration of war will depend

upon whether the supply of arms and munitions to China continues, and we attach little importance to legalistic discussions of the kind mentioned above. The Naval Attaché has been informed by the Navy Department that such arms and munitions are still flowing into China through Soviet Russia, Indochina, and Hong Kong, and that already several hundred trucks and forty airplanes have come from Soviet Russia. If the present blockade of China is found to be ineffective in controlling the flow of such supplies into China an opportunity to lay down an effective naval blockade through a declaration of war would be offered by the establishment of Imperial Headquarters.

6. For the present it is evident to us in view of the foregoing considerations that the determination of the Imperial Headquarters project will probably be governed almost entirely by the problem of completing the China campaign.

7. We are doubtful of the accuracy of the suggestion of Mr. Byas that the Japanese anti-British agitation has been artificially stimulated in order to render more palatable to the Japanese people the Italian pact. The resentment against Great Britain, as we have frequently reported, is based on the thought that the efforts to form a common front against Japan have been led by Great Britain and it is undeniable that a pact at the present time is an outward and visible sign of an inward and spiritual force by which the three strong powers now allied against the democracies are animated. We do not yet know how public opinion is reacting to the Italian pact because there is a press ban on that subject but we venture to predict that when the pact is finally announced the Japanese people will strongly approve of it as having lifted Japan out of its position of isolation in international affairs.[54]

[54] On November 6, 1937, a spokesman for the Japanese Foreign Office gave out a statement concerning the conclusion of a three power protocol: "At 11 A.M. (7 P.M. Japan time) today, November 6, a Protocol concerning the participation of Italy in the Japanese-German Agreement against the Communist International has been signed in Rome between delegates of Japan, Germany and Italy, and has immediately come into effect. . . .

"The cordial relations now subsisting between Japan, Germany, and Italy will, I believe, be further promoted through the conclusion of the present Protocol, which means the realization of the aims of the anti-Comintern policy which the Japanese Government has ever been consistently pursuing." For the full text of this statement and the unofficial translation of the Protocol between Japan, Germany, and Italy, see *China Year Book 1938*, pp. 381–82.

8. It is our belief that the reported Chinese proposal to Soviet Russia for the abrogation of the recent treaty with Outer Mongolia has probably brought about the increase of Japanese forces in Inner Mongolia and Manchuria.[55] The Japanese press about three weeks ago carried a report to this effect. The extension of the Japanese military lines from North China as stated in paragraph three above increases the vulnerability of Japan's right flank to attack from the direction of Outer Mongolia. There is of course a significance of warning to Russia in the north and northwest movement of Japanese troops but this movement is more probably dictated by military expediency than by Japanese diplomatic objectives.

9. That a situation might arise in which the offer of American good offices to the two combatants to bring an end to the hostilities could be advanced with reasonable prospects of success was envisaged in the Embassy's 321, August 27, 4 P.M., and it is suggested that the thought of the acceptability of the opening by the United States of a way toward peace discussions is gradually forming in Japan. We trust, however, that our Government will not presume that the time is yet ripe for any such step.

10. Replying to the Department's specific question as to

[55] The history of the friendly relations between the Soviet Union and Outer Mongolia dated from the time of the Russian Revolution. In 1921, shortly after the revolution, a treaty of friendship was signed between the two countries. Although the relations between the Mongol People's Republic and the U.S.S.R. were close, in 1924 the Soviet Union had specifically recognized that "Outer Mongolia is an integral part of the Republic of China and [the U.S.S.R.] respects China's sovereignty therein."

In 1935, 1936, and 1937 frontier disputes between Manchukuo and Outer Mongolia often occurred, and the President of the Council of Ministers of Mongolia opined in 1936 that Japan had intentions of making a second Manchukuo out of Mongolia. In March, 1936, Stalin was reported to have said that a Japanese attack upon the Mongolian Republic would be met by Russian aid to the Mongols. In this situation the Protocol of Mutual Assistance was signed on March 12, 1936, between the Soviet Union and Outer Mongolia.

China at once protested this protocol, because she felt no foreign state had a right to make such an agreement directly with Mongolia, which China considered "an integral part of the Chinese Republic." On November 1, 1937, the American Embassy at Nanking reported that Chen Li-fu, Chinese Minister of Mass Training and Propaganda, had visited Moscow and discussed the question of the recognition of full Chinese sovereignty over Outer Mongolia. Harriet L. Moore, *Soviet Far Eastern Policy 1931–1945* (Princeton: Princeton University Press, 1945), pp. 56–69, 185–86.

whether foreign rights and interests in China would be respected in case of declaration of war, we may say that there are as yet no indications of the attitude which might be taken by Japan in the event of such a contingency. It is to be presumed that Japan, having in mind the emphasis placed by foreign countries on the observance of international law, will not be inclined to abandon in principle any rights accruing to her as a belligerent and we believe that Japan's relations with each nation concerned would influence such consideration as she might give to foreign rights and interests.

11. The present telegram, we fully realize, is partly speculative in nature but it must be emphasized that Japan's objectives are almost completely shrouded in silence and that only by weighing imponderable factors which change from day to day can our appraisals be formulated.*

On the 8th we reported:

The renewed invitation to Japan to participate in the Nine Power Conference was delivered to the Minister for Foreign Affairs by the Belgian Ambassador at 5 o'clock yesterday afternoon. As it was Sunday and no interpreter present the Ambassador was obliged to read to the Minister an impromptu summarized translation in English of the French note. Hirota replied that he would have to consult his colleagues but would give an answer at the earliest possible moment. He said he could not be optimistic that a favorable reply would be returned.

I added that in the opinion of Baron de Bassompierre, the Belgian Ambassador, the Japanese Government would base its refusal of the invitation on the fact that the Conference had violated Article 7 of the Nine Power Treaty by inviting non-signatory nations to participate and that no reason was perceived why Japan should enter into "full and frank communication" with noncontracting countries.†

With regard to Italy's adherence to the Anti-Comintern Pact on November 6 we telegraphed:

* Telegram No. 524, November 6, 6 P.M.
† Telegram No. 527, November 8, noon.

1. The news of the adherence of Italy to the anti-communist pact is being enthusiastically received in Japan. Reports were carried by the papers yesterday in banner headlines, parades were held through decorated streets, and the German and Italian flags, along with the Japanese flag, were placed over the gates of the Foreign Office.

2. The press without exception express approval. Editorials for the most part stress the ostensible purpose of the pact and the added vigor given to it by the adherence of Italy, but the real reasons for Japanese satisfaction are also revealed, as indicated by following excerpts:

Hochi: "It is not to be expected that the practical benefits of the new instrument will materialize at once, but it is obvious that the intangible benefits of the German-Japanese pact will be greatly enlarged. In connection with the present conflict with China, Japan stands surrounded by a group of unfriendly nations, and it has been greatly inspired by the mere existence of the pact with Germany; so that no words are necessary to indicate how greatly the adherence of Italy will contribute toward strengthening Japan's international position."

Yomiuri: "From the general international situation, the three powers have a common characteristic: Japan and Germany have withdrawn from the League of Nations, while Italy, though still nominally a League member, since the Ethiopia affair is no longer bound by the League; each of them is following objectives which lie in directions different to the objectives of countries revolving around the League. It cannot be denied that this common characteristic has promoted the conclusion of the anti-communist pact, and it may be anticipated that the conclusion of the pact will also promote agreement among the three nations on a variety of questions."

Nichi Nichi: (After argument that the democratic powers are using Soviet Russia to resist any change in the status quo) "There is no doubt but that the close association of Japan, Germany, and Italy raises the curtain on a new scene in international politics. The so-called Rome-Berlin axis boldly challenges the fictitious peace maintained in Europe and the selfish policy of preserving the status quo pursued by the 'have' nations, as Germany and Italy believe that only by so doing can there be realized the right of every country to exist and to develop. Japan is in the same position as Germany and Italy. The three nations have common national tendencies and national aspirations. It is, therefore, a logical result that they should together pursue national policies designed to break down by rational processes the status quo and to create an order of real international justice." *

The text of Italy's adherence to the pact was published in the Japanese press on November 7.†

With regard to reports of German mediation in the Sino-Japanese conflict the Department cabled us on the 9th summarizing Berlin's 266, November 5, and 267, November 6, to the effect that definite denials that any such plan was afoot were elicited through inquiry at the German Foreign Office on the afternoon of November 5 and the British Embassy in Berlin was also without information with regard to these reports. It was, however, stated by the Embassy in Berlin that a stalemate at Brussels was apparently envisaged by party radicals and that under these circumstances Germany might be invited, perhaps at the instance of Italy, to mediate on the ground of Germany's friendly relations with both parties to the conflict. According to the views of our Embassy in Berlin it was not possible to estimate how much of this was due to wishful thinking and how much might prove to be the basis for new tactics of an international nature, especially as the hope was being encouraged among German authorities that, faced with the strength of the association of Germany, Italy, and Japan, Great Britain might consider first approaching Germany as the easiest power and the most logical one with which to come to terms.‡ [56]

Still on the subject of a possible peace, and with reference to the Embassy's 510 — November 2 — and 524 — November 6, we reported on the 11th to the following effect: (Paraphrase)

---

* Telegram No. 528, November 8, 5 P.M.
† Telegram No. 529, November 9, noon.
‡ Department's telegram No. 291, November 9, 5 P.M.
[56] See James T. C. Liu, "German Mediation in the Sino-Japanese War, 1937–38," *The Far Eastern Quarterly*, February, 1949, pp. 157–71.

1. In conjecturing to us as to prospects for peace, a Japanese official who is responsible and very reliable stated *inter alia* that the High Command of the Japanese Army decided that the "challenge" presented by the Chinese Army to transfer the primary seat of operations to the Yangtze district and Shanghai from North China would be met. To penetrate far into China from the North would be a mistake because Japan's right flank would thus be dangerously vulnerable to a Russian attack. He likewise alluded to the fact that the Chinese Army's best troops were at Shanghai, and in order to destroy the will to fight, it would first be necessary to wipe out these elements.

2. That additions have been made to the Japanese Army's forces at Shanghai by units from the Northern front is confirmed by the Military Attaché. It has just been established that a division known to have been functioning on the Peiping-Hankow line down to Chengting participated in the landing operations near Shanghai recently. It is only by protracted investigation of such piecemeal information as casualty lists that conclusive evidence of Japanese units' activities can be obtained. It is our belief that additional research will reveal a large-scale movement to Shanghai of units from the North China field of operations.

3. Our informant's opinion of the prospects for peace boiled down to the fact that the Japanese Government cannot now consider any peace proposition other than from the Chinese Government which would allow for direct negotiations between them.*

Referring to our 524 we cabled on the 12th:

The papers announce this morning that Imperial Headquarters will be established within the next few days on the basis of a new ordinance applicable to the existing *de jure* condition of affairs. It is also reported that the Headquarters will be purely an organ to coordinate military and naval operations and will have no political or other civil functions.

We added that assuming the foregoing report to be correct it was evident that the headquarters question and the question as to whether war would be declared had been disassociated,

* Telegram No. 532, November 11, 7 P.M.

and we therefore believed that there would be no declaration
of war in the immediate future.*

With reference to the Embassy's 527 — of November 8 —
concerning the Brussels Conference we cabled on the 12th the
following Foreign Office translation of the note handed that
afternoon to the Belgian Ambassador:

Note Verbale
The Imperial Government have the honor to acknowledge the
receipt of the *Note Verbale,* dated the 7th November, concerning the Brussels Conference.

While they are pleased to take cognizance of the fact that the
opinion of the participating Powers set forth in the said Note is
the result of careful consideration, the Imperial Government regret that this opinion is not sufficient to persuade them to modify
the views and policy clearly expressed in their last answer, dated
the 27th October, and in their public statement of the same date.
It is stated by the participating Powers that they would be prepared to designate representatives of a small number of Powers
for an exchange of views with one or several representatives of
Japan within the scope of the Nine Power Treaty and in conformity with its provisions. However, the Imperial Government
adhere firmly to the view that their present action, being one of
self-defense forced upon Japan by the challenge of China, lies
outside the scope of the Nine Power Treaty, and that there is
no room for any discussion of the question of its application.
It is certainly impossible for them to accept an invitation to a
conference convened in accordance with the stipulations of that
treaty after Japan has been accused of having violated its terms.

Since the present affair has its origin in the special conditions
of East Asia, the most just and equitable solution can be reached
through direct negotiations between the two parties who are directly and immediately interested. It is the firm conviction of
the Imperial Government that an attempt to negotiate within the
framework of a collective organ such as the present Conference,
would only arouse popular feelings in both countries and hinder
a satisfactory solution of the affair. The Imperial Government
would be glad if the Powers, appreciating fully the above-men-

* Telegram No. 533, November 12, noon.

tioned view, should contribute to the stabilization of East Asia in a manner consonant with the realities of the situation.

The participating Powers state that all the Powers having interests in the Far East are affected by the present hostilities and that the whole world views with apprehension the repercussions of these hostilities on peace and on the security of the members of the family of nations. As regards this consideration, the Imperial Government desire to point out that, as has been made clear in Japan's successive declarations, they are doing everything in their power to respect the rights and interests of Foreign Powers in China, and that they have the deepest concern for the firm establishment of peace in East Asia through a satisfactory conclusion of the present affair.* . . .

From this point on there was continual correspondence with the Department and the Foreign Office concerning the bombing by Japanese planes of American property, particularly mission property, in China. These various attacks and their results and, in some cases, the settlement of the cases by the payment by Japan, wholly or partially, of reparation for the damage caused were subsequently listed by the Embassy and should appear in this survey at a later date. Such correspondence, except in outstanding cases, will therefore not be set forth in this day to day report.

On November 13 we telegraphed:

The press states this morning that in line with the desire of the Japanese Government to implement the anti-communist pact, consideration is being given to Japan's recognition of the Franco Regime.

In connection with the negotiations which have been taking place for several months with regard to the new commercial convention between Japan and Italy, there are persistent indications that the possibilities of a trade arrangement among Japan, Germany and Italy are being examined. It has been suggested that such an arrangement would cover only raw and semi-manufactured materials, but this is probably conjecture.†

* Telegram No. 535, November 12, 7 P.M.
† Telegram No. 540, November 13, 11 A.M.

On November 15 I cabled the Secretary in strictest confidence that I had been asked to call on the Foreign Minister at his residence at 9.30 A.M. on the following day and that I had reason to believe that Mr. Hirota's purpose in wishing to see me was to discuss possible peace approaches.[57] Therefore, until

[57] On November 16, 1937, Mr. Grew and the Japanese Minister for Foreign Affairs held a conversation of which the following paraphrase is included in the diary: "The draft resolution submitted to the conference at Brussels apparently provides for united action against Japan, unless the draft was altered before passed by the Conference. If this provision remains, the Minister fears that the effect on Japanese public opinion will be most unfortunate. If 'united action' means sanctions such as economic boycott, the Minister said such action would have the effect rather of prolonging the hostilities indefinitely than of helping to bring them to a termination.

"According to information received by the Minister through the diplomatic representative of 'a certain Power,' the United States took the initiative in convoking the Brussels Conference and is now taking a leading role there. (At this point I interrupted to give the Minister the information the Department sent us, and to point out Mr. Eden's statement in the House of Commons that the suggestion for calling the Conference arose within the League of Nations, of which the United States is not a member, and that it was merely the suggestion of Brussels as the location of such a conference which came from the United States. Hirota insisted however that he had been informed that the United States had been the real leader since the beginning.) The Minister expressed the hope that I would bring to the attention of representatives at Brussels the views set forth in the first paragraph.

"The Minister went on to say that these rumors of the United States' initiative which would be sure to be published soon in the newspapers here would affect Japanese public opinion most adversely. Up until now the Japanese people have felt that it was Great Britain who had been most active in trying to form a solid front against Japan, but that this onus would be transferred to the United States if the Japanese press reported that our country was taking the lead at Brussels.

"Mr. Hirota said he greatly 'feared' what might result from such a change in opinion here, and that, as he had often before stated to me, his fundamental policy was to maintain good relations with the United States.

"The Japanese had felt that the United States was the only genuinely impartial country during the hostilities between Japan and China, until the moment of the President's Chicago speech on October 5. The impartiality of all other countries had been doubted, because of their special interests in China. The Japanese public felt however that the position of the United States as the most impartial of all Japan's friends might make it [possible] for the United States to play a similar role in helping to bring the present hostilities to an end as it had in the Russo-Japanese war. Although the speech at Chicago had temporarily altered this view, the Japanese people feel that the attitude of the United States may perhaps not be so rigid as feared since the President

my report of the conversation should be received, I suggested that Mr. Hull might wish to hold up any final decision concerning any contemplated action by our Government towards implementing the final Resolution of the Nine Power Conference at Brussels.* 58

made no reference to the Far Eastern situation in his recent speech opening Congress.

"The movements of the Japanese military in China are, Mr. Hirota said, progressing favorably and the army has gone as far as it needs to, although if they consider it necessary to go further they are perfectly able to do so. It is time now to bring about peace in China's own interest. The Minister said that the move which the Chinese Government is considering of moving the Government from Nanking would be very foolish. General Chiang's position is not secure and opposition is already being formed by some of the principal generals. Japan's demands would be 'reasonable' if peace is made now, and Japan would not take a foot of Chinese territory. Later, because more sacrifices would be involved, the attitude of the Japanese Government may change, resulting in more drastic terms being imposed.

"The best thing the United States could do to help would be to persuade the Chinese Government to enter into direct negotiations. Immediately indication is given that the Chinese would be willing to open such negotiations the Minister would send a representative to talk with a Chinese representative in Shanghai, secretly or publicly as the Chinese prefer. (As Mr. Hirota had mentioned that the Chinese Ambassador continues in Tokyo, I inquired whether it might not be possible to use existing diplomatic channels in this connection. Mr. Hirota made no comment, merely assenting that such channels did exist.)

"I repeated Mr. Hirota's statement, point by point, when he had finished and obtained his assent that I had correctly understood everything, saying that I would promptly send to Washington a report of the conversation. I then expressed the hope that the Minister would do his best to keep out of the Japanese press unconfirmed rumors about the American attitude, and that, in any case, he would — at least until I had ascertained my Government's reaction to this conversation — try to calm such adverse press reactions as might occur against the United States. Mr. Hirota agreed with me that this was [of] importance and promised to use his best efforts."

* Telegram No. 543, November 15, 7 P.M.

58 The Conference at Brussels adjourned on November 24. Two declarations were adopted by the Conference. The text of the statement of November 15 was published in *Foreign Relations, Japan: 1931–41*, I, 410–12, and the second declaration appeared in the same volume, pp. 421–22. The declaration of November 24 denounced the use of force as a means to achieving a settlement of the dispute, suggested that China and Japan obtain the assistance of and consult with other powers in order to facilitate the achievement of a lasting agreement, reaffirmed belief in the principles of the Nine Power Treaty, and urged suspension of hostilities in the Far East.

XXXIII

From *Panay* to Konoye's "Greater East Asia"

DECEMBER 12, 1937 – SEPTEMBER, 1941

On September 21, 1941, Ambassador Grew commented in his diary that he was busily engaged in writing the history of his mission to Japan. "I suppose the job will take three months at least depending on how much time I can give to it," he noted. "If a break between the United States and Japan is eventually to occur I hope very much to get this magnum opus *finished first." Unfortunately the press of events that autumn made it impossible for Mr. Grew to complete the history of his mission to Japan.*

Mr. Grew's manuscript stopped just before the sinking of the Panay *in the Yangtze River. On December 1, 1937, Mr. Grew had written in his diary that he had requested the Japanese Foreign Office to inform the Japanese military and naval authorities of the location of the* Panay. *On December 12, a clear and sunny day, six Japanese planes attacked the American ship and three oil tankers which it was convoying. The* Panay *was sunk, and the crew and passengers attempting to escape in lifeboats were strafed by the Japanese planes. Two Americans were killed, and a large number were wounded.*

During the afternoon of the day of the attack on the Panay, *the Minister for Foreign Affairs, Mr. Hirota, who took the unusual step of coming in person to the American Embassy, told Mr. Grew of the sinking and said: "I can't possibly express how badly we feel about this." Although the Japanese, at first, claimed that the attack was unintentional and the visibility had been bad, Mr. Grew pointed out on December 17 to Mr. Hirota that the evidence demonstrated that the Japanese were "clearly guilty of deliberate attack." According to Mr. Grew's record of this conversation the "Minister said that he was totally unaware of the facts which I had presented and that he would immediately take up the matter with the naval and military authorities. He was visibly upset by the facts communicated and the gravity of the manner in which I presented them."*

On December 24, Mr. Hirota handed Ambassador Grew the Japanese note on the incident admitting responsibility, expressing regret, and offering amends. Mr. Grew noted in his memorandum of this meeting that "Hirota said rather sadly: 'I am having a very difficult time. Things happen unexpectedly.' "

The day after Christmas Mr. Grew observed in his diary: "This was an eminently happy day and it showed that wisdom and good sense of two governments who refused to be stampeded into potential war in spite of the tendency of the one side to 'save face' at almost all costs, and in spite of an outrageous affront offered to the other. The Japanese Government had expressed the most abject apologies for the sinking of the Panay *and we, without a moment's delay, accepted those apologies. I thought that our Government's note was a masterpiece."*

To Admiral H. E. Yarnell, Commander in Chief,
U.S. Asiatic Fleet, from Tokyo, January 10, 1938

Your letter of January 2 came to me today and not only am I very glad to hear from you directly but the contents of your letter are of great interest. We all realize here what a strain you have undergone these past months and we all admire the sound well-balanced way in which you have dealt with the difficult problems which have come before you. I hope that you will soon be able to get a change of scene and find some relief from your strenuous duties. The atmosphere which surrounds you in Shanghai must be a tremendous strain on the nerves, much more so than in Tokyo, because here we are at least dealing with people who would like to a certain extent to control the irresponsible elements in the Army if they could only do so, but they seem to be powerless. In our representations to the Foreign Office we feel that in general we are making rather futile gestures — not entirely, of course, because some of our representations seem to be effective, but generally speaking our efforts count for little. After trying for five years to build up a solid structure of Japanese-American friendship, it is very discouraging to have the edifice tumbling about our ears.[1] What you say about the inability of General Iwane Matsui [Commander of the Japanese forces in Shanghai] to control his younger officers explains many things and confirms my belief that there is an appalling lack of discipline in the Japanese Army. This situation is the antithesis of conditions in the German Army during the Great War where the younger officers observed perfect discipline while the higher-ups tended to act as they pleased.

If it were not for the irresponsibility of these younger Japanese officers I would have felt that the *Panay* incident might be a blessing in disguise because it certainly jolted the Government into a realization of the dangers into which Japan was running with regard to the United States. Our action in accepting their apologies, offer of indemnification and assurances for the future must have been a very great relief to them. As for the civilian population, I have been really touched by the depth and genuineness of their feeling of shame which has been expressed to me in countless visits and letters from people in all walks of life. The donations for the survivors and the families of the dead already amount to more than fifteen thousand yen, but this sum will be turned over to some Japanese individual or organization to devote to some constructive purpose in the interests of Japanese-American friendship as our Government does not wish it to go to any American nationals. Nevertheless I cannot for a moment look into the future with any feeling of confidence. I do not think that our Government or people would be willing to go to war to protect our tangible interests in China, but I do think that some act constituting a

[1] On December 10, 1937, Mr. Grew had written in his diary: "The morning papers report that the hostilities in China must continue because China refuses to show 'sincerity.' Henceforth I shall always hate that word because it will always remind me of the Japanese connotation of it: if I hit you and you hit back, you are obviously insincere."

derogation of American sovereignty, or an accumulation of affronts such as the *Panay* incident, might well exhaust the patience of both our Government and people and might place us in a position where war would become inevitable. I think that the President's recent determination to strengthen the American fleet is undoubtedly his answer to the sinking of the *Panay,* and there can be no doubt that the determination is eminently wise. I have steadily advocated such action ever since coming to Japan in 1932. That is the only language that the Japanese fully understand, and if we are to avoid war, that is the very best way to do so. . . .

Throughout 1938 Japan proceeded to consolidate its economic control of China. In July of the same year the United States applied pressure on the Nipponese by inaugurating a "moral embargo" on the export of aeronautical equipment. After the conclusion of the Munich agreement in September, 1938, Japan became even more aggressive. On November 2, 1938, the proclamation of the "New Order" was issued by the Japanese Government: "What Japan seeks is the establishment of a new order which will insure the permanent stability of East Asia. . . .

"This new order has for its foundation a tripartite relationship of mutual aid and co-ordination between Japan, Manchukuo and China in political, economic, cultural and other fields. Its object is to secure international justice, to perfect the joint defence against Communism, and to create a new culture and realize a close economic cohesion throughout East Asia. . . .

"Japan is confident that other Powers will on their part correctly appreciate her aims and policy and adapt their attitude to the new conditions prevailing in East Asia. . . ." [2]

American protests over the closing of the Open Door in China were futile. The new Foreign Minister, Mr. Arita, made clear to Ambassador Grew that the Japanese Government's attitude could be described as follows: "A new situation has arisen in East Asia; Japan must, for her own strategic and economic

2 *Foreign Relations, Japan: 1931–41,* I, 477–78.

safety, control certain sources of raw material in China and certain industrial opportunities. Those particular things you foreigners can no longer enjoy."

December, 1938

December saw further indications of a strengthening of Japanese policy to push forward her "immutable" program in China, while at the same time endeavoring to fortify the anti-Comintern Pact, and simultaneously a noticeable tendency on the part of the democratic Powers, especially Great Britain and the United States, to give more intensive consideration to the question of financial aid to Chiang Kai-shek and of economic pressure on Japan. On December 1, I had a long and important talk with an influential colleague [3] anent these subjects. He feels that there is little time to be lost if assistance to Chiang Kai-shek is to be effective, and he also feels that unless Anglo-American measures are taken against Japan, preferably supported by France, the discrimination against foreign interests in China will be progressive. He also believes that economic sanctions, or merely the definite threat of them, would rapidly force Japan to come to terms. With that thesis I disagree. . . . You cannot prove such a thesis on the basis of statistics alone; there are important psychological factors involved which may be imponderable but which nevertheless should be carefully considered before reaching conclusions. In any event, I told him, first, that while the United States and Great Britain have many common interests and concerns in the broad field of principles and policy in China, there are other considerations both of an economic and political nature which do not affect our two countries in an equal degree, and that such defensive measures as the British might feel it incumbent upon them to take against Japan might not commend themselves in the same degree to us. Second, I said that my Government is in a far better position than am I to survey the whole scene with its many conflicting currents and especially to estimate the

[3] Occasionally Mr. Grew insisted that phrases such as "an influential colleague" be substituted for the name of the individual.

desires and restraints of American public opinion, and that these factors alone, even if I believed in the efficacy and wisdom of sanctions, would deter me from making such recommendations as he proposed. He was good enough to recognize the justice of my position and said that he had no desire to press me. It was his feeling that there is now no time to be lost and his deep sense of the gravity of impending developments that had prompted his proposals to me. Of course this conversation was fully reported to Washington.

In the meantime the Japanese Government and press take the position that they have done their best to explain to us the New Order in East Asia, and that it is not their desire or intention to close the Open Door (entirely), but that we still don't understand. Alas for our obtuseness! . . .

With regard to the credit of $25,000,000 extended through the Reconstruction Finance Corporation to the Chinese National Government, the Foreign Minister said to the foreign press correspondents on December 19 that such reported loans will necessarily prolong the hostilities to the consequent embarrassment and inconvenience of foreign nationals; that this is a regrettable act on the part of the United States which has hitherto acted with discretion and understanding in Chinese affairs; and if it is a political gesture of the United States towards Japan, Arita thinks there will be "nothing more dangerous." The Japanese people, he said, may consider that the present loan is really intended as economic pressure by a powerful economic unit, and its results will prove quite the contrary to what is expected in America. At least the Japanese people will undoubtedly find new grounds for strengthening the proposed new order in East Asia. "But personally" he added, "I am not inclined to regard the loan as a political gesture towards the activities of Japan." . . .

My conversation with the Foreign Minister on December 26 has been covered elsewhere.[4] . . . After Arita had assured me that Japan has no intention whatever of closing the Open Door in China, I replied that as regards principles, our two Govern-

4 *Ibid.*, pp. 818–20.

ments are in disagreement. As regards actualities, Japan cannot expect the American Government or public or press to appraise his statements of intention until they become patent in practice. . . . The Minister said that he was doing his best to bring about results to meet our wishes. . . . In the same breath he added that according to his information Chiang Kai-shek will collapse very soon. It was tantamount to saying: "Don't throw your money away." Anyway, whether or not as a result of the American action, the atmosphere and tone of this conversation were noticeably more conciliatory and resilient than in our former talks. . . .

April 15 [1939]

. . . Attended Count Soyeshima's dinner at the Tokyo Club for Avery Brundage [Chairman of the U.S. Olympic Association]. Afterwards I took Takaishi, editor of the *Nichi Nichi*, aside and said that I deplored the articles which appeared so often, advocating a close tie-up with the totalitarian powers. I said that if a European war should break out, the United States would inevitably be drawn into it sooner or later, and if Japan were in the German camp, it would be difficult for our two countries to remain at peace. Germany and Italy might sweep through Europe in the beginning, but in the long run the unlimited resources and determination of the United States would bring victory to the democratic powers just as they had done in the World War. I appealed to Takaishi to look at the long haul rather than at the present setup. Who could be Japan's best and most helpful friend from every point of view, finance, trade, commerce, business, sentiment, in the long run? What could Germany and Italy do for Japan? Our present difficulties are temporary and should be overcome in time and it would be sheer stupidity to shape a course which might render our future friendship impossible. (This is the tack I have been taking with my influential Japanese friends, knowing that my remarks would be repeated all the way up to the top.)[5] Takaishi

[5] On April 26, 1939, Mr. Grew wrote in his diary: "I had a talk with Prince Chichibu after dinner and talked about Japan's future and the pro-

listened politely but made no comment. The country and many of the prominent papers are so thoroughly anti-British that their attitude and policies are likely to be against the democracies in general. . . .

May 7 [1939]

The Tokyo Golf Club (Asaka), which is generally so hard-boiled where diplomats are concerned in refusing special privileges granted in every other country, surprised me by staging a golf match in my honor;[6] it was listed on the printed monthly program of events as a "Sayonara" match for the American Ambassador, and there was a tremendous sign posted at the entrance. It called out the biggest attendance I have almost ever seen there, about 160 I should think, and after the match everyone sat down to a cocktail party at decorated tables with the big club room gay with Japanese and American flags. Count Kabayama, who presided, made a nice little speech in which he compared me to George Washington (God save the mark!) on the ground that I never told lies to anyone, that he didn't think that I hacked down cherry trees but at least, like Washington's being first in the hearts of his countrymen, I was the foreigner first in the hearts of the Japanese. He then made some pleasant allusions to Alice and presented us on behalf of the club with a very beautiful Imari plate. In my reply I admitted that I hadn't hacked down cherry trees but had made up for it by hacking a great deal of turf at Asaka which so pleased the crowd that some of them referred to it days afterwards, and then I spoke of what the club had meant to me, of my philosophy at golf, of the friendships I had made there and a little about what I had been trying to do in Japan these past seven years. This gathering, the first of its kind so far as I know, was all the more surprising when one remembers that only a

posal to enter an alliance with the totalitarian states just as frankly as I had talked to many others, using the same arguments against it. Whether the matter is finally settled or not, the opportunity was useful and I made the most of it."

6 It was a good-bye party staged shortly before our departure to the United States on leave of absence.—J. C. G.

few years back even our best Japanese friends at the club sheered off from us and were afraid to be seen sitting at the same table with any foreigners. In some respects it was the most touching event of our entire stay in Japan because so totally unexpected; it was certainly a demonstration of real friendship. . . .[7]

[No date]

We were absent from Tokyo from May 19 until October 10. Having been away from the United States since 1936 it was essential that we get back into the home atmosphere again for it doesn't do to let too long go by without the home contacts, official, public and personal.[8]

Officially I obtained the usual modicum of information but very seldom is one able to get a clear-cut definition of policy or any definition of policy except in broad and general terms. There is however an unmistakable hardening of the Administration's attitude toward Japan and a marked disinclination to allow American interests to be crowded out of China. In both my talks with the President I brought out clearly my view that if we once start sanctions against Japan we must see them through to the end, and the end may conceivably be war. I

[7] *Japan News-Week* observed on November 19, 1938: "The United States Government is most ably represented in Tokyo by one of its outstanding career diplomats, Mr. Joseph C. Grew, American Ambassador to Japan. Although Mr. Grew is a representative of the American government who truly represents the best type of American, an extremely busy man in his capacity as head of the United States diplomatic organization in one of the most difficult posts in the world, he still finds time to keep in contact with the American community's business and social activities in as intimate a manner as no other Ambassador to this country has been able to achieve."

[8] The *Yomiuri Shimbun* on May 6, 1939, commented: "It is understood that Ambassador Grew who is 60 years of age will retire from the Diplomatic service after his return home. This is the reason why many Japanese regret the Ambassador's return home this time. It is true that Ambassador Grew is highly respected by all classes of Japanese." *The Japan Times*, on the other hand, wrote on May 18, 1939: "We wish he will tell his people with what grim determination we are carrying on to fight the Affair to the finish, no matter what may or may not happen. We are fighting by staking everything and nothing short of a complete crushing of the Chiang regime and the establishment of a New Order in East Asia will halt our operations."

also said that if we cut off Japan's supply of oil and if Japan then finds that she cannot obtain sufficient oil from other commercial sources to ensure her national security, she will in all probability send her fleet down to take the Dutch East Indies. The President replied significantly: "Then we could easily intercept her fleet." Meanwhile we have denounced our Treaty of 1911 and have sent several extra ships and planes to Pearl Harbor and to Manila.[9] I think it is going to be up to me to let this American temper discreetly penetrate into Japanese consciousness. Sparks may well fly before long. . . .

October, 1939

The month of October has been an important one in American-Japanese relations. It became clear to me last summer in the United States that some sort of major operation must be performed in Japan if those relations were to be prevented from getting steadily worse. One major operation, the denunciation of our treaty of 1911, had already been performed in Washington and there was and is every probability that a second one, in the shape of an embargo against Japan, will take place next winter unless the disease of Japanese depredations against our rights and interests in China is arrested before then. It seemed to me that the operation in Japan had better take the form of a speech before the America-Japan Society rather than another comprehensive note to the Japanese Government because, as we have seen, published notes have a way of causing merely irritation without constructive results. A frank speech, by its very unusualness (because diplomats in Japan are accustomed to talk only platitudes of eternal friendship), might give the necessary stimulus needed and cause not only the people but the Government to take notice.[10] I knew of course that

[9] On July 26, 1939, Secretary Hull announced that the United States intended to abrogate the Commercial Treaty of 1911. Under the terms of the Treaty, the abrogation did not become effective until January 26, 1940.

[10] Mr. Grew wrote in his diary on the day of the speech, October 19, 1939: "As we were on our way to the luncheon I was handed the first section of a telegram from the Department cautioning me, in effect, not to 'pussyfoot.' The second section of the telegram arrived after the luncheon and speech were

such a speech would cause a broadside of vituperative comment in the Japanese press but believed that when that initial barrage had cleared away the net results might and probably would be salutary. The fact is that the Japanese people, including many influential people, simply don't know what their army has been doing in China, and nobody had yet dared to tell them.

The matter was buzzing in my head in Hancock and was first broached in a letter to Max Hamilton [Chief of the Division of Far Eastern Affairs] on July 30. The Department and the President reacted favorably [11] and during my subsequent stay in Washington a good many able cooks, including Stanley Hornbeck [Adviser on Political Relations to the Department of State], Max Hamilton, Joe Ballantine [Assistant Chief of the Division of Far Eastern Affairs], and Larry Salisbury [of the Division of Far Eastern Affairs], worked on the drafting of the speech or made helpful contributions thereto. On the voyage to Japan and after arrival in Tokyo I rewrote the whole thing in my own words, pruning ruthlessly and adding new points but retaining the fundamental substance while aiming to give the speech a friendly and purely objective slant, avoiding any tone of threat or rancor or Jovian preaching but hammering home the "brass tacks." Someone who heard the delivery of the

over. I imagine that the Department, after reading my recent telegram saying that I had toned down certain parts of the speech, feared that I might have toned it down too much. But there was no pussyfooting, as the eventual reaction to the speech indicated. It is my feeling, and the feeling of all of us in the Embassy, that the speech went as far as it could go without defeating its own object through overplaying the hand. I had submitted the final draft to Dooman, Creswell, Smith-Hutton, Williams and Crocker separately; a few minor points were helpfully raised and all of their suggestions were incorporated in the text but they all expressed complete concurrence in the tone, balance and substance of the address upon which I had put in a great deal of work and thought, much as one paints a picture and keeps retouching it to get the proper color tones and perspective. In any case, the speech is mainly for current consumption and effect rather than for complete and permanent record as in the case of a note. A good deal of the Department's drafting was retained and it was most helpful, but also a good deal of it was discarded for the reasons hereinbefore stated."

[11] President Roosevelt wrote Mr. Grew on October 23, 1939: "I liked your address and the Secretary and I agreed that you did it in the right way and at the right time."

speech said that this was precisely the impression conveyed —
hammering the tacks home. It was highly important, however,
to avoid overplaying the hand and thus defeating the whole
purpose of the speech.

After the speech was made, some of the American newspaper
correspondents were using such terms as "dumbfounded,"
"astounded," etc., in describing the reaction of the audience.[12]
As a matter of fact only Thompson of the United Press was
present and he scooped all the others, who had expected the
usual diplomatic platitudes, but Relman Morin of the A.P.,
and Hugh Byas very quickly began to receive calls from New
York for voluminous reports. The Japanese press reacted just
as I had expected, some of the papers accusing me of arrogance,
impertinence and surprising lack of diplomatic propriety. The
general trend was that in spite of what I said, the American
people simply don't know the facts and have construed a few
unintentional "accidents" into wholesale depredations. Also
that we still don't understand the "New Order in East Asia."
But a few of the papers, notably the *Yomiuri*, which in the beginning had castigated me personally for arrogance, eventually
were courageous enough to intimate in veiled language that
there might be some merit in the American point of view and
that it should be carefully examined. Such attitudes here are

[12] The American press reaction was immediate. *Time*, October 30, 1939,
described the speech as "virtually unprecedented in ambassadorial usage. The
Ambassador gave his distinguished audience an earful which made many of
them wish for deafness." Hugh Byas in the *New York Times Magazine*, November 12, 1939, stated: "When an Ambassador can rise in a foreign country in
wartime and speak unpleasant truth about the war that country is waging
and yet do so without giving offense, he has acquired the last touch of diplomatic virtuosity. . . . His argument was unfolded smoothly enough, but it
had the effect a slow-motion thunderbolt might produce." The Washington
Post, October 20, 1939, commented: "Ambassador Grew's straight-from-the-
shoulder speech . . . should go a long way in bringing home to the Japanese
the realities of American public opinion and of American policy in the Far
East." The San Francisco *Chronicle*, October 20, 1939, observed: "This action
of Ambassador Grew is a new departure in methods of overcoming censorship
in a foreign country. From the American point of view it was needed." The
Chicago *Tribune*, October 23, 1939, commented, however, that "the administration in Washington is picking a quarrel with Japan for reasons it does not
disclose."

generally regarded as sheer heresy and it showed that the inoculation was "taking." Many influential and important Japanese told me or conveyed to me their high approbation of the speech and said that it was sorely needed and perfectly timed. Many commendatory letters from Japanese were received. One prominent Member of the Parliament said to me: "You have started the ball rolling and we shall keep it rolling." [13]

When an oil well is drilled it sometimes happens that the oil will not spout. A small dynamite bomb is then dropped down the shaft and the oil promptly begins to gush. I am hopeful that this will be the effect of the speech.

While the text of the speech was promptly given to the A.P. and U.P. I refrained from giving it out to the Japanese press, in spite of Count Kabayama's advice to do so, because I wanted the Foreign Office to know that I had observed this minimum of discretion in not going over the heads of the Japanese Government in that respect. . . . I was banking on a public demand for publication of the text and, sure enough, two days later the Foreign Office itself asked me to release the text to the local press and it was promptly done. This was perhaps a small point but such points loom large in Japan and it was duly noted. . . .

STRAIGHT FROM THE HORSE'S MOUTH [14]

. . . In America, as I have already said, I did my best to show various angles of the Japanese point of view. Without careful

[13] Count Kabayama read the speech before it was delivered, and Mr. Grew recorded in his diary on October 19, 1939: "He observed . . . that this was the least I could say and he thought it would be helpful." On October 25 Mr. Grew wrote that Takechiyo Matsuda, a member of Parliament, had told him that he and his colleagues in the Minseito Party had liked the speech. Then Mr. Grew added: "Count Kabayama came in during the afternoon and said that ever since my 'epoch-making' speech he had been discussing it with the highest officials, notably the Prime Minister, the Foreign Minister, Kurahei Yuasa [Lord Keeper of Imperial Seal] and Count Makino, all of whom had been studying the speech in detail. . . . The speech, he said, had made a very deep impression."

[14] An address delivered before the America-Japan Society on October 19, 1939. This speech was published in *Ten Years in Japan*, pp. 289–94.

consideration of both points of view we can get nowhere in building up good relations. I wish you could realize how intensely I wish for that most desirable end and how deeply I desire, by pure objectivity, to contribute to a successful outcome. Let me therefore try to remove a few utterly fallacious conceptions of the American attitude as I think they exist in Japan today.

One of these fallacies is that the American approach to affairs in East Asia is bound by a purely "legalistic" attitude, a conception which widely prevails in this country today. What is meant by a "legalistic" attitude? If we mean respect for treaties, official commitments, international law, yes; that respect is and always will be one of the cardinal principles of American policy. But the very term "a legalistic attitude," as it has often been used in my hearing in Japan, seems to imply a position where one cannot see the woods for the trees, where one's vision of higher and broader concepts is stultified. Let me therefore touch briefly on a few of the cardinal principles of American policy and objectives, molded to meet the requirements of modern life, which, it is true, are fundamentally based upon but which seem to me far to transcend any purely "legalistic" approach to world affairs.

The American people aspire to relations of peace with every country and between all countries. We have no monopoly on this desire for peace, but we have a very definite conviction that the sort of peace which, throughout history, has been merely an interlude between wars is not an environment in which world civilization can be stably developed or, perhaps, can even be preserved. We believe that international peace is dependent on what our Secretary of State has characterized as "orderly processes" in international dealing.

The American people desire to respect the sovereign rights of other people and to have their own sovereign rights equally respected. We have found by experience that the successful approach to the resolving of international disputes lies not so much in merely abstaining from the use of force as in abstaining from any thought of the use, immediately or eventually, of the methods of force. Let cynics look about them and contemplate the consequences of resort to menacing demands as a process in the conduct of international relations! Is it being purely "legalistic" to put to wise and practical use the finer instincts common to all mankind?

The American people believe that the day is past when wars can be confined in their effects to the combatant nations. When national economies were based upon agriculture and handicraft, nations were to a large extent self-sufficient; they lived primarily on the things which they themselves grew or produced. That is not the case today. Nations are now increasingly dependent on others both for commodities which they do not produce themselves and for the disposal of the things which they produce in excess. The highly complex system of exchange of goods has been evolved by reason of each nation's being able to extract from the ground or to manufacture certain commodities more efficiently or economically than others. Each contributes to the common good the fruits of its handiwork and the bounties of nature. It is this system of exchange which has not only raised the standard of living everywhere but has made it possible for two or even three persons to live in comfort where but one had lived in discomfort under a simple self-contained economy. Not only the benefits of our advanced civilization but the very existence of most of us depends on maintaining in equilibrium a delicately balanced and complex world economy. Wars are not only destructive of the wealth, both human and material, of combatants, but they disturb the fine adjustments of world economy. Conflict between nations is therefore a matter of concern to all the other nations. Is there then any stultification through "legalistic" concepts when we practice ourselves and urge upon others the resolving of international disputes by orderly processes, even if it were only in the interests of world economy? How, except on the basis of law and order, can these various concepts in international dealing be secured?

The American people believe in equality of commercial opportunity. There is probably no nation which has not at one time or other invoked it. Even Japan, where American insistence on the Open Door is cited as the supreme manifestation of what is characterized as a "legalistic" American attitude — even Japan, I say — has insisted upon and has received the benefits of the Open Door in areas other than China, where, we are told, the principle is inapplicable except in a truncated and emasculated form. That highly complicated system of world economy of which I have just spoken is postulated upon the ability of nations to buy and sell where they please under conditions of free competition — conditions which cannot exist in areas where pre-emptive rights are claimed and asserted on behalf of nationals of one particular country.

I need hardly say that the thoughts which I have just expressed are of universal applicability.

Another common fallacy which I am constrained to mention is the charge that the American Government and people do not understand "the new order in East Asia." Forgive me if I very respectfully take issue with that conception. The American Government and people understand what is meant by the "new order in East Asia" precisely as clearly as it is understood in Japan. The "new order in East Asia" has been officially defined in Japan as an order of security, stability and progress. The American Government and people earnestly desire security, stability and progress not only for themselves but for all other nations in every quarter of the world. But the new order in East Asia has appeared to include, among other things, depriving Americans of their long-established rights in China, and to this the American people are opposed.

There's the story. It is probable that many of you are not aware of the increasing extent to which the people of the United States resent the methods which the Japanese armed forces are employing in China today and what appear to be their objectives. In saying this, I do not wish for one moment to imply that the American people have forgotten the long-time friendship which has existed between the people of my country and the people of Japan. But the American people have been profoundly shocked over the widespread use of bombing in China, not only on grounds of humanity but also on grounds of the direct menace to American lives and property accompanied by the loss of American life and the crippling of American citizens; they regard with growing seriousness the violation of and interference with American rights by the Japanese armed forces in China in disregard of treaties and agreements entered into by the United States and Japan and treaties and agreements entered into by several nations, including Japan. The American people know that those treaties and agreements were entered into voluntarily by Japan and that the provisions of those treaties and agreements constituted a practical arrangement for safeguarding — for the benefit of all — the correlated principles of national sovereignty and of equality of economic opportunity. The principle of equality of economic opportunity is one to which over a long period and on many occasions Japan has given definite approval and upon which Japan has frequently insisted. Not only are the American people perturbed over their being arbitrarily deprived of long-established rights, including those of equal opportunity and fair treatment, but they feel that the present trend in the Far East if continued will be destructive of the hopes which they sincerely cherish of the development of an orderly world. American rights and interests in China are being impaired or destroyed by the policies and actions of the Japanese authorities in China. American property is being damaged or destroyed; American nationals are being endangered and subjected to indignities. If I felt in a position to set forth all the facts in detail today, you would, without any question, appreciate the soundness and full justification of the American attitude. Perhaps you will also understand why I wish today to exercise restraint.

In short, the American people, from all the thoroughly reliable evidence that comes to them, have good reason to believe that an effort is being made to establish control, in Japan's own interest, of large areas on the continent of Asia and to impose upon those areas a system of closed economy. It is this thought, added to the effect of the bombings, the indignities, the manifold interference with American rights, that accounts for the attitude of the American people toward Japan today. For my part I will say this. It is my belief, and the belief of the American Government and people, that the many things injurious to the United States which have been done and are being done by Japanese agencies are *wholly needless*. We believe that real security and stability in the Far East could be attained without running counter to any American rights whatsoever.

Mr. Chairman, Ladies and Gentlemen: I have tried to give an accurate interpretation of American public opinion, most carefully studied and analyzed by me while at home. The traditional friendship between our two nations is far too precious a thing to be either inadvertently or deliberately impaired. It seems to me logical that from every point of view — economic, financial, commercial, in the interests of business, travel, science, culture and sentiment — Japan and the United States forever should be mutually considerate friends. In the family of nations, as between and among brothers, there arise inevitable controversies, but again and again the United States has demonstrated its practical sympathy and desire to be helpful toward Japan in difficult times and moments, its admiration of Japan's achievements, its earnest desire for mutually helpful relations.

Please do not misconstrue or misinterpret the attitude which has prompted me to speak in the utmost frankness today. I am moved first of all by love of my own country and my devotion to its interest; but I am also moved by very deep affection for Japan and by sincere conviction that the real interests, the fundamental and abiding interests of both countries, call for harmony of thought and action in our relationships. Those who know my sentiments for Japan, developed in happy contacts during the seven years in which I have lived here among you, will realize, I am sure, that my words and my actions are those of a true friend.

One Japanese newspaper queried, on my return from America, whether I had concealed in my bosom a dagger or a dove. Let me answer that query. I have nothing concealed in my bosom except the desire to work with all my mind, with all my heart and with all my strength for Japanese-American friendship.

Today I have stated certain facts, straightforwardly and objectively. But I am also making a plea for sympathetic understanding in the interests of the old, enduring friendship between our two great nations. In a world of chaos I plead for stability, now and in the long future, in a relationship which, *if it can be preserved*,[15] can bring only good to Japan and to the United States of America.

The troubled situation in the Far East was greatly aggravated in May, 1940, when Hitler launched his Blitzkreig *against Western Europe. French Indochina and the Netherlands Indies were now easy prey for Japan. On April 17, Secretary Hull, however, had warned that intervention "in the domestic affairs of the Netherlands Indies or any alteration of their* status quo *by other than peaceful processes would be prejudicial to the cause of stability, peace, and security . . . in the entire Pacific area."* [16]

During June, Ambassador Grew had four private conversations with Foreign Minister Arita. He wrote in his diary for July 2, 1940: "It is obvious that we cannot expect very much from a mere debating match between the Foreign Minister and myself, although we hear from a reliable source that the Prime Minister, Admiral Yonai, was annoyed with Arita for not giving me more encouragement. American-Japanese relations have got into a vicious circle. On the one hand, we ourselves take the position that there are three main obstacles to an improvement in our relations, namely (1) Japan's use of force as an instrument of national policy; (2) Japan's failure to respect treaty commitments, and (3) Japan's multifarious interferences with American rights and interests in China. On the other hand, Japan takes the position that these various obstacles cannot be removed as long as the hostilities in China are in progress, and that even after the termination of hostilities, only some but not all of our grounds for complaint can be

15 That phrase "if it can be preserved" was purposely emphasized in my speech as a straightforward warning.—J. C. G.
16 *Foreign Relations, Japan: 1931-41,* II, 282.

removed. Furthermore, she takes the position that the absence of a commercial treaty between the United States and Japan is in itself an important obstacle to an improvement in our relations. The vicious circle is complete, and how to break it is a puzzle which taxes imagination."

In a conversation on June 10 the Foreign Minister objected to the bulk of the American fleet being stationed at Hawaii and stated that the continued stay of our Navy there "constitutes an implied suspicion of the intentions of Japan vis-à-vis the Netherlands East Indies and the South Seas," and he desired categorically to assert that Japan entertained no territorial ambitions. Mr. Grew commented in his report of this conversation that the "emphasis which the Minister placed upon this matter is an indication of the important effect on Japanese consciousness of the stay of our naval forces in Hawaii."

Hitler's victories in Europe in the summer of 1940 and the impending attack on Great Britain led the United States to take steps to improve its national defenses. On July 2, 1940, President Roosevelt issued a decree prohibiting the export of materials needed for America's defense. Late in July the requirement for export licenses was applied to petroleum, aviation gasoline, tetraethyl lead, and No. 1 scrap steel.

Relations with the United States deteriorated even further in August when the Konoye Cabinet, with Yosuke Matsuoka as Foreign Minister, assumed control in Japan. The Japanese immediately made demands on Vichy France for special concessions in Indochina, and by the end of the month the Japanese were granted permission to use ports, cities, and airports for "troop movements."

On August 1, 1940, Prince Konoye redefined Japan's "New Order" to include "Greater East Asia" (China, Indochina, and the Netherlands Indies). Then, on September 27 the Japanese signed the Tripartite Pact with Germany and Italy. This treaty was aimed mainly against the United States. Germany and Italy recognized Japan as the leading power in the Orient, and all three agreed to aid each other "in case of an attack by a power not already engaged in war."

On September 12, 1940, Mr. Grew sent to the Department of State a most significant telegram on the Japanese situation. Unlike two years before when he had opposed applying economic sanctions to Japan, he now had reached the conclusion that such a step was vitally necessary. Testifying in 1945 before the Congressional Investigation of the Pearl Harbor Attack, Mr. Grew explained his reversal of position in the following statement: "The Japanese Army was steadily encroaching further into the Far East and into East Asia. They were potentially threatening our vital interests. And from that point of view the situation had very much changed indeed. That, I think, was the main reason why I sent that telegram, but one must remember that my so-called green-light telegram was not something which had developed in a question of a few hours or a few days. It meant a progressive line of thinking over a period to the crux of the situation." [17]

September 12 [1940]

A *magnum opus* finally went off to the Department today in a message of more than twelve pages. It was a general analysis of the situation and represented a sort of focusing of my thoughts during the fifty days since the new Government took office in Japan. As a hook to hang it on I took a recent survey of the situation in Japan as seen by A. T. Steele, China correspondent of the Chicago *Daily News*, during his recent visit to Tokyo, in which he holds that a firm policy by the United States would be effective in restraining Japanese expansionist policies and would not, as is generally believed in the United States, lead to a Japanese-American war.[18] My thesis was more an analysis than recommendation as to policy, because policy must be developed in Washington on the basis of its broader viewpoint and its knowledge of many factors that may not be

[17] U.S. Congress, *Pearl Harbor Attack*, Hearings before the Joint Committee on the Investigation of the Pearl Harbor Attack, 79th Cong., 1st Sess., Pursuant to S. Con. Res. 27 (Washington: Government Printing Office, 1946), Part 2, p. 638.

[18] For a summary of Mr. Steele's views, see *ibid.*, Part 4, pp. 1712–15.

apparent to us here, and it therefore discussed first the hazards involved in a firm policy and then proceeded to discuss the hazards involved in a laissez-faire policy. My first draft met with the concurrence of the Naval, Military and Commercial Attachés and Edward Crocker [First Secretary], but was too strong for the stomachs of Stuart Grummon [First Secretary], William Turner [Second Secretary], and Max Schmidt [Third Secretary], but my second draft secured unanimous approval and it went out in that form. As a matter of fact, it was a great deal better than the first draft which contained too many unsupported hypotheses. So far as I can see, the final message was as sound and as well balanced as it could be made, and it will at least show the Administration the present trend of my thoughts which are not happy ones. . . .

The "Green light" Message, September 12, 1940

1. The observations of Mr. A. T. Steele concerning Japan, recently received here by mail, have had my careful attention. In general terms I believe that Mr. Steele's observations are well-founded and sound, a belief which applies equally to the important considerations advanced in the final two paragraphs of the summary of Mr. Steele's statement. His thesis that "firmness is the soundest and safest American naval policy" and that "the risks involved are much less than is commonly supposed in the United States" is however of such far-reaching gravity as to deserve carefully studied analysis and comment. In presenting the present trend of my thoughts on this general subject I have constantly in mind the fact that the shaping of our policy vis-à-vis Japan must depend upon the broader viewpoint of the Administration in Washington and upon many factors which may not be apparent to this Embassy.

2. The situation and circumstances which led to the series of exploratory conversations with the former Foreign Minister Arita and to the recommendations for considering steps leading toward the negotiation of a new treaty of commerce with Japan have now obviously passed. I earnestly hope that the time will come when I shall feel justified in renewing those recommenda-

tions, but with the fall of the Yonai Cabinet and the radically altered policy and outlook of the present setup in Japan, further initiative on our part in proposing conciliatory measures at the present time would appear to be futile and unwise.

3. Whatever may be the intentions of the present Japanese Government, there can be no doubt that the army and other elements in the country see in the present world situation a "golden opportunity" to carry into effect their dreams of expansion; the German victories have gone to their heads like strong wine; until recently they have believed implicitly in the defeat of Great Britain; they have argued that the war will probably end in a quick German victory and that it is well to consolidate Japan's position in greater East Asia while Germany is still acquiescent and before the eventual hypothetical strengthening of German naval power might rob Japan of far flung control in the Far East; they have discounted effective opposition on the part of the United States although carefully watching our attitude. The ability of the saner heads in and out of the Government to control those elements has been and is doubtful.

4. Now, however, I sense a gradual change in the outburst of exhilaration which greeted the new Government on its inception. The Japanese Government, the army and navy and the public are beginning to see that Germany may not defeat Great Britain after all, a hypothesis which I have constantly emphasized to my Japanese contacts in the plainest language and now to add to that dawning realization, they see the United States and Great Britain steadily drawing closer together in measures of mutual defense with the American acquisition of naval bases in British possessions in the Atlantic and with our support of the British fleet by the transfer of fifty destroyers. They hear reports of our haste to build a two-ocean navy and of our considering the strengthening of our naval bases in the Pacific and even rumors of our eventual use of Singapore. These developments and rumors are having their logical effect on Japanese consciousness. On the one hand they tend to emphasize the potential danger which Japan faces from eventual

positive action by the United States and Great Britain acting together (the danger of combined Anglo-American measures has long been appreciated in Japan as evidenced by efforts to avoid irritating the United States and Great Britain simultaneously) or by the United States alone. On the other hand they furnish cogent arguments for those elements in Japan who seek economic and political security by obtaining markets and sources of raw materials wholly within the control of Japan. As for Germany, the Japanese are beginning to question whether even a victorious Germany would not provide a new hazard to their expansionist program both in China and in the southward advance. Meanwhile the future position and attitude of Soviet Russia is always an uncertain factor in their calculations. These various considerations are beginning to give them concern.

High-pressure diplomacy, especially in the Netherlands East Indies, will continue, but the fact that the Japanese Government was able even temporarily to restrain the military forces from their plans for a headlong invasion of Indochina indicates a degree of caution which I do not doubt was at least partially influenced by the attitude of the United States. What Mr. Steele describes as the "nibbling policy" appears likely to continue until the world situation, and especially the attitude of the United States, becomes clearer.

5. In previous communications I have expressed the opinion that sanctions by the United States would set Japanese-American relations on a downward curve. It is true that our own newly instituted program of national preparedness now justifies measures which need not fall within the realm of outright sanctions. On the other hand we must envisage the probability that drastic embargoes on the export of such important products as petroleum, of which the United States is known to possess a superabundance would be interpreted by the Japanese Government and people as actually sanctions which might and probably would lead to some form of retaliation. The risks which Mr. Steele sees as "much less than is commonly supposed in the United States" will depend less upon the careful calcu-

lations of the Japanese Government than upon the uncalculated "do or die" temper of the Army and Navy in case they should attribute to the United States the responsibility for the failure of their expansionist plans. Such retaliation might take the form of countermeasures by the Government but there would be even greater likelihood of some sudden stroke by the army or navy without the Government's prior knowledge or authorization. These risks constitute an imponderable factor which cannot at any given moment be weighed with assurance. It would be shortsighted, however, to deny their existence or to proceed with the formulation of policy and the adoption of measures without giving these potential risks full consideration and determining the wisdom of squarely facing these risks.

6. In the ensuing observations I am carefully considering both of the fundamental purposes of my mission, namely the protection and advancement of American interests and the maintenance of good relations between the United States and Japan. When these two desiderata conflict, the preponderant emphasis to be placed on the one or the other is a matter of high policy which does not lie within my competency. My object is merely to place before the Administration in Washington the outstanding factors in the situation as we see them from the angle of this Embassy. Having carefully set forth the inevitable hazards involved in a strong policy I now respectfully turn to the hazards involved in a laissez-faire policy.

7. In discussing the specific question of American-Japanese relations it is impossible to view that problem in its proper perspective without considering it as part and parcel of the world problem which, briefly, presents the following aspects:

(a) The United States and Great Britain are the leaders of a great group of English speaking nations around the world standing for a "way of life" which is being appallingly threatened today by a group of Germany, Italy, Soviet Russia and Japan whose avowed purpose is to impose by force of arms their will upon conquered peoples. In attempting to deal with such powers the uses of diplomacy are in general bankrupt.

Diplomacy may occasionally retard but cannot effectively stem the tide. ,Force or the display of force can alone prevent these powers from attaining their objectives. Japan today is one of the predatory powers; she has submerged all moral and ethical sense and has become frankly and unashamedly opportunist, seeking at every turn to profit by the weakness of others. Her policy of southward expansion is a definite threat to American interests in the Pacific and is a thrust at the British Empire in the East.

(b) American security has admittedly depended in a measure upon the existence of the British fleet which in turn has been, and could only have been, supported by the British Empire.

(c) If we conceive it to be in our interest to support the British Empire in this hour of her travail, and I most emphatically do so conceive it, we must strive by every means to preserve the status quo in the Pacific at least until the European war has been won or lost. In my opinion this cannot be done nor can our interests be further adequately and properly protected by merely registering disapproval and keeping a careful record thereof. It is clear that Japan has been deterred from taking greater liberties with American interests only out of respect for our potential power; it is equally clear that she has trampled upon our rights to a degree in precise ratio to the strength of her conviction that the American people would not permit that power to be used. Once that conviction is shaken it is possible that the uses of diplomacy may again become accepted.

(d) If then we can by firmness preserve the status quo in the Pacific until and if Britain emerges successfully from the European struggle, Japan will be faced with a situation which will make it impossible for the present opportunist philosophy to maintain the upper hand. At a moment it might then be possible to undertake a readjustment of the whole Pacific problem on a fair, frank, and equitable basis to the lasting benefit of both the United States and of Japan. Until such time as there is a complete regeneration of thought in this country, a show of force, together with a determination to employ it if need be, can alone contribute effectively to the achievement of such an outcome and to our own future security.

8. Passing from the general to the specific problem that now confronts us, and with the foregoing picture in mind, I applauded the timeliness of the instructions from the Department concerning the Shanghai defense sectors. The Department will have seen from my report of September 4 that the Foreign Minister's complaint as to alleged threats on our part was met with the statement that what we have in mind is "a logical reciprocal adjustment of international relations." I feel that the appropriate time has come to proceed, gradually but progressively with that adjustment. In the present situation and outlook I believe that the time has come when continued patience and restraint on the part of the United States may and probably will lead to developments which will render Japanese-American relations progressively precarious. It is my hope that if the Japanese Government and people can be led to believe that their hand is being overplayed, there will eventually ensue a reverse swing of the pendulum in which a reconstruction of good relations between the United States and Japan will be possible. The alternative seems to me to be hopeless.

9. The foregoing analysis, which has been drafted with care over a period of several days, has the expressed complete concurrence of the Naval, Military and Commercial Attachés and all other members of the immediate staff of this Embassy.

November, 1940

A letter from Washington, dated October 14, says that the dominant subject in certain quarters of the Department in September was our so-called "green light" message of September 12, that there was some little difference of opinion over the significance of one or two passages, and that the dominant school of thought considered that I was of the opinion that threat on the part of the United States to use force against Japan would not be attended by any risk of war and would be effective. . . .

American policy is formulated in Washington, not in Tokyo. All that we do, and what we aim to do, is to report and analyze and, occasionally, to recommend. Our message of September 12 aimed to present what the Department was later good enough to characterize as a "cogent argument and penetrating analysis." In brief it aimed to express the opinion that while a strong American policy would inevitably involve the risk of war, a laissez-faire policy, on the other hand, risked bringing American-Japanese relations into an increasingly precarious state and was therefore "hopeless." International developments since that telegram was sent have served only to confirm and to strengthen our views as expressed. The program of the Japanese extremists, who today are definitely in the saddle and are supported by at least a substantial section of the public, is to sweep on through "Greater East Asia including the South Seas," gaining provisional economic and ultimate political control, as fast and as thoroughly as circumstances permit. Among those retarding circumstances are, first and foremost, the fear of Soviet Russia, Great Britain and the United States, and the greatest of these is the fear of Anglo-American action. The evidence to justify such an assertion is plain for all to see, and I am ready to adduce it if necessary but shall not go into it here. The Department possesses that evidence and has undoubtedly weighted it correctly. We do not yet know just where Soviet Russia is going to stand, or sit; probably, if she is wise, on the fence. We do not know with any certainty how long Chiang Kai-shek can hold a great part of the Japanese Army from participating in the forward drive. But we do know, with almost mathematical certainty, that if the United States follows a policy of laissez-faire, allowing that forward sweep to continue as fast as it can continue in the light of other obstacles, it will sooner or later constitute for us a problem not merely of maintaining our intangible interests in the

Far East but of preserving the safety of our outlying possessions. . . .

The precise problem facing our Government, as I see it, is to determine not *whether* we are going to act, but at just what point in the Japanese advance we are going to act. I do not presume to suggest what that action should be, except that it should aim to provide an effective deterrent to the Japanese advance. And let no one say that I think we can act with impunity — without the *risk* of war — but that the alternative to positive action, namely a laissez-faire policy, will lead to conditions of far greater ultimate danger to our country than now confronts us. Positive action may in itself conceivably serve to avert war. With Mr. Matsuoka I "shudder" to contemplate war between the United States and Japan; I have worked for eight years to minimize the possibility of war; but I recognize that under present circumstances, our unwillingness to contemplate war might well lead to a future catastrophe of far greater proportions than any catastrophe which now confronts us. "Peace in our time," alas, is a temporarily soothing but highly dangerous formula which under present circumstances should find no place in our philosophy, and in the Far East we should profit by Mr. Chamberlain's bitter experience in Europe. We know by experience out here that Japan's word of honor can be trusted no farther than Hitler's word of honor could or can be trusted. Japan has associated herself with a team or system of predatory Powers, with similar aims and employing similar methods. It will be the better part of wisdom to regard her no longer as an individual nation, with whom our friendship has been traditional, but as part and parcel of that system which, if allowed to develop unchecked, will assuredly destroy everything that America stands for.

The letter from Washington, mentioned at the beginning of the foregoing exposition, brought out three points in connection with the situation in the Far East.

1. Japan does not seek "appeasement." If Great Britain falls, they can get appeasement, and more. If Germany falls, no provisional settlement by way of appeasement will stand. (The truth of this is patent.)

2. Our supplying Great Britain with arms is for Britain a critical matter. If our continued supply of arms enables Britain to stand and ultimately to win, we shall be able to have an accounting in the Far East under such terms and at such a time as we may choose. On the other hand, if we become involved in war in the Far East and withhold the supplies that Britain needs, this in itself may bring about Britain's collapse, and even though we might have brought Japan to her knees, our position would then be precarious. (I am not sure of the cogency of this argument. It obviously depends upon our strategy and tactics in the event of war with Japan and to what extent our strategy and tactics would compel us to withhold supplies from Great Britain. Presumably our strategy would involve a long-range blockade, a partial concentration of the fleet at Singapore and a strengthening of our defenses in the Philippines. This of course would entail the sending of a strong air force to Manila, but whether this would involve our entire output of planes, as production increases, is an open question. My guess is that our withholding supplies from Great Britain would be but temporary. However, the point is well taken and must be given careful consideration in determining at just what point in Japan's southward advance we should call a halt. Can we afford to see Japan occupy progressively Hong Kong, the Malay States and Burma and the Dutch East Indies while awaiting Britain's ultimate victory in order to drive Japan out with Britain's help? I doubt it.)

3. Would Japan avoid war with the United States at the cost of abandoning the campaign in China? If she had to choose between retreating ignominiously from China or fighting the United States and Great Britain, would she not choose the latter? (Yes, I think so. We need not aim to drive Japan out of China now. That can be taken care of, perhaps, if and after Britain wins the war with Germany. But stopping Japan's proposed far-flung southward advance and driving her out of China are two different matters. We can tolerate her occupation of China for the time being, just as we have tolerated it for the past three years. I doubt if we should tolerate any

great extension of the southward advance, even while the outcome in Europe is still doubtful.) . . .

January 27, 1941

. . . There is a lot of talk around town to the effect that the Japanese, in case of a break with the United States, are planning to go all out in a surprise mass attack on Pearl Harbor. I rather guess that the boys in Hawaii are not precisely asleep.[19]

To Count Michimasa Soyeshima, a former member of Parliament, Tokyo, September 1, 1941

I well know how deeply the present situation in international affairs is paining you, just as it is paining me. It is a dark and critical period that we are passing through, but during the past nine years I have seen our two countries pass through several crises and surmount them, and I firmly believe that we shall eventually surmount the present one. I cannot visualize the utter stupidity of war ensuing between Japan and the United States, and if ever a break should occur I feel convinced that it will not come as a result of any deliberated act on the part of either of our Governments but rather through some unfortunate act brought about by extremist elements. I know very well that Prince Konoye and Admiral Toyoda, and the President and Mr. Hull, are doing their utmost to avoid war and are dealing with the situation with the highest statesmanship, courage and farsighted vision. Pray God that they may be allowed to achieve success and that their enlight-

19 Before the Congressional Committee investigating Pearl Harbor, Mr. Grew explained that the Peruvian Minister in Japan was the main source for this report. When Senator Clark criticized Mr. Grew for not asking the Minister where he had learned this information, Mr. Grew replied: "To have gone to my Peruvian colleague and said, 'I would like to know the source from which you received that information,' would have put him in a very difficult position, because most of those pieces of information were received from Japanese friends who would have been endangered by the knowledge that they had passed that information on. I think in all probability if I had asked my colleague for the source he probably would have felt that he could not give it to me. In any case, it is a rather difficult thing to do, to ask for such a thing as that." *Ibid.*, pt. 2, p. 572.

ened efforts will not be wrecked by shortsighted and intransigent elements in either country.

But many things have been done over the past several years and are being done today which are not permitted to come to the knowledge of the public in Japan, and therefore it is very difficult, I should say impossible, for the Japanese people to view the situation objectively and to weigh all the factors which have led to the present unhappy pass in our relations. Merely as an illustration, I doubt if many Japanese know of the serious incidents which occurred only recently, when Japanese aviators attacked our Embassy and our navy ship the *Tutuila,* sister ship of the ill-fated *Panay,* in Chungking on several occasions; our Embassy was damaged, fortunately without loss of American lives, and a bomb missed the *Tutuila* by only a few yards, but damaged her.[20] Our Embassy and our ship are in a safety zone, recognized by the Japanese Government, and no military objectives are near them. Three American officers who witnessed the attack on the *Tutuila* from a near-by hill have officially expressed their opinion that the attack was deliberate or, at the very least, due to criminal negligence. The Japanese planes came over in perfectly clear weather; one plane left the others and took a course directly over the *Tutuila,* dropping its bomb as it passed over the ship and missing her only by a split-second of time. If the ship had been sunk, or if our Ambassador had been killed, as might easily have occurred, I do not think that the present status of our relations could have stood the strain because the entire American people would have become inflamed. I said this to Mr. Matsuoka early in June after the first attack on our Embassy, when the buildings had been actually hit; I said that never during my nine years in Japan had I been more anxious over any situation than these obviously deliberate attacks on our Embassy and ship, and that of all the difficult problems with which the Min-

[20] The *Tutuila* had been superficially damaged by bombs on July 30 during a Japanese raid on Chungking. On the following day Japan expressed official regret for the incident and agreed to pay for damages. *New York Times,* August 1, 1941, p. 1.

ister was faced, I felt certain that he was confronted with no more serious problem than this one. Mr. Matsuoka replied "I agree with you," yet the attacks continued, three or four of them within a few weeks. By such hair-breadth escapes are America and Japan still hoping and working to avoid a break.

You write of the desirability of our recognizing Japan's legitimate interests and aspirations. Indeed our Government has time and time again, and only recently, expressed its full appreciation of Japan's legitimate interests and aspirations, realizing that Japan, restricted as she is in her islands, must have access to raw materials, markets for the products of her industries and a free flow of trade and commerce. Nevertheless, unless Japan is willing to abandon aggression by force there can be no hope for an improvement in our relations. We know by sad and bitter practical experience that Japan's so-called "New Order in East Asia" and "Co-Prosperity Sphere" visualize no neighborly relations on the basis of reciprocity and a free give-and-take but rather an order in which Japanese interests, or what one conceives to be her interests, are to be predominant and to be exercised to the exclusion of the legitimate interests of other countries. We have watched the gradual but inexorable elimination of our own legitimate interests over these past several years, our long-standing and patiently-established business, commercial, industrial, banking and cultural interests, all legitimate and co-operative activities, progressively ousted first from Manchuria, and then, in turn, from North China, the ports, the Yangtze, and now they are in process of being excluded from Indochina, in spite of the most categorical assurances and promises that the Open Door and equal opportunity would be scrupulously observed everywhere. Every Foreign Minister — especially Hirota, Arita, Nomura — has given us such promises but not one of those promises has been carried out. Why? Those promises were unquestionably given in good faith. But the military would not permit their implementation. Japanese armed force has prevented their implementation. Is it surprising that when Admiral Toyoda assures me of Japan's peaceful intentions, I am obliged to recount to him those past bitter experiences? How, in the light of those experiences, can my Government believe any such promise or assurance given us by any Japanese Government?

Highly placed Japanese are constantly talking and writing about Anglo-American imperialism in East Asia, about Anglo-American encirclement. Please look at the record. So far as the United States is concerned, we have always wished Japan well, have proved our friendship by concrete acts. In the old days we protected Japan from unequal treaties which other nations attempted to foist upon her. We counseled and actively helped Japan in her splendid efforts to become a great modern Power. At the time of the Great Earthquake we did everything in our power, spiritually and materially, to show our friendship for Japan and to support and aid her in her hour of trial. Up until the invasion of Manchuria in 1931 we were negotiating with China for the abrogation of the unequal treaties, ready and willing to abandon our extraterritorial rights, including our extraterritorial judicial, commercial and customs rights, and this would unquestionably have come to pass if Japan had not set out on her long course of aggression and the use of armed force as an instrument of national policy. The Exclusion Clause of our Immigration Act of 1924 cast a dark shadow on our relations, but do you know that prior to 1931 our Government had been steadily working to have that clause cancelled? In a few months that obnoxious clause, which naturally wounded your proud and sensitive people (even though it was a domestic measure, taken for the same economic protection that Japan has been continually invoking and acting upon during recent years), would almost certainly have been withdrawn. But then came Japan's invasion of Manchuria, and we then knew that further efforts at that time to withdraw the exclusion clause were hopeless.

I do not believe that you, my dear friend, or many of your friends, have any detailed knowledge of the patience and forebearance exercised by the American Government and people in the face of the truly outrageous treatment of our own legitimate interests at the hands of Japanese authorities, both mili-

tary and civil, during these past years. Our missions throughout China, including churches, hospitals, universities and
schools, have been ruthlessly bombed and wrecked and American missionaries and their families have been killed or injured in spite of the fact that such buildings were clearly
marked by American flags both flying and painted on the roofs
and their precise location marked on maps submitted to the
Japanese military authorities, showing that they were seldom
if ever in the neighborhood of any military objectives. There
can be no shadow of doubt that these cruel and brutal attacks
were planned and executed with careful intention. Accidents
can happen, but not two or three hundred accidents of the
same kind. It is a saying among the Chinese that when a Chinese city or town is bombed by Japanese aviators, the most
dangerous spot and the one to get far away from is the American mission. It is perfectly clear that the Japanese bombers
were following a concerted plan to drive American missionary,
educational, medical and cultural activities out of China permanently. We might have broken relations with Japan on this
issue alone, but we didn't; we remained patient and, permit
me to say, long-suffering. Yet you write: "Even an incident
one-tenth as bad as that of the bombing of Iran will never take
place in this our part of the world." [21]

The same concerted drive against our business firms, banks,
industrial interests, commercial and shipping activities, has
steadily and inexorably progressed, first in Manchuria, then in
North China, the ports, the Yangtze valley, and now in Indochina where American-owned cargoes have been ruthlessly
seized and shipped away. Is this the Open Door and equal opportunity, of the scrupulous safeguarding of which I so often
received the most categorical assurances from successive Japanese governments?

Meanwhile the southward advance progressed step by step,
one step at a time, first occupation, then consolidation, a pause
to watch its result, and then another forward step. All this

[21] Between August 25 and 29, 1941; British and Russian forces invaded Iran
and aided in the establishment of the regime of Muhammed Riza Pahlevi.

time many of your leading men, Admirals, Generals, retired Ambassadors, prominent writers, publicists and politicians, were contributing articles to the daily press and magazines advocating the rapid pushing of the southward advance and the elimination of the Americans and Europeans and all of their interests and activities from the entire sphere of "Greater East Asia including the South Seas." And this advance was to be pursued first by high-pressure diplomacy and then, if necessary, by force. Can you possibly believe that if France had not been powerless she would have allowed the occupation of bases, both naval and aviation, in Indochina? Or can you possibly believe that Great Britain, completely occupied as she is with the war in Europe, where her own national life and the safety of the British Isles are at stake, would or could start a program of unprovoked aggression and invasion against Indochina or Thailand, or that the United States or the Netherlands would ever even consider such aggression? The fallacy of the alleged ABCD "encirclement" is too patent to fool even a schoolboy — if he knows the facts. But in the light of Japan's recent actions and the clear intentions of so many of Japan's prominent men as expressed by them in their articles in the daily newspapers and magazines, is it surprising that the ABCD Powers realize beyond a shadow of a doubt that it is they who are being "encircled" and that Malaya, Burma, Singapore, the Netherlands East Indies and the Philippines themselves are in direct line for future aggressive moves by Japan in establishing and consolidating the so-called "New Order in Greater East Asia including the South Seas" and that defensive measures had therefore to be taken? From all that has passed and from all that is being said and written and done, the evidence is clear for all to see that what is euphemistically called the "Co-Prosperity Sphere" means eventual Japanese hegemony over all the areas therein contained. From all the evidence, is it not abundantly clear that we in the United States must now and in future be guided alone by facts and actions and that we can no longer rely on words or assurances of peaceful intentions? I have stated this fact categorically to Admiral Toyoda, after recounting to him our past bitter experiences when we did rely on such assurances.

To turn to the China Affair. Few people know, but I know, that about ten days or a fortnight after the outbreak of hostilities in July, 1937, Chiang Kai-shek sent a message through the British Embassy here to the Japanese Government, offering an immediate armistice and the withdrawal of all Chinese troops if the Japanese troops would likewise withdraw to a given line pending negotiations. Mr. Dodds was then the British Chargé d'Affaires, and when he received that message from the British Ambassador in Nanking he came to ask my advice as to whether he ought to deliver it to the Japanese Government without instructions from London because his own Government might regard the step as in the nature of offering mediation, yet the message was too urgent for him to wait for instructions. I told him that he could not possibly take the responsibility of *not* delivering the message immediately, so he did so and later London approved. The message was delivered to Mr. Horinouchi who was then Vice Foreign Minister. But it died, alas, and nothing came of it. History will most certainly take full cognizance of that effort of Chiang Kai-shek for peace. The Japanese forces didn't want an armistice. They have now had war for over four long years with no end in sight. Chiang Kai-shek, a brave and farsighted man, is still the legitimate head of the Chinese Government, is still fighting against ruthless aggression against his country, and Wang Ching-wei could not live a day if Japan's bayonets were withdrawn.[22] How can he therefore be regarded as representative of China or, in fact, anything more than a puppet? I know well Japan's former troubles in China and with China, but those troubles could have been smoothed out eventually by peaceful negotiation. They have not and never will be smoothed out by war which, unless terminated on terms acceptable to the Chinese — also a proud and sensitive people — will make real friendship between Japan and the Chinese impossible for generations to come.

[22] On March 30, 1940, a puppet Chinese government under Wang Ching-wei was set up at Nanking with Japanese support.

Another and essential aspect of the situation is this. We believe, with abundant reason, that Germany, as controlled by the Nazis, seeks world domination by force and that once in control of Europe and the British Isles it would be only a question of time before the Western Hemisphere was attacked. Hitler has said as much in published statements. We believe that the Nazis seek to control and to alter our whole way of life. Therefore, as a reasonable and sensible measure of self-defense, we determined to help Great Britain to avoid defeat. When Japan allied herself with Germany we inevitably came to associate Japan with the same general program, so far as the Far East is concerned, and we thereupon determined to assist not only Great Britain but all other victims of aggression, including China. In pursuing that policy we feel that it would be utterly shortsighted to pour supplies into Great Britain across the Atlantic while complacently watching the potential cutting off of Great Britain's other great lifeline to the East which would be accomplished by the fall of Singapore to any Axis Power. Therefore, whatever threatens Singapore, directly concerns the United States. The occupation of bases in Indochina definitely does threaten Singapore. The occupation of bases in Thailand would constitute a still more serious threat. Therefore, if Japanese forces should now undertake a further move on the line of the southward advance (and many Japanese openly advocate such a move), I question whether our relations could stand the strain involved.

Incidentally, you mention Iran. The British began to fight this war as amateurs perhaps, but at least like gentlemen. They trusted like gentlemen to Germany's pledged word. But gradually they saw what they were encountering, an enemy whose pledged word counted for nothing. In spite of nonaggression pacts and the most solemn assurances given on the very eve of aggression they saw one country after another fall to the absolutely ruthless invader and to the work of fifth columnists within those countries — Austria, Czechoslovakia, Poland, Belgium, Holland, France, Luxemburg, Denmark, Norway, Rumania, Hungary, Bulgaria, Yugoslavia, Albania, Greece, and now Soviet Russia — as Churchill has so aptly said, "one by one." Do you remember what Hitler said after the seizure of Austria, and after Munich, and after the seizure of Czechoslovakia: "I am now completely satisfied. This is the last territorial readjustment I will seek." In every case Great Britain was too slow and too late. At last she has wisely learned by bitter experience, and it is that experience which prompted her very wise occupation of Syria and Iran — before Hitler could get there and could threaten the Suez Canal and the whole Mediterranean area. But note the difference: Hitler aims to control all of Europe and has so stated; Great Britain has pledged herself, and the world by experience can rely on her pledges, to withdraw from Iran and to restore her complete sovereignty the moment the necessity for these measures of self-defense has passed. I applaud her action. I cannot admire the action of Japan's allies.

Incidentally we now learn that the bombing of Iranian cities by either the British or Soviet forces has been officially denied. I am inclined to believe that the bombing report was merely Nazi propaganda.

International relations, if they are to be stable and secure, must be based upon the scrupulous observance of international commitments. Breaking of the pledged word between nations can lead only to international anarchy. Was it not the breaking of the Nine Power Treaty that constituted the first step in this long line of breaches of international commitments by certain nations? It is maintained in Japan that Japan did not break the Nine Power Treaty. Yet look at the text and the facts, which speak for themselves. It is held in Japan that under changed conditions that treaty had become obsolete. Very well, our Government has stated in categorical terms that it is ready at all times to consider the effect of changed conditions upon international commitments and to modify or modernize those commitments by peaceful negotiations. We do not regard and never have, as charged, regarded the *status quo* as permanently unalterable. Our negotiations with China for abandoning our extraterritorial rights proves the point, just as does our willingness to surrender our permanent leases in Japan and many other legitimate but outmoded rights. But once Japan resorted to force as an instrument of national policy in breaching an important international treaty, from which Japan had gained much when it was concluded because it was a carefully balanced undertaking, entered into by Japan freely and, at that time, gladly, a precedent was set and an example was created which were soon followed by other nations, beginning, as you will remember, by Italy's action in Ethiopia. This was the beginning of international chaos of which we see the sad result today.

Through the process of publicity and propaganda in Japan, largely stimulated from Axis sources, the Japanese people are today told that the Anglo-Saxon countries propose to "encircle" Japan by their imperialistic ambitions, to obtain complete hegemony in East Asia, to control commerce and trade and sources of raw materials, and to drive Japan to the wall. How untrue is this picture you, my dear friend, know only too well, yet how can we hope to improve our relations so long as the Japanese people are made to believe these preposterous charges? My Government believes, and I believe, that Japan's legitimate interests and aspirations should be given the fullest recognition.

As you know, I am no defeatist. I believe that in spite of present difficulties we can still guide our relations into healthy channels, and for that high purpose I am constantly thinking and working. Below are four points which my Government regards as essential for our future good relations. We confidently believe that Japan would achieve the greatest happiness, security, prosperity and contentment by following a policy of peaceful and productive expansion based on the principle of free and equal treatment for all nations, a policy which would have the full support of the United States, while we believe that the continued use of armed force will lead eventually to social, economic and financial disaster. These are the points:

1. Respect for the territorial integrity and the sovereignty of each and all nations.
2. Support of the principle of noninterference in the internal affairs of other countries.
3. Support of the principle of equality, including equality of commercial opportunity.
4. Nondisturbance of the *status quo* in the Pacific except as the *status quo* may be altered by peaceful means.

On such a basis and, I fear, only on such a basis will the United States "ultimately come to sympathize with us in our efforts and, if possible, co-operate with us."

If Japan will mould her policy and actions on the basis of the foregoing four points and will abandon aggression, I see a happy outlook for the development of a new era in Japanese-American relations, contributing to Japan's future prosperity and welfare through a free flow of trade and commerce, access to the needed raw materials and a successful continuation of industrial development, resulting in a progressive raising of the standard of living of her people and a return to the old cultural values of life which have so brilliantly illuminated her background and history.

We should at all times be aware that the facts of geography are immutable. For better or for worse Divine Providence has placed our respective nations on either side of the Pacific; we are neighbors for all time to come; and nothing that anyone can do can alter that fact. Since the beginning of relations between our two countries — almost ninety years ago — we have maintained peace between ourselves, and with the exception of the past ten years, our relations have been marked by friendship, good will, and respect, the one for the other. The tradition of good neighborly relations must be restored, for if we fail in that task, there will be introduced into the Pacific the tradition of war which has cursed Europe since the beginning of history. We who are charged with the accomplishment of this task, who are working for the welfare not only of this generation but of those yet unborn, need your help and the help of all other men of good will.

XXXIV

Pearl Harbor: From the Perspective of Ten Years

*While Mr. Grew was under detention in Japan in the months
following the Japanese attack at Pearl Harbor, he and his staff
assembled memoranda of conversations with Japanese officials
and copies of Embassy despatches to the Department of State
and prepared extensive notes to throw light on their activities
in the crucial months before the outbreak. Working from this
material, Mr. Grew in 1951 compiled the following Preface,
Survey, and Postscript, which present the record as known in
Tokyo in the closing period of his Mission to Japan.*

*Mr. Grew not only had available to him this key material,
which he and his staff had collected within a few months of
the occurrence of the events that led to the break with Japan,
but in addition, with the perspective of ten years he presents
from this material a challenging interpretation of this crucial
period in American diplomacy.*

Preface to the Survey

The fact should be emphasized that in recording our impressions and views in the period leading up to the outbreak
of war on December 7, 1941, we did so with the clear understanding of the limited field of observation then available to
the Embassy. We in the Embassy recognized the fact that a far
broader field of intelligence, including the world picture, had
been open to the Government in Washington. This intelligence included the important Japanese telegrams to and from
the Japanese Embassies in Washington and other capitals bearing the code name "Magic" which enabled our Government,
through the interception of these telegrams and the breaking
of the Japanese cipher codes, to learn that the Japanese Government was rapidly going ahead with its plans of conquest
even while talking peace with us.

The subsequent uncovering of Prince Konoye's "Memoirs" shed further light on this situation.

In spite of these revelations, unknown to our Embassy in Tokyo prior to our return to Washington, it still seems proper from the viewpoint of history to tell the story as it appeared from all angles. Indeed, the story is still being told in books and papers by both Americans and Japanese. It will be the duty of the historians to separate the wheat from the chaff as best they may, and the more material provided them on which to work, the clearer will the ultimate picture emerge. War is too serious a matter to accept as an inevitable misfortune without an exhaustive examination into the facts and causes of its incidence.

It is this thought that leads me, even while realizing that we in Tokyo were "seeing through a glass darkly" during the pregnant period under consideration, to sketch in this survey the thoughts of our Embassy in Tokyo at that time.

It is right to add that on arriving in Washington on August 26, 1942, I discussed with Mr. Hull the conversations between the American and the Japanese Governments which had taken place in the spring, summer and autumn of 1941, as well as the proposal for a Konoye-Roosevelt meeting. Mr. Hull explained to me the point of view of the Administration: in brief, that in the absence of a preliminary agreement between the two Governments covering basic principles, a meeting between the responsible heads of the two Governments would have been fraught with serious dangers, and that regardless of the assurances given me by Prince Konoye in Tokyo it had been impossible to reach such a preliminary agreement in the conversations held in Washington. The proposal for holding such a meeting had therefore lapsed.

FINAL DEVELOPMENTS IN TOKYO LEADING
TO THE OUTBREAK OF WAR BETWEEN
THE UNITED STATES AND JAPAN

During the summer and autumn of 1941 the conversations between the United States and Japan had become to all intents and purposes deadlocked. From time to time there appeared to be some small progress in the efforts to find mutually acceptable formulas for agreement, but at other times the discussions appeared to be regressive. Our government felt that little acceptable ground had been found for proceeding to formal negotiations.

In the early autumn of 1941, before the fall of the Konoye Cabinet on October 16, Admiral Teijiro Toyoda, the Foreign Minister, had told me of his wish to send a prominent Japanese diplomat to Washington to assist Admiral Nomura in conducting the conversations with our Government.[1]

Incidentally, it may be said that as a general rule, when telegrams were received by the Embassy reporting conversations between the Japanese Ambassador and the President or the Secretary of State or other officials in Washington, I gave or sent paraphrases of such telegrams promptly to the Foreign Minister with a view to ensuring accuracy and comprehensiveness in the reporting of such conversations and as a check on the reports received by the Foreign Office from Admiral Nomura. Admiral Toyoda told me that this method of checking was helpful to him and that he welcomed this practice, of which the Department was duly informed.

Prince Konoye had told me in strict confidence at our meeting on September 6, 1941, that he proposed to include in his staff, when proceeding to meet the President, the Japanese Ambassador to Great Britain, Mr. Mamoru Shigemitsu, then on leave of absence from his post in London, and when delay occurred in the proposed meeting of Prince Konoye with the President, we believed that it might be Mr. Shigemitsu whom Admiral Toyoda had in mind to send to Washington. The Konoye Cabinet, however, fell before this plan was carried out, and under the government of General Hideki Tojo, Mr. Shigenori Togo replaced Admiral Toyoda.

[1] Herbert Feis in *The Road to Pearl Harbor* (Princeton: Princeton University Press, 1950), p. 306, states that as early as August 4 Admiral Nomura had cabled to the Japanese Foreign Office asking that some member of the Foreign Service be sent to assist him, because he was "quite at a loss what to do."

Admiral Toyoda's plan had presumably been passed on to Mr. Togo because on November 4 the new Minister for Foreign Affairs informed me of his wish to send to Washington Mr. Kurusu, formerly Ambassador to Italy and later to Germany, one of Japan's outstanding diplomats with a well-nigh perfect grasp of the English language and with a past record as a successful negotiator.[2]

Incidentally, Mr. Togo, from the moment of assuming office, insisted on regarding the Washington conversations as full-fledged "negotiations" which in his view had already entered upon their final phase, and he habitually referred to them as such despite the fact that our own Government maintained the position that the exploratory and informal conversations had not yet led to a basis upon which formal negotiations could begin.

With the prompt and effective co-operation of our Government, immediate accommodations for Mr. Kurusu and his secretary, Mr. Shiroji Yuki, were found on the plane from Hong Kong for San Francisco, the departure of which was delayed for two days to permit the Japanese officials to reach that port of embarkation on November 7, 1941. Soon thereafter Mr. Kurusu arrived in Washington and from that moment participated in the meetings of Admiral Nomura with the President and Mr. Hull.

On November 26 Mr. Hull handed to Admiral Nomura and Mr. Kurusu the ten-point draft proposal of our Government for adjusting the whole situation in the Far East,[3] and during

---

[2] See *Foreign Relations, Japan: 1931–41*, II, 704–5, for a despatch concerning Ambassador Grew's conversation with Kurusu on November 4.

[3] On November 26, 1941, Secretary Hull handed a document to Admiral Nomura described as "Strictly Confidential, Tentative and Without Commitment." After pledging both Governments to support the basic principles which the United States had been advocating, the draft proposal listed ten steps to be taken: the negotiation of a multilateral nonaggression pact; the conclusion of an agreement to respect the territorial integrity of and the equality of economic opportunity in Indochina; the withdrawal of Japanese armed forces from China and Indochina; the agreement of both countries to support the National Government of China; the renunciation of all extraterritorial rights in China; the negotiation of a trade agreement; the removal of freezing re-

the period from November 29, when we were first informed
of the proposal, I left nothing undone to point out to our influential Japanese contacts that this broad-gauge, objective and
statesmanlike program offered to Japan, provided that she
would abandon her policy of aggression, the principal desiderata for which she had ostensibly been fighting — access to
needed raw materials on the basis of equal opportunity, freedom of trade and commerce, financial co-operation, economic,
strategic and social security with a rising standard of living,
together with a withdrawal of the freezing orders and the prospect of the opportunity to enter upon negotiations for a new
treaty of commerce and navigation with the United States. If
the face of the military must be saved, I suggested that the
Japanese Government could tell the Japanese people, through
the press, that their Government had won a diplomatic victory in achieving without further force of arms the precise
objectives for which they had allegedly been fighting. They
were offered, in effect, a bright future of security, prosperity
and contentment which could be achieved in no other way.
To continue their policy of aggression would be to court sure
disaster in the long run.

These observations appeared to fall upon deaf ears. The
American ten-point draft proposal, although it had been presented as a basis for discussion, was generally regarded as an
ultimatum;[4] general pessimism was expressed; Japanese troops

strictions; adoption of a plan for stabilizing the dollar-yen rate; the decision
to interpret no prior treaty or commitment in a way which conflicted with
the purpose of establishing and preserving peace in the Pacific; and influencing
other nations to adhere to the political and economic principles of this document. For the full text see *ibid.*, pp. 768–70.

4 Mr. Grew did not consider that the November 26 proposals constituted an
ultimatum. In his testimony before the Army Pearl Harbor Board Mr. Grew
said: "The reaction of the Japanese military people and also of probably the
majority of the civil government officials, who took their cue from the military
at that time, was that they characterized that memorandum as an ultimatum. . . .
It was in no respect an ultimatum, either in tone or in substance." Before the
Committee investigating Pearl Harbor Mr. Grew added the following comment:
"The VICE CHAIRMAN. Although the message itself was not an ultimatum, the
Japanese officials in charge of the Government at that time sought to con-
vey the information to the Japanese people that it was an ultimatum?

"Mr. GREW. That is true, and in the case of one prominent Japanese, a

and supplies continued to be poured into southern Indochina; and from all indications the situation was generally regarded as well-nigh hopeless for avoiding war with the United States and Great Britain. At this increasingly tense moment the Prime Minister, General Tojo, saw fit to deliver a public address on November 30 which could only be described as bellicose both in tone and substance, and while the address was read by proxy during the absence of the Prime Minister from Tokyo, and while we were later informed that the speech had been written by some official other than the Prime Minister himself and that General Tojo had not seen it in advance, the effect abroad was in no way softened by such explanations.[5]

On the evening of December 7, Tokyo time, the radio from San Francisco announced that the President had sent a message to the Emperor of Japan but gave no information as to its substance or the channel of transmission, but later the same evening I received a brief triple priority message from Mr. Hull stating that a telegram was then being encoded containing a message which I was to communicate to the Emperor at

very prominent Japanese, after I had told him the contents of the memorandum he said that if that were so, as I had related, he felt that the Japanese people if they knew those facts would be very much opposed to an intransigent attitude on the part of their Government." See U.S. Congress, *Pearl Harbor Attack*, Hearings before the Joint Committee on the Investigation of the Pearl Harbor Attack, 79th Cong., 1st Sess., Pursuant to S. Con. Res. 7 (Washington: Government Printing Office, 1946), pt. 2, pp. 575, 772. For a discussion of the November memorandum from differing points of view, see Charles A. Beard, *President Roosevelt and the Coming of the War* (New Haven: Yale University Press, 1948), pp. 557 ff., and Basil Rauch, *Roosevelt from Munich to Pearl Harbor* (New York: Creative Age Press, 1950), pp. 475–77.

[5] On December 1 the Imperial Conference decided on war. The day before Premier Tojo had told the Imperial Rule Assistance Association and the Dai Nippon East Asia League: "The fact that Chiang Kai-shek is dancing to the tune of Britain, America, and communism at the expense of able-bodied and promising young men in his futile resistance against Japan is only due to the desire of Britain and the United States to fish in the troubled waters of East Asia by putting [*pitting?*] the East Asiatic peoples against each other and to grasp the hegemony of East Asia. This is a stock in trade of Britain and the United States.

"For the honor and pride of mankind we must purge this sort of practice from East Asia with a vengeance." *Foreign Relations, Japan: 1931–41*, II, 148–49.

the earliest possible moment. The message itself was received at about 10.30 P.M. I immediately informed the Foreign Minister that I might desire to see him urgently around midnight but that the appointment would depend upon the nature of a telegram from Washington which was then being decoded. The appointment was shortly thereafter confirmed and I called on Mr. Togo at his official residence at about 11.50 P.M. I requested the Minister to arrange an audience for me with the Emperor at the earliest possible moment in order to present the President's message which I then read aloud and a copy of the text of which I handed to Mr. Togo.[6] Mr. Hull had left to my discretion the appropriate method of communication, and I felt it important to give the message maximum weight by asking to see the Emperor himself and to make sure that it got to the Emperor personally. The Minister at first said that he would study the document, but when I inquired if that observation implied some doubt as to whether he would ask for an audience for me, he replied that he would present my request to the Throne.[7]

The fact should here be recorded, as of important significance, that when Mr. Dooman telephoned on the night of December 7 to Mr. Tomoda, the Foreign Minister's private secretary, to make a tentative appointment for me to see Mr. Togo around midnight, Mr. Tomoda said that the Minister wished to retire as soon as possible and he wondered whether it would not be possible to defer my call until the following morning, to which Mr. Dooman replied that I would not think of disturbing the Minister at that late hour unless the matter in hand were of extreme importance and urgency. Furthermore, when Mr. Ohta of the Foreign Office called at the Em-

[6] For the text of the President's message to Emperor Hirohito, see *ibid.*, pp. 784–86.

[7] Mr. Grew explained to the Congressional Committee investigating the attack at Pearl Harbor, that the President's telegram reached Tokyo at noon and was not delivered to Mr. Grew for transmittal to the Emperor until 10.30 P.M. Mr. Grew stated that he believed the Japanese military authorities held up the delivery of the President's message to him in order to delay its presentation to the Emperor. *Pearl Harbor Attack,* pt. 2, pp. 692–93.

bassy on December 9 he referred to the foregoing telephone conversation, and Mr. Dooman asked whether the Foreign Minister, in expressing reluctance to stay up very late to receive me on the night of the 7th, was trying to avoid seeing me again after the beginning of the hostilities. Mr. Ohta burst out spontaneously and with considerable feeling: "Not at all. The Foreign Minister knew nothing about the attack on Hawaii until early the next morning." [8]

At 7 A.M. on December 8, Tokyo time, I received a telephone call from Mr. Kase, the Minister's secretary, who asked me to come to see the Minister as soon as possible. He said that he had been trying to telephone to me ever since 5 A.M. but could not get through to the Embassy. I hurriedly dressed and arrived at the official residence at about 7.30. Mr. Togo entered the reception room almost immediately. He was in formal dress and his manner was equally formal and grim, but as Mr. Togo's manner is habitually somewhat sphinx-like I received no impression of unusual developments. He slapped a document on the table, clearly a gesture of finality, and made to me the following oral statement (in Japanese, interpreted into English by Mr. Kase, who later sent me the text in handwriting):

His Majesty has expressed his gratefulness and appreciation for the cordial message of the President. He has graciously let known his wishes to the Foreign Minister to convey the following to the President as a reply to the latter's message.

"Some days ago, the President made inquiries regarding the

[8] The Imperial Conference had approved a statement of policy on September 6 which said, in part, that if "by the early part of October there is no reasonable hope of having our demands agreed to in the diplomatic negotiations mentioned above, we will immediately make up our minds to get ready for war against America." A resolution of November 5 adopted by the Conference called for the placing before the Emperor of the final decision to go to war, if no agreement had been reached between the United States and Japan by November 25. On December 1 at a meeting of the Imperial Conference, in the presence of the Emperor, the decision to go to war was transmuted into the "way of the Emperor." Foreign Minister Togo knew the plans for the surprise attack, although he had protested ineffectively in the period between December 1 and 7 against the decision to give no advance notice of the beginning of war. See Feis, *op. cit.*, pp. 265, 295, 330, 332.

circumstances of the augmentation of Japanese forces in French Indochina to which His Majesty has directed the Government to reply. Withdrawal of Japanese forces from French Indochina constitutes one of the subject matters of the Japanese-American negotiations. His Majesty has commanded the Government to state its views to the American Government also on this question. It is, therefore, desired that the President will kindly refer to this reply.

"Establishment of peace in the Pacific and consequently of the world has been the cherished desire of His Majesty for the realization of which He has hitherto made the Government to continue its earnest endeavors. His Majesty trusts that the President is fully aware of this fact."

The Minister then said that the document which he was about to hand me, a memorandum of thirteen pages in English, dated December 8, had been communicated by Admiral Nomura to Mr. Hull, breaking off the conversations. The final paragraph of the memorandum read:

The Japanese Government regrets to have to notify hereby the American Government that, in view of the attitude of the American Government, it can not but consider that it is impossible to reach an agreement through further negotiations.[9]

Mr. Togo said that he had seen the Emperor (at 3 A.M., I understand) and that the memorandum constituted the Emperor's reply to the President's message. I asked the Minister if this meant that my request for an audience had been refused and I advanced three points to substantiate the request: (1) the privilege of an Ambassador, according to international usage, of access to the Sovereign to whom he is accredited; (2) the fact that the Japanese Ambassador in Washington frequently is received at his request by the President; and (3) the critical situation then obtaining, justifying such a step. The Minister merely replied that he had no desire nor intention to stand between the Throne and myself. He then made a little speech,

9 This document is given in full in *Foreign Relations, Japan: 1931-41*, II, 787-92.

thanking me for my co-operation during the conversations and for my efforts toward the maintenance of Japanese-American friendship, and he came downstairs, as usual, to see me off at the door. The curtain then dropped, but I was not aware of it until an hour or so later when a *Yomiuri* bulletin was received, announcing that armed conflict had occurred between Japan and the United States and Great Britain.

At about eleven o'clock on the same morning, Mr. Ohno of the Foreign Office drove to the Embassy and asked to see Mr. Dooman, but as the latter had been for the moment refused admittance to the Embassy compound, the gates having already been closed by the police, Mr. Ohno saw Mr. Crocker, took a document from his pocket, and said: "I am instructed to hand to you, as representing the Embassy, the following document which I shall first read to you." He then proceeded to read in English the following note:

> I have the honor to inform Your Excellency that there has arisen a state of war between Your Excellency's country and Japan beginning today.
> I avail myself of this opportunity to renew to Your Excellency the assurances of my highest consideration.

When the reading of the foregoing note was finished Mr. Crocker said: "This is a very tragic moment," to which Mr. Ohno replied: "It is; and my duty is most distasteful."

Mr. Ohno then proceeded to read an English translation of the following statement in Japanese, concerning the Embassy and the suspension of its functions:

> 1. That functions of the Embassy and the Consulates will be suspended as of today.
> 2. That members of the Embassy and Consulates be accorded protection and living facilities in accordance with international usages.
> 3. That in order to secure protection and facilities aforementioned it is recommended that all the members of the Embassy be congregated in the Embassy compound.

4. That communication with the outside including telephone and telegraph be suspended. In the case anyone desires to go out permission must be obtained from the Gaimusho through the officer who will be posted in front of the Embassy, liaison officer Mr. Masuo. He has come here with me.

5. As soon as a country representing your interests is nominated contact between your Embassy and representatives of the said country will be allowed as is necessary for the purpose of representing your interests.

6. That due attention is being paid to protecting the citizens of the United States.

7. That all wireless transmitting sets be surrendered at once.

8. That all short-wave wireless receiving sets private as well as official the use of which will no more be acquiesced to be handed over.

9. That *en clair* telegrams informing your Government of having been notified of a state of war will be allowed through the liaison officer.

From that moment we were locked in the Embassy compound and kept interned there, until our release to sail to the United States on the exchange ship the following June.

FAR EASTERN POLICY OF THE UNITED STATES

At the outset of this survey, it is essential to define the main objectives of the Far Eastern policy of the United States during the period covered by this record, since a clear understanding of immediate as well as of long-range objectives is essential to the conduct of diplomacy.

Prior to the outbreak of the Second World War, it could be said that there existed "a Far Eastern problem," and that within the limits of this specific problem it was possible to pursue certain traditional American objectives in the Far East, which need not be elaborated here. With the outbreak of the Second World War, and more urgently following Japan's adherence to the Axis group in September, 1940, it became evident that the Far Eastern problem had ceased to be even practically a separate question but had become an integral part of the world crisis created by Adolf Hitler's bid for world domination. This fundamental fact necessitated a thorough re-examination of our approach to the problems of the Far East and a redefinition of the main immediate objectives to be pursued by American diplomacy.

The distinction should here be clearly drawn between the ultimate goal and the immediate objectives of our foreign policy. Our long-range objectives are based on our belief in the wisdom and efficacy of the universal adoption and maintenance of certain fundamental principles in the conduct of international affairs, principles which had been enunciated on numerous occasions by the President and the Secretary of State.[10] Obviously, the attainment of this goal was of its nature not an immediate possibility and was predicated upon the existence in the world of certain conditions which most emphatically did not and could not obtain until the termination of the European war. The immediate objectives of our foreign policy, on the other hand, vary of necessity in accordance with shifting conditions and may be defined as the protection and maintenance of those vital national interests without whose preservation there could be no hope of attaining our ultimate goal.

In order to avoid confusion on this point and to ensure unanimity of outlook and procedure between the Administration and the Embassy, I had written to the President on December 14, 1940, in the course of direct correspondence initiated at his suggestion, my own conception of the problem:

Tokyo, December 14, 1940

I would give a great deal to know your mind about Japan and all her works. It seems to me to be increasingly clear that we are bound to have a showdown some day, and the principal question at issue is whethe⁀ it is to our advantage to have that showdown sooner or to have ⁀ later.

The chief factorₔ in the problem would seem, from this angle, to be:

10 See, for instance, *ibid.*, I, 325–26, 379–83; II, 406–10.

(1) whether and when Britain is likely to win the European war;
(2) whether our getting into war with Japan would so handicap our help to Britain in Europe as to make the difference to Britain between victory and defeat; and
(3) to what extent our own policy in the Far East must be timed with our preparedness program and with respect to the relative strength of the American and the Japanese navies now and later.

Those are questions which, with our limited information here, I am not qualified even approximately to answer.

From the Tokyo angle we see the picture roughly as follows:

After eight years of effort to build up something permanently constructive in American-Japanese relations, I find that diplomacy has been defeated by trends and forces utterly beyond its control, and that our work has been swept away as if by a typhoon with little or nothing remaining to show for it. Japan has become openly and unashamedly one of the predatory nations and part of a system which aims to wreck about everything that the United States stands for. Only insuperable obstacles will now prevent the Japanese from digging in permanently in China and from pushing the southward advance, with economic control as a preliminary to political domination in the areas marked down. Economic obstacles, such as may arise from American embargoes, will seriously handicap Japan in the long run, but meanwhile they tend to push the Japanese onward in a forlorn hope of making themselves economically self-sufficient.

History has shown that the pendulum in Japan is always swinging between extremist and moderate policies, but as things stand today we believe that the pendulum is more likely to swing still further toward extremes than to reverse its direction. Konoye, and especially Matsuoka, will fall in due course, but *under present circumstances* no Japanese leader or group of leaders could reverse the expansionist program and hope to survive.

Our own policy of unhurried but of inexorable determination in meeting every Japanese step with some step of our own has been eminently wise, and that policy has sunk deep into Japanese consciousness. But while important elements among the Japanese people deplore the course which their leaders are taking, those elements are nevertheless inarticulate and powerless and are likely to remain so. Meanwhile the Germans here are working overtime to push Japan into war with us. I have told Matsuoka point-blank that his country is heading for disaster. He has at least seen that his efforts to intimidate us have fallen flat and have had an effect precisely the reverse of that intended.

It therefore appears that sooner or later, unless we are prepared, with General Hugh Johnson, to withdraw bag and baggage from the entire sphere of "Greater East Asia including the South Seas" (which God forbid), we are bound eventually to come to a head-on clash with Japan.[11]

A progressively firm policy on our part will entail inevitable risks — especially risks of sudden uncalculated strokes such as the sinking of the *Panay* which might inflame the American people — but in my opinion those risks are less in degree than the far greater future dangers which we would face if we were to follow a policy of *laissez-faire*.

In other words, the risks of not taking positive measures to maintain our future security are likely to be much greater than the risks of taking positive measures as the southward advance proceeds. So far as I am aware, the great majority of the American people are in a mood for vigorous action. The principal point at issue, as I see it, is not whether we must call a halt to the Japanese program, but when.

It is important constantly to bear in mind the fact that if we take measures "short of war" with no real intention to carry those measures to their final conclusion if necessary, such lack of intention will be all too obvious to the Japanese who will proceed undeterred, and even with greater incentive, on their way. Only if they become certain that we mean to fight if called upon to do so will our preliminary measures stand some chance of proving effective and of removing the necessity for war — the old story of Sir Edward Grey in 1914.

If by such action we can bring about the eventual discrediting of Japan's present leaders, a regeneration of thought may ulti-

11 Before the Pearl Harbor Investigating Committee Mr. Grew further explained this paragraph by stating: "Now, that clash need not have been a military clash. In other words, it was always my hope that the economic measures which we had taken against Japan would finally bring Japan to a position where she might come to a reasonable agreement with us." *Pearl Harbor Attack,* pt. 2, p. 617.

mately take shape in this country, permitting the resumption of normal relations with us and leading to a readjustment of the whole Pacific problem.[12]

In a nutshell that is about the way I regard the present and future situation. No doubt you have seen some of my telegrams which have tried to paint the picture as clearly as has been possible at this post where we have to fumble and grope for accurate information, simply because among the Japanese themselves the right hand often doesn't know what the left hand is doing. Their so-called "New Structure" is in an awful mess and the bickering and controversy that go on within the Government itself are past belief. Every new totalitarian step is clothed in some righteous-sounding slogan. This, indeed, is not the Japan that we have known and loved.

If you are willing to give me even a cue to your thoughts, either in a personal ultra-confidential letter or orally by some trustworthy person coming out here, it will be of tremendous help.

I cabled you my enthusiastic and affectionate congratulations on your re-election. You are playing a masterly hand in our foreign affairs and I am profoundly thankful that the country is not to be deprived of your clear vision, determination and splendid courage in piloting the old ship of state.

President Roosevelt had replied: "I find myself in decided agreement with your conclusions." In his letter the President wrote me in complete frankness his concept of the objectives of our policy in the Far East in the light of the changed conditions brought on by the European war and by Japan's association with the Axis and his views on what he termed the vital national interests of the United States in the Far East at that time:

[12] Before the Pearl Harbor Investigating Committee Mr. Grew elaborated this statement: "My thought was that by taking these measures we would eventually bring at least the thinking, the sane-minded statesmen in Japan to the realization that unless they stopped in their tracks they were going to have war with the United States and Great Britain and other countries. . . .

"In other words, I think at that time some of those more intelligent statesmen in Japan realized that they were on the brink of an abyss and it was my belief at that time that they tried their best to reverse the engine. It was too late to do it but they tried to do it." *Ibid.*, p. 640.

Washington, January 21, 1941

I have given careful consideration to your letter of December 14.

First, I want to say how helpful it is to have your over-all estimates and reflections — based as they are upon a rare combination of first-hand observation, long experience with our Japanese relations, and masterly judgment. I find myself in decided agreement with your conclusions.

I also want you to know how much I appreciate your kind words of congratulation on my re-election and your expression of confidence in my conduct of our foreign affairs.

As to your very natural request for an indication of my views as to certain aspects of our future attitude toward developments in the Far East, I believe that the fundamental proposition is that we must recognize that the hostilities in Europe, in Africa, and in Asia are all parts of a single world conflict. We must, consequently, recognize that our interests are menaced both in Europe and in the Far East. We are engaged in the task of defending our way of life and our vital national interests wherever they are seriously endangered. Our strategy of self-defense must be a global strategy which takes account of every front and takes advantage of every opportunity to contribute to our total security.

You suggest as one of the chief factors in the problem of our attitude toward Japan the question whether our getting into war with Japan would so handicap our help to Britain in Europe as to make the difference to Britain between victory and defeat. In this connection it seems to me that we must consider whether, if Japan should gain possession of the region of the Netherlands East Indies and the Malay Peninsula, the chances of England's winning in her struggle with Germany would not be decreased thereby. The British Isles, the British in those Isles, have been able to exist and to defend themselves not only because they have prepared strong local defenses but also because as the heart and the nerve center of the British Empire they have been able to draw upon vast resources for their sustenance and to bring into operation against their enemies economic, military and naval pressures on a world-wide scale. They live by importing goods from all parts of the world and by utilizing large overseas financial resources. They are defended not only by measures of defense carried out locally but also by distant and widespread economic, military, and naval activities which both contribute to the maintenance of their supplies, deny certain sources of supply to their enemies, and prevent those enemies from concentrating the full force of their armed power against the heart and the nerve center of the Empire. The British need assistance along the lines of our generally established policies at many points, assistance which in the case of the Far East is certainly well within the realm of "possibility" so far as the capacity of the United States is concerned. Their defense strategy must in the nature of things be global. Our strategy of giving them assistance toward ensuring our own security must envisage both sending of supplies to England and helping to prevent a closing of channels of communication to and from various parts of the world, so that other important sources of supply will not be denied to the British and be added to the assets of the other side.

You also suggest as chief factors in the problem the questions whether and when Britain is likely to win the European war. As I have indicated above, the conflict is world-wide, not merely a European war. I firmly believe, as I have recently declared publicly, that the British, with our help, will be victorious in this conflict. The conflict may well be long and we must bear in mind that when England is victorious she may not have left the strength that would be needed to bring about a rearrangement of such territorial changes in the western and southern Pacific as might occur during the course of the conflict if Japan is not kept within bounds. I judge from the remarks which appear at the bottom of page 4 and at the top of page 5 of your letter that you, too, attach due importance to this aspect of the problem.

I am giving you my thoughts at this length because the problems which we face are so vast and so interrelated that any attempt even to state them compels one to think in terms of five continents and seven seas. In conclusion, I must emphasize that, our problem being one of defense, we can not lay down hard and fast plans. As each new development occurs we must, in the light of the circumstances then existing, decide when and where and how we can most effectively marshal and make use of our resources.

In stressing the integral relationship of certain aspects of the Far Eastern situation to the world crisis occasioned by the Nazi threat of world domination, the President pointed out the inconsistency of our bending our national efforts to ensure the continued efforts of Great Britain, with which we felt our own national interests to be indissolubly linked, while at the same time permitting Japan to occupy or to threaten areas in the Pacific which were equally vital to the continued existence of the British Empire and the British Isles. From the President's letter and his concurrence in my own presentation, the implication was clear that he regarded the essential objectives of American diplomacy in the Far East under the conditions then obtaining as aimed: (1) to prevent Japan in our own national interests, by diplomacy if possible, from pursuing her southward advance to a point where she would either actually control or would be in a position seriously to threaten those areas in the southern Pacific essential to the life of the British Empire (areas defined by the President as the Netherlands East Indies, the Malay Peninsula, and adjacent regions); and (2) to achieve this aim if possible without becoming involved in a war with Japan, obliging the United States to wage war on two fronts, for which we were still inadequately prepared.

On the basis of the President's incisive letter, I assumed that our views in regard to the main lines of our Far Eastern policy were in complete accord with those of the Administration. In fact, Mr. Dooman and I, in our talks with prominent Japanese, had continually emphasized the salient points brought out by the President even before his letter had been received, and all our efforts, and our reports and recommendations to our Government, were made with these objectives constantly in mind. Let it be made clear, however, that the concentration of our efforts on the achievement of the foregoing two immediate objectives, which could properly be classified as among the vital national interests of the United States, did not in any sense mean to lose sight of the long-range objectives of our foreign policy as a permanent concept. It was, therefore, the task of diplomacy to ensure that the attainment of our immediate objectives should in no way involve any sacrifice whatever of the fundamental principles upon which our foreign policy is and must be based, or any impairment whatever of the possibility of their eventual attainment. It is for this reason that at no time did I advocate, nor would I have advocated, our entering into any agreement with Japan which would run counter to our principles or which would be made at the ultimate expense of any friendly country.

It was our conviction that in the late summer and autumn of 1941 a unique opportunity was presented to the United States to safeguard our vital national interests in the Far East, as outlined by the President, without sacrifice of principle or at the ultimate expense of any friendly country, and without incurring war with Japan. The term "any friendly country" refers chiefly to China and calls to mind the frequent statement by American speakers and in the American press, that whatever happens "we must not sell China down the river." This thought is implicit in Mr. Hull's four principles [13] which were accepted by Prince Konoye in principle as a basis for a settlement between Japan and the United States in September, 1941. Indeed, far from being to the detriment of the Chinese Republic, the type of agreement with the Japanese which we in the Embassy visualized and believed possible and practicable would not only have been of immediate benefit to the Chinese but would, in the opinion of the Embassy, have been a long step on the road to the eventual rectification of the manifold injuries inflicted upon China by Japan.

History will determine whether this opportunity was missed by an attempt to achieve at once our long-range objectives, an utter impossibility under the circumstances then obtaining, at the expense of the immediately vital and essential interests of our country. There is indeed tragic truth in the old proverb, "The better is the enemy of the good."

JAPAN'S POSITION IN 1941

In the late summer and autumn of 1941 the strong policy of the United States toward Japan in meeting every aggressive

[13] *Infra*, p. 1326.

move by Japan with a countervailing measure of our own, culminating in our freezing order of July 26, in conjunction with the impact of other developments abroad, had rendered the political soil of Japan fertile for the sowing of new seeds. Japan's efforts to conquer China by force of arms had reached virtually a stalemate; her economic situation and future economic outlook were becoming progressively and rapidly hopeless; her people were dispirited and war-weary; the reputation of her armed forces was in eclipse; evidence of their failure or of their comparative incapacity to succeed in China was obvious. Mr. Matsuoka, the Foreign Minister who had been active in leading Japan into the alliance with the Axis, was discredited and forced to retire from the Government on July 16, 1941.

Under these circumstances, Japan was faced with two alternatives. One road pointed to an all-out, do-or-die attempt on the part of her armed forces to render their country impervious to foreign economic pressure by spreading to the south and by conquering and permanently controlling those areas which were capable of supplying the necessities of life but of which Japan was being partially or wholly deprived through foreign pressure, notably oil, rubber, tin and adequate foodstuffs. The other road pointed toward a peaceful adjustment of the whole Far Eastern problem by which, through a peace settlement with China, to be effected by negotiations initiated through the good offices of the United States, and through economic settlements with the United States, Great Britain, the Netherlands East Indies and other nations having possessions in East Asia, Japan would be assured *inter alia* of a free flow of trade and commerce and of free access to raw materials on a basis of equality in commercial opportunity, thus serving her future safety, prosperity, and well-being. The necessity of choosing between a program of war and a program of peace, and of achieving success in whichever program might be selected, was urgent and inescapable.

During this critical period the Embassy, which was in close touch with the highest responsible Japanese leaders, made clear in repeated telegrams to Washington the following considerations: [14] the political soil in Japan was for the first time in ten years ripe for the sowing of new seeds which should be planted with constructive wisdom; we believed that Prince Konoye was in a position to carry the country with him in a program of peace and was prepared to enter commitments with our Government which would ensure, eventually if not immediately, an adjustment of the whole Far Eastern problem in conformity with the four principles laid down by Mr. Hull as the basis for such an adjustment and for the rehabilitation of Japan's relations with the United States; we believed, for reasons hereinafter presented, that this problem could never be solved by formulas drawn up in the exploratory conversations; we believed that it could and would be solved if the proposed meeting between Prince Konoye and the President should take place; in his efforts Prince Konoye needed positive encouragement by the American Government, especially certain steps recommended by the Embassy, to facilitate the immensely difficult problem with which he was faced in meeting dissident elements in his own country; Prince Konoye's name was associated with many of Japan's past misdeeds,[15] but he was the only Japanese statesman then capable of reversing the engine, and this, we believed, he tried to do, his efforts being born of dire necessity; at the same time, while endeavoring to find a way out of the crisis by negotiation and compromise, Japan was preparing a program of war in case the peace program should fail, and in the event of failure it was virtually certain that the Japanese armed forces would take control and would go all-out in a do-or-die attempt to conquer the entire area of Greater East Asia including the South Seas.

This is essentially a survey requiring intensive study by the historians at a time in future when war passions shall have

---

[14] See, for instance, *Foreign Relations, Japan: 1931–41*, II, 565, 603–4, 645–50.

[15] Feis has written in *The Road to Pearl Harbor*, pp. 282–83, of Konoye, that as "Prime Minister (in 1937) he was responsible before the Emperor for the war in China, even though the Army had run its own course; and as Prime Minister (in 1941) he was responsible before the Emperor for the program adopted on September 6. The past had him by the heels."

abated and when this whole tragic subject can be examined objectively, impartially, and in proper perspective.

The Point of View of This Discussion

The fact should be emphasized that, while fully realizing that the world situation as a whole, covering the five continents and seven seas, must be viewed as a single problem, we in the Embassy approached this subject from the angle of our observation post in Japan. Having long been out of close contact with Washington, I could not and did not presume to claim a comprehensive and intimate perception of the whole international picture resulting from current developments in the war in the West as that picture may have been viewed by the Administration. What I did claim was a comprehensive and intimate perception of the situation in the Far East, derived from nearly ten years of official residence in Japan, and it was the development of that picture that we in the Embassy endeavored to paint clearly and precisely to the Administration in Washington, from month to month, from week to week, and from day to day, during the progressively critical period leading up to the outbreak of war between the United States and Japan.

A second point should be clarified, namely, that the responsibility for the progressive deterioration in our relations, culminating in the outbreak of war, rested squarely upon Japan. Whatever efforts may have been made by successive Japanese Governments since the invasion of Manchuria in 1931 and the commencement of hostilities with China in 1937 to stem the intermittent tide of aggression by the armed forces of the country, these efforts proved futile.

Japan's So-called "Monroe Doctrine"

The Japanese in the years prior to the outbreak of war had invoked a so-called "Monroe Doctrine" for Japan; [16] yet between such a doctrine and our own Monroe Doctrine, as we

16 *Supra,* pp. 957–62.

have interpreted and applied it uniformly since 1823, there was no more resemblance than between black and white. As pointed out by our Government, our Monroe Doctrine contemplates only steps for our physical safety, while the Monroe Doctrine as practiced by Japan was seemingly applicable to all other purposes, economic, social and political, and had implicit in it a doctrine of expansion. Japan in 1931 had applied her Monroe Doctrine to Manchuria and then to China, and had finally indicated that it related economically to Greater East Asia including the South Seas, implying the assumption of leadership and special influence in the Eastern Hemisphere without limitation as to functions or purposes, while the United States and other western countries were to be denied equality of trade and industrial opportunity in every Chinese port. Japan herself had demanded equality of trade opportunities in every part of the world, yet had undertaken to spread herself out over the huge Republic of China and had indicated, at least in the press and in articles and speeches by prominent men, that she would not be content unless she extended herself three thousand miles beyond, to embrace the great archipelago comprising the East Indies, evidently with a view to shutting out all equality of trade opportunity among nations.

American Objectives

The attitude and measures of the Government of the United States during the critical period under discussion were based primarily upon the objective of ensuring the maintenance of our lawful rights and legitimate interests in the Far East; the maintenance of the principles of general equality of opportunity in terms of nondiscriminatory treatment and fair play; respect for national sovereignties everywhere and the abandonment of aggression by force; respect for treaties and for the maintenance of the territorial and administrative integrity of China under the mutual commitments freely entered into by Japan in the Washington treaties of 1922. We sought no new territory nor special privileges, nor did we seek in any way whatsoever to curb the legitimate rights and interests of the Japanese Empire. It was indeed highly in our own interests that Japan should remain a strong, prosperous and productive country under conditions of peace, justice, stability and security, and that our mutual trade and other relations should flourish in the future as they had in the past. At the same time we earnestly sought and worked for the maintenance of peace between our two countries as well as for a return to conditions of peace throughout East Asia. The allegations in the Japanese press and in frequent bellicose speeches and articles by Japanese throughout this period that the position and measures of the United States were based upon imperialistic ambitions and upon a desire and intention to thwart Japan in the pursuance of her own legitimate rights and interests were wholly childish and untenable. In Japan's conception of a "new order in Greater East Asia" and a "co-prosperity sphere" there was no room for a continuance of the legitimate rights and interests of the United States or of any other western power. The war guilt rested squarely and exclusively upon Japan.

On the other side of the picture the fact should be recognized, although in no respect by way of condonement, that Japan over the years had been forced to submit to many harsh and hard discriminatory obstacles to its trade, shipping, investment and migration.

Diplomacy and Constructive Conciliation

A third point should furthermore be clarified. There are those who are inclined to regard the efforts of diplomacy as so-called appeasement. Appeasement is an unfortunate and much overused and ill-used term. It seems inevitably to have become closely associated with Munich, and considering the aftermath of Munich it is perhaps not surprising that any term associated with that fiasco must necessarily be tainted in the public mind. But let us not forget that diplomacy is essentially our first line of national defense, while our Navy is but the second line and our Army, let us hope, only the third line. If the first line, diplomacy, is successful, those other reserve lines need not be called into action, and it is the first line that must bear the responsibility for avoiding the necessity of ever using those reserves. Elihu Root said that the main object of diplomacy was "to keep the country out of trouble . . . in the right way." [17]

A better and more accurate term to describe the efforts of diplomacy is "constructive conciliation," and that word "constructive" is important. It connotes building, and no one is going to be foolish enough to try to build any structure, if it is to be a permanent structure, on an insecure foundation. The foundation for any international building must rest on certain basic principles in international dealing, and with those principles there should be no compromise. *Methods* of building, however, may be flexible. Some degree of flexibility, without sacrificing any point of principle, was we felt, needed in dealing with Japan during the critical period under reference.

THE FAR EASTERN PROBLEM AS RELATED TO THE EUROPEAN WAR

It was our view in the Embassy in Tokyo that the current war would bring finally and conclusively to an end an era which had its beginnings in the industrial revolution or possibly earlier. How the world would be reconstituted, internally within each country and as a community of nations, would depend on the outcome of the war. When the war was finally won by the democracies, an eventuality of which I had not the slightest doubt, we believed it was certain that there would be no slavish reversion to the economic and political concepts of an epoch which would have gone forever. In all probability there would, we felt, be a pooling, in some form, of the sovereignty of the individual nations to the extent that their security and welfare would demand, for the irresistible logic of facts had again proved that national isolation is no longer a political reality. In these circumstances, and having in view the im-

[17] From Philip C. Jessup, *Elihu Root* (New York: Dodd, Mead & Co., 1938), II, 4.

measurably grave consequences of a defeat for the democracies, it seemed to us of the highest importance that, once the war in Europe had broken out, our primary objective in the Far East should have been to diminish, so far as it was possible, consistently with American security and honor and the principles to which we were committed, the creation of obstacles to the ultimate victory of those democracies having a common interest in the defeat of the one nation sufficiently powerful to threaten the world with domination, namely, Germany. The Japanese people had become thoroughly dispirited over the failure, notwithstanding years of effort, to conquer China — claimed by Japan and admitted by her friends to be militarily a backward nation — while Japan's economic position had sadly deteriorated, and her own allies had shown themselves to be thoroughly untrustworthy. A unique opportunity then presented itself, we believed, not only to promote an end to the China conflict and to employ the substantial resources of both China and Japan in the war effort of the democracies against Germany, but also to diminish the chances of Japan's adding her weight to that of Germany.

If a permanent stabilization of the Far East in conformity with our principles could not be found during the period of the European war, such stabilization would have been automatically a concomitant of eventual victory by the democracies, or it could have been achieved thereafter by force when the resources of the democracies could have been concentrated exclusively on that effort. The outcome of the war in Europe was bound to determine, for as long as it was possible to foresee, the conditions under which men were to live, and it was for that reason that I conceived the opportunity presented in Japan in 1941 as a challenge to the utmost in foresight, imagination, and statesmanship. It was significant that Japan chose to declare war against the democracies, not when victory seemed to be in Germany's grasp but when that eventuality appeared to be more remote than at any other time since the war in Europe began.

APPEASEMENT ABSENT FROM OUR RECOMMENDATIONS

We in the Embassy did not favor a course of so-called appeasement toward Japan. For several years we had pointed out, objectively, the fact that the imposition of economic sanctions against Japan would start American-Japanese relations on a downward course which might eventually end in war, and that such sanctions would never, in themselves, bring about the collapse of Japan. But as time went on and Japan's encroachments against American interests in the Far East increased, we made clear our opinion, especially in telegram No. 827, September 12, 9 P.M., 1940, that the question at issue was not whether we must take steps to call a halt to the expansionist moves of Japan, but when. Furthermore be it recorded that my speech before the America-Japan Society in Tokyo on October 19, 1939,[18] shortly after returning from leave of absence in the United States, was prepared and delivered on my own initiative. The phrase "straight from the horse's mouth" was used because I was at that moment in a position to express directly the views of the American Administration which had been consulted in Washington, and the Department had been helpful in drafting certain passages; but the speech as a whole was written by me on the voyage back to Japan and the plan for its preparation and delivery had originated in my own mind as a result of a summer of careful thought in the peaceful surroundings and atmosphere of the hills of New Hampshire. The delivery of the speech, from which any thought of appeasement was markedly absent, created something of a sensation in Japan, but its net result was at that time considered by prominent Japanese to have been constructive and helpful. There was not a shadow of doubt that the time had come for a strong policy by the United States in dealing with Japan, nor, in our opinion, was there a shadow of doubt that it was this policy, in conjunction with the impact upon Japan of other foreign developments, that brought temporarily to the top in Japan those elements favoring a policy of conciliation with the United States.

18 *Supra,* pp. 1211-21.

If by such (strong) action we can bring about the eventual discrediting of Japan's leaders, a regeneration of thought may ultimately take shape in this country, permitting the resumption of normal relations with the United States and leading to a readjustment of the whole Pacific problem.[19]

JAPAN'S WAR GUILT, CERTAINTY OF OUR ULTIMATE VICTORY

Adverting once again to the subject of war guilt, there can be no condemnation more categorically unqualified and emphatic than the condemnation by my staff and myself of the depredations of the armed forces of Japan during those ten years. It will be difficult in future ever to forget or to forgive the invasion of Manchuria and other portions of China and Indochina, the rape of Nanking, the sinking of the *Panay*, the continual and obviously intentional bombing by Japanese planes of our missions and other property in China, or the truculent interference by Japanese authorities with our manifold and long-established interests — religious, cultural, educational, medical, financial, industrial, commercial — throughout that entire area, these various and widespread depredations culminating in the dastardly and unprovoked attack on Pearl Harbor on December 7, 1941, while the conversations between our two Governments were still in progress. We returned to our country to take whatever part we might properly be called upon or find opportunity to take toward contributing to the certain ultimate victory of the United States in the war of the nations, and with the firm conviction that in spite of initial successes by the Axis Powers, a terrible reckoning in the eventual defeat of those powers was as mathematically certain as was the law of gravity. For her own good, for the future safety and welfare of the United States, and for the future security and welfare of world civilization, we believed that Japan must be overwhelmingly beaten, for only thus could her armed

[19] From the "green light" telegram of September 12, 1940, the full text of which is given *supra*, pp. 1224–29.

forces, her military machine and system, be wholly discredited and liquidated, and the Japanese nation be turned permanently into paths of peace. However long this process might take, however much it might involve American "blood, sweat and tears," there must be no relinquishing of this essential task until it was finally and effectively completed. There was not room in the Pacific area for a peaceful America and a swashbuckling Japan.

Our Reports

My duties as Ambassador, as in the case of all diplomatic envoys, involved *inter alia* periodic reporting and interpreting to my Government of the political situation as it developed. In spite of serious difficulties in the way of submitting accurate reports, due to the chauvinistic and suspicious attitude of the Japanese authorities toward all foreigners which had set in during the final period of my mission, thus greatly restricting our reliable Japanese sources of information so that at times we were left groping in the dark, the fact remains that certain sources of information of unquestioned reliability were still available to us up to the end.

In the course of our reporting, recommendations toward shaping the course of United States policy were continually submitted, but those recommendations in connection with the outstanding issues during the final months were largely ignored, or at least discarded, by our Government.

Lack of Close Co-ordination with Washington

During this critical period it is regrettable that the Administration in Washington, subsequent to the President's letter to me of January 21, 1941, hereinbefore mentioned, gave me little or no information as to its thoughts and intentions, and no information whatever, save in a few comparatively unimportant instances, as to the confidential intelligence and advice which must have been flowing in to Washington from various sources other than the Embassy and upon which the course of our Government appears to have been based. Furthermore, little or no reaction was received from Washington by way of comment on our periodic reports. Our telegrams, save when specific instructions were asked, seldom brought response; they were rarely even referred to, and reporting to our Government was like throwing pebbles into a lake at night; we were not permitted to see even the ripples. For all we knew, our telegrams had not in any degree carried conviction. Obviously I could only assume that our recommendations were not welcome; yet we continued to express our carefully considered judgment on the developing situation.

In contrast, my British colleague, with whom I maintained the closest touch and whose helpful collaboration during this difficult period I highly valued, received from his Government prompt reaction to his reports and recommendations, stating whether London agreed with him or not, and if not, why not; while the policy, thoughts, intentions and information of his Government, much of which information he was good enough to communicate in confidence to me, were continually made clear to him. Furthermore, Sir Robert Craigie passed on to me confidential and important information emanating from my own Government through the British Ambassador in Washington, information of which I was deprived by direct communication.

This situation proved so heavy a handicap to our work in Tokyo that on July 10, 1941, I sent the following telegram to the Acting Secretary, Sumner Welles, explaining the great disadvantage to us of being deprived of the prompt confidences of our Government and of the current intelligence in its possession:

On July 9 I was shown by Sir Robert Craigie a "most secret" cablegram from Lord Halifax giving a detailed report of what purported to be the enlightening and important talk which he had had with you on July 3 and an equally important report on a conversation between the Director of Naval Intelligence in

Washington and the British Naval Attaché. It is my very strong feeling that I should have been promptly informed by the Department of the information revealed in the conversations under reference.

Please remember that in Tokyo few of our Japanese friends now dare come to see us at the Embassy or to meet us elsewhere and that many of them have received warnings from the police to keep away from us. It is now exceedingly difficult to know what is going on behind the scenes in Japan and we are often groping and fumbling in the dark. The appraisal of developments and situations in Japan is of course one of my fundamental duties, and yet in the case of many issues which I am asked to appraise or deal with here I am deprived of clues and intelligence pertinent to those issues which are available in Washington. Sir Robert Craigie generally reports to me sooner or later the talks which Lord Halifax has with you or other high officials in the Department or the White House, but to learn the expressed views and information of my own Government from that source seems to me to be distinctly *infra dignitatem*. It should also be noted that such information when forwarded by pouch is seldom of more than academic value, especially in rapidly developing situations, because it arrives much too late to be of current use.

Without indicating my real discouragement at being deprived of the prompt confidences of Mr. Hull and yourself, I have emphasized the foregoing consideration in many former communications and in talks which I had with you in the Department two years ago. At that time I was told that it was not so much due to formulated policy as to inadequate machinery in the Department that we in the field were deprived of such prompt reports. If it is the inadequacy of departmental machinery that is responsible for this unfortunate situation I earnestly recommend that steps be taken to rectify it. If on the other hand this deprivation is due to a matter of policy, then I hope that you will explain my point of view fully to the President and let him know of the great discouragement and handicap with which I as his Ambassador am confronted. Unless a motor is hitting on all cylinders it cannot function effectively.

Mr. Welles' reply was received on July 19, a considerate message pointing out the Department's reluctance to entrust certain types of information to the cable or radio and indicating that, other things being equal, there was no intention to withhold from me prompt information of the most confidential nature.

The excessive caution of our Government against entrusting ultraconfidential information to our secret codes was in principle no doubt wise; yet if the British could place confidence in their ciphers, repeating their telegrams all over the world, it seems surprising that we ourselves were unable to do so in ours.[20] We had certain codes which we in the Embassy believed to be secure enough for even the most secret communications, codes that were used for all ultraconfidential communications with Washington. This belief was in effect confirmed to us by a friendly Japanese in high position, the Prime Minister, Prince Konoye, who warned us against entrusting certain types of information to any but our most secret codes, adding that according to his understanding we did possess "one code" which was unbreakable. We had little doubt that Prince Konoye was reflecting information received from the Japanese military police, and was passing it on to us in view of certain types of intelligence which it was not in his interest to have known to the police. I duly communicated this statement to the Department.

The exchange of telegrams with Mr. Welles was helpful only to the extent that from that moment the Department cabled me reports of important conversations between our Government and the Japanese Ambassador in Washington, and in a very few cases with other foreign envoys, instead of, as formerly, sending such reports by mail with a resultant delay of from one to two months, by which time the information was only of academic interest. Nevertheless, information as to the Administration's thoughts and intentions and its reactions to our

[20] In Tokyo during the months just before the outbreak of war Mr. Grew did not know that the United States Government had broken the Japanese code. See *Pearl Harbor Attack*, pt. 2, p. 563. For a discussion of the breaking of the Japanese code and the messages, "Magic Intercepts," which Washington was receiving, see Rauch, *Roosevelt from Munich to Pearl Harbor*.

own reports and to the developing political situation, save in a very few specific instances, continued to be withheld. We were given no clear conception whatever of the thoughts of our Government and its reaction to the rapidly moving political scene. I consequently felt very much out of touch with Washington during this critical period. I wish to make it clear, however, that such implications as may be drawn from the ensuing discussion are subject to a close and thorough understanding of the reliability of the information, and of the purposes, incentives or compulsions, which guided our Government, factors that were inadequately known to us in the Embassy. I wish, also, here to make clear the fact that until the end of August, 1941, I found myself in accord with the general course and measures of the Administration, as is revealed from time to time in our official correspondence as well as in my diary. In fact, I frequently wrote and spoke of my feeling of great pride in the Administration's conduct of our foreign affairs.

Possible Premises

Unless the course of our Government toward Japan was haphazard and undeliberated in advance, an untenable hypothesis, it appeared to have been based upon one of two premises, either:

(a) that Japan was bluffing, would eventually back down and would not fight; or

(b) that Japan's expansionist program, which she had no intention of abandoning, rendered war with the United States eventually inevitable.

There might logically have been an important difference in our national position and plans if predicated upon premise (a) rather than on premise (b).[21]

These two premises were of course open to various qualifica-

21 For a memorandum prepared in the Department of State, concerning the informal conversations between the United States and Japan, see *Foreign Relations, Japan: 1931–41*, II, 325–86.

tions. Premise (*b*) might be developed to include the thought that only through the discrediting of the armed forces of Japan by military defeat could they be permanently curbed in their plans for expansion by force, and that if we were to help Japan to extricate herself from the conflict in China through a patched-up peace, her armed forces would merely be given a breathing spell to reorganize and to prepare for further aggression at a later time. Yet even if the foregoing argument was sound, was it not, with time so clearly on our side in building up our armaments, in our national interest to stave off war as long as possible? In any case, it was not perceived that our Government's course, if it were not a haphazard course, could have been based upon any fundamental third alternative to those under (*a*) and (*b*) above — either the conviction that Japan would not fight or the conviction that she would fight. Obviously neither of the foregoing premises could be a matter of certainty, but the courses of governments are habitually formulated upon what they conceive, from the intelligence in their possession, to be reasonable probabilities, and it is those conceptions which inevitably influence, if they do not wholly control, the courses followed.

THE PREMISE THAT JAPAN WOULD NOT FIGHT

The Embassy was aware that at least one school of official thought in Washington maintained that it was altogether improbable, in the circumstances existing during the period under consideration, that Japan would deliberately take action in response to any action which the United States was likely to take in the Pacific which action if taken by Japan would mean war between that country and the United States. In the light of the attack on Pearl Harbor on December 7, 1941, the fallacy of this judgment was patent. The Embassy had no way of knowing whether or to what extent this theory was accepted by the Administration, nor is it within the province of this discussion to examine the arguments advanced within the Administration upon which the policy and course of the Administration were based. Nevertheless it is pertinent to stress the fact that in various telegrams to the Department the Embassy took issue with the foregoing thesis and expressed its opinion in no uncertain terms to the contrary. For example, in our telegram No. 1736, November 3, 3 P.M., I made clear our conviction that if the then Japanese Government should fail in its efforts to reach a settlement with the United States, Japan would go all-out in a do-or-die effort to render herself invulnerable to foreign economic pressure, even to the extent of committing national hara-kiri rather than cede to pressure from abroad; that it would be shortsighted on our part to predicate our policy on the speculative theory that Japan's preparations for war were only bluff, designed to reinforce Japan's diplomacy; that Japan was preparing a program of war in case her program of peace should fail; and that action by Japan which would render unavoidable armed conflict with the United States might come *with dangerous and dramatic suddenness.* This important telegram, be it noted, was despatched to Washington over a month before the outbreak of war. As the telegram presents a clear and concise statement of the Embassy's position and attitude at that time, a complete paraphrase is set forth below. It should be carefully studied in connection with the present discussion.

1. A full translation of a leading article which appeared in the *Nichi Nichi* on November 1 under the headline "Empire Approaches Its Greatest Crisis" was telegraphed in full on November 1. This article preceded a news despatch from New York which summarized statements said to have been made to the *New York Times* by a member of the Japanese Embassy at Washington concerning the necessity for bringing the economic war between Japan and the United States to an end. The article in question and the editorial in the same newspaper, which also was telegraphed to the Department in full, are typical of the present atmosphere in Japan as sensed by the Embassy.

2. I have nothing to add to the evaluation of the various factors which are instrumental in determining the policy of Japan as set forth in the Embassy's telegrams during recent months, nor

do I perceive any reason for altering in any important aspect the views expressed therein. The present position of Japan can, I believe, best be understood by setting forth the following considerations which seem to bear directly on the development of the present situation:

(a) It is impossible for Japan to dissociate either herself or the China Incident from either the War in Europe or the varying phases of that war.

(b) In contrast to public opinion in democratic countries where there is a uniform set of principles which guide or affect foreign policy and where differences of views are more apt to relate to questions of means rather than of basic principles, in Japan where political development runs from liberalism to medievalism public opinion is a variable element and at any particular moment there is predominant only that body of opinion which has come to the surface as a result of the impact of developments outside of Japan. The victories of Germany in western Europe last year had the effect of bringing into power pro-Axis elements in Japan. The inability of Germany to launch an invasion against England, which gave rise to uncertainty as to an ultimate German victory, was among the various factors which tended to strengthen the hands of the more moderate elements in Japan; while the German assault on the Soviet, which abolished the basis of normal relations and peace between Germany and the Soviet Union, brought with it the realization that the political leaders who had led Japan into the Tripartite Pact had been guilty of misleading the country.

(c) The endeavors of the previous Cabinet of Prince Konoye, which the Tojo government apparently intends to continue, to bring about an adjustment of relations with the United States and thus afford a possibility of putting an end to the China conflict constitute an attempt to undo the errors of the previous year. Should these endeavors fail of their purpose and should German military successes continue, I anticipate that Japan will definitely align herself more closely with the Axis Powers.

(d) We have never shared the view of certain outstanding economists that the deterioration of Japan's economic and financial resources would within a short time cause Japan as a militaristic power to collapse, in view of the fact that predictions of this nature rested on the unconscious assumption that Japan would under any circumstances seek to retain her capitalistic system. The prediction contained in these forecasts has not come about in spite of the fact that Japan has lost the greater part of her trade and has suffered a severe drain on her natural resources and a drastic reduction of her industrial production. Indeed, to the contrary, the program of consolidating and of integrating Japan's national economy, without which the anticipated collapse might well have come about, is being carried forward with great vigor. Up to the present the facts have failed to support the view that Far Eastern conflict can best be avoided by the continued imposition of embargoes on trade and, as has been suggested, by the blockading of Japan.

3. At this juncture I venture to draw the Department's attention to the Embassy's telegram No. 827, September 12, 9 P.M., 1940, which was despatched under circumstances and at a moment when measures of conciliation on the part of the Government of the United States appeared to be not only inadvisable but useless. The adoption by the United States subsequently of the strong policy recommended in the telegram under reference, plus the effect on Japan of world political developments, as has previously been indicated, impelled the Government of Japan to seek an adjustment of its relations with the United States. In the event that these endeavors should fail of their purpose, in all probability Japan will revert once again to her previous position or go even further, leading to the adoption of what we have termed a "do-or-die" or "all-out" effort to make Japan invulnerable to foreign economic measures, even to the point of risking national suicide rather than yield to pressure from abroad. It is apparent to us who are in daily contact with the sentiment here that such an eventuality is not only a possibility but a probability.

4. In view of the national temperament and character of the Japanese people, the hypothesis that the imposition of progressive measures of economic pressure while involving some risk of armed conflict may probably avert such a conflict, is a perilously unsure basis upon which to predicate the policy of the United States. It is our belief that war would not be averted by the adoption of such measures. However, the conflicting views on this question constitute no more than opinion and we therefore

hold the view that it would not be in conformity with American national interests to assume as a certainty the validity of either opinion and to base thereon a final policy since so to do would be to reverse cause and effect. The main question to be decided would seem to be whether or not the national interests, aims and policies of the United States are such as to justify a war with Japan should diplomacy, the first line of national defense, fail, for only in conformity with a decision of this character could the Government of the United States pursue a course of policy devoid, in so far as possible, of uncertainty, hypothesis and opinion. I have no doubt that the decision in question, which might well be irrevocable, has already been considered in its entirety and reached, for the sands are running fast.

5. I trust that the Department will realize that as, in touching on a subject of such momentous gravity, I am not conversant with the views and intentions of the Administration on the subject, I have no thought whatsoever of implying that the Administration is following an unconsidered policy, nor is it my desire in any way to suggest either the adoption of a policy of so-called appeasement on the part of the United States or that we should depart in the slightest degree from the basic principles which our Government has set forth as the only foundation for our relations with foreign countries, including those with Japan. While means may be flexible, there must be no compromise with principles. *My only purpose is to make sure that my country does not become involved in war with Japan as* a result of any possible misunderstanding of the ability or readiness of this country to plunge into a suicidal war with the United States.* Such action on the part of Japan would be contrary to dictates of national reason, but our standards of reason cannot be applied to the Japanese. There is no necessity for us to become unduly anxious at the present warlike tone of the press in Japan which has in past years assailed the United States in successive degrees of intensity, but it would be lacking in perspicacity to disregard or underestimate the fact that Japan is clearly preparing for war in the event that her alternative program of peace should not succeed. It would likewise be shortsighted on our part to predicate our policy on the view that these warlike preparations are nothing more than bluff designed to supplement Japa-

nese diplomacy. Action by Japan which might render unavoidable an armed conflict with the United States may come with dangerous and dramatic suddenness.[22]

WARNINGS BY THE EMBASSY

As further indications of the warnings continually conveyed to the Administration by the Embassy, certain paraphrased excerpts from our telegrams from month to month are likewise cited below, as well as certain excerpts from my diary, a copy of which was sent regularly to a Stanley Hornbeck, Chief of the Division of Far Eastern Affairs, with expressed authority to communicate in his discretion to any other officials in Washington any information contained therein which might be regarded as of interest or as helpful to those officials. While the diary was in no respect an official document, and while it frequently contained comment, as do all diaries, based on the thoughts and information only of the moment, a copy was habitually sent to Dr. Hornbeck every month by pouch in the belief that all intelligence, even from unofficial source material, might be of value to those concerned with the shaping of the policy of our Government. That the diary was regularly and carefully read by Dr. Hornbeck was evinced by his acknowledging the receipt of each monthly batch with incisive comment on various points raised therein, and he frequently alluded to its helpfulness.

The underlining in the following passages written in 1941 was not originally included and has been inserted by the writer.

[22] The substance of the Embassy's telegram of November 3, 1941, is given in *Foreign Relations, Japan: 1931–41*, II, 701–4. In *The Road to Pearl Harbor*, p. 298, Herbert Feis has written that the "incoming reports from Grew were somber and his diary even more so. War, they said, was near unless the American government granted a reprieve by relaxing economic restraints. His message carrying the surest forecast was that of November 3. . . .

"It was hard for Grew, a person of buoyant belief that any situation could be straightened out if the try was hard enough, to admit that this one could not be. There was regret, even reproach, between the lines of this cable of November 3, of which later he wrote in his diary, 'I hope that history will not overlook this telegram.' "

JANUARY

There is a lot of talk around town to the effect that the Japanese, in case of a break with the United States, are planning to go all-out *in a surprise mass attack on Pearl Harbor.* I rather guess that the boys in Hawaii are not precisely asleep.[23]

FEBRUARY

Apparently the conservative elements in the army and navy counsel delaying any action against Singapore until the European situation is favorable, and yet it must be remembered that *the reckless do-or-die spirit of the military extremists may force the issue* before Great Britain or the United States could or would intervene.[24]

MAY

A progressive deterioration of relations between the United States and Japan *eventually leading to war* might well be the alternative (to the successful conclusion of the current conversations). The risk of failure would appear to be more than offset by the possibility if not the probability of success.[25]

JUNE

On the one hand I feel that either the Cabinet would fall or moderate and restraining influences would prevail if an attack on the (Netherlands East) Indies were surely subject to exhaustive calculation and careful deliberation by the Cabinet, but on the other hand we should not forget that as in the case of the invasion of Manchuria in 1931 *the Japanese Army is capable of sudden and surprise action . . .* and *we*

[23] From the diary, January 27, 1941.
[24] *Ibid.,* February 7, 1941, and telegram No. 180 of the same date to the Department of State.
[25] From telegram No. 743 of May 27, 1941, to the Department of State.

should therefore be ready for all eventualities. For the present I believe it highly unlikely that anything more than high-pressure diplomacy will be exerted on the Netherlands East Indies, but we should keep constantly in mind the foregoing considerations *and be prepared for any and all developments however unexpected.*[26]

JULY

We and the British, who also seem to have done with so-called appeasement, immediately met the move into Indo-China with retaliatory steps, and Japan responded in kind. The vicious circle of reprisals and counterreprisals is on. *Facilis descensus Averno.* Unless radical surprises occur in the world, it is difficult to see how the momentum of this downgrade movement in our relations can be arrested, nor how far it will go. *The obvious conclusion is eventual war.*[27]

It seems to me preposterous to believe that while still deeply involved in China Japan will undertake another major war on the Asiatic continent unless or until there is evidence of a collapse of the Soviet regime. . . . (but) *It is also always possible that the war may be extended to the Pacific* through Japan's interpretation of her common interests with Germany, although I know of no evidence to support the view that Japan will risk war with the United States unless she sees no other way of terminating the China conflict or carrying out what she conceives to be her honorable commitments under the Tripartite Pact.[28]

We must not allow any possible misconception by the Japanese as to our determination to take decisive action in certain circumstances let Japanese-American relations *proceed one step further on the road to potential war.*[29]

26 From the diary, June 10, 1941.
27 *Ibid.,* July, 1941.
28 *Ibid.,* July 17, 1941, and a telegram to the Department of State of the same date.
29 From the diary, July 22, 1941, and reported by cable to the Department of State on or about July 22, 1941.

AUGUST

... to halt the present growing momentum toward *a head-on collision* between the United States and Japan. ...

And finally it is almost mathematically certain that we must be prepared to accept the thought that if the proposed meeting between the President and Prince Konoye, which is an outstanding and very likely final effort on the part of the Japanese Government, should not take place, the alternative would be a reconstitution of the present Government or a formation of a new Government for the purpose of confiding Japan's future destiny to the armed forces for a do-or-die all-out attempt to establish the hegemony of Japan over all Greater East Asia, which would *carry with it the inevitability of war with the United States.*[30]

While in Japan there are groups who are entirely cognizant of the perilous possibilities inherent in the present positions and who are ready to make far-reaching efforts in an endeavor to avoid an armed clash with the United States, the possibility that the constructive statesmen of Japan will be able to counteract the increasing psychology of desperation is at present diminishing daily. Traditionally in this country *a national psychology of desperation develops into a determination to risk all.* ...

From the vantage point of this Embassy it appears that time is the essential factor if the Government of the United States still is willing to give consideration to a Japanese approach. There are events in process of development which if not forestalled in the very near future *might do away with the only remaining hope, however faint, of keeping war out of the Far East.*[31]

SEPTEMBER

If an adjustment of relations is to be achieved, some risk must be run, but the risk taken in pursuance on our part of

[30] From telegram No. 1271 of August 19, 1941, to the Department of State.
[31] From telegram No. 1319, August 27, 1941, to the Department of State.

a course which would not only provide inducements to the Japanese to honor their undertakings but would also leave to the United States Government a certain leverage of compulsion would appear to be relatively less serious than *the risk of armed conflict* entailed in the progressive application of economic sanctions which would result from a refusal to accept these proposals.[32]

I firmly believe that the opportunity is now presented to halt that program without war or the immediate risk of war, *and that we shall be confronted with the greatly augmented risk of war if the present opportunity fails us. . . .*

[And] a situation might well be created through measures of reprisal and counterreprisal in which *it would be very difficult to avoid war.*

Unless we are ready to impose a reasonable degree of confidence in the sincerity of intention and the professed good faith of the Prime Minister and his supporters in Japan to mold the future policy of the country on the fundamental principles *which they have expressed their readiness to accept,* and to carry out measures by which those principles shall be loyally if gradually implemented, I do not believe that we shall be successful in creating a new turn of thought in this country which will justify the hope of a general improvement in Japan's relations with the United States *and of the avoidance of eventual war in the Pacific.*[33]

OCTOBER

Why on earth should we rush headlong into war? When Hitler is defeated, as he eventually will be, the Japanese problem will solve itself.[34]

NOVEMBER

In the event that these endeavors should fail of their purpose, in all probability Japan will revert once again to its previous

[32] From telegram No. 1405, September 5, 1941, to the Department of State, printed in *Foreign Relations, Japan: 1931–41,* II, 600–3.

[33] From the paraphrase of telegram No. 1529, September 29, 1941, to the Department of State, the substance of which is printed in *ibid.,* pp. 645–50.

[34] From the diary, October 19, 1941.

position or go even further, leading to the adoption of what we have termed an "all-out, do-or-die" effort to make Japan invulnerable to foreign economic measures, even to the point of risking national hara-kiri rather than yield to pressure from abroad. It is apparent to us who are in daily contact with the sentiment here that such an eventuality is not only a possibility *but a probability*. . . .

[The] hypothesis that the imposition of progressive measures of economic pressure while involving some risk of armed conflict may probably avert such a conflict is a perilously unsure basis upon which to predicate the policy of the United States. *It is our belief that war would not be averted by the adoption of such measures*. . . . The main question to be decided would seem to be whether or not the national interests, aims and policies of the United States are such as to justify a war with Japan should diplomacy, the first line of national defense, fail, for only in conformity with a decision of this character could the Government of the United States pursue a course of policy devoid, in so far as possible, of uncertainty, hypothesis and opinion. I have no doubt that the decision in question, which might well be irrevocable, has already been considered in its entirety and reached, *for the sands are running fast*. . . .

My only purpose is to make sure that my country does not become involved in hostilities with Japan as a result of any possible misunderstanding *of the ability or readiness of this country (Japan) to plunge into a suicidal war with the United States*. . . .

It would be shortsighted on our part to predicate our policy on the view that these warlike preparations are nothing more than bluff designed to reinforce Japanese diplomacy. Action by this country which might render unavoidable an armed conflict with the United States may come *with dangerous and dramatic suddenness*.[35]

[35] From the Embassy's telegram of November 3, 1941, printed in *Foreign Relations, Japan: 1931–41*, II, 701–4. On November 17 Mr. Grew telegraphed the Department of State, as printed in *ibid*., pp. 743–44: "The Ambassador, referring to his previous telegram No. 1736 of November 3, 3 P.M., final sentence, emphasizes the need to guard against sudden Japanese naval or military actions in such areas as are not now involved in the Chinese theater of operations. He

It should be noted that the foregoing excerpts are far from a complete record of the warnings submitted by the Embassy. At the moment of the outbreak of war, all confidential cor-

is taking into account, therefore, the probability of the Japanese exploiting every possible tactical advantage, such as surprise and initiative. He advises his Government accordingly of the importance of not placing the major responsibility in giving prior warning upon the Embassy staff, the naval and military attachés included, since in Japan there is extremely effective control over both primary and secondary military information. The Embassy would not expect to obtain any information in advance either from personal Japanese contacts or through the press; the observation of military movements is not possible by the few Americans remaining in the country, concentrated mostly in three cities (Tokyo, Yokohama, Kobe); and with American and other foreign shipping absent from adjacent waters the Japanese are assured of the ability to send without foreign observation their troop transports in various directions. Japanese troop concentrations were reported recently by American consuls in Manchuria and Formosa, while troop dispositions since last July's general mobilization have, according to all other indications available, been made with a view to enabling the carrying out of new operations on the shortest possible notice either in the Pacific southwest or in Siberia or in both.

"The Ambassador expresses the Embassy's full realization that the present most important duty perhaps is to detect any premonitory signs of naval or military operations likely in areas mentioned above and states that every precaution is being taken to guard against surprise. He adds that the Embassy's field of naval or military observation is restricted almost literally to what could be seen with the naked eye, and this is negligible. Therefore, the United States Government is advised, from an abundance of caution, to discount as much as possible the likelihood of the Embassy's ability to give substantial warning."

Before the Congressional Committee investigating the Japanese attack at Pearl Harbor, the following statements were made: "Mr. GREW. I said in that telegram: 'In emphasizing need for guarding against sudden military or naval actions by Japan in areas not at present involved in the China conflict I am taking into account as a probability that the Japanese would exploit all available tactical advantages, including those of initiative and surprise.'

"I think that is the passage that you have in mind.

"Senator FERGUSON. So you think that that more nearly conveys the idea that they may strike without a declaration of war?

"Mr. GREW. Very definitely.

"Senator FERGUSON. And you had in mind what they had done at Port Arthur?

"Mr. GREW. I think that word 'surprise' comprises that thought.

"Senator FERGUSON. And you conveyed that to our Government on the 17th of November?

"Mr. GREW. I did, sir.

"Senator FERGUSON. Do you think that that strengthened your former message of November 3?

respondence in Tokyo, including copies of confidential telegrams, was immediately destroyed, so that only these few passages quoted above were included in my diary and are immediately available to me. The foregoing passages, however, appear to be adequate to indicate the estimate of the Embassy as to the probability of a Japanese attack under certain given circumstances — "with dangerous and dramatic suddenness" — estimates which were before our Government when shaping its course toward Japan. In the light of these appraisals by its official representatives on the spot, it would appear to be an untenable hypothesis that the Administration could have continued to formulate its course on the premise that Japan was bluffing and would not fight unless those appraisals by the American Ambassador, who had been sent to Japan for the purpose of keeping his Government accurately informed, were regarded as unsound and discarded.

The Premise that Japan Would Fight

I now turn to the second premise upon which the course of our Government may have been based, namely, that Japan's expansionist program, which she had no intention of abandoning, rendered war with the United States eventually inevitable.

"We are satisfied in our own minds," Colonel Frank Knox, Secretary of the Navy, was quoted in the evening edition of the *Japan Times and Advertiser* of October 25, 1941, as having stated that *"the Japanese have no intention of giving up their plans for expansion,"* adding, "If they pursue that course, *collision there is inevitable."* Such a public statement by a prominent member of the American Cabinet, if correctly reported, would appear to indicate that our Government's course was being definitely shaped on the basis of premise (*b*).

From documentary evidence, for instance, the confidential memorandum of the Department of State of April 18, 1941, the

"Mr. Grew. I think it supplemented it.

"Senator Ferguson. Supplemented it. You felt that you were conveying this knowledge that you had to the Government in as direct language as you could?

"Mr. Grew. That is correct." See *Pearl Harbor Attack*, pt. 2, p. 683.

Embassy was aware that one school of official thought within the Administration in Washington held that the first essential toward renunciation of an objective of conquest by force was the development within the nation which cherished that objective of a real conviction of the futility of the effort which it was making, and that this could be brought about only on the basis of evidence of failure or of comparative incapacity to succeed. It was furthermore held that as is the case with Germany, Japan's program of imperialistic expansion (which had long been cherished and which had been projected to extend far into the future) would not suddenly be abandoned by Japan; and Japan's militant leaders would continue to take advantage of every opportunity which developed for a further advance by Japan — until Japan's militant leadership had been shown to its own people to be not possessed of the capacity to take and to hold.

It was our belief that the Emperor, the Government of Prince Konoye and the militant leaders of Japan (the leaders then in control) had come to accept the status of the four-year unsuccessful conflict in China, in conjunction with our freezing measures and of Japan's economic condition, as evidence of failure or of comparative incapacity to succeed, and while this opinion was not susceptible of proof, concrete evidence in support of this opinion appears in the memoranda hereinafter set forth of conversations with the highest officials of the country, notably my conversation with Prince Konoye himself on September 6.

The Embassy could not escape the impression that the view expressed as to the improbability that any action by the United States in the Pacific would lead to counteraction by Japan which would mean war between our two countries, and the view expressed immediately above that Japan would not in the near future abandon in any sense whatever her existing doctrine of military conquest by force, were by implication contradictory and mutually irreconcilable.

Efforts of Japan to Effect a New
Orientation of Policy

I revert at this point to the discussion of the basic issues between the United States and Japan which were raised by the actions of Japan during a term of years. No one who was so close to the ground as I was during those critical years, and who was daily presented with incontrovertible evidence of calculated implementation of a policy so sinister as that of Japan's militarists, could ever entertain any view other than that "the war guilt must rest and does rest exclusively upon Japan." The objective and impartial historian will not overlook the merits of the case for Japan as her case may have stood ten years ago. He will likewise not overlook the grim record of Japan's policy and actions during the intervening decade. The purpose of this comment is not to examine the circumstances which led to the seizure of Manchuria in 1931, nor to weigh the incentives which brought about the conflict with China in 1937 but to discuss the course and methods of our own Government as well as the efforts of the Japanese Government, as revealed by the evidence hereinafter set forth, during the months prior to the outbreak of war with the United States to effect a new orientation of policy and to start the country along paths of peace while professing readiness, provided that peace with the Chinese Government could be brought about by negotiations instituted through the good offices of the United States, to relinquish in due course her ill-gotten territorial gains since the outbreak of the conflict with China in 1937.

Baron Hiranuma's Proposal

As a preface to the efforts on the part of the Konoye Government in 1941 it appears pertinent to consider briefly the similar efforts of Baron Hiranuma when he was Prime Minister in 1939, having in mind the fact that the latter visualized not only the avoidance of eventual war with the United States but the avoidance of the world war which later developed.

On May 16, 1939, a few days before my departure on leave for the United States, I was a guest at a luncheon given by Baron Harada who, while holding no official position, was a close friend and confidant of many high personages close to the Emperor. My host spoke to me substantially as follows:

> Although the Japanese Government had decided not to conclude a military alliance with Germany and Italy, strong pressure was being exerted, not only by Germany and Italy, but by reactionary elements in Japan, toward the conclusion of some arrangement which would link together nations whose policies were opposed by the democratic powers. The argument which was most difficult to meet of those Japanese who favored a political link with Germany and Italy was that Japan could not afford to be isolated. Germany and Italy were urging Japan "to come over to their side," while the democratic nations were turning to Japan a cold shoulder. It would greatly strengthen the hands of those Japanese who were working for restoration of good relations between Japan and the United States, if the democratic Powers could indicate that the way was open for Japan to align herself with the democratic camp.

I informed my host that, although the United States earnestly desired that good relations between our two countriees be restored, I did not believe that the United States could make the indication of welcome which had been suggested unless Japan's peace terms with China could be reconciled with the peace terms of China.

During an interview with Mr. Arita, the Minister for Foreign Affairs, on May 18, 1939, the day before my departure for the United States on leave of absence, the Minister handed me a message from the Prime Minister, Baron Hiranuma, which he requested that I convey to the Secretary of State.[36] The message, which was couched in vague and obscure language, gave expression to Japan's desire to contribute toward the maintenance of peace and contained a suggestion that there be some form of collaboration between the United States and Japan for the furtherance of that objective.

[36] The text is given in *Foreign Relations, Japan: 1931–41*, II. 1.

In response to an invitation extended by Baron Hiranuma, Mr. Dooman, then Chargé d'Affaires in my absence, on May 23 called on the Prime Minister at his private residence. Baron Hiranuma said that the possibility of a war arising in Europe was one which he contemplated with horror. Such a war would inevitably result in the total destruction of civilization, as no nation, however remote from the seat of war, could hope to escape the eventual consequences even though it might be so fortunate as to avoid direct involvement. There were, he continued, elements in Japan which believed that Japan could not afford to maintain a condition of isolation and that her security demanded that she enter into "special relations" with Germany and Italy. He deplored the practice of statesmen attempting to gain favorable tactical positions, which were, after all, ephemeral. It was essential that those responsible for the welfare of nations seek long-term objectives, one of the most important of which was a stabilized peace to replace interludes of preparation for the next war. Japan and the United States were not directly involved in the troubles of Europe, and it was his thought that these two nations were in a position to exercise a moderating influence on Europe.

The position of Japan, Baron Hiranuma continued, was not unlike that of Germany and Italy. The objectives which Japan had pursued in China were essential for Japan's security in a world of sanctions, embargoes, lack of access to markets and to raw materials. If conditions could be brought about which would assure to all nations markets for the world's goods on the basis of equality and price, and supplies of the materials which they need, the importance to Japan of seeking a market and sources of raw materials in China would greatly diminish, and similarly there would not be the urge on Germany to expand at the expense of weaker and smaller nations. Baron Hiranuma stated that the conditions which had brought about the situation in the Far East were not local but universal in character. The Prime Minister concluded his presentation by saying that there could be no confident hope that a permanent peace could be established until the world-wide economic and political conditions which bring about unrest in Europe and in the Far East were corrected. He proposed that the President of the United States approach the British and French Governments with a view to the calling of an international conference which would consider the causes of political unrest, he (Baron Hiranuma) to approach the German and Italian Governments, and that if there were returned favorable replies by all the nations; the President call the conference. He requested that the Chargé d'Affaires urgently and confidentially communicate his proposal to the Secretary of State.

OUR GOVERNMENT'S REPLY

In August, some three months later, there was received by mail a reply to the message which had been communicated by the Prime Minister to the Secretary of State through me, to the effect that the American Government would be interested to receive a further statement from the Japanese Government on the possibility of collaboration between the United States and Japan to maintain conditions of peace, but that in the meantime Japan could make a material contribution to peace by withdrawing her forces from China.[37] The Chargé d'Affaires was directed at the same time to convey to the Prime Minister a copy of this message as a response to the proposal which he had confidentially made to Mr. Dooman on May 23.

The nature of this reply to Baron Hiranuma's momentous step was interpreted by him as in no way an encouragement but, on the contrary, as a rebuff, and the matter was not pursued.

THE SITUATION IN JAPAN IN 1941

To understand the situation in Japan as it had developed throughout the summer of 1941 we must go back to the month of April when the so-called "conversations" between the two

[37] The Department of State's answer to Baron Hiranuma was dated July 8, 1939 and is printed in *ibid.*, pp. 5–8.

Governments commenced.[38] Prince Konoye was Prime Minister, with Mr. Matsuoka holding the portfolio of Foreign Affairs. The alliance of Japan with the Axis had been consummated in the previous September on the initiative of Mr. Matsuoka himself, thus aligning Japan with the totalitarian Powers as opposed to the democracies. There existed, however, in Japan powerful elements who were reluctant to see a progressive worsening of Japan's relations with the United States, and it was these elements who initiated the conversations in Washington for the purpose of bringing about a readjustment of Japan's relations with the United States, commencing informally and unofficially in April and continuing intermittently with an increasing degree of formality up to the moment of the outbreak of war.[39]

The unexpected attack by Germany on Soviet Russia on June 22, 1941, following Mr. Matsuoka's neutrality pact with the latter, had rendered the position of that official untenable owing to his egregious miscalculation and brought about his fall. The Cabinet was reconstructed, still under the premiership of Prince Konoye; Admiral Toyoda, an officer with marked pro-Anglo-Saxon sympathies, was appointed Minister for Foreign Affairs, and the new Government immediately set about to bring the Washington conversations to some successful conclusion. Japan's ties with the Axis at this time underwent a distinct weakening, and while lip-service was publicly and officially paid to Japan's determination to fulfill her obliga-

---

[38] On March 8, 1941, Hull and Nomura had begun the series of informal talks which were to continue until the attack on Pearl Harbor.

[39] In January, 1941, two Catholic priests, Bishop Walsh and Father Drought, who had just returned from Japan, where they had talked with influential Japanese including Matsuoka, obtained an interview with the President and Mr. Hull. They told President Roosevelt and the Secretary that Matsuoka wanted to improve Japanese-American relations and that certain elements of the Japanese Government wished to reach an agreement with the United States. Walsh and Drought were asked to continue their conversations with the Japanese and to put in writing their ideas and proposals. Two Japanese, Colonel Iwakuro of the young officer's clique and Wikawa, President of the Co-operative Bank, came to the United States in February to continue the talks begun in Tokyo. Feis, *op. cit.*, pp. 174–75; Rauch, *op. cit.*, pp. 377–78.

tions under the Alliance, a new emphasis was laid upon her equal determination to follow a course of complete independence. Mr. Matsuoka's interpretation of Article 3 [40] of the Axis Pact as rendering virtually certain a state of war between Japan and the United States in the event that war should occur between the United States and Germany was repudiated by Prince Konoye, and abundant evidence appeared that while Japan would remain faithful to the letter of the Pact, nevertheless the new Government was prepared to reduce the Alliance virtually to a dead letter, provided that a settlement with the United States could be reached.[41] The outlook for a successful conclusion of the Washington conversations at that time appeared to be auspicious, as well as the opportunity to wean Japan effectively away from the Axis.

ABILITY OF THE JAPANESE GOVERNMENT TO CARRY OUT ITS COMMITMENTS

At this point it is pertinent to note that on May 24, 1941, the Department, with reference to the current exploratory conversations, asked my opinion as to whether the Japanese Gov-

[40] Article 3 of the Three-Power Pact said that "Germany, Italy and Japan agree to co-operate in their efforts on aforesaid lines. They further undertake to assist one another with all political, economic and military means if one of the three contracting Powers is attacked by a Power at present not involved in the European War or in the Chinese-Japanese conflict." Matsuoka, when Foreign Minister, had interpreted this to mean, that if war occurred between Germany and the United States, Japan would join Germany. See S. Shepard Jones and Denys P. Myers (eds.), *Documents on American Foreign Relations,* III (Boston: World Peace Foundation, 1941), 304–05, and Feis, *op. cit.,* pp. 119–21, 280.

[41] Over the interpretation of Article III, Feis has written in *The Road to Pearl Harbor,* pp. 280–81, the "Konoye Cabinet lived in an agony of division." The Japanese Government never gave any definite repudiation of the tie. On September 18, 1941, however, Konoye's secretary, Ushiba, told Mr. Dooman "that an understanding had been reached among the various influential elements in Japan which would enable Prince Konoye to give orally and directly to the President an assurance with regard to the attitude of Japan which, he felt sure, would be entirely satisfactory to the President." Feis comments that, thus, "the American government could gather that devotion to Germany probably would not stand in the way of an accord that Japan found desirable."

ernment — any Japanese Government — would and could carry out in good faith such provisions for a settlement with the United States as might be agreed upon. I replied in telegram No. 743 of May 27, 1941, (in paraphrase) as follows:

1. There is no reason to doubt that any Government of Japan which undertook a bilateral commitment of the kind referred to with the Emperor's approval and that of the Cabinet and probably of the Privy Council would implement in good faith and to the best of its ability the provisions of any such agreement.

2. The armed forces or certain elements in the Army and Navy are the only groups in Japan which could offer any effective opposition to the implementation of such commitments, and it may be assumed that the Japanese Government would not accept any such commitments without having obtained the prior approval of the Navy and War Ministers who in their turn would not give their approval unless they were assured of the agreement of the more important groups in their respective services. We have good grounds for believing that both the Navy and War Ministers are, in general, in favor of a settlement along the lines of that under consideration.

3. If the Emperor in an Imperial Rescript should publicly confirm the conclusion of such an agreement, the provisions thereof would then become the definite policy of Japan. In our view the Japanese people would greet such a settlement with a deep feeling of relief.

4. Without attempting to analyze in detail the suggested terms of the settlement, it would appear that the commitments which the United States is to assume are primarily either of a negative or abstentious character or envisage actions of a nature which would be considered as forming a normal part of relations with a friendly country, whereas certain of the commitments which Japan is to assume would be of a type necessitating positive action. Should the Japanese after agreeing to these terms fail to carry them out in good faith, the United States would then be absolved from the obligation which it had assumed under the agreement and consequently there is no ground for believing that the position of the United States in the Far East would be materially worsened during the process of implementation. It follows therefore that the United States has

a great deal to gain from such an agreement and that even in the event of a failure on the part of Japan satisfactorily to implement its commitments, which we do not think will occur, American interests would not necessarily suffer to any serious extent. The *status quo ante* could still be maintained in the meantime without any important sacrifice.

5. The views put forth in this telegram should be considered in conjunction with the Embassy's telegram No. 741, May 26, 9 P.M. I consider that our Government should from the point of view of constructive statesmanship continue the conversations with the object of bringing about an agreement along the proposed lines. A progressive deterioration of relations between the United States and Japan eventually leading to war might well be the alternative. The risk of failure would appear to be more than offset by the possibility if not the probability of success. I have real hope that if an agreement can be worked out on paper it will not fail to be carried out.

In another telegram on the same day I reported:

We are unable to say whether fear of war with the United States, economic difficulties, and other factors are powerful enough to overcome the opposition to the removal of the Japanese forces from China, but it does appear to us that if a settlement on paper should result from the negotiations between Japan and the United States, it would be up to Japan to give validity to that settlement by fulfilling this particular condition in advance.

In summation, the foreign policy and diplomacy of Japan are especially influenced by world events and developments. At the present moment I am of the opinion that we are unable to report any important advance in influence by either the moderate or the extremist elements in Japan, although we consider that the trend for the moment is in favor of the moderates. The progress of the European war, as well as developments in the actions and policy of the United States, will inevitably affect future trends. It is therefore wholly impossible to predict the outcome in Japan but I would express the opinion that *under present conditions Japan is highly malleable.*

On June 5, 1941, the following passage occurs in a telegram sent by the Embassy to the Department:

In this regard the British Ambassador showed me on May 24 the telegrams exchanged between the British Ambassador in Washington and Mr. Eden concerning the conversations in Washington. My British colleague asked me my views on the subject of these conversations. I told him that personally I was impressed with the statement of Secretary Hull to the effect that even if the chances of obtaining a *reasonable* agreement were only one in twenty-five, it would be unwise to miss that one chance by declining to investigate its possibilities.

JAPAN'S MOVE INTO INDO-CHINA

In July American-Japanese relations, in spite of the fall of Mr. Matsuoka, took a pronounced turn for the worse as a result of the movement of Japanese armed forces into French Indo-China with the specious argument that the step was taken as a measure of self-defense against the alleged encirclement of Japan by the ABCD powers. (American, British, Chinese, Dutch.)

THE PRESIDENT'S PROPOSAL

On July 24 the President made to the Japanese Government through the Japanese Ambassador in Washington a proposal of the highest statesmanship, offering to use his good offices to bring about the international neutralization of Indo-China, and later of Thailand, provided that the Japanese forces should abstain from entering the former country or, if they had already disembarked, that they should withdraw.[42] Washington's telegram informing me of this proposal was received in Tokyo on July 27. Immediately, although it was a Sunday, I sought on my own initiative an appointment with the Foreign Minister

42 For a copy of Sumner Welles' memorandum concerning the conversation of President Roosevelt with Ambassador Nomura, see *Foreign Relations, Japan: 1931-41*, II, 527-30.

and urged with all the force at my command that Japan was hereby afforded a supreme opportunity to reorientate her policy along paths of peace with the certain guarantee that no threat could be offered by the alleged ABCD "encirclement"; the President's broad-gauge gesture effectively met Japan's alleged problem; and Admiral Toyoda, as I said to him, was here presented with an opportunity to go down in history as one of Japan's greatest statesmen, while offered at the same time a solution of the grave situation which faced him at the outset of his ministry. I told the Department what I had done and said that although I had exceeded all authority I felt after careful thought that three considerations justified my step: (1) the prime importance that Admiral Toyoda should completely and accurately understand the President's proposal, (2) the importance of the time element which made it impossible for me to ask for authority from Washington in advance, and (3) my belief that the President would wish nothing to be left undone to ensure that maximum consideration should be given to his proposal and that the Japanese Government should fully recognize its far-reaching and enlightened import because upon its rejection or acceptance might depend the future peace of the Pacific.[43] The Acting Secretary, Sumner Welles, was later good enough to inform me that he regarded my action at that time as of the greatest assistance and value and that both the President and he himself had approved of what I had done.

To my astonishment, in that Sunday morning interview, Admiral Toyoda pleaded total ignorance of the President's proposal, which had been communicated to Admiral Nomura three days earlier, and it later appeared that the latter's full report had been delayed owing to the Ambassador's departure from Washington to New York. Possibly Admiral Nomura attached little importance to the proposal in the belief that nothing could then restrain the Japanese armed forces from their plans, and, as things turned out, the proposal came to nothing since the Japanese suggestions for the usual "compromise,"

[43] *Ibid.*, pp. 534–37.

presented on August 6, were quite properly held by our Government as not responsive to the President's gesture.[44] The President's effort nevertheless placed the United States at that moment in an unassailable position from the point of view of history.

SUSPENSION OF THE WASHINGTON CONVERSATIONS

As a result of the Japanese invasion of Indo-China, Mr. Hull informed Admiral Nomura that the American Government could see no ground for continuing the Washington conversations, and if no further favorable developments had intervened, we in the Embassy would have shared what was apparently the opinion of the Administration that an adjustment of American-Japanese relations was then impossible.

THE PROPOSAL OF PRINCE KONOYE
TO MEET THE PRESIDENT

Favorable developments, as stated hereinafter, did however intervene. The first suggestion for a meeting between Prince Konoye and the President was communicated to me as a definite proposal by the Japanese Government by Admiral Toyoda in our long two-and-a-half-hour conversation on August 18,[45] and, according to our records, was conveyed to the

---

[44] On August 6 Nomura replied that Japan would agree not to station troops in other areas of the southwest Pacific excepting Indo-China and would be willing to withdraw from Indo-China after the war in China had been ended. In return for these and other concessions from Japan the United States must agree to cease military measures in the southwest Pacific, to resume normal trade relations with Japan, to aid Japan in obtaining raw materials from the southwest Pacific area, to use its good offices for the initiation of direct negotiations between Japan and the Government of Chiang Kai-shek, and to recognize Japan's special status in Indo-China, even when Japanese forces had been withdrawn. *Ibid.*, pp. 527-30, 548-50.

[45] Mr. Grew commented in his diary for August 18, 1941: "Apropos of this conversation, it was a fearfully hot day, and as I wrote down his remarks, it was drip, drip, drip, so after the first hour Admiral Toyoda ordered cold drinks and cold wet towels to swab off with. . . . Today the talk was so im-

President by Admiral Nomura on August 23. Admiral Toyoda told me that he had sent these instructions to Admiral Nomura on August 7, but it appeared that the President was at that time absent from Washington.

For a Prime Minister of Japan thus to shatter all precedent and tradition in this land of subservience to precedent and tradition, and to offer to come, hat-in-hand so to speak, to meet the President of the United States on American soil seemed to us in the Embassy a gauge of the determination of the then Japanese Government to undo the vast harm already accomplished in alienating our powerful and progressively angry country.[46] In our telegram No. 1529 of September 29,

portant that I wrote down everything he said, about a dozen pages of foolscap and I almost had writer's cramp at the end. He is a sympathetic and very human type and I think I like him more than any other Foreign Minister I have ever dealt with. Our personal relationship is very friendly. Today, while we were swabbing off with the cold towels, I said: 'Admiral, you have often stood on the bridge of a battleship and have seen bad storms which lasted for several days, but ever since you took over the bridge of the Foreign Office you have undergone one long continuous storm without any rest. You and I will have to pour some oil on those angry waves.' The Minister laughed heartily and I guess he will relate that remark in Cabinet, but he missed the opportunity to say: 'All right, but if you stop sending us the oil, what are we going to do about it?' "

On August 18 Mr. Grew telegraphed Hull: "The Ambassador urges, however, with all the force at his command, for the sake of avoiding the obviously growing possibility of an utterly futile war between Japan and the United States, that this Japanese proposal not be turned aside without very prayerful consideration. Not only is the proposal unprecedented in Japanese history, but it is an indication that Japanese intransigence is not crystallized completely owing to the fact that the proposal has the approval of the Emperor and the highest authorities in the land. The good which may flow from a meeting between Prince Konoye and President Roosevelt is incalculable. The opportunity is here presented, the Ambassador ventures to believe, for an act of the highest statesmanship, such as the recent meeting of President Roosevelt with Prime Minister Churchill at sea, with the possible overcoming thereby of apparently insurmountable obstacles to peace hereafter in the Pacific." *Foreign Relations, Japan: 1931–41*, II, 565.

[46] In his "Memoirs" Prince Konoye described the circumstances surrounding the formulation of the proposal for the Roosevelt-Konoye meeting: "During this time, I was considering every means by which to surmount the Japanese-American crisis. Finally, I made up my mind to personally meet with the President, and on the evening of August 4th, I told both the Ministers of War and of Navy about this for the first time. My words were as follows: . . .

" 'The Prime Minister should meet personally with the President and ex-

1941,[47] I pointed out that the current efforts of the Japanese Government to bring about a new orientation in policy, involving conciliation with the United States, were due in part to

press straightforwardly and boldly the true intentions of the Empire. If the President still does not understand, I shall, of course, be fully prepared to break off the talks and return home. It is, therefore, an undertaking which must be carried out while being fully prepared for war against America. If, after a direct meeting with the President, an understanding cannot be obtained, the people will know that a Japanese-American war could not be avoided. This would aid in consolidating their determination. The world in general, also, would be made aware that the primary factor is not aggression and invasion. It will know that great efforts were made in behalf of maintaining peace in the Pacific. . . .

" 'Japan will insist, of course, on the firm establishment of the Greater East Asia Co-Prosperity Sphere. American claims will be based on the provisions of the Nine-Power Pact. The contents of these are at odds with each other. However America has stated that "it is ready at any time to discuss making revisions to the Nine-Power Pact through legal means." Japan's ideal, of course, is to bring about the firm establishment of the Greater East Asia Co-Prosperity Sphere. In view of the national potential it is too much to expect this ideal to be fulfilled at once. Therefore, I do not believe that Japanese-American talks are an impossibility if they are carried out with broadmindedness. . . .'

"Both the War and Navy Ministers listened to me intently. Neither could give me an immediate reply but before the day was over, the Navy expressed complete accord and, moreover, anticipated the success of the conference. . . .

"The War Minister was of the opinion that 'failure of this meeting is the greater likelihood.' After considering the matter from all angles, the Foreign Minister concluded that 'matters should be carried out expeditiously.' On the morning of the 6th, immediately after the joint conference, I was granted an audience, and I conveyed my intentions to the Emperor. During the afternoon of the 7th, I was summoned to his presence and was advised: 'I am in receipt of intelligence from the Navy pertaining to a general oil embargo against Japan by America. In view of this, the meeting with the President should take place as soon as possible.' Instructions were despatched to Ambassador Nomura during the morning of the 7th.

"The first impression made on America by even this major proposal, was discouraging. The President was absent from Washington at the time, having gone to meet with Prime Minister Churchill. Ambassador Nomura called on Secretary Hull on the 8th, and relayed the proposal to him. As stated before, however, this coincided with our receiving the American reply to Japan's proposal of August 4th. With regard to this most important new proposal, Hull's comment was: 'As long as there is no change in Japan's policy, I lack confidence in relaying this proposal to the President.' Ambassador Nomura did not press the matter further but suggested by telegraph that the matter be taken up in Tokyo with Ambassador Grew." *Pearl Harbor Attack*, pt. 20, pp. 3999–4000.

[47] The telegram of September 29, 1941, is printed in *Foreign Relations, Japan: 1931–41*, II, 645–50.

the fact that our Government had followed precisely the strong policy which we had advocated in previous telegrams, notably in an important message, which we in the Embassy called our "green light" telegram, in the autumn of 1940. The discrediting and downfall of Mr. Matsuoka was due primarily to his miscalculations in connection with Germany's attack on Soviet Russia, but it was the strong policy of the United States — that of meeting every aggressive Japanese step with a step of our own — that led indirectly to his fall.[48]

OUR FREEZING ORDER

The Japanese agreement with Vichy by which Japanese armed forces were given authority to occupy certain strategic bases in French Indo-China was announced in Vichy on July 24; [49] on July 26 our Government announced the freezing of Japanese assets in the United States, obviously as a retaliatory step, while Mr. Hull, as stated above, had informed the Japanese Ambassador through Mr. Welles on July 23 that he could not see that any basis was now offered for continuing the Washington exploratory conversations.[50] In the light of these unfavorable developments, had no favorable developments then occurred, as already stated, it might well have been held that our Government had abandoned all hope and further efforts toward reaching an adjustment of American-Japanese relations.

A NEW AND FAVORABLE OUTLOOK

This, however, proved not to be the case because on August 28, *a full month after Japan's agreement with Vichy and*

48 See Feis, *op. cit.,* pp. 219–26, for a discussion of the circumstances surrounding the resignation of Foreign Minister Matsuoka.

49 On July 21, 1941, France and Japan had reached a joint-defense agreement concerning Indochina. See *Contemporary Japan,* August, 1941, pp. 1105–6.

50 President Roosevelt issued on July 26 an Executive Order freezing Japanese assets in the United States. Retaliatory measures were taken by Japan on July 28 to control all assets and transactions of Americans in Japan. See Leland M. Goodrich (ed.), *Documents on American Foreign Relations,* IV (Boston: World Peace Foundation, 1942), 501, 503–6, for the texts of the President's press release announcing the freezing and of the statement by the Japanese Department of Finance in August, 1941.

the occupation by Japanese armed forces of bases in Indochina, the President received Admiral Nomura at the latter's request and a conversation took place, from which the following excerpts from the Department of State's telegram of August 29, 1941, are given:

> The President received Admiral Nomura at the latter's request on August 28. . . . Admiral Nomura delivered to the President a message from Prince Konoye [51] . . . Prince Konoye was of the opinion that the continuation of the conversations previously held, to be subsequently confirmed by the responsible heads of the American and Japanese Governments, would not be sufficient to cover the requirements of the swiftly developing conditions in which unpredictable events might occur.
>
> After reading the message the President expressed admiration for both its spirit and tone. He said that the time required to reach the Hawaiian Islands might make it difficult for him to proceed there in order to meet Prince Konoye and suggested Juneau, Alaska, which would necessitate on his part an absence from Washington of not more than two weeks including a period of three or four days for the meeting itself, as a possible place. . . .
>
> After promising to study the communication from the Japanese Government the President told Admiral Nomura *that the Ambassador might state to his Government that the President was very optimistic* as he regarded the latest communication from the Japanese Government *as a step in advance.* The President went on to say that *he looked forward with real interest to the possibility of conferring for several days with the Japanese Prime Minister.*

[51] In his communication to Roosevelt, Konoye said that Japan and the United States were the last two Powers holding the key to world peace and to the preservation of world civilization. Misunderstandings, he felt, had brought about the present strained relations between the two countries. He thought that a meeting between Roosevelt and himself might facilitate an adjustment of Japanese-American relations. "I consider it, therefore, of urgent necessity," he continued, "that the two heads of the Governments should meet first to discuss from a broad standpoint all important problems between Japan and America covering the entire Pacific area, and to explore the possibility of saving the situation. Adjustment of minor items may, if necessary, be left to negotiations between competent officials of the two countries, following the meeting." *Foreign Relations, Japan: 1931–41,* II, 572–73.

Here, then, was a clear indication that the Administration had by no means abandoned its hope and efforts for a settlement with Japan, and with the foregoing concrete encouragement by the President, Prince Konoye and Admiral Toyoda undertook intensive efforts to bring about the meeting of the Prime Minister with the President at the earliest possible moment.

A Settlement with China Essential

Throughout the conversations in Tokyo, which were conducted in a way parallel to the conversations in Washington, it was clear that apart from a settlement with the United States, the concern uppermost in the mind of the Japanese Government was a settlement with China, which must necessarily be a primary requisite for any adjustment of American-Japanese relations. A country at war, whatever may be thought by the world at large of the antecedents and purposes of that war, can hardly be expected to cease its military campaign until an armistice is reached, and in my talk with Admiral Toyoda on August 18 he emphasized the Japanese contention that the stationing of Japanese forces in Indo-China had been undertaken for the purpose of solving the China Affair, obviously in order to be in position eventually to interrupt the supplies which were flowing to Chungking over the Burma road and to conduct a possible incursion into Yunnan Province. This occupation of bases in Indo-China was of course also one further step on the so-called "southern advance"; it was furthermore another step in preparing a program of war if the program of peace should fail; and it obviously involved a further threat to the countries to the south.

Effect in the United States of Japan's Southward Advance

We had left the Japanese Government under no misapprehension concerning the effects on the United States of the progressive expansion of Japan into Southeast Asia. On February 14, 1941, the Counselor, Mr. Dooman, who had just returned from the United States, called on the then Vice Minister for Foreign Affairs, Mr. Ohashi, and spoke to him substantially as follows, setting forth a point of view which I had continually been emphasizing in my talks with prominent Japanese:

The Japanese Government had no doubt taken note of the view emphasized by the American press that the intrusion of the Japanese Army into French Indochina was a step in the direction of a possible future move by Japan into the Netherlands East Indies and Malaya, and that a Japanese threat to occupy areas from which the United States procured essential primary commodities would not be tolerated. Although the assuring of supplies of such commodities was an important factor, there was another consideration of even greater importance to the United States: it was the fixed policy of the United States to contribute, from the point of view of its own defense, such assistance as would be necessary for the continued existence of Britain. To that end the United States was in process of mobilizing its industrial resources in order to provide Britain with needed munitions and war materials to withstand Germany. Britain, however, relied on the other component units of the British Empire for supplies of foodstuffs and of man power, and her very existence depended on sea communications between the various elements of the Empire being kept open. If Japan were to occupy Singapore or the Netherlands East Indies, she, as an ally of Germany and Italy, would be able to prey on, if not to destroy, British shipping in the South Pacific and the Indian Ocean, and thus compromise the safety of the British Empire. The ultimate purpose of the United States in providing Britain with munitions and war materials, namely, to promote the defenses and safety of the United States, thus would not have been accomplished. It could not be supposed that the United States on the one hand would exert every effort to prevent the conquest of Britain by Germany while on the other hand viewing with equanimity action by Japan which would equally be destructive of British resistance.

WAR OR PEACE?

We were well aware that during this entire period the Japanese armed forces were steadily engaged in preparing a program of war in case the program of peace should ultimately fail, and, as appears from the records, I continually warned our Government that the risk of war was constantly and progressively present. Prince Konoye and his Government nevertheless gave every indication of desiring a peaceful settlement.

In the course of my conversation with Admiral Toyoda on August 18 he had said, *inter alia:*

> . . . the breakdown of peace between both countries which has long been cherished with the accomplishment of cordial friendship between both peoples would itself be an extremely miserable matter, and not only that but because both Japan and the United States which are the last two countries which hold the key for maintaining world peace in their hands under the present world situation without showing statesmanship, that would leave the greatest black spot on human history and would be nothing but making future historians unable to understand the nature of the breakdown; and lastly because allowing the situation to come to that pass would mean that we as statesmen had not fully fulfilled our responsibility for the benefit of both peoples.[52]

The following excerpt from the memorandum of my conversation with the Foreign Minister on September 27 is pertinent:

> All details of preparation for the proposed meeting (between the Prime Minister and the President) have been completed by the Japanese Government: the personnel of the Prime Minister's suite, including full admirals and generals, have been confidentially appointed and the ship to carry the party has been put into momentary readiness to sail. (Admiral Toyoda here remarked that Mr. Hull had mentioned to the Japanese Ambassador his fear that the Japanese Government might not be allowed by the Japanese Navy and Army to venture upon any

[52] *Ibid.*, p. 562.

course of peace. The Foreign Minister stated that in order to dissipate doubt as to the collaboration of the Japanese Navy and Army with the Prime Minister's undertaking, high-ranking naval and military officers would accompány Prince Konoye.) A reply from the United States Government is being momentarily awaited. . . . From every point of view, time is of the essence.[53]

Final Efforts of Japan for Peace

These final efforts of the Japanese Government for a settlement were initiated in the long conversation between the Foreign Minister and myself on August 18.

Just before the meeting, Mr. Terasaki, Chief of the American Bureau of the Foreign Office, asked Mr. Dooman to call and spoke to him as follows:

The interview between the Foreign Minister and the Ambassador, to be held at four o'clock this afternoon, would be of the greatest importance. He hoped that it would initiate a series of conversations between them which would eventually yield a satisfactory adjustment of American-Japanese relations. If these conversations should prove unsuccessful, he did not believe that another attempt could be made. If a Cabinet under the leadership of Prince Konoye should prove unable to adjust relations with the United States, it would be inconceivable for any other Japanese statesman to succeed where he had failed.

The prime requisite in accomplishing the end which he had in mind was high statesmanship on both sides — an undue alertness on the part of either side to criticize the actions and policies of the other should be avoided and each should make effort to appreciate the position of the other.

The third point stressed by Mr. Terasaki was that *whereas Japan was ready to respond to any action by the United States intended to bring the conflict in the Far East to an end,* it would under no circumstances give in to any form of pressure.[54]

In proposing the meeting between Prince Konoye and the President, the Foreign Minister said:

53 *Ibid.,* pp. 643–44.   54 *Ibid.,* pp. 559–60.

The only way to eliminate this critical situation, the Minister thinks, is that the responsible people of both countries should directly meet each other *and express their true intentions toward each other* and thus to study the possibility of remedying the present situation, trying to discover the methods for contributing toward mankind and the peace of the world.[55]

Admiral Toyoda added:

Needless to say, the Premier's going abroad would have no precedent in Japanese history and the Prime Minister, Prince Konoye, has made up his mind with an extremely strong determination to meet the President notwithstanding the fact that he is fully aware of the objections in certain parts of this country. This determination of Prince Konoye is nothing but the expression of his strongest desire to save the civilization of the world from ruin, as well as to maintain peace in the Pacific by making every effort in his power, and the Minister firmly believes that the President will also be in harmony with this thought and will give his consent to the proposal of the Japanese Government.

It is firmly believed that in the conversations between the Prime Minister and the President it will be possible to reach a just and equitable agreement on the general question of Japanese-American relations from the broadminded point of view as a result of the expressions of the highest degree of statesmanship of both leaders.[56]

A complete report of the foregoing conversation was of course cabled by me to Washington the same evening.

THE URGENCY FOR ARRANGING PRINCE KONOYE'S PROPOSED MEETING WITH THE PRESIDENT

On the next day, August 19, the following appraisal was sent by the Embassy to the Department:

In considering the proposal of the Prime Minister to meet President Roosevelt in Honolulu it is important to give due

[55] *Ibid.,* pp. 562–63.   [56] *Ibid.,* p. 563.

weight in so far as we can to the full significance of this proposal. In the first place the Prime Minister's offer reveals a high degree of courage since, should it become prematurely known or should it fail of its purpose, it would very likely bring in its train further attempts at assassination. In the second place it represents a supreme attempt on the part of the Japanese Government to remain at peace with the United States, with the knowledge that the suggested meeting with the President would be entirely fruitless *unless the Japanese Government were ready to make far-reaching concessions.* In the third place it shows that the present Japanese Government is determined to free itself from the control of the extremist elements.

It is possible also that the Japanese Government has been forced to take this unprecedented step by virtue of the fact that Japan is economically nearing the end of her strength and is not in a position to live through a war with the United States. Conversely, even if Japan were faced with an economic catastrophe of the first magnitude, there is no reason whatever to doubt that the Government however reluctantly would with resolution confront such a catastrophe rather than yield to pressure from a foreign country.

Prince Konoye's proposal to journey to a foreign country to confer with a foreign Chief of State will, if carried out, be considered by many groups in Japan as a loss of face and, if unsuccessful, will very likely bring down the Government; but in my opinion his proposal should be viewed less as a final desperate gamble than as an act of the highest statesmanship. Considered in that light it merits a magnanimous response and Prince Konoye deserves whatever support we may properly give him in his valiant effort to surmount the extremist elements in Japan and, if necessary, to sacrifice his own life as well as his political future and that of the Government of which he is head.

As to what concessions Japan might be prepared to make in order to meet the views of the United States, there is little doubt that Prince Konoye would first of all request the co-operation of the United States in terminating the China Affair and he would probably be ready to accept far-reaching commitments on this point entailing as well the eventual removal of Japanese armed forces from French Indo-China. From an observation of the Foreign Minister, reported in my telegram No. 1267,

August 18, 9 P.M., I am inclined to believe that the Japanese Government expects that one of the first requisites from the point of view of the American Government for a settlement between the United States and Japan would be Japan's withdrawal from the Axis.

The element of time is important since the steady deterioration of economic conditions in Japan resulting in part from the measures which the United States has adopted will have a tendency progressively to reduce rather than to increase the influence of the present Cabinet and of the moderate elements in the country and to strengthen the hand of the extremist elements.

Even though the constructive results of the proposed meeting between the President and Prince Konoye might not be entirely favorable and at best slow in materializing, its most important aspect is that it provides a real opportunity to prevent a rapid deterioration of the situation in the Pacific and at least to halt the present growing momentum toward a head-on collision between the United States and Japan. This possibility would in itself seem sufficient to justify a favorable reception of Prince Konoye's proposal. While it is not in my province to attempt to forecast the reaction in domestic political circles in the United States to such a meeting, it appears to me to offer great possibilities.

And finally it is almost mathematically certain that we must be prepared to accept the thought that if the proposed meeting between the President and Prince Konoye, which is an outstanding and very likely final effort on the part of the Japanese Government, should not take place, the alternative would be a reconstitution of the present Government or a formation of a new Government for the purpose of confiding Japan's future destiny to the armed forces for a do-or-die all-out attempt to establish the hegemony of Japan over all Greater East Asia, *which would carry with it the inevitability of war with the United States.*

Unsuccessful Exploratory Conversations

In spite of all efforts to bring about the meeting between the Prime Minister and the President, the conversations in Washington dragged on futilely, various proposals and counterproposals being submitted by both sides, some of which appeared to indicate progress while other proposals by the Japanese Ambassador were held by the Department to have been of a retrograde nature. The position of our Government was that there would be no purpose in the proposed meeting between the responsible heads of the two Governments unless and until the exploratory conversations had produced what our Government would regard as a substantial basis for entering upon formal negotiations.

The Problem Unsolvable through Formulas

I do not for a moment wish to imply that our Government was at this time following obstructive tactics or that it was not the earnest desire of our Government to bring the conversations to a point where formal negotiations would be considered appropriate. There can be no question but that exhaustive efforts were being made in Washington to find mutually satisfactory formulas to cover the various issues outstanding in our relations with Japan and to bring about a practical adjustment of the whole situation in the Pacific area. I do not doubt that our Government felt that its most painstaking efforts were devoted throughout this period to that high purpose. The essential point is that during this period I expressed to the Department the carefully considered opinion that it would be idle to expect the Japanese to commit themselves in advance of the proposed meeting to such clear-cut undertakings as would be wholly satisfactory to the United States in point both of principle and concrete detail.

It was the Embassy's impression that one of the prime purposes of our Government in the exploratory conversations, although such a demand was never, so far as I am aware, formally presented, was to obtain from the Japanese Government a definite commitment dissolving Japan's ties with the Axis, a logical desideratum in the light of the wholly wise and justified efforts of the Administration to educate our people to the dangers to our country which would inevitably be involved in an Axis victory. Yet this was the one commitment, above all others, which the Japanese Government, in the preliminary conversations, could not afford to undertake. An Imperial Rescript, given by the Emperor, had sanctioned the Tripartite Alliance, and in the face of that Rescript, a matter of almost holy sanctity in Japan, no Japanese Government which had committed itself to a unilateral dissolution of the alliance could have expected to survive. The best that we could hope was that as a result of the proposed meeting of the Prime Minister with the President the alliance would become inoperative, in other words a dead letter, while remaining for the time being technically in force, and this, we were given good reason to believe, would be the case. In any event, an agreement with the United States would in fact automatically have created such a situation. The point is furthermore pertinent that the United States, which is committed to supporting the principle of the sanctity of treaties, could not well have requested Japan to betray her own treaty commitments.

The problem, indeed, could never satisfactorily be solved through formulas. The reason for this lay in the constant fear by the Japanese Government of the extremist and pro-Axis elements in the country. Even among the Japanese, who are past masters at secrecy, such commitments were bound to leak and rapidly to become known in military and political circles, and while imbued with every desire to meet the view of our Government in the exploratory conversations, the Japanese Government was reluctant to afford to the opposition such ammunition as would be derived from the far-reaching provisional commitments which we desired. The Japanese State, be it remembered, was far from that of totalitarian Germany under the Nazis where opposition to the Government could be ruthlessly crushed. In Japan, the opposition had to be reckoned with, and when that opposition believed that the Government's policy was contrary to what the opposition conceived to be in the best interests of the nation, either the Government could be overturned or, if that failed, wholesale assassination of members of the Government and their supporters was the traditional method by which the opposition sought to express its belief and impose its will. Prince Konoye and his associates were courageous men; they did not fear assassination, while taking every proper precautionary step, but what they did fear was the overturning of their Government, through assassination or otherwise, before they could accomplish their program of conciliation with the United States, ensuring for their country a policy of peace with its attendant outlook of future national security, welfare and prosperity. The standpoint of the Japanese Government in the early autumn of 1941 was that the meeting of the Prime Minister with the President would produce a *fait accompli* of so dramatic a nature that the Japanese people as a whole would be swept into new channels of thought and would readily accept Prince Konoye's program as a progressive and enlightened achievement, having in mind the momentous advantages to Japan which would accrue therefrom, the nature of which could and would be made clear to the Japanese people. Under such circumstances, the opposition, it was believed, would be overwhelmed. The situation was well and accurately expressed to one of my reliable colleagues, the Polish Ambassador, Mr. de Romer, by a former Japanese Prime Minister, Mr. Hirota, influential in military and political circles, who said that if Prince Konoye should meet the President it would be unthinkable for him to return to Japan from a mission which had ended in failure, and that therefore the American terms would perforce have to be accepted by the then Prime Minister who would and could carry the entire Japanese nation, including the military, with him.

These facts and views were presented to our Government in general terms in repeated telegrams from the Embassy,[57]

57 On September 22 Mr. Grew wrote the following letter to Franklin D. Roosevelt: "I have not bothered you with personal letters for some time for the good reason that letters are now subject to long delays owing to the infrequent sailings of ships carrying our diplomatic pouches, and because developments in American-Japanese relations are moving so comparatively rapidly

notably in our telegram No. 1529, September 29, noon, which it appears to me desirable here to set forth in full, since it epitomizes our views on the entire situation and deals specifically, in paragraphs 7 to 10, inclusive, with the problems of the exploratory conversations and the desirability of bringing about the meeting of the Prime Minister with the President *before* the force of the initial impetus of these efforts should be lost and *before* the opposition, which we believed would steadily and inevitably increase in Japan, might intervene and overcome those efforts.

1. With a view to bringing about as soon as possible the proposed meeting between the President and the Prime Minister of Japan, the steadily increasing and lately intensified efforts of the Japanese Government are revealed by reviewing the con-

that my comments would generally be too much out-of-date to be helpful when they reach you. But I have tried and am constantly trying in my telegrams to the Secretary of State to paint an accurate picture of the moving scene from day to day. I hope that you see them regularly.

"As you know from my telegrams, I am in close touch with Prince Konoye who in the face of bitter antagonism from extremist and pro-Axis elements in the country is courageously working for an improvement in Japan's relations with the United States. He bears the heavy responsibility for having allowed our relations to come to such a pass and he no doubt now sees the handwriting on the wall and realizes that Japan has nothing to hope for from the Tripartite Pact and must shift her orientation of policy if she is to avoid disaster; but whatever the incentive that has led to his present efforts, I am convinced that he now means business and will go as far as is possible, without incurring open rebellion in Japan, to reach a reasonable understanding with us. In spite of all the evidence of Japan's bad faith in times past in failing to live up to her commitments, I believe that there is a better chance of the present Government implementing whatever commitments it may now undertake than has been the case in recent years. It seems to me highly unlikely that this chance will come again or that any Japanese statesman other than Prince Konoye could succeed in controlling the military extremists in carrying through a policy which they, in their ignorance of international affairs and economic laws, resent and oppose. The alternative to reaching a settlement now would be the greatly increased probability of war, — *Facilis descensus Averno* — and while we would undoubtedly win in the end, I question whether it is in our own interest to see an impoverished Japan reduced to the position of a third-rate Power. I therefore most earnestly hope that we can come to terms, even if we must take on trust, at least to some degree, the continued good faith and ability of the present Government fully to implement those terms."

fidential telegrams with regard to the exploratory conversations in Washington and Tokyo which we have exchanged since last spring. My role in this connection is principally that of an agent of transmission but I naturally desire to help in any constructive manner, first by persuading the Japanese Government to adopt such measures and policies as the Government of the United States regards as essential for a mutual understanding or agreement between the two countries, and second in endeavoring to convey to the President and yourself an accurate conception of the factors and conditions in this country which directly or indirectly influence this whole subject. It is true that through force of circumstances American diplomacy in Japan has been temporarily in abeyance ever since the fall of the Cabinet of Admiral Yonai but a new and very active lease of life has been given to that diplomacy with the advent of the Konoye-Toyoda Government, and I earnestly hope that we shall not allow this favorable period to pass without establishing a new foundation of such stability that we can place a reasonable degree of confidence in the permanency of whatever structure we can gradually but progressively build upon it.

2. I have pointed out in times past that the pendulum in Japan has always been swinging between moderate and extremist policies; that under past circumstances any Japanese leader or group of leaders who tried to reverse the program of aggressive expansion could not hope to live; and that the pushing of the southward advance and the permanent digging in of the Japanese in China could be avoided only if insuperable obstructions should intervene. The risks of failing to take positive measures for the maintenance of the future security of the United States, as I have pointed out, would probably be much greater than such risks as might accrue by our taking positive measures. I have furthermore pointed out that Japan could be deterred from pushing her program of aggressive expansion only by a show of force on our part and a manifestation that we are willing to use that force if necessary, and that it is only out of respect for our potential power that Japan has hesitated from taking greater liberties with American interests than she has taken. I have made it clear that if Japan's leadership could eventually be discredited by such action on the part of the United States, there might finally take shape in Japan a regeneration of thought

which would permit the adjustment of relations between our two countries and which might bring about a resumption of normal relations throughout the Pacific Area.

3. I respectfully submit that our Government in its wisdom has followed precisely this policy and in conjunction with other developments in the world at large, the discrediting of Japan's leadership, notably that of Mr. Matsuoka, has thereby been brought about. First of all among these world developments was the positive reaction of our Government to the conclusion by Japan of the Tripartite Pact, followed by Japan's recognition of the regime of Wang Ching-wei and followed later by Hitler's attack on Soviet Russia. Japan had joined the Axis chiefly to safeguard her security against Soviet Russia and thus to avoid the risk of being caught between the U.S.S.R. and the United States. The basis on which Japan had joined the Tripartite Alliance had thus been completely upset and this country is now endeavoring to get out of a very dangerous position in which it has enmeshed itself by pure miscalculation. The impact of foreign developments, as I have pointed out to our Government, inevitably reacts on the foreign policies of Japan and I have indicated that the liberal elements in this country might well be brought to the top through the trend of events abroad. This situation has now come and I believe that there is a favorable chance that *under these new conditions* Japan may be induced to fall into line in a program of world reconstruction on the basis of the Roosevelt-Churchill declaration. For many years we have followed a policy of patient argument and forbearance toward Japan while at the same time making clear our determination to take positive measures as they might be called for, and this policy, in conjunction with the impact upon Japan of developments abroad, has rendered the political soil of this country hospitable to the sowing of new seeds. If these seeds are now carefully planted and fostered, the anticipated regeneration of thought in Japan and a complete readjustment of the relations between our two countries may be brought about.

4. There has been advanced from certain quarters, and I have no doubt that the thought is prominently in the mind of our own Government, the belief that an American-Japanese understanding at this particular moment would merely afford Japan a breathing spell and that after Japan had untangled herself

from the hostilities in China with the help of the United States she would use this opportunity to recuperate and strengthen her military forces in order to continue, at the next favorable moment, her program of aggressive expansion. That thought cannot with certainty be gainsaid. This school of thought also maintains that if the United States, Great Britain and the Netherlands now follow a policy of progressively intensifying their economic sanctions against Japan, this country will be obliged to give up her program of expansion owing to the deterioration of her domestic economy and the danger of social, economic and financial disaster. If all this is true, our Government has been faced with the dilemma of choosing between two methods of approach to obtain our desiderata, on the one hand the method of strangling Japan through progressive economic measures and on the other hand the method of constructive conciliation which is quite different from so-called appeasement. When our Government accepted in principle the proposal for a meeting between the responsible heads of the two Governments and when the exploratory conversations began in Washington, it became clear that the latter procedure had definitely been chosen by the Government of the United States. In our note of December 30, 1938, we agreed to negotiate with Japan on any issues, even though this country had already at that time started on a program of forceful expansion, and we have, indeed, never departed from that willingness. From the point of view of far-sighted statesmanship it would appear that the wisdom of our choice could not be questioned. If either now or subsequently this method of constructive conciliation should fail we would always be in a position to enforce the other method of economic pressure, and we may be sure that our country will have to remain in a state of preparedness for a long time to come no matter what trends our relations with Japan may now assume, whether for better or for worse. In the meantime we may have in mind, and we may take whatever encouragement therefrom that would seem to be justified, the thought that many problems would be automatically solved by a British victory in the world war.

5. Whatever course we may pursue in dealing with Japan must admittedly and inevitably involve certain risks, but I firmly believe after the most careful study that if our exploratory con-

versations can be brought to a head by the proposed meeting
between the President and the Prime Minister, substantial hope
will be held out, if not of securing definitely constructive results, at the very least of preventing the Far Eastern situation
from moving from bad to worse. In times past I have expressed
the opinion that in our relations with Japan the fundamental
point at issue is not whether we must call a halt to the Japanese
expansionist program but when. I firmly believe that the opportunity is now presented to halt that program without war
or the immediate risk of war, and that we shall be confronted
with the greatly augmented risk of war if the present opportunity fails us.

6. Under existing circumstances certain quarters maintain the
improbability that any action by the United States in the Pacific
would lead to counteraction by Japan which would mean war
between our two countries, but I cannot agree that public opinion in either country might not be so enflamed by acts by elements in either country, whether irrational or deliberate, as to
render war inevitable. Let us remember the *Maine* and the
Panay.

7. Japanese psychology is basically different from the psychology of any nations in the West; we cannot gauge Japanese
actions by any Western measuring rod or predict the reactions
of these people to any given set of circumstances (this fact is
hardly surprising in the case of a country so lately emerged from
feudalism) and I feel that it is most important for us to understand that psychology in connection with the present problem.
During the past several months and years I have aimed in my
reports to the Department to interpret this psychology as one
of my principal duties, and having that thought constantly in
mind I venture even at the risk of repetition respectfully to
advance the following observations.

8. If we expect and wait for Japan to undertake in the exploratory conversations such clear-cut commitments as would
be satisfactory to the United States in point both of principle
and concrete detail, there is grave risk that these conversations
will almost surely continue unproductively and indefinitely to a
point where the conclusion will be reached by the Japanese
Government and by those elements which support the Government in aiming at an understanding with the United States that

the outlook for such an understanding is hopeless and that we are merely playing for time. When we consider the abnormal sensitiveness of this country and the abnormal results of a loss of face, such a contingency might and probably would bring about a serious reaction here resulting in a revulsion of feeling against our country and the discrediting of the Konoye Cabinet. Such a situation might well bring about irrational acts the eventual cost of which would not be taken into consideration and the nature of which would be very likely to have an inflammatory effect on the American people, and a situation might well be created through measures of reprisal and counter-reprisal in which it would be very difficult to avoid war. In such a contingency the fall of the present Government and the coming into power of a military dictatorship which would have neither the disposition nor the temperament to avoid a clash with the United States would be the logical result. It seems quite possible that such a situation might prove to be even graver than if the proposed meeting between the President and the Prime Minister should take place and should fail to bring results of an entirely satisfactory nature. To put the matter in other words, the question arises whether a demonstrated unwillingness of the United States to enter upon such negotiations at all might not be more serious than the failure to attain complete success in negotiations entered upon in good faith.

9. The Japanese Government has constantly emphasized to me, and I am convinced that their declarations on this point must be accepted as sound, that it is impossible for the Government to give us assurances and future commitments more definite than those already advanced in anticipation of the proposed meeting between the President and the Prime Minister and the entry upon formal negotiations. In the strictest confidence I have been informed that one reason for this attitude is based on the fact that when Mr. Matsuoka had retired from the Gaimusho he told the German Ambassador all the details of the Washington conversations up to that moment, and the fear has been expressed that many of Mr. Matsuoka's supporters who are still in the Foreign Office would not hesitate to impart to the Germans and to the extremists whatever information might render untenable the position of the present Government. It is true that although the Government has accepted certain

fundamental principles provisionally, the definitions of Japan's future objectives and policy and the formulae which have up to the present been advanced in the exploratory conversations are open to very wide interpretation and they are so equivocal or abstruse as to create confusion rather than to clarify the undertakings which Japan would be prepared to enter upon. We are informed at the same time, however, that in the proposed direct negotiations Prince Konoye is in a position to offer to the President far-reaching assurances which could not fail to satisfy us. I have no way of knowing whether this is so, but with regard to the specific case of Japan's relations with Germany I would point out the fact that by indicating its readiness to enter upon formal negotiations with us, the Japanese Government has shown itself prepared to reduce to a dead letter Japan's membership in the Axis although she has consistently refused overtly to renounce that membership. It therefore seems quite possible that at the proposed meeting with the President Prince Konoye might be in a position to undertake commitments more satisfactory and explicit than those already undertaken in the exploratory conversations.

10. Having in mind the foregoing observations and my conviction as to their soundness, I feel that we shall not obtain our desiderata by continuing to insist on Japan's giving us in the exploratory conversations the sort of clear-cut specific undertakings which we would expect to see included in any formal and final agreement. Unless we are ready to impose a reasonable degree of confidence in the sincerity of intention and the professed good faith of the Prime Minister and his supporters in Japan to mould the future policy of the country on the fundamental principles which they have expressed their readiness to accept, and to carry out measures by which those principles shall be loyally if gradually implemented, I do not believe that we shall be successful in creating a new turn of thought in this country which will justify the hope of a general improvement in Japan's relations with the United States and of the avoidance of eventual war in the Pacific. It would of course be understood that we ourselves would implement our own commitments *pari passu* with the measures taken by Japan. Only by complete military defeat, of which there is at present no prospect, can the Japanese military machine be wholly discredited, and I be-

lieve that the only wise alternative is to endeavor to bring about through constructive conciliation, along the lines of our present efforts, a regeneration of outlook and thought in this country. I believe that it is in accordance with the highest traditions of statesmanship and wisdom that we bring our present efforts to a head before the force of their initial impetus shall be lost and before the opposition, which we believe will steadily and inevitably increase in Japan, may intervene and overcome those efforts.

11. My approach to this problem is of course restricted to the viewpoint of this Embassy and I submit the foregoing discussion in all deference to the far broader field of view of the President and yourself.[58]

Special emphasis should be placed on the views expressed in the foregoing telegram that:

(1) . . . the question arises whether a demonstrated unwillingness of the United States to enter upon such negotiations at all might not be more serious than the failure to attain complete success in negotiations entered upon in good faith.

(2) I firmly believe that the opportunity is now presented to halt that program (the expansionist program of Japan) without war, and that we shall be confronted with the greatly augmented risk of war if the present opportunity fails us.

(3) I believe that it is in accordance with the highest traditions of statesmanship and wisdom that we bring our present efforts to a head before the force of their initial impetus shall be lost and before the opposition, which we believe will steadily and inevitably increase in Japan, may intervene and overcome those efforts.

THE DIFFICULTIES FACING PRINCE KONOYE

The difficulties of the Japanese Government in the face of the extremist and pro-Axis opposition were vastly increased by the publicity given to the fact that Prince Konoye had sent a

[58] A paraphrase of telegram No. 1529, September 29, 1941, the substance of which appears in *Foreign Relations, Japan: 1931–41*, II, 645–50.

conciliatory message to the President (delivered by Admiral Nomura on August 28) and it is surprising that this publicity, instead of emanating from the White House or the State Department, appears to have been given out in Washington by the Japanese Ambassador himself who might have been expected to realize the unfortunate effects of such publicity in affording ammunition to the opposition in Japan.[59] It was indeed of the utmost importance that Prince Konoye's efforts toward conciliation be conducted so far as possible in the strictest secrecy until the Japanese public could be faced with a *fait accompli* and informed of the far-reaching advantages of that *fait accompli* to the interests of Japan as a whole and to every Japanese individual, thus effectively taking the wind out of the sails of the opposition. Admiral Toyoda told me that the message had been conveyed to Admiral Nomura in confidence, but once the announcement had come over the wires to Domei, it was found impossible to suppress the news in Japan.

CONVERSATION WITH PRINCE KONOYE

On September 6 there took place a meeting and conversation of prime importance, the nature of which should be carefully studied and weighed in any appraisal of the sincerity of the Japanese Government in its determination to reach a settlement with the United States *at almost any price,* provided that the proposed meeting between Prince Konoye and the President should take place.[60] Traditionally in Japan the Prime

---

59 The *New York Herald Tribune,* August 29, 1941, p. 1, for instance, headlined its article "Tokyo Bid for U.S. Accord On East Seen as Konoye Sends Note to Roosevelt." Wilfrid Fleisher went on to say that a message had been given to the President from the Prime Minister "by which it is believed the Japanese Premier seeks to pave the way for a Pacific settlement."

60 At 10 A.M. on September 6 — on the evening of which Mr. Grew met the Prime Minister — an Imperial Conference was held at which the following plans for prosecuting the policy of the Japanese Government were adopted: "1. Determined not to be deterred by the possibility of being involved in a war with America (and England and Holland) in order to secure our national exist-

Minister has no contact, either official or social, with foreign envoys except on State occasions, yet Prince Konoye on this night broke that tradition by inviting me to dine with him in strict secrecy at the house of a personal friend, Baron Ito, and by talking to me with the utmost frankness for a period of some three hours, only Mr. Dooman and Mr. Ushiba, the Prime Minister's confidential secretary, being present.[61] A full report of this conversation was, of course, promptly cabled by me to Washington the same evening.

Mr. Hull's Four Principles Accepted by Prince Konoye

At this point it is important to have in mind Mr. Hull's four enunciated principles which the American Government re-

ence, we will proceed with war preparations so that they be completed approximately toward the end of October.

"2. At the same time, we will endeavor by every possible diplomatic means to have our demands agreed to by America and England. . . .

"3. If by the early part of October there is no reasonable hope of having our demands agreed to in the diplomatic negotiations mentioned above, we will immediately make up our minds to get ready for war against America (and England and Holland)." As Konoye has said in his "Memoirs," after the meeting of September 6 "as far as Japan was concerned a point had been established beyond which negotiations could not proceed." *Pearl Harbor Attack*, pt. 20, pp. 4006, 4022.

T. Kase has written in *Journey to the Missouri* ed. David Nelson Rowe (New Haven: Yale University Press, 1950), p. 52, that of "all the decisions made before the war, that of September 6 was the worst. Konoye cannot be absolved of responsibility in recommending it to the throne, for he should have been fully aware of what was implied by such a momentous step. He had little liking for the decision. He should have resisted the military with more vigor and resigned then and there if his views were overruled. Instead he temporized, trusting to luck."

[61] Mr. Grew explained to the Committee investigating the Pearl Harbor attack that Konoye took great precautions to prevent the Japanese military extremists from hearing about this meeting. Mr. Grew said: "Ordinarily a Japanese Prime Minister does not consort with diplomats. The contact is always with the Foreign Minister. Most prime ministers stay off it completely. But in this case Konoye wanted to talk the thing over directly. So we proceeded to the house of a mutual friend, and automobile tags on diplomatic and official automobiles were changed so nobody could recognize us. We had the dinner. All the servants were sent out and the dinner was served by the daughter of the house. We talked for 3 hours." *Pearl Harbor Attack*, pt. 2, p. 663.

garded as an essential basis for any rehabilitation of relations between the United States and Japan, and the fact that at that evening's meeting Prince Konoye "conclusively and wholeheartedly" accepted these principles:

(1) Respect for the territorial integrity and sovereignty of other nations;

(2) Non-interference in the internal affairs of other nations;

(3) Equality, including equality in commercial oportunity; and

(4) Non-disturbance of the *status quo* except as the *status quo* may be altered by peaceful means.[62]

The memorandum of my conversation with Prince Konoye follows:

This evening the Prime Minister invited me to dine at a private house of a friend. Only Mr. Dooman and Mr. Ushiba, the Prime Minister's private Secretary, were also present. The conversation lasted for three hours and we presented with entire frankness the fundamental views of our two countries. The Prime Minister requested that his statements be transmitted personally to the President in the belief that they might amplify and clarify the approach through diplomatic channels which he had made in Washington through Admiral Nomura. The following is a brief summary of the salient points as they emerged in the course of our discussion.

1. Prince Konoye, and consequently the Government of Japan, *conclusively and wholeheartedly agree with the four principles enunciated by the Secretary of State* as a basis for the rehabilitation of relations between the United States and Japan.

2. Prince Konoye recognizes that the responsibility is his for the present regrettable state of relations between our two countries but, with appropriate modesty as to his personal capabilities, he likewise recognizes that only he can cause the desired rehabilitation to come about. In the event of failure on his part no succeeding Prime Minister, at least during his own lifetime,

[62] See the memorandum of April 16, 1941, by Secretary of State Hull, *Foreign Relations, Japan: 1931–41*, II, 406–10.

could achieve the results desired. Prince Konoye is therefore determined to spare no effort, despite all elements and factors opposing him, to crown his present endeavors with success.

3. The Prime Minister hopes that as a result of the commitments which the Japanese Government is prepared to assume as communicated to me by Admiral Toyoda, a rational basis has been established for a meeting between the President and himself. The Prime Minister, however, is cognizant of the fact that certain points may need clarification and more precise formulation, and *he is confident that the divergencies in view can be reconciled to our mutual satisfaction,* particularly by reason of the favorable disposition on the part of Japanese naval and military leaders who have not only subscribed to his proposals but who will also be represented at the suggested meeting. The Prime Minister stated that *both the Ministers of War and of the Navy have given their full agreement to his proposals to the United States.*

4. The reports which the Prime Minister has received from the Japanese Ambassador concerning the latter's conversations with the President and the Secretary have led the Prime Minister to think that the Administration in Washington entertains serious doubts as to the strength of the present Cabinet and that the Administration is not certain that in the event that the Cabinet should adopt a peaceful program it could successfully resist the attacks of opposing elements. Prince Konoye told me that from the inception of the informal talks in Washington *he had received the strongest concurrence from the responsible chiefs of both the Army and the Navy.* Only today he had conferred with the Minister of War who had promised to send a full General to accompany the Prime Minister to the meeting with the President; the Minister of the Navy had agreed that a full Admiral should accompany the Prime Minister. Prince Konoye added in confidence that he expected that the representative of the Navy would probably be Admiral Yoshida, a former Minister of the Navy. In addition the Premier would be accompanied by the Vice Chiefs of Staff of the Army and the Navy and other high-ranking officers of the armed services who are in entire accord with his aims. He admitted that there are certain elements within the armed forces who do not approve his policies, but *he voiced the conviction that since he had the full support of*

the responsible chiefs of the Army and Navy it would be pos-
sible for him to put down and control any opposition which
might develop among those elements.[63]

5. *Prince Konoye repeatedly stressed the view that time is*
of the essence. It might take half a year to a year to work out
all the details of the complete settlement and since resentment
is daily mounting in Japan over the economic pressure being
exerted by other countries, he could not guarantee to put into
effect any such program of settlement six months or a year from
now. *He does, however, guarantee that at the present time he*
can carry with him the Japanese people to the goal which he
has selected and that should difficulties be encountered in working out the details of the commitments which he may assume,
these difficulties can be overcome satisfactorily because of the
determined intention of his Government to see to it that its
present efforts are fully successful.

6. In the course of our discussion I outlined in general terms
the bitter lessons of the past to our Government as the result of
the failure of the Japanese Government to honor the promises
given to me by former Japanese Ministers for Foreign Affairs
apparently in all sincerity, as a result of which the Government
of the United States had at long last concluded that it must place
its reliance on actions and facts and not on Japanese promises
or assurances. The Prime Minister did not attempt to refute this
statement but stressed the fact that his Government now wished
to bring about a thoroughgoing reconstruction of American-
Japanese relations and he assured me that any commitments
which he would undertake would bear no resemblance to the

[63] In commenting on Konoye's emphasis upon the fact that Japanese military men were supporting his proposal to meet Roosevelt, Herbert Feis, *Road*
to Pearl Harbor, p. 276, has said: "Konoye stressed first, that his ideas were
approved by the Army and Navy; and second, that senior officials (Vice-Chiefs
of Staff) of both branches would accompany him on his mission. If and when
he said 'Yes,' they would say 'Yes'; and thus the United States could count
upon unified execution of any accord. But it seems to me far more likely
that the Army and Navy had other thoughts in mind on assigning high officials to go along with him. They would be there to see that Konoye did not
yield to the wish for peace or the will of the President. The truer version
of the bond is expressed in the title of one of the subsections of Konoye's
'Memoirs: The Independence of the Supreme Command and State Affairs from
Each Other: The Anguish of Cabinets from Generation to Generation.'"

"irresponsible" assurances which we had received in the past and that such commitments if given would be observed. The Prime Minister concluded his presentation of this point by giving me to understand that given the will the way can be found.

7. Prince Konoye stated that should the President desire to communicate any kind of suggestion to him personally and confidentially he would be glad to arrange subsequent secret meetings with me, but he expressed the earnest hope that in view of the present internal situation in Japan the projected meeting with the President could be arranged with the least possible delay. Prince Konoye feels confident that all problems and questions at issue can be disposed of to our mutual satisfaction during the meeting with the President, and he ended our conversation with the statement that he is determined to bring to a successful conclusion the proposed reconstruction of relations with the United States regardless of cost or personal risk.[64]

Prince Konoye said that the ship which was standing by to take him and his party to the proposed meeting had been specially equipped with radio of such power as to enable him to communicate directly with Tokyo from the meeting place, wherever that might be, and that as soon as he had reached agreement with President Roosevelt and had so reported to the Emperor, the Emperor would immediately issue a rescript ordering the suspension forthwith of all hostile operations.

The fact that the peace party led by Konoye, and including even influential figures in the Army and Navy, was ready to resort to the unprecedented and highly hazardous device of causing the Emperor to intervene — the device used four years later with complete success to accomplish Japan's surrender — is strong proof that Prince Konoye was ready to use all possible means to accomplish his objectives of avoiding war with the United States and reorienting Japan. Whether there was sufficient support to carry through these plans to success is not a matter on which I could express any intelligent opinion. All I can say is that Prince Konoye seemed confident that there was such support, and that the intervention of the Emperor

64 *Foreign Relations, Japan: 1931–41*, II, 604–6.

four years later, in incomparably more difficult circumstances owing to the opposition of the Army, was effective.[65]

The Phraseology of Prince Konoye's Commitments

In connection with Prince Konoye's statement that he and consequently the Japanese Government "conclusively and wholeheartedly agree with the four principles enunciated by the Secretary of State as a basis for the rehabilitation of relations between the United States and Japan," it will be noted that in our conversation of October 7 the Foreign Minister, Admiral Toyoda, referred to my conversation with Prince Konoye on September 6 and especially to the Prime Minister's

[65] In 1949 in an interview with the editor of these volumes, Mr. Grew said that on his return from Japan in 1942, he had talked to Hull and asked why Konoye's proposal of a visit with Roosevelt had not been accepted. Mr. Grew felt that such a meeting might have brought peace. Mr. Hull replied, "If you thought so strongly, why didn't you board a plane and come to tell us?" Mr. Grew reminded the Secretary of the daily telegrams which he had sent explaining the situation and his feeling about it. It was at this point, Mr. Grew said, that he wondered whether Mr. Hull had been given and had read all of the despatches from Tokyo.

In 1951 Mr. Grew wrote: "At various times during the critical period described in this survey I had carefully considered whether anything was to be gained by my requesting authorization to fly to Washington for personal conference with the President and the Secretary in order to explain the situation as we in the Embassy appraised it. I, however, discarded such a step for the following reasons:

"(1) Even in personal conversation nothing could have been added to the voluminous and detailed reports and expressions of views which throughout this period I had been telegraphing at brief intervals to the Department as partially set forth in this survey.

"(2) Up to the fall of the Konoye Government I was given no reason to believe that the conversations in Washington might not still take a favorable turn and lead to an eventual agreement between the two Governments.

"(3) At such a critical moment, when time was of the essence, I felt that it would be highly dangerous for me to absent myself from my post for the considerable period required for a flight via Hong Kong or Manila to Washington and return. My departure from Tokyo at that time would have been universally interpreted as a first step toward a break of relations, regardless of explanations, and might have hastened the war.

"(4) Under these circumstances I felt that my place of duty lay continuously in Tokyo in case developments should occur in which my personal influence with the Konoye Government might conceivably sway the issue."

"personal and private message" to the President, the phraseology of which appeared to differ in our own record and in the record on file in the Foreign Office.[66] Mr. Hull had told Admiral Nomura in Washington that Prince Konoye, as reported by us, had "fully subscribed" to the Secretary's four principles, while the Foreign Office record indicated that the Prime Minister had accepted the four points "in principle" and had indicated that some adjustment would be required in the matter of applying the four points to actual conditions. Admiral Nomura had therefore, in view of the disparity in the records, been instructed to inform the Secretary of State that the phrase "in principle" should modify the words "fully subscribed" in attributing to the Prime Minister the foregoing statement, which had been made privately. The Foreign Minister was reluctant to have Prince Konoye's "private" statement incorporated in a public official document which would have to be circulated to various Japanese officials who had no knowledge of my meeting with the Prime Minister or of his statements at that meeting.[67]

Here again was illustrated the Japanese Government's fear of formulas and its painstaking care in limiting the phraseology of the official records. There can be no doubt whatsoever that the observations of the Prime Minister to me on September 6,

[66] *Foreign Relations, Japan: 1931–41*, II, 663–65.

[67] Konoye has written in his "Memoirs": "We came more and more to feel that we were approaching a show-down. By this time we were largely aware of the difficulties confronting the negotiations, as well as the intentions of the United States. In other words, when it came to fundamentals, the difficulty was the 'Four Principles,' and when it came to more concrete obstacles, we were faced with the problems of the stationing of troops in China, the establishment of a principle of equal economic opportunity, and the problem of the Tripartite Pact. America seemed for the present to feel that Japan had no objections to the 'Four Principles.' And since I myself had told Ambassador Grew that they were 'splendid as principles,' it could well be imagined that this did not represent a real obstacle. Nevertheless, among certain elements of both the Army and the Foreign Ministries, there was undeniably powerful opposition even to agreeing upon these as principles. . . . However, since it was evident that to reject the 'Four Principles' would be to doom the American-Japanese negotiations to failure, I was hard put to know how best to handle this problem." *Pearl Harbor Attack*, pt. 20, p. 4006.

which were made in Japanese and translated by Mr. Dooman, who was born in Japan and who had a complete and accurate grasp of the Japanese language, were accurately set forth in my telegram of September 6, 1941, to Mr. Hull reporting that conversation. It should not be overlooked that Prince Konoye had qualified his statement with the observation that certain points at issue would require clarification and more precise formulation, and that it might take half a year to a year to work out all the details of the complete settlement. He had, however, expressed his confidence that the divergencies in view could be reconciled to our mutual satisfaction and that he could carry the Japanese people, including the military, to the goal selected. The wholeheartedness and completeness of Prince Konoye's conviction and assurances impressed us as being far above any question of phraseology or formulas.

Risk of Assassination

The risk to Prince Konoye's life was real, not imaginary. An attempt to assassinate Baron Hiranuma, who was known to favor a settlement with the United States, had taken place earlier in the summer and he was so seriously wounded in the throat as to render him unfit for a long period for further active service. At about this time, as we were informed on reliable authority, an attempt on Prince Konoye's life was made by four men who jumped on the running-board of his car with daggers and short swords as he was about to leave his private residence at Ogikubo. Fortunately the doors of the car were locked inside and the would-be assassins were quickly overpowered by plainclothes police.[68]

Impressions of Conversation with Prince Konoye

Mr. Dooman and I returned to the Embassy from that historic meeting with the firm conviction that we had been deal-

[68] On August 14, 1941, extremists attempted to assassinate Baron Hiranuma, Minister for Home Affairs. On September 18, 1941, four men had attacked the car in which Konoye was riding. The Prime Minister was not injured.

ing with a man of unquestioned sincerity, a point which need not be labored when one considers the high traditions of Prince Konoye's background and family, extending back into the dim ages of Japanese history.

In considering the question of Prince Konoye's sincerity in our meeting of September 6, the term "sincerity" requires qualification. His sincerity in the situation under discussion was born of dire necessity. No statesman, however high his standard of integrity, can be expected to adopt a policy which he conceives to be contrary to the best interests of his own nation. Prince Konoye could have been no less sincere in permitting his country to join the Axis and thereby to take a position opposed to the position of the United States, or later in at least tacitly countenancing the invasion of Indo-China. It was unquestionably the strong measures taken by the United States, culminating in the freezing order of July 26, 1941, that had led him to see the handwriting on the wall and to realize that the best interests of his country then lay in conciliation with America. It was in this conviction, and in the measures which he was consequently willing to take to carry this conviction into effect, and in his certainty that he could take such measures effectively, that his sincerity lay. Historians can nevertheless not overlook the fact that Prince Konoye was still Prime Minister when the decisions of July 2 and September 6 were taken.

Uncompromising Attitude of Our Government

In the light of the foregoing appraisal by the American Ambassador on the spot and in personal touch with the highest Japanese authorities, all of which was duly and fully reported to our Government, we in the Embassy felt that the burden of proof would appear to lie upon those in our Government who may have doubted the possibility of reaching a mutually satisfactory agreement with Japan or the ability of the Japanese Government to implement that agreement when reached. There are some things that can be sensed by the man on the spot which cannot be sensed by those at a distance, at home.

My belief that such doubt did exist in Washington, and that this doubt was a controlling factor in the pursuance of the subsequent policy of the Administration, springs logically from the fact that from the moment of the foregoing conversation with Prince Konoye, little or no evidence is apparent in the official correspondence of a desire or of efforts on the part of our Government to simplify Prince Konoye's difficult task or to meet him even part way. So far as we in the Embassy could perceive, the policy of the Administration during this critical time was almost completely inflexible.[69]

[69] Cordell Hull has written in his *Memoirs* (New York: The Macmillan Co., 1948), II, 1025–26, about the proposed Konoye-Roosevelt meeting: "During the next few weeks we received numerous appeals from Tokyo to hasten the Roosevelt-Konoye conference. Ambassador Grew recommended it. But Grew, who had an admirable understanding of the Japanese situation, could not estimate the over-all world situation as we could in Washington.

"President Roosevelt would have relished a meeting with Konoye, and at first he was excited at the prospect. But he instantly agreed that it would be disastrous to hold the meeting without first arriving at a satisfactory agreement.

"At no time did we return a refusal to Japan's proposal for a meeting. We simply laid down the condition that we should arrive at a basic agreement before the meeting. Japan could have had the conference at any time by negotiating an agreement that would really have brought peace in the Pacific and prosperity to her as well as to the other countries interested in the Orient.

"As for me, I was thoroughly satisfied that a meeting with Konoye, without an advance agreement, could only result either in another Munich or in nothing at all. I was opposed to the first Munich and still more opposed to a second Munich.

"We did not know it at the time, but four years later, with the uncovering of Premier Konoye's memoirs, there came a striking confirmation of the wisdom of our refusal to hold the conference unless an agreement had been reached. Konoye sets forth in his memoirs that on August 4, 1941, he presented his project for the meeting to the Japanese War and Navy Ministers. He proposed that, if the President failed to 'understand' the Japanese position, he would quit the meeting, and that the Japanese people would then understand that war was inevitable and would consequently have a firmer determination. He felt that haste was necessary because Germany might not come out well with her war in Russia, in which event the United States might take a stronger attitude toward Japan.

"Konoye's memoirs say further that the Navy supported his view. The Army, however, made a conditional acceptance in writing, to which Konoye would have to agree before setting out to meet the President. The Army first stated that the meeting would be calculated inevitably to weaken the Empire's diplomacy founded on the Tripartite Alliance and was likely to cause considerable domes-

FUTILE EFFORTS OF JAPANESE GOVERNMENT TO ELICIT
OUR CONCRETE TERMS FOR A SETTLEMENT

Continual efforts were subsequently made both by Prince Konoye and Admiral Toyoda to find out precisely, in concrete terms, the conditions which our Government regarded as essential to an agreement; our Government stated those conditions, yet in abstruse and general terms. We knew that one of the guiding considerations in the policy of our Government in dealing with Japan was to refrain from laying down any specified "conditions" as requirements to be met by Japan, yet we in the Embassy strongly felt that the time had come to state those conditions. The earnest efforts of the Japanese Government to learn, before it was too late, the expectations of our Government in concrete terms, and the unresponsiveness of our Government to these requests, are clearly revealed by the following excerpts from official conversations which are worthy of most careful study:

. . . Mr. Ushiba went on to say that pessimism in Japanese official quarters had been strengthened by failure on the part of the American Government to lay any of its cards on the table. It was true that the American Government had given a full - presentation of its principles, *but it had not precisely specified what it wanted the Japanese Government to undertake.* Although several months had elapsed since the conversations began, the apparently great care being taken by the American Government not to give the Japanese any specifications was extremely dis-

tic ripples, and was therefore considered by the Army to be inappropriate. Then came this condition:

" 'If the Prime Minister intends, while attending the conference, to adhere to the fundamental policy contained in the Japanese revised plan and, in the event that the American President fails to understand the real intentions of this country and is resolved to go on with his present policy, to quit the place of rendezvous with a determination to make war on the United States, the Army will not oppose the Prime Minister's having a direct talk with the President.'

"Konoye thus had to promise to go to the meeting and demand a Yes or No answer from the President to the Japanese proposals which would have given Japan the overlordship of the Orient; and, if the President said No, to return to Japan determined to make war on the United States."

couraging. Since the receipt of the last American memorandum (October 2) an increasing number of persons in Japanese Government circles were of the opinion that Japan had fallen into a trap, the argument running somewhat as follows: the United States never had any intention of coming to any agreement with Japan; it has now got from Japan an exposition of Japanese policies and objectives; those policies and objectives are not in line with American policies and objectives, and there is therefore justification for refusing to make an agreement with Japan and for continuing to maintain an attitude of quasi-hostility against Japan. . . .

Mr. Ushiba (the Prime Minister's secretary) asked whether we had received the actual text of the memorandum (the American memorandum of October 2).[70] The summary (which I had allowed him to read on October 4) was businesslike and objective in tone, but the actual memorandum was, he said, "extremely disagreeable." It was argumentative and preceptive, it was quite uncompromising, and it contained no suggestion or indication calculated to be helpful to the Japanese Government toward meeting the desires of the American Government. Citing the reference to attitudes toward the European war, he put the rhe-

[70] The Oral Statement of October 2, although reaffirming the desire of the Government to have Roosevelt and Konoye meet, explained that the interpretation of certain principles and the application of these principles to specific problems would have to be clarified first. The statement expressed disappointment with the Japanese proposals of September 6, professing not to understand the qualifications which Japan attached to its assurances of peaceful intent toward other nations, or the Japanese restriction upon the principle of nondiscrimination in commercial relations to the Southwest Pacific area and the limitation of the principle in regard to China. The American Government in this document stated its disfavor with the proposal to station troops in China for an indefinite period and called for some open sign of Japan's intention to withdraw from Indo-China and China. ". . . this Government has endeavored to make clear that what it envisages is a comprehensive program calling for the application uniformly to the entire Pacific area of liberal and progressive principles. From what the Japanese Government has so far indicated in regard to its purposes this Government derives the impression that the Japanese Government has in mind a program which would be circumscribed by the imposition of qualifications and exceptions to the actual application of those principles.

"If this impression is correct, can the Japanese Government feel that a meeting between the responsible heads of government under such circumstances would be likely to contribute to the advancement of the high purposes which we have mutually had in mind?" *Foreign Relations, Japan: 1931–41*, II, 656–61.

torical question, Why was there not provided some indication of the kind of undertaking the Japanese Government was expected to give? . . .[71]

The Minister began by saying that although he had given careful study to the Secretary's memorandum of October 2 he had encountered some difficulty in seizing the point of the memorandum. He had, however, come to the conclusion that the three questions concerning which the American and Japanese Governments held divergent views were as follows: (1) the maintenance of Japanese armed forces in China, (2) the respective attitude of the United States and Japan in regard to the war in Europe, and (3) equal opportunity in China. The Minister added that on October 3 he had instructed the Japanese Ambassador in Washington to ask the Secretary *whether the United States Government would set forth in precise terms the obligations which the United States Government wished the Japanese Government to undertake* with reference to the three questions mentioned above. Having heard nothing from the Japanese Ambassador, he had again on October 6 instructed Admiral Nomura to approach the Secretary in the above sense. On October 9 the Japanese Ambassador had telegraphed the Foreign Minister that he had seen the Secretary on that date but that the Ambassador was unable to provide the information which had been requested by the Foreign Minister. Admiral Toyoda added that a week of very valuable time had been wasted in an endeavor to elicit through the Japanese Ambassador information which, had it been received, would have measurably accelerated the present conversations. The Foreign Minister had today sent further instructions to Admiral Nomura to continue his efforts to obtain the desired information, but at the same time, in order to prevent further delay, he was requesting that I ask my Government to provide the desired information in reply to the following statement:

"The Government of Japan has submitted to the Government of the United States with reference to certain questions proposals which are apparently not satisfactory to the Government of the United States. *Will the American Government now set forth*

---

[71] From the memorandum of a conversation held between Mr. Ushiba and Eugene Dooman, October 7, 1941, printed in full in *ibid.,* pp. 662–63.

to the Japanese Government for its consideration the undertak-
ings to be assumed by the Japanese Government which would be
satisfactory to the American Government?" . . .[72]

All of these conversations were of course promptly reported by cable to our Government, yet not until November 26, six weeks later and long after the fall of the Konoye Cabinet, was Mr. Hull's 10-point draft proposal submitted to the Government of General Tojo. This draft proposal for a comprehensive settlement of Pacific problems was a broad-gauge, statesmanlike document, but it came too late. Had it been presented to the Konoye Cabinet, in reply to the continual requests of that Government for just such a comprehensive and detailed statement, privately and without publicity, or had it been presented to Prince Konoye at the proposed meeting with the President, there would, in our opinion, have then been every probability that an agreement would be reached. It is true that the draft proposal was not presented as an ultimatum, but coming when it did, after the conversations had dragged on futilely for some seven or eight months, permitting the pro-Axis and extremist forces of opposition in Japan to organize and consolidate their strength and allowing them to convey to the Japanese public the impression that the United States was merely playing for time and had no real intention of reaching a settlement, it was definitely regarded in Japan as an ultimatum, and it consequently was followed by the almost immediate outbreak of war.[73]

72 From the memorandum of a conversation between Mr. Grew and the Japanese Minister for Foreign Affairs, October 10, 1941, printed in *ibid.,* pp. 677–79.

73 Cordell Hull has written in his *Memoirs,* II, 1084–85, that the moment he handed the November 26 proposals to Nomura: "[The] Tokyo Government's military preparations for launching widespread attacks throughout the Pacific were nearing completion. The Japanese fleet was already steaming toward Pearl Harbor. It was Tokyo that intended to attack if the negotiations failed — not Washington. We had no plans for an attack on Japan. Japan was prepared for war in the Pacific, we were not. We wanted peace. We wanted nothing to interrupt the flow of our aid to Britain, Russia, and other Allies resisting Hitlerism. It was Japan, not the United States, who took the offensive eleven days later and made war, not alone on the United States who, she said, had delivered an ultimatum, but also upon Great Britain, Australia, and The Netherlands.

"Nomura and Kurusu themselves recognized that the responsibility for a rup-

The uncompromising attitude of our Government during this period was clearly revealed in the Department's telegram No. 542, August 27, 5 P.M. Mr. Terasaki had complained of the anti-Japanese tone of the American press and of the impression created on the Japanese public that Japan was being "encircled" by the ABCD powers, and he had expressed the hope that this unfortunate impression could be modified. The Department replied:

> It will be noted from the Department's 527, August 23, 11 A.M., which was sent before your telegram 1290, August 22, 6 P.M., was received, that the Government of the United States has endeavored publicly to make it clear that there is no intention on its part to bring about the encirclement of, or otherwise to menace, any nation.
>
> In your discretion you may point out to officials of the Japanese Government that the tone of recent press comment in the United States concerning the Far East reflects the natural reaction to the policies and actions of Japan which would have an adverse effect on American interests. The Department believes that *some positive action on the part of the Japanese Government* in response to the representations of the United States Government designed to ensure respect by Japan for the rights and interests of the United States in the Japanese Empire and the areas under its control might be more instrumental in changing the trend of public opinion in the United States to which Mr. Terasaki objects than would any statement which the Government of the United States could make.

ture with us would be Japan's, and in a message to Tokyo on that same day, November 26, which our Army and Navy intercepted and decoded, suggested an attempt be made to shift that responsibility. 'Should we,' they said, 'during the course of these conversations, deliberately enter into our scheduled operations, there is great danger that the responsibility for the rupture of negotiations will be cast upon us. There have been times in the past when she [the United States] could have considered discontinuing conversations because of our invasion of French Indo-China. Now, should we, without clarifying our intentions, force a rupture in our negotiations and suddenly enter upon independent operations, there is great fear that she may use such a thing as that as counter propaganda against us.' "

Mr. Hull has also written in the same book, p. 1091: "I saw the President at the White House at noon, following his return, and went over the situation with him. We both agreed that, from all indications, a Japanese attack was in the immediate offing."

The foregoing telegram, in conjunction with the fact that no action was taken on the important recommendation presented in my telegram of August 30, 6 P.M., rendered it clear that the Administration expected "positive action" on the part of the Japanese Government while withholding any helpful step by the United States of a nature to assist Prince Konoye in his efforts to create a situation where such "positive action" by Japan could eventually be brought about without wrecking his Government. When the Prime Minister offered to come to confer with the President of the United States, while at the same time assuring us that at such a conference Japan would meet the desires of the United States in a way to give full satisfaction, the rebuff implied in the unhelpful attitude of the American Government as revealed in the foregoing telegram and in the virtual stagnation of the Washington conversations,[74] as well as in the failure of our Government to accept Prince Konoye's proposal to come to the United States to meet the President, led logically to the fall of Prince Konoye.[75]

[74] Konoye has written: "On October 13th, Minister Wakasugi, who had returned from Tokyo to his post of duty, called upon Under-Secretary Welles on receipt of telegraphic instructions, and spoke intimately with him on the entire range of Japanese-American negotiations. He tried somehow or other to draw out positive expressions of opinion from the American side, but although Welles did say that 'There is no change at all on the point that the President and Hull desire a meeting with Premier Konoye, just as soon as the three problems that are outstanding are settled,' as regards the question, 'If that is so, what is the opinion of America on those problems?' there was only an insistence on the point, that, 'This also is fully taken up in the memorandum of October 2nd, and a clarification beyond this is unnecessary.'

"In the end, the Japanese side insisted that 'It is now the United States' turn to say something,' and to this the Americans continued to say stubbornly, 'It is Japan's turn.' The negotiations had now reached a complete deadlock." *Pearl Harbor Attack,* pt. 20, p. 4008.

[75] The Konoye Cabinet resigned on October 16. In his letter of resignation the Prime Minister said: "War Minister Tojo has come to believe that there is absolutely no hope of reaching an agreement with America by the time we specified, (Namely, the middle or latter part of October). . . . He thus concludes that the time has arrived for us to make up our minds to get ready for war against America. However, careful reconsideration of the situation leads me to the conclusion that, given time, the possibility of reaching an agreement with

AMERICAN PUBLIC OPINION UNINFORMED

As for the question of public opinion in the United States toward Japan, an important if not a controlling factor in shaping the course of our Government, it is submitted that the American public was totally unaware of the details of the proposals, efforts and assurances of Prince Konoye, or of my own reports and estimates, and that in the absence of such knowledge our public was hardly in a position to pass mature judgment in a matter of such vital and critical importance to the future welfare of our national interests and of our country.

RECOMMENDED PROCEDURE

Our views as to the method of procedure which should govern the working out in practice of any agreement reached with the Japanese Government were succinctly presented in a telegram to the Department on September 5, 1941, stating *inter alia*:

> It is obvious in this connection that no Japanese undertakings whether oral or in written form can be accepted as giving a complete guarantee that such undertakings can or will be carried out to our entire satisfaction. It is clear that the first step toward a return to the *status quo ante* in the Far East or the establishment of a situation in that area which would conform to the principles which we believe should govern decent relations between states involves the cessation on the part of Japan of its progressive acts of aggression. It would appear that the commit-

the United States is not hopeless. . . . To plunge into a great war, the issue of which is most uncertain, at a time when the China Incident is still unsettled would be something which I could not possibly agree to, especially since I have painfully felt my grave responsibility for the present state of affairs ever since the outbreak of the China Incident. . . . I have had four serious conversations with him [Tojo] on this subject but was unable to change his position. It is therefore clear to me that my ideas will not prevail and that I shall be unable to carry out my responsibilities as an advisor to the Throne." *Ibid.*, pp. 4025–26. For a discussion of the circumstances surrounding Konoye's resignation, see Feis, *op. cit.*, pp. 282–85.

ments contained in the latest Japanese proposal, if implemented, would fulfill this requirement. Since it is presumed that a detailed formulation of a general plan of reconstruction of the Far East could not probably be worked out in advance, it would be eminently desirable that the military and economic measures of the United States which are now inexorably pressing on Japan be relaxed point by point *pari passu* with the actions of the Japanese Government in the direction of implementing its proposed commitments. If our Government followed this suggested course it would always retain in its hands the leverage which would contribute to Japanese implementation of its commitments. If an adjustment of relations is to be achieved some risk must be run, but the risk taken in pursuance on our part of a course which would not only provide inducements to the Japanese to honor their undertakings but would also leave to the United States Government a certain leverage of compulsion would appear to be relatively less serious than the risk of armed conflict entailed in the progressive application of economic sanctions which would result from a refusal to accept these proposals.[76]

RECOMMENDATION FOR SPEECH BY PRESIDENT UNHEEDED

One of my most important recommendations to our Government, the Embassy's telegram No. 1355, August 30, 6 P.M. was ignored, or at least not acted upon. I told the Department that the Japanese public had never been given a clear conception of the concrete advantages which would accrue to Japan through a settlement with the United States on the basis of Mr. Hull's four principles, namely, *inter alia,* free access to raw materials on a basis of equality of commercial opportunity, a free flow of trade and commerce, financial co-operation, markets for Japan's industries, future strategic and economic safety, prosperity and a rising standard of living. The United States was pictured to the Japanese public as trying to drive Japan to the wall, economically and in every other way, and our alleged imperialistic ambitions, together with those of Great Britain, were characterized to the Japanese public, largely at German instigation, as aimed at securing an economic strangle-

[76] *Foreign Relations, Japan: 1931–41,* II, 602–3.

hold on the countries of East Asia. The only sure way of getting the true intentions of our country to the knowledge of the public in Japan was through a speech by the President which would have to be published here, and I said that I would take good care to see that it was published. Here was an important opportunity to bring about a regeneration of thought in Japan. I suggested that the President deal with this subject in his Labor Day speech. If this subject would not fit into that particular speech, an early opportunity should have been taken to bring it out in another speech. But it was never done. Of course this general theme had been touched upon by Mr. Hull and others in various utterances, but, as I told the Department, this aspect of the whole subject had never been brought forcibly to the attention of the public in Japan. Such a speech as I had in mind and recommended would have immeasurably strengthened Prince Konoye's hand at a moment when he terribly needed strengthening. It might well have turned the whole trend in Japan at this critical time. Why was my recommendation not carried out? History will wish to know.

The telegram under reference is of such importance in portraying this situation and in setting forth the foregoing considerations that it is here given, in paraphrase, in full.

As in other critical periods in the relations between our two countries which have arisen in the immediate past, all happily tided over, at this moment of crisis I conceive it of the greatest importance that I should neglect nothing in order to bring to the President and to you an entirely clear understanding of the different elements in this country which control or influence to an important degree the formulation of Japanese public opinion and consequently the motives which exert a controlling or important influence on the determination of the policies and actions of the Government of Japan. In the absence of such a complete and close understanding, measures may be adopted or constructive steps passed over by the United States which may influence to an important degree for good or evil the situation as a whole. There is little that I can add in broad outline to the accumulated knowledge of our Government which has been obtained from the regular reports from this Embassy and from elsewhere. At this particular moment, however, I shall endeavor to focus clearly this knowledge in its application to the problems before us now and to put forth in relation thereto, for what value they may possess, certain recommendations.

As the Department is fully aware, the view widely held outside of Japan that this country may be classified as a totalitarian power is untrue. The Japanese Government exercises a considerable but in no manner a controlling effect on Japanese public opinion by working through the police and the press. The answer may be found in the fact that the Japanese Government for its own part is continually beset by pressure groups and different powerful though ununified elements which must to varying extent be pacified and to whose opinions consideration must be given in the determination of official policies and actions. As the past has demonstrated, the alternate course would lead to political murders and the fall of the Government. There is of course always a possibility that a military Government of a totalitarian nature may be set up which would be able and willing to govern along purely dictatorial lines. As I have indicated on previous occasions, under certain circumstances there is always the possibility, perhaps greater now than at any previous time, of such a development, but it has yet to occur and may perhaps never materialize should the Government now in power be able to steer Japan successfully through the present critical period.

The Prime Minister is considered by liberals to be weak but doubt may be expressed whether those liberal elements have a clear understanding of the basic difficulties and perils with which he is faced from the pro-Axis and extremist groups. The Prime Minister, as pointed out in the last paragraph of my 1347, August 29, 9 p.m., cannot avoid the grievous responsibility for having permitted his country to reach its present position, but it is equally true that Prince Konoye is now with great energy endeavoring to find a solution. It is likely that the writing on the wall is already perceptible to the Prime Minister and his associates in the Government; it is clear that they now recognize the basic mistake that Japan made in joining the Axis, but having encouraged and fostered the growth of pro-Axis feeling in this country the Prime Minister and his colleagues are at the present time confronted with serious difficulties in surmounting that feeling and in inaugurating a new course both in policy and in public sentiment, particularly in the direction of a reconstruction of relations between the United States and Japan. In the circumstances would it not be in our interest and for the sake of opposing pro-Axis influence in Japan for the Government of the United States to try to assist the Prime Minister in his endeavors, so far as that is possible without sacrificing the principles for which the United States stands, and indeed with the hope that he will be able to bring about a change of course on the part of Japan which may in good time lead Japan itself to subscribe to these principles?

Propaganda activities emanating from Nazi sources, for which the Konoye Government must accept a large share of responsibility, have implanted in the consciousness of the greater portion of the Japanese a regrettably false picture, of which the following is a brief outline:

> England and America, allegedly having everything, have consistently despoiled for selfish ends the nations of the Far East; the aim of Great Britain and the United States is to establish their dominance in the Orient, to bring under their control the raw materials, trade, and commerce of this area, thus shutting off Japan from access to materials essential to her national existence and, through a policy of so-called encirclement, to crush her. Following a German victory (which is considered as certain), the resulting collapse of Great Britain and preoccupation of America which would then be required to move the United States fleet into the Atlantic, would give Japan a free hand to carry out the southward advance and to set up the co-prosperity sphere and the new order in East Asia, including the liquidation of the China Affair, unhampered by the occidental imperialists.

The picture sketched above could be indefinitely elaborated but in broad terms and in brief it sets forth what the greater portion of the Japanese people believe at the present time.

As against the foregoing, the Japanese public have not had presented to them the real aims of the United States nor the advantages which the United States would be in a position to make available to Japan if the latter were to accept the American view-point by giving up the employment of force in her national policy and by subscribing to the principles outlined by the United States as a basis of reconstruction in the relations between our two countries. The Japanese people have been afforded no idea of the advantages which would accrue to Japan as a result of such a change of action and policy. The press of this country has certainly given no hint of such possible advantages and any information along those lines as may be received by officials and governmental departments is usually segregated from other officials and kept from the general public.

I venture therefore with due respect to inquire whether our Government might not fruitfully give consideration to the benefits which might result from a public expression of views on this general topic emanating from an official source, dealing not with the present or the past but with what the future might hold, possibly beginning with the four points appearing in the document delivered to you on April 16 by the Japanese Ambassador as a foundation for a reconstruction of relations between the United States and Japan, followed by a review of some of the practical advantages which would redound to Japan if that country were at the present time to embark upon a new course of policy consistent with these broad principles. I am aware that the subject in general has been on numerous occasions discussed in public statements by high officials of the United States Government, but rarely if ever have these statements reached the Japanese people and those which in the past may have been given publicity in Japan are at this moment buried and forgotten under the mass of anti-American propaganda.

The time element is an essential factor. The Japanese people as well as the press are intensely interested, whether pro or con, in the outcome of endeavors to reconstruct relations with the United States arising from Prince Konoye's letter to the President. The present juncture appears to be favorable. Should the President find it possible to deal, however briefly but in a constructive manner, with this general subject in his speech to be delivered on Labor Day, stressing the benefits which the future could hold rather than dwelling on the regrettable past and in so far as practicable leaving out observations which could be utilized by pro-Axis groups here, it is my opinion that the President's comments could be given publicity in this country (naturally I would spare no effort to have his remarks appear in the press here) and that a new line of reasoning might as a result be opened up to the public which would tend to reinforce the hand of the Prime Minister and his associates in their attempts to work for conciliation with the United States in the teeth of the pro-Axis groups and extremist elements who will stop at nothing to wreck these endeavors.

Another Recommendation Unheeded

Another and previous important recommendation of mine in July, in connection with reports of a possible invasion of French Indochina by Japanese forces, namely, that if our Government was prepared to apply economic reprisals in case of such an invasion, the Japanese Government should be privately informed of such an intention *before* the occupation of bases in Indochina should occur, was also, so far as I am aware, not acted upon.[77] The subject is dealt with in the following excerpt from my diary for July 22. Our freezing order against Japan was announced and went into effect on July 26.

Information has come to me from a secret source that continued pressure on Vichy is being exerted by the Japanese Government to cede bases in Indochina with an indication that these bases will be taken by force if a favorable reply is not given before July 24 (extended from July 20). The British Commander in Chief in the Far East feels very strongly that both the British and American Governments should warn Japan *in advance* that certain economic sanctions will be imposed if these bases are taken. By occupying these bases the Japanese would greatly improve their strategic position for an attack on American, British and Dutch possessions and also would be able to bring overwhelming pressure on Siam. Once these bases had been occupied it is unlikely that any threat would induce the Japanese to withdraw, but a warning in advance might serve to deter them. . . .

Craigie feels that such a warning will now be too late but that

77 See Feis, *op. cit.*, pp. 227–41, for a discussion of the circumstances surrounding the issuance of the freezing order.

if it is to be issued at all it would have greater effect if given out exclusively in London and Washington rather than by us in Tokyo.

In passing this information on to the Department I said that I had no reason to alter my previous opinion that the reports of a possible descent on Indochina should be taken seriously, but I still felt that the new report should be taken with a certain degree of caution. If, however, our Government is prepared to apply economic reprisals I felt sure that careful consideration would have to be given to the thought that some private intimation to the Japanese Government of that fact would be desirable rather than to take such action after the bases in Indochina had been taken with or without the permission of Vichy. If an occupation were once effected, the question of saving face would render subsequent withdrawal difficult, but a deterrent effect might conceivably be exerted by a clear and unambiguous statement of our intentions in advance. We must not allow any possible misconception by the Japanese as to our determination to take positive action in certain circumstances let Japanese-American relations proceed one step further on the road to potential war.

JAPAN'S CRIMINALITY

The implications revealed by the foregoing discussion and the documents cited are obvious. Japan had broken the law of nations and was properly regarded as an international criminal. Yet when successive Japanese Governments pleaded for the assistance of the United States in the creation of conditions which would supply the necessary incentive to a complete reorientation of policy and an undoing of her international misdeeds (not, it is true, admitted by herself as misdeeds), such assistance was coldly withheld. Thus two of Japan's foremost statesmen, Baron Hiranuma in 1939 and Prince Konoye in 1941, were tacitly rebuffed in their far-sighted efforts to turn their country into new channels in which good relations with the United States and the other democracies could, for them, become practicable. Up to the autumn of 1941 Japan had found that crime does not pay. Nevertheless it was the old story of the criminal permanently suspected by the police, unable to attain rehabilitation because untrusted and unaided in his efforts toward reform, and unable to alter the conditions which had originally turned him to criminality. But in international affairs, given what we have every reason to believe were sincere efforts toward reform, was this position and attitude of the United States one of far-seeing and constructive statesmanship?

Crime, by definition and of its nature, is never justifiable or capable of being condoned. There are crimes committed gratuitously and out of sheer perversity or lust, but cases sometimes occur when the crime might have been averted by the exercise of foresight and imagination on the part of those associated in some way with the circumstances out of which the crime has arisen. It seemed to us in the Embassy that the attitude toward the offender — Japan — of our Government until the end of August, 1941, was one in which readiness to extend a helping hand and promise of stern retribution if the offender should resort to further crimes were wisely balanced. However, that far-seeing and enlightened attitude appeared to be suddenly abandoned, and according to Secretary Knox, if correctly reported, the conclusion was reached that the offender was incorrigible and that he should, in the fullness of time, be summarily dealt with.

INTERNATIONAL CONCILIATION

The soil of Japan, through the stagnation of the conflict in China and the impact of other developments abroad, had become, as we pointed out to our Government, fertile for the sowing of new seeds, and we felt the importance of our Government's sowing those seeds with constructive wisdom. The greatest obstacle to international conciliation is the inability of one Government to put itself in another Government's place and to comprehend the difficulties with which that Government is faced, and, when practical, to assist that other Government in overcoming those difficulties for the ultimate good of both countries, when there exists any evidence whatever that the second Government genuinely intends to adopt new policies and to undo past iniquities. International conciliation is not a one-way street. It must work both ways. To explain these things, mutually and reciprocally, namely the point of view of both Governments and the specific difficulties with which each Government is faced, is one of the primary reasons why ambassadors are sent abroad. I continually told the Japanese Government of the attitude of American public opinion; I continually told our own Government of the attitude of Japanese public opinion; and I continually told both Governments of the attitude of official opinion in our respective countries.

A Dramatic Gesture Needed

What was needed in the summer or early autumn of 1941 was a dramatic gesture, something that would electrify the people both in Japan and in the United States and would give impetus to an entirely new trend of thought and policy. The proposed meeting of the President with the Prime Minister of Japan would, in our opinion, have accomplished this had it taken place, and the new orientation desired by the Konoye Government would have been accepted by the Japanese people as a whole with a profound sense of relief, for they were tired of war and of the economic hardships resulting directly and indirectly from war. The primary purpose of Prince Konoye's proposal to meet the President was to learn our Government's point of view at first hand, no less than to explain the point of view of Japan. It lay entirely with the Government of the United States to say the word that would have brought Prince Konoye, whose ship and staff, composed of the highest military and naval officers of the country, were ready and waiting, promptly to meet the President in Alaska or anywhere else that he might designate.[78]

[78] As late as the end of August, 1941, President Roosevelt was seriously considering meeting Prince Konoye. In Mr. Hull's memorandum reporting the

URGENCY OF THE SITUATION

The Japanese could not have been playing for time, as was reported in the American press. The Japanese needed to bring about a relaxation of our freezing order at the earliest possible moment, and both Prince Konoye and Admiral Toyoda were constantly emphasizing to me that time was of the essence and that Japan could not afford to permit the negotiations to be drawn out. Japan had been cut off from sources of supply of most of her basic raw materials, she was each day diminishing her stocks of these materials, and the time would inevitably come when these stocks would become depleted and she would be impotent. These facts were continually emphasized in our telegrams to Washington.

ABILITY OF THE JAPANESE GOVERNMENT TO CONTROL ITS ARMED FORCES

Our Government was in possession of information which had convinced it that the armed forces of Japan, which were busily engaged in preparing a program of war if the peace

meeting of the President with Admiral Nomura and himself on August 28, 1941, the following significant points are brought out: "He then handed to the President a communication from the Prince Premier of Japan to the President of the United States. . . . The President read it with interest and complimented the tone and spirit of it.

"The President then spoke somewhat as he did at the last meeting a week ago Sunday about the idea suggested by the Japanese Prime Minister of a personal meeting between the President and the Prime Minister at as early a date as possible for the purpose of having a frank discussion of all important affairs existing between the two countries. The President again spoke of the difficulty of going as far as Hawaii and elaborated on the reasons why it would be difficult to get away for twenty-one days. He then turned to Juneau, Alaska, as a meeting place, which would only require some fourteen or fifteen days, allowing for a three or four days' conversation with the Japanese Prime Minister. The only point raised by the Ambassador in this connection was that the conversation be held as early as possible.

"At the conclusion of the reading of the communication, the President said to the Ambassador that he could say to his Government that he considered this note a step forward and that he was very hopeful. He then added that he would be keenly interested in having three or four days with Prince Konoye, and again he mentioned Juneau." *Foreign Relations, Japan: 1931–41*, II, 571–72.

program should fail, could not be controlled by the Japanese Government. We in Tokyo were closer to the scene than was the Administration in Washington, and we believed, on the basis of the highest possible evidence, and so reported, that the Japanese Government at that time *was* in a position to control the armed forces of the country. We explained in several of our telegrams to our Government that Germany's attack on Soviet Russia had given those elements in Japan which controlled national policies further and convincing evidence that confidence could not be placed in Germany's promises; that the Japanese public at large had become apathetic over the four-year effort to conquer China; and that the loss of the major portion of Japan's foreign trade through operation of the economic sanctions against Japan, following as it did a progressive depletion of her economic and financial resources, was bringing home to the Japanese people the desperate position into which the pursuit of their Government's policies had led them. That the Japanese Government was in a position at that time to control its forces is an affirmation of belief which can never be conclusively proven; but no one, I think, would contest the view that the Japanese Government was in a far better position to control its forces in the summer of 1941 than it was in December, 1938, when the American Government indicated to the Japanese Government willingness to consider changes by process of negotiation of treaties which were declared by Japan to be outmoded.

THE WORLD PROBLEM

Without speculating on the question whether, prior to the conclusion of the Tripartite Alliance on September 27, 1940, the Far Eastern conflict could be dissociated from the European war, it became obvious from the moment that Japan allied herself with Germany and Italy — if not before — that the Far Eastern conflict had become an integral part of a much wider problem, involving military as well as political considerations of the first order of importance. What were the probabilities of the United States becoming involved in war with Germany and Italy? Was the United States in a position to justify our country in engaging in war at the same time with Germany and Japan? If war with Germany were probable or inevitable, was it in our national interests to take a position which would simultaneously make war with Japan probable or inevitable? These were questions which preoccupied us. We assumed that the Administration had given them the most careful study and had reached conclusions based on information far more extensive than that available to us. However, we were given no indication of the character of these conclusions, and without such indication it was impossible for us intelligently to appraise the purely factual information which was furnished us on the progress of the conversations with the Japanese. I therefore ventured to remind the Department that the formulation and carrying out of a program with regard to future relations with Japan should properly be postulated on the answer to the question whether war with Japan, if not considered to be inevitable, was at this time in the national interests. I observed in effect that, if war with Japan were considered to be neither inevitable nor desirable, it would not be the better part of wisdom to shape our course, which increasingly reduced the prospects of an adjustment of relations with Japan, on an estimate or opinion that Japan in no circumstances would risk a war with the United States.

THE UNITED STATES HAD EVERYTHING TO GAIN, NOTHING TO LOSE, BY THE PROPOSED MEETING OF THE PRESIDENT AND THE PRIME MINISTER

We now know that our Government felt that a meeting between the President and the Prime Minister, should it fail to yield all of our desiderata, would be ultimately more dangerous to our interests than if no meeting were held at all. With such a premise we in the Embassy could not agree. We were convinced in any case that *most* of our desiderata then and all of our desiderata later would be met and eventually implemented; we felt strongly that the ultimate effects of rebuffing Prince Konoye by continual delay in arranging the meeting, even if the preliminary conversations failed to produce all that we desired of them, would be far more serious than if the meeting were held with only partial immediate success, and we so reported.

In considering the foregoing point, we had in mind the fact that whatever results might emerge from the proposed meeting, the United States could and would still hold the leverage necessary to bring about the implementation of whatever commitments should be undertaken, relaxing our economic measures only as that implementation should proceed. We had, it appeared to us in the Embassy, nothing to lose, everything to gain. The United States was committed to the support of the Government of China, but it was not committed to invite war with Japan in order to obtain China's total desiderata immediately. It was our belief in the Embassy that had the meeting with the President taken place, Prince Konoye, in the face of the concrete advantages to Japan which the President would have been able to offer, could never have afforded to allow the conference to result in failure.[79]

---

[79] Herbert Feis, former State Department official, has written in *The Road to Pearl Harbor,* pp. 274–76: "The world may long wonder what would have happened had the President agreed then to meet with Konoye. Grew and Dooman, at the time and later, had a sense that the refusal was a sad error. To them it seemed that the American government missed a real chance to lead Japan back to peaceful ways. Konoye, they thought, was sincere in his acceptance of those principles of international conduct for which the American government stood, and with the support of the Emperor would be able to carry through his promises. In words which Grew confided to his diary:

" 'It is my belief that the Emperor, the Government of Prince Konoye and the militant leaders of Japan (the leaders then in control) had come to accept the status of the conflict in China, in conjunction with our freezing measures and Japan's economic condition as evidence of failure or comparative incapacity to succeed.'

"Our attitude, he thought (and others since have thought the same), showed a lack both of insight and suppleness, if not of desire. The mistake sprang, in this view, from failure to appreciate why Konoye could not be as clear and conclusive as the American government wished; and to admit that Japan could

WITHDRAWAL OF JAPANESE TROOPS FROM
INDOCHINA AND CHINA

We in the Embassy had no doubt that the Prime Minister would have agreed, at his meeting with the President, to the eventual withdrawal of Japanese forces from all of Indochina and from all of China with the face-saving expedient of being permitted to retain a limited number of troops in North China and Inner Mongolia temporarily. In this connection it is pertinent that in the proposals of the Japanese Government communicated by Admiral Toyoda to me on September 4 (and

correct its course only in a gradual and orderly way. Wise American statesmanship, thus, would have bartered adjustment for adjustment, agreeing to relax our economic restraints little by little as Japan, little by little, went our way. Instead, the judgment ends, it was dull and inflexible. By insisting that Japan promise in black and white, then and there, to conform to every American requirement, it made Konoye's task impossible.

"It will be always possible to think that Grew was correct; that the authorities in Washington were too close to their texts and too soaked in their disbelief to perceive what he saw. That the American government was as stern as a righteous schoolmaster cannot be denied. Nor that it was unwilling either to ease Japanese failure, or to provide any quick or easy way to improve their hard lot. But the records since come to hand do not support the belief that a real chance of maintaining peace in the Pacific — on or close to the terms for which we had stood since 1931 — was missed. They do not confirm the opinion that Konoye was prepared, without reserve or trickery, to observe the rules set down by Hull. Nor that he would have been able to do so, even though a respite was granted and he was allowed to grade the retreat gently.

"If Konoye was ready and able — as Grew thought — to give Roosevelt trustworthy and satisfactory promises of a new sort, he does not tell of them in his 'Memoirs.' Nor has any other record available to me disclosed them. He was a prisoner, willing or unwilling, of the terms precisely prescribed in conferences over which he presided. The latest of these were the minimum demands specified by the Imperial Conference of September 6, just reviewed. It is unlikely that he could have got around them or that he would have in some desperate act discarded them. The whole of his political career speaks to the contrary....

"Konoye could have honestly agreed that Japan would stop its southern advance and reduce its forces in China to the minimum needed to assure compliance with its wishes. That is really all. To the seekers of the New Order in East Asia this seemed much; to the American government it seemed too little. The error, the fault, in American policy — if there was one — was not in the refusal to trust what Konoye could honestly offer. It was in insisting that Japan entirely clear out of Indo-China and China (and perhaps out of Manchukuo) and give up all exclusive privileges in these countries."

by Admiral Nomura to the Secretary of State on September 6) section (d) stated:

> that Japan will endeavor to bring about the rehabilitation of a general and normal relationship between Japan and China, upon the realization of which *Japan is ready to withdraw its armed forces from China as soon as possible* in accordance with the agreements between Japan and China.[80] . . .

Soviet forces were in occupation of Outer Mongolia; garrisons of several foreign powers, including the United States, were still present in various parts of China. As for Manchuria, it was our understanding that General Chiang Kai-shek himself had declared in July, 1937, that China was determined to give up *no more* of its territory, a tacit admission that the return of Manchuria to China could not at that time be expected.[81]

Point 3 of the Japanese terms for peace with China, as handed to me by the Foreign Minister on September 22, 1941, referred to "Co-operation between Japan and China for the purposes of preventing communistic and other subversive activities which may constitute a menace to the security of both countries and of maintaining the public order in China," and it provided for the "stationing of Japanese troops and naval forces in certain areas in the Chinese territory for a necessary period for the purposes referred to above and in accordance with the existing agreements and usages." When I asked Admiral Toyoda the precise purport of the term "existing agreements and usages," he replied that these words must be understood as written; however, he referred in this connection to the presence in China of American marines merely by way of an illustration of the phrase in question.[82]

The following excerpt from my conversation with the Foreign Minister on October 7 is especially pertinent:

[80] *Foreign Relations, Japan: 1931–41*, II, 608.
[81] See *supra*, p. 1055, n. 9.
[82] See the record of this conversation printed in *Foreign Relations, Japan: 1931–41*, II, 631–33.

The Foreign Minister said that in so far as the Secretary's memorandum of October 2 was concerned, he would like to make one brief comment, namely, that it was his impression that the Government of the United States wished the Japanese Government to revert at once and unqualifiedly to the *status quo* which prevailed four years ago. Since that time Japan had been involved in warfare on a large scale demanding hardships and sacrifices of the people of Japan who had been led to support such trials as a patriotic duty. The Japanese Government *was willing and prepared to return to the situation prevailing four years ago* but it was essential that the Government of the United States should understand that to undo virtually at a moment's notice the work of the past four years is an undertaking of tremendous scope and one entailing basic adjustments.[83]

Also the following excerpt from certain observations made to me by a reliable Japanese informant, Count Kabayama, on October 25:

The belief is current among Japanese leaders that the principal difficulty in the way of an understanding with the United States is the question of *the removal of Japanese armed forces from China and Indochina,* but these same leaders are confident that, provided Japan is not placed in an impossible position by the insistence on the part of the United States that all Japanese troops in these areas be withdrawn at once, *such a removal can and will be successfully effected.*

The informant, who is in contact with the highest circles, went on to say that for the first time in ten years the situation at present and the existing political setup in Japan offer a possibility of a reorientation of Japanese policy and action.[84]

I have little doubt that the view was strongly supported in the Administration in Washington that an agreement with Japan under which assent would be given to Japan's stationing troops in certain parts of China for an unspecified period would have compromised a principle adopted by the United States. Had it been possible for us immediately to meet one of the

[83] *Ibid.*, p. 665.   [84] *Ibid.*, p. 698.

fundamental purposes which had led Japan to seek an agreement with the United States, namely Japan's free access to certain critically needed raw materials on a basis of commercial equality, the objection might have been valid. The facts were, nevertheless, that such a program could not have been implemented in its entirety under wartime conditions, for the raw materials of which she had greatest need were the very materials which we ourselves were obliged to conserve in our defense efforts against Germany. It would not have been possible for the United States, while carrying out its rearmament program and manufacturing war materials for Great Britain, to have provided Japan with full access to the materials required. So long, therefore, as the obligation of the United States to accord to Japan one of the fundamental advantages which she was to gain through an agreement with our country would have had to await full implementation until after the European war had ended, assent to the stationing of Japanese troops in specified parts of China until such time as the plan could be fully carried out would not, it seemed to us, have compromised the position of the United States on a matter of principle.

WHAT THE EMBASSY BELIEVED

We in the Embassy believed that the proposed meeting between the President and Prince Konoye should have taken place in spite of the failure of the exploratory conversations to yield all that we desired of them; we believed that at that meeting the Administration might have placed our cards face-up on the table along the general lines of the 10-point draft program of November 26 while at the same time emphasizing the benefits which Japan would unquestionably derive from an acceptance of that program, benefits which might helpfully have been stressed in an earlier speech by the President. We believed that at the same time sympathetic study might have been accorded to the problems facing the Japanese Government which Prince Konoye would then have presented, and that the latter might have been informed that the Government of the United States recognized the inherent difficulties which would confront the Japanese Government in meeting completely and immediately such commitments as Prince Konoye had already professed himself willing to undertake, but that the relaxation of our economic sanctions could take place only gradually and *pari passu* with the implementation of those commitments. In the meantime, as a gauge of our own good faith and with a view to affording Prince Konoye some concrete achievement to take home to the Japanese people, our Government might well have offered to commence negotiations at an early date for a new treaty of commerce and navigation with Japan, on the distinct understanding that the signature of such a treaty and its ultimate ratification must depend upon the effectiveness of the measures taken by the Japanese Government toward implementing such commitments as might have been undertaken at the conference.

The crux of this whole situation, as it existed in the early autumn of 1941, was clearly expressed to me by a former Japanese Prime Minister, Mr. Hirota, having important influence in the highest political circles. He said, on October 1, that the proposal of Prince Konoye to meet the President of the United States on American soil was generally approved, even among the military, in view of the absolute necessity of arriving at a settlement with the United States because of the economic situation; that delegations representing important political groups had met with Prince Konoye and had given him assurances that his endeavors to attain an agreement with the United States would be supported by the Japanese nation as a whole; *and since, if the proposed conference were held, it would be unthinkable for Prince Konoye to return to Japan from a mission which had ended in failure, the American terms would perforce have to be accepted by the Prime Minister who would and could carry the entire Japanese nation, including the military, with him.*

We believed that the American embargoes and freezing order had created precisely the situation in Japan which they were intended to create, but that our Government failed to profit by the situation thus produced by its own carefully calculated measures. We believed that in the perpetual tug-of-war between the military extremists and the moderate elements in Japan, those moderate elements, as represented by Prince Konoye and his Government, which desired and aimed to avoid at almost any cost a war with the United States, for the first time in ten years predominated, and that the American Government should have accorded to Prince Konoye all reasonable support and assistance in achieving his difficult but enlightened task. We believed that had the proposed conference between Prince Konoye and the President been held it would have led, without our sacrificing any point of principle or interest whatsoever, to a rehabilitation of the relations between the United States and Japan, and to an ultimate settlement of the whole problem of the Pacific.

THE FACTS ASSEMBLED

War is too serious a matter to accept as an inevitable misfortune without an exhaustive examination into the facts and causes of its incidence.[85] An attempt has herein been made, from the standpoint of the Embassy in Tokyo, to present the facts and to examine the causes of the outbreak of war between the United States and Japan. The record as presented in the documents in this survey speaks for itself.

It is natural that certain questions should have arisen in the mind of the objective observer. For purposes of clarity, it is felt desirable at this point to assemble, at the expense of some

[85] In the hearings before the Congressional Committee investigating the attack at Pearl Harbor, Mr. Grew was asked when he had reached the conclusion that war was inevitable. He replied: "Mr. Chairman, I think my position on that is perhaps somewhat similar to the position of a candidate for political office who knows that he is going to be defeated but he does not admit it until it is all over.

"Our foreign service is our first line of national defense and our duty is to hold that line if we can do it. For any diplomatic officer in the foreign service or for any foreign-service officer to go abroad and throw up his hands and say 'War is inevitable' might as well go home because he would be a discredit to the service in which we are members." Pearl Harbor Attack, pt. 2, p. 566.

repetition, the outstanding factors in the situation as they appeared to the Embassy:

1. In the summer and autumn of 1941, the restrictive financial and economic measures of the United States, added to the impact of other foreign developments including the virtual stagnation of the conflict in China, had brought Japan to a precarious position. In that position, the Japanese Government was faced with two urgent and inescapable alternatives: either an all-out do-or-die attempt to render herself invulnerable to foreign pressure by conquering the areas to the south which could supply her essential commodities, or a settlement with the United States, involving a settlement with China.

2. Prince Konoye, as Prime Minister, chose to pursue a program of peace. He accepted Mr. Hull's four fundamental principles for a settlement, he proposed that he come to meet the President of the United States on American soil, and he gave definite assurances that he was prepared fully to meet the views of the American Government and to conclude an agreement which would be satisfactory to the United States. His position and attitude were born of dire necessity.

3. While endeavoring to follow and to effectuate a program of peace, the Japanese Government was steadily preparing a program of war in case the peace program should fail.

4. The American Government meanwhile took the position that unless or until the exploratory conversations with the Japanese should produce what it considered a satisfactory basis to commence formal negotiations, there would be no purpose in the meeting between the responsible heads of the two Governments.

5. The Embassy, however, pointed out that the problem could never be solved by formulas drawn up in the exploratory conversations, and that the Japanese would not commit themselves in those conversations to the maximum concessions which Prince Konoye would be willing and able to yield in his proposed meeting with the President. The reason for this was that they feared the effect on the opposition of the certain leakage of such commitments as might be undertaken in the preliminary conversations, whereas, when faced with a final *fait accompli* and a complete agreement with the United States as a result of the meeting between Prince Konoye and the President, the op-

position in Japan would be overwhelmed by the enthusiasm and general sense of relief of the Japanese people as a whole.

6. The Japanese Government repeatedly and urgently begged that the meeting take place and an agreement be concluded before the initial impetus of Prince Konoye's efforts be lost and the internal situation in Japan should force the Government, or a successor Government, to abandon the program of peace and revert to a program of war. The Japanese Government meanwhile continually begged our Government to state concisely and completely its terms for an agreement. This was not done until Mr. Hull's 10-point draft proposal was submitted to the Japanese Ambassador in Washington on November 26, 1941, long after the fall of the Konoye Cabinet. The proposal came too late and war almost immediately intervened.

7. Prince Konoye and his Government knew beyond peradventure that it would be unthinkable to allow the proposed meeting with the President, had it taken place, to result in failure, and they knew, and so informed us, that they must accept our terms, for *time was on our side* and our defense program was daily growing in strength.

8. Japan's invasion of French Indochina indicated the strength of the momentum of the southern advance, as did the Japanese refusal to accept the President's proposal for the neutralization of that country. With the peace talks still continuing in Washington, Prince Konoye had either approved of the invasion of Indochina, or did not wish or was unable to prevent it. Could he have been expected one month later suddenly to "reverse the engine," which had gathered speed over the space of a decade, as a result of a few days' conversation with the President?

In July, when Indochina was invaded, Prince Konoye could hardly yet have seen the handwriting on the wall. We had not officially warned him that freezing measures would be immediately imposed should Japan take over Indochina. In August and September the picture was clearer, and by that time Japan's growing distrust of Germany following her attack on Soviet Russia, our freezing measures, and the added necessity, imposed by those developments, for the early termination of the conflict with China, had convinced him of the imperative necessity of reaching an agreement with the United States. By such an agreement he could and would have reversed the engine of Japanese military aggression.

WHAT THE UNITED STATES HAD TO GAIN

The question furthermore poses itself as to what the United States had to gain, or what to lose, from the proposed meeting between the President and the Prime Minister, instead of allowing our relations with Japan to proceed without an agreement, permitting our economic measures against Japan to work their results unchecked.

(*a*) It was believed by the Embassy that the United States had everything to gain, nothing to lose, by the proposed meeting between the President and Prince Konoye. The step-by-step *pari passu* arrangement by which an agreement would be implemented by the United States had been explained to the Konoye Government which could have labored under no illusion that Japan could trick our country into any unilateral surrender of an advantageous position. Our restrictive measures need have been relaxed only step-by-step with Japan's implementation of her own commitments, and could immediately have been reapplied if those commitments were not carried out.

(*b*) There could be no reason to believe that our position would have been any less favorable had Japan taken advantage of an agreement with the United States to regain and reorganize her strength and later to have sent to the south or to the north the troops withdrawn from China through American assistance. Since it would have been absurd for us to attempt to require or to expect Japan to disarm in a world at war, it would have been necessary for us, also, to remain completely prepared in this area whether an agreement were reached or not. We could not for a moment have thought of weakening our Pacific fleet. With our defense effort much further along, the Philippines better defended, Singapore reinforced, and Japan out of southern Indochina and possibly Hainan, we would have been far better prepared to fight later than we were in December, 1941.

(*c*) The fact that Japan's alliance with the Axis would have had to be rendered immediately inoperative following an agreement with the United States is important for even though the letter of the Pact with Germany and Italy must have remained, its spirit would have disappeared. Japan's ties with the Axis would inevitably have been weakened and pro-Axis sentiment would rapidly have cooled. It is even conceivable that Germany, disgruntled by Japan's defection toward the United States, might herself have abrogated the Alliance.

(d) Had Japan, after withdrawing from China and abandoning her southward advance, later attacked Soviet Russia, a country which we were then aiding as a matter of expediency and major strategy, we would have been in a far more favorable position to offer effective assistance to Soviet Russia than we were under the circumstances.

OUR POSITION AS REGARDS CHINA

During the Washington conversations, the American press and public had constantly expressed anxiety lest an agreement with Japan should involve our "selling China down the river." Such anxiety was reflected, for instance, in two editorials in the *New York Herald Tribune* from which the following excerpts are significant and illustrative of widespread editorial comment throughout the United States:

No Peace at China's Expense
Almost all that is definitely known about the Japanese government's approach to an adjustment of relations with this country is that gossip about it in Tokio has aroused high hopes of a return to normal commercial relations with the United States. One or two guesses are also warranted by such officially proclaimed developments as the Emperor Hirohito's assumption of direct command over the Army. It appears that the Konoye government may be getting ready to offer peace terms to China, or a modus vivendi to the United States, which would be distasteful, to put it mildly, to the Japanese Army. It looks as though somebody might have to give orders, precedent to an understanding with either China or the United States, which the army would take from no one but the Emperor. Even if this were a

correct interpretation of the Emperor's personal intervention between government and army it would not mean that contemplated orders to the army, which might infuriate that organization would necessarily create conditions in the Far East which would satisfy long-tortured China or appeal to this country as a convincing Japanese repudiation of armed aggression as an instrument of policy. We feel that within the last few days reactionary spokesmen and homing militarists from China and Korea have been getting grimly busy with an organization of opinion in defiance of a policy of conciliation which is going to make things very hard for the Konoye Government.

Yet we cannot ignore all published gossip about Japanese efforts to negotiate a peace between Chungking and puppet Nanking, and all reports from Tokio about Japan's readiness to admit the United States to a junior partnership in the exploitation of the greater East Asia co-prosperity sphere, without saying that the American people have ideas about Japan's war guilt in China and about the price she should pay for the cruel damage already done, which the Administration dare not ignore if it would. We have no reason to think, indeed, that the Administration is inclined to whitewash Japan for expediency's sake at a lower price than public opinion would exact.

We are confident, indeed, that so far as the State Department is concerned it will win no more appeasement from the United States government than it would win from the man in the street, whose one fixed idea about the situation in the Far East is that, after the hideous agonies that China has suffered, to take care of herself and to keep the Japanese busy, nothing, not even a consideration of self-preservation, would move us to let the Chinese down.[86]

Talk of Japan's Appeasement

The number of China's active, alert, keenly sympathetic and influential friends in this country runs into many thousands. The body of China's American well-wishers, who expect their government to be satisfied in the long run with nothing short of the complete restoration of China's administrative integrity, and with nothing less than Japan's complete discomfiture, makes

[86] *New York Herald Tribune,* September 16, 1941, p. 22.

up an overwhelming majority of those who have any opinion at all on foreign affairs.

We cannot believe that that is likely, or even possible. But it must be admitted that a close study of Japanese official publicity, during the last few days, when coupled with the fact that Tokio expects conversations to be renewed when its Minister to Washington gets back here, warrants one of two conclusions. Either the Japanese have persuaded themselves that a resumption of normal trade relations can be bought from the American government, with a modification of policy in the Orient that would fall far short of satisfying American public opinion; or that the Administration is actually trying to appease Japan and win at least temporary surcease from worry in the Pacific, so that this nation can give its whole attention to the Atlantic. Of these two possible interpretations of current events, we are strongly inclined to favor the first, not because of any special information, but chiefly because we know that Mr. Hull is a man of principle, because he has only recently said that these exploratory talks with Japan are leading up to no compromise with his principles, and because an American recognition of any Japanese advantage gained by armed aggression, or by cajolery backed by force, in Manchuria or China would be flagrantly inconsistent with Mr. Hull's recorded principles. . . .

All such Japanese bombast and gossip, taken in conjunction with Washington's inclination to let Japan talk on and on under cover of strict secrecy, is naturally hard on the nerves of a great body of Americans who would as lief see Hitler feted on Broadway as have their government condone Japan's continental exploits. We are confident, however, that these disquieting conversations are designed on Washington's part to give Japan the fairest possible scope to express herself; and that, if this expression is obstinately consistent with her record, she will be invited to make what she likes of an ever-tighter encirclement.[87]

In the second of the foregoing editorials one is inevitably struck by the asseveration that the overwhelming majority of the American people who have any opinion at all on foreign

[87] *Ibid.*, September 21, 1941, II, 8.

affairs would be satisfied with nothing short of Japan's "complete discomfiture." There are two kinds of sanctions: corrective and purely punitive. The distinction may be said to lie in the method of application. Corrective sanctions aim to create a situation where the object of the sanctions is forced to seek conciliation and such sanctions are, or should be, accompanied by efforts toward conciliation. The application against Japan of purely punitive sanctions, unaccompanied by efforts toward conciliation, must inevitably have led to war. It is believed that the foregoing discussion has demonstrated that our own sanctions against Japan, if wisely and constructively followed up, were capable of bringing about the desired corrective effect without war. If it is to follow a purely punitive policy, diplomacy is defeated at the start. Our own corrective sanctions had produced precisely the situation which they were intended to produce, and efforts toward conciliation were undertaken in Washington on Japanese initiative. Those efforts, however, were not carried through to their logical conclusion.

In connection with our position toward China, the following points appear to be worthy of consideration:

(a) Had the settlement of the China question along the general lines proposed by Prince Konoye been effected, that country would, without cost and in the space of a few months, have achieved far more than she could possibly have achieved by force of arms over a long period, even assuming that the Burma Road could have been kept open and American aid rendered available in ever-increasing degree. It is believed that no military expert would question this contention.

(b) Inasmuch as we would have been unable for an indefinite period of years, by force of circumstances, to implement some of the most important provisions of our side of an agreement, no sacrifice of principle could have been involved in our permitting Japan temporarily to maintain garrisons in North China and Inner Mongolia as a guarantee of good faith. And not even the most ardent sympathizer with the cause of China could logically have contended that such an arrangement could be anything but temporary, or that any real danger existed that we would have been unable or unwilling to insist upon removal of those garrisons after the world war. For if Japan should then have demonstrated an indisposition to co-operate with the democracies by refusing fully to relinquish her hold on China, or by failure to co-operate in other directions, Japan, no more than any other nation, could have expected to survive as a great Power in a world economy such as we may expect to see set up following the defeat of the totalitarian Powers.

(c) None of the self-denying pledges and multilateral treaties which we have concluded with China require us to *guarantee* her administrative or territorial integrity. All we have ever done is to engage, in an international commitment, not to violate them ourselves. Japan's advance to the south, including her occupation of portions of China, constituted for us a real danger, and it was definitely in our national interest that it be stopped, by peaceful means if possible, by force of arms if necessary. American aid to China should have been regarded, as we believe it was regarded by our Government, as an indirect means to this end, and not from a sentimental viewpoint. The President's letter of January 21, 1941, shows that he then sensed the important issues in the Far East, and that he did not include China, purely for China's sake, among them.

(d) The failure of the Washington Administration to seize the opportunity presented in August and September, 1941, to halt the southward advance by peaceful means, together with the paramount importance attached to the China question during the conversations in Washington, gives rise to the belief that not our Government but millions of quite understandably sympathetic but almost totally uninformed American citizens had assumed control of our Far Eastern policy.

American Principles

American policy in the Far East, as elsewhere, is based upon certain fundamental principles which we cannot allow to be undermined for the sake of temporary expediency and the point is essential in considering whether an agreement with Japan — the sort of agreement that was possible — would have involved the sacrifice of those principles.

(*a*) In the larger sense, at least, it cannot but be agreed that we are more seriously compromising our fundamental principles when we place in jeopardy our hopes for their eventual acceptance by the world at large than when we set before all other considerations the protection of our vital national interests, to the end that we may some day in future be in a position to see those principles made operative throughout the world.

(*b*) The two phrases "expediency" and "a larger strategy" have acquired in the public mind much the same taint as the word "appeasement," simply through a failure to grasp their true meaning and significance. When our national future, if not the future of the whole civilized world, is at stake, it is imperative that we play what cards we have to the best advantage. To stop, without war, Japan's southern advance at the expense of a few temporary garrisons in a once more peaceful China would certainly have been an expedient move, but that is no reason to condemn it. Britain's former occupation of Iran, our own occupation of Iceland, as well as American and British support of their ally, Soviet Russia, were all moves of expediency dictated by a larger strategy.

(*c*) No thinking American, with all of the facts before him, could claim that an agreement with Japan such as that contemplated by the Embassy could have impaired our moral position in the slightest degree.

JUNEAU AND MUNICH

Would the President's departure for Juneau to negotiate with Prince Konoye have suggested to the minds of the American people, necessarily ignorant of many of the important aspects of the situation, another case of "Chamberlain to Munich," with China instead of Czechoslovakia in this case to be offered up in sacrifice? Would the immediate political repercussions from such a step have been seriously unfavorable?

The most superficial examination of the two cases reveals that there could be no comparison whatever between them. For the President would have been meeting the Japanese Prime Minister at the latter's suggestion on American soil. Had the meeting been unsuccessful, the President at its conclusion would have had simply to announce that he had listened to the best that Japan had to offer and had found it insufficient, while, had an agreement been reached, its immediate publication would inevitably have carried conviction as to the immense advantages accruing from it to the United States, to China, and to the Allies' cause. And if doubts had been expressed as to the ability of the Japanese Government loyally to implement its part of the agreement, or the willingness of the Japanese to withdraw entirely from China when it had become possible for us to implement fully our own commitments, the President had facts at his disposal more than ample to convince the doubtful and to enlist the support of the entire country in his far-sighted and enlightened action. By accepting the Japanese proposal for the meeting we had, as pointed out in this survey, nothing to lose, everything to gain. It is believed that the facts spoke for themselves, and that when logically marshalled and presented to the American public, along the general lines of this survey, those facts would have overwhelmingly convinced our people that the Administration had once again, as in many previous instances, acted with consummate wisdom in the vital interests of our nation.

THE FUTILITY OF WAR

The question must finally be posed whether our Government, convinced by our naval and military experts that a war with Japan would be both brief and victorious, had decided that such a war would provide the most effective solution of the entire Far Eastern problem, and that it had better come now than later.

(a) It is difficult to believe that this could have been the case. The record indicates beyond question that the Embassy, in the summer and autumn of 1941, believed such a solution to be wholly unnecessary. Any unnecessary war, whether it be won or lost, must be averted if humanly possible. Situations may arise in which no self-respecting nation can afford to maintain peace, but it was our profound conviction that such a situation had not arisen, and need not arise, in our relations with Japan.

(b) The possible tactical advantages to be gained in an unnecessary war with Japan, even were it brief and American arms victorious, and even were it to result in the total destruction of the Japanese fleet, freeing our Pacific fleet for action in the Atlantic, could not have warranted the sacrifice of American lives, or the ever-present risk, no matter how remote, that our plans might go awry and the position of the democracies in their life-and-death struggle with the Axis powers be perhaps irreparably weakened. War, at best, is a futile method of solving disputes.

THE LESSONS OF HISTORY

History is properly based upon facts and upon such contemporary comment as may tend to clarify those facts. Yet a study of history is futile unless, from the lessons of history, mankind derives constructive guidance in the art of statesmanship. The rapidly accelerating progress in certain phases of civilization, notably in science, economics, communication and transit, has rendered national isolation an anachronism. The nations of the world have become so closely integrated and knitted together that, as frequently stated by our Government in recent years, any war between any two or more nations disturbs a delicately balanced world economy and is, therefore, of concern to all other nations. For that reason our Government has consistently manifested its concern in situations in various parts of the world which threatened to, or did in fact, lead to war.

The right to intervene morally or physically in such situations carries with it, however, a corollary in the way of an obligation: we cannot logically on the one hand exercise the right of intervention, morally or physically, in situations between other nations which might lead to war on the ground that our national interests are affected thereby, while on the other hand manifesting indifference to the conditions creating such situations. It is a fact and not a theory that the nations are today interdependent: in a world so closely integrated as it is today, the policies and actions of every nation carry consequences which reach the world's five continents and seven seas. We cannot permit nations to seize and pre-empt by processes of conquest areas whose resources should be available to all. Nevertheless, so long as any nation follows policies designed exclusively for the protection and furtherance of its own interests and is not solicitous to assist in resolving the problems of other nations whose well-being is equally necessary for the operation of a world economy such as we have today, just so long will the progress of civilization and the welfare of mankind be retarded through unnecessary and futile wars.

In the world of today and tomorrow, no nation can afford simply to "mind its own business," for the problems of its neighbors, all its neighbors, must inevitably become an important part of its business, and sound statesmanship must recognize that the practical logic of "splendid isolationism," or bloc isolationism, has gone forever. And so long as we, in our future diplomatic, political and legislative policies and actions, fail to perceive the lessons of history and the lost opportunities of the past, just so long shall we as a nation continue to overlook opportunities to employ our limitless strength, both material and moral, toward the development of civilization and of the welfare of our own country and people without the dissipation of lives and wealth in useless wars.

The cumulative factors, extending back over the years, have in this survey been touched upon only superficially. It is the immediate factors of the final months and weeks prior to the outbreak of war that are the chief concern of this discussion, and it is believed that the facts herein presented may serve to give precision to the eventual historiography of this pregnant period. In an issue of such transcendent gravity to the people of the United States, and in the interests of the future statesmanship and policy of our country, it appears to be obvious that all factors which have controlled this momentous problem must ultimately come before the American people. I have presented the evidence as known to the Embassy in Tokyo. The verdict must be left to history.

POSTSCRIPT TO THE SURVEY

In all the published material bearing upon the proposed Konoye-Roosevelt Meeting that has emerged both in our country and in Japan in recent years, I have been especially impressed by the objective discussion in Herbert Feis's book *The Road to Pearl Harbor.* For Mr. Feis himself, with whom I was formerly associated in the Department of State, I have high regard and admiration. His approach to this problem is scholarly and he has clearly familiarized himself with all available published evidence to justify his findings, namely that "the records since come to hand do not support the belief that a real chance of maintaining peace in the Pacific — on or close to the terms for which we had stood since 1931 — was missed."

This point can never be proven to everybody's satisfaction. Probably even Prince Konoye himself, before his untimely death, could not have given a categorical answer.

On one point, however, I feel competent to comment. It was held by our Government in its consideration of the wisdom of the proposed meeting, and it has been advanced by commentators since, that Prince Konoye's record was bad and that in the light of that record he could not be trusted. Konoye was responsible, as Prime Minister, for the invasion of China in 1937 and for joining the Axis in 1940. At all times he was under terrific pressure. In such matters one has to be guided by impressions. Certainly no one who was present at that three-hour meeting on the evening of September 6, 1941, could have doubted the sincerity of his determination to reach an agreement with the United States. He frankly admitted his responsibility for allowing his country to move into its then predicament but he said with equal frankness that he was the only statesman in Japan capable of reversing the engine. He knew that Japan could not afford to go to war with the United States. He knew beyond peradventure the only basis on which an agreement could be reached, namely the withdrawal of Japanese forces from Indochina and China. He knew that only on the general basis of Mr. Hull's four points could such an agreement be had. These things he admitted to me and said he was prepared and able to carry them out. Whether he could have done so is a question which can probably never be answered with entire satisfaction, but he himself at that time expressed to me complete confidence that he could — and that he was the only person who could.

From the records it is a simple matter to prove that Prince Konoye, in his assurances to me, had his tongue in his cheek. In such cases the impressions of the moment are not controlling but they cannot be brushed off. Mr. Dooman and I were convinced at that moment that he meant what he said. I still believe he did.

As for the records, Konoye's position at that time was one of the most difficult ever encountered by a statesman. In the Imperial Conference of September 6, 1941, he assured the War Minister that if President Roosevelt failed in the Juneau meeting to "understand" Japan's policy, he would turn around and come home. Unless Konoye could get the leaders of the armed forces to play along, he knew very well that his proposed meeting with the President would be futile and that there would be no purpose in going to meet Roosevelt at all. If Konoye was capable of deliberately misleading the American Ambassador, he was equally capable of misleading his own military leaders on the ground that the end justified the means. Is it beyond the bounds of reason to believe that what Konoye hoped to accomplish was to obtain from Roosevelt an agreement of so dramatic a character in the best interests of the future welfare of his country, even though it might put a stop to further aggression, to the southern advance and to the conquest of China, that the Japanese people would be swept off their feet and, with the support of the Emperor and of the many influential "moderates" in Japan who were tired of the years of war and fighting could have blocked the path even of the military extremists? Even in Japan, public opinion could be a powerful weapon. This is approximately what Konoye told me he expected to do.

I may as well close this Postscript with a single sentence from Mr. Feis's book, taken out of context it is true, but in my ex-parte view it is the crux of the whole story. "It will always be possible," he writes, "to think that Grew was correct; that the authorities in Washington were too close to their texts and too soaked in their disbelief to perceive what he saw." [88]

[88] Feis, *op. cit.*, p. 275.

PART SIX

Wartime Service

1942–1945[1]

THE PERIOD from our return from Japan in 1942 until my retirement from office in 1945 was one of constant turmoil, for these were war years, and I think that my most important service was rendered during that pregnant time. In some respects it was a period beset with grim frustrations; in other respects, opportunities occurred here and there to influence policy and action in a definitely constructive way. There is, however, very little pleasure to be found in looking back on those difficult years.

I shall not try in these memoirs to deal with that period chronologically. I was far too intensively busy to keep up the diary, although official records are of course available, and, at least while I was Under Secretary of State, my staff kept a sort of running diary for me. It seems to me better, however, to pick out, with the assistance of my editor, a few significant highlights regardless of chronological sequence, and to tell what I knew of those specific situations.

We returned on the exchange ship *Gripsholm* from Japan in August, 1942, having spent two full months traveling pretty much all around the world. The Japanese exchange ship *Asama Maru* left Yokohama on June 25, 1942, stopped at Shanghai, Hong Kong and Saigon to pick up our interned fellow countrymen, slipped down through the Soenda Strait, and finally brought us to Lourenço Marques in Mozambique where the Americans were transferred to the *Gripsholm* and the Japanese officials moved over to the *Asama*.

[1] Mr. Grew wrote the following statement in 1950.

An incident occurred here which caused me regret. Admiral Nomura and Saburo Kurusu, the two Japanese Ambassadors in Washington, were both old and respected friends of mine of long standing. Admiral Nomura was generally regarded as a genuine friend of our country and strongly opposed to war. Not so Kurusu. In the fully justified heat of public opinion over the attack on Pearl Harbor, it was generally believed that Kurusu had come to Washington for the purpose of lulling us into a sense of false security — "to pull the wool over our eyes" until the Pearl Harbor attack could be brought about. I have always disagreed with that thesis. I had known Kurusu fairly intimately over many years. I had negotiated with him, played golf with him, played poker with him, and he, his American wife and charming daughter Jaye, now married to Lieutenant William Maddox of our Army, had often been under our roof in Tokyo. Such close association helps one to size up any man. I have always regarded Kurusu as an intellectually honest man. I so regard him today.

Long before Pearl Harbor, indeed long before the Japanese had determined on war, the Foreign Minister, Admiral Toyoda, told me that he was going to choose a Japanese diplomat with a thorough command of English to help Admiral Nomura in Washington in the conversations which were then taking place. He said that Nomura was "tired" and needed assistance, but I knew the real reason for the move. Nomura's command of English was limited. One evening, considerably later, Kurusu came to see me in Tokyo and told me that to his complete surprise and consternation he had been ordered to proceed immediately to Washington. He said he knew nothing of the details of the American-Japanese conversations, except what he had been able to pick up that afternoon from reading the Foreign Office files, and he said that he was frankly aghast at the difficulties of the job. He, however, made clear his attitude to the effect that he intended to do everything in his power to bring the conversations to a successful conclusion. No one who knew Kurusu intimately and who heard him talk that night could believe that he was anything but sincere. In order to help him get to Washington at the earliest possible moment, I had the American plane held up for forty-eight hours in Hong Kong.

Whether the Japanese Government sent Kurusu to Washington "to pull the wool over our eyes" without his knowledge, I doubt. Apart from the extreme militarists, there was an earnest hope on the part of many highly placed Japanese, including the Emperor, that the Washington conversations would succeed and that war would be avoided. It was felt that Kurusu, with his American background and his complete command of English, could help to that desirable end. In actual fact, however, Kurusu in Washington, regardless of his own attitude, was powerless. He, like Admiral Nomura, was on the end of a telegraph wire from Tokyo and all he could do was to report developments and minutely obey the instructions received.[2]

As to the incident mentioned, when our respective ships drew up, nose to stern, at the dock at Lourenço Marques, Admiral Nomura sent me a message asking me to meet him for a talk. Had I agreed to such a meeting, which in any case would have been to no purpose except to go into post mortems, it is obvious how it would have been played up by the press in our two countries. My refusal to meet Admiral Nomura was in no sense intended as a snub. It hurt me to have to say no to an old friend, now an enemy, but acceptance of his invitation could only have been harmful. I passed Nomura and

[2] Herbert Feis in *The Road to Pearl Harbor* (Princeton: The Princeton University Press, 1950), pp. 296–97, has this to say about Kurusu's mission: "Finally he [Admiral Nomura] was informed that in view of the gravity of the situation Ambassador Kurusu was leaving Japan by clipper at once. The message from Togo telling him of this went on to state that 'he (Kurusu) is carrying no additional instructions — so please tell him all.' But there can be little doubt that Kurusu knew of the Japanese program and schedule of action. But he probably was uninformed of the plan to dispose of the American fleet at Pearl Harbor." Feis goes on to state on p. 307, that Kurusu's mission "was unpromising, even if not false. His purpose, looked at in the best light, was to persuade the American government to accept the latest Japanese terms in preference to war. Looked at in the worst light, it was to engage American interest while the assault plans were being secretly completed."

Kurusu on the dock one day when coming out of town and merely raised my hat. There was really nothing else to be done.

The *Gripsholm* rounded the Cape of Good Hope, stopped for a day at Rio de Janeiro where my wife left us to fly to Chile to visit our daughter, Elsie Lyon, in the Embassy in Santiago, and we arrived at New York on August 25.[3] On the dock at New York I was asked to make an extempore radio address over CBS which appears to have been heard by a good many people, as it was referred to all over the country when I soon started my nation-wide talks.

Very soon after our return from Japan I found that our people were woefully, if not dangerously, misinformed about Japan's fighting power. They had been told by high officials that as soon as Hitler had been defeated we would "clean up the Japs in a matter of weeks." While I had not the slightest doubt from the beginning or at any time, even during the darkest days of Japan's early successes, that we would win the war in the long run,[4] I knew very well that the Japanese were going to give us a much tougher and longer fight than most of our public believed. It seemed to me highly dangerous to allow our people to bank on any such unsound illusion as they had been allowed to develop, and that my most effective war effort would be to go around the country and tell the facts. Having just returned from Japan after ten years there, I believed that people would listen and that I might influence editorial and other press comment, as well as people themselves, in a helpful way.

Mr. Hull approved of this program and gave me appropriate

[3] For an account of the voyages of the *Asama Maru* and the *Gripsholm*, see *Exchange Ship* (New York: Farrar & Rinehart, 1942), by Max Hill, an Associated Press correspondent on board. There were over 1,500 people on the *Gripsholm* with lifeboat accommodations for less than half that number. — J. C. G.

[4] Mr. Grew, for instance, had written Sir Robert L. Craigie on June 14, 1942, just before leaving Japan: "My own faith in our final victory is complete and unwavering as no doubt is yours. The results of the Coral Sea and Midway battles are a tremendous encouragement and clearly mark the turn of the tide, but as long as so many of our warships are needed in European waters I suppose that we must not expect decisive results for some time to come."

standing as Special Assistant to the Secretary of State. My jour-
neys afield, North, South, East, West, from Montreal to New
Orleans and from Maine to California, were undertaken partly
under the sponsorship of the Office of War Information, partly
on behalf of Civilian Defense and partly on my own initiative
on the basis of invitations received. For the next two years,
therefore, my life was one of almost perpetual motion. I talked
to groups of all political and social hues, labor groups, Cham-
bers of Commerce, colleges and universities, army and navy
groups, round-table discussions arranged by Foreign Policy Associations, in churches, in industries, in civic auditoriums.[5]
I think my record was seven speeches in two days at Nashville,
Tennessee, and that the largest gathering was of 10,000 people
in the auditorium in San Francisco. The net result of these
talks was difficult to evaluate, but a marked change in the attitude of the press gradually became noticeable, and this alone
encouraged me to feel that these efforts were not waste motion.
They were certainly very strenuous efforts. At least I learned
something about what must be the strain of a political campaign, even although I was running for no office.

At commencement at Harvard in the spring of 1943 one of
the highest honors of my life suddenly and most unexpectedly
came to pass. Even today that tremendous experience still
fills me with wonder. What happened was that in the winter
of 1941 I was informed in Tokyo that Harvard wished to give
me an honorary degree at Commencement in June. Here was
the materialization of a dream of many years, but a dream that
I never really expected to see realized. Since Harvard gives
no honorary degrees in *absentia*, I asked the State Department
if it felt that I could properly take a brief leave of absence for
that purpose. The permission was duly accorded. But I began
to question whether I had the right to leave the throttle of the
engine — and a very important engine it was — at that time.
Eugene Dooman, who would become Chargé d'Affaires in my
absence, was fully competent to deal wisely and effectively with

[5] See Chapter XXXV for an example of one of Mr. Grew's speeches during
this period.

any developments, but there are some situations where the voice of an ambassador can be all-important. The temptation to go was the biggest with which I had ever had to wrestle, but I finally decided to pass up the degree and stay on the job.

On our arrival in Mozambique on the exchange ship in the summer of 1942 the first news to greet me was that at Commencement that spring the announcement had been made that I had been elected President of the Harvard Alumni Association. That news was big enough to surprise me, but not long thereafter I learned that the degree offered in 1941 had been held over, and that I was to be the recipient of the honorary degree of LL.D. from Harvard at Commencement in 1943.[6] Mine was the only honorary degree given that year.

One of the duties of the President of the Alumni Association who presides at the big Alumni meeting on Commencement afternoon is to read the results of the elections to six-year terms on the Harvard Board of Overseers. When my name came first with the biggest vote, my cup of embarrassment and happiness certainly ran over.[7] Later I had to make the alumni address, which was probably the most difficult, but to me the most inspiring speech of my life.[8] Indeed, I know of no more inspiring occasion than Commencement at one's own Alma Mater, especially in wartime, when so many of my fellow

[6] In 1942 Mr. Grew received the honorary degree of LL.D. from Norwich University, Colgate University, and Trinity College. The following year the same degree was bestowed upon him by Bates College, Tufts College, Princeton University, Clark University, and Bethany College, as well as the degree of D.C.L. and Honorary Chancellor by Union College, and L.H.D. by Denison University. He had received his first honorary LL.D. degree from George Washington University in 1926. In 1943 he was also the recipient of the Howland Memorial Prize from Yale, the Roosevelt Distinguished Service Medal, and the Holland Society Gold Medal for Distinguished Service.

[7] That situation seemed to call for a little piece of raw deception and of unrehearsed acting, if I was capable of it. Of course, I had been told the result of the vote for Overseers, but I simply hadn't the nerve to face those 15,000 people with that smug announcement, as if I knew it all already. So I sealed the results in an envelope, opened it ostentatiously before the crowd and then read the names and number of votes while feigning astonishment. Whether I got away with it, I don't know to this day. — J. C. G.

[8] For Mr. Grew's speech see the *Harvard Alumni Bulletin*, June 12, 1943, pp. 648–51.

alumni were fighting for our nation's freedom, and when so many of those Harvard men had already given their "full measure of devotion."

On May 1, 1944, I was assigned as Director of the Office of Far Eastern Affairs in the Department of State, a post which I held until December, 1944. Joe Ballantine, my wise and well-fitted Deputy, ran the office most of the time because of other duties assigned to me. For a time I presided over our delegation in bilateral negotiations for civil aviation treaties, including the negotiations with the Russians and the Chinese, and in that job I ran into considerable acrimony with various Senators who declined to accept the viewpoint of the Administration that these agreements could be approved merely by Executive Order. They held that they must be confirmed by the Senate as fullfledged treaties.

In the midst of these activities I was suddenly appointed a member of the United States delegation to the Dumbarton Oaks Conference to lay the basis for an eventual United Nations, and this work was, of course, a full-time job. The question of the veto came up here and the consensus of our delegation and advisers, especially the military and naval advisers, was that without the principle of the right of veto by the principal powers in the projected Security Council in disputes in which one of them was a participant, no international agreement for an international body such as the United Nations could ever pass the United States Senate. I myself was wholly opposed to the veto, while recognizing the importance of Senate approval of whatever document might emerge.[9]

On December 20, 1944, after eight months of service as Director of the Office of Far Eastern Affairs, I took the oath of office as Under Secretary of State.

The way in which this job was offered to me was amusing. I had gone to the office of the Secretary, Edward Stettinius

[9] See U.S. Department of State, *Postwar Foreign Policy Preparation 1939–1945* (Washington: Government Printing Office, 1949), and Edward R. Stettinius, Jr., *Roosevelt and the Russians: The Yalta Conference*, ed. Walter Johnson (Garden City: Doubleday & Co., Inc., 1949).

(always "Ed" to his close associates), to congratulate him on his appointment as Secretary of State and then started to withdraw. He said: "Wait a minute; I want to tell you of my plans." So we sat down on the sofa, and he sketched out his proposals to bring new blood into the old Department and to sweep away some of the cobwebs. His team of Assistant Secretaries were to be Dean Acheson, Jimmie Dunn, Will Clayton, Nelson Rockefeller, Archie MacLeish, and General Julius Holmes. I told Stettinius of my enthusiastic support of his plans and then again started for the door. He said again: "Wait a minute. I have lots more to say. You know where you are going, don't you?" I replied in the negative, while visions of some far-flung post abroad flitted across the mental horizon. He said: "You are staying right here as my partner. I want you to be my Under Secretary of State." It was I who now said: "Wait a minute. I held that job twenty years ago and I know by bitter experience what a terrific job it is. I am much too old to go through that experience again." Stettinius replied: "This is not going to be the same thing at all. You and I are going to keep our desks clean and develop a system in which we shall avoid all routine work and have time, when we need it, just to sit and think. When one of us is tired, he will be free to go away for a week or ten days, or for any time he needs to rest up. When I am here, I shall tell you not only what I am doing but what I am thinking, so that when I have to be absent, as I shall have to be much of the time, you can simply slip into my chair and carry on just as I would have done. I want our relationship to be of the most intimate character."

Of course I accepted. He meant it all, and he did his very best to keep me in touch with every detail of his thoughts and actions. Whenever he saw the President or some other high official or diplomat he invariably called for his stenographer and myself at the same time and had me listen while he dictated the memorandum of his talk. How different my position as Under Secretary would have been, if my other chiefs had done the same and had consulted with me at every step! But alas, human or rather official nature is seldom built that way. Little did Ed then realize that no high official can ever keep his desk clean or avoid the mass of problems that must daily come to him, no matter how effective the system. In all my service in Washington I never saw the Department better organized than during the Stettinius regime, and Billy Phillips, who also had twice been Under Secretary, agreed with me on this. But the number of problems that must come to the top are un-controllable regardless of system, and no Secretary or Under Secretary can ever under any circumstances avoid the terrific strain of his office or the mass of papers that must inevitably flow across his desk day in and day out. I generally got to the Department at eight in the morning and left after seven in the evening for a night of work at home, always including Saturdays and often Sundays. My wife used to say that I re-turned looking like a piece of Gorgonzola cheese which, al-though perhaps not a particularly happy figure of speech, was probably accurate. Little does the public realize what those jobs entail.

My reasons for assuming this arduous office, I explained to the Senate Foreign Relations Committee on December 12, 1944:

". . . Mr. Chairman, and members of the committee, when the President and the Secretary of State offered me the position of Under Secretary of State, I said frankly that under other circumstances I would have hesitated to accept the position. I have served our country for 40 years. I have always been prepared to go where I was asked to go, and I have done so. I am no longer a young man. The job of Under Secretary of State is a hard-slogging job — I know that, because I held the position for more than 3 years, 20 years ago — but I accepted the position, Mr. Chairman, for the following reason:

"First, because our country is at war.

"Second, because I believe in the President. I highly admire the grit and vision with which he has been and is conducting the war, and I heartily support his determination that effective machinery shall be erected to insure future international peace and security.

"Third, because I believe in Mr. Stettinius and am profoundly happy to follow his dynamic and inspiring leadership. He is 'the man who gets things done.'

"Fourth, because the job of Under Secretary is a very different proposition from 20 years ago. Now a new and liberal pattern is emerging. A newspaper sketch of me — presumably based on the thought that, like the late George Apley, I hail from conservative New England — said that I am 'inhospitable to change.' Well, if I were inhospitable to change, I would certainly not have been asked or have been willing to join this team. I think that this new pattern is going to commend itself to the Congress and to our people. The world is in flux and malleable. It can be a better world and we shall try to make constructively helpful our contribution toward building it anew.

"Fifth, because I want to see the work begun at Dumbarton Oaks carried through to a successful conclusion and, with your help, we intend to do it. No work in the world can be of greater importance.

"This is all, Mr. Chairman. . . ." [10]

10 U.S. Congress, Senate, *Nominations — Department of State,* Hearing before Committee on Foreign Relations, 78th Cong., 2d Sess. (Washington: Government Printing Office, 1944), p. 13. As Under Secretary of State from December 20, 1944, to August 12, 1945, Mr. Grew found himself as Acting Secretary of State for 166 days out of the total of 240 days. The Yalta, Chapultepec, and San Francisco Conferences necessitated Secretary Stettinius' absence from Washington, and the Potsdam Conference required Secretary Byrnes' absence.

XXXV

The Strength of the Japanese Enemy

Address over the Columbia Broadcasting System
from Washington D.C., August 30, 1942

First of all, I should like to say how deeply we have been
moved, my associates and myself, who have just returned on the
exchange ship, *Gripsholm,* by the many greetings of friends
and the great volume of messages of welcome which have
come to us from all over the country. The welcome given us
has warmed our hearts, and it is one that we can never forget,
nor can we ever forget the really inexpressible joy of coming
home after the difficult months and moments through which
we have passed in Japan and Japanese-occupied territories. It
may be impossible to answer all those messages individually.
Please let me express now to all who hear me our most grateful
thanks for them.

Never before has my native land looked to me so beautiful.
Never before has a homecoming meant so much. I think you
will realize a little of what it meant to us when I tell you of
those last seven days at anchor off Yokohama before our evacuation vessel finally sailed from Japanese waters. We were
awaiting the completion of the negotiations for our exchange,
not knowing whether those negotiations would be successful
and whether, if they were unsuccessful, we might not all be
returned to our imprisonment in Japan. Among us were many
Americans — missionaries, teachers, newspaper correspondents,
businessmen — who had spent the preceding six months in
solitary confinement in small bitterly cold prison cells, inadequately clothed and inadequately fed and at times subjected
to the most cruel and barbaric tortures. . . .

And then came one of the greatest of all moments. I awoke
at 1.00 A.M. on June 25 sensing that something was happening.

I looked out of the porthole and saw a piece of wood slowly moving past in the water. Another piece of wood moved faster. We were at last under way, slowly accelerating until the ship was finally speeding at full steam, away from Yokohama, away from Japan, pointing homeward. Ah, what a moment that was, even though we had 18,000 miles to cover and seventy days in all before we should pass the Statue of Liberty in New York harbor and repeat to ourselves, with tears pouring down many a face,

> Breathes there the man with soul so dead
> Who never to himself hath said,
> This is my own, my native land? . . .

And now, before closing, I should like to tell you something about the Japanese military machine against which we are fighting today. That machine has been trained and perfected through many years, for it has always had in view, even before the invasion of Manchuria in 1931, the prospect of eventually sweeping not only to the north against Russia, but to the west and south in order to control what the Japanese have latterly termed "The Co-Prosperity Sphere of Greater East Asia including the South Seas." It need hardly be said that the phrase "Co-Prosperity Sphere" denoted in fact the intention to exert Japanese control, politically, economically — absolutely — over all those far-flung territories.

In 1931 came their invasion of Manchuria. In 1937 came their invasion of China south of the wall, and while their Army eventually floundered in China, due to the magnificent fighting spirit of Chiang Kai-shek, his courageous armies, and his determined people, nevertheless the warfare which then ensued proved a practical training for the Japanese soldiers and sailors, who tirelessly developed and perfected the tactics which they subsequently used in their landings and conquests to the south.

The idea should not for a moment be entertained that the failure of the Japanese forces in China has discouraged the Japanese people. It has instead served to steel them for still greater sacrifices and to prepare them better for the war of deadly purpose to conquer, upon which they have finally embarked. As the realization came home to them of the need for greater and greater efforts, they accepted the inevitable war-footing reorganization of the country's life with characteristic calmness and determination.

Probably no other factor has contributed more heavily to the preliminary victories achieved by the Japanese in this war than the offensive spirit which permeates all of the armed forces of the Empire. This spirit, recognized by competent military men as the most vital intangible factor in achieving victory, has been nourished and perpetuated since the foundation of the modern Japanese Army. The Japanese High Command has counted heavily upon the advantages this would give them over less aggressive enemies. They have put great store in what they consider to be the white man's flabbiness. They look upon us Americans as constitutional weaklings, demanding our daily comforts and unwilling to make the sacrifices demanded for victory in a war against a military machine which has prepared and trained itself in Spartan simplicity and the hardness and toughness demanded by war. They attach great importance to the former disunity in the United States over the war issue, and they still count on an appreciable interval before an aroused nation can find itself and develop a fighting spirit of its own. By that time, they feel, Japan will be in complete control of all East Asia. When they struck, they made no provision for failure; they left no road open for retreat. They struck with all the force and power at their command. And they will continue to fight in the same manner until they are utterly crushed.

We shall crush that machine and caste and system in due course, but if we Americans think that, collectively and individually, we can continue to lead our normal lives, leaving the spirit of self-sacrifice to our soldiers and sailors, letting the intensification of our production program take care of itself, we shall unquestionably risk the danger of a stalemate in this war of ours with Japan. I say this in the light of my ten years' experience in Japan, my knowledge of the power of the Japanese Army and Navy and of the hardness and fighting spirit of the Japanese. I feel it my bounden duty to say this to my fellow countrymen. I know my own country even better than I know Japan and I have not the slightest shadow of doubt of our eventual victory. But I do not wish to see the period of our blood, sweat and tears *indefinitely and unnecessarily prolonged.* That period will be prolonged only if our people fail to realize the truth of what I have just said, that we are up against a powerful fighting machine, a people whose morale cannot and will not be broken even by successive defeats, who will certainly not be broken by economic hardships, a people who individually and collectively will gladly sacrifice their lives for their Emperor and their nation, and who can be brought to earth only by physical defeat, by being ejected physically from the areas which they have temporarily conquered or by a progressive attrition of their naval power and merchant marine which will finally result in cutting off their homeland from all connection with and access to those outlying areas — by complete defeat in battle.

I need say no more. I have told you the truth as I see it from long experience and observation. I have come home with my associates in the Far East to join our war effort with yours and I realize, perhaps better than anyone else, that nothing less than the exertion of our maximum capacities, individually and collectively, in a war of offense will bring our beloved country safely through these deep waters to the longed-for haven of a victorious peace.

We are fighting this war for the preservation of righteousness, law and order, but above all for the preservation of the freedoms which have been conferred upon us by the glorious heritage of our American citizenship, and for these same freedoms in other countries of the United Nations, and while we are fighting against the forces of evil, lawlessness and disorder in the world, we are primarily fighting to prevent the enslavement which actually threatens to be imposed upon us if we fail. I am convinced that this is not an overstatement. Surely ours is a cause worth sacrificing for and living for and dying for if necessary. "Though love repine and reason chafe, there came a voice without reply; 'tis man's perdition to be safe, when for the truth he ought to die."

Address before the Cleveland, Ohio, Foreign Affairs Council, February 5, 1943

. . . Let me tell you about two things: the nature of the enemy, and the dangers of a false, treacherous peace. In speaking of the enemy, I shall describe the Japanese. I knew the Germans in the First World War and the Japanese in the present war. Both have been infected by the virus of militarism which has begun to rage again until the world is sick with it. Both the German and the Japanese Governments took advantage of our humanity, our love of peace, to betray and conquer their neighbors, and to prepare for war against us. Both are equally dangerous. I happen to have come from Tokyo most recently, and will for that reason tell you about Japan. You must remember, however, that what I say of Japan applies most of the time to the Germans as well.

Let me tell you, therefore, about the part of this war which I know best, the Japanese war against America. I have watched it brew for years, and feel that I have taken the measure of our Japanese enemies. I do not for a moment presume to touch upon questions of high policy and strategy in the fighting of this war nor upon the relative emphasis to be placed on the various theatres of war. Our highest leaders are taking care of that. I speak merely of the Japanese war machine as I have known it and have seen it grow, in power and determination and overweening ambition, during the past ten years of my mission to Japan.

Let me paint for you the picture as I see it, for you Clevelanders might in other wars have had the right to feel protected by the massive continent which shields you on all sides. In this age of air power, no mere geography will shield you; and if American planes can hit the enemy in the Solomon Islands, in Africa, and in innermost China, the enemy must be awaited everywhere and anywhere. I shall not overstate the case nor overdraw the picture. Let us look at that picture as it faces us today.

Even before Pearl Harbor, Japan was strong and possessed a military machine of great power — and when I speak of that military machine I include all branches of the Japanese armed forces, the army, the navy, and the air force. That military machine had been steadily strengthened and developed during many years, especially since Japan's invasion of Manchuria in 1931, an act of unprovoked aggression which, in effect, commenced the expansionist movement of Japan in total disregard of the rights and legitimate interests of any nation or of any people that might stand in the way of that movement.

In 1937 came Japan's invasion of North China and Shanghai, which led to the past six years of Sino-Japanese warfare. During all these years of their unavailing effort to conquer China and to bring about the surrender of the Chinese National Government, those Japanese armed forces were using China as a training ground in preparation for the greater war, already carefully planned, for their eventual conquest and intended permanent control of all of so-called "Greater East Asia including the South Seas" and for the imposition upon the peoples of those far-flung areas of what Japan is pleased to refer to as the "New Order" and the "Co-Prosperity Sphere."

We know what that euphemistic slogan "Co-Prosperity" means: it denotes absolute hegemony — economic, financial, political — for Japan's own purely selfish interests, and the virtual enslavement of the peoples of those territories to do the bidding of their Japanese masters. This statement is not a figment of the imagination; it is based on practical knowledge of what happened in other regions already subjected to Japan's domination. Such a regime will be imposed in *every* area that may fall under Japan's domination.

During all of this period of preparation the Japanese military machine has been steadily expanded and strengthened and trained to a knife-edge of war efficiency — in landing on beaches, in jungle fighting, and in all the many different forms of warfare which it was later to encounter.

Add to that intensive training the native courage of the Japanese soldiers, and sailors, and airmen, their determined obedience to orders even in the face of certain death and their fanatical joy in dying for their Emperor on the field of battle, thus acquiring merit with their revered ancestors in the life to come, and you get a grim conception of the formidable character of that Japanese fighting machine. Furthermore, in war Japan is wholly totalitarian; her economy is planned and carried out to the last detail. No word of criticism of the Government or its acts is tolerated; the so-called "thought control" police take care of that. Labor unions are powerless. In war Japan is a unit, thinks and acts as a unit, labors and fights as a unit.

With that background, and having in mind the strength and power of Japan even before Pearl Harbor, consider for a moment the scene as it has developed in the Far East. Consider the tremendous holdings of Japan today — Korea, Manchuria, great areas in China Proper, Formosa, the Spratly Islands, Indochina, Thailand, Burma, and the Andamans, the entire Malay Peninsula, Hong Kong and Singapore, the Philippines, the Netherlands East Indies and, farther to the south and to the east, myriads of islands many of which are unsinkable aircraft carriers.

Those areas contain all — mind you, all — the raw materials essential to the development of national power; rubber, oil, tin, metals and foodstuffs — everything that the most comprehensive economy can desire; and they contain furthermore millions of native inhabitants who, experience has proved beyond peradventure, will be enslaved as skilled and unskilled labor by Japan to process those raw materials for immediate and future use. There you have a recipe and the ingredients for national strength and power that defeat the imagination even approximately to assess.

Now to this recipe and these ingredients add one further element of grimly ominous purport. During all of my ten years in Japan I have read the books, the speeches, the newspaper and magazine articles of highly placed Japanese, of

Generals and Admirals, of statesmen and diplomats and politicians. Sometimes thinly veiled, sometimes not even veiled, has
emerged their overweening ambition eventually to invade and
to conquer these United States. In their thinking, even the
megalomania of Hitler is surpassed. Fantastic if you will, but
to them it is not fantastic. . . .

It might be one year or two years or five or ten years before
that Japanese military machine would find itself ready to undertake an all-out attack on this western hemisphere of ours;
they themselves have spoken of a hundred-year war; but one
fact is as certain as the law of gravity; if we should allow the
Japanese to dig in permanently in the far-flung areas now occupied, if we should allow them to consolidate and to crystal-
lize their ill-gotten gains, if we should allow them time to
fortify those gains to the nth degree, as they assuredly will
attempt to do, it would be only a question of time before they
attempted the conquest of American territory nearer home.
In no respect do I overstate this case. My judgment is based on
no wild surmise nor upon any far-fetched and imaginative hypothesis. It is based on facts, which are there for all to see, and
upon ten long years of intimate experience and observation.

What worries me in the attitude of our fellow countrymen is
first the utterly fallacious prewar thinking which still widely
persists, to the effect that the Japanese, a race of little men,
good copyists but poor inventors, are incapable of developing
such power as could ever seriously threaten our home shores,
our cities and our homes, a habit of mind which is reinforced
by the great distance separating our homeland from the Far
Eastern and Southern Pacific battlefronts today.

I am also worried by the reaction of our people to the current successes of our heroic fighting men in the Solomons and
New Guinea, for after each hard won victory the spirits of
our people soar. Moral stimulation is good but moral complacency is the most dangerous habit of mind we can develop,
and that danger is serious and everpresent. I have watched the
intentional sinking of the *Panay,* the attempts on the *Tutuila*
and on our Embassy in Chungking, and other efforts on the

part of those military extremists to bring on war with the United States for the very purpose of leading up to the eventual carrying out of their fell designs; and I say to you, without hesitation or reserve, that our own country, our cities, our homes, are in dire peril from the overweening ambition and the potential power of that Japanese military machine — a power that renders Japan *potentially* the strongest nation in the world — potentially stronger than Great Britain or Germany or Russia or the United States — and that only when that military caste and its machine have been wholly crushed and destroyed on the field of battle, by land and air and sea, and discredited in the eyes of its own people, and rendered impotent either to fight further or further to reproduce itself in the future, shall we in our land be free from that hideous danger and be able once again to turn to paths of peace.

You see that I promise no end to war through the simple formula of defeating the enemy today. Totalitarian aggression must be smashed first, and then its stump must be uprooted and burned. It is not enough to win now only, in the course of war; we must win the peace as well. To win the peace, we must be sure that it is our kind of peace, and not a peace which compromises with German or with Japanese militarism.

It is with regret, not unmixed with humility, that I repeat to you today words which I addressed to a similar audience in January 1918 — twenty-four years ago last month. I said then, after describing the enemy Germany, from which I had recently returned: "That is the Germany of today with which we are at war and which we have got to defeat; otherwise, as surely as the immutable laws of nature control the movement of this earth, our future generations will have to take up what we now leave off, facing the same problem which now confronts us, perhaps unaided. If we do not want to leave this heritage to our unborn sons, if this country is not to remain an armed camp permanently, Germany, as she is now organized, controlled, and governed, must be defeated." Those words are even more true today, and they are true as well of that other Germany in the Pacific — the Japanese Empire. We failed then to rid the world of the militarism which is our enemy; we must not fail again.

We must not tolerate Japanese or German militarism under new names and new flags. We must not drive the forces of imperialism, totalitarianism, and aggression underground. We must annihilate these evil forces, and show that the age of imperialism is ended. We cannot afford to treat with those enemies whose ruin we have pledged. We cannot afford — should they ask it — to make peace with the fanaticism which we have sworn to exterminate. We must watch vigilantly for the dangerous signs of a German or Japanese peace offensive, designed to let us win the war but to lose the peace. Let me tell you about such a move, as it could come from Japan; the same general tactics would hold true of German militarism.

In my various talks around the country I have repeatedly stressed the view that the Japanese will not crack. What I mean is exemplified in the tenacity with which their armed forces have been holding out in New Guinea and in Guadalcanal. That is to say, the Japanese military code does not admit of surrender, even when it is the only alternative to annihilation, but this does not mean that the Japanese will stand up to be shot down to the last man when some other alternative presents itself, such as running away to fight another day. Despite their sentimentality and fanaticism the Japanese are fundamentally a practical people. When they find that they cannot win on the field of battle, that they are bound to be beaten there, and that they therefore are in danger of losing all of their so-called "co-prosperity sphere," rather than accept a conclusive defeat, rather than take loss of all of their gains, it is altogether likely that they will look about for ways of effecting a compromise whereby they might avoid the disgrace of defeat and might hope to retain a part of their gains.

At the present time, of course, the Japanese leaders, and even more so the people, are far from convinced that they cannot manage to retain substantially all of their gains. But when the Allied offensive gains momentum and Japanese self-confidence is shaken by successive reverses and loss of territory then we may look for a development of new tactics. The Japanese art of self-defense, jujitsu, gives us a clue as to what these tactics are likely to be. The essence of this art is that by letting the adversary take the initiative and by giving way and simulating defeat the adversary may be lulled into dropping his guard; then when the adversary has advanced too far and is off balance, he is destroyed by a quick recovery and a lightning attack where he is weakest.

I have no fear that our military authorities are likely to be taken in by any military application of the jujitsu principles. I do feel, however, that the American people and the people of nations united with them in war on Japan should be forewarned against the possibility of a jujitsu feint in the realm of diplomacy — namely, a peace offensive. The Japanese are capable of preparing the ground for such an offensive with elaborate care. That is to say, the military leaders might begin by bringing forth from retirement some former statesman with a liberal label and placing him at the head of a puppet civilian cabinet. This step would be heralded as representing the overthrow of military dictatorship in favor of liberalism. The scene would then be set for a peace move. There might be an announcement by the new premier intimating that Japan was ready to conclude a peace on a fair and just basis. If the United Nations were willing to rise to the bait before awaiting at least the clearing of the Japanese armed forces from the territories that they have seized, so much the better for Japan, but even if the United Nations should insist on such withdrawal as a prerequisite to a peace parley such a Japanese move would still seem to its authors worthwhile if it should have chance of deceiving some of the peoples among the United Nations and rendering them lukewarm toward the further prosecution of the war. The Japanese might well calculate that by the time they were ready to launch such a peace offensive their peace-loving enemies would be so weary of the war that they would be receptive to peace offers; that once an armistice had been declared and negotiations begun it would be difficult to get their enemies to resume fighting again even if the Japanese were to hold out for partial retention of their gains.

It is believed that the American people in being forewarned

against deceptive Japanese peace moves should be made to realize that the only safe course for the United Nations to take in the presence of such moves will be to keep in mind the President's words to Congress on December 8, 1941, that "we will not only defend ourselves to the uttermost but will make very certain that this form of treachery shall never endanger us again," and that we continue to press our operations against Japan until she has no alternative to admitting defeat and submitting to disarmament. If the United Nations were to begin discussing peace with Japan or Germany while she is still armed, the only peace to which such a procedure could lead would be an armed truce to be followed by even more bitter warfare.

The President and the Prime Minister made it plain at Casablanca that they were not to be deceived by such tactics. "Unconditional surrender" is the complete summary of the terms which we of the United Nations shall and must offer the aggressor powers. To do less would be to temporize with murder and to negotiate with treachery embodied in human flesh. We have everything to lose and nothing to gain in a peace which fails to assure freedom throughout the world, on the terms which an aroused and civilized mankind demands. To barter or bargain with the substance of freedom would be to deny the cause for which our men are dying.

I have shown you what happens under the militarism which has corrupted Germany and Japan, and which now threatens the world. I have described for you how the Axis wages war, and why the Axis wages war. Truly may it be said: "Their object is crime and their method, death." And I have sought to warn you against the insidious menace of a shameful "peace," an armistice which would allow militarism to flower again in the next generation, when a new crop of infantrymen — sons of oppressed, ignorant mothers — would be ready for the harvest of war.

We are faced with an immense task. This war is the greatest war ever fought. The United Nations are the greatest coalition of free peoples ever formed; our ranks in this war are immeasurably strengthened by the *active* aid and partnership of the three largest countries of the world — China, Britain and Russia. We shall control all the seas and the air of the world. We shall be able to do this only by virtue of putting forth our maximum efforts here in America. We can, and we must mold the world of the future. But to do this we must discipline ourselves in self-denial, we must exert ourselves to the full extent of our several capacities. We must work and save and unite; we must day in and day out cultivate patience, determination, endurance and courage.

The war is here, confronting me and confronting you. It is in the air about us. The war is not something far away on the other side of the world. The war against us consists of immense physical forces in the hands of men who are brave, furious, implacable enemies. This violence and power is being kept out of your homes, here in Cleveland, only by the sacrificial efforts of our allies and of our American men overseas. Let these relax, and the Germans and Japanese will be here. . . .

To Brigadier General William J. Donovan, June 26, 1944, Office of Strategic Services

I have received reports from Colonel K. D. Mann [of the O.S.S.] and from Mr. Dooman, a member of the Far East panel, with regard to projects which have been presented to the panel for study, and I am now moved to lay before you certain thoughts in the hope that they may be helpful in the carrying out of your operations as they apply to the Far Eastern enemy, Japan.

Except for certain brief periods, the political and moral concepts of the Japanese people from the time of their origin in remote antiquity until their entry into the family of nations have developed under a society and a moral system to the creation of which the experiences of mankind as a whole have contributed little or nothing. Their social system and behavior pattern are essentially those developed under tribal conditions. They have the good characteristics of a tribal community — cohesiveness and subordination to a central authority, loyalty to the community, and courage — but they have also the defects of a tribal community: lack of initiative, resistance to change, at least in many aspects of their social life, and fear of tribal sanctions. The introduction of Chinese culture of the Tang and Sung dynasties, the introduction of Christianity in the sixteenth and seventeenth centuries, and more recently the importation of western knowledge since the middle of the last century have had little effect on the fundamental concepts of the Japanese as a nation. The Japanese have perhaps colored these concepts but have in no way altered their form or pattern. Their impact on the individual has been at times noticeable but ephemeral. Thus, the Japanese nation today presents itself to the world as a unique paradox. In its outward and visible aspects — in the possession of a well-disciplined social organization, a formidable army and navy, a modernized industry, and a merchant marine and foreign commerce which distributed Japanese goods to all quarters of the world — it seemed qualified to take a place among the great powers. Yet, in the general fields of morals, in the sense of principles regulating human conduct, and of intellectual speculation in an effort to fix the final objectives of man, it has shown itself peculiarly impervious to foreign ideas.

It is during time of war that the characteristics of the Japanese developed under tribal conditions are conspicuously present. Japan today is a united nation, both in appearance and fact, on the home front. It is undivided in its determination to prosecute the war, and both the people at home and the soldiers at the front show every evidence of willingness to make extreme sacrifices. But every society has some weaknesses, although they may be more difficult to discern in some cases than in others. There are weaknesses in the Japanese individual and in the social structure which, if properly exploited at the appropriate time, might well bring about cleavages among the Japanese sufficiently profound to contribute substantially to Japan's military defeat and eventual collapse.

I stated on a certain occasion: "The Japanese military machine can and will be discredited in the eyes of the Japanese people — and we, the United States of America, will bring that about." A cleavage between the people and the Japanese militarists would, in my view, be the ultimate objective to be aimed at, but there are a number of mutual antipathies and antagonisms within Japanese society which should be exploited as soon as possible to contribute toward the bringing about of that objective. I refer here to such jealousies and antagonisms as those between the Army and the Navy, between factions within the Army itself, between big business and militarists, between the agrarian and industrial elements, and so on.

Address at the Washington, D.C., Navy Day Dinner, October 27, 1944

Our Navy and a Warning to Japan [1]

In the life of every nation, as in the life of every individual, there come occasions when it is good to pause for a moment in the midst of great endeavor to take stock of the road already traveled, and of the road ahead. Navy Day, 1944, is such an occasion. And if the Japanese are listening in, let them take stock, too.

First, the road already traveled. The darkest day in the naval history of our country was December 7, 1941, the day of infamy. There we were on the threshold of a two-ocean war, a war which rapidly spread to the seven seas, confronted with what then appeared to be the ruins of a substantial part of our one-ocean navy. The Japanese had done their despicable work well; just as at Port Arthur at the opening of the Russo-Japanese War in 1904, they struck without a declaration of war. Perhaps we ought to have remembered that every seasoned criminal has a special technique of his own, and is likely to follow the same technique in successive crimes. But that is all water over the

---

[1] Admiral William D. Leahy has written of this speech in *I Was There* (New York: Whittlesey House, 1950), p. 274: "Under Secretary of War Robert Patterson and Assistant Secretary of State Joseph Grew were the speakers. The latter gave a very informative analysis of the Japanese situation and prospects, a subject on which he was undoubtedly the best informed official of the American Government."

dam now. The Japanese gangster is not going to be given the opportunity to commit further international crimes, if the present temper and determination of our people and of our allies are any criterion.

At any rate, there we were, on December 7, 1941, momentarily stunned in contemplation of what then appeared to be the smoking ruins of our once proud Pacific fleet, and in contemplation of our dead. Had the Japanese at that moment been prepared to land in force on the island of Oahu and to occupy Pearl Harbor, we might now have been very far from entering upon what we confidently believe are the decisive phases of the Pacific war. Fortunately for us, they hadn't the vision to follow through. Vision is not one of their strong points. If it had been one of their strong points, they would never in the world have attacked us anywhere.

Then came the American miracle. It *was* a miracle by every standard of experience and of history. Had the Japanese military and naval High Command been told at that time what we were to do, they would have scoffed with their hilarious but mirthless humor. But now they know. No dream castle ever erected could have surpassed the construction in these three years of the greatest, most powerful and certainly the most efficient and effective navy that the world has ever seen. Yes, now they know. They began to know in the Coral Sea, and they continued to learn at Midway, at Guadalcanal, in the Kula Gulf, at Attu, at Kwajalein and Saipan, at Tinian and Guam and Palau, and now, at last, in the Philippines themselves, in what may prove to have been a decisive naval battle and one of the greatest victories in history, rivaling Trafalgar itself. They have not only continued to learn of the fighting power of our ships and of the aggressive spirit of our officers and men, whether in the Army or Navy, the Marine Corps or the Air Forces — a quality in which the Japanese believed themselves paramount and to which they attached the greatest importance in their own fighting machine — but they have discovered one other essential truth, namely, that our American fighting men do not go into battle like regimented automatons: they use their heads as well as their guns and thus constantly outguess and outmaneuver the enemy.

The Japanese navy, *without* a declaration of war, exploited the tactical advantage of initiative and surprise. They had their day, but now they are learning to their sorrow that initiative and surprise — when war is on — are no Japanese monopoly. The glories of our victories and those of our Allies already achieved will ring down through the ages in the annals of military and naval history.

So much for the past and present. Now for the road ahead. This is no time for our people to sit back in smug contentment. Pride in past and present achievements should be but a spur to future effort. This Navy Day should be not a day of exultation, but a day of rededication — rededication to the mighty task of winning the war against both Germany and Japan. And when we think and speak of winning the war, let us not again fall into the fatal error of believing the enemy finally defeated just because he asks for an armistice and a peace conference.

I wish to take this important occasion to repeat, with all possible force, the warning which I have continually tried, all over the country, to drill home into the consciousness of our people, namely, that we must not, under any circumstances, accept a compromise peace with Japan, no matter how alluring such a peace may be or how desirous we may become of ending this terrible conflict. An enticing peace offer may come from Japan at any time. The facts of the situation are beginning to seep into the consciousness of the Japanese people. Some of them — perhaps only a few at the present time, but the number will grow steadily — know beyond peradventure that they are going to be defeated, that their merchant fleet is being whittled down to the vanishing point, that their war plants are gradually being blotted out of existence, and that their gangster loot will eventually be taken away from them. They know that, if the war continues long enough, their military machine and cult will be — to use the word so much loved by our enemies — liquidated, and that their nation will then be reduced to the status of a third-class power. . . .

There is, however, still an alternative open to Japan, and I address these words directly to the more intelligent elements in that misguided country. There is one way by which the Japanese *can* keep their homeland free from further aerial attack. If the Japanese leaders can read the handwriting on the wall and can come to the realization that for them the war is already lost and that their situation is hopeless; if they can realize that the determination of the United Nations to carry through, regardless of time or cost, to complete and unequivocal victory is inflexible, and that no temporizing or compromise is conceivable, let them unconditionally surrender now. That alternative is open and will remain open. The Japanese cannot avert defeat by postponing the inevitable. If they act now, they will avoid useless sacrifice of lives and wholesale devastation. Let *them* call it a day.

Now, what of the future of our Navy? May I quote from a recent article in the *Saturday Evening Post* by Secretary Forrestal a passage which should be the fundamental creed of the American people in the difficult years that lie ahead? "In spite of this war," he wrote, "we shall continue to be a peace-loving nation, with neither greed nor desire for world domination. The very concept of imposing our rule upon other people is not consistent with our national character and would be repugnant to our people. Therefore, it is good and desirable that we keep the dream that someday, somehow, a framework of permanent peace will be evolved by men of sense and good will throughout the world.

"In the meantime, we dare not forget an anonymous admiral's words after the last war: 'The means to wage war must be in the hands of those who hate war.' "

May our country take those words to heart. At Dumbarton Oaks we have tried to lay a firm foundation upon which that framework can and will be built. I believe that never before have the peoples of the world been more determined that such a structure *shall* be built, that it shall be effective and that it shall endure.

"The means to wage war must be in the hands of those who

hate war." Behind our day-to-day diplomacy abroad there lies a factor of prime importance, namely, national support, demonstrated and reinforced by national preparedness. With such a background, and only with such a background, can we pursue our diplomacy with any confidence that our representations will be listened to or that they will lead to favorable results. General Douglas MacArthur, when Chief of Staff of the United States Army, said: "Armies and navies, in being efficient, give weight to the peaceful words of statesmen, but a feverish effort . to create them when a crisis is imminent simply provokes attack." We need thorough and permanent preparedness not in the interests of war but of peace. Let us constantly have in mind the eminently wise advice of Theodore Roosevelt: "Speak softly *and carry a big stick.*"

Let our people appreciate the tremendous importance of learning the lessons of history for future guidance. We intend, with all the determination and energy that is in us, to contribute to the erection of a world organization for the maintenance of peace and security that will some day render superfluous the great armaments that now so heavily handicap the development of peaceful economies. But until that day comes, I wish that every American would consider it a patriotic duty to familiarize himself with Secretary Forrestal's article entitled "Will We Choose Naval Suicide Again?" [2] and let his warning become a fundamental concept in our national thinking, our future action, and our inexpressible pride in the American Navy.

[2] James V. Forrestal, *Saturday Evening Post,* June 24, 1944, p. 9 ff.

XXXVI

The Emperor of Japan and Japan's Surrender [1]

THROUGHOUT the war I took the position that propaganda by any branch of our Government against the Emperor of Japan, or any effort to bomb the Emperor's palace, should be withheld. I knew very well that when the time came for Japan's surrender, the Emperor was the only one who could bring it about, and that by issuing an Imperial Rescript, a document sacred to all Japanese, he alone could put it into effect. The Japanese militarists regarded themselves as superior to any civilian Prime Minister or Government and, as has been shown, they could wreck any Government merely by withholding support for any War Minister.

This is just what happened in August, 1945. The Japanese army, a considerable proportion of which had never fought and was fresh, wanted to fight to the last ditch. Had our own army been forced to bring about the final military defeat by invading first the island of Kyushu, and later the Kwanto plain on the main island of Honshu, the strategy envisaged, the Japanese would have fought on the beaches and in the streets and houses of the towns and villages, and finally in the caves in the higher land where our casualties would have been very high. Even when the Emperor finally ordered surrender, military elements in Tokyo rebelled and entered the Imperial Palace in an effort to kidnap the Emperor and to destroy the record presenting the Emperor's orders in his own voice, which was to be broadcast to the nation and to the forces afield. In this effort they failed, and the Emperor's Imperial Rescript calling upon the entire nation to surrender brought the war to an end.

As Acting Secretary of State I was fortunately able to influence this situation at home in the face of considerable difficulty

1 Mr. Grew wrote this statement in 1950.

with certain agencies of our Government and certain sections of the press and with certain radio commentators who charged me with desiring to preserve the old feudal system in Japan. My position in the controversy seemed to me to be sound. I advocated waiting until we got to Tokyo to determine whether the Emperor would be a liability or an asset in turning Japan toward democracy. In the last analysis I felt that the Japanese people themselves must ultimately decide what sort of system they wanted. This was in accordance with the principles laid down in the Atlantic Charter and by many statesmen in the Allied countries. We could certainly not occupy Japan permanently.

As things turned out, the Emperor proved to be a very important and substantial asset to General MacArthur, and he cooperated effectively in bringing about the transition from the old to the new.

The Emperor had been charged with responsibility for the war, because he gave his approval to the attack on Pearl Harbor. Only those who are fully conversant with the former Japanese system of government can understand why the Emperor who, from all available evidence was bitterly opposed to the war, could not have stopped the attack. In actual fact the Emperor was no totalitarian dictator. Throughout history the Emperor has followed the influences in the Government and country of the predominantly powerful elements. Had the Emperor opposed the military determination on war and had he refused to approve the order for the Pearl Harbor attack, there would seem, in the light of the facts as we now know them, little doubt that he would either have been by-passed by the armed forces, or actually held in restraint, so that the military could have their way. This does not relieve the Emperor of the technical responsibility for the war, but it indicates clearly that the Emperor himself was powerless to prevent the war.

So far as my own attitude and efforts were concerned, the following admission in an article on June 10, 1950, by Drew Pearson, one of the most prominent and influential columnists and broadcasters in our country, who had continually attacked me during the war, gave me a considerable degree of satisfaction:

> Grizzled Joe Grew has spent a lifetime working for his country. He began as a young career diplomat many years ago, worked his way to be Ambassador to Turkey, Undersecretary of State, Ambassador to Japan.
> There were times during those days when I, as a reporter covering the State Department, used to be critical of Joe Grew. He was diffident, hard to understand, and, of course, it wasn't as hard for him to get ahead as for some, since he had a slice of the J. P. Morgan millions behind him.
> In retrospect, however, I am convinced that some of my criticism of Joe Grew was wrong. Certainly he was right and I was wrong about the Emperor of Japan, who he felt would be a healthy influence, first toward surrender, second toward making Japan a democratic nation after surrender.

This was a very gratifying statement. But even in such a generous eulogy, myths, I suppose, will always persist. How helpful that illusory "slice of the J. P. Morgan millions" would have been! Jack Morgan did marry one of my cousins, a very dear cousin, but no Morgan millions or any other millions ever came my way. I still remember my invariable rule at my first post in Cairo: a ten-cent instead of the usual five-cent cigar only on Saturday nights.

To Cordell Hull [April, 1944]

POSTWAR PLANNING COMMITTEE

In view of the fact that I am to take over the direction of the Division of Far Eastern Affairs on May 1, I am glad to have this opportunity to express certain views with regard to the shaping of our Government's plans for dealing with Japan after the war.

The problem seems to me to envisage two fundamental desiderata: (1) To render Japan incapable of ever in future threatening the peace; (2) to establish order in Japan with the least possible delay and with the least possible foreign personnel.

In order to achieve these desiderata we shall do well to avail ourselves of whatever elements in Japan may lend themselves to the attainment of one or both of those ends.

In anticipation of our invasion and occupation of areas in Japan, we cannot with certainty foresee what, if any, such elements we may find. Many imponderable factors are involved. Probably, for instance, we shall not know in advance what the effect of the impact of the war and of defeat may be on the thinking and attitude of the so-called liberal elements in Japan who originally were opposed to the war, and of the Japanese people as a whole. We have no yardstick to measure by, for Japan has never lost a war in modern times. We probably shall not be able to foresee with any certainty, prior to invasion and occupation, whether the Japanese people as a whole will follow guerrilla tactics or whether they will co-operate in maintaining order, thus greatly reducing the number of military and civil personnel necessary to enforce order. We shall have to be prepared for anything. But we can make at least a reasonable estimate of probabilities based on our knowledge of the psychology and tendencies of the Japanese people.

The Japanese people, through long-inculcated habits of regimentation and discipline, are somewhat like sheep in following leaders. Without intelligent leadership, they tend to disintegrate. Without intelligent leadership, chaotic conditions might develop.

At the outset, after invasion and occupation, that leadership will necessarily devolve upon the foreign military command, and the amount of actual force necessary to maintain order will depend in large measure upon the wisdom of the measures which the military command may take and the manner in which those measures are effected. Face saving is a powerful factor in Japan. If the co-operation of the Japanese metropolitan police, as distinguished from the Japanese military police, could be secured at the outset, the maintenance of order would probably be ensured at the start with a minimum of foreign military personnel. If a reasonable degree of tact is employed, it seems to me probable that such co-operation will be forthcoming. But we must not depend on it.

Once the initial measures are put into effect by the military command, the logical second step will be to explore the possibilities of enlisting the co-operation of Japanese civil authorities in providing the necessary leadership. Such co-operation, in my judgment, will in all probability be forthcoming if a statesmanlike manifesto is issued by the foreign military command at the outset. Such a manifesto should, in forceful terms, make clear to the Japanese people three fundamental purposes of the command: first, the maintenance of order; second, the carrying out of measures designed to render Japan incapable of undertaking future military aggression; third, the desire and intention of the occupying force to ensure to the Japanese people subsistence and an adequate livelihood. In such a manifesto the Japanese people should be told that they will have much to gain by co-operation, much to lose by recalcitrance. The determination to punish Japan's military leaders and those responsible for acts of cruelty and brutality not essential to military operations in war would fall within point two and might well be set forth in the manifesto.[2]

The enlistment of the co-operation of Japanese civil leadership will be of prime importance if we are to avoid the necessity of maintaining for a long period a vast military and civil army of occupation. Some degree of foreign occupation will no doubt be necessary for a long time to come, but it should obviously be one of our primary aims to reduce so far as possible the number of personnel required merely for the maintenance of order and to shift that burden as soon and as far as possible to the shoulders of the Japanese themselves.

In considering the question of available Japanese civil leadership, the potential use of the institution of the Throne immediately presents itself.

---

[2] See the Statement of the Supreme Commander for Allied Powers on Occupation Policy of September 9, 1945. Raymond Dennett and Robert K. Turner (eds.), *Documents on American Foreign Relations*, VIII (Princeton: Princeton University Press, 1948), 273–75.

In approaching this question we should be very careful to divorce ourselves from the prejudices and much of the unsound and uninformed thinking of the great majority of our people with regard to Japan. In the light of Pearl Harbor and especially of the barbaric cruelty and brutality of the Japanese military, those prejudices are wholly reasonable, and to the extent that those prejudices guide us in rendering Japan utterly incapable of ever again threatening world peace, we shall do well to keep them constantly before us. On the other hand, we must not let those sometimes blind prejudices deter us from attaining the ends we seek by adopting the most practical means of achieving those ends. In our democracy, Government must constantly listen to public opinion, but sometimes it is wise, in the best interests of our country, to lead rather than to follow public opinion when that opinion is uninformed as to facts. During my ten years in Japan I very often had occasion, especially when my recommendations based upon intimate knowledge were ignored, to wish that this could have been done. . . .

The prejudice in our country today against the Emperor of Japan is intense. The artificiality of the absurd myths of the Emperor's divine origin and the artificiality of the Shinto cult are just as well known to the thinking people in Japan as they are to you and me. These things are accepted by the Japanese much as our people as a whole accept the standardized myths about George Washington as set forth by Parson Weems. But regardless of the artificiality of those myths, which of course have a profound influence upon all Japanese thinking and action, the fact remains that the institution of the Throne in Japan is a cornerstone and a sheet anchor. If, after final victory, we wish to avail ourselves — as common sense would dictate — of any assets that we find in Japan which can be used for the maintenance of order as distinguished from the maintenance of the military cult, we would in my judgment, simply be handicapping the pursuit of our ultimate aims by any attempts to scrap or to by-pass the institution of the Throne. Should we insist on so doing, I can see only chaos emerging from such a decision.

The point has been advanced in some quarters that merely

by bombing the Imperial residence we would rid the Japanese people of the myth of the invincibility of the Emperor and of his alleged protection by the Sun Goddess and that the Emperor would thereby lose caste and be discredited in the eyes of the people. This in my opinion is a very shortsighted view and a view based on an inadequate understanding of Japanese psychology. On the contrary, I believe that such an act on our part would weld the Japanese people together more firmly than ever in a solid wall of hatred and would rally all shades of opinion against us. On my return from Japan, when General Doolittle [Commander of the Eighth Air Force] told me that he had been under great pressure to bomb the Emperor's palace but that he had discarded the plan, and asked me what I thought, I told him that he had made a most fortunate decision. The Japanese military authorities have tried, through propaganda, to create such hatred against the United States and the American people, but it seems to me highly doubtful if any genuine hatred of us is universal or perhaps even widespread in Japan today. At any rate, it is certain, in my judgment, that far from discrediting the Emperor the intentional bombing of his palace would render our future efforts to secure the co-operation of the Japanese people in creating order and peace a thousandfold more difficult.

Another point that has been advanced is that just as long as the Emperor is retained in postwar Japan, he will personify and perpetuate the myth of Japan's racial predominance and manifest destiny to rule the world, and therefore the cult of military aggression.

We must carefully examine that argument. It is very difficult for our people to understand the place of the Emperor in the Japanese picture. He has been and is surrounded by an aura of mythology, propaganda and regimented abject obeisance. Yet in practice he is nothing more than a symbol, and it is perhaps not without significance that not only are his personal wishes continually ignored but efforts have more than once been made in modern times to assassinate him. The cult of manifest destiny and of military aggression has been artificially developed, and the Emperor has quite simply been used as a convenient facade to justify and to consecrate that cult in the eyes of the people. I therefore say, without qualification, that the Emperor can be used equally well — indeed far more easily — to justify and to consecrate, if you will, a new order of peaceful international co-operation.

As for Hirohito himself . . . we have no adequate yardstick to help us foresee what he might do under unprecedented circumstances, and it is unwise ever to predict with certainty any Japanese action or reaction. We know, as clearly as anything can ever be known of what goes on behind the screen in Japan, that Hirohito was always opposed to war with the United States. He himself chose the name for his administration, namely "Showa" — "enlightened peace." I find that the opinion of substantial foreigners who have lived long in Japan almost unanimously share that view, and I was interested in reading the following item in the London *Times* of March 24, 1944:

> Sir Robert Craigie, British Ambassador in Japan until the outbreak of war, who was the chief guest of the Over-Seas League at luncheon yesterday, said that he was convinced that the Emperor of Japan, who acted on the advice of his counsellors, was never in favour of the present war. During the time Sir Robert Craigie was in Tokyo the Emperor showed many indications of his personal desire to avoid plunging his country into war.

This is all water over the dam now, and I repeat that we cannot with any certainty foresee what the effect of the impact of the war and of defeat may be on the thinking and attitude of the so-called liberal elements in Japan, including the Emperor himself. Until we learn these things, some of our plans for occupation of Japan must necessarily be only tentative. But unless the Japanese themselves wish to abolish the institution of the Throne on the ground that it has failed to achieve victory and has therefore let them down — an unlikely contingency, I think — it would seem to be common sense on our part to preserve and to support any nucleus in Japan which

may serve as a rallying point for the preservation and maintenance of order as opposed to the preservation and maintenance
of the military cult. If Hirohito fades out of the picture, his
Oxford-educated brother, Prince Chichibu, or his minor son,
the Crown Prince, might step into his shoes. It is the institution rather than the individual that is important.

In this connection, I should like to repeat a statement made
in my address to the Illinois Educational Association in Chicago on December 29, last [1943]. Parts of that address were mis-
reported and distorted in the press and aroused considerable
editorial controversy, including the following passage as actually delivered:

> There are those in our country who believe that Shintoism is
> the root of all evil in Japan. I do not agree. Just so long as
> militarism is rampant in that land, Shintoism will be used by the
> military leaders, by appealing to the emotionalism and the super-
> stition of the people, to stress the virtues of militarism and of war
> through emphasis on the worship of the spirits of former military
> heroes. When militarism goes, that emphasis will likewise dis-
> appear. Shintoism involves Emperor-homage too, and when once
> Japan is under the aegis of a peace-seeking ruler not controlled
> by the Military, that phase of Shintoism can become an asset, not
> a liability, in a reconstructed nation. In his book *Government by
> Assassination* [published in New York, in 1942] Hugh Byas
> writes: "The Japanese people must be their own liberators from
> a faked religion."

It seems to me, and to many students of Japan with whom
I have conferred, including Admiral Harry Yarnell [former
Commander in Chief of the Asiatic Fleet], whose thinking and
policy have been about as hardheaded as those of any of us, that
the foregoing thought is sound and makes sense. Any cult
which has been artificially created, as has the Shinto cult, can
always be molded to suit new conditions, and if the institution
of the Japanese Throne can in future be turned toward peaceful international co-operation, as it was in the days of the
Shidehara diplomacy, Shintoism, since its essence is support of

the Throne, can and may prove to be an asset rather than a liability in a healthy postwar reconstruction. The Japanese are past masters at executing the maneuver of right-about-face.

At the Senate Foreign Relations Committee's hearings on the appointment of Mr. Grew as Under Secretary of State on December 12, 1944, Senator Joseph Guffey said: [3] *"Mr. Ambassador, the newspapers have reported that you favor keeping Hirohito in power after the war. Were you correctly quoted? ..." Mr. Grew replied:*

"I appreciate the courtesy of the committee in allowing me to set straight certain distortions of fact contained in an article from the Philadelphia Record of December 6, which was published in the Congressional Record on that date. In that article the statement occurs:

" 'Since Pearl Harbor and his return to the United States, Mr. Grew has frequently advocated a policy of doing business with Emperor Hirohito after the war. He says we must preserve the Mikado as a Japanese symbol around which a stable, peaceful government can be built.'

"Permit me to say, Mr. Chairman, that never since my return to the United States after our 6 months of internment in Japan have I made such statements or advocated such a policy as are attributed to me in the article under reference. I should like to take this opportunity very briefly to set forth my precise attitude on this question, especially as the misquotation and distortion of 1 or 2 of more than 250 public speeches which I have made in our country, trying to tell our people something about what we are up against in fighting Japan, have been widely published and have conveyed an entirely erroneous impression of my position.

"My position, in a nutshell, is this: When we get to Tokyo — and we certainly will get there, in due course — our main objective will be to render it impossible for Japan again to

[3] See *Nominations — Department of State,* Hearings, Committee on Foreign Relations, 78th Cong., 2d Sess., pp. 17–19.

threaten world peace. We shall first have to maintain order, primarily to provide our army of occupation with conditions which will facilitate their task and safeguard the lives of its personnel, and, secondarily, to conduce toward the attaining of our main objective. We shall then have to take specific measures to demilitarize Japan, both physically and intellectually. This will obviously include, among other things, the destruction of the Japanese military machine and the destruction of their tools of war and the paraphernalia for making those tools of war in future.

"The accomplishment of these objectives in the post-surrender period in the shortest practicable space of time will be a matter of first importance. The American people will not only expect but will demand a high degree of perfection in our planning, so that the achievement of our security aims as they relate to Japan and therefore the repatriation of our soldiers in the army of occupation will not be unnecessarily prolonged. But many still imponderable factors inevitably enter into that planning. Japan has never lost a war in modern times. We therefore have no yardstick to measure the eventual impact on the Japanese mind of the cataclysm of destruction and defeat. Before we allow any Japanese authority to emerge in the post-surrender period, we can, and I hope we will, require it to demonstrate that it will be co-operative, stable, and trustworthy. But if we were to prescribe in advance the eventual Japanese political structure that will follow military occupation, thus severely circumscribing the compass within which such structure could take shape, we would necessarily have to assume the responsibility for any delay in achieving our security objectives and in bringing home our soldiers. We shall have to be governed by facts and realities rather than by theories when the time comes to act, and in taking measures for the attainment of our objectives, we shall wish to avail ourselves of whatever may appear to be assets and to eliminate as far as practicable whatever may prove to be liabilities. This seems to me to be plain common sense.

"But now with regard to the institution of the Emperor, I do not think that anyone is yet in a position to determine definitely whether it is going to be an asset or a liability. Whatever decisions are made they should certainly be made on a purely realistic basis and on the basis of intimate contact with the various current factors involved in the problem. It must be remembered today, if we are not to repeat the errors of the past, that Japanese attitudes and reactions have not conformed in a single important respect to any universal pattern or standard of behavior. We shall have learned nothing from the past if we assume that Japanese reaction in any specific instance is going to conform to a universal pattern.

"I have never held and have never stated that the Japanese Emperor should be retained after the war, nor have I ever held or stated that the Japanese Emperor should be eliminated after the war. I believe that the problem should be left fluid until we get to Tokyo and our authorities and the authorities of those of the United Nations directly concerned can size up the situation and can determine what will best conduce to the attainment of our objectives. I do not believe that the solution of this problem can intelligently or helpfully be reached until we get to Tokyo.

"I have a feeling that the importance of the Emperor institution, especially as a factor in the dynamic aspects of Japanese policies and actions, has been greatly exaggerated. It is argued that it is the existence of this institution that made possible Japanese militarism and aggression. This argument must be examined in the light of the fact that during the preceding period of Japanese aggression in the sixteenth century, when the ruling war lord tried to conquer Korea and China, the imperial family had been barely maintaining a shadowy existence for several centuries. Unlike the war lords of today, whose conquests, they proclaim, are due to the 'august virtues of the Emperor,' whose instruments they proclaim themselves to be, it was Hideyoshi, the shogun or military dictator, and not the Emperor, who said that when he had conquered China and

Korea he would make himself and not the Emperor the master of the world.[4]

"The Emperors in those days were completely overshadowed by the shoguns and were usually hard put to it to maintain a bare living. My point is, therefore, that the Japanese do not need to have an emperor to be militaristic and aggressive, nor is it the existence of an emperor that makes them militaristic and aggressive. There are conditions more deeply rooted in their social structure and concepts growing out of that social structure which have to be exorcised in one way or another. It will be one of our fundamental objectives to remove those conditions. As I have said, no one today can predict what effect the impact of the cataclysm of defeat will have on the Japanese mind. There might be a complete revulsion from all the archaic concepts of the past. The Emperor institution might on the other hand be the only political element capable of exercising a stabilizing influence. To understand the position of the Emperor in the Japanese political structure it might be useful to draw a homely parallel.

"As you know, the queen bee in a hive is surrounded by the attentions of the hive, which treats her with veneration and ministers in every way to her comfort. The time comes, however, when a decision of vital importance to the hive must be made. The hive vibrates as though in excited debate, and finally the moment arrives when the queen is thrust forth into the outside world, and the hive follows her to its new home.

[4] The date, 1192, has often been chosen to mark the beginning of the Shogunate. In that year the title of shogun, generalissimo, was bestowed upon Yoritomo, the first of the line of military rulers to bear the title. The end of the Shogunate came in 1868, when the Tokugawa shogun was defeated in civil war, and sovereign power was restored to the Emperor. At various times during this period of over six hundred years the shoguns were as impotent in wielding power as were the emperors. In the sixteenth century, for instance, the feudal lords, Nobunaga and Hideyoshi, exercised in succession the real power in Japan, completely dominating the figurehead shogun. Kenneth Scott Latourette has written that those "who had proved their capacity by seizing the actual power constituted the real government and ruled either through old titles given in practice a new meaning or through new offices created to fill a felt need." *A Short History of the Far East* (New York: The Macmillan Co., 1947), p. 217.

It was not the queen which made the decision; yet, if one were to remove the queen from the swarm, the hive would disintegrate.

"I do not wish to push the parallel too far, but I believe it describes with substantial accuracy the position in the past of the imperial institution. If a new condition has arisen, so much the better, but if the other possibility eventuates and the Emperor remains as the sole stabilizing force, I would not wish to have ourselves committed to a course which might conceivably fix on us the burden of maintaining and controlling for an indefinite period a disintegrating community of over 70,000,000 people.

"That, Mr. Chairman, represents in brief my position on this subject. That is why I have never advocated either the retention or the elimination of the Japanese Emperor after the war. I want to wait and see. I believe this to be plain common sense.

"It may be pertinent to add in this connection the statement of Chiang Kai-shek in his New Year's message to the Chinese armies and people on January 1, 1944, that in his opinion the question of what form of government Japan should adopt after the war should be left to the awakened and repentant Japanese people to decide for themselves. . . ." [5]

[5] In his radio address of New Year's Day, 1944, Chiang Kai-shek reported a conversation which he had held with President Roosevelt: "When President Roosevelt asked my views, I frankly replied, 'It is my opinion that all the Japanese militarists must be wiped out and the Japanese political system must be purged of every vestige of aggressive elements. As to what form of government Japan should adopt, that question can better be left to the awakened and repentant Japanese people to decide for themselves.'

"I also said, 'If the Japanese people should rise in a revolution to punish their war mongers and to overthrow their militarist government, we should respect their spontaneous will and allow them to choose their own form of government.' President Roosevelt fully approved of my idea. This opinion of ours is entirely based on the spirit of the joint declaration of the United Nations in 1942." Chinese Ministry of Information, *The Collected Wartime Messages of Generalissimo Chiang Kai-shek 1937–1945* (New York: The John Day Co., 1946), II, 779.

To Randall Gould, Editor of the American Edition
of the Shanghai *Evening Post* and *Mercury,*
April 14, 1945

... The really important point in all this, however, seems to me to be just this: if, after we get to Tokyo, some Japanese Government surrenders, that will be no guarantee whatsoever that the millions of Japanese soldiers throughout East Asia will stop fighting, and the mopping up of those tremendous areas would of course be a very long and costly process. If at that time however the Emperor could be led to issue an Imperial Rescript, which is sacred to all Japanese, ordering the Japanese Armies to lay down their arms for the future good of the country, that is the one thing that might do the trick and it might save the lives of tens of thousands of our own fighting men. That of course is a pure gamble, but it is a gamble worth considering, and I think we would make a great mistake to render such action impossible by determining in advance to eliminate the Emperor merely through prejudice. In other words, I would like to wait and see, and this seems to me to be plain common sense. . . .

Of course there is a great deal more to be said on this whole subject, which would take a book in itself. I am certain that we could not graft our type of a democracy on Japan because I know very well that they are not fitted for it and that it could not possibly work. If the Japanese themselves want to keep their emperorship we had better let them do it, while taking very good care that they never be allowed in future the paraphernalia for building the tools of war. If we were to eliminate the emperorship I have little doubt that the Japanese themselves would take it right back again as soon as our backs were turned, and we cannot very well occupy Japan permanently. There will be other ways of controlling their capacity to make war and, after what is coming to them in the present war, I don't believe the Japanese people will have much stomach for recreating a military caste and a military machine for a long time in the future.

Our views on this matter of the treatment of the emperorship in the post-defeat period are consistently supported by every type of evidence that we can get of the actual and present-day thinking of the Japanese masses. It is significant that the Japanese communists in China make no reference whatever to the emperorship in their propaganda directed at Japanese troops in China and the Japanese people at home. Again, those Japanese prisoners of war who have been collaborating in our psychological warfare against Japan have, in every known instance, insisted that they shall not be required to say anything derogatory of the Emperor. Still again, polls taken among Japanese civilian internees at Saipan and elsewhere have elicited an overwhelming desire that the emperorship be retained. The Japanese involved in all these cases are almost entirely those belonging to the lower and lower-middle classes — peasants, partisans, shopkeepers and clerks. In the face of the clear evidence, it would seem unrealistic to plan today the elimination by fiat of a concept which appears still to be firmly rooted in the Japanese mind. . . .

JAPAN'S SURRENDER [6]

Much light has been shed since the war, in books, articles and reports from Americans in Japan during the occupation, on the developments leading up to Japan's surrender in August, 1945.[7] For a long time I had held the belief, based on my intimate experience with Japanese thinking and psychology over an extensive period, that the surrender of the Japanese would be highly unlikely, regardless of military defeat, in the absence of a public undertaking by the President that unconditional surrender would not mean the elimination of the present dynasty if the Japanese people desired its retention. I furthermore believed that if such a statement could be formulated and issued shortly after the great devastation of Tokyo by our B-29 attacks on or about May 26, 1945, the hands of the Emperor and his peace-minded advisers would be greatly

[6] Mr. Grew wrote this statement in 1950.
[7] See especially Toshikazu Kase, *Journey to the Missouri.*

strengthened in the face of the intransigent militarists and that the process leading to an early surrender might even then be set in motion by such a statement. Soviet Russia had not then entered the war against Japan, and since the United States had carried the major burden of the war in the Pacific, and since the President had already publicly declared that unconditional surrender would mean neither annihilation nor enslavement, I felt that the President would be fully justified in amplifying his previous statement as suggested.[8] My belief in the potential effect of such a statement at that particular juncture was fully shared and supported by those officers in the Department of State who knew Japan and the Japanese well, especially by Eugene H. Dooman, formerly Counselor of the American Embassy in Tokyo, Joseph W. Ballantine, Director of the Office of Far Eastern Affairs in the State Department, Professor George Hubbard Blakeslee, Chairman of the Far Eastern Area Committee of the State Department, all of whom I regarded as among our soundest experts on Japanese affairs, and others.[9]

[8] In a statement issued to the press on May 8, 1945, President Truman had said: "Our blows will not cease until the Japanese military and naval forces lay down their arms in *unconditional surrender*.

"Just what does the unconditional surrender of the armed forces mean for the Japanese people?

"It means the end of the war.

"It means the termination of the influence of the military leaders who have brought Japan to the present brink of disaster.

"It means provision for the return of soldiers and sailors to their families, their farms, their jobs.

"It means not prolonging the present agony and suffering of the Japanese in the vain hope of victory.

"Unconditional surrender does not mean the extermination or enslavement of the Japanese people." U.S. Department of State, *The Department of State Bulletin*, May 13, 1945, p. 886.

[9] Dr. Alexander H. Leighton in his book, *Human Relations in a Changing World* (New York: E. P. Dutton & Co., 1949), p. 55, wrote that "during the winter and spring of 1945 the analysts [of the Foreign Morale Analysis Division of the OWI] strongly advised the policy makers against employing attacks on the Emperor or the imperial institution in psychological warfare. It was believed that such lines would at best be wasteful and could well harden enemy resistance. On the other hand, the analysts thought that the Emperor might be

Then, on my own initiative, as Acting Secretary of State, I called on President Truman on May 28, 1945, and presented this thesis as set forth in a memorandum prepared immediately after that meeting, a copy of which I read aloud at a further conference in the Pentagon Building on May 29, 1945, in the presence of the Secretaries of War and Navy and the Chiefs of Staff. I also handed the President on May 28 a draft of a proposed statement which we in the State Department had prepared after long and most careful consideration.

In my own talk with the President on May 28, he immediately said that his own thinking ran along the same lines as mine, but he asked me to discuss the proposal with the Secretaries of War and Navy and the Chiefs of Staff and then to report to him the consensus of that group.[10] A conference was

turned to good use in lowering resistance if the enemy were told that the decision regarding his fate after an Allied victory would be up to the Japanese themselves." Leighton also stated, p. 126, that it "is evident from what has been presented here that as early as May, 1945, the Division had concluded that the Japanese determination to fight was seriously undermined. . . . The first indicators of the downward trend had been noted as early as January."

In *Great Mistakes of the War* (New York: Harper & Bros., 1950), pp. 92, 95, Hanson Baldwin wrote: "It is therefore clear today — and was clear to many even as early as the spring of 1945 — that the military defeat of Japan was certain." The United States "demanded unconditional surrender, then dropped the bomb and accepted conditional surrender, a sequence which indicates pretty clearly that the Japanese would have surrendered, even if the bomb had not been dropped, had the Potsdam Declaration included our promise to permit the Emperor to remain on his imperial throne."

"More important, however," wrote Admiral Ellis M. Zacharias in *Secret Missions* (New York: G. P. Putnam's Sons, 1946), p. 335, "were recent intelligence reports disclosing a definite Japanese trend which could be exploited to move the Japanese toward surrender, or at least a termination of hostilities prior to our invasion of Japan proper. Among these was a very significant report given in the utmost secrecy to one of our intelligence officers in a neutral capital. It outlined in great detail the course Japan intended to take and stated that General Koiso would soon resign and permit the appointment as prime minister of Admiral Suzuki, an old confidant of the Emperor and leader of what I even then had come to call the 'peace party.' Moreover, the document indicated that the Emperor himself was leading a group of influential personalities desirous of obtaining peace terms under the most favorable circumstances."

[10] James Forrestal on page 69 of the book *The Forrestal Diaries* (New York: The Viking Press, 1951), edited by Walter Millis with the collaboration of

therefore called and was held in the office of the Secretary of War in the Pentagon Building on May 29, 1945, and the issue was discussed for an hour. According to my memorandum of that meeting it became clear in the course of the discussion that Mr. Stimson, Mr. Forrestal, and General Marshall (Admiral King was absent) were all in accord with the principle of the proposal but that for certain military reasons, not then divulged, it was considered inadvisable for the President to make such a statement at that juncture. It later appeared that the fighting on Okinawa was still going on, and it was felt that such a declaration as I proposed would be interpreted by the Japanese as a confession of weakness. The question of timing was the nub of the whole matter, according to the views expressed. I duly reported this to the President, and the proposal for action was, for the time being, dropped.

When Mr. Byrnes became Secretary of State over a month later, I endeavored to interest him in the importance and urgency of a public statement along the lines proposed, but during those few days he was intensely occupied in preparing for the Potsdam Conference, and it was only on the morning of his departure for Potsdam that I was able to hand him a draft on which a declaration might be based. This was the draft I had shown to the President. Mr. Byrnes was already on his way out of his office to drive to the airport, and his last action before leaving was to place our draft in his pocket. Mr. Stimson was then already in Europe and I urged Jack McCloy, Assistant Secretary of War, when he met him over there, to tell Mr. Stimson how strongly I felt about the matter.

Mr. Stimson did take energetic steps at Potsdam to secure the decision by the President and Mr. Churchill to issue the

E. S. Duffield, says, "Mr. Grew was of the impression that the President had indicated that he was not in accord with this point of view" (that we should indicate now that the Japanese, after surrender, should be allowed to retain their own form of government). Mr. Forrestal was clearly mistaken in this conception of what I had said. I made it quite clear in the meeting in Secretary Stimson's office on May 29, 1945, attended by numerous witnesses, that on this point the President had assured me that "his own thinking ran along the same lines as mine" but that he wished me to consult our military and naval authorities. — J. C. G.

proclamation. In fact, the opinion was expressed to me by one American already in Potsdam, that if it had not been for Mr. Stimson's wholehearted initiative, the Potsdam Conference would have ended without any proclamation to Japan being issued at all. But even Mr. Stimson was unable to have included in the proclamation a categorical undertaking that unconditional surrender would not mean the elimination of the dynasty if the Japanese people desired its retention.

The main point at issue historically is whether, if immediately following the terrific devastation of Tokyo by our B-29s in May, 1945,[11] "the President had made a public categorical statement that surrender would not mean the elimination of the present dynasty if the Japanese people desired its retention, the surrender of Japan could have been hastened.

"That question can probably never be definitively answered but a good deal of evidence is available to shed light on it. From statements made by a number of the moderate former Japanese leaders to responsible Americans after the American occupation, it is quite clear that the civilian advisers to the Emperor were working toward surrender long before the Potsdam Proclamation, even indeed before my talk with the President on May 28, for they knew then that Japan was a defeated nation. The stumbling block that they had to overcome was the complete dominance of the Japanese Army over the Government, and even when the moderates finally succeeded in getting a decision by the controlling element of the Government to accept the Potsdam terms, efforts were made by the unreconciled elements in the Japanese Army to bring about nullification of that decision. The Emperor needed all the support he could get, and in the light of available evidence I myself and others felt and still feel that if such a categorical statement about the dynasty had been issued in May, 1945, the surrender-minded elements in the Government might well have been afforded by such a statement a valid reason and the necessary strength to come to an early clear-cut decision.

"If surrender could have been brought about in May, 1945, or

11 The following quotation is taken from a letter to Mr. Henry L. Stimson, February 12, 1947.

even in June or July, before the entrance of Soviet Russia into the war and the use of the atomic bomb, the world would have been the gainer.

"The action of Prime Minister Suzuki in rejecting the Potsdam ultimatum by announcing on July 28, 1945, that it was 'unworthy of public notice' was a most unfortunate if not an utterly stupid step. Suzuki, who was severely wounded and very nearly assassinated as a moderate by the military extremists in 1936, I believe from the evidence which has reached me was surrender-minded even before May, 1945, if only it were made clear that surrender would not involve the downfall of the dynasty. That point was clearly *implied* in Article 12 of the Potsdam Proclamation that 'The occupying forces of the Allies shall be withdrawn from Japan as soon as . . . there has been established in accordance with the freely expressed will of the Japanese people a peacefully inclined and responsible government.' This however was not, at least from the Japanese point of view, a categorical undertaking regarding the dynasty, nor did it comply with your [Henry L. Stimson's] suggestion that it would substantially add to the chances of acceptance if the ultimatum should contain a statement that we would not exclude a constitutional monarchy under the present dynasty.[12] Suzuki's reply was typical of oriental methods

12 See Henry L. Stimson and McGeorge Bundy, *On Active Service in Peace and War* (New York: Harper & Bros., 1948), pp. 619–27, where Mr. Stimson has written: "I wrote a memorandum for the President, on July 2, which I believe fairly represents the thinking of the American Government as it finally took shape in action. This memorandum was prepared after discussion and general agreement with Joseph C. Grew, Acting Secretary of State, and Secretary of the Navy Forrestal, and when I discussed it with the President, he expressed his general approval." In this memorandum Mr. Stimson said that he felt that a statement should be issued to the Japanese, assuring them among other things of the "withdrawal from their country as soon as the above objectives of the Allies are accomplished, and as soon as there has been established a peacefully inclined government, of a character representative of the masses of the Japanese people. I personally think that if in saying this we should add that we do not exclude a constitutional monarchy under her present dynasty, it would substantially add to the chances of acceptance."

In an article in the February, 1947, issue of *Harper's Magazine* Mr. Stimson further explained his position in 1945. *On Active Service* contains quotations

in retaining his supposed bargaining position until he knew precisely what the Potsdam Proclamation meant in that respect. The Asiatic concern over the loss of assumed bargaining power that might arise from exhibiting what might be

from this *Harper's* article with Stimson's and Bundy's further comments and explanations.

" 'Many accounts have been written about the Japanese surrender. After a prolonged Japanese Cabinet session in which the deadlock was broken by the Emperor himself, the offer to surrender was made on August 10. It was based on the Potsdam terms, with a reservation concerning the sovereignty of the Emperor.'

"This Japanese reservation precipitated a final discussion in Washington. For months there had been disagreement at high levels over the proper policy toward the Emperor. Some maintained that the Emperor must go, along with all the other trappings of Japanese militarism. Others urged that the war could be ended much more cheaply by openly revising the formula of 'unconditional surrender' to assure the Japanese that there was no intention of removing the Emperor if it should be the desire of the Japanese people that he remain as a constitutional monarch. This latter view had been urged with particular force and skill by Joseph C. Grew, the Under Secretary of State, a man with profound insight into the Japanese character. For their pains Grew and those who agreed with him were roundly abused as appeasers.

"Stimson wholly agreed with Grew's general argument, as the July 2 memorandum shows. He had hoped that a specific assurance on the Emperor might be included in the Potsdam ultimatum. Unfortunately during the war years high American officials had made some fairly blunt and unpleasant remarks about the Emperor, and it did not seem wise to Mr. Truman and Secretary of State Byrnes that the Government should reverse its field too sharply; too many people were likely to cry shame. Now, in August, the Americans were face to face with the issue they had dodged in previous months. The Japanese were ready to surrender, but, even after seeing in dreadful reality the fulfillment of Potsdam's threats, they required some assurance that the Potsdam Declaration 'does not comprise any demand which prejudices the prerogatives of His Majesty as a Sovereign Ruler.'

"August 10 was hectic in Washington. Radio reports from Japan announced the surrender offer before official notification reached Washington by way of Switzerland. At nine o'clock Stimson was called to the White House where the President was holding a conference on the surrender terms. All those present seemed eager to make the most of this great opportunity to end the war, but there was some doubt as to the propriety of accepting the Japanese condition.

" 'The President then asked me what my opinion was and I told him that I thought that even if the question hadn't been raised by the Japanese we would have to continue the Emperor ourselves under our command and supervision in order to get into surrender the many scattered armies of the Japanese who would own no other authority and that something like this use of the Emperor must be made in order to save us from a score of bloody

interpreted as a sign of weakness is always uppermost in Japanese mental processes. He can seldom be made to realize that the time for compromise has passed if it ever existed. This explains but certainly does not excuse Suzuki's reply, and the result of his reply was to release the atom bomb to fulfill its appointed purpose. Yet I and a good many others will always feel that had the President issued as far back as May, 1945, the recommended categorical statement that the Japanese dynasty would be retained if the Japanese people freely desired its retention, the atom bomb might never have had to be used at all. . . ."

The memorandums of Mr. Grew's conferences with President Truman on May 28 and at the Pentagon on May 29, as well as further documents on the surrender of Japan, follow:

May 28, 1945

This morning, on my own initiative as Acting Secretary of State, I asked for an appointment with President Truman and went to see him at 12.35 P.M., accompanied by Judge Samuel Rosenman [Special Counsel to the President] with whom I had talked the matter over in advance. I set forth the purpose of our visit as follows:

In waging our war against Japan it is an elementary and fundamental concept that nothing must be sacrificed, now or in future, to the attainment and maintenance of our main objective, namely to render it impossible for Japan again to threaten world peace. This will mean the destruction of Japan's tools for war and of the capacity of the Japanese again to make those tools. Their military machine must be totally

Iwo Jimas and Okinawas all over China and the New Netherlands. He was the only source of authority in Japan under the Japanese theory of the State.' (Diary, August 10, 1945)

"The meeting at the White House soon adjourned to await the official surrender terms. Meanwhile Secretary Byrnes drafted a reply to which Stimson gave his prompt approval. In a later meeting this masterful paper was accepted by the President; it avoided any direct acceptance of the Japanese condition, but accomplished the desired purpose of reassuring the Japanese."

destroyed and, so far as possible, their cult of militarism must be blotted out.

With the foregoing fundamental concepts as a premise it should be our aim to accomplish our purpose with the least possible loss of American lives. We should, therefore, give most careful consideration to any step which, without sacrificing in any degree our principles or objectives, might render it easier for the Japanese to surrender unconditionally now.

While I have never undertaken to predict with certainty anything that the Japanese may do, we must remember that the Japanese are a fanatical people and are capable of fighting to the last ditch and the last man. If they do this, the cost in American lives will be unpredictable.

The greatest obstacle to unconditional surrender by the Japanese is their belief that this would entail the destruction or permanent removal of the Emperor and the institution of the Throne. If some indication can now be given the Japanese that they themselves, when once thoroughly defeated and rendered impotent to wage war in future, will be permitted to determine their own future political structure, they will be afforded a method of saving face without which surrender will be highly unlikely.

It is believed that such a statement would have maximum effect if issued immediately following the great devastation of Tokyo which occurred two days ago. The psychological impact of such a statement at this particular moment would be very great.

In a public message to his troops sometime ago Chiang Kai-shek, whose country has suffered more from the Japanese than any other country, said that in his opinion a defeated and penitent Japan should be permitted to determine its own future political structure.

The idea of depriving the Japanese of their Emperor and emperorship is unsound for the reason that the moment our backs are turned (and we cannot afford to occupy Japan permanently) the Japanese would undoubtedly put the Emperor and emperorship back again. From the long range point of view the best that we can hope for in Japan is the development of a constitutional monarchy, experience having shown that our system of democracy in Japan would never work.

Those who hold that the Emperor and the institution of the Throne in Japan are the roots of their aggressive militarism can hardly be familiar with the facts of history. For approximately 700 years the Japanese Emperors were deprived of their throne in practice and were obliged to eke out a precarious existence in Kyoto while the Shoguns who had ejected them ruled in Tokyo, and it was the Shogun Hideyoshi, not the Emperor, who in the sixteenth century waged war against China and Korea and boasted that he would conquer the world.

The Emperor Meiji who brought about the restoration of the Throne in 1868 was a strong man who overcame the militaristic Shoguns and started Japan on a moderate and peaceful course. The Emperors who followed Meiji were not strong men and it became relatively easy for the military extremists to take control and to exert their influence on the Emperors. If Hirohito had refused to support the military and approve the declaration of war in 1941 he would in all probability have suffered the fate of his predecessors. In any case whether he was or was not war-minded he would have been powerless to stem the tidal wave of military ambition.

The foregoing facts indicate clearly that Japan does not need an Emperor to be militaristic nor are the Japanese militaristic because they have an Emperor. In other words, their militarism springs from the military clique and cult in the country which succeeded in gaining control even of the Emperor himself and rendered powerless the Emperor's advisers, who in the years before Pearl Harbor were doing their best to restrain the hotheads. The assassinations in February, 1936, were undertaken by the military extremists for the specific purpose of purging the peace-minded advisers around the throne. General Tojo and his group who perpetrated the attack on Pearl Harbor were just as much military dictators as were the Shoguns in the old days and the Emperor was utterly powerless to restrain them regardless of his own volition.

The foregoing facts do not in any way clear Hirohito from responsibility for the war for, having signed the declaration of war, the responsibility was squarely on his shoulders. The point at issue is that the extremist group would have had their way whether the Emperor signed or not. Once the military extremists have been discredited through defeat the Emperor, purely a symbol, can and possibly will be used by new leaders who will be expected to emerge once the Japanese people are convinced that their military leaders have let them down. The institution of the Throne can, therefore, become a cornerstone for building a peaceful future for the country once the militarists have learned in the hard way that they have nothing to hope for in the future.

I then submitted to the President a rough draft of a statement which he might wish to consider including in his proposed address on May 31. The President said that he was interested in what I said because his own thoughts had been following the same line. He thereupon asked me to arrange for a meeting to discuss this question in the first instance with the Secretaries of War and Navy, General Marshall and Admiral King and that after we had exchanged views he would like to have the same group come to the White House for a conference with him. I said that I would arrange such a meeting at once for tomorrow morning and I asked Judge Rosenman to join us, which he said he would do. (The meeting was arranged in Mr. Stimson's office in the Pentagon Building for 11.00 A.M. tomorrow.)

Judge Rosenman thought that our draft statement could be somewhat tightened up and suggested three or four points which we shall endeavor to include in the statement.

Draft Proclamation by the Heads of State
U.S. — U.K. — [U.S.S.R.] — China

[Delete matters inside brackets if U.S.S.R. not in war]
(Completed in Department of State May, 1945)

(1) We, — The President of the United States, the Prime Minister of Great Britain, [the Generalissimo of the Soviet

Union] and the President of the Republic of China, representing the hundreds of millions of our countrymen, have conferred and agree that the Japanese people shall be given an opportunity to end this war on the terms we state herein.

(2) The prodigious land, sea and air forces of the United States, the British Empire and of China, many times reinforced by their armies and air fleets from the west [have now been joined by the vast military might of the Soviet Union and] are poised to strike the final blows upon Japan. This military power is sustained and inspired by the determination of all the Allied nations to prosecute the war against Japan until her capitulation.

(3) The result of the futile and senseless German resistance to the might of the aroused free peoples of the world stands forth in awful clarity as an example to the people of Japan. The might that now converges on Japan is immeasurably greater than that which, when applied to the resisting Nazis, necessarily laid waste to the lands, the industry and the method of life of the whole German people. The full application of our military power backed by our resolve *will* mean the inevitable and complete destruction of the Japanese armed forces and just as inevitably the utter devastation of the Japanese homeland.

(4) Are the Japanese so lacking in reason that they will continue blindly to follow the leadership of those self-willed militaristic advisers whose unintelligent calculations have brought the Empire of Japan to the threshold of annihilation? The time has come *for the Japanese people* to decide whether to continue on to destruction or to follow the path of reason.

(5) Following are our terms. We will not deviate from them. There are no alternatives. We shall brook no delay.

(6) There must be eliminated for all time the authority and influence of those who have deceived and misled the people of Japan into embarking on world conquest, for we insist that a new order of peace, security and justice will be impossible until irresponsible militarism is driven from the world.

(7) Until such a new order is established *and* until there is convincing proof that Japan's war-making power is destroyed,

Japanese territory shall be occupied to the extent necessary to secure the achievement of the basic objectives we are here setting forth.

(8) The terms of the Cairo Declaration shall be carried out and Japanese sovereignty shall be limited to the islands of Honshu, Hokkaido, Kyushu, Shikoku and such minor islands as we determine.

(9) The Japanese military forces, after being completely disarmed, shall be permitted to return to their homes, with the opportunity to lead peaceful and productive lives.

(10) We do not intend that the Japanese shall be enslaved as a race or destroyed as a nation, but stern justice shall be meted out to all war criminals, including those who have visited cruelties upon our prisoners. Democratic tendencies among the Japanese people shall be supported and strengthened. Freedom of speech, of religion and of thought, as well as respect for the fundamental human rights shall be established.

(11) Japan shall be permitted to maintain such industries as are determined to offer no potential for war but which can produce a sustaining economy and permit the Japanese to take their part in a world economic system, with access to raw materials and opportunities for peaceful trade.

(12) The occupying forces of the Allies shall be withdrawn from Japan as soon as these objectives have been accomplished and there has been established beyond doubt a peacefully inclined, responsible government of a character representative of the Japanese people. This may include a constitutional monarchy under the present dynasty if the peace-loving nations can be convinced of the genuine determination of such a government to follow policies of peace which will render impossible the future development of aggressive militarism in Japan.[13]

(13) We call upon the Japanese people and those in au-

[13] This last essential sentence of paragraph 12 was omitted from the Potsdam Declaration. — J. C. G. For the text, as released to the press, see U.S. Department of State, *The Department of State Bulletin,* July 29, 1945, pp. 137–38, and *infra,* p. 1437, n. 15.

thority in Japan to proclaim now the unconditional surrender of all the Japanese armed forces and to provide proper and adequate assurances of their good faith in such action. The alternative for Japan is prompt and utter destruction.

May 29, 1945

At the President's request in our talk yesterday I called a meeting this morning in Secretary Stimson's office in the Pentagon Building. The following were present:

> Mr. Stimson, Secretary of War;
> Mr. Forrestal, Secretary of the Navy;
> General Marshall, Chief of Staff;
> Mr. Elmer Davis, Director of OWI;
> Judge Samuel Rosenman, Counsel to the President;
> Mr. Eugene H. Dooman, Department of State;
> Joseph C. Grew, Acting Secretary of State.

Admiral King, Chief of the Bureau of Naval Operations, was absent. I brought Mr. Davis, Judge Rosenman and Mr. Dooman with me.

The purpose of the meeting which I explained at the start, was to discuss the question as to whether the President, in his forthcoming speech about our war with Japan, should indicate that we have no intention of determining Japan's future political structure, which should be left to the Japanese themselves, in the thought that such a statement, which had already been made by Mr. Hull and by Chiang Kai-shek, might render it easier for the Japanese to surrender unconditionally instead of fighting fanatically for their Emperor. The meeting lasted for an hour and in the course of the discussion it became clear that Mr. Stimson, Mr. Forrestal, and General Marshall were all in accord with the principle but for certain military reasons, not divulged, it was considered inadvisable for the President to make such a statement just now. The question of timing was the nub of the whole matter according to the views presented. I undertook to inform the President of the consensus of the meeting.

To Samuel I. Rosenman, June 16, 1945

The campaign in Okinawa is likely to be finished in the not distant future and I am wondering whether, with the announcement of its fall, a suitable opportunity would not be presented for us to make some sort of public statement again calling upon the Japanese to surrender. As we are bearing the brunt of the war in the Pacific, I am not convinced that there is any good reason to defer such action until the meeting of the Big Three, and in my opinion the sooner we can get the Japanese thinking about final surrender the better it will be and the more lives of Americans may ultimately be saved.

As I have said to the President and to you, we must at every step make it abundantly clear that we propose to cut out the cancer of militarism in Japan once and for all. Having stated our position in that respect in no uncertain terms, and the tougher the language we employ the better, I think it will be a matter of plain common sense to give the Japanese a clearer idea of what we mean by unconditional surrender. The President has already stated that this does not mean extermination or enslavement, but there are two further points which would make it vastly easier — if they could be specifically announced — for a peace movement to get started in Japan, and I have no doubt that there are elements in Japan today who clearly realize that they have everything to lose and nothing to gain by continuing the war. The foregoing arguments are amply confirmed by the Psychological Warfare Branch of the Army on the basis of the interrogation of intelligent prisoners selected for their reliability after a long process of screening.

The two points which I have in mind are, first, the fact that once we have rendered the Japanese incapable of again building up a military machine and once they have convinced us of their intention to fulfill their international obligations and to co-operate for the furthering of common peace and security, the Japanese will then be permitted to determine for themselves the nature of their future political structure. Chiang Kai-shek said just this in his address on New Year's Day, 1944. The second point is that we have no intention, when the foregoing matters have been taken care of, to deprive the

Japanese of a reasonable peacetime economy to prevent starvation and to enable them gradually to work their way back into the family of nations. These things have never been clearly brought out and, while there are many people in our country who will not be in sympathy with any such assurances, I believe that the more intelligent elements in our press and public will recognize that it is plain common sense to save perhaps tens of thousands of American lives by bringing the Japanese to unconditional surrender as soon as possible. They will presumably also recognize the fact that we cannot occupy Japan permanently and that it is not going to be in our long-range interests to create permanent festering sores anywhere in the postwar world so long as we do not recede an inch from our determination to render the Japanese impotent to bring about future breaches of the peace. . . .

I understand that the President is to have a talk with the Joint Chiefs of Staff on Monday afternoon and it may be that he would wish to bring up these points at that time. I cannot see any advantage in indefinitely delaying some sort of a public statement along the general lines suggested.

P.S.

One consideration which leads me to attach special importance to the making of a proposed statement at the end of the Okinawa campaign, and in any event before the landing in Japan, is the likelihood that the very large casualties which we are likely to suffer during the assault operations in Japan might create a state of mind in the United States which would be wholly unreceptive to a public statement of the character now proposed. I have received competent military opinion to the effect that the military operations in Japan cannot be anything but costly in terms of human lives, and if we had refrained previously from taking any action which would create a condition favorable to the making of peace advances by the Japanese, I would expect no possible alternative than to let matters take their course until the bitter end.[14]

---

[14] For a statement as to the number of casualties expected from a landing on Japan, see *ibid.*, p. 619.

Date: June 18, 1945
SUBJECT: Appointment with the President, 9.30 A.M.
PARTICIPANTS: The President; The Acting Secretary,
Mr. Grew.

I went to the President at 9.30 this morning and took up the following matters:

1. The President said that he had carefully considered yesterday the draft statement which I had given to Judge Rosenman calling on Japan for unconditional surrender to be considered for release at the moment of the announcement of the fall of Okinawa but that while he liked the idea he had decided to hold this up until it could be discussed at the Big Three meeting. I said to the President that I merely wished to square my own conscience at having omitted no recommendation which might conceivably result in the saving of the lives of thousands of our fighting men so long as we did not recede an inch from our objectives in rendering Japan powerless to threaten the peace in future. I wanted to see every appropriate step taken which might encourage a peace movement in Japan and while it was all guesswork as to whether such a statement would have that effect I nevertheless felt very strongly that something might be gained and nothing could be lost by such a step and in my opinion the sooner it was taken the better. The President having ruled against the step at this time, there was of course nothing more to be done but I felt that this question should be kept prominently in mind. The President asked me to have the subject entered on the agenda for the Big Three meeting and I so informed H. Freeman Matthews [Director of the Office of European Affairs].[15]

15 At Potsdam on July 26, 1945, the following statement was issued by the United States, Great Britain, and China: "We do not intend that the Japanese shall be enslaved as a race or destroyed as a nation, but stern justice shall be meted out to all war criminals, including those who have visited cruelties upon our prisoners. The Japanese Government shall remove all obstacles to the revival and strengthening of democratic tendencies among the Japanese people. Freedom of speech, of religion, and of thought, as well as respect for the fundamental human rights shall be established.

"Japan shall be permitted to maintain such industries as will sustain her

Memorandum for the Secretary of State, from
Joseph C. Grew, August 7, 1945

Ambassador Patrick Hurley [in China] in his telegram of August 4 requested the views of the Department on the position to be taken by the American delegate on the Far Eastern and Pacific Subcommission of United Nations War Crimes Commission, now sitting in Chungking, in the event that the question of listing the Japanese Emperor as a war criminal is brought up in the Subcommission.

Mr. Green Hackworth of the Department in his appended memorandum of August 6, brings up the point that the Department would probably be subjected to considerable criticism if the impression should go out that we are hedging or are not clear in our own minds with respect to the Emperor. He feels that our decision can be taken now as well as later. He recognizes the fact that political expediency might have to be taken into account but he feels that in the administration of justice we should not be influenced by expediency.

I have given a good deal of thought to this subject and am inclined to feel that if Japan refuses to heed the Potsdam Proclamation and declines to surrender unconditionally, necessitating our invasion of the main Japanese islands by force and the inevitable loss of life which will occur among the Allied forces in the event of such invasion, the Emperor of Japan might well be treated as a war criminal in order that full justice should be done. The listing of the Emperor does not mean that he will be convicted. This will depend upon the evidence, part of which will relate to the question whether the Emperor has taken part in the planning and carrying on of the war with all of its atrocious aspects or whether he is a mere

economy and permit the exaction of just reparations in kind, but not those which would enable her to re-arm for war. To this end, access to, as distinguished from control of, raw materials shall be permitted. Eventual Japanese participation in world trade relations shall be permitted.

"The occupying forces of the Allies shall be withdrawn from Japan as soon as these objectives have been accomplished and there has been established in accordance with the freely expressed will of the Japanese people a peacefully inclined and responsible government."

symbol without power to control or influence his military leaders.

In this particular problem, however, I do not think that we can afford to disregard the factor of political expediency. We have good reason to believe that important elements in Japan, including some of their elder statesmen as well as high officers in the Army and Navy, are trying to bring about an acceptance of the terms proposed in the Potsdam Proclamation. We know, for instance, from secret but unimpeachable information, that Sato, the Japanese Ambassador to Moscow, formerly Minister of Foreign Affairs, has been earnestly recommending this course and we believe it possible although by no means certain that this movement may gain headway to a point where the advocates of peace will be able to overcome the opposition of the military extremists and their present control of the Emperor. If they succeed in persuading the Emperor to issue an Imperial Rescript, which is regarded throughout Japan as a sacred document, ordering all Japanese armies to lay down their arms for the future good of the country, the war might thereby be brought to an end. Short of fighting to the last ditch within Japan itself it is not believed that the war is likely to come to an end in any other way as it is improbable that the Japanese armies in China, Manchuria and elsewhere would obey such an order from any Japanese Government without the sanction of the Emperor.

If it now becomes known that we have agreed to the listing of the Emperor as a war criminal — and if we take such a position it will almost certainly leak to the public in short order — the effect in Japan would in all probability be to nip in the bud any movement toward unconditional surrender and peace. The result, in all probability, would be to consolidate the determinaton of the Japanese people as a whole to fight on to the bitter end. Our decision therefore will be of prime importance and many thousands of American lives may depend on its nature.

I have not had an opportunity, owing to their absence from Washington, to discuss this question with Mr. Stimson and Mr.

Forrestal but from what I know of their thinking I believe that they will probably share my views. I believe that in any case you will wish to discuss this matter with them as well as with the President. In the meantime I recommend that the appended telegram be sent to Ambassador Hurley directing him to inform the Department if the question of listing the Emperor as a war criminal is raised in the Subcommission and expressing the Department's desire that the American delegate should not himself raise this question.

To Mrs. J. Borden Harriman, September 9, 1945

. . . As for the future, my guess is that the Emperor may prove to be an asset rather than a liability in stamping out the whole military caste and cult in Japan — and it will have to be a thoroughly radical surgical operation. . . . Once we rid him of the control of the militarists, my guess is that he will develop strength and will become a powerful asset in steering Japan into peaceful and constructive channels. But whether Hirohito remains or not — and I can't help feeling that he will have to take the responsibility for the war . . . the throne can and probably will become the safest guarantee against the rise of militarism in future. Without the future stabilizing influence of the throne, the field will be open for military dictators to maneuver themselves into power the moment our occupation ceases.

Let us remember, too, that the fable about the divinity of the Emperor is an artificial creation of the last eighty years — certainly not believed by intelligent Japanese — and whatever is artificial can be corrected over a period of time. MacArthur will have a difficult job of reconstruction and re-education, but it can be done, and once the Japanese people come to realize where their militarists have led them, I believe there will be an automatic reaction against the whole feudal system and that we shall find plenty of co-operation in starting that misguided country towards a New Deal. I should expect some kind of a constitutional monarchy to develop in due course. Any attempt to impose an outright democracy on the

Japanese would result in political chaos and would simply leave the field wide open for would-be dictators to get control. One can't live in a country for ten years without knowing these things.

But what I want to see first of all is the arrest, trial and punishment of every Japanese, high or low, who has been responsible for the utterly barbarous treatment of our prisoners. Until that has been done — and thoroughly done — we can know no rest.

At the same time we must set about destroying the whole military system, their tools of war and all their machines capable of making the tools of war.

The Japanese judicial system must be revamped and their courts and judges completely freed from the baneful control of the military police who directed the judiciary and dictated both convictions and sentences.

Free speech and a free press must be ensured, as well as free religion.

Finally the whole feudal system must be disintegrated and the Zaibatsu — the six or seven families who held control of the financial and economic life of the country through enormous cartels and great wealth — broken up and the farmers assured a higher standard of living.

Then, of course, re-education must be developed from the kindergarten to the university, with new text books and new curricula.

The job will be tremendous but it can and will be done. Meanwhile the Japanese, not more than some 60% of whom could subsist on the produce of their home islands, will have to be allowed access to but not control of raw materials afield and the development of light industry and peaceful trade abroad. If they ever in future try to rebuild a military machine — and we shall have to be on the watch for a long time to come — control of their imports of oil, iron and coal would make it impossible for them ever again to threaten any nation or the world with war. . . .

To Mr. and Mrs. Cecil B. Lyon,
September 30, 1945

. . . You can have no idea how happy I am to be free, with no office hours.[16] The press and public called for a clean sweep in the Department and an entire reorganization and it is great fun to watch the new setup working, from the outside. The old Department never had been, and probably never will be, so well organized as during the Stettinius regime. I am told that there hasn't been a single meeting of the Secretary's Staff Committee since we left, yet that committee, which was composed of the ten highest-ranking officers, met every morning while we were there, discussed every important problem and co-ordinated all our activities, so that everyone knew what every-one else was doing. Yet the press and public insisted on the contrary and called for a complete change. Alas, they will be doing the same a year or so from now.

Another amusing sidelight is that the press and public in-sisted on getting rid of the so-called "Japan crowd" and "soft peace boys" in the Department. This was thoroughly done: Dooman resigned and Ballantine was replaced by John Carter Vincent, while Erle Dickover [Chief of the Division of Japa-nese Affairs] I believe is trying to get a foreign assignment. The funny thing about this is that our plan for the postwar treatment of Japan was a great deal more drastic than the plan finally sent by Byrnes to MacArthur. The "Japan crowd" and the "soft peace boys" wanted to go a lot farther than was finally done. . . .

16 Mr. Grew had submitted his letter of resignation to the President on August 15, 1945.

XXXVII

The United States and the Soviet Union

Shortly after the Yalta Conference the unity that had been achieved during the war and in the Crimea began to disintegrate. The Soviet Union, within two weeks of Yalta, started to violate commitments. The Russians delayed, for instance, the execution of certain military agreements. In the case of plans for the postwar control of Germany, the Soviet Union impeded the formation of the German Control Commission agreed to at Yalta.

The violation of the Polish agreement, however, caused the most concern. This agreement required that "the Provisional Government which is now functioning in Poland should therefore be reorganized on a broader democratic basis with the inclusion of democratic leaders from Poland itself and from Poles abroad." Foreign Minister Molotov delayed invitations to Polish leaders from London and Poland to come to Moscow to reorganize the Polish Government, and he tried merely to enlarge the puppet Lublin Government.

The Soviet Union also violated the "Declaration on Liberated Europe" in Rumania thirteen days after the agreement had been signed. The "Declaration on Liberated Europe" pledged the United States, Great Britain, and the Soviet Union to "jointly assist the people in any European liberated state or former Axis satellite state in Europe . . . to form interim governmental authorities broadly representative of all democratic elements in the population. . . ." Instead of joint action in Rumania, the Soviet Union unilaterally forced the King to appoint a government formed by pro-Communist leader Peter Groza.

President Roosevelt and Prime Minister Churchill protested these violations of the Yalta agreements. Already before the

President's death the Department of State, with Mr. Roosevelt's approval, had drafted some very strong messages to Moscow on the Polish question. One message of April 1, 1945, Churchill described as a "grave and weighty" document, and threw the full weight of the British Cabinet behind it. "We must be firm, however, and our course thus far is correct," President Roosevelt telegraphed Winston Churchill on the day that he died. When these messages are fully released, it is believed that they will show how sharp was Roosevelt's reaction to Soviet violations of the Yalta agreements.

SOVIET RUSSIA [1]

Although the Secretary of State, Mr. Stettinius, was present at Yalta, we in the State Department had very little if anything to do with the proceedings and results contained in the Far Eastern Agreement signed there. In fact, it was only long afterwards that we were able to learn the whole story, most or all of which has now been published. The Yalta agreement on the Far East was squarely based on a military estimate of the war against Japan. It was an act of military policy, a deal in which the United States military people thought they were getting more than an adequate *quid pro quo*. I do not think now and I did not think then that there was any possibility of keeping Soviet Russia out of the war against Japan. The world would be in a far happier state today if we could have done so. Actually the Far Eastern Agreement was not so much to ensure Soviet participation in the war as to ensure participation at a time when it would benefit United States military plans for landing on the Japanese main islands. I believe that the Yalta action was based on a badly mistaken military estimate of Japan's ability to continue the war after the German surrender.[2]

[1] Mr. Grew wrote this statement in 1950.

[2] Edward R. Stettinius, Jr., in *Roosevelt and the Russians*, pp. 90–98, 304–5, and Admiral William D. Leahy in *I Was There*, pp. 293, 311–12, and 318, explain President Roosevelt's signature of the Far Eastern Agreement as being the result of pressure from the Joint Chiefs of Staff — particularly the Army —

We should remember that it has been Soviet violations of the Yalta agreements rather than the agreements themselves that have been the main trouble. It is reasonable to question whether the Yalta agreements could be regarded as so favorable to the Soviet Union when later, at every step, the Soviets had grossly to violate the agreements reached.

At the height of this difficult era, I passed a sleepless night while Acting Secretary of State, mulling over the difficult international problems that then faced us. At five o'clock in the morning of May 19, 1945, I dressed, came down to my desk and tried to concentrate my thoughts in concise form in a memorandum for my purely private use. That morning I read my memorandum to two high American officials competent in Russian affairs, W. Averell Harriman and Charles E. Bohlen, and then locked the statement in my private despatch box at home, in a place where nobody would have access to it, and there it lay for a long time. When I took it out and reread it two or three years later, it was interesting to see how developments had occurred along the general lines predicted.

This was the memorandum. It has not hitherto been published.

Washington, May 19, 1945

This war, so far as the interests of the United States are concerned, will have achieved one purpose and one purpose only, namely protection from the military expansion of Germany and Japan. For that purpose we had to fight, for had we not fought, our nation itself would have been in direst peril. It was and is, so far as our own interests are concerned, purely a war of self-defense, forced upon us.

But as "a war to end wars," the war will have been futile, for the result will be merely the transfer of totalitarian dictatorship and power from Germany and Japan to Soviet Russia which will constitute in future as grave a danger to us as did the Axis.[3]

that Russia be brought into the Japanese war in order to shorten the war and reduce American casualties.

[3] According to Admiral Leahy, *I Was There*, p. 336, Mr. Grew had asked him "on March 6 [1945] to suggest to Roosevelt that he act slowly on a Russian

The world organization for peace and security now being built at San Francisco will be incapable of preserving peace and security because, through the agreement at Yalta to give the right of veto to the great powers against the use of force in disputes to which one of them is a party, the organization will be rendered powerless to act against the one certain future enemy, Soviet Russia. In practice the main purpose of the organization will be annulled. We shall be able to place no confidence in it whatsoever. Its power to prevent a future world war will be but a pipe dream.

Already Russia is showing us — in Poland, Rumania, Bulgaria, Hungary, Austria, Czechoslovakia and Yugoslavia — the future world pattern that she visualizes and will aim to create. With her certain stranglehold on these countries, Russia's power will steadily increase and she will in the not distant future be in a favorable position to expand her control, step by step, through Europe. The Near East and the Far East will in due course be brought into the same pattern. Once Russia is in the war against Japan, then Mongolia, Manchuria, and Korea will gradually slip into Russia's orbit, to be followed in due course by China and eventually Japan. . . .

A future war with Soviet Russia is as certain as anything in this world can be certain. It may come within a very few years. We shall therefore do well to keep up our fighting strength and to do everything in our power to strengthen our relations with the free world.

Meanwhile we should insist upon the control of strategic air and naval bases. The most fatal thing we can do is to place any confidence whatever in Russia's sincerity, knowing without question that she will take every opportunity to profit by our clinging to our own ethical international standards. She regards and will continue to regard our ethical behavior as a weakness to us and an asset to her.

As soon as the San Francisco Conference is over, our policy toward Soviet Russia should immediately stiffen, all along the line. . . .

request for the loan of some naval vessels in lieu of receiving some of the Italian warships. Grew apparently wanted to use this request to bargain with Moscow to obtain Russian cooperation in some of our European political problems, particularly in Rumania."

That paper was obviously private and unofficial. It was in no sense a state document. Its purpose was merely to set down in brief form, and solely for my own private records, my views on the danger confronting us by Soviet expansion. It was written before Russia had come into the war against Japan, and before the use of the atomic bomb. Had it been prepared as an official memorandum, certain statements in it would have been qualified. In the fourth paragraph, for instance, the assertion that Japan would eventually slip into the Soviet orbit and in the fifth paragraph that a future war with Soviet Russia is as certain as anything in this world can be certain would have been qualified with the proviso *"unless we recognize the danger and take steps to meet it in time."*

During this era I felt that the great majority of the American people as well as elements in the Government were woefully blind to the fundamental philosophy and doctrine of the Soviets. Few had studied or even read those Soviet bibles, the works of Marx and Engels, Lenin and Stalin himself, on which that philosophy and doctrine are firmly based. Our people as a whole were blind to the Soviet doctrine that the end always justifies the means, that the Soviets feel warranted in entering any commitment, making any promises, concluding any treaty or agreement without the slightest intention of honoring such commitments when they run counter to what Moscow considers to be the best interests of the Soviet Union. They were blind to the utter ruthlessness of the Kremlin toward the individual and to the savage cruelty with which any defection from the communist "line" is punished. They were blind to the Soviet doctrine that communism and capitalism cannot continue to exist peaceably side by side, and that war between the two camps is eventually inevitable. They were blind to the patent fact that the only language understood by the Kremlin is the language of strength, force and power; that friendly appeasement in any form is regarded as a clear sign of weakness and an invitation to further demands or encroachments.

President Truman, on assuming office, felt bound by his predecessor's commitments and to a large extent by the general policy of continuing to "get along" with our difficult ally. But even before his death, Roosevelt began to see the handwriting on the wall, and it was not long before the true picture began to take shape in Truman's mind if it was not there at the very start of his Administration. Concrete steps began to be taken to meet the Soviet menace.

Politically I myself have been about as nonpartisan as any American could conscientiously be. The fundamental attitude of officers in the Foreign Service of the United States is and must be nonpartisan. We serve whatever Government is in office, and we must be prepared to readjust our loyalty if not our thinking when changes in administration and in general policy occur. In effect, we serve the United States. If we can't conscientiously carry out the policy laid down by the Government, we should resign. I have loyally served under many Presidents in both parties: Theodore Roosevelt; Taft; Wilson; Harding; Coolidge; Hoover; Franklin Roosevelt; and Truman. Now, in retirement from office, even though not a party man, I am free to support or to oppose the policies and acts of any Administration.

In the case of the Truman Administration, it is not difficult to find flaws, many of them. But the memory of our people is short. They forget the vitriol poured on such high-principled outstanding men as Grover Cleveland and Theodore Roosevelt in our own lifetime. Today the same public vitriol is poured on Harry Truman and his adviser in foreign affairs, Dean Acheson. The Truman Administration has followed some unwise policies and has been guilty of grievous errors. Most administrations have. But so far as Soviet Russia is concerned our people tend to forget the constructive acts of the Truman Administration in recognizing the Soviet menace and in taking steps to meet it. I list a few of them: the Truman Doctrine and its corollary of aiding Greece and Turkey; the Marshall Plan; E.C.A.; the Berlin airlift; the North Atlantic Pact; the rearming of western Europe; the head-on meeting of aggression in Korea; the peace treaty with Japan; and the undertaking to create a foundation for collective security in the United Nations alternative to the veto-bound Security Council.

In the case of every Administration there is a balance sheet. Let's not overlook or forget the whole record. We might reasonably ask ourselves where would we be today if these steps had not been taken, and we might remember that each of these steps required vision, imagination, courage, and determination. We might wish that similar vision had been shown in certain other problems and certain other areas. History should however not forget this credit side of the ledger. History alone can find the proper balance and give the proper answer.

In the light of my paper of May 19, 1945, people might well ask: "What did *you* do to implement the policy you advocated? You were in a position of authority." That is a fair question. It was once asked me a few years ago at a big public meeting, at which I had expressed some of the foregoing views about the Soviet menace. I do not now remember my reply but the facts. as I probably then stated them, were these:

An Under Secretary, even when Acting Secretary of State, can influence, but he cannot dictate foreign policy. He can take action only with the approval of the President of the United States who is primarily responsible for the conduct of our foreign relations. The President, for his part, must constantly listen to, even if he be not guided by, the predominant feeling in Congress and the public, and by the consensus of the members of his Cabinet. As the war was not yet over during the several months that I was Acting Secretary in 1945, the views of the Secretary of War, that wise and long experienced elder statesman, Henry Stimson, played an important part in influencing policy. Every Tuesday morning I met the Secretaries of War and Navy — Stimson and Forrestal with Jack McCloy as recorder — and compared notes and opinions. Almost every morning I conferred with President Truman, sometimes several times a day. He was available at any hour. I used to go over with him the usually large batch of important telegrams to our ambassadors and ministers abroad, conveying instructions which often involved matters of important policy. The great majority of these telegrams the President approved after I had explained them. Once in a while he would keep one on his desk for further study and consideration. I have served few chiefs who were more genuinely considerate and willing to discuss a problem even when initial difference arose in our respective views. His mind was always open.

Thus I was able to exert at least some small influence toward implementing the policies in which I believed. I recollect today no fundamental difference between the President and myself on any issue. In the case of the step I recommended on May 28, 1945, for hastening Japan's surrender, the President said: "My mind goes along with yours," but he added that we would have to get the approval of the Secretaries of War and Navy and of the Joint Chiefs of Staff before acting. They, unfortunately, disapproved, not the principle but the timing. That story is told in the chapter on Japan's surrender.[4]

In the case of China, our fundamental incentive was to avoid civil war, and for that purpose to explore the possibility of some sort of co-operation between the Nationalists and the Communists. The China picture was far from clear in those early days. At that time, in the light of such intelligence as was available, the evidence that the Chinese Communists throughout the land were to be wholly controlled from Moscow was not yet compelling. I did not know China intimately, but I did know that three concepts fundamental in the philosophy of the Chinese people were basically opposed to the Soviet line, namely the dignity of the individual, the importance of the family unit and the sacredness of the individual's possession of his plot of ground. It was difficult at that time to believe that even Soviet regimentation and terror could undermine those concepts.

On May 14, 1945, T. V. Soong, Chiang Kai-shek's Foreign Minister, said to the President and myself that the National

---

[4] Sumner Welles in his book, *Seven Decisions that Shaped History*, pp. 124–25, records that he was opposed to the policy adopted by the Administration of postponing agreements on territorial adjustments or political settlements until the war had ended, when they could be handled by a peace conference of the United Nations. "I was profoundly impressed with the gravity of the problem," he wrote. "And there was little I could do. The decision was based almost entirely on military factors in whose evaluation I played no part." Welles goes on to state that he "was convinced that our wisest course would be to try to work out with our allies now, before V-Day, as detailed an agreement as possible."

Government would like to have the Communists join in but could do so only if the Communists recognized that the National Government was in supreme control in China. On May 21, 1945, the War Department wrote me that "some sort of understanding between the Chinese Communists and the Generalissimo seems to be in order as of first importance."

On June 14, 1945, the President, in my presence, told Dr. Soong that after reading the minutes of Harry Hopkins' conversations in Moscow he was able to tell Dr. Soong that Stalin's assurances with respect to the sovereignty of China in Manchuria and elsewhere had been even more categorical than he had told Dr. Soong the last time he saw him. The President said that Marshal Stalin had stated that he had no territorial claims of any kind against China and that furthermore he intended to work with Chiang Kai-shek, since he considered that Chiang was the only Chinese leader capable of bringing about the unification of China; that none of the Communist leaders was capable of unifying China; and that the Soviet Government was prepared to lend its help to bring about China's unity. He added that Marshal Stalin had further stated he would be quite prepared to have representatives of the Central Government come to the areas of Manchuria or China where the Soviet armies might be operating in order to set up immediately Chinese Administration of the liberated areas. Dr. Soong expressed his gratification at this news.

Once the utter impracticability of such a coalition became apparent, as it very soon did, I doubt very much if I could have gone along very far in supporting or even in condoning the policy subsequently followed and intensified, for I firmly believed in supporting Chiang Kai-shek. It is easy to be wise after the event. But the horrors of possible civil war in China faced us, and certainly an initial effort to obviate that situation in the light of all the evidence then before us, if only by way of exploration, seemed to be justified. Anyway, the effort failed and my retirement from office in August, 1945, left me no further opportunity to try to influence that situation one way or the other.

I suppose I should at least touch on the Amerasia case although I cannot contribute very much to the story. What happened was that in the spring of 1945 General Julius Holmes, then Assistant Secretary of State, informed me as Acting Secretary of State that the FBI was in possession of evidence tending to implicate six persons, one of whom was a Foreign Service Officer of the United States, in the theft of confidential documents from the State and Navy Departments. General Holmes had asked the FBI to prepare a statement on the cases which he said he had shown to Dean Acheson, then Assistant Secretary of State, in view of his experience and background in matters of law and that Acheson, after examining the papers, had said that in his opinion the evidence appeared to show a case against the six individuals. General Holmes said that he simply wished my authorization to tell the Department of Justice that from the point of view of the Department of State there was no reason why it should not proceed, pointing out that the responsibility for arrest and prosecution lay squarely on our police and judicial authorities.

I asked General Holmes if he considered the evidence sufficient to ensure indictment and conviction if the cases were carried through to which he replied in the affirmative on the basis of the opinion of the Department of Justice. I then said that I knew of no reason why the Department of Justice should not proceed. It was only after this that I learned of the names of the six persons involved and I was very much surprised and shocked that the names included a prominent officer of our Foreign Service. The arrests were then carried out and the subsequent presentation of evidence and the results of the action of the court are publicly known.

The next development was when General Holmes informed me somewhat later that a hitch had occurred in the prosecution of the six persons, allegedly based on instructions from the White House. General Holmes and I immediately went to see the President who, as it was late in the evening, had already left his office and was in his private sitting room upstairs in the White House. I have seldom seen a man more angry than the President when he heard that somebody, allegedly in the White House, was trying to hold up the prosecution of the six persons mentioned. The President had the telephone off the hook while we were still with him and he told Justice in no uncertain terms that he wished nothing whatever to interfere with the prompt and thorough prosecution of the cases. It was abundantly clear that the President knew nothing whatever about any White House directive to stop the prosecution.

It has subsequently appeared, and this is confirmed by *The Forrestal Diaries*, page 65, that the action to hold up the prosecution was based on the belief that the inevitable consequence of such action now would be greatly to embarrass the President in his current conversations with the Soviet Government because of the anti-Russian play-up the incident might receive out of proportion to its importance. I presume that this point was made to someone in the White House who communicated the "hold-up" instruction to the FBI which was promptly countermanded by the President when General Holmes and I brought the matter to his attention. In any event the case was entirely out of the hands of the State Department from the moment the FBI was called in. The results of the prosecution are now a matter of history.

Date: April 30, 1945

PARTICIPANTS: The President; Acting Secretary of State Grew; Mr. William Phillips [Special Assistant to the Secretary of State]; Mr. H. Freeman Matthews.

Mr. Grew told the President that a government had been set up in Austria obviously under Russian instigation. The only information which we had other than that contained in the press was a notification received on April 27 from the Soviet Government to the effect that Renner, a well-known Austrian Socialist leader and former Chancellor, was planning to form a government and that the Soviet did not intend to oppose his administration.[5] Mr. Grew continued that the Brit-

5 A despatch from Moscow was printed on page one of the *New York Times*, April 30, 1945. The despatch recorded the fact that an Austrian Provisional Government had been set up in Vienna under Dr. Karl Renner, a Social Democrat. Three Communists were included in the Cabinet of 13, holding the positions of Minister of the Interior, Minister of Public Instruction and Religion, and Minister without Portfolio. The *Times* quoted Tass as saying that the

ish Foreign Office had already issued a statement declining to recognize the new government (he read the ticker report) and he thought we should get out a statement along similar lines. Mr. Grew then read a draft statement which the President promptly approved (without change) and it was subsequently issued by the Department.

Mr. Grew continued that the Prime Minister proposed to register a strong protest at Moscow and asked the President to join him in a message to Stalin. Mr. Grew asked whether the President agreed that we should make some representations to Moscow. He outlined briefly to the President the composition of the Austrian Government and the fact that Moscow-trained Communists seemed to hold the key positions of Minister of Interior and Minister of Education and Religion. The President said that he agreed that we should protest against the procedure of the Soviet Government in acting unilaterally without consultation but not to comment on the composition of the Government. He requested that this protest be delivered by our Embassy at Moscow and a copy sent to John Winant [American Ambassador to Great Britain] to communicate to Prime Minister Churchill. He told Admiral Leahy to reply to the Prime Minister's personal message to the President merely stating that we were taking it up through our Moscow Embassy and that Mr. Winant was being directed to give him a copy of our telegram. (These directions were carried out this afternoon.)

Date: May 2, 1945

SUBJECT: Interview with the President, May 2, 11.15 A.M.

PARTICIPANTS: The President; Acting Secretary, Mr. Grew

(1) PRESENTATION TO THE PRESIDENT OF MAJOR GENERAL CRANE AND BRIGADIER GENERAL SCHUYLER

I introduced to the President Major General John Crane and Brigadier General Cortlandt Schuyler, the American Repre-

new Austrian government represented "the will of the majority of Austrian people."

sentatives on the Allied Control Commission in Bulgaria and Rumania respectively. General Schuyler spoke on behalf of both officers, General Crane making it clear that the situation in both countries was very similar. General Schuyler gave a clear statement with regard to Soviet policy in both those countries clearly carrying out a determination to control through Communist governments in a completely totalitarian way. The methods by which this policy is being carried out were explained in detail by General Schuyler, who added that Rumania and Bulgaria were test cases and if the Soviets were able to get away with their program in those countries they would be encouraged to try the same game in every other country in Europe as far as they could penetrate. The President asked why, under these circumstances, it would not be better to withdraw our representatives entirely. I said that I did not think we ought to allow the matter to go by default and that there were some advantages in retaining our representatives at least for the present. . . .

May 12, 1945

Memorandum for the Secretary of War,[6] from Mr. Grew, Acting Secretary of State

In order to determine the policy of the United States Government in the Far East in connection with the political effects of the expected Soviet entry into the Pacific War and the relationship of the Yalta Agreement [7] on this subject, I would ap-

---

[6] The same memorandum was sent to the Navy Department.

[7] The Far Eastern Agreement signed at Yalta by President Roosevelt, Prime Minister Churchill, and Marshal Stalin stated:

"The leaders of the three Great Powers — the Soviet Union, the United States of America and Great Britain — have agreed that in two or three months after Germany has surrendered and the war in Europe has terminated, the Soviet Union shall enter into the war against Japan on the side of the Allies on condition that:

"1. The status quo in Outer-Mongolia (the Mongolian People's Republic) shall be preserved;

"2. The former rights of Russia violated by the treacherous attack of Japan in 1904 shall be restored, viz.:

"(a) the southern part of Sakhalin as well as all the islands adjacent to it shall be returned to the Soviet Union,

"(b) the commercial port of Dairen shall be internationalized, the preeminent

preciate receiving from you the views of the War Department on the following questions:

1. Is the entry of the Soviet Union into the Pacific war at the earliest possible moment of such vital interest to the United States as to preclude any attempt by the United States Government to obtain Soviet agreement to certain desirable political objectives in the Far East prior to such entry?

2. Should the Yalta decision in regard to Soviet political desires in the Far East be reconsidered or carried into effect in whole or in part?

3. Should a Soviet demand, if made, for participation in the military occupation of the Japanese home islands be granted or would such occupation adversely affect our long term policy for the future treatment of Japan?

In the opinion of the Department of State it would be desirable politically to obtain from the Soviet Government the following commitments and clarifications regarding the Far East prior to any implementation on our part of the Yalta Agreement:

1. The Soviet Government should agree to use its influence with the Chinese Communists to assist this Government in its endeavors to bring about the unification of China under the

interests of the Soviet Union in this port being safeguarded, and the lease of Port Arthur as a naval base of the U.S.S.R. restored,

"(c) the Chinese-Eastern Railroad and the South-Manchurian Railroad, which provides an outlet to Dairen, shall be jointly operated by the establishment of a joint Soviet-Chinese Company, it being understood that the preeminent interests of the Soviet Union shall be safeguarded and that China shall retain full sovereignty in Manchuria.

"3. The Kurile Islands shall be handed over to the Soviet Union. It is understood that the agreement concerning Outer-Mongolia and the ports and railroads referred to above will require concurrence of Generalissimo Chiang Kai-shek. The President will take measures in order to obtain this concurrence on advice from Marshal Stalin.

"The Heads of the three Great Powers have agreed that these claims of the Soviet Union shall be unquestionably fulfilled after Japan has been defeated.

"For its part the Soviet Union expresses its readiness to conclude with the National Government of China a pact of friendship and alliance between the U.S.S.R. and China in order to render assistance to China with its armed forces for the purpose of liberating China from the Japanese yoke." Stettinius, op. cit., pp. 351–52.

National Government headed by Chiang Kai-shek. The achievement of Chinese unity on the basis considered most desirable by the United States Government should be agreed to by the Soviet Union before the United States Government should make any approach to the Chinese Government on the basis of the Yalta Agreement. The difficulties in regard to Sinkiang should be settled by amicable agreement between the Soviet and Chinese Governments.

2. Unequivocal adherence of the Soviet Government to the Cairo Declaration regarding the return of Manchuria to Chinese sovereignty and the future status of Korea.[8]

3. Definite agreement of the Soviet Government that when Korea is liberated, whether before final capitulation of Japan or after, it be placed immediately under the trusteeship of the United States, Great Britain, China, and the Soviet Union. This agreement should make clear that the four trustees are to be the sole authority for the selection of a temporary Korean Government.

4. Before giving final approval to the annexation by the Soviet Union of the Kurile Islands it might be desirable to receive from the Soviet Government emergency landing rights for commercial planes on certain of these islands.

From the War Department to Joseph C. Grew,
May 21, 1945

Following are the views of the War Department on the ques-

---

[8] At Cairo in 1943, Roosevelt, Churchill, and Chiang Kai-shek had agreed that the "Three Great Allies are fighting this war to restrain and punish the aggression of Japan. They covet no gain for themselves and have no thought of territorial expansion. It is their purpose that Japan shall be stripped of all the islands in the Pacific which she has seized or occupied since the beginning of the first World War in 1914, and that all territories Japan has stolen from the Chinese, such as Manchuria, Formosa, and the Pescadores, shall be restored to the Republic of China. Japan will also be expelled from all other territories which she has taken by violence and greed. The aforesaid three great powers, mindful of the enslavement of the people of Korea, are determined that in due course Korea shall become free and independent." U.S. Department of State, *The Department of State Bulletin,* December 4, 1943, p. 393.

tion contained in your memorandum of 12 May regarding the Soviet Union in the Far East.

1. The War Department considers that Russian entry into the war against Japan will be decided by the Russians on their own military and political basis with little regard to any political action taken by the United States. The War Department's view is that while the U.S.S.R. will seek and will accept any political inducement proffered by the United States as a condition to her entry into the war against Japan, such political inducements will not in fact affect the Russian decision as to when, if ever, she will enter the war. Russian entry will have a profound military effect in that almost certainly it will materially shorten the war and thus save American lives.

Military considerations therefore do not preclude an attempt by the United States Government to obtain Soviet agreement to desirable political objectives in the Far East prior to the entry of the Soviet Union into the Pacific war.

2. The concessions to Russia on Far Eastern matters which were made at Yalta are generally matters which are within the military power of Russia to obtain regardless of U.S. military action short of war. The War Department believes that Russia is militarily capable of defeating the Japanese and occupying Karafuto, Manchuria, Korea and Northern China before it would be possible for the U.S. military forces to occupy these areas. Only in the Kuriles is the United States in a position to circumvent Russian initiative. If the United States were to occupy these islands to forestall Russian designs, it would be at the direct expense of the campaign to defeat Japan and would involve an unacceptable cost in American lives. Furthermore, the Russians can, if they choose, await the time when U.S. efforts will have practically completed the destruction of Japanese military power and can then seize the objectives they desire at a cost to them relatively much less than would be occasioned by their entry into the war at an early date.

From the foregoing, it appears we can bring little, if any, military leverage to bear on the Russians in so far as the Far East is concerned, unless we choose to use force. From the military point of view it would be desirable to have a complete understanding and agreement with the Russians concerning the Far East. If it is believed that the reconsideration of the Yalta agreement will assist such a complete understanding and agreement, then the War Department would favor it, but it is not believed that much good will come of a rediscussion at this time.

3. With regard to Soviet participation in the military occupation of the Japanese homeland, the War Department considers this to be a matter for political decision. From one military standpoint, this participation appears desirable, since it would reduce the military requirements of the U.S. for occupation purposes. On the other hand, our experiences with the Russians in the occupation of Germany may in the future lead to considerations which would point to the wisdom of exclusive occupation by our own forces. The discussion of this subject prior to Russian entry into the Japanese war does not appear necessary at this time.

The War Department concurs in the desirability of obtaining the four commitments and clarifications desired of the Soviet Government by the Department of State. If the present schism in China continues and, at the same time, Russian forces advance to areas giving them close contact with the Chinese Communists, our present problems in China will become more complicated, unless a prior satisfactory understanding has been reached with the Russians. However, as a preliminary, some sort of understanding between the Chinese Communists and the Generalissimo seems to be in order as of first importance.

As to emergency landing rights for commercial planes in the Kuriles, it would probably be best to make a specific proposal on this matter to the Russians in case it is desired to discuss the subject with them. However, Russia has the military capability of implementing unilaterally the Yalta Agreement (except possibly the Kuriles). Hence, as pointed out above, measures other than U.S. military assistance must be found to persuade the Russians to give their agreement to the four points listed in the State Department memorandum.

Date: May 14, 1945

SUBJECT: Conference with the President, 2.00 P.M.

PARTICIPANTS: The President; Mr. T. V. Soong, Minister for Foreign Affairs of China; Acting Secretary, Mr. Grew.

At the President's request, I attended this afternoon at two o'clock a meeting between the President and T. V. Soong, Foreign Minister of China. Nobody else was present.

Mr. Soong took up the following problems:

(1) Brunt of driving out Japanese forces from China by sustained effort falls on China, hence:

(a) Continuation of military supplies to Chinese Army via India and Burma.

The President said that we had every intention of continuing these supplies.

(b) Opening up of a port on the Chinese coast to bring adequate military supplies, transports, and industrial equipment in order to strengthen Chinese economy for final war effort. It follows that appropriate Lend-Lease arrangement must be made now to prepare for supplies when port is opened. Which U.S. agency to apply to?

The President said that Mr. Soong should discuss this matter with Leo Crowley [Foreign Economic Administrator] and I suggested that William Clayton [Assistant Secretary of State] might also be helpful. The President concurred and advised Mr. Soong to see both Mr. Clayton and Mr. Crowley.

(c) Implementation of 1943 Agreement to supply gold to check Chinese inflation.

Mr. Soong said that he had discussed this matter with Secretary Morgenthau, who had suggested the use of Chinese gold in the United States, but Mr. Soong advanced various reasons why he felt this would not be practical. The President said that he was not familiar with these technical financial matters and would like to consult Secretary Morgenthau before giving Mr. Soong an answer yes or no.

(2) Arrangement, in the event of American landings, to hand over enemy-held Chinese territory and territories that under the Cairo Agreement are to be returned to China.

Mr. Soong produced a map of China and said that Manchuria and Formosa should be handed back to China. The President concurred.

(3) Understanding with Russia generally, and particularly if she enters war. Chinese internal situation.

Mr. Soong sketched the relations of the National Government with the Communists and said that the National Government would like to have the Communists join in but could do so only if the Communists recognized that the National Government was in supreme control in China. He discussed at some length the attitude of Soviet Russia, which during the early stages of the Sino-Japanese war when China alone was holding off the Japanese forces, was very friendly and had helped the Chinese Government with a supply of arms and ammunition. This had continued for some time but latterly there had been a change and the Soviet Government seemed to be supporting the Chinese Communists rather than the National Government. Mr. Soong said he thought it very important that he should proceed to Moscow to discuss this situation with the Soviet authorities and that at the termination of the San Francisco Conference he would like to proceed first to Chungking, then to Moscow, and then back to Washington via London to report further to the President. He said that no Chinese planes were available for such a journey and he asked the President if he could have an American Army plane for this purpose. The President assented but I said that before committing ourselves on this I would like to look into it a little further and to report further to the President. The President assented to this procedure. Mr. Soong said that the Soviets were using American planes and that, as for the political implications involved, he thought it would be helpful to have the Russians know that he was returning to Washington to talk to the President after the meeting in Moscow. This matter was left open. . . .

In the course of the conversation the President said that the United States desired to see a strong, united and democratic China. Mr. Soong observed that the maintenance of Chinese sovereignty was the most important thing of all. The President concurred.

Date: May 15, 1945

PARTICIPANTS: The President; the Acting Secretary of State [Mr. Grew]; Ambassador W. Averell Harriman [Ambassador to the U.S.S.R.]; and Charles Bohlen [Assistant to the Secretary of State].

. . . THE ACTING SECRETARY then said there was another matter which he would ask Ambassador Harriman to explain in detail, namely, that we all felt in the Department of State that it was of the utmost importance that the Big Three meeting should take place as soon as possible and not be postponed until July.

AMBASSADOR HARRIMAN said that the problem of our relations with Russia is the number one problem affecting the future of the world and the fact was that at the present moment we were getting farther and farther apart. In addition to the general picture there were the specific and immediate questions such as the treatment of Germany on a tripartite basis, setting up of the Control Council, etc., on which no progress had been made with the Russians. There was, of course, the Polish question and many others. He said he felt that the establishment of a basis for future relations with Russia and the settlement of these immediate issues could only be done at a tripartite meeting, that the longer the meeting was delayed the worse the situation would get, and that while he assumed of course that we were not prepared to use our troops in Europe for political bargaining nevertheless if the meeting could take place before we were in a large measure out of Europe he felt the atmosphere of the meeting would be more favorable and the chances of success increased. He said he felt that Stalin was not getting accurate reports from Molotov or any of his people and as a result had grown deeply and unjustifiably suspicious as to our motives which he probably thought were designed to deprive him of the fruits of victory.

THE PRESIDENT said that he agreed with that and felt that a meeting as soon as possible was most desirable. He added that he agreed with what the Ambassador said but that his difficulty was that he had a number of pressing domestic questions particularly the preparation of a budget message before the end of the fiscal year which made it difficult for him to leave before then. AMBASSADOR HARRIMAN said that he felt the President would be confronted with a much more difficult situation two months from now than he would if the meeting could be arranged within the next few weeks. THE PRESIDENT said that he did not favor a meeting in Germany since he thought this time that Stalin should come over to meet us and he had in mind Alaska as a possible meeting place, and he was not favorably inclined to a prior meeting with the British which would give the Russians the impression that we were "ganging up" on them. He asked Mr. Bohlen's opinion on these two points.

MR. BOHLEN replied that he felt that somewhere nearer Moscow whether it be Germany or somewhere else would be preferable since it was of great importance that Stalin be able to communicate quickly and securely with Moscow; otherwise there might be delay or at least greater difficulty in having any agreements reached stick once Stalin had returned to Moscow. . . . In regard to the second point MR. BOHLEN said that he did not feel that the fear of an impression of "ganging up" was very dangerous since he believed that the Russians considered it in the logic of things that a prior meeting with the British on the way to the Big Three meeting or in any other manner that could be arranged might on the contrary have a salutary effect and make Stalin more reasonable.

THE ACTING SECRETARY then asked the PRESIDENT what he thought of Vienna as a meeting place. THE PRESIDENT did not appear to be unfavorably impressed with this idea and added that while these pressing domestic matters made it difficult for him, if the foreign situation really required he would of course be prepared to go very soon. He added that he had just had a message from the Prime Minister saying that the latter had taken up with Stalin the question of a meeting. AMBASSADOR HARRIMAN asked then would the President consider having the meeting in the early part of June to which THE PRESIDENT replied that he would certainly consider it if the other two wanted it then.

THE PRESIDENT asked Ambassador Harriman when he was

going back and said that he felt someone should be in Moscow who could talk to Stalin. THE AMBASSADOR said he would of course go back whenever the President wanted him to but that he thought he should have a clear idea of what he was to say to Stalin and also some definite information as to the time and place of meeting. He added furthermore that in connection with the Yalta agreement on the Far East, as the President knew, Mr. Grew had been having meetings with the Secretaries of War and Navy as to the Yalta Agreement and other questions affecting the Soviet Union in the Far East. He added that there were two subjects which had been discussed only orally at Yalta which should be clarified, namely the question of Chinese unity and the question of a trusteeship for Korea. THE PRESIDENT said that he thought provided the Ambassador was not delayed too long it would be wise for him to go back to Moscow with clarity on those subjects.

In conclusion THE PRESIDENT said that he would await word from Churchill as to Stalin's reply before we would decide definitely in regard to the meeting.

Date: June 4, 1945

SUBJECT: Meeting with the President, 12.15 A.M.
PARTICIPANTS: The President; Acting Secretary,
Mr. Grew; Ambassador Lane.

I went to the President this morning with Ambassador Arthur Bliss Lane [American Ambassador to Poland] who wished to talk over some of the issues with regard to Poland. Mr. Lane feels that our attitude towards Soviet Russia in connection with the Polish issue should be integrated with the many other issues in Central Europe, particularly the Soviet blackouts in the Balkan states and the states of Central Europe. The President said that he had precisely the same opinion and that this would be the fundamental subject which he intended to discuss at the Big Three meeting. There was some further talk with regard to the arrest of the 16 Poles and the choice of Poles for consultation in setting up a unified Polish government. It was felt that, while Mr. Hopkins is still negotiating in Moscow and while the San Francisco Conference is still going on it would be desirable not to exert too much pressure.[9] The President, however, left Mr. Lane in no doubt as to his intention to insist on the eventual removal of the Soviet blackout in the countries mentioned. . . .

                                              Date: June 9, 1945

SUBJECT: China.
PARTICIPANTS: President Truman; Dr. T. V. Soong; Acting Secretary Grew; Admiral Leahy.

I went to the President this morning at eleven o'clock and attended the interview between the President and Dr. T. V. Soong, Foreign Minister of China, which lasted for a full hour. Admiral Leahy was also present. The President told Dr. Soong of the agreements reached at Yalta with regard to the Far East and he showed the Minister the telegram which we are about to send to Ambassador Hurley on this subject. There was a long discussion of every point, the President making it clear that he was definitely committed to the agreements reached by President Roosevelt.[10] It is understood that Dr. Soong will

[9] Sixteen Polish underground leaders were arrested on March 27, 1945, by the Russians. Led by General L. Bronislaw Okulicki, commander of the underground "Home Army," and Jan Jankowski, Deputy Premier of the London Cabinet, they pleaded guilty to spreading anti-Soviet propaganda and to responsibility for acts leading to the death of men of the Soviet Army in Polish territory. On June 21, 1945, the sentences were pronounced against them. Okulicki received a ten-year sentence, Jankowski — eight years, and ten others lesser penalties. Three were acquitted, and one trial was postponed because of illness.

Harry Hopkins was in Moscow from May 25 to June 7. The results of his discussions are in Robert E. Sherwood, *Roosevelt and Hopkins* (New York: Harper & Bros., 1948), pp. 887–912.

[10] See Admiral Leahy, *I Was There*, p. 381, for his account of the meeting. Leahy records that the "Chinese statesman told me privately that his country could not agree to permit Russia to exercise the degree of control in Manchuria that was possible under the Yalta agreement. He said China would prefer to settle the controversy by military action when forces should become available.

" 'When do you think you would be in a position to do that?' I asked, having in mind the existing deplorable state of Chiang's armies.

" 'Well,' replied Soong reflectively, 'that might be any time in the next five hundred years.' "

leave Washington on June 15 to go first to Chungking, where he will discuss this matter with the Generalissimo, and then to Moscow to talk to Marshal Stalin.

At the end of the conference, the President asked me to send to Dr. Soong a copy of the telegram to Ambassador Hurley. I said that I would have the telegram paraphrased and would then have it sent by safe hand to place in Dr. Soong's hands personally. Dr. Soong undertook not to telegraph this information to Chungking as we impressed on him very forcefully the serious results which would flow from any leaks. This was mentioned twice in the conference.

Date: June 14, 1945

PARTICIPANTS: The President; Dr. T. V. Soong; Acting Secretary, Mr. Grew; Mr. Charles E. Bohlen.

I called on the President this morning and after a preliminary talk with the President and Chip Bohlen, Dr. Soong was shown in and the following conversation took place:

The President said that after reading the minutes of Mr. Hopkins' conversations in Moscow he was able to tell Dr. Soong that Stalin's assurances with respect to the sovereignty of China in Manchuria and elsewhere had been even more categorical than he had told Dr. Soong the last time he saw him. The President said that Marshal Stalin had stated that he had no territorial claims of any kind against China and that furthermore he intended to work with Chiang Kai-shek and the central government since he considered that Chiang Kai-shek was the only Chinese leader capable of bringing about the unification of China; that none of the Communist leaders was capable of unifying China; and that the Soviet Government was prepared to lend its help to bring about China's unity. He added that Marshal Stalin had further stated he would be quite prepared to have representatives of the Central Government come to the areas of Manchuria or China where the Soviet armies might be operating in order to set up immediately Chinese Administration of the liberated areas.

Dr. Soong expressed his gratification at this news and then said that he had a number of points he would like to clarify with the President. He said that the information the President had given him concerning the Yalta understanding had referred to the re-establishment of Russian rights in Manchuria which had been lost as a result of the Russian-Japanese war of 1904. He said these rights had been quite sweeping in their scope and had been based upon concessions made to Russia by China after the Chinese-Japanese war in 1895. Dr. Soong then pointed out that in the Soviet-Chinese Treaty of 1924 and the Soviet Treaty of 1924 [11] made with Chang Tso-lin [the *de facto* ruler of Manchuria at that time] the Soviet Government had specifically renounced all these special concessions, leases, and privileged position including extraterritoriality by its own free will. He said it would be necessary to clarify all these points with Stalin when he went to Moscow and also the meaning of the term "pre-eminent interest" of the Soviet Union in the port of Dairen. He added that for China the most difficult feature of the Soviet desires was the lease on Port Arthur since after all the suffering in this war the Chinese Government and people were very much against the re-establishment of the system of special leased ports in China.

With the President's permission Dr. Soong then asked Mr. Bohlen if he thought the Russians intended to sign a definite agreement with him when he was in Moscow with particular reference to the Treaty of Friendship and Mutual Assistance referred to in the Yalta Agreement. Mr. Bohlen said he had no information on that specific point and thought that that would naturally depend on the course of Dr. Soong's discussions in Moscow. He added that he thought, however, that if the Soviet Union were to enter the war against Japan it would desire to do so on the basis of complete agreement with China and as an ally with China, Great Britain, and the United States.

Dr. Soong then inquired whether the President contemplated

11 See H. G. W. Woodhead (ed.), *The China Year Book 1924-5* (Tientsin: The Tientsin Press, 1924), pp. 1192–2000, and H. G. W. Woodhead (ed.), *The China Year Book 1925-6* (Tientsin: The Tientsin Press, 1925), pp. 797–800.

some general agreement in regard to the surrender terms for Japan among the principal allies in the Pacific war. The President said that the terms of surrender would be imposed on Japan by the Allies and that he thought some such general agreement would be both necessary and desirable but he thought it should be done when the Soviet Union entered the war. He added that his chief interest now was to see the Soviet Union participate in the Far Eastern war in sufficient time to be of help in shortening the war and thus save American and Chinese lives. Although this was his chief preoccupation at the moment he said he wished to assure Dr. Soong that he would do nothing which would harm the interests of China since China was a friend of the United States in the Far East. The President continued that just as in Europe the United States desired above all to see these postwar questions settled in such a way as to eliminate any tinderboxes both in Europe and in the Far East which might cause future trouble and wars. He said for example we had no selfish interest in Poland but a very vital interest in seeing the Polish question settled in such a manner as to insure tranquillity and stability.

Dr. Soong expressed agreement with the President's remarks and said there was no nation in the world that China regarded as more of a friend than the United States. He asked the President if he had any message other than those already given to him for the Generalissimo. The President replied only that he might tell the Generalissimo that he hoped some day to have a meeting with him so they might talk face to face. . . .

Date: June 18, 1945

SUBJECT: Soviet-Turkish Relations.
PARTICIPANTS: British Chargé d'Affaires, Mr. John Balfour; Acting Secretary, Mr Grew.

Mr. Balfour of the British Embassy called on me this afternoon and left with me the appended text of a telegram from the British Minister at Istanbul to the Foreign Office of June 13 and an *aide-mémoire* from the British Embassy to the Department of June 18 setting forth a conversation between Mr.

Molotov and the Turkish Ambassador to Moscow in which the former stated that before proceeding to the negotiation of a new Soviet-Turkish Treaty it would be best to solve outstanding questions between Turkey and Russia as follows:

(*a*) Russo-Turkish treaty of 1921. Molotov stated that cessions of territory made by Russia to Turkey under this treaty were made under duress and required revision,

(*b*) The cession of bases by Turkey to Russia in the Straits,

(*c*) An agreement between Turkey and Russia as to the revision of the Montreux Convention.[12]

The Turkish Ambassador stated to Mr. Molotov in reply that his Government was not prepared to reopen the question of the Russo-Turkish Treaty of 1921 which they considered to have been freely negotiated nor could they even consider granting Russia bases in the Straits. As regards the Montreux Convention the Turkish Ambassador repeated that this was not a matter which could be discussed between the two Governments alone. The Turkish Government has approved its Ambassador's attitude.

The British Government, especially in view of the Anglo-Turkish Treaty, proposes to support the Turkish position particularly as the position taken by Mr. Molotov appears to be in direct conflict with statements made by Marshal Stalin at Yalta.[13] The British Government hopes that the United States Government will agree to a joint Anglo-American approach along the lines of its *aide-mémoire* and that this approach be made to the Soviet Government prior to the meeting of the

12 The Montreux Convention was signed July 20, 1936. For the full text see James T. Shotwell and Francis Deak, *Turkey at the Straits* (New York: The Macmillan Co., 1940), pp. 124–27, 154–67.

13 See Stettinius, *op. cit.*, pp. 267–69. Stalin stated that a revision of the Montreux Convention "should be done in such a way as not to harm the legitimate interests of Turkey," and that Turkey should be assured that its independence and integrity would be guaranteed. Stalin also proposed at Yalta that the Foreign Ministers of the Big Three discuss the Montreux Convention at their next meeting and added that the Soviet Union would transmit its views on the subject to the United States and Great Britain. Russia had not done so when the talk between Molotov and the Turkish Ambassador to Russia took place on June 7, 1945.

Big Three at which it may well be necessary to discuss this whole question.

I said to Mr. Balfour that I would give immediate attention to the British Government's proposal but that I could make no commitment until this whole subject had been given careful study here. In any case, I said I thought it would be preferable to withhold action until the end of the San Francisco Conference which it was now hoped might be brought to a close on or about June 23 and that if action were to be taken there would presumably be plenty of time between the close of the San Francisco Conference and the meeting of the Big Three. Mr. Balfour said he agreed with me and as he understood that the Big Three meeting would not take place before July 15 he also thought that it would be well to delay action until after the San Francisco Conference had been concluded. He said he was further asked to say to me that even if we should not feel in a position to make a joint approach with the British Government, his Government hoped that we would at least support the British action with some step of our own.

Date: July 7, 1945

SUBJECT: Soviet-Turkish Relations.
PARTICIPANTS: Turkish Ambassador, Mr. Huseyin
Ragip Baydur; Acting Secretary, Mr. Grew.

The Turkish Ambassador called on me this morning with his secretary, who acted as interpreter, and, after some preliminary talk concerning the success of the San Francisco Conference, the Ambassador said that the Turkish Foreign Minister wished him to express to me his great regret that, owing to the early sailing from Boston on a ship on which he had found accommodations, he had been unable to stop in Washington and this had been a great disappointment to him as he had looked forward to his visit here. I thanked the Ambassador for his message and said that I fully understood the reasons which had obliged his Foreign Minister to abandon his plans to stop in Washington.

The Ambassador then turned to the conversation which had

taken place in Moscow some three weeks ago between Mr. Molotov and the Turkish Ambassador in which the former had stated the Soviet demand for (1) a rectification of the Turco-Soviet frontier, (2) a demand for bases on the Dardanelles, and (3) a bilateral modification of the Montreux Treaty. Subsequently Mr. Molotov had added that there might be also certain requirements from the Balkan states, which the Ambassador interpreted as some sort of a territorial demand from Bulgaria.

The Ambassador said that he had come to see me for the purpose of ascertaining the attitude of the American Government towards this situation.

I said to the Ambassador that this Government is very definitely concerned with any threat to the peace which might fall within the purview of the United Nations organization. For the present we understood that the conversations had been a friendly exchange of views and that no concrete threats had been made. The Ambassador asked me whether, if the Soviet Government should demand that we cede to the Soviet Union the cities of Boston and San Francisco, we would not consider such a demand as a threat, and he also asked whether we felt that such a demand could be a matter for negotiation. I replied definitely in the negative but I asked the Ambassador whether the Soviet Government had specified the nature of the frontier rectification which it desired and whether the demands were yet of such a concrete nature as to be regarded as open threats. The Ambassador replied that Mr. Molotov had stated that the Treaty of 1921 had been negotiated at a time when Soviet Russia was weak and he had added, "Now we are strong." The obvious implication was that Soviet Russia desired the return of the Vilayets of Kars and Ardahan.

The Ambassador then said he wished me to know — and he felt sure that in the light of my own friendship for and knowledge of the Turkish Republic I would know this myself — that Turkey would not cede one inch of territory and that if Soviet Russia should appropriate such Turkish territory Turkey would immediately fight. A situation would thus be created which was totally contrary to the spirit and letter of all that had been achieved at San Francisco.

The Ambassador then went on to say that the Turkish Government felt very strongly that strong representations by the United States in advance of possible trouble would have a powerful effect on the Soviet Government. He understood that I had told Lord Halifax [British Ambassador] that the American Government would support the proposed démarche of the British Government in Moscow but that later Ambassador Edwin C. Wilson [American Ambassador] at Ankara had informed the Turkish Foreign Office that the matter would be further studied and had implied that I had made no such statement.

I immediately told the Ambassador that Mr. Wilson was quite right; I had had no conversation on this subject with Lord Halifax, whom I had not seen officially since his return from San Francisco. (The Ambassador was clearly referring to my conversation with Mr. Balfour in which I had said that we would prefer to delay action on this matter until after the San Francisco Conference and that if action were to be taken there would presumably be plenty of time between the close of the San Francisco Conference and the meeting of the Big Three. Mr. Balfour, however, said that his Government hoped that we would at least support the British action with some step of our own. Mr. Balfour happened to call on me a few moments after my conversation with the Turkish Ambassador and definitely corroborated my understanding of what I had said to him. He said he had reported my position accurately to his Government and that no indication had been given of any commitment whatever on my part.)

I then said to the Ambassador that he must know very well himself that we have been following this situation with concern; that I hoped that the subject might be discussed at the coming meeting of heads of government and that, for that purpose, the President had been fully briefed on all the information in our possession. I personally believed that much more could be accomplished by a direct talk between the President and Marshal Stalin than could be accomplished by any formal representations made in Moscow. In any case, I thought that the matter could better be left without action on our part until we could learn whether it will have been discussed at the Berlin meeting, and the results. I said that this Government, as a friend both of Turkey and the Soviet Union, would naturally be glad to be of assistance in arriving at a peaceful solution of the problem. The Ambassador must understand that this was in no respect an offer of mediation but merely a statement of our general attitude in all such situations. The Ambassador said that he understood my position perfectly but he wished to repeat with all possible emphasis that Turkey would cede no territory and was prepared to fight if necessary.

My attitude in the conversation clearly indicated my sympathy with Turkey's position but no commitment of any kind was made or implied.[14]

14 When this issue was raised at the Potsdam Conference, Stalin said that the Montreux Convention was "inimical" to the Soviet Union. Furthermore, he added that Turkey was too weak to give any effective guarantee of free passage, and it was only right that the Soviet Union should have bases to defend the Straits. President Truman declared that while the United States agreed to a revision of the Montreux Convention, "We believe, however, that the Straits should be a free waterway open to the whole world and guaranteed by all of us." Secretary of State Byrnes has commented on this interchange: "That presented the issue. The Soviets wanted the free navigation of the Straits guaranteed by the Soviets, or by the Soviets and Turkey. This meant their armed forces would be on Turkey's soil. We wanted the free navigation of the Straits guaranteed by the United Nations." James F. Byrnes, *Speaking Frankly* (New York: Harper & Bros., 1947), pp. 77–78.

XXXVIII

American Relations with Tito

On April 30, 1945, it was announced that Yugoslav forces had entered Trieste. A May 1 communiqué from Belgrade reported that "our troops continued their glorious offensive drive for the liberation of our brothers in the towns of Trieste, Istria and Gorica. No strength could hold our army and prevent the liberation of our brothers pining under a foreign yoke." The reaction in Italy to these Yugoslav despatches was immediate. On April 30, the Italian government demanded that Trieste and Venezia Giulia be governed by Allied military authorities. Italian students paraded through the streets of Rome shouting that "Trieste is Italian!"

A despatch of May 3 to the New York Times *stated that the New Zealand Second Division of the British Eighth Army had joined with the Yugoslav Partisans in occupying Trieste, Lieutenant General Freyberg having accepted the surrender of the German garrison there on the previous day. On May 4, the Yugoslavs warned that the New Zealanders had come into Trieste "without permission," and such entry might result in "undesirable consequences." On May 7, it was reported that American troops also had moved into the area. The* New York Times *noted that the "Partisan men and women in varied uniforms all bearing the red star of Tito were stationed in all of the villages throughout this territory and they still are moving in today past the long convoys of American troops taking up their positions in roughly the same area."*

Mr. Grew, as Acting Secretary of State, was deeply concerned about the problem of the Yugoslav occupation of Trieste. As he later stated, this "problem is far more than a mere frontier controversy between two claimants. It raises the issue of the settlement of international disputes by orderly process rather than unilateral action." [1]

Date: April 30, 1945

SUBJECT: Memorandum of Conversation at the White House.

PARTICIPANTS: The President; Mr. Grew; Admiral Leahy; Mr. Phillips; Mr. Matthews.

Mr. Grew stated that he had asked to see the President to discuss a problem which had arisen with regard to Venezia Giulia and the Prime Minister's telegram (No. 22) to the President on this matter. He said that there were two phases to the problem which the Prime Minister seemed to confuse: first, the operational phase resulting from the desire of Field Marshal Alexander [Supreme Allied Commander in the Mediterranean Theatre] to establish his control over Trieste and Pola in order to protect his lines of communication to Austria, and second, the question of future administration of the Istrian peninsula by Allied Military Government. Reports had just come in, Mr. Grew continued, indicating that the Yugoslav Partisans have already occupied Trieste and Pola. We might, therefore, be faced with the question of whether to use American troops to compel Tito's forces to withdraw. He said that the Department felt that it would be most unwise to employ American forces to fight the Yugoslavs. The President promptly said that he did not intend to have American forces used to fight Yugoslav forces nor did he wish to become involved in Balkan political questions. Admiral Leahy said that he felt that Field Marshal Alexander has all the guidance he needs in FAN No. 536 from the Combined Chiefs of Staff. Mr. Grew pointed out to the President that in NAF 932, Alexander expressly stated his intention of telling Marshal Tito of his plans and of stating that if any of Tito's forces remain in that area they must come under Alexander's command. Mr. Grew said that while it seemed unlikely that Tito would comply with

1 See the *New York Times'* reports of the following dates for material on the Trieste situation: May 1, 1945, p. 3; May 2, 1945, p. 2; May 4, 1945, pp. 1, 8; May 7, 1945, p. 4; May 13, 1945, pp. 1, 7.

Alexander's wishes, FAN 536 specifically directs Alexander to communicate with the Combined Chiefs of Staff before taking further action in the area in question if the Yugoslav forces there fail to co-operate. The President was likewise informed that the Department felt that we could concur with the Prime Minister's suggestion that obtaining prior Russian consent to Alexander's operations was not necessary. It was pointed out as a pertinent fact that under his present general directive, Alexander has the authority to use American forces under his command for operational purposes anywhere in Italy; consequently it would require further instructions from the Combined Chiefs of Staff to alter or limit this authority. Alexander, however, had ordered the 15th Corps composed only of British forces to head east towards Trieste and there seemed, therefore, no need to raise the question of his operational directive at this time.

In conclusion, the President gave instructions for the Department to prepare a draft telegram in reply to the Prime Minister and submit it to Admiral Leahy, the telegram to emphasize that American forces should not be used to fight Yugoslav forces or for political purposes in the Balkans. (The attached draft was subsequently prepared, taken to Admiral Leahy and approved and despatched by the President.)

Telegram from the President to the Prime Minister, April 30, 1945

Your Number 22, April 30.

It seems to me that Field Marshal Alexander has all the guidance he needs in FAN No. 536 from the Combined Chiefs of Staff. I agree that in the operational phase when he is endeavoring to establish his lines of communication to Austria and to establish his control over Trieste and Pola, there is no need for obtaining prior Russian consent. I note from NAF 932 that before his task force enters Venezia Giulia Alexander will inform Marshal Tito of his intentions and explain to Tito that if any of his forces remain in that area they must necessarily come under Alexander's command. FAN 536 directs Alexander to communicate with the Combined Chiefs of Staff before taking further action in the area in question if the Yugoslav forces there fail to co-operate. I think this is important for I wish to avoid having American forces used to fight Yugoslav forces or being used in combat in the Balkan political arena.

Date: April 30, 1945

SUBJECT: Occupation of Northern Italy.
PARTICIPANTS: The Secretary of War, Mr. Stimson;
the Acting Secretary, Mr. Grew.

Mr. Stimson telephoned me today and said he had just received my letters of April 26 and 28 concerning Northern Italy. He said he was sending over to me immediately a reply and read to me the following excerpt from his letter:

> The policy in your letter raises the question as to whether you propose United States forces implement it by using force against Yugoslav forces in case they fail to co-operate. Since present plans indicate the United States will have little or no military interest in the areas considered in CCS 739/1 once the Germans are eliminated therefrom, the continued presence of United States forces in these areas and their operations become a political matter. The problem of just how much force will be used against the Yugoslavs and against the Russians, if they co-operate with the Yugoslavs, may quickly become pressing and it is requested that the State Department furnish clear-cut guidance at once.

Mr. Stimson stated that the Staff is very much troubled about the whole matter. He said we had kept our people out of the Eastern Mediterranean and we were carefully limiting them from going into Italy except for certain purposes. On the other hand he said Churchill wanted to go around into the Eastern Mediterranean. Mr. Stimson said that he had talked this matter over with General Marshall, who is very worried about it. Mr. Stimson said he had told the Staff that at present they should follow the State Department policy on this matter and said he read my letter which gave the policy. He stated that this was a reasonable policy to follow but that it does bring up serious dangers and he thought the War Department was entitled to know what they should do in case things should begin to move quickly. Mr. Stimson said he made the policy against the views of the Staff. He said they think we are taking chances in following Alexander in what he is to do and are inclined to stay off completely. The Staff thought we are very likely to clash primarily with Tito, and they feel also that the Russians are backing up Tito on this matter. Mr. Stimson stated that our friends, the Russians, are very quick to make different decisions than what we make. . . . He stated further that the War Department had kept our troops confined to the leg of the peninsula and said that when we started on the landing at Salerno the only American strategic policy as far as Italy was concerned was to get bases far enough up in Italy to bomb southern Germany. Mr. Stimson said it was all right as long as things went properly and if everybody understood that we were there simply for the time being and were waiting for the peace conference decision. He said that Woodrow Wilson's hand was forced the last time in the same locality.[2]

Date: May 10, 1945

SUBJECT: Interview with the President, 9.30 A.M.
PARTICIPANTS: The President; General Julius C. Holmes, Assistant Secretary of State; Mr. William Phillips; Acting Secretary, Mr. Grew.

. . . 2. The Situation in Venezia Giulia and Trieste

I said to the President that the most disturbing problem be-

[2] In the Treaty of London of 1915, Fiume had been reserved for the Austrian province of Croatia, which became a part of the new Yugoslav state. Fiume had, however, been occupied and claimed by Italy after the First World War. When Woodrow Wilson decided that Italy had no "legal or moral" right to Fiume and appealed to the Italian people to support his view, Orlando and Sonnino, Italian representatives, left the Peace Conference. In 1920, Italy and Yugoslavia signed a treaty recognizing Fiume as a free state "in perpetuity." Four years later another treaty was negotiated under terms of which Italy received Fiume. See Thomas A. Bailey, *Woodrow Wilson and the Lost Peace* (New York: The Macmillan Co., 1944), pp. 257–70.

fore us today is the situation in Venezia Giulia and especially in Trieste which the Yugoslavs had largely occupied, had raised their own flags and had changed the names of the streets from Italian to Yugoslav. I told the President of my deep concern regarding this situation which was growing more serious hourly, that Tito was not only proceeding to dominate the entire region which he admitted he intended to keep under the Peace Treaty, that Russia was undoubtedly behind Tito's move with a view to utilizing Trieste as a Russian port in the future, that the Socialists and Communists — in Italy — argued that the United States and Great Britain are no longer able to oppose the Soviet Union in Europe and that Ivanoe Bonomi's [Italian Premier and Foreign Secretary] position as President of the Council was endangered.

The President replied that he had been giving the most serious consideration to this matter and had finally come to the conclusion that the only solution was to clear Trieste. He realized that this was a reversal of his former position but that developments were such that it left no alternative.

I expressed relief and satisfaction and said that I would have prepared immediately a memorandum for the President to use in his communication to the Joint Chiefs. (This memorandum will lay down the so-called Alexander Line which includes Trieste and Pola as the eastern boundary to be occupied by the Allied forces.)

We are also drafting a telegram from the President to Churchill on this subject. . . .

Date: May 11, 1945

SUBJECT: Interview with the President, 10.45 A.M.
PARTICIPANTS: The President; General George C. Marshall; Fleet Admiral William D. Leahy; Mr. William Phillips; Acting Secretary, Mr. Grew.

At a conference this morning at the White House which I attended with General Marshall, Admiral Leahy, and Mr. Phillips, the Venezia Giulia problem was again discussed. General Marshall felt the importance of a strong joint communication to the Yugoslav Government by the American and British diplomatic representatives in Belgrade before General Alexander was given any definite instructions with regard to action. Accordingly we are preparing a message from the President to the Prime Minister which, after expressing the President's deep concern at Tito's extravagant claims and actions in Italian territory, will suggest the type of instruction which both the American and British Governments might well send to their representatives in Belgrade. The President agreed that these representations should be very strong. He hoped, as we all do, that the influences around Tito will be able to modify his intransigent attitude as a result of the joint representation to the Yugoslav Government.[3]

Date: May 14, 1945

SUBJECT: Conference with the President, 2.30 P.M.
PARTICIPANTS: The President; Mr. Anthony Eden;
Mr. Clement Attlee; Mr. John Balfour; and Admiral
Leahy; Acting Secretary, Mr. Grew.

. . . (3) TRIESTE

The conversation then turned to the situation in Italy, and especially in Trieste, and there was a general exchange of views as to the best method of dealing with Tito and whether it

[3] In a statement issued to the press on May 12, 1945, Mr. Grew said that it had been decided some time earlier to set up an Allied Military Government in this area until an equitable solution of the problem could be found by the United Nations. "Aware of Yugoslav interest in the Venezia Giulia area, proposals along the above lines were presented to, and accepted by, Marshal Tito last February." Mr. Grew went on to say that claim had now been put forward by Yugoslavia to the right to occupy and control this area, and reports stated that a "National Federal Government of Slovenia" was being set up by Yugoslavs in Trieste. ". . . this Government reiterates its view that a disinterested military government is essential in Venezia Giulia in order not to prejudice, through sudden unilateral action taken in the flush of victory, a final solution corresponding to the problems and the principles involved. . . . The disposition of Venezia Giulia, as of other disputed territories, must therefore await a definite peace settlement in which the claim of both sides and the peoples concerned will receive a full and fair hearing." U.S. Department of State, *The Department of State Bulletin*, May 13, 1945, p. 902.

would be possible to secure our rightful position in Venezia Giulia without hostilities with the Yugoslavs. It was generally agreed that Tito was not very sure of himself and it was not believed that Stalin would give him unlimited support. The Yugoslavs were however already in occupation of most of the disputed area and it was not seen how the Yugoslav forces could be ejected without hostilities. I asked Mr. Eden whether the outbreak of hostilities with one of our Allies would not have a deplorable effect on the San Francisco Conference. Mr. Eden replied that it seemed to be equally deplorable to allow ourselves to be pushed around without taking a position. Reference was made to the continual exchange of telegrams between the President and the Prime Minister and the fact that our respective Ambassadors in Belgrade were working together under identic or similar instructions. . . .

Date: May 15, 1945

SUBJECT: Our attitude toward Tito; meeting of Big Three.
PARTICIPANTS: Mr. Anthony Eden; Mr. Balfour; Ambassador Harriman; Mr. William Phillips; Acting Secretary of State, Mr. Grew.

I opened the conversation by stating our considered views with regard to the importance of presenting a firm attitude to Tito, otherwise we would be faced in the future with a number of similar problems. I mentioned the rather unfortunate publicity which had been given out in London and appeared in this morning's press and said I hoped that in the future it could be so arranged that such publicity could be given simultaneously by the two governments.[4] Mr. Eden expressed his regret and promised to send a telegram to London at once on the subject. Mr. Eden agreed with my conclusion about the

---

[4] On the first page of the *New York Times* of May 15, a despatch from London was printed which revealed that the United States and Great Britain had sent similar notes to Tito. These notes were reported to ask for the withdrawal of Yugoslav troops from Trieste, which "must remain under the Allies' control until its future has been decided at the peace table."

importance of a firm attitude and murmured that otherwise problems by the hundreds would arise in the future. We asked whether there were any new developments today. Mr. Phillips read telegrams 2154, portions of 2156 and 2158, all May 14, from Caserta. I said that we had been considering consulting the Soviet Government at this point, having in mind the Yalta Agreement, but had come to the conclusion that this was not necessary since as long ago as March we had asked the Soviet Government for its views on our plans for the establishment of a temporary military government in that area and had never received any response. Mr. Eden appeared to agree to this decision. Later in the conversation Mr. Harriman raised the point (without recommending action) that should Tito refuse to back down from his present intransigent attitude, we might then ask the Soviets whether they would use their influence to persuade Tito to see reason. Eden took note of this suggestion but made no comment. Mr. Harriman then spoke of the importance of clarifying the relations of our two governments to the Soviets before his return to Moscow. He pointed out that with regard to Poland we had laid down our present position very definitely but had not sufficiently planned our future course. Mr. Eden agreed to its importance. . . .[5]

Date: May 15, 1945
SUBJECT: The situation in Venezia Giulia.
PARTICIPANTS: The President; the Acting Secretary of State; Ambassador Harriman; and Mr. Bohlen.

THE ACTING SECRETARY said he wished first of all to bring the President up-to-date on the Venezia Giulia; they had looked

[5] The Soviet Union was delaying on the agreement reached at Yalta concerning Poland. On April 1, President Roosevelt had sent an urgent cable to Stalin on the Polish issue, and he had pointed out to Stalin that a mere enlargement of the Lublin Government could not be reconciled with the agreement. Edward R. Stettinius, *Roosevelt and the Russians: The Yalta Conference,* ed. Walter Johnson (New York: Doubleday and Co., Inc., 1949), pp. 313–14. On May 23, President Truman sent Harry Hopkins to Moscow to discuss a number of issues, including Poland.

into the question of consultation with the Soviet Government so as to avoid any charge from that quarter that we had not lived up to that principle. The record was that as far back as March we had together with the British pointed out the desirability on this question of the maintenance of Allied Military Government until the conflicting claims could be adjudicated and although we had requested Soviet views on this point no reply had been received. He added, therefore, that our record is entirely clear on this point.

MR. GREW then asked the President if his understanding was correct that before Field Marshal Alexander took any action against the Yugoslav forces, in the event of Tito's refusal of our diplomatic approach, he would have to refer back to the Combined Chiefs of Staff. The President confirmed this understanding but said that he had asked Admiral Leahy to discuss with the Joint Chiefs of Staff the question of making available to Field Marshal Alexander the necessary forces should that be required. He added that Field Marshal Alexander had 4 divisions in the vicinity of Trieste and in all 18 divisions in the theater with possibly some additional forces in Austria. He said he had made it plain to the Prime Minister that United States forces would not start shooting since we could not become involved in another war but that they should, of course, defend themselves if attacked by Tito's troops. . . .

Date: May 19, 1945

SUBJECT: Conference with the President, 2.30 P.M.
PARTICIPANTS: The President; Acting Secretary, Mr. Grew.

I called on the President at 2.30 this afternoon and took up with him the following points. . . .

TRIESTE

I told the President that, in view of Marshal Tito's rejection of our demands that an Allied Military Government be set up in Venezia Giulia and in view of the fact that the press is clamoring for information as to the nature of Tito's reply which the correspondents know has been sent us from Belgrade,[6] I thought the thing for us to do is to come out with a definite statement to the effect that Tito has failed to meet our position and reiterate what that position is as stated in my press release of May 12. I then handed to the President our proposed release, which he read carefully and approved.[7] I said that at the same time we are drafting, for the President's consideration, a proposed telegram to be sent direct by the President to Marshal Stalin explaining the present situation and asking for his support of the position that we and the British have taken. The President said he thought this was just the right thing to do. I said that I hoped to have the telegram ready for him this afternoon and that then he might wish to tell Churchill what he had done and suggest that Churchill take similar action. The President concurred. . . .[8]

[6] The text of Marshal Tito's reply was given to the press on May 19. He said, in part, that the "honor of our army and the honor of our country demand the presence of the Yugoslav Army in Istria, Trieste and the Slovene coastline," and that the "decisions of the peace conference, which will be the final decisions as regards the apportioning of the region concerned, are in no way prejudiced. With regard to this the federation of Yugoslavia is opposed to all unilateral declarations." *New York Times*, May 20, 1945, p. 16.

[7] In a press conference held on May 19, Mr. Grew stated that Marshal Tito's reply had not been satisfactory, and "it could not be reconciled with the American position as outlined" on May 12. He went on to say that it had been decided previously that the control of Trieste and the adjacent area should rest with Allied Military Government until a settlement could be reached after consultation by the parties involved. The Trieste situation, moreover, "involved the issue of due process as opposed to unilateral action that challenges agreements made among several powers." *Ibid.*, p. 18.

[8] On the same day on which Mr. Grew held this conference with the President, Tito's commanders moved their main headquarters out of Trieste, although not abandoning their military control of the city. On the next day, May 20, it was disclosed that Yugoslav forces had agreed to evacuate the disputed Austrian province of Carinthia. A despatch dated May 22 announced that Tito had accepted "in principle" the Allied proposals regarding Trieste and Venezia Giulia, although the terms of the compromise were not yet known.

On June 9, an agreement was finally signed by the United States, Great Britain, and Yugoslavia according to which that part of Venezia Giulia including Trieste was placed under "command and control" of the Supreme Allied Commander. Two thousand Yugoslav troops were to be permitted to remain in

The President, as usual, was exceedingly affable and, as usual, he expressed full appreciation of my recommendations and advice. He said that he welcomed all my recommendations and that if at any time he disagreed with them he would tell me so with complete frankness but, whether he agreed with them or not, he welcomed having them made. Among all the Presidents under whom I have served, I have never known one who seems so genuinely grateful for advice on any subject.[9]

the area in a section assigned to them by the Commander. Allied Military Government was to govern the area.

Yugoslav troops began to move out of Trieste on June 10, and two days later Allied military authorities took over control of the city. See *ibid.*, May 21, 1945, pp. 1, 5; May 23, 1945, p. 1; June 10, 1945, pp. 1, 6; June 11, 1945, p. 8; and June 13, 1945, p. 7.

[9] In a letter of May 2, 1945, to Cecil Lyon Mr. Grew stated: "If I could talk to you about the new President you would hear nothing but the most favorable reaction. I have seen a good deal of him lately and I think he is going to measure up splendidly to the tremendous job which faces him. He is a man of few words but he seems to know the score all along the line and he generally has a perfectly clear conception of the right thing to do and how to do it. He is personally most affable and agreeable to deal with but he certainly won't stand for any pussyfooting in our foreign relations and policy, all of which of course warms my heart. When I saw him today I had fourteen problems to take up with him and got through them in less than fifteen minutes with a clear directive on every one of them. You can imagine what a joy it is to deal with a man like that and my admiration and liking for him daily increase."

XXXIX

Diplomacy and Power

UNIVERSAL MILITARY TRAINING [1]

SECRETARY GREW. Mr. Chairman and gentlemen, I come before you as an advocate of military training for the young men of America. I believe profoundly that our young men should have this training. I do not believe that there is anyone in our country, in the armed forces or in civilian life, who feels this more strongly than I do, and my attitude is based on the experience gained in 40 years of foreign service, especially the 10 years I spent in Germany before and during the last war and the 10 years I spent in Japan before the war we are fighting now.

I believe it is an essential part of our share in the United Nations proposals for world security. And I am glad to know that young men who now make up the Army and the Navy of the United States themselves favor military training to defend and maintain, in the perilous years that lie ahead, the liberty they have preserved.

We have never lost a war, and pray God we never shall. But I believe there are wars we should not have had to fight if we had been properly prepared in time, if we had shown the aggressors what might we were equipped to wield.

A great charter of security for mankind is being created by the United Nations at San Francisco. The plans for a world organization for peace call for a series of steps to be taken by the Security Council before force is used to deal with those who would plunge the world into war.

[1] This statement was made on June 4, 1945. See the U.S. Congress, House, *Universal Military Training*, Hearings before Select Committee on Postwar Military Policy, 79th Cong., 1st Sess., Pursuant to H. Res. 465 (Washington: Government Printing Office, 1945), pp. 1–5.

But we must be prepared to contribute our complement of armed force to the United Nations pool if we should be called upon to do so when all other steps have failed to preserve the peace.

The precise numbers and components of the forces and facilities would be determined by agreements among the member states under the auspices of the Security Council. But it is obvious that such agreements cannot be made until after the international organization is under way.

It is impossible today to foresee the whole future and say exactly what our responsibilities may be in providing our share of force to keep the peace. Yet it is decidedly clear that if we are to have that force ready when it is needed it will have to be provided by whatever peacetime military and naval plan we decide beforehand to carry out. Modern armies and navies do not spring into being overnight.

We should accept, therefore, the judgment of our highest military authority. And that authority holds that unless a system of universal military training is put into effect we shall not have available the reserve of trained men required to make our air and sea and land forces adequate to meet any possible future threats to our freedom.

Above all, if our young men are ever again to be called on to defend our freedom it will be better for them and better for us if they are well-trained. We have an obligation to them and to the Nation to give them the best possible training, that they, and the Nation, may survive. Their chances of survival will be infinitely greater if they are trained.

The foreign policy of the United States, in Mr. Hull's classic definition, is —

the task of focusing and giving effect in the world outside our borders to the will of 135,000,000 people through the constitutional processes which govern our democracy.

Behind our day-to-day diplomacy in fulfilling that policy lies a factor of prime importance: National determination demonstrated and backed by national preparedness. Without adequate preparedness our diplomacy becomes weak and ineffective. If our diplomacy abroad is to achieve favorable results, our country should be constantly prepared to meet all eventualities. As General MacArthur said when he was Chief of Staff:

> Armies and navies in being efficient give weight to the peaceful words of statesmen, but a feverish effort to create them when once a crisis is imminent simply provokes attack.

Looking back to the old days, before 1914, in Berlin, I remember seeing German officers banging their glasses on the table and singing Der Tag. They were boastful and arrogant, contemptuous of the weak.

We are bound to attack France some day — they said:

> When we attack France we may have to go through Belgium, of course. But the Belgians won't fight; they are weak and spiritless. As for the British, they are all shot up with their Irish and labor troubles; we can count England out of the picture.

That represented the thinking of those Prussian military officers before 1914.

And it has always seemed to me that if, at that time, England had been prepared, even moderately prepared, in those years before 1914, and if, when Germany threatened France, Sir Edward Grey had been able to say to Von Bethmann-Hollweg, "If you attack France, Great Britain will come into the war within an hour," I have serious doubts as to whether the German would ever have ventured upon that war; and the scene goes on 10 years to Japan.

In 1932 I went to Japan. Not long after taking up my duties as Ambassador, I wrote to the Secretary of State, then Mr. Stimson, saying, the Japanese military machine —

> has been built for war, feels prepared for war, and would welcome war. It has never yet been beaten and possesses unlimited

self-confidence. I am not an alarmist, but I believe we should have our eyes open to all possible future contingencies.

I was constantly urging preparedness, not in the interests of war but in the furtherance of peace, because might was the only language the Japanese could understand. Military weakness simply invited contempt.

I remember especially my talks with Mr. Matsuoka, the then Japanese Minister of Foreign Affairs, in the late thirties and 1940. I knew him very well, and instead of going to the Foreign Office, I used to go to his house to see him, and he would walk up and down the garden, we would walk together, sometimes by the hour, and I remember very well one conversation in which he said to me:

"War has now broken out between Great Britain and Germany, and the Atlantic Ocean is a war zone. If you insist on sending your ships into that war zone, and you get into a shooting match with a German submarine, and as a result of that war breaks out between the United States and Germany, we will have to come in, on the basis of the tripartite pact as a member of the Axis."

I said:

"Mr. Minister, do you mean to say that you are willing to place the entire future destiny of your country in with those of the Axis, where they would be 2 to 1 against you?"

He said:

"That is my interpretation of the tripartite pact."

Then he said to me:

"You had better watch your step, because you in America could not fight a total war. Germany will undoubtedly win this war and will control all of Europe, and we in Japan are the stabilizing force in East Asia."

Of course, he had to use the usual familiar phrase about "stabilizing influence."

He said:

"Democracy is bankrupt and this is the day of totalitarian powers. Your people have been brought up in the lap of luxury; they are dependent on their daily comforts, and with your labor troubles, your strikes, your pacifism and isolationism, you would be incapable of waging total war. Your people won't let you. They would not allow you to come in even if your Government wanted to."

Now, that was the thinking of Matsuoka at that time, and it was the general thinking of most of those aggressive militarists over there. They did not understand our country.

Matsuoka, himself, rather surprisingly, was born in this country, in Oregon, and grew up in our schools and always prided himself on his understanding of our country and our way of thought, and thought that he knew our psychology, and after that I remember saying to him:

"It is surprising that you pride yourself on being an expert on America and should be so wide of the mark."

I said:

"It is true that we in our country are not prepared for war."

It is not perhaps surprising, I must say, that the Japanese thought that we were ruled by our isolationists and pacifists, because the only speeches in our country that the Japanese were allowed to read in their papers in the prewar years were the speeches of our ultraisolationists and pacifists, and whenever a strike occurred in America it was always headlined in Japanese papers.

The Japanese people got the idea that it was the majority thinking in our country.

I said:

"Mr. Minister, you little understand our country. You don't seem to know our history. If you did, you would realize that we are a pretty inflammable people when something is done against us."

I said:

"We go into war, when a war is forced on us, as amateurs. We are not prepared, and the wheels may grind in the early stages, but gradually we will move up through the different gears, and when we get into top gear, as we have always done and always will, nothing in the world can stop us."

I remember the minister's looking at me as if to see if I was joking, and seeing that I was not, he shook his head, as if he were talking to a child.

I tell you that story, Mr. Chairman, merely to give you an idea of the thinking of the people in Japan at that time, and the thinking that led into war.

If at that time we had been prepared, if we at least had had a pool of trained men in our country to draw from, if the Japanese understood that, as they would have had to understand it — I question seriously whether they would ever have dared to attack.

If during those years before Pearl Harbor our people had been able to see the handwriting on the wall, if we had been even reasonably prepared at that time, I don't believe for a moment that Japan would have attacked us.

We must not, we dare not, let it happen again. That's why we cannot afford to wait.

I have said that I believe a year's military training is necessary because of our obligations under the world security organization; because in the world of things as they are, our international policy to be effective must have strength behind it; and because my experience has taught me that aggressors are not deterred by latent superior strength but shrewdly try to obtain their ends by attacking when they consider their potential opponents unprepared and therefore at a disadvantage.

There is one further aspect of the problem which I considered before giving my unreserved support to the demand for a year of military training for our young men in peace as well as in war, and that is the effect on our young men themselves.

During my life I have been intensely interested in education and I have been in close touch with educators, universities, and colleges, and I am a staunch believer in the value of academic training. I know there are some who believe that the requirement of a year's military training would take our young men away from colleges and schools, from academic life.

I am convinced, on the contrary, that if this system were to go into effect it would be the greatest possible stimulus to our young men to go into educational life. They are going to realize the disadvantages of a lack of education. They will be in contact with educated men.

It is my view that the plan would be in the best interests of our educational institutions throughout the country. It would also give our young men physical conditioning, discipline, an understanding of teamwork, fair play, and that sort of thing, which would be permanent assets to them throughout their lives.

And when those who continued their academic work went back to it, their approach would be more mature and the harvest would be richer. In sum, our young men would gain rather than lose by a year's training to fit them to be members of a civilian army.

These are some of the reasons why I earnestly recommend the adoption of the plan for a year of military training of our youth. Without qualification, I believe it to be in the best interests of our Nation and our people. We must be strong if we would be free. . . .[2]

Address at the Commencement of the School of Advanced International Studies, Washington, D.C., June 23, 1945

THE RESPONSIBILITY OF POWER

This new School of Advanced International Studies answers an urgent practical need. The choice of Washington as a background for your study of international relations was an act of wisdom and imagination. The choice of students with both a theoretical and a practical interest in foreign affairs is recognition of the new scope and character of relations among peoples. And the selection of a faculty who are at once artisans and students of history is nothing short of an inspiration.

Here in Washington there are many artisans but few students

[2] For another statement by Mr. Grew urging Universal Military Training, see a speech read into the *Congressional Record, Appendix*, 80th Cong., 2d Sess. (Washington: Government Printing Office, 1948), pp. A910–A912.

of history. Too many go about their business in this great storehouse of the living past with unseeing eyes and minds obsessed with the emergency of the moment.

You have had the privilege of living with both the present and the past on intimate terms — of listening to debates in the Congress that have shaped the course of history and then stepping across the street to the great library where Magna Carta, the Declaration of Independence, the Constitution and other historic documents of human freedom are housed; of passing from the Supreme Court down Pennsylvania Avenue to the Archives Building on which Confucius' admonition "Study the past" and Shakespeare's reminder that "What is past is prologue" are etched in stone.

I hope that, wherever you may be, your eyes and ears will never become insensitive to the reminders of history. I hope you will never lose the most precious gift this school has to offer — an understanding of the present founded on a sense of the past.

I spoke a moment ago of the new character of relations among peoples. To say that scientific progress in communications has changed the scope and content of foreign relations is perhaps to state a platitude. Yet there is danger that platitudes may be accepted without being fully understood. We are apt to take for granted the wartime developments in short-wave radio, facsimile newspapers and international radio photos. We have become accustomed to radio programs that circle the earth instantaneously and planes that span it in a matter of hours. "The Parliament of Man" is no longer a phrase, but a fact. The volume of communication among governments is now but a tiny trickle compared with the mighty torrent of conversation among peoples.

In the same way, the whole concept of the foreign services of nations is in process of revision. The United States is, at the moment, represented abroad by some six million men and women. I venture to say that these representatives of ours in the uniform of the armed forces are doing more, in a brief space of time, to shape foreign attitudes toward the United

States than all our diplomatic and commercial missions have done, or could have done, in the past 25 years.

Through them our friends and our enemies abroad are learning at firsthand about America — its power and its character, its diversity and unity, its aims and intentions. The abnormal conditions under which they are learning these things, the fact that this sudden migration is temporary makes no difference. For years to come the work of American civilians who follow in the wake of our armed forces overseas after the war will be conditioned by the impression our forces have left behind.

The effects of this current migration cannot be assessed in terms of the last war. We have no precedent with which to compare it. Instead of the two million men concentrated in the countries of Western Europe in 1918, we have had, during this war approximately three times that many Americans — both men and women — scattered over five continents and countless islands — from Burma to Brazil, from Iran to Iceland, from Aden to Australia. The total impact of their presence is the sum of millions of small impacts, millions of seemingly unimportant situations — the ragged Indian urchin sitting on the steps of the Taj Mahal, singing "Deep in the Heart of Texas" and collecting coins from delighted Yanks; the wounded Russian heroes examining with intense interest the wrapping on a package of American cigarettes; the Sergeant from Kansas billeted with an English family, helping to wash the dishes and sharing his chewing gum and his chocolate ration with the children. These things, as well as the policies being determined in Washington and San Francisco are the stuff of which international relations are made. And these things will have to be studied and taken into account from here on.

Those of us who go abroad in the Foreign Service of the United States in the months and years ahead will be carrying on from where our servicemen and women leave off, and like them, each of us will hold in our hands responsibility for a tiny segment of the foreign relations of the United States, whether we go in the service of our Government, or to buy and sell abroad, to study or teach, to write or to travel.

In the light of these new facts, let us re-examine the old question "How shall we represent America abroad? How can we best serve the interests — the highest interests of our people?" That is a complicated question to which I think there is a simple answer. It has been a tradition and an age-old principle of the Foreign Service of our Government that we can represent America best by representing it truthfully. But I think it is not always fully realized that in order to do that we must *know* America: not just the State or region in which we have lived; not just the segment of society in which we have been raised, but the broad sweep of the land and the complex of human beings who live and work in it.

From now on I wish it were possible for anyone who undertakes to represent America abroad, in any capacity whatsover, to have traveled the length and breadth of this nation, to have understood the meaning of the melting pot in American life, the power that is uniquely American of welding people of many national origins together in the service of an idea; to have appreciated the contribution of many European cultures to our own national culture; to have experienced our sense of unity, and our capacity for infinite variety within that unity. In other words, I want everyone who represents America to have the *feel* of America in his bones, as well as the love of America in his heart. Remember, you who today cross the threshold of this school and pass into the outer world, that America will be judged by what you say, what you write, what you do and what you are. Your responsibility is very great.

All this, our representatives in foreign lands should have. All this is, of course, in addition to a sound knowledge of our domestic history and foreign relations, as well as a high competence in the field of work that sends them abroad.

Perhaps this is too much to ask of the people who represent America, but I believe we should ask it. The dangers that lie ahead, the problems that confront us in our dealings with the rest of the world demand it. The new position and the new role of the United States in the community of nations make it essential.

That position is the position of the most powerful nation on earth; that role is, as I see it, a role of service and of leadership, the only role that befits a leading player on a world stage.

We should not be afraid to talk about our power as a nation, but we should take care neither to whisper nor to shout about it, neither to boast nor to apologize. Our power is a fact. It must be recognized by ourselves, as it is recognized by the rest of the world. Our friends abroad fear, not that we will recognize the fact, but that we shall fail to recognize it. For that failure would undoubtedly lead to our failure to accept the responsibilities that power inevitably imposes.

The tragedies of history are the tragedies of the misuse of power, and historians never tire of pointing out that the decline of nations and civilizations inevitably and logically follows from the fatal possession of great power without the exercise of great leadership. Arnold Toynbee, one of the wisest of modern historians, warns that "Power is a force which is perhaps rarely brought into play without being abused. In any event, the tenure of power is an abuse in itself, if those who hold the power have lost the faculty of leadership."

In a mood of discouragement over the trials of the 1919 Peace Conference, Harold Nicolson bewailed the fact that "human nature can, like a glacier, move but an inch or two in every thousand years." I would not wish to quarrel with a distinguished diplomatist, nor to quibble about small measurements, but I cannot share the pessimism or the fatalism that that observation implies.

Human nature does move. Men and nations do learn by hard experience. We are and shall remain the masters of our fate.

I have always subscribed to the philosophy of man's free will, and in this belief I am encouraged by the findings of historians such as H. A. L. Fisher who spent a lifetime journeying through the past and returned with this final testament:

"Men wiser and more learned than I," he said, "have discerned in history a plot, a rhythm, a predetermined pattern. These harmonies are concealed from me. I can see only one emergency following upon another as wave follows upon wave, only one great fact with respect to which, since it is unique, there can be no generalizations, only one safe rule for the historian: that he should recognize in the development of human destinies the play of the contingent and the unforeseen. This is not a doctrine of cynicism and despair. The fact of progress is written plain and large on the page of history. But progress is not a law of nature. The ground gained by one generation may be lost by the next. The thoughts of men may flow into the channels which lead to disaster and barbarism."

But history provides us also with examples of survival of virile and mature cultures and peoples through the wise use of power. We have, among others, the example of the British people, who would be the first to acknowledge their own mistakes in the period of acquiring and assimilating power, but who have learned and practiced moderation and concession in retaining and consolidating their power.

We can profit, we must profit, by the lessons of history, but in the end, we shall have to solve the problems of our own power in our own particular way. That we shall solve them I do not for a moment doubt. But I believe that these problems of power confront the American people with the greatest challenge in all their history.

If, as I have suggested, our first duty lies in recognizing the power of the United States, our second duty is to understand in what it consists. In its most obvious form, of course, it consists in military power — in planes, ships, tanks, guns, and men who are skilled in the organization and use of them. We have also, what is even more important under conditions of modern warfare, a vast military potential in terms of industrial plant and scientific and technological skill.

We have been accused of many things, but never of being a militaristic people. It would therefore be not only untrue but mischievous to suggest that we shall ever use our military power to threaten the peace of the world. We shall use it as we have used it in two world wars — in the service of law and justice and human freedom — in other words, in the service of peace on earth, without which we cannot serve our own highest interests.

We are about to enter into a compact with the other peace-loving nations to make sure that military power — *ours and theirs* — will be used and used only for that high purpose. Our military power exists. It will continue to exist as a force for the common good. It will be a threat only to the violators of international peace and justice.

If our military power is the product of grim necessity, our economic power provides us with a glorious opportunity. But let us not confuse economic power with gadgets, machines, and assembly lines. It is essentially a human, not a material thing. It consists in the vitality, the creative genius, the capacity for patient, hard work of a people. If our land had been devastated in this war, if our entire industrial plant had been leveled to the ground, it would have meant the interruption, but not destruction of our economic progress. And that, incidentally is one of the problems we face in conquered Germany and Japan: how to prevent the Germans and Japanese who are also productive people from ever again acquiring economic power which might be used again as a threat to world peace?

We know the extent of our economic power; we know that it can and must be used to strengthen the peace of the world. In the hands of the American people, it must be used, in the first instance, to raise our own standard of living and our own level of employment. Never again can we afford to have domestic depressions which cause untold misery at home and are felt around the world.

More than that, we must plan our production of goods and services and their distribution abroad in such a way as to enable our friends, whose countries have been devastated, to get back on their feet again, to employ their own people so that they can produce goods for us, and buy goods from us in ever increasing volume. In other words we must find ways of cooperating with our friends so as to increase the volume of world trade and promote the general prosperity, month by month and year by year. If in the years to come we should think narrowly and in purely national terms of the so-called "danger of competition from abroad" there will be no revival in Europe, no sound prosperity at home, no growth of world trade, nothing but recurrent depression, political instability and perhaps another world conflict.

After the last war we embarked on the dangerous and inconsistent policy of erecting high tariff walls and insisting on payment of war debts, while lending huge sums abroad. We were a creditor nation, but we refused to act like one. Now we are again in the position of a creditor, and we propose to face up to the implications of that fact. The extension of the system of our reciprocal trade agreements is one proof of that intention. The plan for a World bank and an international stabilization fund agreed upon at Bretton Woods constitute another step in the right direction — a long step. We shall pursue the path of economic co-operation through the organization of the United Nations, whose Economic and Social Council promises to be one of the most hopeful contributions to the future well-being of nations.

On the basis of our past record, our economic power is distrusted and even feared abroad. It will be to our own interest to dispel those fears not by statements of good intentions, but by concrete examples of co-operation.

The war has, I think, clearly demonstrated the extent of our economic power to produce, to convert and reconvert, and to distribute what we produce in bottoms and planes of our own making.

What we do not fully understand, what in my opinion we have never appreciated and understood is the extent of our moral and spiritual power among other peoples. In order to do that, we would have to do what is virtually impossible — see ourselves as others see us.

Each foreigner's idea of America is, of course, conditioned by his personal experience, by his contact with the printed or spoken word, with the motion pictures, by his personal acquaintance with an American, or in the cases of millions of Europeans, by the experiences of a brother, a cousin or an uncle who has emigrated to the United States.

At the risk of overgeneralizing, I would say that, in the main, the rest of the world has the impression that we are tremendously big, incredibly rich and extraordinarily lucky. There is an idea abroad, a rather remarkable idea that we have achieved this happy state not through hardship, stamina and courage, but through the workings of divine providence. Not by hard work, but by sheer good luck. And that is one reason why our friends abroad are not unduly impressed by expressions of high ideals and principles that may come to them from this side of the Atlantic.

They are, however, deeply impressed by the qualities of character and integrity which they have found in some of our leaders. They are also impressed by acts of statesmanship — concrete acts that have shown concrete results. I should like to give you, as examples, the power of two men and two actions.

One example is the regard, verging on reverence, that was felt for Franklin D. Roosevelt by millions of humble people in every part of the world. These people looked upon our late President as their friend. They saw him as the champion of all humanity in a hard and ruthless world. And, in the eyes of these foreigners, all other Americans somehow shared in the reflected glory of the great man whom they had chosen as their President.

General Eisenhower is another example of an American who has earned the affectionate admiration of millions of Europeans. One might expect him to be worshipped primarily as a great architect of victory, but the people have shown remarkable insight by recognizing the simplicity and humanity of the man no less than the genius of the general.

It is, of course, natural that the moral power of America should become personified in our leaders. But I have in mind also two acts of statesmanship which have enhanced that power. I am thinking of the policy of Philippine independence and the way in which it has contributed to our prestige in the Orient. I am thinking also of the Lend-Lease Act, whose passage historians may well point to as one of the decisive victories of this war — even though the United States was not at war at the time. For by that Act America, with all her moral, economic and military power, underwrote the defeat of the Axis and the survival of freedom in the world.

Lend-Lease was, in my opinion, a classic example of the use of power to strengthen the hands of our friends, the peace-loving peoples, and to ensure the downfall of the enemies of peace. Only by such uses of power, by such examples of statesmanship and enlightened self-interest can we hope to preserve the greatness of America as a people and an idea.

It may be said that it is only in moments of great national peril that nations are capable of bold and imaginative acts of statesmanship — acts such as Lend-Lease and Prime Minister Churchill's offer of union to France. But the fact is, there is a continuing peril in dealings among nations, peril that a selfish, ill-considered action, or neglect to act, or denial of responsibility by a nation may start a chain of events that leads to disaster. We cannot for a moment relax our vigilance. We cannot for a moment surrender to what Winston Churchill called "the craven fear of being great." Power cannot for a moment be left idle like money in an old sock.

It must be used constantly and wisely to fortify the friends of peace everywhere in the world, and thereby to fortify ourselves.

The problem of the exercise of power over a defeated enemy is complicated in the extreme, but it is relatively simple compared with the problem of blending the power of friends and allies. General Eisenhower developed a successful pattern for doing this in wartime. We shall have to learn how to do it in creating peace. The road will be hard. If we should ever become fainthearted or cynical at any step along the way, then our power would become a curse instead of a blessing to mankind.

Abraham Lincoln was speaking even more for our time than for his when he said, "the dogmas of the quiet past are inadequate to the stormy present. The occasion is piled high with difficulty, and we must rise with the occasion. As our case is new, so we must think and act anew. We must disenthrall ourselves and then we shall save our country."

I wish for every one of you what you yourselves may conceive as success. If you build your lives on the unmovable
foundation of principle, if you set your objectives high and
swerve not from the road that leads to their attainment, and if,
in pursuing those objectives you keep constantly before you
the long-range picture of life, the right kind of success will be
yours.

Good luck!

XL

The United States and France

Relations between President Roosevelt and General Charles de Gaulle were tense and unsatisfactory throughout the war. It was not until October 23, 1944, that the United States, after consultation with Great Britain and the Soviet Union, recognized the de Gaulle de facto authority as the Provisional Government of the French Republic. About three and one-half months later the Big Three held a conference at Yalta. De Gaulle was incensed because he had not been invited to attend. The Big Three, however, did agree at Yalta to invite France to be a sponsoring power for the forthcoming United Nations Security Conference to be held at San Francisco on April 25.

Date: February 11, 1945

SUBJECT: United Nations Security Conference.

PARTICIPANTS: French Ambassador, Mr. Henri Bonnet; Acting Secretary, Mr. Grew.

The French Ambassador called at my house at my request this Sunday evening at 10.30 and I read to him, for his information, the telegram being sent this evening to Ambassador Jefferson Caffery [American Ambassador to France] setting forth plans for the United Nations Conference. I emphasized to the Ambassador the great urgency of the matter and expressed the hope that he might feel like sending a flash telegram to his Government urging that a reply be given to us at the earliest possible moment. I pointed out that after the communiqué agreed upon by the United States, Great Britain, and the Soviet Union is issued on Tuesday morning, February 13, there will be great speculation in the press with regard to the details of the agreement on voting procedure in the Security Council.[1]

---

[1] Edward R. Stettinius, *Roosevelt and the Russians: The Yalta Conference,* ed. Walter Johnson (New York: Doubleday and Co., Inc., 1949), pp. 140–50.

We therefore hoped that our consultation with the Provisional Government of France could be carried through with the greatest possible despatch.

The Ambassador asked me several questions regarding certain points in our communication which I clarified for him and he then expressed serious doubt as to whether a reply from his Government could be forthcoming within several days. He said that the question of voting in the Security Council, as well as other points, would have to be submitted to the Council of Ministers in Paris and that this would take time. It was also pointed out that according to press reports General de Gaulle was absent from Paris. Mr. Bonnet also pointed out the adverse feeling on the part of his Government which had been aroused by the fact that General de Gaulle had not received an invitation to attend the Big Three Conference.

I once again urged the Ambassador to do his best to ensure our receiving a reply from his Government at the earliest possible moment.

                              Date: March 5, 1945, 11.45 A.M.
SUBJECT: Issuance of Invitations to United Nations. Conference at San Francisco.
PARTICIPANTS: Mr. George Conn [Administrative Assistant in the State Department]; Acting Secretary, Mr. Grew.

Mr. George Conn telephoned from Mexico City this morning and said that the Secretary had just left for the meeting to make his speech and that he was going to hold a press conference right afterwards.[2]

Mr. Conn then read to me the following off-the-record remarks of Mr. Stettinius on the French situation:

2 Secretary Stettinius was attending the Chapultepec Conference on Inter-American Affairs. After three weeks of waiting for the French to take action on sponsorship of the San Francisco Conference, Great Britain, the Soviet Union, China, and the United States issued the invitation in the name of the Big Four.

The reasons why France did not join in sponsoring the San Francisco Conference:

1. The Provisional Government of France first asked that its own suggestion for the world organization be given an equal place on the agenda at San Francisco with the Dumbarton Oaks proposals.

2. France then asked that the invitation be amended so that the Dumbarton Oaks proposals would be a matter for discussion instead of being considered as the basis for the charter.

3. At no time did France indicate to us the substance of its reservations to the Dumbarton Oaks proposals.

I told Mr. Conn that I had issued a statement myself this morning but that I hadn't gone nearly as far as the Secretary. I said I merely told the press for background that the consultations have not resulted in France being willing to become a sponsoring power. I then read my off-the-record statement, as follows:

At the time that the Provisional Government of the French Republic first replied to the invitation to join the United States, Great Britain, and the Soviet Union in sponsoring the San Francisco Conference, the Provisional Government made clear that it would be glad to participate in the Conference. The Provisional Government, however, which had not participated in the conversations at Dumbarton Oaks, placed conditions upon its joining in sponsoring invitations to the Conference. The four Governments sponsoring the Conference welcomed the assurance that the Provisional Government of the French Republic would participate in the Conference but were unable, after consultations among themselves, to agree upon the conditions of the Provisional Government with regard to the latter's becoming a sponsoring Government.

Mr. Conn said that the above statement had been received by them last night. He said that the two statements were not contradictory, to which I agreed, but I added that the Secretary went farther than I did. . . .

Date: May 17, 1945

SUBJECT: French Situation.

PARTICIPANTS: President Truman; Acting Secretary Grew.

I saw the President at two o'clock today and said I felt it would be very helpful in improving our relations with France if after his conversation with Mr. Bidault [French Minister of Foreign Affairs] tomorrow he would issue a statement to the press covering the points touched upon in the conversation. I then handed him a draft for such a press release and asked the President if he would be willing to cover, in his talk with Mr. Bidault, each of the points raised in the proposed release. The President read it over and indicated that he liked it. He put it on his desk for more careful reading later.

I then said to the President that we have reports of a growing anti-American campaign by the Communists in France, and as Mr. Bidault is a Catholic I thought it would be very helpful if the President in his talk with the Minister tomorrow would allude to this campaign and give Mr. Bidault some ammunition for fighting it.

I then handed to the President a memorandum setting forth some of the things we are doing for France, especially the Lend-Lease program of $1,600,000,000 to be used in France in spite of the termination of hostilities in Europe. The memorandum also set forth the sacrifices which the American people are accepting in the way of restricted commodities in order to help feed people in the liberated areas in Europe, especially in France. The President took the memorandum and indicated that he agreed with my suggestion.

The President then referred to the two memoranda which I had sent him last night briefing him on the two points which we knew Mr. Bidault would raise, namely, the desire of General de Gaulle to be invited to attend the next meeting of the Big Three, and also General de Gaulle's desire that French forces should fight alongside our forces in the war against Japan. I asked the President if it was his wish to be briefed in this way before conferences with foreign statesmen. He replied that he very definitely did wish to be so briefed and that our memoranda were a great help to him. He said he had carefully read the two which I had sent him last night. . . .

Date: May 19, 1945

PARTICIPANTS: The Acting Secretary of State; Mr. George Bidault; Mr. Henri Bonnet; Mr. William Phillips; Mr. Freeman Matthews.

I received Mr. Bidault and the French Ambassador in my office at 10 o'clock this morning and opened the conversation by saying how much Mr. Stettinius had appreciated all that Bidault had done in contributing to the success of the Conference. The Minister seemed pleased and thanked me, adding that he had enjoyed his association with Mr. Stettinius.

THE PRESIDENT'S PRESS RELEASE

Mr. Bidault then referred with great satisfaction to the President's press release following his call at the White House yesterday afternoon.[3] The statement, he said, had gone even further than he had hoped, and he was certain that it would have a most excellent effect in France.

FRENCH MILITARY ASSISTANCE IN THE FAR EAST

I mentioned that among the points which had been touched upon at the White House was that of French military assistance in the Far East in the war against Japan. I reminded Mr. Bidault that while the President had expressed his general approval to French military association with us in this theater, he had emphasized that the problem was a military one and would necessarily have to be judged on its merits by the military authorities. I said that in the circumstances it was up to General MacArthur to decide just how much and where the French military contribution could be best utilized. The Minister mentioned that there were two French divisions ready for immediate transportation to the Far East. In reply to my inquiry as to whether there are Senegalese troops among them, he

[3] See the *New York Times*, May 19, 1945, p. 7.

admitted that this was probably so, although there were also substantial numbers of white French. He made it clear that the French divisions could be utilized anywhere in the Far East, and there was no intention of limiting their contribution to attacking the enemy in Indochina. I reiterated that this matter would be placed before our military authorities immediately.

SYRIA AND LEBANON

I said that we were considerably disturbed over reports which were coming to us from Syria and Lebanon, and that a rather explosive situation seemed to be developing as a result of French troops which were being sent to the Levant States.[4] We realized that some of these troops were merely replacements, but our reports indicated that in addition to replacements the forces were being augmented. I then read to the Minister a paraphrase of the instructions which I had sent to Ambassador Caffery on April 30th for presentation to the French Government. This message expressed the various reasons for the interest and concern of this Government.

(a) That it would be extremely unfortunate for disorders to occur in the Levant States when a supreme effort is being made by the Allied forces, or in the near future, when redeployment to the Far Eastern theater of war will make the Near East a highly important avenue;

(b) That an effect out of proportion to its intrinsic importance might be created at this time by an even minor act

[4] In the early part of 1945, Syria and Lebanon demanded that France transfer to them the Levantine troops which had been conscripted into the French territorial forces. In May, treaty negotiations were begun among the three countries. At the same time that French treaty proposals were being presented by General Paul-Etienne Beynet, France was landing additional troops in the area. France stated that these new troops were only routine reinforcements, but the Syrians regarded them as a threat. A joint note was sent by Syria and Lebanon breaking off negotiations. On May 27, street fighting broke out at Hama, and the following day similar incidents occurred at Homs. The French retaliated by bombing a Syrian stronghold at Damascus and firing on the Syrian Parliament building. At this juncture Churchill sent a note to General de Gaulle informing him that British forces in the Middle East had been ordered to intervene.

of a great power which might be regarded as provocative, and this in turn might be an issue of first importance at San Francisco;

(c) That the application or even threat of force by France would give rise to doubts throughout the world in regard to the intention of the major United Nations to support their enunciated principles by force.

The message concluded with the statement that we consider that any increase in French forces in the Levant States could not in the absence of military necessity be more ill-timed. Mr. Bidault listened attentively, and the Ambassador summarized the entire despatch in French in a remarkable piece of interpretation. The Minister did not answer specifically the points raised. He spoke of the responsibility of the French to maintain order. He referred to the presence of nearby British troops and that if any foreign troops were to be withdrawn they should all be withdrawn simultaneously. I interrupted by assuring him that I was not referring to a withdrawal of French troops but merely the dangers involved by augmenting their present forces. . . .

GERMANY

M. Bidault said that he would like to set forth his ideas with regard to the treatment of Germany. He said that he understood that the thinking of the United States and of the British on the long-term treatment of Germany — he was not referring merely to the occupation period — had not crystallized but was still in a fluid state. He said that he himself had formerly thought that Germany should be divided up into a number of pieces but that he had revised his thinking on this. He has, however, some definite ideas; the Rhineland and the Ruhr and Westphalia should, he was convinced, be separated from the rest of Germany. On the other hand, there were certain definite objections to putting that whole area into a single state. He thought the separate parts of it should be treated differently:

(1) As to the Saar region, France did not desire to annex it but was determined to have the Saar coal.

(2) North of the Saar there is an agricultural area over which

France feels she must have definite control for security reasons. This area included only the left bank of the Rhine up through Cologne and possibly one or two bridgeheads across the river. It was the area through which France had so often suffered military invasion. If it is placed in the hands of some international organization, the occupation of it might end by some "majority vote" against France. He emphasized that what France wanted was control and not annexation (though he did not define this difference). He said this would not mean slavery or deportation for the population. While some elements of the population, such as Gestapo members or those who might preach a German resurgence and unification, might be deported from the area, it was his expectation that the local population would remain there. The French, he said, again wish to control this agricultural area north to Cologne without any restrictive international supervision.

(3) He then came to the Ruhr. This region, he said, was the source of power and wealth of Germany and he felt should be definitely placed under the control of an international regime.

If a single Rhineland-Ruhr-Westphalia state is created, M. Bidault said, the standard of living in that area would probably be higher than the rest of Germany, its population would be privileged and it would attract more people from other regions of Germany. It conceivably could become another Prussia or Piedmont and form the nucleus or rallying point for a new strong, unified Germany. Under an international control, if such control were set up, the Russians might not agree with the western Europeans as to the policy to be applied. Therefore, as he had said before, he was opposed to the creation of a single Rhine-Ruhr state under international control. Germany will, he believes, in the nature of things, look to the west for hope and particularly to the Rhine area and he does not wish to see a powerful state established which will play one country off against another in typical German fashion, thus dividing the Allies.

In reply to a question, M. Bidault said that it might not be necessary to distinguish between the Saar and his agricultural area on the left bank of the Rhine though apparently what he wants in the Saar is only the control or ownership of the mines, whereas he wants complete security control in the area north of it. He admitted that he has not yet thought out the details. He did not specify what the nature of the international regime to govern the Ruhr should be but he did say in reply to a question that he was opposed to Germany having heavy metallurgical and machine-tool industries or any substantial chemical industry. He said the Germans should be allowed to have industries such as textiles and in general "enough to let them live."

His views with regard to the treatment to be applied to the remainder of Germany have not developed. The German people, he said, are badly shocked and there will be no elements prepared to take over a government of the country. He believes that we should wait some months to see how conditions develop before deciding whether the country should be divided into more than one state.

In reply to a question as to whether France desired to utilize German labor as a form of reparation, he said that he had not definitely made up his mind. He thought, however, that a number of Germans, particularly those military elements who knew the job, should be utilized for clearing France of the many thousands of mines which have been laid throughout the country. He said that Raoul Dautry, the Minister of Reconstruction, had estimated that it would cost ten billion francs, ten years labor and fifty thousand dead finally to clear France of mines.

In concluding his remarks on Germany, M. Bidault reiterated that he had merely wanted to present these strong views of his Government with regard to the Rhineland and he did not seem to expect an immediate answer as to the American position. He was told that, as he had intimated, our ideas on the long term territorial treatment of Germany have not yet crystallized.

FRENCH PENETRATION IN THE VAL D'AOSTA

After discussing the question of French reinforcements being sent to Syria and the Lebanon, I said that there was another question I should like to bring up. We are much disturbed at the situation prevailing along Italy's northwest frontiers and the resulting unrest and the tension there. General Eisenhower has asked the French military authorities, I said, to withdraw French forces in northwest Italy across the Franco-Italian border as Field Marshal Alexander's forces assume control of the area. The French commander in that region has received orders from General Jacob Devers [Commander of the Sixth Army Group] to withdraw his troops to the frontiers but he states that he is awaiting instructions from the French Government. Meanwhile, reports indicate that French troops in the province of Turin have increased and that French troops continue to be infiltrated under military cover in the Val D'Aosta region. There are also reports of annexationist propaganda being carried out in the several regions occupied by the French troops. Alexander has considered the situation sufficiently serious to recommend that the question be taken up with the French on a governmental level.

I said that Ambassador Caffery had spoken to General de Gaulle and the latter has assured him that France has no territorial ambitions in this region other than very minor frontier adjustments which he hoped to take up amicably through regular channels with the Italian Government at a later date. . . . The Department had instructed him to take this action at the request of SHAEF. I emphasized our concern over these developments particularly in view of the situation in the Istrian peninsula and the importance we attach to the application to this area of the principles of pacific adjustment of territorial plans as set forth in my public statement of May 12 which M. Bidault had presumably seen. What is needed, I said, is that the French Government should send instructions for the withdrawal of French forces in northwest Italy and endeavor to stop any irresponsible French annexationist activities in that area.

M. Bidault replied that the question was largely one of "amour propre" in view of Italian occupation of France in 1940, and the fact that France was invaded through those valleys. He said he came from the region in question and was familiar with the situation there. He agreed completely with General de Gaulle that France should have no annexationist claims to the area and referred to the plebiscite of 1860 and the fact that part of the region had been given to the King of Italy as a hunting preserve. He said that he thought there should be a minor rectification affecting two villages but not the Val D'Aosta itself. He said that France wants to establish friendly relations with Italy and that such a policy is the only sensible one for both countries. Therefore, any claims the French may have would be adjusted through normal channels. He endeavored to make light of the present situation and spoke of the habits of intelligence officers — French, American, British, Italian Partisans, et cetera, who circulated throughout the area reporting all sorts of rumors and implied that such reports should not be exaggerated. I reiterated that what is needed to solve the present tense situation there is for the French Government to send instructions to the French military commander to withdraw to the frontier. M. Bidault promised to look into the question immediately.

Date: May 21, 1945

SUBJECT: French Situation.

PARTICIPANTS: President Truman; M. Bidault; Mr. Henri Bonnet; Acting Secretary Grew.

I saw the President this morning at about 10.25 and suggested that in the course of his second conversation with Mr. Bidault, the French Foreign Minister, it would be well to refer to the fact that French troops are still occupying areas in northwestern Italy contrary to the directions of the Commander in Chief and that they have apparently refused to move. The French in this case are doing just about what Tito is doing in Trieste and Venezia Giulia and it might be helpful if the President would point this out with complete frankness. The President concurred.

Mr. Bidault and the French Ambassador then came in at 10.30. Mr. Bidault said to the President that he wished to thank him heartily for the President's statement to the press after their last conversation. He said that this statement had made a very fine impression in France and had greatly strengthened Mr. Bidault's hand, as well as the relations between the two countries. The President said that he was very glad to know this and that it had been gratifying to receive Ambassador Caffery's report of the French reaction to the statement. The President said that he is interested in France and feels very strongly that the friendship between France and the United States should be steadily strengthened, and he wished to do whatever he could to that end. Mr. Bidault expressed appreciation.

The President then said that even among friends it is best to place one's cards face up on the table, and that he wished to explain to Mr. Bidault the unfortunate effect on our relations of the fact that French forces are still occupying areas in northwestern Italy contrary to the orders of the Commander in Chief. The French are in fact doing very much what Marshal Tito is doing in Venezia Giulia and in Trieste, in other words they are occupying territory, the ultimate possession of which is under dispute, and they are thereby prejudicing the ultimate settlement of these matters at the eventual peace conference. This, the President said, gives ammunition to those in our country who may be trying to stir up trouble between the United States and France, and he would be very glad if the Foreign Minister would take steps to overcome this situation. The President said that there had been other incidents of a similar nature, notably in the French occupation of Stuttgart.

Mr. Bidault listened carefully to the President's remarks, which were accurately translated by the French Ambassador, and then said that he himself knew nothing about this situation except what he had seen in the newspapers, but that he would take the matter up immediately upon his return to France.

Mr. Bidault then said that he did not feel that he need

trouble the President with the various troubles he had in mind as he had been able to explain the French point of view to me in our two-hour conversation on May 19. He hoped that the President was familiar with the points he had taken up with me, especially with regard to certain French desiderata in Germany. The President immediately indicated that he was in entire sympathy with the French point of view and thought there would be no difficulty about arranging matters as the French desired. Mr. Bidault expressed great gratification at the President's statement, whereupon I felt obliged to make sure that the Foreign Minister was not taking this as an official commitment concerning the ultimate disposition of the Saar, the Ruhr, and the Rhineland, which Mr. Bidault had mentioned in his talk with me. I therefore said that I thought the President was referring to the French desire to have part of the American zone in Germany and not to the other areas mentioned, as the President had not yet had time to study the record of my own talk with the Foreign Minister, although I would see that a full statement of the points raised by Mr. Bidault would come to the President's attention. Mr. Bidault immediately replied that he fully understood this and realized that the President was not in a position to make a definite commitment at this time. . . .

Date: June 1, 1945

SUBJECT: Cabinet meeting, 2 P.M.
PARTICIPANTS: The President; Acting Secretary,
Mr. Grew.

At Cabinet meeting today I gave the following brief summary of the situation in the Levant:

The landing of French troops in the Levant States concurrently with the presentation of demands for concessions of a political and military nature which the Syrian and Lebanese Governments regarded as incompatible with their independence, resulted in an outbreak of disorders which quickly spread through Syria, culminating in the indiscriminate bombing of several Syrian cities, including Damascus, by the French in an effort to intimidate the public.

We foresaw the potential danger of the French action in sending troops to the Levant States in the prevailing highly charged political atmosphere, and implored the French Government to refrain from such a course.[5] The British Government, which was equally alive to the danger, did likewise.

Neighboring Arab countries became aroused as the situation deteriorated and there was every indication that the trouble would shortly involve the whole Near East. Mr. Stettinius informed us that the Levant crisis was seriously disturbing the atmosphere of the Conference in San Francisco. The British Military, who are responsible for over-all security in the Near East, intervened May 31 and have now apparently put an end to the fighting and restored order. We have been in the closest touch with the British Government throughout and we gave our approval to their action to prevent further bloodshed.

I added that this situation had caused us much concern during the past week but fortunately positive action had now been taken and we believed that the serious aspects of the affair were now probably under control. I said that the Near East is a powder keg, that the French action might well have resulted in blowing off the lid and that a general conflagration might have resulted throughout the Arab world. I stated further that, in my opinion, the position we had taken had greatly increased our prestige among the Arab states and that this prestige had

[5] On May 28, Ambassador Caffery delivered the following note to the Provisional French Government: "I have been instructed by my Government to convey to the Government of France the deep concern which my Government feels with regard to recent developments in Syria and Lebanon.

"An impression has been created in the United States and elsewhere that French representatives have been using the threat of force to obtain from Syria and Lebanon concessions of a political, cultural, and military nature. . . .

"The Government of the United States, therefore, in a most friendly spirit earnestly urges the Government of France carefully to review its policy toward Syria and Lebanon with the purpose of finding a way to make it clear to those countries and to all the world that, in its dealings with the Levant States, France intends to treat them as fully sovereign and independent members of the family of nations." U.S. Department of State, Department of State Bulletin, June 8, 1945, p. 1013.

been enhanced by the visit of the Regent of Iraq. The President referred to his having conferred on the Regent this morning the Legion of Merit and I added that this had gone far to balance the effect of President Roosevelt's gift of a plane to King Ibn Saud. The President said that, choosing between the plane and the decoration, he himself would have preferred the plane. . . .

Date: June 8, 1945

PARTICIPANTS: President Truman; Acting Secretary Grew.

I called on the President this morning at 9.30 and took up the following matters:

1. I said that I brought good news regarding the French position in northwest Italy. Ambassador Caffery had delivered the President's letter to de Gaulle yesterday afternoon and shortly thereafter Bidault had telephoned to Caffery that the matter had been arranged, and that General Juin would leave at once for Caserta with appropriate instructions. Caffery said that he would get more on this from Bidault in the morning. I said that the President's technique had evidently been successful and had caused de Gaulle to climb down. . . . I therefore thought that the tactics of the President's sending a private letter to de Gaulle was, at least in the first instance, very much wiser than to carry out the first plan of giving the whole story to the press. The President said he thought I was right "as usual" — a remark to which I smilingly took exception. . . .

Date: June 8, 1945

SUBJECT: Cabinet meeting, 2 P.M.
PARTICIPANTS: The President; Acting Secretary, Mr. Grew.

At Cabinet meeting today the President was in his place a few minutes before two o'clock and had to wait some time before all the members appeared and took their places. When the President turned to me I spoke without notes approximately as follows:

Mr. President, I don't believe as a rule in crowing before the sun is really up but I may say that the international scene is a great deal brighter today than it was even two days ago.

In the first place, the Russians have met our position on the voting procedure in the Security Council and the San Francisco Conference has thus been saved.[6] It is now practically certain that a charter will be produced furnishing a structure which can be developed and strengthened in future with time and experience. This achievement will be a great monument to you and your Administration and Secretary Stettinius. The President immediately interposed with the observation that the credit should go to President Roosevelt who had done the spade work.

I then said that with regard to the situation in Venezia Giulia and Trieste, Marshal Tito and Marshal Alexander were this afternoon to sign an agreement establishing Allied Military Government throughout those areas. I said that we had passed many anxious days and nights over this problem and while we must judge by practical results rather than written commitments it now looked as if the problem would be satisfactorily settled.

With regard to northwestern Italy, French forces had settled down in Italian areas and we had been faced there with very much the same problem as that existing in Venezia Giulia where we had stood firmly on principle. General Doyen at the instance of General de Gaulle had adopted a highly arrogant attitude and had disobeyed the orders of his Commanding Officer, Marshal Alexander, in refusing to budge from the occupied territory in Italy. Now, however, as a result of the President's masterly note to de Gaulle, the latter had informed the President that he would yield and General Juin was already on his way to confer with Marshal Alexander in order to reach a settlement. The President interposed "masterly is not quite the word; the note was a sledge hammer."

I was about to speak of improvement in the situation in the

6 See Stettinius, *op. cit.*, pp. 319–21.

Levant [7] but at this point the President turned to the Secretary of the Treasury and the succeeding remarks and discussions were exclusively of a domestic nature. . . .

Date: June 26, 1945

PARTICIPANTS: Fawwaz Shaalan; Faour el Faour; Ali el Atrash, Syrian Emirs; Syrian Chargé d'Affaires; Mr. Grew; Mr. Loy Henderson [Director of the Office of Near Eastern and African Affairs].

This afternoon the Syrian Chargé d'Affaires presented to Mr. Grew three Emirs, Fawwaz Shaalan, Faour el Faour, and Ali el Atrash, prominent Sheikhs who are members of the Syrian Paliament.

These three Sheikhs are at present making a tour of the United States in a private capacity and the call was more a matter of courtesy than of business.

The Sheikhs did however express, on behalf of the members of the Syrian Parliament and of the Syrian people, their deep appreciation of the attitude which they said the United States had consistently shown to Syria. They said that Syria owed to the United States a great debt because of the manner in which the Government and people of the United States had supported the independence and sovereignty of Syria. They expressed particular gratitude for the attitude which the American Government has been showing during the present crisis in Syria and said that they were confident that the United States, which was well known as the champion of small nations and weak peoples, would continue to support Syria in the struggle for Syrian independence.

[7] By the early part of June order had been largely restored in the Levant. A cease fire had been sent by France to her troops. In July, 1945, the French agreed to hand over the Levantine troops to Syria and Lebanon within forty-five days, and by October it was reported that about twenty-four thousand troops had been transferred. On December 13, 1945, an agreement was signed by Great Britain and France according to which both were to withdraw their troops from Syria and to regroup them in Lebanon, pending a decision by the United Nations on the organization of collective security in that area.

Mr. Grew thanked the Sheikhs for their friendly remarks which, he said, indicated that they had a correct understanding of American policy with regard to Syria. The United States recognized Syria as an independent country and wished to see peace maintained and mutually helpful relations with the United States developed in Syria as in all other countries in the Near East. . . .

XLI

Ending Government Service

When President Harry S. Truman assumed office, Mr. Grew submitted his resignation as Under Secretary of State, but it was not accepted. Later, when James F. Byrnes replaced Edward R. Stettinius Jr. as Secretary of State, Mr. Grew in a conversation with the President on July 1, 1945, reminded the President of his letter of resignation: "I then said to the President that when I had my first talk with the new Secretary of State, Mr. Byrnes, I would say to him that he would probably wish to choose his own Under Secretary and that I wished him to know that my resignation was on the President's desk and was equally available to Mr. Byrnes at any time that he might wish to avail himself of it. I said that having served the Government for forty-one years and having passed the age of retirement I would be very happy at any time to retire from public life. The President very kindly said that if Mr. Byrnes should accept his advice he would make no change in the Under Secretaryship. I thanked the President for his attitude and said I wished him to know that I would go along with him anywhere as I had for him great admiration and personal affection. I did not, however, know Mr. Byrnes well and I knew nothing of his policies or methods, but that I would certainly not let anyone down, and if Mr. Byrnes should wish me to stay at least for a time I would not be unwilling to do so. The matter was, however, to remain open until I could discuss it with Mr. Byrnes himself. The President, with a twinkle in his eye, asked if I thought Mr. Byrnes' nomination would be confirmed by the Senate, to which I replied that I thought it would unquestionably be confirmed in very short order.

"The President as usual thanked me in very cordial terms for my call."

On August 16, 1945, however, President Truman accepted Mr. Grew's resignation. A few days after his resignation had been accepted, Mr. Grew wrote the following letters throwing light on the background of the resignation and on his attitude toward his second period of service as Under Secretary of State.

To Elizabeth Sturgis Lyon, September 2, 1945

. . . I can't remember whether I sent you a letter after my resignation telling you the facts, but anyway I'll tell you now and you'll have to forgive me if I'm repeating. When Mr. Byrnes became Secretary of State I told him immediately that my resignation had been on the President's desk ever since he took office and that it was equally available to Byrnes, and I assumed that he would wish to choose his own Under Secretary in view of the intimate relationship that must exist. Byrnes asked me to remain at least until after the Potsdam Conference as he didn't want to consider personnel questions then. The moment he returned and Japan had announced the intention to surrender I again went to Byrnes and showed him a letter I had written to the President asking him to accept my resignation, as I had signed up under Stettinius only "for the duration" and had passed the age of retirement after 41 years of service. I knew very well that Byrnes wanted a change anyway and I wished to relieve him of all embarrassment.[1]

Byrnes was very nice about it, even affectionate, and asked if I would go out to Japan as General MacArthur's political adviser. I declined for three reasons. First I knew very well that . . . MacArthur would not want much advice and I didn't want to be in a position of seeing things done of which I disapproved, with the implication that I was responsible for them. Second I certainly didn't want to face our old friends in Japan as a conqueror. Third I knew that there would be no chance to diet and that my gallstones might flare up again and I would

[1] After a month of the Byrnes regime, Mr. Grew later commented, he saw that an inner group was making the major decisions, and that he was not being consulted. Mr. Grew, therefore, informed Mr. Byrnes that he as Secretary of State should have a man of his own choice in the post of Under Secretary.

simply crack up. The first two arguments might have been overcome but not the third and Byrnes immediately recognized that fact and said he thought I was right in declining to go. Anyway, so far as I am aware, MacArthur has never asked for a political adviser. I think he will probably handle things very well himself, and he has a lot of officers who have lived in Japan and know the language and the mentality of the people.

So that was that. Both the President and Byrnes wrote me very generous letters which were published in the *New York Times*,[2] the former being very affectionate and addressing me as "Dear Joe." I was immensely happy to get out, feeling that my job was really done in having started the ball rolling for the Potsdam Proclamation which leaves to the Japanese people themselves to determine the future political structure of the country, and in having persuaded the Administration to keep the Emperor, at least for the present, as the only man who could stop war and avoid the needless loss of thousands of our soldiers, if we had had to invade Japan itself. I think that my position has been thoroughly vindicated in spite of all the attacks on me these past years, which I have had to accept in silence. So my conscience is clear and I am really very happy at the outcome. I think that history will show that we were right all along the line. What I want to see now is the ferreting out and the trial as war criminals of every last man responsible for the barbarous treatment of our prisoners. . . .[3]

[2] *New York Times*, August 17, 1945, p. 9.

[3] Charges were made in 1945 and have been repeated since, as, for instance, in the Chicago *Tribune*, July 14, 1950, that Mr. Grew was forced out of office by "left wing" pressure. "Myths have arisen about that point," Mr. Grew stated on July 21, 1950. "Actually I resigned on my own initiative and had to exert a little pressure to get my resignation accepted. The left wingers chortled that they had pushed me out, but they really had nothing to do with it." On August 19, 1945, *PM* had stated in an editorial that the "old Stettinius team that took over the State Dept. last December after a hot Senate confirmation fight is melting away rapidly," and that there "is no use undervaluing what has happened. Grew . . . belonged to the Department's most reactionary group." *The New Republic* on August 27, 1945, concluded that the "second reorganization of the Department of State in less than a year is under way. This one promises to be much more thorough, and to mean a great deal more, than the reorganization last December by Roosevelt and Stettinius," because

To Robert J. Lynch, Special Assistant to Edward
R. Stettinius Jr., September 28, 1945

Your letter came while we were away on a month's motor
trip in New England, and I appreciated it greatly. Your generous appraisal of my service is intensely gratifying, coming
from one who had an opportunity to observe from close quarters. You well know of my devotion to Ed Stettinius which
will always be the same even though we can work together no
longer. The press and the public wanted a clean sweep in the
Department, but you and I know that the old Department had
never in all its history (and Billy Phillips confirms this) been
so effectively organized as under the Stettinius regime. He understood teamwork better than any chief I have ever served
under.

I have enjoyed our own association and hope that our respective roads may meet often in future. I fully appreciate and am
grateful for all the fine support you gave me during sometimes
difficult days. . . .

From James F. Byrnes to Joseph C. Grew, August
16, 1945

I am indeed sorry that you are leaving the Department to
which for more than two score years you have given distin-

already "two extreme conservatives placed in the Department by Mr. Roosevelt
— Under-Secretary Joseph C. Grew and Assistant Secretary Julius C. Holmes
have been retired."

In May 1952 Mr. Grew added: "I have read the constantly recurring myths
in current books, magazine articles and newspaper stories about my allegedly
enforced retirement as Under Secretary of State in August 1945. Probably
nothing that I may say or write will stop those myths. The fact is, however,
that I intensely wished to retire at that time for the following reasons:

  "1. The war was over.
  "2. I had agreed with Secretary Stettinius to serve as Under Secretary only
     for the duration of the war.
  "3. I had passed the Foreign Service age limit.
  "4. I had served the government for 41 years.
  "5. I was then not in good health and was facing a possible major surgical
     operation.

"These facts should be sufficient to dispel the reports that anyone had to
push me out. If certain elements and influences wanted to get me out, they
certainly chose just the right time from my point of view."

guished and devoted service of the highest order. In those years you have made most notable contributions to the development of our foreign policy and to the improvement of the Foreign Service. In those years you have acquired knowledge and experience, particularly of the problems in the Far East, which have been of inestimable value to our country in the critical war period.

I appreciate that you desire and are entitled to some rest from active service. But I am glad to have your assurance that I may freely call upon you for advice and counsel which I am sure will be most helpful to me.

I also want you to know how very much I personally appreciate your constant helpfulness to me during the brief period we have worked in close association in the Department.

To Harry S. Truman from Joseph C. Grew,
August 15, 1945

When President Roosevelt and Mr. Stettinius as Secretary of State asked me last December to take the position of Under Secretary of State, I accepted, with high appreciation, for the duration of the war. The war now being over, I respectfully request that my resignation, submitted when you became President, be accepted. Having served our Government for forty-one years and having passed the age of retirement from the Foreign Service, I feel that the proper time has come to lay down the responsibility of public office.

Please permit me, Mr. President, to express to you my enduring gratitude for the confidence you have placed in me, the deep satisfaction which I shall always retain in the privilege of working closely with you during the months when I was Acting Secretary of State, and my full appreciation of the fine support you gave me at difficult moments in the conduct of our foreign relations.

From Harry S. Truman to Joseph C. Grew,
August 16, 1945
Dear Joe:

Replying to your letter of the fifteenth, I am regretfully acceding to your request that you be permitted to resign as Under Secretary of State. I know that after more than two score years of service you are certainly entitled to some rest and relief from the burdens of government.

I am delighted, however, that you have assured the Secretary of State that you are going to be available to him for advice and consultation, and for any service that he may require.

May I on behalf of the nation give you this personal word of thanks for your long, faithful and efficient service during all these years. I am sure that you can look back with great satisfaction on your long career of public service.

I shall miss our close personal relationship of the past few months and hope you will come to see me from time to time.

Very sincerely yours,

HARRY S. TRUMAN

INDEX

Index

1544

INDEX

American institutions in Turkey, 766–67, 854–55; forms cabinet (1930), 871 and n. 9
Ishii, Viscountess, 987
Ishii, Kikujiro, Viscount, 698, 936–37 and n. 11, 944, 949, 987, 1156
Istanbul. *See* Constantinople
Istria, 1475 ff., 1512
Ito, Baron, 1325
Ives, Ernest, 716, 719, 722, 729, 731, 734, 761, 763, 767, 792
Ives, Mrs. Ernest, 718–19, 790
Iwakuro, Colonel, 1295 n. 39
Izvolsky, Alexander, Russian Minister of Foreign Affairs, 54, 56

Jackson, John B., 204, 258
Jackson, Mrs. John, 202
Jacquart, M., 803
Jadwin, General Edgar, 390 n. 11
Jagow, von, German Minister for Foreign Affairs, 70, 184, 273, 287; on *Lusitania* and the blockade, 193–94, 195–96; on *Hesperian* case; Grew's comment on position of, 220; on Gerard's note on submarine question, 222–23; conveys to Gerard Emperor's wish to see him, 223; before Budget Committee, 245, on German willingness to consider terms of peace, 251; retirement, 253
James, Edwin, 517
Jancovici, 614
Japan, brief survey of history of (1894–1932), 921–25; relations between U.S. and (1932–35), 927–86; anti-American propaganda in, 934; recognizes Manchukuo, 935; secedes from League of Nations, 938–40; mobilization of national resources, 940; petroleum resources, 942–43; relations with Soviet Russia (1933), 945; the Press in, 946–48; attitude to American recognition of Soviet Government, 950–51; oil conservationism, 956–57; naval limita-

tions ratio, 964–65; preliminary naval conversations and abrogation of Washington Treaty, 966–67; proposed oil monopoly in Manchuria and Petroleum Industry Law, 967–70, 976–78, 1023–26; "The February 26 Incident," 987–996; relations with America (1935), 997–1003; relations with China, 1003–14; control of automobile industry in, 1020–21; trade dispute with Australia, 1021 n. 26; U.S. duty on cotton textiles from, 1021; relations with Soviet Russia, 1026–28; commercial secrecy in, 1030; abrogation by U.S. of Commercial Treaty of 1911, 1212 and n. 9; outbreak of war with U.S., 1245–54; efforts of, to effect new orientation of policy, 1291–94; situation in (in 1941), 1294–99; surrender of, 1421–42. *See also* Japanese Government
Japanese assets, freezing of, in U.S., 1304; Grew's recommendation concerning, 1347–48
Japanese Government, ability of, to carry out its engagements, 1296–98; futile efforts of, to elicit from U.S. concrete terms for settlement, 1335–39; ability of to control its armed forces, 1351–52
Jardine, William, 15 n.
Jay, DeLancey, 656
Jay, Peter, 26, 169, 186–87, 189, 412, 443; appointed Ambassador to the Argentine, 654–55; letter to, from Grew, 663
Jillson, Jeannie, 762, 774
Joachim, Prince, 106
Johns, Clayton, 135
Johnson, Herschel, 446
Johnson, General Hugh, 1257
Johnson, Nelson, Chief of Division of Far Eastern Affairs, 659–60, 691–92; U.S. Ambassador in China, 1076, 1079, 1093–94, 1101,

1554